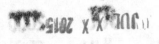

AN ANNOTATED
SECONDARY BIBLIOGRAPHY SERIES
ON ENGLISH LITERATURE
IN TRANSITION
1880–1920

HELMUT E. GERBER

GENERAL EDITOR

W. SOMERSET MAUGHAM

JOSEPH CONRAD

THOMAS HARDY

E. M. FORSTER

JOHN GALSWORTHY

GEORGE GISSING

D. H. LAWRENCE

H. G. WELLS

WALTER PATER

G. B. SHAW

THE CONTRIBUTORS

PIERRE COUSTILLAS
University of Lille

PAUL GOETSCH
University of Freiburg

MADELINE BERGEROVA LONG
Western Maryland College

MIRJANA N. MATARIĆ
National Serbian Library (Belgrade)

EARL E. STEVENS
Rhode Island College

H. RAY STEVENS
Western Maryland College

John Galsworthy

AN
ANNOTATED
BIBLIOGRAPHY
OF WRITINGS
ABOUT HIM

COMPILED AND EDITED BY

EARL E. STEVENS

AND

H. RAY STEVENS

NORTHERN ILLINOIS UNIVERSITY PRESS
DE KALB, ILLINOIS

Earl E. Stevens is Professor of English at Rhode Island College.
H. Ray Stevens is Professor of English at Western Maryland College.

Library of Congress Cataloging in Publication Data

Main entry under title:

John Galsworthy: an annotated bibliography of writing about him.

(An Annotated secondary bibliography series on English literature in transition, 1880–1920)
Includes indexes.
1. Galsworthy, John, 1867–1933—Bibliography.
I. Coustillas, Pierre.   II. Stevens, Earl E.,
1925–   III. Stevens, Harold Ray, 1936–
IV. Series: Annotated secondary bibliography series on English literature in transition, 1880–1920.
Z8321.45.J63   [PR6013.A5]   016.823'9'12   78-60456
ISBN 0-87580-073-4

for
Ruth Ann
and
Twila

Preface

Our approach to the editing of the John Galsworthy volume of the Annotated Secondary Bibliography Series has been simple: we have tried to include all of the extant secondary bibliographical materials relating to Galsworthy. This task has consumed a large portion of our waking hours since 1969 and has provided some memorable nightmares. We have recognized that the paradise of the bibliographical world, completeness, is as unattainable as was Mr. Stone's dream of Universal Brotherhood in *Fraternity*. But because it is more comprehensive than any of the earlier bibliographies, the present volume will, it is hoped, add significantly to the work begun by H. V. Marrot (A BIBLIOGRAPHY OF THE WORKS OF JOHN GALSWORTHY, 1928), expanded in the bibliographies found in the pages of ENGLISH FICTION IN TRANSITION: 1880–1920 and ENGLISH LITERATURE IN TRANSITION: 1880–1920 (all of which have been useful in compiling the present volume), and continued in the work of E. H. Mikhail (JOHN GALSWORTHY THE DRAMATIST: A BIBLIOGRAPHY OF CRITICISM, 1971).

Of the difficulties encountered in preparing this volume because of the limitations of time, funds, and available data little need be said, for those who are familiar with the demands of the bibliographer's job know what is involved. Perhaps the following two examples will serve to illustrate the particular kinds of problems we encountered. *A Man of Devon* (1901), the last of four volumes published by Galsworthy under the pseudonym John Sinjohn, is recorded by H. V. Marrot (THE LIFE AND LETTERS OF JOHN GALSWORTHY) as having received more than forty notices when it appeared. Yet Marrot's BIBLIOGRAPHY lists only one review of the work, and he quotes from only one other in his discussion of *A Man of Devon* in *Life and Letters*. An inquiry to the publisher, William Blackwood, brought news that the building on Paternoster Row in London which housed all of the press clippings of *Devon* was destroyed in the bombing of London in December 1940. Letters to Galsworthians uncovered no new items, and two intriguing but rather frustrating days spent in the stacks of the Library of Congress by one of the coeditors reading through the book sections of the various periodicals and newspapers for the appropriate year uncovered only two additional items. Probably many of the forty notices mentioned by Marrot were of the publisher's notice variety or were short comments of a few lines that appeared in the omnibus reviews common at the turn of the century. To be sure, such cursory remarks would in all likelihood have added little of appreciable value to the canon of Galsworthy criticism, but their inclusion would have helped to make this volume more complete.

The second example concerns the East European language entries. Mirjana N. Matarić of the National Serbian Library in Belgrade generously supplied the bibliographical listings of the Galsworthy materials found in the various libraries in eastern Europe, and she also provided reprints of several important publications. George V. Starosolsky, head of the East European section of the Library of Congress, and Sheila Penners and Ellen Zolas, who are also associated with the Library of Congress, have assisted in translating, and where appropriate, in transliterating almost all of the Bulgarian, Czech, Polish, Russian, and Slovene entries. Unfortunately, some of the articles from eastern Europe have not been annotated because of the unavailability of materials and because we were unable to locate, over a period of more than seven years, a sufficient number of people who had the time and the linguistic skills and who were willing to contribute their services for a project such as this. In spite of this handicap, a sampling is provided which represents the work done by students of Galsworthy in eastern Europe. And even for the unannotated items, the subject of a particular entry can often be determined from the available bibliographical data.

In all of our entries we have tried to be consistent both within this volume and within the context of the whole Annotated Secondary Bibliography Series. We have not always been successful, especially with non-English language entries, because all of the bibliographical data has not always been available; but rather than omit items in order to maintain a perhaps too narrow consistency, we have included all of the information given us. This course of action has seemed the most reasonable, given the fact that entries from eighteen languages in addition to English have been included and that contributions have been received from people schooled in bibliographical procedures different from ours. Except for foreign doctoral dissertations that have been published in monograph series, we have included Ph.D. dissertations without annotation. When such information has been available, we have given the appropriate listing for abstracts that have appeared in DISSERTATION ABSTRACTS or similar series. We have excluded undergraduate honors papers and M.A. theses in almost all cases.

As with the other volumes in the Series, we have tried to be objective in our annotations, saving critical comment or supplemental information for bracketed insertions at the conclusion of the annotation. Some annotations have only brief bracketed comments such as "inconsequential book review"; such an item is usually a review of a paragraph or less (like those that appear in the A.L.A. BOOKLIST), and it consists of a simple statement of theme or a brief plot summary, without critical or interpretative comment. All items not specifically seen or read by the coeditors or by those listed on the contributors page have been clearly marked "not seen." We have consciously avoided trying to catalogue all of the articles written about the British Broadcasting Corporation's televised adaptation of *The Forsyte Saga* that began to appear about the time that plans for this volume were made. Instead, a representative sampling of the comments found in some of the various publications has been included. Most of the comments that appeared were, if not plot summary, a rehash of viewpoints which had become standardized for more than a generation in the canon of Galsworthy criticism.

Entries are listed under the date of first publication and include data regarding reprintings, revisions, and translations. Translations are listed only under the original author's name. Within the listing for each year all entries are alphabetized. In order to give this volume the greatest usefulness for a variety of research purposes, five indexes are provided.

Concerning Galsworthy's work as a dramatist, it must be noted that many of the reviews of the plays included in this volume are theater reviews rather than reviews of the publication of the various plays in book form. Obviously, some of the theatrical reviews are as concerned with the stage business and the quality of the acting as with the play as literature. We have tried to capture the diversity of comments and approaches of the various theater critics, but our controlling emphasis has been in focusing on the significance of Galsworthy as author. As a consequence, the main thrust in the annotations of theatrical reviews has been to record how the critics have responded to the work of Galsworthy as a dramatist. At the same time, however, we have included the reactions of various critics to the productions and to the quality of the acting, as, for example, in the case of John Barrymore, who in 1916 attracted widespread attention in the United States with his performance of Falder in *Justice*.

Of all endeavors in literary study, the job of the bibliographer is the one most open to reproof and to discernible error. A misspelled word or a footnote incorrectly numbered in a critical study is distressing, but such errors are usually self-limiting and they can be silently corrected by the reader as he notes with an inward smile another's fallibility. In bibliographic studies there is probably no such thing as a minor error, as we have learned too well while tracking down and trying to verify the entries for this volume. An incorrect citation perhaps because of a faulty volume number, a date that was mistyped, or the wrong pagination has diabolical possibilities that could arouse the dedication of Browning's Grammarian. Any information that may help us to reduce the omissions and correct the errors of this volume will be welcome; as there is no end to the making of books, the time may come when a revised edition is needed.

ACKNOWLEDGMENTS

A work such as this is the result of the willingness of many colleagues, here and abroad, to give generously of their time and talents, and to all of them—those who have already been named in the list of contributors or elsewhere in the preface and to the nameless many—we wish to express our deepest gratitude for their indispensable assistance and encouragement.

The resources of libraries throughout the United States and Europe were utilized, and in almost all cases the responses were generous, helpful, and prompt. The heaviest burdens fell on George Bachmann and Carol Quinn, librarian and reference librarian of Western Maryland College, and on Beth Perry, Louise Sherby, and Frank Notarianni, reference librarians, and Linda Catino of the Interlibrary Loan Department of the James P. Adams Library, Rhode Island College. Their patience and skills seem inexhaustible, and we are especially grateful to them. Ruth Ann Stevens assisted in various ways with typing and editorial matters, and Rhonda Kiler, Lola Mathias, and Crystal Bellinger, secretaries at Western Maryland College, assisted in preparing the manuscript. Nancy Phoebus and Fred Rudman helped to collect data from some American newspapers.

We are grateful to the Research and Creativity Committee of Western Maryland College for two grants that aided in acquiring some materials, in assisting with secretarial costs, and in enabling one of the coeditors to spend a portion of his sabbatical leave pursuing elusive bibliographic material at the British Museum and at the Library of Congress. We wish also to express our gratitude to the Faculty Research Committee of Rhode Island College for two research grants that helped to provide some of the support and resources necessary to the success of this project.

Finally, we are grateful to Ruth Ann and Twila who, while enduring much, continue graciously to endow others with their riches and strengths.

EARL E. STEVENS
H. RAY STEVENS

Contents

Titles of Galsworthy's works appear in italic type; titles of his stories, in roman capitals and lower case with quotation marks. Titles of books by other authors, collections of stories and letters edited by other writers, and names of periodicals and newspapers appear in capitals and small capitals. The translations appearing in parentheses are confined to meanings of the phrases; however, it should be noted that the titles of translations are seldom literal ones.

John Galsworthy

AN ANNOTATED BIBLIOGRAPHY
OF WRITINGS ABOUT HIM

A Checklist

OF THE WORKS OF JOHN GALSWORTHY
CITED IN THIS BIBLIOGRAPHY

I. FICTION
A. SEPARATE WORKS

From the Four Winds. John Sinjohn. [pseud.] Lond, 1897. Contents: "The
Running Amok of Synge Sahib"; "Dick Denver's Idea"; "Ashes";
" 'Tally-Ho'—Budmâsh"; "The Doldrums"; "The Capitulation of Jean
Jacques"; "The Spirit of Karroo"; "A Prairie Oyster'; "According
to His Lights"; "The Demi-Gods."
Jocelyn. John Sinjohn. [pseud.] Lond, 1898. NY, 1977.
Villa Rubein. John Sinjohn. [pseud.] Lond, 1900.
A Man of Devon. John Sinjohn. [pseud.] Edinburgh and Lond, 1901.Contents:
"A Man of Devon," 1900; "The Salvation of Swithin Forsyte," 1900; "The
Silence," 1901; "A Knight," 1900.
The Island Pharisees. Lond and NY, 1904.
The Man of Property. Lond and NY, 1906.
The Country House. Lond and NY, 1907.
A Commentary. Lond and NY, 1908. Contents: "A Commentary"; "The Lost
Dog"; "Demos"; "Old Age"; "The Careful Man"; "Fear"; "Fashion";
"Sport"; "Money"; "Progress"; "Holiday"; "Facts"; "Power"; "The
House of Silence"; "Order"; "The Mother"; "Comfort"; "A Child";
"Justice"; "Hope."
Fraternity. Lond and NY, 1909.
A Motley. Lond and NY, 1910. Contents: "A Portrait," 1908; "A Fisher of Men,"
1908; "The Prisoner," 1909; "Courage," 1904; "The Meeting," 1904; "The
Pack," 1905; "Compensation," 1904; "Joy of Life," 1899; "Bel Colore,"
1899; "A Pilgrimage," 1900; "The Kings," 1904; "Apotheosis," 1903;
"The Workers," 1909; "A Miller of Dee," 1903; "A Parting," 1909; "A

3

Beast of Burden," 1905; "The Lime Tree," 1909; "The Neighbours," 1909; "The Runagates," 1900; "A Reversion to Type," 1901; "A Woman," 1900; "The 'Codger' "; "For Ever," 1906; "The Consummation," 1904; "The Choice," 1910; "The Japanese Quince," 1910; "Once More," 1910; "Delight," 1910.

The Patrician. Lond and NY, 1911.

The Inn of Tranquillity. Lond and NY, 1912. Contents: CONCERNING LIFE: "The Inn of Tranquillity," 1910; "Quality," 1911; "Magpie over the Hill," 1912; "Sheep-shearing," 1910; "Evolution," 1910; "Riding in Mist," 1910; "The Procession," 1910; "A Christian," 1911; "Wind in the Rocks," 1910; "My Distant Relative," 1911; "The Black Godmother," 1912; "The Grand Jury," 1912; "Gone," 1911; "Threshing," 1911; "That Old-time Place," 1912; "Romance—Three Gleams," 1912; "Memories," 1912; "Felicity," 1912; CONCERNING LETTERS: "A Novelist's Allegory," 1909; "Some Platitudes Concerning Drama," 1909; "Meditation on Finality," 1912; "Wanted—Schooling," 1906; "On Our Dislike of Things as They Are," 1905–1912; "The Windlestraw," 1910; "About Censorship," 1909; "Vague Thoughts on Art," 1911.

The Dark Flower. Lond and NY, 1913.

The Little Man and Other Satires. Lond and NY, 1915. Contents: "The Little Man," 1913; "Hall-marked," 1913; "The Voice of——!" 1908; "The Dead Man"; "Why Not?"; "Hey-Day"; STUDIES OF EXTRAVAGANCE: "The Writer"; "The Critic"; "The Plain Man"; "The Superlative"; "The Preceptor"; "The Artist"; "The Housewife"; "The Latest Thing"; "The Perfect One"; "The Competitor"; "Abracadabra"; "Hathor: A Memory," 1914; "Sekhet: A Dream"; "A Simple Tale," 1914; "Ultima Thule," 1914.

The Freelands. Lond and NY, 1915.

Beyond. Lond and NY, 1917.

Five Tales. Lond and NY, 1918. Contents: "The First and the Last," 1914; "A Stoic," 1916; "The Apple Tree," 1916; "The Juryman," 1916; "Indian Summer of a Forsyte," 1917.

The Burning Spear. A. R. P—M. [pseud.] Lond, 1919. NY, 1923.

Saint's Progress. Lond and NY, 1919.

Tatterdemalion. Lond and NY, 1920. Contents: Part I.—OF WAR TIME: "The Grey Angel," 1917; "Defeat," 1916; "Flotsam and Jetsam," 1917; "The Bright Side," 1919; " 'Cafard'," 1917; "Recorded"; "The Recruit," 1917; "Peace Meeting," 1917; " 'The Dog It Was that Died'," 1919; "In Heaven and Earth"; "The Mother Stone," 1903; "Poirot and Bidan"; "The Muffled Ship," 1919; "Heritage"; " 'A Green Hill Far Away'," 1918; Part II.—OF PEACE-TIME: "Spindleberries," 1918; "Expectations," 1919; "Manna," 1916; "A Strange Thing," 1916; "Two Looks," 1904; "Fairyland," 1912; "The Nightmare Child," 1917; "Buttercup Night," 1913.

In Chancery. Lond and NY, 1920.

Awakening. Lond and NY, 1920.

To Let. Lond and NY, 1921.

The Forsyte Saga. Lond and NY, 1922. Contents: *The Man of Property;* "Indian Summer of a Forsyte"; *In Chancery;* "Awakening"; *To Let.*

Captures. Lond and NY, 1923. Contents: "A Feud," 1921; "The Man Who Kept His Form," 1920; "A Hedonist," 1920; "Timber," 1920; "Santa Lucia," 1921; "Blackmail," 1921; "The Broken Boot," 1922; "Stroke of Lightning," 1921; "Virtue," 1922; "Conscience," 1922; "Salta Pro Nobis," 1922; "Philanthropy," 1922; "A Long-ago Affair," 1922; "Acme," 1923; "Late—299," 1923; "Had a Horse," 1923.

The White Monkey. Lond and NY, 1924.

Caravan: The Assembled Tales of John Galsworthy. Lond and NY, 1925. Contents: "Salvation of a Forsyte"; "A Stoic"; "A Portrait"; "The Grey Angel"; "Quality"; "The Man Who Kept His Form"; "The Japanese Quince"; "The Broken Boot"; "The Choice"; "Ultima Thule"; "Courage"; "The Bright Side"; "The Black Godmother"; "Philanthropy"; "A Man of Devon"; "The Apple Tree"; "The Prisoner"; "A Simple Tale"; "The Consummation"; "Acme"; "Defeat"; "Virtue"; "The Neighbours"; "Stroke of Lightning"; "Spindleberries"; "Salta Pro Nobis"; "The Pack"; " 'The Dog It Was That Died' "; "A Knight"; "The Juryman"; "Timber"; "Santa Lucia"; "The Mother Stone"; "Peace Meeting"; "A Strange Thing"; "The Nightmare Child"; "A Reversion to Type"; "Expectations"; "A Woman"; "A Hedonist"; "A Miller of Dee"; "Late—299"; "The Silence"; "A Feud"; "A Fisher of Men"; "Manna"; " 'Cafard' "; "The Recruit"; "Compensation"; "Conscience"; "Once More"; "Blackmail"; "Two Looks"; "A Long-ago Affair"; "The First and the Last"; "Had a Horse."

The Silver Spoon. Lond and NY, 1926.

Two Forsyte Interludes. Lond, 1927. NY, 1928. Contents: "A Silent Wooing"; "Passers By."

Swan Song. Lond and NY, 1928.

A Modern Comedy. Lond and NY, 1929. Contents: *The White Monkey;* "A Silent Wooing"; *The Silver Spoon;* "Passers By"; *Swan Song.*

On Forsyte 'Change. Lond and NY, 1930. Contents: "The Buckles of Superior Dosset, 1821–1863"; "Sands of Time, 1821–1863"; "Hester's Little Tour, 1845"; "Timothy's Narrow Squeak, 1851"; "Aunt Juley's Courtship, 1855"; "Nicholas-Rex, 1864"; "A Sad Affair, 1867"; "Revolt at Roger's, 1870"; "June's First Lame Duck, 1876"; "Dog at Timothy's, 1878"; "Midsummer Madness, 1880"; "The Hondekoeter, 1880"; "Cry of Peacock, 1883"; "Francie's Fourpenny Foreigner, 1888"; "Four-in-Hand Forsyte, 1890"; "The Sorrows of Tweetyman, 1895"; "The Dromios, 1900"; "A Forsyte Encounters the People, 1917"; "Soames and the Flag, 1914–1918."

Maid in Waiting. Lond and NY, 1931.

Flowering Wilderness. Lond and NY, 1932.

Forsytes, Pendyces and Others. Lond and NY, 1933. Contents: "Danaë," 1905–1906; "Water," 1924; "A Patriot," 1927; "Told by the Schoolmaster," 1925; "The Smile," 1922; "The Black Coat," 1926; "The Mummy," *ca.* 1924; "The Gibbet," 1914–1918; "The Doldrums," 1895–1896; "Memorable Moments," *ca.* 1920; NOTES ON FELLOW-WRITERS PAST AND PRESENT: "Tributes to Conrad: ['Address Given at Warsaw and Cracow'], 1930; 'Preface to Conrad's Plays,' 1924; "Homage to Anatole France," 1924; "John Masefield and His Narrative Poems," 1912; "Note on 'The Portrait of a Lady' "; "Preface to 'Green Mansions'," 1915; "Note on W. H. Hudson," 1924; "Note on Edward Garnett," 1914; "Foreword to 'Jeanne D'Arc,' (Play by Edward Garnett)" *ca.* 1928; "Note on Meggie Albanesi," 1924; "Note on R. B. Cunninghame Graham"; "Foreword to 'The Assembled Tales of Stacy Aumonier' "; "Preface to 'The Spanish Farm,' (R. H. Mottram) 1924; "Introduction to 'Bleak House,' (Waverley Edition [Charles Dickens]) 1912; "Preface to 'Anna Karenina,' (Centenary Edition [Leo Tolstoi]) 1926; "The Great Tree," 1915; FOUR DRAMATIC PIECES: "The Winter Garden," *ca.* 1908; ESCAPE, Episode VII, 'The Foxhunter,' 1926; "The Golden Eggs," 1925–26; "Similes," 1932.

Over the River (American Title, *One More River*) Lond and NY, 1933.

End of the Chapter. NY, 1934. Lond, 1935. Contents: *Maid in Waiting, Flowering Wilderness; Over the River.*

B. COLLECTED EDITIONS

The Works of John Galsworthy. Lond, 1921–1925. 18 vols. (called Popular Edition; also known as the Uniform Edition.)

The Works of John Galsworthy. The Manaton Edition. NY, 1922–1936; Lond, 1923–1936. 30 vols.

The Novels, Tales, and Plays of John Galsworthy. Devon Edition. NY, 1926–1927. 18 vols.

The Works of John Galsworthy. Grove Edition. Lond, 1927–1934. 24 vols.

Works. Compact Edition. NY, 1929. 6 vols.

Works. Nobel Prize Edition. NY, 1934. 7 vols.

II. ESSAYS, SATIRES, AND MISCELLANEOUS WRITINGS

A Sheaf. Lond and NY, 1916. Contents: MUCH CRY—LITTLE WOOL: "On the Treatment of Animals"; "Concerning Laws"; "On Prisons and Punishment"; "On the Position of Women"; "On Social Unrest"; "On Peace"; THE WAR: "Valley of the Shadow"; "Credo"; "France"; "Reveille"; "First

Thoughts on this War"; "The Hope of Lasting Peace"; "Diagnosis of the Englishman"; "Our Literature and the War"; "Art and the War"; "Tre Cime di Lavaredo"; "Second Thoughts on this War"; "Totally Disabled"; "Cartoon"; "Harvest"; AND—AFTER?: "Prelude"; "Freedom and Privilege"; "The Nation and Training"; "Health, Humanity, and Procedure"; "A Last Word"; "The Islands of the Blessed."

Another Sheaf. Lond and NY, 1919. Contents: "The Road"; "The Sacred Work"; "Balance Sheet of the Soldier Workman"; "The Jewel Fund"; "Impressions of France, 1916–17"; "Englishman and Russian"; "American and Briton"; "The Drama in England and America"; "Speculations"; "The Land, 1917"; "The Land, 1918"; "Grotesques."

Addresses in America. Lond and NY, 1919. Contents: "At the Lowell Centenary"; "American and Briton"; "From a Speech at the Lotus Club, New York"; "From a Speech to the Society of Arts and Societies, New York"; "Address at Columbia University"; "To the League of Political Education, New York"; "Talking at Large."

International Thought. Cambridge, Eng., 1923.

Abracadabra and Other Satires. Lond, 1924. Contents: "Abracadabra"; "The Voice of ——!"; "A Simple Tale"; "Ultima Thule"; "Studies of Extravagance"; "For Love of Beasts"; "Reverie of a Sportsman"; "Grotesques."

On Expression. Lond, 1924.

Castles in Spain and Other Screeds. Lond and NY, 1927. Contents: "Castles in Spain. An Address," 1920; "Where We Stand," 1920; "International Thought," 1923; "On Expression. An Address," 1924; "Reminiscences of Conrad," 1924; "Time, Tides, and Tastes," 1925; "Foreword to 'Green Mansions'," 1915; "A Note on Sentiment," 1922; "Preface to Conrad's Plays," 1924; "Burning Leaves," 1921; "After Seeing a Play," 1903; "Six Novelists in Profile. An Address," 1924; " 'Books as Ambassadors' " 1924; "Faith of a Novelist," 1926.

A Rambling Discourse. Lond, 1929.

The Creation of Character in Literature. The Romanes Lecture, 21 May 1931. Oxford, 1931.

Literature and Life. Princeton, NJ, 1931.

Candelabra: Selected Essays and Addresses. Lond, 1932; NY, 1933. Contents: "Some Platitudes Concerning Drama"; "Vague Thoughts on Art"; "Meditation on Finality"; "Diagnosis of the Englishman"; "France, 1916–1917. An Impression"; "Speculations"; "Castles in Spain. An Address"; "A Note on Sentiment"; "Six Novelists in Profile: An Address"; "International Thought"; "On Expression: An Address"; "Reminiscences of Conrad"; "Books as Ambassadors"; "Time, Tides, and Taste"; "Faith of a Novelist"; "Four More Novelists in Profile: An Address"; "Literature and Life: An Address"; "The Creation of Character in Literature: Romanes Lecture: 1931."

III. DRAMA
A. SEPARATE WORKS

The Silver Box. Lond, 1910.
Joy. Lond, 1910.
Strife. Lond, 1910.
Justice. Lond and NY, 1910.
The Little Dream. Lond and NY, 1911.
The Eldest Son. Lond and NY, 1912.
The Pigeon. Lond and NY, 1912.
The Fugitive. Lond, 1913.
The Mob. Lond and NY, 1914.
A Bit O' Love. Lond and NY, 1915.
The Foundations. Lond and NY, 1920.
The Skin Game. Lond and NY, 1920.
Loyalties. Lond, 1922.
A Family Man. Lond and NY, 1922.
Windows. Lond, 1922.
The Forest. Lond and NY, 1924.
Old English. Lond, 1924; NY, 1925.
The Show. Lond and NY, 1925.
Escape. Lond, 1926.
Exiled. Lond, 1929.
The Roof. Lond, 1929; NY, 1931.

B. COLLECTED EDITIONS

Plays: The Silver Box; Joy; Strife. NY and Lond, 1909.
Plays. Second Series: The Eldest Son; The Little Dream; Justice. Lond, 1912; NY, 1913.
Plays. Third Series: The Fugitive; The Pigeon; The Mob. Lond and NY, 1914.
Plays. Fourth Series: A Bit O' Love; The Foundations; The Skin Game. Lond and NY, 1920.
Six Short Plays. Lond and NY, 1921. Contents: "The First and the Last" [adaptation of the short story], 1917; "The Little Man," 1913; "Hall-marked," 1913; "Defeat," 1917; "The Sun," 1918; "Punch and Go," 1920.
Plays. Fifth Series: A Family Man; Loyalties; Windows. Lond, 1922; NY, 1923.
Plays. Sixth Series: The Forest; Old English; The Show. Lond, 1925; NY, 1926.
Plays. Seventh Series: Escape; Exiled; The Roof. Lond, 1930.
Four Dramatic Pieces, first published in *Forsytes, Pendyces and Others.* Lond and NY, 1933. Contents: "The Winter Garden," *ca.* 1908; *Escape,* Episode VII, "The Foxhunter," 1926; "The Golden Eggs," 1925–1926; "Similes," 1932.

IV. POETRY

Moods, Songs and Doggerels. Lond and NY, 1912.
The Bells of Peace. Lond, 1921.
Verses New and Old. Lond and NY, 1926.
Collected Poems of John Galsworthy. NY, 1934.

V. LETTERS

Autobiographical Letters of John Galsworthy: A Correspondence with Frank Harris. NY, 1933.
Letters from John Galsworthy, 1900–1932. Edited and introduction by Edward Garnett. Lond and NY, 1934.
My Galsworthy Story, by Margaret Morris; introduction by Marjorie Deans. Lond, 1967.
John Galsworthy's Letters to Leon Lion, ed. and annotated by Asher Boldon Wilson. The Hague, 1968. Studies in English Literature, XV.

Introduction

In contrast to many of the writers who are the subjects of other volumes in this series of annotated secondary bibliographies, the situation of John Galsworthy is singular. For the other writers, a major emphasis in the review of the scholarship focuses on what has already been well done. In Galsworthy's case, however, the review of the scholarship indicates that major concern must be on what yet needs to be done. In his own time he earned a worldwide reputation as a novelist, dramatist, and humanitarian; as a matter of fact it is a cliché of Galsworthy criticism that he won the Nobel Prize in 1932 at least as much because of who he was as because of what he had written. Galsworthy's fall from grace has probably been more spectacular than that of any other famous writer of the early twentieth century. One suspects that no other writer of comparable stature has been the subject of so few in-depth studies over the past four decades. What is disturbing is not that he has been dutifully ignored since his death in 1933; it is, rather, that he has often been mentioned but seldom read critically. There appears to be no sensible, compelling reason why this critical neglect should continue.

A brief review of the five principal reasons for the continuing critical indifference by many to Galsworthy's work may help to clear the air and thereby establish a better perspective or basis for the overdue reassessment of his work and its importance.

First, the criticisms of his work have been intoxicatingly contradictory. Beginning in 1897 when he published *From the Four Winds,* and continuing throughout his career, reactions have been mixed and often antithetical. He has been faulted for being too Forsytean and for failing to understand what the Forsytes are really like; for being too fanciful and too realistic or naturalistic; for being too sensitive or too insensitive; for being too sensual and too coldly objective in portraying human emotions; and for being too compassionate and too coldly calculating. The sorting out of these Procrustean dicta is still to be done.

Second, Virginia Woolf and D. H. Lawrence were enormously influential in shaping modern literary values, and they both found reasons for relegating John Galsworthy's work to the dustheap. Mrs. Woolf's ex cathedra dismissal, in 1924, of his work as materialistic and propagandistic found ready acceptance. Her assessment, which was published in the essay "Mr. Bennett and Mrs. Brown," was originally a lecture presented to the Heretics Club at Cambridge; she faulted the work of Galsworthy, H. G. Wells, and Arnold Bennett by saying that these authors never looked at the characters in their novels, "never at life, never at human nature." According to her, they were content to enumerate the surface realities and accept the superficial. The oversimplification is of course extreme, and she admitted as much in the apologia that went with her attempt to present an invigorating challenge to her audience. Some four years later, D. H. Lawrence published in *Scrutinies* his essay disposing of Galsworthy once and for all. Although the Forsytes of *The Forsyte Saga* are human enough, they are not, Lawrence asserts, vividly so. Galsworthy's characters are social beings without a free soul among them. There is a doggishness in his treatment of passion that deteriorates into the "nastily sentimental." His later novels have sold only because of his earlier work; John Galsworthy is, in fact, actually a cynic.

To be sure, Lawrence and Woolf were asserting their independence from the older forms of the novel and from the older established novelists, but the gap between the Edwardians and the Georgians seems to have been more than an ordinary generation gap. It seems likely that the cataclysm of World War I divided the past, with its values and traditions, from the present—the modern, the new, the different, the experimental, and the shocking—in ways that accentuated the differences and thus made the break particularly decisive. Human nature did not change, as Mrs. Woolf had claimed, but the artist's perceptions of it had. The artistic worlds of Joyce, Woolf, Lawrence, and their successors were exciting and modern, and by comparison Galsworthy's work seemed terribly old-fashioned.

Third, "old-fashioned" is quite probably an accurate term to apply to Galsworthy's work. In his writings he followed generally in the footsteps of the major Victorians; his philosophy was most fully embodied in the humanitarian and courtly ideals of the gentleman; moreover, his work was limited in range and subject matter. The worlds of the gentleman, of the oppressed unhappy wife, and of the ineffectual intellectual did not seem really important in the 1920s when works like *Ulysses, Jacob's Room, The Waste Land,* and *Women in Love* were breaking new ground.

Fourth, Galsworthy's reputation depended on his role as a literary gadfly. His work was seen by many as essentially that of a reforming reporter, a sociological photographer, and a critic of society. His success lay in his stirring things up and in the various reforms he suggested. Accordingly, as society changed and reforms were made, Galsworthy's works lost their value except as quaint tidbits for social historians. *The Man of Property,* so this argument goes, became irrelevant when the divorce laws were changed to allow women like Irene to free themselves from incompatible, hopeless marriages.

Fifth, Galsworthy's reputation in his own time was so inflated that when the inevitable reaction set in, the dismissal of his work, by way of compensation, was carried to the other extreme and has continued for more than forty years.

This discussion of the several reasons for the continued lack of serious interest in Galsworthy has concentrated on the unfavorable, and perhaps not always valid, judgments about his artistic merits. Such a view is obviously too limiting, too one-sided. There are many positive aspects to his work that must not be overlooked. In 1933, for instance, most of the approximately 150 items that appeared emphasized various positive aspects of his work.

Henry Seidel Canby's "Galsworthy: An Estimate" in the *Saturday Review of Literature* (NY) is typical. To Canby, Galsworthy was "liberal, [an] intellectual aristocrat, spiritual, sensitive, humanitarian, proud," who presented a "bourgeois aristocracy" that modified old codes of behavior while keeping responsibility to state, class, chivalry, and duty. He was, Canby continues, a great realist in the way realism really mattered to early twentieth-century England. He was especially popular on the Continent because he expressed the "living explanations of what England was in the period of her dominating greatness," and because those on the Continent recognized that his work, despite faults of sentiment and diffuseness, was epic in scope. Galsworthy gave to his readers the "moral meaning of a generation." Like most critics Canby preferred Galsworthy's novels to his dramas. The theater did not give Galsworthy enough room; he was best "pageant-wise, not drama-wise"; his strength was in the slow tenacity of descriptive narration, not in quick symbols or isolated events.

Between 1933 and the mid-1960s there was little significant, new critical insight into the works of Galsworthy; but perceptions appear to be gradually and tentatively changing. Within recent years some of the assumptions made by Woolf and Lawrence and their followers have come to be reexamined and challenged. Sufficient time has passed so that the term "old-fashioned" when applied to things Victorian need no longer be automatically damning. In 1964 Evelyn Waugh, in commenting on *The Man of Property,* observed that property usurps the traditional role of the Greek Nemesis in Soames's life, thereby affirming Professor Gilbert Murray's 1922 comment that Galsworthy's "queer poetical method . . . simulates realism in order to attain beauty." In his introductory essay to *The Galsworthy Reader* (1967), Anthony West noted the close interrelationship between Galsworthy's life and a psychological interpretation of his work. Much earlier André Chevrillon *(Trois Études de la Littérature Anglaise,* 1921) had perceptively studied some of the psychological implications found in the novels. A careful and complete exploration of the psychological implications in Galsworthy's works is yet to be done, despite the lengthy discussions of several of the novels in William Bellamy's *The Novels of Wells, Bennett, and Galsworthy 1890–1910* (1971).

For the past two decades the strongest interest in Galsworthy has been found in the countries of eastern Europe, especially in the Soviet Union. One of the main reasons for his popularity in the USSR is the fact that the government allows Galsworthy's novels to be printed there. Access to Galsworthy was greatly enhanced by the appearance in 1962 of the sixteen-volume translation into Russian of Galsworthy's works by M. Lorie. Typical of the reaction of Russian critics to Galsworthy is N. D'iakanova's *Dzohn Golsuorsi: 1867–1933*

(1960), the thesis of which is that Galsworthy condemned the cruelty of the capitalistic leaders and foresaw the coming destruction of the old order. D. Zhantieva's article in *Literaturnaia Gazeta* (1967) emphasized, as had D'iakanaova, that Galsworthy attacked a bourgeois society that was paralyzed by complacency and privileged stability.

It was inevitable that the advent of the Galsworthy centenary and the impact of the BBC's televised version of *The Forsyte Saga* would arouse a great deal of attention. The success of the television series led in sound Forsyte fashion to a number of reprints of the volumes of the *Saga*. In England alone, from the time the series began until 1971, some 1,300,000 volumes of the Forsyte novels were sold. Although the series enjoyed worldwide success, the critical comments generated by the Forsytes were conventional and unoriginal. The clichés of old wives were taken out of mothballs for the occasions at hand.

Up to this point consideration has been given to Galsworthy's career as a novelist, but he was also a successful and highly competent playwright. Of Galsworthy as dramatist, Allardyce Nicoll, in *World Drama from Aeschylus to Anouilh* (1950), wrote that Galsworthy outdistances Pinero and Jones in dramatic power because of his "perfect mastery of naturalism . . . compassionate depiction of humanity . . . [and] fine humanitarianism of spirit." Albert Edward Wilson, in *Edwardian Theatre* (1951), emphasized Galsworthy's importance to the Vedrenne-Barker management of the Court Theatre. Lynton Alfred Hudson, in *The English Stage: 1850–1950* (1951), has argued that among English dramatists Galsworthy is the first to achieve "complete realism" in his dramatic presentations. More recently, J. William Miller, in *Modern Playwrights at Work* (1968), called Galsworthy a "master of naturalism," and Allardyce Nicoll, in *English Drama: A Modern Viewpoint* (1968), has argued that Galsworthy is really more Brechtian than Brecht and deserves to be studied more seriously than he has been by modern playwrights.

By their very nature, the abstracts and annotations given in this volume are unable to indicate fully the methods of the various critics involved in the study of Galsworthy, and they do not always indicate the depth with which the texts of the novels and dramas have been studied. With relatively few exceptions in the criticism of the past forty years, evidence of close textual analysis of Galsworthy's works simply does not exist, except perhaps in some of the unpublished doctoral dissertations. Thus what is needed is a renewed critical study or studies based on close textual analysis which will examine the extent to which the generalities of Galsworthy criticism are valid, and which will explore anew the ways in which Galsworthy speaks in light of the developments in criticism of the past forty years.

Some of the directions such studies need to take are as follows: a new biography; a look at what Galsworthy did, rather than what another writer handling the same material might have done; a new study of Galsworthy's critical theory and of his reputation as an essayist; a critical analysis of the novels to see precisely how he created the effects that he did; and a reexamination of his contributions to the drama, especially in the light of the dramas of the 1960s and 1970s, much of which seem to have developed in ways similar to Galsworthy's both in production and theme.

When a restudy of Galsworthy has been completed, and his faults properly deplored—his poor paragraph construction in the novel, his aggravating habit of concluding some of his plays with stage directions rather than dialogue, his occasional sentimentality, his occasional lapse of stylistic control, his tendency to rely too much on the chronicling of events, his tendency to melodrama in some of his plays, his inability to come to grips in the way that Joyce did with twentieth-century methods of working with psychology, and so forth—it is most probable that Galsworthy will be found to have much of sterling worth, the worth that some critics have perceived in his writings from the beginning. Clearly Galsworthy will not oust Woolf or Lawrence from their preeminent places as masters of the English novel, or Shaw from his as dramatist, and yet his place as the last major Victorian novelist and as a provocative, compelling playwright should be secure.

The Bibliography

1897

---

1 *"From the Four Winds,"* ACADEMY (Lond), LII (17 July 1897),
Fiction Supplement, 35.

In *From the Four Winds,* the author is "violent, cosmopolitan, knowing"; he
tries to catch up with Kipling in his blend of "smoking-room ethics and Imperialism." "The Running Amok of Synge Sahib" is a "good idea," and
"Tally-ho-Budmâsh" is a "perfect gem . . . delightful from beginning to end."

2 "Novel Notes: *From the Four Winds,*" BOOKMAN (Lond), XII (July
1897), 101.

"Tally-ho-Budmâsh" is a story quite as bad as Kipling's tales of child life in
India.

1898

---

3 *"Jocelyn,"* OUTLOOK (Lond), I (14 May 1898), 471.

Jocelyn, JG's *drame passionnel,* succeeds in part because the main characters in
sin are not really English: Giles Legard is an "unheroic hero" very much like
characters from D'Annunzio's romances, and Jocelyn Ley has something of the
foreign and exotic in her. JG succeeds by focusing on observation of character.
The "delightfully commonplace" Mrs. Travis and Nielson are two of the best
comic characters in recent fiction.

4 *"Jocelyn,"* SATURDAY REVIEW (Lond), LXXXVI (6 Aug 1898), 184.

Jocelyn is above the "common run of fiction." It is a "comedy of manners and a
melodrama worked out with some psychological insight. The principal characters are scarcely more than . . . introspective phantoms" somewhat in the
Henry James manner. JG "puts light insight, [and] humor" into his "stale
materials."

17

1899

[No entries for this year.]

1900

5 *"Villa Rubein,"* ACADEMY (Lond), LIX (3 Nov 1900), Fiction Supplement, 420.
JG demonstrates a "clean, nervous style, and an eye for character" in *Villa Rubein*. [Brief notice of publication.]

6 *"Villa Rubein,"* ATHENAEUM (Lond), No. 3813 (24 Nov 1900), 680.
Villa Rubein is well-written, with a "force and directness . . . [that] outweigh some crudity in . . . method." Mr. Treffrey is convincingly portrayed. Female characters do not have any particular charm; male characters are better drawn, but with too much of the grotesque about them to be totally attractive.

1901

7 *"A Man of Devon,"* ACADEMY (Lond), LXI (26 Oct 1901), 386.
[Brief notice of publication, listing only the titles of the four stories.]

8 *"A Man of Devon,"* ATHENAEUM (Lond), No. 3865 (23 Nov 1901), 697.
"The Salvation of Swithin Forsyte" is superior to other stories in *A Man of Devon*. "Salvation" is grimly lifelike, with suggestions of a "visionary and dual nature of life" to counterbalance life's grimmer realities. JG is superior in this respect to some other realists. [The reviewer does not identify the other realists.]

9 *"A Man of Devon,"* GRAPHIC (Lond), 1901. [not seen].
The four stories of *A Man of Devon* are worthy and tragic. JG seems to borrow from Henry James in reading too much of consequence into "a glance or a trick of habit," but that results from his "insight into the infinite pathos of little things, and never blinds him to the import of the great ones." The works are a pleasure to read critically. [Cited by H. V. Marrot, THE LIFE AND LETTERS OF JOHN GALSWORTHY (Lond: Heinemann, 1935; NY: Charles Scribner's Sons, 1936), pp. 130–31.]

10 "Middling," OUTLOOK (Lond), VIII (7 Dec 1901), 639–40.
JG is more artistic and believable portraying, with a touch of Thackeray's cynicism, the "milder temperaments" of "The Salvation of Swithin Forsyte" than he is portraying the strained temperaments of the title story of *A Man of Devon*. "Devon" fails because: (1) the plot is an unhappy incident rather than a tragedy; (2) characterization is ineffective; (3) Zachary's puzzling adventure is not developed properly; and (4) JG tries too hard to capture the tempestuousness of Brönte's WUTHERING HEIGHTS.

1902

[No entries for this year.]

1903

[No entries for this year.]

1904

---

11 "Eight Novels," NATION (NY), LXXVIII (23 June 1904), 499–501.
The plotless and lengthy *Island Pharisees* is a diatribe against morality that is characterized by "cheap cynicism, labored epigram . . . unconvincing psychology," and destructive criticism.

12 "New Novels. *The Island Pharisees,*" ATHENAEUM, No. 3987 (26 March 1904), 394.
The Island Pharisees—a subtle, sincere, and occasionally humorous satire in light narrative form—emphasizes the British distrust of anything that criticizes them.

13 "Novels," SATURDAY REVIEW (Lond), XCVII (5 March 1904), 305.
A sense of comedy makes *The Island Pharisees* completely readable. The questions Shelton asks are those which most of us asked in our undergraduate days. JG "is a gentle satirist, not an iconoclast. Perhaps he takes his philosophy too seriously."

14 "Novels," SPECTATOR, XCII (16 April 1904), 608.

The hero of *The Island Pharisees* takes such a jaundiced view that he considers "the excellent commonplace people" he meets to be hypocrites. They are not hypocrites; they are bores. Even when the characters are not true to life the "interest of the story lies in the character drawing." Shelton's one intolerable fault is his lack of a sense of humor.

1905

[No entries for this year.]

1906

---

15 B., H. "Stageland," CLARION (Lond), No. 775 (12 Oct 1906), 3.

The work of the Vedrenne-Barker group at the Court Theater is enormously important because there is no pandering "to the idle diversion of bored and satiated Society." Of course, their leader is George Bernard Shaw, but there are others like Granville Barker, St. John Rankin, and now JG whose *The Silver Box* opened last week. The fashionable will find JG's play "disgustingly sordid and vulgar." The play is a gripping, moving drama without theatrical exaggeration; the one incident that is "theatrically repulsive" involves "the crying of the imprisoned charwoman's children outside the rich M. P.'s mansion."

16 B[aughan], E. A. "*The Silver Box:* A Stimulating Play at the Court Theatre," DAILY NEWS (Lond), 26 Sept 1906, p. 4.

The Silver Box has the "stuff of drama" in it despite JG's "needless disregard of the architectural side of the playwright's craft." Characters are well contrasted, and situations rise from the clash of temperaments. The police court scene has "close observation of reality." JG's impartial treatment of the inevitability of injustice theme is new; but he devotes too much time to developing unnecessary scenes.

17 Conrad, Joseph. "A Middle-Class Family," OUTLOOK (Lond), XVII (31 March 1906), 449–50; rptd in JOHN GALSWORTHY, AN APPRE-CIATION (Canterbury: pvtly ptd by H. J. Goulden, 1922); rptd in LAST ESSAYS (Garden City, NY: Doubleday, Page, 1926), pp. 125–37.

It is difficult to get a "critical hold" of *The Man of Property* because JG "gives . . . no opening." "Defending no obvious thesis, setting up no theory, offering no cheap panacea, appealing to no naked sentiment," JG "disdains also the effective device of attacking insidiously the actors of his . . . dramatic comedy." The book is "of a disconcerting honesty, backed by a discouraging skill." There is not one phrase "written for the sake of its cleverness," giving the impression of a "*willed* moderation of thought." "Its critical spirit and its impartial method are meant for a humanity which has outgrown the stage of fairy tales." JG looks at the middle-class Forsyte family with "the individual vision of a novelist seeking his inspiration among the realities of the earth." His art lies primarily in a "remarkable power of ironic insight combined with an extremely keen and faithful eye for all the phenomena on the surface of the life" that he observes. People who read *Property* will find amusement and "something more lasting if they care for it." While some will find JG disappointing, none will find him futile and uninteresting. The only difficult part to justify is Bosinney's tragedy—a minor thing "in the face of his considerable achievement."

18 "Court Theatre: *The Silver Box*," DAILY TELEGRAPH (Lond), 26 Sept 1906, p. 10.
The Silver Box portrays "stern and gaunt" realism, with photographic detail and accuracy.

19 deS., H. "Drama. Court Theatre: *The Silver Box*," ACADEMY (Lond), LXXI (29 Sept 1906), 312.
The commonplace story of *The Silver Box* is treated powerfully because of JG's use of contrasts and "savagely correct" detail. It indicts stupidity but lacks color and expansiveness.

20 "The Drama: *The Silver Box*," TIMES LITERARY SUPPLEMENT (Lond), V (28 Sept 1906), 330.
JG is a rare breed because he can dramatize facts without distorting them; the object of *The Silver Box* at the Court Theatre is "to show how circumstances alter cases." The praiseworthy drama is really an "anecdote" elevated to dramatic success by skillful use of "patiently observed, unforced detail."

21 Ellis, Anthony L. "Actors and Acting: The Price of Truth—Signs from 'Old Drury Drury'—*The Silver Box*," STAR (Lond), 26 Sept 1906, p. 1.
[Part of a tripartite review briefly commenting on the Court Theatre's production of *The Silver Box*. The plot summary emphasizes the reality of injustice.]

22 Grein, J. T. "Court: *The Silver Box*," SUNDAY TIMES (Lond), 30 Sept 1906, p. 4.
JG is a kinsman to Granville-Barker, for both are realists. A true realist like JG pays no heed to plot. The one flaw in the realism is the police-court scene "because it lacks that touch of imagination which segregates art from craft." As is usual at the Court Theatre the performances are excellent. A new playwright and acting equal to the best found on the Continent indicate that there still is life in the British theater.

23 "London Theatres. The Court," STAGE (Lond), No. 1332 (27 Sept 1906), 16.

The Silver Box is original and unconventional with traces of Ibsen. The episodic "stage silhouettes" in Act I are unconventional, but MP John Barthwick is quite conventional. [Primarily a plot-summary review of a performance.]

24 *"The Man of Property,"* ACADEMY, (Lond) LXX (31 March 1906), 309–10.

The Man of Property is an excellent work because JG takes the leaden material of the Forsyte family in its "massive unimportance" and creates separate human beings. The writing is skilled, delicate, and effortless, with excellent and distinct character drawing and narrative technique. Some vivid scenes are: Soames listening to the peacocks at dawn; George following Bosinney through the fog; Irene returning to Soames. The book has strength without sensation. JG has only two unhappy instances in *Property:* (1) he occasionally belabors the Forsytes; and (2) in one instance he mistakes brutality for strength.

25 *"The Man of Property,"* EVENING STANDARD (Lond), 1906 [not seen].

Irene in *The Man of Property* "hardly has a speaking part, but a whole tragedy lies in her silence, and in her influence over the carefully moral, well-fed animals around her." [Cited by H. V. Marrot, THE LIFE AND LETTERS OF JOHN GALSWORTHY (Lond: Heinemann, 1935; NY: Charles Scribner's Sons, 1936), p. 186.]

26 *"The Man of Property,"* OUTLOOK (NY), LXXXIV (15 Dec 1906), 941.

The Man of Property is an "unusually thoughtful novel of English social life," with sly humor and surface cynicism that emphasize generosity and high ideals.

27 *"The Man of Property,"* SCOTSMAN (Edinburgh), 1906 [not seen]. "Irene is a remarkable study in impressive silence." Even though she seldom speaks in *The Man of Property,* she always has the last word. [Cited by H. V. Marrot, THE LIFE AND LETTERS OF JOHN GALSWORTHY (Lond: Heinemann, 1935; NY: Charles Scribner's Sons, 1936), p. 186.]

28 *"The Man of Property,"* SPECTATOR (Lond), XCVI (14 April 1906), 587–88.

The Man of Property is "unacceptable for general reading" because of repellent details, which nevertheless are presented in a "cold dispassionate manner." The "instinct of self-preservation" is developed with "ruthless logic and an almost uniformly sardonic humour." JG lashes out at law and order. His remarkable talent has both geniality and dignity. [The reviewer believes that Bosinney committed suicide.]

29 *"The Man of Property,"* TIMES LITERARY SUPPLEMENT (Lond), V (30 March 1906), 116.

In *The Man of Property* JG comments rather than lets characters develop. One does not move with Irene or Soames or Bosinney; rather one watches as a member of the Forsyte family. "Hero, heroine, and villain are all one" to the Forsyte family's point of view. The novel ends, perhaps unnecessarily, a "little brutally." *Property* is a new type of novel, showing thought, determination, and alertness.

30 "New Novels. *The Man of Property,"* ATHENAEUM, No. 4094 (14 April 1906), 446.

The Man of Property is an intelligent, sound, and equable work, worth rereading. Plot is subservient to characterization and precise pictures.

31 "Novel Notes: *The Man of Property,"* BOOKMAN (Lond), XXX (June 1906), 116.

The Man of Property is "unquestionably a brilliant book." It has characterization, wit, subtlety, literary charm; but it lacks vitality. The erring wife and her lover are "insupportably tiresome." JG "is happier in his cynical portraiture of the Forsyth [*sic*] family."

32 Pierre. "The Diary of a Playgoer: *The Silver Box,"* VANITY FAIR (Lond), 3 Oct 1906, p. 445.

The Silver Box, despite its lack of traditional drama, interests the audience because "real-life" people are interesting—and that is the key to JG's success.

33 "Portrait of Galsworthy," CRITIC (NY), XLIX (Sept 1906), 202–3.

[Unattributed photo with notice of favorable reception of *The Man of Property.*]

34 Rambler. "A New Dramatist: *The Silver Box* at the Court Theatre," EVENING NEWS (Lond), 26 Sept 1906, p. 5.

JG detests middle-class shams and sympathizes with the poor. He maintains interest in *The Silver Box* through clearly drawn characters and lively dialogue.

35 *"The Silver Box.* A Real Comedy Admirably Acted," DAILY MAIL (Lond), 26 Sept 1906, p. 5.

The Silver Box at the Court Theatre delights with its truth, humor, restraint, and "sympathetic studies of the poor." The "slight story" written in the "minor key" is not suitable for a large theater. Satire is less important than the genuine drawing of characters from life.

36 *"The Silver Box:* A Triumph of Realism at the Court Theatre," EVENING STANDARD AND ST. JAMES'S GAZETTE (Lond), 26 Sept 1906, p. 5.

The realistic *Silver Box* has very unheroic protagonists in the Joneses.

37 *"The Silver Box* at the Court," DAILY GRAPHIC (Lond), 27 Sept 1906, p. 13.

The Silver Box is a "curiously interesting and well-written" study of high and low life.

38 *"The Silver Box* at the Court," ILLUSTRATED LONDON NEWS, CXXIX (6 Oct 1906), 467.

The Silver Box is an artistically treated slice of life, showing genuine stage instinct. [The brief review primarily states the theme of *Box.*]

39 *"The Silver Box:* Interesting New Play by Clever Novelist at Court Theatre Matinees," DAILY MIRROR (Lond), 26 Sept 1906, p. 6.

JG's biting wit in the "original and entertaining" *Silver Box* deprecates the middle classes.

40 *"The Silver Box:* Mr. Galsworthy's Comedy at the Court Theatre," STANDARD (Lond), 26 Sept 1906, p. 5.

The court scene of *The Silver Box* is one of the most realistic ever seen on the stage. JG is "faintly ironic concerning the law, strongly satiric in his dramatic comparison of the Philistine Barthwicks with the Barbarian Joneses."

41 *"The Silver Box:* New Dramatist's Experiment in Realism at the Court," DAILY CHRONICLE (Lond), 26 Sept 1906, p. 6.

The Silver Box tries to be earnest, clever, realistic, unsensational, and moral— "altogether different from ordinary, cheap, conventional melodrama." The action, however, is "simply preposterous": melodramatic plays are more interesting because of the dullness of the scenes within the MP's home. The unhappy ending is untrue, inconclusive, and unsatisfactory.

42 Vengerova, Z. "J. Galsworthy, *The Man of Property,*" VESTNIK EVROPY (St. Petersburg and Leningrad), IX (Sept 1906), 407–15 [not seen].

[Review of *The Man of Property.*] [In Russian.]

43 W., J. *"The Silver Box* at the Court Theatre," WESTMINSTER GAZETTE (Lond), 26 Sept 1906, p. 2.

[The plot-summary review of the performance emphasizes JG's photographic sense of realism.]

44 Wylie, J. "Royal Court Theatre: *The Silver Box,*" SPEAKER, XV (6 Oct 1906), 8–9.

JG's art in *The Silver Box* is a "marvel of careful and accurate observation," an "intellectual joy," that fascinates with its "quiet unobtrusive realism"; but he strains credulity with the magistrate's gentle treatment of the MP's son in the witness box. The actors, especially Irene Rooke and Norman McKinnell, are excellent.

1907

45 B[aughan], E. A. "Inconclusive Play. John Galsworthy's *Joy* at the Savoy," DAILY NEWS (Lond), 25 Sept 1907, p. 8.

The real drama of *Joy* never gets expressed because JG tries too hard to capture a certain type of English society, frittering away the chance for good drama: a whole act is devoted to developing an atmosphere that a great dramatist could have created immediately. *Joy* "strikes a very unpleasant dissonance. . . . it is inconclusive, vague, and . . . extraordinary in its dullness." Although his minor characters are alive, he has not succeeded in handling a subtle theme.

46 Beerbohm, Max. "At the Savoy Theatre," SATURDAY REVIEW (Lond), CIV (28 Sept 1907), 389–90.

Joy, despite its fertile theme, falls short of greatness because JG fails to interpret as well as to portray: his art fails to portray significance.

47 Cecil, George. "Stage Vanities: *Joy,*" VANITY FAIR (Lond), LXXIX (2 Oct 1907), 430.

JG's aim in *Joy,* now playing at the Savoy Theatre, is to write advanced views on marital infidelity. The play stops rather than concludes.

48 "Comment on Current Books," OUTLOOK (NY), LXXXVI (1 June 1907), 254–56.

In the "clever" *Country House* JG conveys a "convincing impression of the almost unconscious, impelling, noble power" that moves Mrs. Pendyce amid the distasteful complications of her life.

49 Cooper, Frederic Taber. "The Fallacy of Tendencies in Fiction," FORUM (NY), XXXIX (July 1907), 110–20.

The Country House follows the best tradition of fictional realism, focusing on a local domestic problem but going beyond to detail the disruption of the established social order. George Pendyce's complicity in a divorce suit is portrayed with indulgent irony, human understanding, and mastery of fictional technique.

50 Cooper, Frederick Taber. "The Social Fabric and Some Recent Novels," BOOKMAN (NY), XXV (July 1907), 497–98.

JG, one of the few contemporary British novelists taking fiction seriously, is producing works that are in the "finer sense criticisms of life." *The Country House* says much in brief but precise and illuminating phrases.

51 *"The Country House,"* ACADEMY, (Lond) LXXII (9 March 1907), 251.

The Country House has qualities of greatness, but is not great. JG's "taint of personal bitterness . . . blunts the fine edge of irony." Mrs. Pendyce is the most interesting character because her human instincts have not been strangled by the "tentacles of tradition." JG falsifies balance in favor of Mrs. Pendyce, while he is unfair to the "stupid and coarse" George. A tendency to bitterness and sentimentality blemishes an otherwise well-written novel.

52 *"The Country House,"* CATHOLIC WORLD, LXXXV (Aug 1907), 680.

The Country House excels in the depiction of traditional prejudices and types portraying them, not in the development of individual characters. JG's observations are tolerant, with a touch of "kindly cynicism." [Brief review.]

53 *"The Country House,"* NATION (NY), LXXXIV (2 May 1907), 414–15.

The Country House satirically and humorously treats the themes of entail and primogeniture in the evolution of character. Setting and atmosphere suggest Thackeray, Trollope, and other "stable English writers." The interesting novel comments on divorce laws, treatment of animals, and—with a "certain hostility"—the rights of the landed gentry. Development is workmanlike, with "brisk, competent narrative" and description.

54 *"The Country House,"* NEW YORK TIMES SATURDAY REVIEW OF BOOKS AND ART, 20 July 1907, p. 451.

The Pendyces, the rector, Vergil, and Paramor are admirably portrayed but too minutely described. [The review of *The Country House* concentrates solely on characterization.]

55 *"The Country House,"* SATURDAY REVIEW (Lond), CIII (6 April 1907), 433.

JG fails to sustain the cross-section of England promised in the first chapters of *The Country House;* his chief characteristics are deft drawing, impressionistic touches, and swift dramatic definition.

56 *"The Country House,"* SPECTATOR (Lond), XCVIII (30 March 1907), 503–4.

The Country House should be praised because JG makes some concessions to public taste in avoiding scandal and averting catastrophe. JG likes to present systems; here the system is the domestic, patriarchal tyrant, Pendyce. Mrs. Pendyce is a "crypto-Bohemian," on whom the story centers because of her "unexpected self-assertion" and "tenacity." Mrs. Pendyce's "powerful and impressive" story is told with a "cold and mordant irony." The spaniel is adorable.

57 *"The Country House,"* TIMES LITERARY SUPPLEMENT (Lond), VI (8 March 1907), 77.

JG writes about one of the varieties of the wealthy classes in *The Country House,* focusing on Pendyce, the self-satisfied country gentleman who, unaware of his own unreality, is the passive recipient of wealth and misfortune. The siren Mrs. Bellew, a "mere means of exposing the futility of others," does not really live. Mrs. Pendyce reacts to society through feeling rather than thought or action. The well-written novel "stops short" rather than ends, when all but Mrs. Pendyce are proven incapable of acting. Plot loses symmetry as Mrs. Pendyce emerges as the strongest character.

58 "The Current Plays," THEATRE MAGAZINE (NY), VII (April 1907), 114.
The scrubwoman in *The Silver Box* (at the Empire Theatre) is completely unimaginative; Ethel Barrymore as Mrs. Jones is unequal to the task of playing a pathetic and stupid woman. [Reviewer disputes JG's contention that the poor and distressed are necessarily unimaginative.]

59 "A Doubtful *Joy:* Mr. Galsworthy's New Play at the Savoy," EVENING STANDARD AND ST. JAMES'S GAZETTE (Lond), 25 Sept 1907, p. 4.
The title *Joy* is sardonic and cynical; the lack of dramatic construction is apparent; and some of the episodes are tedious. The success of the play comes in character development, especially that of the minor ones.

60 Dunbar, Olivia Howard. "New Books Reviewed. *The Country House,"* NORTH AMERICAN REVIEW, CLXXXV (2 Aug 1907), 777–80.
JG's portraits are "almost precise literary equivalents of good cartoons—strong, eloquent strokes, relentlessly unflattering, indisputably true and . . . unambiguous." English society in *The Country House* is depicted uncompromisingly and unsentimentally through a series of brilliant impressions without great depth, except for the characterization of Mrs. Pendyce. Quotable epithets abound, and, although the style is occasionally choppy, the overall effect is of sturdiness and power. JG's permanent value will be assured when his characters develop greater consciousness and greater unity.

61 E., A. L. "Savoy Theatre, *Joy,"* STAR (Lond), 25 Sept 1907, p. 1.
Joy is "extremely unsatisfying." The theme demands virile treatment, but JG "moves delicately, politely, his voice pitched to a shrill feminine 'Yellow-book' note" that is inappropriate. The successful method of *The Silver Box* is not suited to *Joy.* Despite weakness of "dialogue and action, there are subtleties of characterization worthy of the author at his best."

62 Fyfe, H. Hamilton. "The Theatre: Mr. Galsworthy's *Joy,"* WORLD (Lond), 1 Oct 1907, p. 544.
There is nothing in *Joy* "to awaken emotion, to stimulate thought, to quicken the pulses." JG is not "really real," just real enough to be tedious. His characters, fine for novels, fail on the stage. [Fyfe's condescending plot summary gives little substance to back up the detrimental comments.]

63 Grein, J. T. "Savoy: *Joy,*" SUNDAY TIMES (Lond), 29 Sept 1907, p. 4.

JG's *Man of Property* and *The Silver Box* make him one of our best authors, but *Joy* is an error. The theme overtaxed JG's strength, and the labored acting of Dorothy Minto as Joy was not an asset. Comedy is a misnomer, but perhaps JG was thinking of French *Comédie,* a term which is much broader in meaning.

64 H., K. "*Joy:* Ladylike Entertainment at Savoy Theatre," DAILY MAIL (Lond), 25 Sept 1907, p. 2.

Joy is "child's play—a flimsy, emasculate, tea-party concoction." JG spends too much time drawing character, forgetting the necessity to make every word have bearing on the story.

65 Hueffer, Ford Madox [Ford Madox Ford]. "Literary Portraits: Mr. John Galsworthy," TRIBUNE (NY), 10 Aug 1907, p. 2.

The English suspect the novel of being useless and a waste of time. Hypothetically, a novel could have sociological value and yet be written so as to give pleasure: e.g., JG's work. JG is a typical Englishman. He became atypical by thinking for himself and by turning to writing. He apprenticed himself to French and Russian literary models until with *Villa Rubein* he showed "signs of having achieved method, style, construction—Art, in fact." But his being English will guarantee that he will use his art for the betterment of society. "The artist is a simple collector, collecting effects as another man collects cigar labels. Mr. Galsworthy is a man of enthusiasms and indignations." He has wisely turned to drama, a form which is better suited to the presentation of his indignations. The "value of his novels as Art" may be less, but his method "does tremendously help them as sociological sidelights. Hence our great pleasure at finding that an artist so careful as Mr. Galsworthy can yet find such a very considerable public."

66 "*Joy* at the Savoy," ILLUSTRATED LONDON NEWS, CXXXI (28 Sept 1907), 438.

One leaves *Joy* asking "What has happened?" Its great possibilities are only partly realized—a disappointment after the success of *The Silver Box*. [Review of performance.]

67 "*Joy* at the Savoy: New Comedy by Mr. John Galsworthy," DAILY CHRONICLE (Lond), 25 Sept 1907, p. 6.

Joy is just another inconclusive treatment of the mother–child–lover triangle that leaves too many unresolved threads. Like *The Silver Box, Joy* has merit in the quiet unstrained observation of the middle class. The love scene between Joy and her beau is "daringly silly" and refreshing enough to relieve the tension of the last act.

68 "*Joy* at the Savoy. Vedrenne-Barker Matinées," DAILY GRAPHIC (Lond), 25 Sept 1907, p. 3.

Joy is "commendably brief, exceeding slight, and . . . not very entertaining." The faults of *The Silver Box,* but not the merits, are developed in *Joy.*

69 "Literature: Three English Novels," INDEPENDENT (NY), LXIII (11 July 1907), 96–97.

The Country House is better constructed and better written than either *The Island Pharisees* or *The Man of Property:* its plot, apparently slight, in reality is firm and of close texture. Each character study is carefully developed.

70 "London Theatres: The Savoy," STAGE (Lond), 26 Sept 1907, p. 16.

The comedy *Joy* mixes sentimentality and cynicism. Miss Beech is decidedly the most happily drawn and performed character.

71 McCarthy, Desmond. THE COURT THEATRE, 1904–1907; A COMMENTARY AND CRITICISM (Lond: A. H. Bullen, 1907); ed by Stanley Weintraub, and rptd (Coral Gables, Fla: University of Miami P, 1966), p. 22.

The Silver Box attacks social injustice by showing how rich and poor people commit the same crime, the rich son going free, the poor workman being punished. The merit of the play lies in the "complex exactness of the parallel between the two cases"; the parallel is so carefully drawn that the moral does not occur to the spectator until the last act, which is the "highest compliment" that can be paid to a "play with a purpose."

72 Melville, Lewis. "Some New British Novelists," NEW YORK TIMES SATURDAY REVIEW OF BOOKS AND ART, 15 June 1907, p. 394.

JG's psychological novels *The Man of Property* and *The Country House* are admirable in style, incisive in humor, and splendid in descriptions of unpleasant characters; but JG lacks tenderness. The satirist's theme is pursued admirably and inexorably. JG will influence other writers.

73 "Mr. Galsworthy's New Play. *Joy* at the Savoy Theatre," MANCHESTER GUARDIAN, 25 Sept 1907, p. 6.

JG attempts the "illusion of reality" in *Joy,* but his realism only chronicles "some very small beer." Some theatrical tricks are cheap; Joy's love scene is the best in an interesting but artificial play.

74 "Mr. Galsworthy's New Play: Mines and Morals at the Savoy," PALL MALL GAZETTE (Lond), 25 Sept 1907, p. 9.

The preliminaries of *Joy* are leisurely enough, but when the real business of the play comes along, the playgoer is not prepared for it. [Primarily a plot summary review.]

75 "Mr. John Galsworthy," BOOKMAN (Lond), XXXII (Aug 1907), 154–56.

[Short, general biographical sketch in *"The Bookman* Gallery" series.]

76 "Mr. John Galsworthy's *Joy,*" NATION (Lond), I (28 Sept 1907), 1085–86.

JG fails to present the characters of *Joy* clearly enough to be understood, and one is baffled rather than convinced by Joy's reaction to her mother's affair. The play is performed with clarity and insight, and some of the middle-class characters are true to life, especially Colonel Hope. But the performance is too slow and deliberate, and Mrs. Gwyn is not drawn definitely enough.

77 "New Novels. *The Country House,*" ATHENAEUM, No. 4143 (23 March 1907), 348–49.

JG presents in the self-deluding community of Worsted Skeynes, especially Horace Pendyce, the embodiment of habit and tradition: *The Country House* mirrors the truth of life through sharp insight, irony, and satire that is occasionally mordant.

78 "The New Play, *Joy,* at the Savoy Theatre," DAILY MIRROR (Lond), 26 Sept 1907, pp. 8–9.

[Four stills of scenes in Vedrenne's production of *Joy* at the Savoy, with sentence explanations.]

79 Payne, William Morton. "Recent Fiction," DIAL (Chicago), XLIII (1 Aug 1907), 61–66.

The Country House is interesting because of precision in phrasing and in delineating character. JG gives reality to commonplace people and their environs.

80 Pratt, Cornelia Atwood. "The Epidemic of Idealism in Fiction," PUTNAM'S MONTHLY, II (May 1907), 183–87.

The Man of Property is the "*reductio ad absurdum* of the materialistic life," arguing for the life of the soul and of beauty by showing their antitheses. JG, like Tolstoy, recognizes the need to get inside a character's mental processes, and he succeeds admirably with Soames, illustrating that temperament rather than logic is the prime reason for our actions.

81 "A Review of the Important Books of the Year," INDEPENDENT (NY), LXIII (21 Nov 1907), 1227.

The Country House "portrays with a humor that does not smile and a bitterness that does not relent the lack of virtue, intelligence, and sympathy in the landed gentry of England."

82 Rover. "Shrivelled Soul's Delight: Mr. Galsworthy's New Play," EVENING NEWS (Lond), 25 Sept 1907, p. 2.

[Caustic and slurring review suggests that *Joy* at the Savoy Theatre will appeal to "flat-chested women" and other "freaks" who lack intelligence.]

83 S., E. F. "*Joy* at the Savoy," WESTMINSTER GAZETTE (Lond), 25 Sept 1907, p. 3.

JG represents the young dramatists who reject the "well made play" and substitute the "slice of life." There is too much "silent business" on the stage—overcompensating for disdain with soliloquy in *Joy.* The conclusion is arbitrary and the title misleading; but it is often "intensely true to life." Miss Beech, Colonel Hope, and Joy are well developed by JG.

84 S., E. F. ["Monocle"]. "The Stage from the Stalls," SKETCH (Lond), LIX (2 Oct 1907), 374.

Joy is clever, truthful, and amusing; but the play is too short, and the ending is enigmatic even though JG is skillful in presentation of character. [Review of *Joy* at the Savoy, accompanied by a photo from the production.]

85 "Savoy Theatre: *Joy,* " DAILY TELEGRAPH (Lond), 25 Sept 1907, p. 9.

Joy is the *reductio ad absurdum* of the tendency away from traditional emphasis on story and construction. The main point of the play seems to be that humans do as they will. JG's attempt to be the "humorous observer" fails; there is none of the "powerful realism and psychological skill" of *The Silver Box.*

86 "Savoy Theatre. *Joy,* " MORNING POST (Lond), 25 Sept 1907, p. 6.

In *Joy,* nothing happens and nothing is concluded. Characters are trespassers, developed for their own interest rather than the interest of the play. Overemphasis on tedious but realistic detail and scenes unrelated to the main action detract from the few intense scenes between the main characters. There is too much talk about the gold mine, and the stage business of the tree is overdone. Dorothy Minto does well as Joy, and Thalberg Corbett is a "suave and well-mannered Lever." Colonel Hope and Miss Beech are "non-essential" characters.

87 Scott, Eric Clement. "Savoy Theatre: *Joy,* " BYSTANDER, XVI, No. 200 (2 Oct 1907), 24.

[Information doubtful. Listed in E. H. Mikhail, JOHN GALSWORTHY THE DRAMATIST: A BIBLIOGRAPHY OF CRITICISM (Troy: Whitson, 1971), p. 73; but the editors cannot verify the entry where cited by Mikhail.]

88 T., R. "Drama: *Joy,* " ACADEMY (Lond), LXXIII (28 Sept 1907), 954.

The simple methods JG adopted for *Joy,* produced at the Court Theatre, lead only to dullness. The story is simply a variation of Maupassant's YVETTE.

1908

89 Borsa, Mario. THE ENGLISH STAGE OF TO-DAY, trans from Italian by Selwyn Brinton (Lond & NY: John Lane, 1908), pp. 116–17.

The Silver Box is well-constructed, restrained, and lucid in expression. JG is original—Shaw has not "contaminated" him—his moral and ideal purposes are

directly revealed in his realistic works. [The original Italian volume IL TEATRO
INGLESE CONTEMPORANEO (Milan: Treves, 1905) [not seen] would not have
referred to *The Silver Box*. Apparently a revised ed appeared between 1905 and
1908, but the editors have been unable to locate it.]

90 Cecil, Eleanor. *"A Commentary,"* LIVING AGE (NY), CCLIX (24
Oct 1908), 240–43.

JG looks at many aspects of society in *A Commentary,* especially human
stupidities and wrongdoings, usually absolving humans of responsibility for
their actions. This creates the forlorn spectacle of men both blameless and
without hope. JG's technique uses both strong confrontation and dim projection
of types to observe various strata of society.

91 *"A Commentary,"* NATION (NY), LXXXVII (1 Oct 1908), 317.

A Commentary is a group of vignettes "of misery and comfort, satiric, ironic,
tragic." The particularized individuals "expand into a type." JG shows bitter
compassion for the ignorant, the infirm, the vicious. The organically related
sketches are better on the whole than comparable material found in *The Island
Pharisees* because JG does not force the reader to see the world through the eyes
of "an unconvincing crank."

92 *"A Commentary,"* SATURDAY REVIEW (Lond), CV (27 June 1908),
826.

"Clearness of thought, fine treatment of circumstance," and a "sane, sardonic
humor" characterize *A Commentary,* but the collection reminds one of a
notebook. To perceive problems is not enough—JG needs to suggest possible
remedies.

93 Cooper, Frederic Taber. "Six Books of the Month: Galsworthy's
Villa Rubein," BOOKMAN (NY), XXVIII (Sept 1908), 47–48.

JG demonstrates in *Villa Rubein* a "keen understanding of human nature . . .
trained powers of observation," and the ability to characterize humans by
selecting "one or two salient tricks of speech or gesture." These qualities keep it
from being an "early immature effort" by a promising artist.

94 Parker, John (ed). "John Galsworthy," THE GREEN ROOM BOOK;
OR, WHO'S WHO ON THE STAGE (Lond: T. Sealey Clark, 1908), p. 179.

[First brief biographical reference to JG in THE GREEN ROOM BOOK series. The
same notice appears in the 1909 volume.]

95 "Literature: Two Notable Volumes of Short Stories," INDEPEN-
DENT (NY), LXV (3 Dec 1908), 1305–6.

A Commentary shows that JG has the balance a good novelist must have, because
he presents situations clearly, not as a "muckraking novelist is sure to do." JG
quotes for the reader literally "the confidences and half articulate philosophy of
the poor."

96 "Mr. Galsworthy's Short Stories," BOOKMAN (Lond), XXXIV (July 1908), 154–55.

Like Earle in the MICROCOSMOGRAPHIE JG succeeds except in one or two cases in *A Commentary* in "generalising his characters, so as to make them types and even personifications." Creating a personification or an "emblem" is the highest achievement of this method, and JG succeeds admirably in "Fear," "Money," "Order," and "Hope." The weakness of this method is that "its social purpose is obvious," and this obviousness weakens the vitality of the book. The author is seen more clearly than are his characters.

97 "Mr. Galsworthy's *Villa Rubein*," NEW YORK TIMES SATURDAY REVIEW OF BOOKS AND ART, 1 Aug 1908, p. 427.

Villa Rubein is impressive, and the characters and delineation are noteworthy, but there are lapses into slipshod work. "It is good enough to make one wish it were better."

98 "Our Library Table. *A Commentary*," ATHENAEUM, No. 4214 (1 Aug 1908), 125–26.

A Commentary contains raw material for JG's philosophy. Selections are sincere and occasionally sentimental, but they lack the quality of art.

99 Scott-James, R. A. MODERNISM AND ROMANCE (Lond: John Lane, 1908), pp. 255–62.

Maurice Maeterlinck, Henry Newbolt, Lucas Malet, and JG may be considered in the light of Frederic Myers's term *borderland,* which refers to "the line which marks off the visible, sensible world from that vague sphere whence and whither all our imaginings, ideals and dreams of perfectibility seem to pass." Although JG is still a developing novelist, there are aspects of his work in *The Country House* that justify reference to his work in this context. His eloquent restraint permits his characters to "develop in the simple, unobtrusive way of real life." His realism is not the sordid realism of a Zola or Gorki; instead, "it takes its cue from the ordinary, unalterable course of real life, [in] that it reflects with fidelity the sombre and the lighter shades of colour, [and] that it does not even shrink from the terrible, unbeautiful reality" of the monotone. There are moments in his work when "his pictures are illumined by the *raison mystique* of which Maeterlinck speaks, the power which makes us wonder and *perceive* in spite of the dulling influences of our pragmatic society, the influences which ordinarily produce the common-sense point of view." Such a moment occurs as Mrs. Pendyce is talking to Captain Bellew (Part 3, chapter 9), hoping to persuade him to drop the divorce proceedings when the thought flashes through her mind " 'My poor dress will be ruined!' " Such a thought at such a moment reveals the hidden realities of our everyday lives.

100 Tonson, Jacob [pseud of Arnold Bennett]. "Books and Persons (An Occasional Causerie)," NEW AGE, nsIII:6 (6 June 1908), 112; rptd in THE AUTHOR'S CRAFT AND OTHER CRITICAL WRITINGS OF ARNOLD BENNETT, ed by Samuel Hynes (Lincoln: University of Nebraska P, 1968), pp. 203–4.

The Man of Property and *The Country House* are not first-rate novels; they are "hard and hostile," lacking a sense of beauty. *A Commentary* is monotonous, characterized by a "strong prejudice against its own subjects." Some sketches are brilliant, but JG must get rid of his hostilities. His tear-shedding over the "weak and the oppressed is a sign of facile emotionalism" rather than of an "ordered and powerful imagination."

101 *"Villa Rubein,"* NEW YORK TIMES SATURDAY REVIEW OF BOOKS AND ART, 13 June 1908, p. 338.

Villa Rubein has sustaining human emotion and absorbing incident.

102 *"Villa Rubein. The Island Pharisees,"* NATION (NY), LXXXVII (6 Aug 1908), 119–20.

The revised *Villa Rubein* and *The Island Pharisees* are much improved—not great but earnest and polished, showing the results of artistic solicitude. Evident are precision, force, and a distinct prose rhythm. [Primarily plot summary.]

103 "The Vital Literary Art of Galsworthy," CURRENT LITERATURE, XLV (Oct 1908), 408–10.

The influences of Flaubert, Turgenev, and Conrad on JG's work are evident. The fearlessness of his art, its satiric humor, and its mystic realism are distinctly Galsworthian. His chief defect is the inflexibility in his work. [This review of the American ed of *Collected Works* published by Putnam (*Villa Rubein, The Island Pharisees, The Man of Property, The Country House, A Commentary*) also cites various reviews and surveys of JG's works and reputation.]

1909

---

104 Archer, William. "Mr. Galsworthy Arrives," NATION (Lond), IV (13 March 1909), 892–93.

With *Strife* JG has arrived as a dramatist. As presented at the Duke of York's Theatre, the play has a symbolic rather than a naturalistic effect. Superficially a just and sober picture of life, it is fundamentally the embodiment of a thought. JG does not, unlike Hauptmann in DIE WEBER, "pile up brutalities and agonies"; rather he allows two principles to confront each other in their "stark simplicity." *Strife* is "a reduction to absurdity . . . of the theory that capitalism can co-exist with personal liberty." JG's development is "natural and probable," never catering to "the tastes or habitual expectations of his audience."

105 "At the Play," OBSERVER (Lond), (14 March 1909), p. 7.
Character-drawing in *Strife* creates live drama, but there is little movement. The board scene is photographic but prosaic. *Strife* is filled with irony. [Review of performance at the Duke of York's Theatre.]

106 B., J. O. "Stage Vanities: *Strife,*" VANITY FAIR (Lond), LXXXII (17 March 1909), 338–39.
[Insignificant personal ruminations pass for review of performance of *Strife*.]

107 Baughan, E. A. "A Dramatist Who Counts: *Strife:* Mr. Galsworthy's New Play at the Duke of York's—A Masterful and Powerful Drama," DAILY NEWS (Lond), 10 March 1909, p. 7.
Strife presents insight into the types of human nature that make labor-management warfare possible. The clash of will and temperament between Anthony and Roberts, who cannot see the implications of human suffering, makes for genuine drama. The play ends pessimistically and with bitter irony, emphasizing the theme that "the lives of men and women should not be at the mercy of a combat of will." The drama is powerful, despite JG's intentional oversight of not clearly developing the background.

108 Baughan, Edward A. "John Galsworthy as Dramatist," FORTNIGHTLY REVIEW, XCI (May 1909), 971–77.
JG's talent is rare because he understands and works well with the basic differences between novel and drama. His novels are analytic, his plays synthetic. Characters in his dramas have their own idiom, and he understands the imaginative challenge of stage business. Characters in *The Silver Box* are human beings; the pessimism results from the circumstances of life. *Strife* has greater depth of pathos than *Box;* the portrayal of John Anthony is a masterpiece of brevity, and the contrast of Anthony and Roberts is skillfully presented; many touches—Roberts and his wife, the board meeting—show JG's mastery of technique. Everything in *Strife* is united organically. His impartiality is admirable but sometimes overdone; his lack of humor is only a minor irritant.

109 Beerbohm, Max. "Two Plays," SATURDAY REVIEW (Lond), CVII (20 March 1909), 367–68.
The ardent socialism of *Strife* does not affect JG's dramatic balance in the well-written play. Anthony fights for "all labour against all capital," with his eye on the universal future.

110 Bennett, Arnold. "A Few Words on Galsworthy," NEW AGE, nsIV:23 (1 April 1909), 461; rptd in THE AUTHOR'S CRAFT AND OTHER CRITICAL WRITINGS OF ARNOLD BENNETT, ed by Samuel Hynes (Lincoln: University of Nebraska P, 1968), pp. 205–6.
Strife consists largely of "good intentions"; it is "nourished on genuine ideas." Even though the play is conventional and is lacking in "first-hand observation,"

it is "scornfully honest" and "free from sentimentality." The attempted realism of Acts I and II does not ring true; but the appearance of John Anthony's daughter appeals to the child in the viewer: from her first appearance on, the play pleases the aesthetic sense. [Review of production.]

111 Bennett, Arnold. "Tendencies of Modern Literature," T. P.'s CHRISTMAS NUMBER [T. P.'s WEEKLY], XIV ([Dec] 1909), 7–10.

In writing plays as well as novels, JG gives authority to the theater and takes it away from the library. Lacking both hero and heroine, *The Country House* has a villain: the land-owning, leisured class. The novel is a sincere, deadly attack written by an "insider."

112 "The Bookman's Table: *Plays: The Silver Box, Joy, Strife,*" BOOKMAN (Lond), XXXVI (May 1909), 98.

JG is one of the two or three acted dramatists "who can be seriously regarded as artists and critics of life." Behind his "grey dramas" there is a "fine mind" with "grave emotion." "There is hardly a speech to be found in his plays which shows intuitive knowledge of his characters; each has been carefully, honestly thought out, with an intellectual insight and an emotional sympathy, but not with that combination of the two which is essential to perfect imaginative and creative work." Such a cavil would only be appropriate if ours were an age of giants, but it is not. JG is one of our giants "if intellectual honesty, moral weight, and artistic form count for anything."

113 Boynton, H. W. "Some Recent Novels," PUTNAM'S MAGAZINE, VI (July 1909), 492–96.

Fraternity, wistfully recording human experience, asks when justice and brotherhood will come to man.

114 "Chronicle and Comment: Apropos of Some Published Plays," BOOKMAN (NY), XXX (Sept 1909), 15–16.

The Silver Box and *Joy* impress with their "intellectual frugality"; interest in *Strife* is maintained by incident rather than the "meagerly sketched, merely typical" characters.

115 "Comment on Current Books," OUTLOOK (NY), XCII (1 May 1909), 19–22.

[Plot-summary review of *Fraternity.*]

116 Cooper, Frederic Taber. "Deliberation and Some Recent Novels," BOOKMAN (NY), XXIX (May 1909), 316–17.

Excellent control and "admirable economy of means" make *Fraternity* a structurally and technically remarkable work.

117 "Drama. *Plays. The Silver Box, Joy,* and *Strife,*" ATHENAEUM, No. 4264 (17 July 1909), 79–80.

Strife and *The Silver Box,* like the novels *The Country House* and *Fraternity,* are mature, thoughtful, and vital art—appealing to brains as well as heart. *Joy* is "unfortunate and unsatisfactory." JG is attuned to two types of audience: the one who wants a message and the one who wants to be thrilled and amused. Because JG has learned well the use of pantomime, his stage directions are copious. Dialogue is natural and usually colloquial, seldom destroyed by rhetorical flights. One fault in his realistic approach is the tendency to let mean characters use dialect above their station.

118 "Duke of York's Theatre: Mr. Galsworthy's New Play: *Strife*," DAILY GRAPHIC (Lond), 10 March 1909, p. 7.
[Plot-summary review of *Strife*.]

119 "Duke of York's Theatre: *Strife*," GLOBE AND TRAVELLER (Lond), 10 March 1909, p. 5.
[Plot summary of *Strife*.]

120 "Duke of York's Theatre. *Strife*," MORNING POST (Lond), 10 March 1909, p. 5.
Strife, one of the most notable plays in years, presents the themes of moderation and conciliation. Bleak, bald, sometimes monotonous in subject matter, and with an occasional but unobtrusive satiric thrust, Granville-Barker's production is admirable. Mr. McKinnell as John Anthony conveys "sullen power."

121 "Duke of York's Theatre. *Strife*," TIMES (Lond), 10 March 1909, p. 10.
Anthony and Roberts in *Strife* are "cast-iron, implacable extremists," refusing to compromise. Two quite effective scenes are those of the "inspissated gloom" of Roberts's house and the men's meeting. JG alternates between opposing camps. The play is of "real importance," treating a theme of social consequence with "the impartiality . . . of all round sympathy and understanding."

122 E., A. L. "Duke of York's Theatre, *Strife*—Mr. Galsworthy's Brilliant Capital and Labor Play," STAR (Lond), 10 March 1909, p. 2.
Strife—to date JG's best play—is "a play of singular power . . . a work of great significance and value, even if that value is more sociological than dramatic." When JG works on the principle that "drama can never be impersonal," he may write "not merely a brilliant play but a great one." JG does not take sides in the conflict; it "is not the dramatist's business to take sides." He fulfills his job by painting a picture of life. There are some passages "in which the human portraiture is blurred, or extravagantly caricatured": e.g., Scantlebury. "The critical value of *Strife* lies in its destructive analysis of modern economic conditions and the pretensions of uncontrolled capital. Its constructive value lies in its insistence on the futility of sectional industrial warfare as a method of industrial progress." The naturalness of the performance "has not been equalled on the London stage since Mr. Granville Barker's former productions at the Court Theatre."

123 "Fine Strike Drama: Mr. Galsworthy's *Strife* at the Duke of York's Theatre," DAILY MIRROR (Lond), 10 March 1909, p. 5.
[Plot summary of *Strife* without commentary.]

124 *"Fraternity,"* A.L.A. BOOKLIST, V (April 1909), 113.
[Brief notice of publication.]

125 *"Fraternity,"* INDEPENDENT (NY), LXVII (9 Sept 1909), 601–2.
In the strange *Fraternity* JG speaks of our time as "in those days, when men were living on their pasts." One reads it with a sense of futility.

126 *"Fraternity,"* NATION (NY), LXXXVIII (6 May 1909), 466–67.
Fraternity is filled with the "leaven of humanitarianism" but leaves the reader's artistic sense unsatisfied because it really has "no hero or heroine, no climax, and no conclusion." JG apparently feels, as Carlyle and Ruskin did late in their careers, that true art cannot appear until the ills of society are cured. Despite this, his achievement is notable. JG has developed "astonishingly" in "breadth, variety, subtlety, charm, and sympathy," with many touches of "grim yet tender irony."

127 *"Fraternity,"* NEW YORK TIMES SATURDAY REVIEW OF BOOKS AND ART, 20 March 1909, p. 160.
Fraternity, great in conception and execution, is a novel of shadows. Hilary and his wife are sophisticated, understanding, and "a little weary of life." The "odor of the great unwashed rises as a barrier between us and our 'shadows.' " JG is a realist of the Turgenev rather than the Zola school.

128 *"Fraternity,"* NEW YORK TIMES SATURDAY REVIEW OF BOOKS AND ART, 12 June 1909, p. 374.
[The brief review recommends *Fraternity,* one of the "greatest novels" of the century, for summer reading.]

129 *"Fraternity,"* OBSERVER (Lond), 21 Feb 1909, p. 4.
JG displays the "analytical subtlety of Balzac" in his "cleverly written" and powerful "sociological disquisition." The milieu is banal, the power realistic.
[Plot-summary review.]

130 *"Fraternity,"* SATURDAY REVIEW (Lond), CVII (13 March 1909), 341–42.
The "revolutionary" *Fraternity* is "very dangerous," calculated to bring contempt upon the governing class. Characters are puppets; JG is a propagandist, whose "class hatred has gone mad."

131 Grein, J. T. "Duke of York's: *Strife,* " SUNDAY TIMES (Lond), 14 March 1909, p. 4.
Strife is a powerful play that belongs on the same plane of "strike-plays" as Hauptmann's THE WEAVERS, Mirabeau's LE MAUVAIS BERGER, and Heijer-

mans's THE GOOD HOPE. JG presents a vehement indictment of the old methods of the limited company, and although he never swerves from his purpose, his heart is with the laborers. This is the kind of drama that will strengthen our theater and our national reputation.

132 "A Guide to the New Books," LITERARY DIGEST (NY), XXXVIII (1 May 1909), 763–64.

In *Fraternity* JG insists that it is impossible for the rich Dallisons to help the indigent Creeds, given present social conditions. Such conditions therefore must change. Interesting character types are presented concisely, cleverly, and with a welcome artistic effect; but JG loses some effectiveness because of his preoccupation with theme.

133 Ignotus. "Mr. Galsworthy's Plays," SPECTATOR (Lond), CII (27 March 1909), 498–99.

Even though it is refreshing to see drama without the usual love interest and rhetorical speeches, JG's plays (*Plays: The Silver Box, Joy, Strife*) have not appealed to wide audiences, despite the fact that his work is directed in a modern way to ordinary men. *Strife* appeals because of stage business and acting; it is unsatisfying as art because the "human soul" is seldom evident in the conflict of "prejudices and ideals of two classes." The play has divided purpose and consequently cannot be true art. [Ignotus does not develop the thesis enough to explain either JG or himself.]

134 "John Galsworthy's *Strife,*" NATION (NY), LXXXIX (25 Nov 1909), 520–21.

Strife is good contemporary drama but lacks greatness because it is "founded on insufficient premises, is specious and illustrative rather than logical in its development and . . . ends inconclusively." Characters are admirable, especially the "veracious" Anthony and Roberts. [Review of performance at the New Theatre.]

135 "London Theatres. The Duke of York's," STAGE (Lond), No. 1460 (11 March 1909), pp. 17–18.

Strife is an excellent and praiseworthy theatrical recovery after the failure of *Joy.* Old Anthony is masterful characterization, and the contrast with Roberts is equally masterful. [Primarily a plot-summary review.]

136 Macartney, M. H. H. "The Novels of Mr. John Galsworthy," WESTMINSTER REVIEW, CLXXI (June 1909), 682–93.

Close, detailed observation is a noteworthy strength of JG's novels. *Fraternity,* his most powerful novel, suggests a shift, in that adverse social criticism may be blending with positive suggestions for reform.

137 Metcalfe, [J. S.]. "*Strife,*" LIFE (NY), LIV (9 Dec 1909), 855.

Strife is a series of episodes rather than a play, a bald example of using the stage to expose economic conditions. The company that performed it deserves better material. [Review of a New Theatre performance.]

138 "Mr. Galsworthy's New Play: *Strife* at the Duke of York's Theatre," MANCHESTER GUARDIAN, 10 March 1909, p. 7.
[Information doubtful. Cited in E. H. Mikhail, JOHN GALSWORTHY THE DRAMATIST: A BIBLIOGRAPHY OF CRITICISM (Troy: Whitson, 1971), p. 56; but the present editors cannot verify the entry where cited by Mikhail.]

139 "Mr. Galsworthy's Plays," OUTLOOK (Lond), XXIII (20 March 1909), 397.
In *Plays. First Series* JG writes with conviction and genuine critical impulse, presenting facts with vitality. *The Silver Box* and *Strife* present truisms about public life; *Joy* treats with delicacy the emotional force of a deeply felt domestic situation. JG's style is concentrated, economic, severe, and intellectual in a way that good drama about real life must be.

140 "Mr. Galsworthy's *Strife* at the Duke of York's," ILLUSTRATED LONDON NEWS, CXXXIV (13 March 1909), 370.
In *Strife* JG adopts "more all-around methods" than does Bergstrom in THE HEAD OF THE FIRM. [The review is primarily a plot summary emphasizing JG's use of detail and impartiality that is "full of a throbbing, tense humanity."]

141 "Mr. John Galsworthy's New Play. A Dramatic Treatise on Strikes," PALL MALL GAZETTE (Lond), 10 March 1909, p. 4.
Photographic reality and brilliant acting characterize *Strife* at the Duke of York's Theatre. The most significant thing in the excellent play and dramatic production is the author's sense of pity.

142 "New Novels. *Fraternity,*" ATHENAEUM, No. 4246 (13 March 1909), 312–13.
JG seems not to be able to decide whether to write narrative or sociological treatise: as a result he does neither successfully. *Fraternity* lacks cohesion, and detail sometimes seems superfluous. The characters revolve around the "clever but painful portrait" of the scientist and philosopher who has outlived human emotions. The old butler surpasses other characters in interest.

143 Payne, William Morton. "Recent Fiction," DIAL (Chicago), XLVI (1 June 1909), 368–72.
JG's master stroke of irony in the ironic *Fraternity* is the portrayal of the futility of the old man who is writing his book on "Human Brotherhood." Pity is evident in the development of the "curious interrelationship" of the two groups—the outwardly respectable and the degraded—that is encapsulated in the philosopher's comment, "Each of us has a shadow in those places—in those streets." JG is too pessimistic. [Payne digresses into moral soliloquy.]

144 "People and Things Theatrical," PEARSON'S MAGAZINE, XXII (Aug 1909), 223–31.
[Plot-summary review of *Strife*.]

145 "Plays," NATION (NY), LXXXIX (19 Aug 1909), 167.
The underlying theme in *Plays* (*The Silver Box, Joy,* and *Strife*) is the seemingly hopeless conflict of ideal justice with natural instincts. *Strife* is the best of the three plays. Confronting the problems of life, JG is groping his way into the drama of class conflict—perhaps the drama of the future. Prescriptions for his future success based on the deficiencies of the current plays: don't invade Shaw's ground, as in *Joy;* don't confuse situation with plot, as in *Strife;* use "Ibsenese symbolism"; but most of all, remember that great drama has great characters.

146 "Plays By Galsworthy," NEW YORK TIMES SATURDAY REVIEW OF BOOKS AND ART, 7 Aug 1909, p. 477.
Plays (*The Silver Box, Strife,* and *Joy*) have ideas, humanity, and a "limpid crystalline" style with color and warmth; yet they do not satisfy because they are inconclusive and because JG is not sufficiently detached.

147 *"Plays: The Silver Box, Joy, Strife,"* A.L.A. BOOKLIST, VI (Sept 1909), 13.
Plays "expose some modern problems but attempt no solution." They are readable and consistent with JG's best work. [Brief review.]

148 *"Plays: The Silver Box, Joy, Strife,"* ILLUSTRATED LONDON NEWS, CXXXIV (10 April 1909), 518.
JG, the "modern of moderns," is beginning to conquer his public, as the publication by Duckworth of the three plays shows.

149 "Reading Plays," INDEPENDENT (NY), LXVII (21 Oct 1909), 931.
[Brief review of *Plays: The Silver Box, Joy, and Strife*.]

150 "Reviews of New Plays. *Strife,* at the New Theatre," NEW YORK DRAMATIC MIRROR, LXII (27 Nov 1909), 5.
Strife presents impartially and without comic relief a study of the conflict between capital and labor.

151 S., E. F. ["Monocle"]. "The Stage from the Stalls," SKETCH (Lond), LXV (17 March 1909), 306.
Strife is a masterly picture that is weakest in the scene (end of Act II) where it should have been the strongest. The drama is intensely concentrated. [Review of performance.]

152 S., E. F. *"Strife* at the Duke of York's," WESTMINSTER GAZETTE (Lond), 10 March 1909, p. 3.

Strife, unconventional and written without regard for the public taste, has "no romance . . . no sickly sentiment, no comic relief, no insincere trickery with sexual questions; it deals powerfully . . . bluntly" with labor strife. The weakest part of the play is the strike scene, because JG does not understand mob oratory.

153 Scott, Eric Clement. "Duke of York's Theatre: *Strife,*" BY-STANDER, XXI (24 March 1909), 590.

Strife is a more forcible exposition of capital-labor friction than the very similar THE HEAD OF THE FIRM. The strike and suffering should not have taken place on the stage: the dying of Annie Thomas could be dispensed with. Consequently, the play does not gain much by use of stage realism.

154 "Sorting the Seeds: A Survey of Recent Fiction," ATLANTIC MONTHLY, CIII (May 1909), 702–12.

Fraternity has a "compact, closely worked-out plot," concentrated on the central incident, with judicious economy in the choice and relation of incidents. Occasionally the movement is retarded because of a tendency to finish elaborate but separate scenes; JG tries too hard "to enforce psychological processes by external effects." Irony is "keen and pungent"; sympathy is poignant; but realism approaches the boundary of an unartistic allegory "through a too shrewd selection of details all of one kind." JG blunders in seeing all of life in one mood.

155 "Stageland: A Labour Play and a New Hamlet," CLARION, 19 March 1909, p. 3.

The story necessary to maintain interest in *Strife* at the Duke of York's Theatre is lacking, and JG's impartiality lacks effectiveness. The play is inept.

156 "*Strife.* Duke of York's Theatre; Capital Against Labour," DAILY TELEGRAPH (Lond), 10 March 1909, p. 9.

The movement of *Strife* is not dramatic action. Although the play is "well drawn," the dialogue is dull. The women (Annie Roberts and Madge Thomas) suffer most in the tragic waste that characterizes the drama.

157 "*Strife:* Mr. Galsworthy's New Play at the Duke of York's," DAILY CHRONICLE (Lond), 10 March 1909, p. 7.

Strife is the finest labor-drama since Hauptmann's WEAVERS, holding interest despite its judicial aspects. The theme of "shame on your strife" develops through "unstrained realism and contrasted character-drawing" to show capital-labor conflicts. Granville-Barker does a fine job with the strike meeting scene.

158 "*Strife:* Mr. Galsworthy's Powerful Strike Drama," DAILY MAIL (Lond), 10 March 1909, p. 5.

Strife at the Duke of York's Theatre commands attention despite its subject matter, lack of comic relief, and romantic interest. The message: in life only the great fighters count, and the only solution to problems comes in "rational, economic compromise."

159 "A Strike on the Stage. A Noteworthy New Play," SCOTSMAN (Edinburgh), 10 March 1909, p. 9.

JG has the courage to deal with the topic of strikes better than anyone else to date. [This inconsequential plot summary of *Strife* serves as a review of the Duke of York's Theatre production.]

160 "A Success for the New Theater," LITERARY DIGEST (NY), XXXIX (4 Dec 1909), 1013.

[Quotes from favorable reviews of performance of *Strife* at NY's New Theater.]

161 Tillinghast, Philip. "Fiction of Some Importance," FORUM (NY), XLI (April 1909), 389–92.

JG is important as a novelist generally because of highly developed technique that is often concealed by his tightly knit structure, his serious interest in life's problems, and realism. *Fraternity*'s theme, "Am I my brother's keeper," is developed in a remarkably concise (fourteen characters, interior scenes of "two or three English dwellings") form with an "extreme nicety" of technique. [The promise of careful analysis of structure in *Fraternity* gives way to plot summary and brief comments on some characters.]

162 Tonson, Jacob [pseud of Arnold Bennett]. "Books and Persons (An Occasional Causerie)," NEW AGE, nsIV:16 (11 Feb 1909), 325–26; rptd in Arnold Bennett, BOOKS AND PERSONS: BEING COMMENTS ON A PAST EPOCH (Lond: Chatto & Windus, 1917; NY: George H. Doran, 1917; NY: Greenwood P, 1968), pp. 94–100; rptd in THE AUTHOR'S CRAFT AND OTHER CRITICAL WRITINGS OF ARNOLD BENNETT, ed by Samuel Hynes (Lincoln: University of Nebraska P, 1968), pp. 78–82.

[Passing references to JG, whose claim to prominence is his "fierce animosity" to the "great stolid, comfortable" novel-reading public. JG belongs to a lower rank of novelist than Henry James; his observations will prejudice him in the eyes of posterity.]

163 Vachell, Horace Annesley. "Concerning Mr. Galsworthy," SATURDAY REVIEW (Lond), CVII (20 March 1909), 368.

[Vachell defends JG's artistic integrity against the harsh attack on *Fraternity* in SATURDAY REVIEW CVII (13 March 1909), 341–42.]

1910

164 "At the New Theater," HAMPTON'S MAGAZINE (NY), XXIV (Feb 1910), 272.

JG's writing is "adept, stern and acerbic"; *Strife* sets the proper path for the New Theater to follow.

165 "At the Playhouses. New Theatre. *Strife,*" THEATRE MAGAZINE (NY), XI (Jan 1910), 2–3.

Because JG does not present meaning dramatically in *Strife,* meaning must be read into it. Except for the strong characterization of Anthony and Roberts and the emphasis on unavailing strife, there is no defined purpose. Action, noise, and talking do not compensate for lack of plotting.

166 B. "The Repertory Theatre. *Justice,*" SPECTATOR (Lond), CIV (26 Feb 1910), 339.

Justice at the Duke of York's Theatre is "merely a record of a series of events," an effective realistic work, whose importance lies in complexity and emotional appeal filled with depression and, occasionally, an almost intolerable "strained horror."

167 B., J. M. [Barrie, James Matthew?]. "Plays for Grown-up People: Two Remarkable New Ventures," GRAPHIC (Lond), LXXXI (26 Feb 1910), 268.

JG builds up a "quiet . . . powerful indictment" in *Justice.* It is the tragedy of the cumulative force of a machine that, once started, cannot stop. Falder, hopeless and morally anemic, is a "danger to himself and society"; society, however, punishes itself by making Falder a permanent criminal. The "grim power" of Falder's demise is the best of the type since TESS OF THE D'URBERVILLES. Mr. Eadie as Falder reacted magnificently to the great play. [Review of performance at the Duke of York's Theatre.]

168 Beerbohm, Max. *"Justice,"* GRAPHIC (Lond), LXXXI (26 Feb 1910), 268.

[Information doubtful. Listed in E. H. Mikhail, JOHN GALSWORTHY THE DRAMATIST: A BIBLIOGRAPHY OF CRITICISM (Troy, NY: Whitson, 1971), p. 23. Most likely it is B., J. M. [Barrie, James Matthew?], "Plays for Grown-Up People: Two Remarkable New Ventures," GRAPHIC (Lond), LXXXI (26 Feb 1910), 268.]

169 Beerbohm, Sir Max. *"Justice,"* SATURDAY REVIEW (Lond), CIX (5 March 1910), 296–97; rptd in AROUND THEATRES (Lond: Heinemann, 1924; NY: Knopf, 1930; Lond: Rupert Hart-Davis, 1953; NY: Simon & Schuster, 1954; NY: Greenwood Press, 1968; NY: Taplinger Publishing Co., 1969), pp. 565–68.

JG is dispassionate in characterization in *Justice* because he pities victims of a "clumsy, mechanical, mischievous" law and penal system. JG's technique is "cinematographic." *Justice* hardly seems to be theater so much as an actual presentation of life. Whereas *Strife* and *Fraternity* seem to present irremediable problems, *Justice* suggests that the British legal system is not beyond redemption. The cell scene in Act III suggests the horror of incarceration better than all the books written on the topic. [Beerbohm's review of the performance at the

Duke of York's Theatre is one of the most perceptive short reviews of JG's drama; his comments are germinal to later critical comments.]

170 Cooper, Frederic Taber. "Some Recent Books: *A Motley,*" BOOKMAN (NY), XXXI (Aug 1910), 642–43.

The sketches in *A Motley* are "so fragile that one hesitates to dignify them even with the name of short stories."

171 "Drama. *Justice,*" ATHENAEUM, No. 4318 (30 July 1910), 136.

Justice is a play with a purpose; and despite the fact that the most appealing scene on stage is the silent one, the play is better suited for the library than many that have never been acted. The real action of the play, Falder's forgery, occurs before the drama begins.

172 "The Dramatic Calendar. *Strife.* By John Galsworthy," MET-ROPOLITAN MAGAZINE (NY), XXXI (March 1910), 815–17.

[Paragraph review of performance at NY's New Theatre, accompanied by five photos of the production.]

173 "Dual Genius of John Galsworthy," CURRENT LITERATURE, XLVIII (Jan 1910), 81–83.

[Recent estimates of JG's work, with particular reference to *Strife,* are quoted.]

174 "Duke of York's Theatre. *Justice,*" TIMES (Lond), 22 Feb 1910, p. 10.

The naturally somber *Justice* is filled with "inspissated gloom." JG, England's "sole tragic writer," writes realistic tragedy without comment or literary decoration.

175 Eaton, Walter Prichard. "*Strife* as a Dramatic Debate," AT THE NEW THEATRE AND OTHERS; THE AMERICAN STAGE: ITS PROBLEMS AND PERFORMANCES 1908–1910 (Bost: Small, Maynard, 1910), pp. 35–40.

JG has a scientist's temperament, a dramatist's sense of character, and a "literary artist's sense of natural incident and human speech." *Strife* as presented at New York's New Theatre appeals to "intellectual faculties" and to a "sense of reality." In his "dispassionate and neuter" approach to the play, JG ignores the audience's tastes.

176 Findlater, Jane H. "Three Sides to a Question," NATIONAL RE-VIEW; rptd in LIVING AGE (NY), CCLXIV: 3426 (5 March 1910), 603–12.

Three authors—H. G. Wells in TONO BUNGAY, JG in *Fraternity,* and Stephen Reynolds in A POOR MAN'S HOUSE—analyze and comment on modern social ills; their conclusions are negative and of little help. The theme of TONO BUNGAY concerns "what is coming into the English mind." Wells show us the evils of the moneyed classes and the miseries of the working classes, and his solution is that a man's salvation will come from whatever a man sets his heart and soul to with all his might; it is the religion of the strong man. In *Fraternity* there are four types who work for social progress: (1) Hilary Dallison, overcultured, overrefined, and sympathetic to the poor; (2) Stephen Dallison, unimaginative, kind-hearted, and willing to be charitable; (3) Old Mr. Stone, a dreamer who writes an unreadable book on universal brotherhood; (4) Martin Stone, a young doctor who works to improve the living conditions of the poor. JG's solution seems to lie with Martin Stone. But this solution with its concern for the physical evils overlooks the more serious obstacle: sin, or man's innate depravity. Reynolds argues that the poor are better off than the educated; the poor have "the courage to live" and their primitive virtues need to be preserved even if material advances must be foregone.

177 "Galsworthy's *Motley,*" NEW YORK TIMES SATURDAY REVIEW OF BOOKS AND ART, 17 Sept 1910, p. 505.

Despite what some critics say, JG is not really a socialist or a propagandist; rather, he is a strong individual writer of "ultra-modern temper" in thought and imagination, observing life rather than prescribing it.

178 Goodman, Edward. "*Strife,*" FORUM (NY), XLIII (Jan 1910), 70–7).

Strife prophesies a harmonious and glorious future. JG does not take sides in the struggle between capital and labor—he stands above, advocating cooperation. [Review of performance has more of Christian zeal than sound criticism.]

179 H., A. "*Justice.* First Play at Repertory Theatre," DAILY MAIL (Lond), 22 Feb 1910, p. 5.

The tragedy *Justice* at the Duke of York's Theatre is the "most dramatic piece of realism" seen in England since the private performance of Gorki's LOWER DEPTHS. JG's staggering realism makes the play fall short of truly great drama. Yet it is "truly fine," with the audience feeling more like participators than theater-goers. The realism is crass and brutal without being cynical.

180 Howe, P. P. THE REPERTORY THEATRE: A RECORD AND A CRITICISM (Lond: Martin Secker, 1910), pp. 81–91, 209, 217–27.

In the Duke of York's Repertory Theatre's seventeen-week season (beginning 21 February 1910), *Justice* was performed twenty-six times. *Justice* indicts "the march of justice" through Falder, the "insect under foot." *Justice* is not the squalid anecdote that others have called it; rather, Falder is the "average Weakling" in justice's impersonal drama. JG's progress as dramatist from *The Silver Box* through *Joy* and *Strife* to *Justice* suggests a loss of "characterizing power" and an increase in the "drama of impersonal forces." JG needs more nobility in his dramatic purges, even though the play apparently effected some changes in the court system in the treatment of people like Falder. [Appendix contains copy of the playbill and a list of dates of performances.]

181 Jackson, Holbrook. "Modern Writers: John Galsworthy," SHEF-
FIELD DAILY TELEGRAPH, 21 Aug 1910, p. 6.

JG is a realist, with criticism of life implied. Early novels are ordinary fiction, but the real JG arrived with *The Man of Property* and *The Silver Box*. JG's success in 1910 is gauged by his popularity with young writers and with the critics, and by the fact that his reputation grows steadily with all classes of readers. *A Commentary* is the key to JG's ideas. His ability to "psychologize" life gives poignancy to his disdain for the "wastefulness and stupidity of modern life."

182 Jingle. "*Justice* at the Repertory Theatre (Duke of York's),"
BYSTANDER, XXV (2 March 1910), 431–32.

JG is deterministic in the presentation of the staggering, grim, and dismal *Justice*. The drama, developed thoroughly and carefully, does not moralize; rather JG lets the presentation speak for itself. [Three illustrations by Norman Morrow accompany the review.]

183 "John Galsworthy," DAILY MAIL (Lond), 22 Feb 1910, p. 6.

JG is unusually successful in his role as novelist and playwright. His success is even more remarkable when one considers that he does not pander to modern tastes—actually writing about unpopular topics: the poor, strikes, thieves, laxity of morals. Like Russian writers, his attitude is "detached, objective though the substance is acrid and pitiless." His plays are intense without being moralizing.

184 "*Justice*," NATION (NY), XCI (27 Oct 1910), 398.

[Brief, favorable review of publication of *Justice*. JG's case is weak, but it is skillfully and powerfully presented.]

185 "*Justice*," REVIEW OF REVIEWS (NY), XLII (Dec 1910), 763.

[Paragraph notice of *Justice*, commenting that the indictment of the British penal system has instigated an inquiry by the British Home Secretary.]

186 "*Justice: A Tragedy in Four Acts*," BOOKMAN (Lond), XXXVIII
(April 1910), 50.

Justice reads better than it acts, because the stage cannot treat properly JG's "exaggeratedly subdued method" and his "singular humour." Unfortunately, individuals are subordinated to thesis.

187 "*Justice* at London's New Repertory Theatre," ILLUSTRATED
LONDON NEWS, CXXXVI (26 Feb 1910), 294.

[The reviewer emphasizes JG's mastery of "a big subject" in an otherwise pedestrian plot summary.]

188 Kellogg, P. U. "*Strife*: A Drama of the Politics of Industry,"
SURVEY, XXIII (12 Feb 1910), 705–8.

[In this review of the American production of *Strife* in New York the reviewer relates the theme of the play to contemporary issues.]

189 "Literature: *A Motley*," INDEPENDENT (NY), LXIX (6 Oct 1910), 774.

In *A Motley* JG is "the refined Socialist who expresses himself with sympathetic understanding rather than in vituperative hysterics." Every "word of analysis or description is poignant with the pain of comprehension, vivid with satire, or tender with humor and pathos."

190 "Literature: *Justice*," INDEPENDENT (NY), LXIX (27 Oct 1910), 931.

Justice is written realistically, impartially, and vividly.

191 "Mr. Galsworthy's *Justice*," NEW YORK TIMES SATURDAY REVIEW OF BOOKS AND ART, 22 Oct 1910, p. 582.

[The plot-summary review of *Justice* debates the point of the extent to which society needs to be protected as it relates generally to a play of "absorbing interest" and stark realism.]

192 "Mr. Galsworthy's Sketches," SPECTATOR (Lond), CV (9 July 1910), 63.

JG's style shows improvement in *A Motley*. Some of the early work is sentimental and melodramatic, and a "too autumnal" mood presents dim plots, pale characters, and desiccated satire; on the whole, however, he is serious, individualistic, and technically competent.

193 *"Motley,"* A.L.A. BOOKLIST, VII (Oct 1910), 59.

The collection of previously published pieces in *A Motley* tells of commonplaces of everyday life with a varying appeal to fancy or pathos. [Brief review.]

194 *"A Motley,"* DIAL (Chicago), XLIX (1 Aug 1910), 70.

All the stories in *A Motley* illustrate JG's ability to use commonplace material to present vivid and delicate pictures, characters, and incidents. He fuses sympathy with sincerity and tenderness with truth in "A Portrait," thirty pages of masterful description almost without incident but filled with life and reality.

195 *"Motley,"* NATION (NY), XCI (7 July 1910), 15.

A Motley's sketches are neatly turned, but wit is occasionally forced, and the sketches are often too brief. JG's power to portray character on various levels of society is evident. JG and Max Beerbohm rank with the "second stratum of British cleverness," below Shaw, Chesterton, and Wells.

196 *"A Motley,"* REVIEW OF REVIEWS (NY), XLII (Sept 1910), 384.

[Paragraph review of the series of "impressionistic sketches," filled with a "haunting literary quality" and "conviction of reality" that are included in *A Motley*.]

197 *"A Motley,"* SATURDAY REVIEW (Lond), CIX (25 June 1910), 827.

[Brief, negative notice of *A Motley*.]

198 "Musings Without Method," BLACKWOOD'S MAGAZINE, CLXXXVII (April 1910), 580–89.

Justice is "a rather squalid anecdote," with characters of no particular interest. JG spares nothing; the painful episodes are presented literally and without pity. The preacher gets the better of the dramatist: prejudice in favor of the weak and neurotic is evident in the prison scene.

199 Nathan, George Jean. "The Dramatic Role of Honor: *Strife,*" BURR MCINTOSH MONTHLY (NY), XXII (Feb 1910), 122–23.

Strife is a drama of talk, tears, and little action, lacking most qualities supposedly required for contemporary drama. It convinces the intellect with its bigness and strength in the conflict between Albert Bruning as Roberts and Louis Calvert as Anthony. [Two photos of production at NY's New Theatre are reproduced.]

200 "One Argument in *Justice,*" PALL MALL GAZETTE (Lond), 23 Feb 1910, p. 7.

[Insignificant comment about the possibility of one's mind going blank—in reference to a barrister's argument in *Justice*.]

201 Pollock, Channing. "Some Old Themes and the New Theatre," THE GREEN BOOK ALBUM (Chicago), III (Feb 1910), 390–96.

[Plot-summary review of a performance of *Strife* at the New Theatre in New York.]

202 Richardson, H. M. "Modern Influences. LI. John Galsworthy," MILLGATE MONTHLY, V (Feb 1910), 273–77.

JG is a judge "who perpetually sums up but never delivers judgment"; his influence extends not only to art but also to morality and economics: perhaps his impartiality results from the desire to avoid the avalanche of verbiage that would follow his first statement of conviction. He reveals "good men fighting good men in the darkness of ignorance." [The article, primarily a general survey of JG's works to 1909, is preceded by a photo of JG and one of his residence.]

203 "Short Stories," ATHENAEUM, No. 4318 (30 July 1910), 122.

The twenty-eight items in *A Motley* vary in coverage from "mere reporting" to "gems of imagination." "The Japanese Quince" shows the finest artistry; two stories about wife-killing experiment with the point of view of the inevitability of crime.

204 "*Strife*. By John Galsworthy," METROPOLITAN MAGAZINE, XXXI (March 1910), 816–17.

[Five illustrations from the New Theatre production of *Strife*.]

205 "*Strife*—John Galsworthy's Powerful Labor Play," CURRENT LITERATURE, XLVIII (May 1910), 537–45.

Irony is central to JG's art. The production at the New Theater is a "distinguished success." Miss Emma Goldman characterizes *Strife* "as the most important labor play since Hauptmann's WEAVERS." The production of *Strife* was suppressed by the mayor of Philadelphia during the strike there. JG has transferred the setting to America: e.g., John Anthony is president of the Ohio River Tin Plate Mills. JG's message seems to say that "society at large . . . will always choose the path of mediocrity and of compromise." [Reprints substantial excerpts from the play.]

206 Tonson, Jacob [pseud of Arnold Bennett]. "Books and Persons (An Occasional Causerie)," NEW AGE, nsIV:11 (14 July 1910), 253–54; rptd as "John Galsworthy," BOOKS AND PERSONS: BEING COMMENTS ON A PAST EPOCH (Lond: Chatto & Windus, 1917; NY: George H. Doran, 1917; NY: Greenwood P, 1968), pp. 214–16; rptd in THE AUTHOR'S CRAFT AND OTHER CRITICAL WRITINGS OF ARNOLD BENNETT, ed by Samuel Hynes (Lincoln: University of Nebraska P, 1968), pp. 209–10.

The Man of Property stands the test of rereading: (1) its sound harmonious design is original; and (2) the tension is never relaxed from the point of view of subject matter. Its finest quality is its "extraordinary passionate cruelty towards the oppressors as distinguished from the oppressed." The Forsytes are universal. *Property* ranks well with Dostoievsky's CRIME AND PUNISHMENT and Björnson's ARNE.

1911

207 [Anthony, Luther B.] *"Justice.* An Example of Overworked Theme," DRAMATIST (Easton, Pa), II (Jan 1911), 128.

The theme of *Justice* is overworked in Act III because it is a harangue rather than a dramatic realization. This in turn gives rise to an arbitrary conclusion. The play is better read than said.

208 [Anthony, Luther B.] *"The Silver Box.* Galsworthy's Nearest Approach to Drama," DRAMATIST (Easton, Pa), II (April 1911), 158.

JG's main problem as a dramatist is that he is a novelist. In *The Silver Box,* theme predominates, resulting in two unnecessary shifts of curtain in Acts I and II. Act II is needlessly subdivided as JG's pen rambles, thus diluting dramatic illusion. Act III in part redeems the play through skillful dramatization and suspense. *Box, Joy,* and *Strife* are filled with an excellent and easy dialogue—and too much doctrine. [Review of *Plays. First Series.*]

209 Bernstein, Eduard. *"Justiz"* (*Justice*), in PAN, ed by W. Herzog (Berlin: P. Cassirer, 1911), pp. 503–8.

While Shaw is too much the preacher and satirist, JG has written two important plays, *Strife* and *Justice,* which thanks to their realism and artistry do much towards the long-needed reform of the English drama and theater. [In German.]

210 Björkman, Edwin. "John Galsworthy: An Interpreter of Modernity," REVIEW OF REVIEWS (NY), XLIII (May 1911), 634–36; rptd in IS THERE ANYTHING NEW UNDER THE SUN? (Lond: S. Swift, 1913), pp. 183–200.

JG "is first of all an artist, not a reformer"; his "aloofness" and unbiased observation are essential to his art. He is masterly in producing real human creatures, and yet "it is not as separate individuals, but as types of such groups, that his characters obtain their utmost significance." His work gives the impression of modernity, of "a time between two ages," a time of "a vain struggle to reach stability between a dying and a coming faith—between the faith in authority, in the god-given destiny of 'the best men,' and the faith in voluntary service and the intrinsic worth of all normal men." His plots are slender. ". . . his impressionism is underlaid with symbolism, so that he constantly uses the superficial reality of the fleeing moment to ensnare and hold the lasting reality of the spirit within." He is a "spiritual realist," and he continues "the formal and spiritual traditions" of Ibsen and Meredith.

211 Browne, Maurice. "The Hull-House Players in *Justice,*" THEATRE MAGAZINE (NY), XIV (Sept 1911), 89–90.

Justice, "the greatest English play since Shelley's *CENCI,*" is a great sermon. The silent scene in Falder's cell (Act III) touches greatness. [Browne praises the rise of English realistic drama.]

212 Burton, Richard. "The Bellman's Bookshelf. Aristocrats— Arguments for Peace," BELLMAN (Minneapolis), X (6 May 1911), 562.

The Patrician exhibits English aristocratic types and their belief in caste by focusing on two pairs of lovers. The richly characterized people are credible and likable; the natural descriptions remind one of George Meredith; and JG's sense of public duty is admirable.

213 "Chronicle and Comment: John Galsworthy," BOOKMAN (NY), XXXIII (April 1911), 116–17.

[A portrait of JG with a brief comparison to Arnold Bennett.]

214 Cooper, Frederic Taber. "The Quest of Novelty and Some Recent Books: *The Patrician,*" BOOKMAN (NY), XXXIII (May 1911), 318.

The Patrician is a "careful and penetrating" study of English social life. While it "lacks the amplitude" of *Fraternity,* it is an admirably proportioned and completed work.

215 Dukes, Ashley. MODERN DRAMATISTS (Lond: F. Palmer, 1911), pp. 141–50; rptd (Freeport, NY: Books for Libraries P, 1967).

JG in his dramas utilizes the common man, a figure frequently overlooked in the

theater except as a clown. JG failed in *Joy* because "the subject did not suit him."
In *Strife, Justice,* and *The Silver Box* one finds "an interplay of forces rather than
of persons." Although JG called *Justice* a tragedy, it is not a tragedy. The play
"arouses anger and pity, not inspiration. And inspiration is the test of tragedy."
Moreover, *Justice* is not "great drama." JG has a place in the modern theater,
even though his "preoccupation is with actuality."

216 Hueffer, Ford Madox. THE CRITICAL ATTITUDE (Lond:
Duckworth, 1911, 1915); rptd as written by Ford Madox Ford (Freeport,
NY: Books for Libraries P, 1967), pp. 94–100.

JG is "the moral observer of the British middle class," who gradually begins to
write more and more with "unimaginative description," his characters vying
"with each other in exhausting the gamut of imbecilities and of want of intellectual courage." JG is now presenting the literature of "agonised materialism."
His narrative method is to state a case and let readers adopt the moral attitude
they think appropriate. [General appreciation.]

217 "Literary Notes," INDEPENDENT (NY), LXXI (6 July 1911), 46.

The Little Dream is enigmatic: at best the fantasy verse is "commonplace," and
there is a conspicuous absence of new ideas.

218 "Literature: *The Patrician,*" INDEPENDENT (NY), LXX (22 June
1911), 1372–73.

JG's "excellent literary manner" in *The Patrician* gives a seriousness to his
patricians that they do not deserve. They do not have the "decency and righteousness" to justify their existence.

219 *"Little Dream,"* NATION (NY), XCIII (21 Sept 1911), 270–71.

The fanciful allegory of the Alpine maiden in *The Little Dream* is obscure,
unsuitable for drama, and trite. [Review displays no understanding of allegory
and symbolism.]

220 *"The Little Dream,"* SATURDAY REVIEW (Lond), CXII (15 July
1911), 88.

The Little Dream has "artificial" rather than "created" beauty. To be a "clever
man of ideas and words" is not necessarily to be a poet, and JG is the former.

221 Maas, William. "Literary Portraits: Mr. Galsworthy," DAILY
CHRONICLE (Lond), 11 Oct 1911, p. 4.

JG is one of Emerson's "symmetrical men." He does not shock: he writes in
"tones" rather than in "colors," usually choosing pleasing images and
metaphors to lessen the shock of man's "rude asperities." JG began to write to
tell a story, but he soon began to probe deeply into character. JG's later attempts
have worked basically the same ground deeper than he did in earlier volumes.
Seeming "trifles" take on meaning, but there is little appeal to the imagination.
Characters are filled with desires but lack the courage to act. JG's art primarily

"represents the cultivated classes perturbed by ideas," and he is thus primarily a "moral" rather than an "aesthetic" writer.

222 Meyerfeld, Max. "John Galsworthy," DAS LITERARISCHE ECHO (The Literary Echo) (Berlin), XV (1911), 1090–94.
JG is a craftsman of the first order and an excellent critic of the middle classes who has written the English BUDDENBROOKS. He deserves more attention in Germany. [A survey of his works.] [In German.]

223 "Mr. Galsworthy's Allegory," NEW YORK TIMES, 5 Nov 1911, p. 704.
The Little Dream is well written and casts a spell of beauty over the reader. The precise meaning of the allegory is uncertain, but this may be its most "elusive charm," since it permits each person to interpret the work according to his own experience and needs.

224 "Mr. Galsworthy's *Patrician,*" NEW YORK TIMES SATURDAY REVIEW OF BOOKS AND ART, 19 March 1911, p. 154; 9 April 1911, p. 222; 11 June 1911, p. 372.
The Patrician is an excellent story of the patrician class affected by things that are not supposed to affect them. The study of the young woman is masterful. JG continues in the tradition of George Meredith and follows Greek dramatic technique by having incidents discussed rather than portrayed. [The 19 March comments appear with minor alterations on 9 April and 11 June.]

225 "New Novels. *The Patrician,*" ATHENAEUM, No. 4356 (22 April 1911), 440.
The Patrician is notable for vigor of intellect and imaginative treatment of women. Characters are well-sketched, but the novel suffers from a conventional ending and a lack of humor.

226 "Notable Novels," OUTLOOK (NY), XCVII (25 March 1911), 629–30.
The Patrician, which demonstrates JG's ability to give "marvelous distinction" to the aristocracy, has advanced "style . . . vitality of characterization, and . . . human interest."

227 *"The Patrician,"* A.L.A. BOOKLIST, VII (May 1911), 396.
A "strong, vital work" for the educated reader, *The Patrician* is a "brilliant and convincing study" of four generations of an English family. The "ascetic but ardent" protagonist renounces happiness to satisfy his sense of honor and duty. *Patrician* shows both the weakness and the influence of the British patrician class.

228 *"The Patrician,"* CATHOLIC WORLD, XCIII (June 1911), 393–94.
The commonplace plot of *The Patrician* glows with "intense, dramatic inter-est." JG's impressionistic approach promises what is not delivered, failing in the

last chapters. *Patrician* recedes into fatalism, offering no solution to the conflict of tradition and authority vs. the heart. External nature voices JG's message interpreting moods and actions; JG cannot present life in depth.

229 *"The Patrician,"* LITERARY DIGEST, XLII (1 April 1911), 634.
The Patrician's theme of "family pride triumphant," in a novel filled with "delightful description" and excellent character development, "grips the reader with realistic power." JG occasionally "explains too much."

230 *"The Patrician,"* NATION (NY), XCII (20 April 1911), 399.
The characters of the dignified and powerful *Patrician* are "immemorial types"; the setting is time-honored. The novel might have bordered on greatness if JG's purpose had not wavered in the last chapters.

231 *"The Patrician,"* NORTH AMERICAN REVIEW, CXCIV (July 1911), 154.
[Favorable brief review of *The Patrician,* with no critical insight.]

232 *"The Patrician,"* SATURDAY REVIEW (Lond), CXI (18 March 1911), 337–38.
Characters in *The Patrician,* and not the author, discuss the possible survival of the hereditary aristocracy. Characters are both visible and understandable; occasional "quaint conceits" of circumlocution do not detract from the well-written and worthwhile novel.

233 *"The Patrician,"* SPECTATOR (Lond), CVI (18 March 1911), 408.
The Patrician, a "most remarkable act of literary homage to the hereditary system," is an act of "reluctant admiration" from a "convinced democrat and humanitarian."

234 Payne, William Morton. "Recent Fiction," DIAL (Chicago), L (1 June 1911), 442–43.
The Patrician is JG's best novel to date because he has mellowed. His indignation has been tempered to allow human nature more justification, while at the same time he "desentimentalizes life by painting its grim realities." The tragedy of the novel lies in the recognition that noble spirits cannot escape the "deadening consequences" of environment. Despite "democratic" tendencies, JG can still view the aristocracy objectively.

235 "Recent Fiction and the Critics," CURRENT LITERATURE, L (June 1911), 675–76.
[A survey of critical reactions to *The Patrician* as found in various publications is provided. Reviewer remarks that in both *The Patrician* and THE NEW MACHIAVELLI the hero is an aristocrat whose parliamentary career is jeopardized by an illicit love affair. The BROOKLYN EAGLE remarks that the passions are mastered by self-control in *The Patrician* and that JG seems to have abandoned his "destructive-critical vein." The London NATION observes that many of the

favorably treated characters in *The Patrician* would have been satirized in his earlier works. Both William Marion Reedy and the editor of the MIRROR (NY) believe that JG is at his best in this new, "almost lyrical mood." Some of the unfavorable critical comments are as follows: A London critic argues that the chief flaw is that Miltoun is saved by a woman, not by himself; the NEW YORK EVENING POST holds that it is not a great novel because of its slackness of nerve; the NEW YORK SUN maintains that Miltoun is a dreary ass; and the NEW YORK HERALD believes that the book is a near miss. It fails to provide an "exposition of patrician qualities," and it takes four hundred pages to go nowhere.]

236 Sherwood, Margaret. "The Makers of Plots," ATLANTIC MONTHLY, CVIII (Oct 1911), 557–68.
Plot is carefully developed in *The Patrician,* and the dramatic motif is always evident in the novel, characterized by classical restraint and finish. Tradition, working through character, develops into action. The strong characters shape their own destiny: JG does not manipulate them; rather he is the amused spectator enjoying the irony. Unfortunately, JG finds no hope in the struggle.

237 *"The Silver Box* at the Coronet," ILLUSTRATED LONDON NEWS, CXXXVIII (4 March 1911), 326.
The Silver Box is the subject of the last week of repertory at the Coronet. [Brief notice of performance, with short comments about major actors.]

238 Skelton, Isabel. "John Galsworthy, An Appreciation," WORLD TO-DAY (Lond), XXI (Aug 1911), 995–99.
[This appreciation covers both the novels and plays.]

239 Tivadić, Bravimiz. "John Galsworthy," SAVREMENIK (Zagreb), VI (1911), 400–408 [not seen].
[In Serbo-Croatian.]

1912

240 Adcock, A. St. John. "John Galsworthy's *Moods, Songs, and Doggerels,"* BOOKMAN (NY), XXXV (Aug 1912), 625.
JG's *Moods, Songs, and Doggerels* is a little constrained, "A little formal, a little artificial." He is unable to let himself go in any "rush of careless rapture."

241 Archer, William. PLAY-MAKING. A MANUAL OF CRAFTSMANSHIP (Lond: Chapman & Hall; Bost: Small, Maynard, 1912); rptd (NY: Dover, 1960), pp. 14, 25, 43, 88, 92, 107, 109, 216, 250, 275, 276, 290.
JG does not write with a scenario, believing that the theme becomes lifeless when

that happens. [JG's name is dropped on various occasions, usually in a life of other dramatists.]

242 Astor, Lenox. "Bibliographies of Younger Reputations: V—John Galsworthy," BOOKMAN (NY), XXXV (April 1912), 203–4.
[A list of JG publications to date, followed by an eight-item secondary bibliography.]

243 Beerbohm, Max. "Endeavour. BY J*HN G*LSW*RTHY," A CHRISTMAS GARLAND (Lond: Heinemann, 1912) pp. 101–14; rptd (1950); rptd in PARODIES: AN ANTHOLOGY FROM CHAUCER TO BEERBOHM—AND AFTER (NY: Random House, 1960), pp. 162–68.
[Beerbohm parodies JG with the following: Mr. and Mrs. Adrian Berridge, surrounded by their accustomed luxuries and their aged canary Amber, are confronted by the problem of a starving robin on the window sill this Christmas morning. They attempt to be principled and to do the right thing—in this case they decide not to feed the robin because "sporadic doles could do no real good"; they realize that their efforts may be futile for their beliefs may be "only a half-truth or not true at all."]

244 Burton, Richard. "The Bellman's Bookshelf," BELLMAN (Minneapolis), XII (30 March 1912), 403.
[Brief, favorable review of JG's "sympathetic" *The Pigeon* presently running at NY's Little Theatre.]

245 Burton, Richard. "Some Recent Dramas," DIAL (Chicago), LII (16 June 1912), 469–70.
The delightful *Pigeon* has no plot in the conventional sense and it proves nothing. As a student of society, JG presents the case and lets the viewer decide. [Review of performance at the Little Theatre.]

246 C., P. "Mr. Galsworthy's New Play," MANCHESTER GUARDIAN, 31 Jan 1912, p. 7.
The Pigeon at the Royalty Theatre loses the individual in the idea. Types are presented sympathetically, humorously, impartially, with pity and with insight. In spirit and detail it is like *Strife* and *The Silver Box* but lacks their design and photographic accuracy.

247 C., P. "Mr. Galsworthy's New Play," MANCHESTER GUARDIAN, 25 Nov 1912, p. 11.
JG's art is that of the historian, striving for completeness of presentation rather than searching for beauty or revealing the depths of human character. Typical scenes rather than dramatic conflict are common in *The Eldest Son*. The rejection scene is excellent theater, but the audience endures much superfluous material before it arrives. [Review of performance at the Kingsway Theatre.]

248 Carew, Kate. "John Galsworthy Really Gave Kate Carew Quite a Shock," NEW YORK TRIBUNE, 29 Dec 1912, Sec. 2, p. 3.

[This report of an interview reveals JG's opinions on censorship, working habits, socialism, women's rights, the philosophy of composition, and literary criticism.]

249 "Charming Comedy Concealing Profound Philosophy," TATLER (Lond), XLIII (14 Feb 1912), 183.

[A full-page photograph of a scene from *The Pigeon* at the Royalty Theatre.]

250 Cooper, Frederic Taber. "John Galsworthy: His Place in Contemporary Letters," BOOK NEWS MONTHLY (Philadelphia), XXX (July 1912), 774–77.

JG ranks high as man of letters because (1) he is a craftsman as seen in his inanimate objects; (2) he has an aptitude for learning as seen in his growth as a novelist from *Villa Rubein* to *The Man of Property* and *The Country House;* and (3) he has a philosophy of life that presents harping attacks on the system. JG's latest work (*The Patrician*) bodes ill for the future because it is a lesser Victorian novel rather than modern fiction.

251 Cooper, Frederic T[aber]. SOME ENGLISH STORY TELLERS: A BOOK OF THE YOUNGER NOVELISTS (NY: Holt; Lond: Richards, 1912), pp. 177–205.

JG's craftsmanship is of a high order; his material is well understood, but his philosophy is puzzling because he puts humanity ahead of the individual. His "carefully veiled exposition of Soames's brief hour of madness in *The Man of Property* [when Soames asserted himself as a husband] touches the limit of what is permissible in fiction." The chapter is "structurally perfect" and is comparable to an analogous scene in Maupassant's UNE VIE (A Life) except that JG gets full value out of the scene, while Maupassant does not. From JG's books one gets the impression that everything is wrong with the world; the focus of his criticism is the system itself. *The Patrician* lacks the vital grip of his earlier work, and it is true, as the ATHENAEUM suggests, that Mrs. Humphry Ward might have written it. JG as a writer of the new school of fiction is already handicapped when his latest work is Victorian in its materials and methods.

252 DeFoe, Louis V. "We Must Have Novelty," RED BOOK MAGAZINE (Chicago), XIX (June 1912), 369–75.

The Pigeon reproduces life realistically, compensating for lack of conflict. Wellwyn does not learn JG's moral: philanthropy will not raise the confirmed vagabond's level of living. [Plot-summary review of NY's Little Theatre production, with two photos of scenes.]

253 Dodd, Lee Wilson. "Book Reviews," YALE REVIEW, nsI (July 1912), 690–93.

The Pigeon is a charming yet profound reading of life, without sentimentality and without bending to the common desire for a well-made play. JG's ability to elevate drama above the masses is "naturalism of the very soul," almost mystical in nature.

254 Eckermann, Karl. "John Galsworthy," DIE NEUEREN SPRACHEN (Marburg), XX (May 1912), 65–93.
[A good discussion of *The Island Pharisees, The Man of Property, The Country House,* and *The Patrician,* concentrating on JG's raisonneurs, his gradual advances in plotting, and his views on social reforms. The plays are considered old-fashioned.] [In German.]

255 "*The Eldest Son* at the Kingsway," ILLUSTRATED LONDON NEWS, CXLI (30 Nov 1912), 792.
The Eldest Son is a realistic comedy of caste, filled with "much thought and observation . . . [a] strong grip on reality . . . a wide . . . sweep of social facts and social conventions." [Brief review of performance.]

256 "*The Eldest Son* by John Galsworthy," GRAPHIC (Lond), LXXXVI (30 Nov 1912), 854.
The Eldest Son at the Kingsway Theatre is the best play in London at the moment for intelligent people. [Moralizing plot summary.]

257 "Essays and Essayists," ATHENAEUM, No. 4435 (26 Oct 1912), 474.
The Inn of Tranquillity appeals most when JG attempts to show the difference between the real world and the world as the wealthy conceive it to be. "Wanted—Schooling" is noteworthy in calling writers and publishers to serve causes greater than themselves.

258 "The Everlasting Renewal," PALL MALL GAZETTE (Lond), 24 Oct 1912, p. 6.
[Editorial comment on *The House [sic] of Tranquillity* has no literary or critical focus.]

259 French, E. B. "Mr. Galsworthy's *Inn of Tranquillity,*" BOOKMAN (NY), XXXVI (Dec 1912), 445–47.
The Inn of Tranquillity is valuable for its sincerity, "fidelity to the author's mood," and unity that comes from a cadenced and "somewhat plaintive style."

260 "Galsworthy and the Labor Problem," OUTLOOK (NY), CI (20 July 1912), 607.
[Quotes passages from JG on the problem of labor.]

261 "The Galsworthy First Night," MANCHESTER GUARDIAN, 25 Nov 1912, p. 8.

[Winston Churchill was at the opening night performance of *The Eldest Son* at the Kingsway Theatre.]

262 "Galsworthy's *Pigeon*," REVIEW OF REVIEWS (NY), XLV (May 1912), 632.

Fantasy in *The Pigeon* is formless, actually an "exposition of a theory in brilliant dialogue"; nevertheless it is "wholly delightful and entertaining." [Photograph of JG accompanies the review.]

263 Hamilton, Clayton. "The Advent of the Little Theatre: *The Pigeon*," BOOKMAN (NY), XXXV (May 1912), 243.

JG's "Olympian aloofness" prohibits him from using his "imaginative sympathy" that might have suggested a solution for *The Pigeon*, an "inconclusive tract." JG draws no clear distinction between hero and villain; consequently the audience cannot identify with the forces of good.

264 Henry, Albert S. "Recent Dramas," BOOK NEWS MONTHLY (Philadelphia), XXXI (Dec 1912), 287–88.

In *The Pigeon* JG demonstrates poetically that human frailties are part of the system of nature. Mrs. Megan is one of JG's most subtle female portraits. *The Little Dream* appeals in its attempt at lyric poetry and careful finish, not as a major dramatic work.

265 "An Intellectual Muse," SATURDAY REVIEW (Lond), CXIII (11 May 1912), 592–93.

Moods, Songs, and Doggerels is poetry that should be read as concise treatments of themes that animate JG's fiction. As an analyst, his use of emotion is "tinged with morality"; and his people are "embodiments of thought and motive." The poems have a "prose excellence": JG is simply too intellectual and reflective to write lyrical poetry.

266 "John Galsworthy," HARPER'S WEEKLY, LVI (6 April 1912), 6.

Arnold Bennett, H. G. Wells, and JG are the most important living writers.

267 "John Galsworthy Denies That He Is a Reformer," NEW YORK TIMES, 10 March 1912, Sec. 5, p. 11.

[This article records an interview with JG, who denies an intent toward social reform in *Justice* and eschews presentation of dogma as the role of the novelist, while at the same time affirming that the novelist must convey his own beliefs and feelings. Rather than a "conscious purpose," the novelist has a "different point of view." The novelist must write about what moves him. JG prefers Dickens and Thackeray to Eliot and believes that Meredith is unpopular because of his too-poetic prose style.]

268 "John Galsworthy's Cure for Industrial Ills: Cooperation the End of the Teachings in His Novels and Plays, He Says—Denies That He Is a

Socialist; Author of *The Pigeon* Tells How Some of His Books Grew—
Likes His *Man of Property* Best," NEW YORK SUN, 10 March 1912, Sec.
4, p. 8.
[Report of an interview.]

269 "John Galsworthy's Latest: A Collection of Sketches and a Discussion of the Naturalistic Drama," SPRINGFIELD REPUBLICAN (Mass),
3 Nov 1912, p. 31.
The Inn of Tranquillity is characteristic of JG in both theme and artistry. More
than any other English author, JG approaches the style of Marguerite Audoux in
his "terse, unaffected, yet poetic simplicity."

270 Knopf, Alfred A. "John Galsworthy," NEW YORK TIMES SUN-
DAY REVIEW OF BOOKS, 13 Oct 1912, p. 582.
"Concerning Life" in *The Inn of Tranquillity* continues the pattern of *A Motley*.
"Quality" reflects JG's ability to "wring our hearts with the veriest commonplaces of everyday life"; "The Grand Jury" reflects his "fighting intellect"
at its best. "Concerning Letters" contains many insightful and beneficial reflections on the art of writing.

271 Lippman, Walter. "John Galsworthy," NEW YORK TIMES SAT-
URDAY REVIEW OF BOOKS AND ART, 24 March 1912, p. 159.
In *The Pigeon* JG reacts both to society's "uplifters" who pursue social problems
to solve, and to forces that attempt to regiment human beings.

272 "Literary Invasion of the Stage," LITERARY DIGEST, XLIV (23
March 1912), 592–93; pub simultaneously in OUTLOOK (NY), C (23
March 1912), 608–9.
[Brief article consists primarily of comments by JG in the NY press, as he is
directing *The Pigeon* at the Little Theatre.]

273 "Literature. *Moods, Songs, and Doggerels,*" ATHENAEUM, No.
4408 (20 April 1912), 429–32.
JG is the Hamlet of modern literature—"grave, melancholy, and questioning—
haunted by the riddle which baffles him." But he is psychologist and "pitiful
explorer" rather than poet. Consequently the "architectural quality" of *Moods,
Songs, and Doggerels* is not delicately woven. Craftsmanship is uneven, the
lyrical quality is seldom eloquent, and there is a sameness of mood; yet JG's
insight, sympathy, subtlety, and humanity recommend his poetry. The "graceful
slightness" of "Land Song of the West Country" and the tender whimsy of "To
My Dog" are superior to JG's more serious attempts.

274 "The Little Theatre Plays," AMERICAN PLAYWRIGHT (NY), I (15
April 1912), 116–18.
The Pigeon, currently under production, does not have enough action to sustain

the play. The last act has no suspense; it becomes a character study, losing dramatic credibility. [The purportedly specific critical and technical study of *The Pigeon* becomes moralistic and general.]

275 "The London Stage," ENGLISH ILLUSTRATED MAGAZINE (Lond), XLVI (March 1912), 608–15.

Despite what some other critics say, *The Pigeon* at the Royalty Theatre—with JG's sensitivity and "sad irony"—is not a failure, although "I was unable to answer exactly" what it "all amounted to."

276 "A Master of Characterization," AMERICAN PLAYWRIGHT (NY), I (April 1912), 142.

Excellent characterization recommends *The Pigeon*. The progressive play is a relief from "morbid and immoral plays" that characterize the newer breed of playwrights. [Review of published play.]

277 "Men and Books," LIVING AGE, CCLXXIII (1 June 1912), 565–67.

[In an article devoted to examining the necessity of reading modern literature, the writer comments that JG's *Justice* and *Strife* "in recent years have called forth the most criticism and interest in intellectual circles."]

278 Metcalfe, [J. S.] "Drama: Showing Good and Bad Tendencies," LIFE (NY), LIX (21 March 1912), 588.

The Pigeon simply presents well-drawn types from low society and restates the truism that the poor are always around. Its primary interest is in the currently popular theorizing about the poor. The Winthrop Ames production at NY's Little Theatre is good.

279 "Mr. Galsworthy and the Labor Problem," OUTLOOK (NY), CI (20 July 1912), 607.

[Summarizes JG's articles on labor appearing in the London DAILY MAIL.]

280 "Mr. Galsworthy's Essays," SPECTATOR (Lond), CIX (2 Nov 1912), 710.

"Mastery over neutral tint is undeniably complete" in *The Inn of Tranquillity*. JG's conclusions in "Concerning Letters" are "restrained, sober, and rusty."

281 "Mr. John Galsworthy," OUTLOOK (NY), C (23 March 1912), 608–9.

[General literary comments incited by JG's visit to the United States.]

282 "Mr. John Galsworthy's Fantasy: *The Pigeon* at the Royalty," PALL MALL GAZETTE (Lond), 31 Jan 1912, p. 5.

The Pigeon raises the question: Should wastrels be allowed to exist as the state seems to insist that they do; or should they, as the professor suggests, be exterminated?

283 *"Moods, Songs, and Doggerels,"* A.L.A. BOOKLIST, VIII (May 1912), 359.
[This brief review consists of quotations from the NEW YORK TIMES SATURDAY REVIEW OF BOOKS AND ART, 31 March 1912, p. 182.]

284 *"Moods, Songs, and Doggerels,"* NEW YORK TIMES SATURDAY REVIEW OF BOOKS AND ART, 31 March 1912, p. 182.
The conservative JG looks unflinchingly and without cheer to the future in *Moods, Songs, and Doggerels.* "A Dream" is too long and too argumentative. The poems generally are vigorous, courageous, healthful, and conventional.

285 *"Moods, Songs, and Doggerels,"* NORTH AMERICAN REVIEW, CXCV (May 1912), 713–14.
JG cannot maintain the lyric emotion necessary to create great poetry in *Moods, Songs, and Doggerels;* but some of the poems, especially "The Dream," show a "high power of moral interpretation."

286 Moses, Montrose. "The Advance Guard of British Dramatists," METROPOLITAN MAGAZINE (NY), XXXVII (Dec 1912), 31–32, 53–54.
JG is an ironic sentimentalist with insight into human nature. His novels have less structure than his plays. [Short general character sketches of various English playwrights.]

287 Moses, Montrose J. "Galsworthy-Dramatist," BOOK NEWS MONTHLY (Philadelphia), XXX (July 1912), 771–74.
JG, unlike most of his contemporaries, has vision, is true to humanity, is a thinker and an artist. Close observation is combined with the spirit of the poet and the reformer. Concern with the "cosmic spirit and with the irony of things" is the keynote to his artistry: this is well-developed in JG's essay on Joseph Conrad. JG is rich in attitude rather than in ideas; his greatest work is yet to come. [Article contains one-sentence comments about JG's best dramas.]

288 "The New Plays. The Little Theatre. *The Pigeon,*" THEATRE MAGAZINE (NY), XV (April 1912), 106–7.
JG, "an ardent Socialist," presents realistic pictures of life whimsically. The excellent and beautifully acted Winthrop Ames production of *The Pigeon* at NY's Little Theatre emphasizes that real charity consists of helping others without criticizing or embarrassing recipients. [Still photo of scene in Act II accompanies review.]

289 Oliver, D. E. THE ENGLISH STAGE: ITS ORIGINS AND MODERN DEVELOPMENTS (Lond: John Ouseley, 1912), pp. ix, xi, 104, 106, 128.
[Oliver briefly mentions the themes of *Strife, Justice,* and *The Silver Box.*]

290 P., H. T. "Galsworthy's Newest Play: *The Eldest Son,* a Review," BOSTON EVENING TRANSCRIPT, 7 Dec 1912, Sec. 3, p. 8.

Graphic narrative and the vivid character revelation in *Eldest Son* are complemented by "strokes of irony, delineation and keen, quick reflection, of which no other English playwright, unless it is Mr. Barrie, is capable."

291 Palmer, John. THE CENSOR AND THE THEATRES (Lond: T. Fisher Unwin, 1912); rptd (NY: Benjamin Blom, 1971), pp. 11, 208–14.

JG emphasized in his appearance before the "Joint Select Committee of the House of Lords and the House of Commons on the Stage Plays (Censorship)" in 1909 the hidden effect of censorship on the writing of plays. He testified that he had "not yet written" a play that he felt was quite acceptable because he believed it would not pass the Lord Chamberlain's Examiner.

292 Palmer, John. *"The Eldest Son,"* SATURDAY REVIEW (Lond), CXIV (7 Dec 1912), 703–4.

JG's reputation rests on the absence of vices rather than the presence of virtues. This is demonstrated by *The Eldest Son,* now being performed at the Kingsway Theatre. *Son* has no outstanding "fancy, humor or character"; it is a scenario rather than a play; the ironic comedy is incompatible with the sentiment. The performance is better than the play. [Palmer's thesis about JG's vices and virtues is developed in more detail in THE FUTURE OF THE THEATRE (Lond: G. Bell, 1913), pp. 149–52.]

293 Palmer, John. *"The Pigeon,"* SATURDAY REVIEW (Lond), CXIII (10 Feb 1912), 169–70.

Acts I and II of *The Pigeon* approach Gorki's THE LOWER DEPTHS in giving "a complete imaginative perception of a certain phase of life": at the end of Act II, *Pigeon* is "imaginatively complete." But JG descends to his usual self in Act III, effectively annulling Acts I and II by lecturing. Even in the first two acts, the characters have a "certain stiffness"; the dramatist's use of imagination has not yet manifested itself.

294 Parsons, Chauncey L. "John Galsworthy, an Unscientific Sociologist," NEW YORK DRAMATIC MIRROR, LXVII (3 April 1912), 5.

JG begins a work by looking for a human type, and, having found it, he looks for a philosophical generalization to develop it. The search crystallizes into expression and the expression into construction. He does not attempt to make his works a pulpit for sociology, but Christopher Wellwyn's tolerance (in *The Pigeon*) is the "right attitude carried to an extreme." [Record of an interview with JG.]

295 Payne, William Morton. "Recent Poetry," DIAL (Chicago), LIII (16 Aug 1912), 100–102.

[Review of *Moods, Songs, and Doggerels* consists of many quotations and a few lines of uncritical commentary.]

296 *"The Pigeon;* a Fantasy in Three Acts," A.L.A. BOOKLIST, VIII (May 1912), 359.

The Pigeon is in turn "pathetic, ironic and playfully imaginative." [Brief review.]

297 *"The Pigeon.* Mr. Galsworthy's Fantasy at the Royalty," DAILY CHRONICLE (Lond), 31 Jan 1912, p. 5.

The Pigeon is a delightful departure for JG, "whimsical, picturesque, mingling farce and philosophy with Shawesque freedom," yet giving the JG tradition of seeing the worst without cynicism and the best without sentimentality. JG's view seems to be that of the French immigrant: "wild birds" do not necessarily play upon tame birds. The play is a cross between a Dickensian Christmas tale and Haddon Chamber's PASSERS BY.

298 "Pigeons and Hawks: Mr. John Galsworthy's New Play at the Royalty," DAILY GRAPHIC (Lond), 31 Jan 1912, p. 6.

JG is "high priest" of the doctrinaire dramatists. *The Pigeon,* under the management of Vedrenne and Eadie at the Royalty Theatre is a farce with the underlying theme that "no public system . . . can save, reform, or transform the individual who is mastered by habit or [is] inherently the slave of his impulses." The street-people are contrasted effectively, realistically, and pointedly to a professor, an MP, and a canon.

299 "The Playhouses. *The Pigeon,* at the Royalty," ILLUSTRATED LONDON NEWS, CXL (3 Feb 1912), 150.

Though the fantasy *The Pigeon* occasionally tends to become farcial, JG never suppresses the serious themes of charity, drunkenness, vagabondage, marriage, and the close association of privation and jail. The slum types who contrast to Wellwyn enliven the play. [Review of performance.]

300 "Plays of the Week," NEW YORK DRAMATIC MIRROR, LXVII (13 March 1912), 6.

Much happens, but nothing changes in JG's *The Pigeon,* a loosely plotted view of the relations of characters to society. [A plot-summary review of performance at the NY Little Theatre.]

301 Pollock, Channing. "The Big Little Theatre," GREEN BOOK ALBUM (Chicago), VII (May 1912), 970–80.

JG, an English Eugene Brieux, tries to show the plight of lower classes. *The Pigeon* is a cross-section of commonplace, sordid, and ugly everyday life. The theme seems to be "what is, is and always will be." [The feature article on NY's Little Theatre devotes pp. 970–73 to the production of *The Pigeon.*]

302 "Recent Verse," SPECTATOR (Lond), CVIII (18 May 1912), 799–800.

JG's *Moods, Songs, and Doggerels* demonstrates a "sensitive joy" in natural beauty; but some courageous and noble poems are written in a manner "too tight-lipped to sing readily." Songs such as "Devon to Me" and "Cuckoo Song" are charming and nearer to essential poetry. [Omnibus review of seventeen volumes of poetry.]

303 Roberts, W. J. "John Galsworthy: An Impression," BOOK NEWS MONTHLY (Philadelphia), XXX (July 1912), 763–70.
[Romanticized record of a trip to visit JG at Manaton, containing seven photographs of JG and his Dartmoor surroundings.]

304 "Royal Court Theatre. CALLISTO and *The Little Dream,*" TIMES (Lond), 29 Oct 1912, p. 9.
The Little Dream's allegory is too light to bear all the scenes and effects.

305 "Royalty Theatre. *The Pigeon,*" TIMES (Lond), 31 Jan 1912, p. 7.
The Pigeon, speaking winningly and whimsically of charity, asks theatergoers to pity, understand, and succor the outcasts of society. The "symmetrical and synchronistical arrangement" of the three advisors' "personified theories" reminds one of Thomas Love Peacock's technique. Wellwyn's charity is that of Oliver Goldsmith rather than that of Samuel Johnson.

306 S., D. "Plucking the Pigeon. Mr. Galsworthy's Latest Social Comedy," DAILY EXPRESS (Lond), 31 Jan 1912, p. 5.
JG is the British Brieux: plays present social problems and incidental comments by artist and observer. *The Pigeon* at the Royalty Theatre, while superficially ending as sardonic tragedy, is "really a courageous and original essay in optimism."

307 "The Slaughter of Animals," JEWISH CHRONICLE (Lond), 20 Dec 1912, pp. 9–10.
[Editorial comment agrees with JG that brutal slaughter of animals is bad (reacting to articles by JG appearing in the DAILY MAIL 16–19 Dec 1912).]

308 "Social Justice in Recent Verse," OUTLOOK (NY), CI (8 June 1912), 290–93.
Moods, Songs, and Doggerels is "a book of courage, of faith in courage, of lovely visions of nature . . . of clear, refreshing song."

309 "Some Books of Verse," INDEPENDENT (NY), LXXII (18 April 1912), 844.
[Brief review of *Moods, Songs, and Doggerels,* emphasizing JG's care in craftsmanship and the British desire to escape into the "quaint English outland."]

310 "The Theatre. *The Eldest Son* at the Kingsway Theatre," ACADEMY (Lond), LXXXIII (7 Dec 1912), 738–39.
The Eldest Son is "sincere . . . realistic . . . well considered, distinguished, profound, and boldly simple."

311 Tridon, André. "An Interview with the Author of *The Pigeon*," THEATRE MAGAZINE (NY), XV (May 1912), viii, 158, 160.
JG, "anonymous" in appearance, knows conventions but scorns them. [Interviewer records some of JG's well-known opinions about drama and the novel.]

312 "Two Books by Galsworthy," INDEPENDENT (NY), LXXIII (26 Dec 1912), 1498–99.
Those who think that *The Pigeon* was JG's best will undoubtedly enjoy *The Inn of Tranquillity;* but those who prefer *Justice* will not be impressed. Nonetheless, it is full of "heartsearching intuition" and "luminous understanding." *The Eldest Son,* "admirable in pungency and cleanliness," has little of the "whimsicality and picturesqueness" of *Pigeon* but "is forceful and moving." *Son* is "more shapely and firm-textured" than most of JG. [Review of *Tranquillity* and *Son.*]

313 "Verses by Galsworthy," REVIEW OF REVIEWS (NY), XLV (May 1912), 636.
[Favorable one-paragraph review of *Moods, Songs, and Doggerels.*]

314 W., H. M. [Massingham, H. W.?]. "Mr. Galsworthy's New Play: A Drama of Caste," PALL MALL GAZETTE (Lond), 25 Nov 1912, p. 7.
[Conventional plot summary and laudatory review of performance of *The Eldest Son* at the Kingsway Theatre.]

315 "The Week: Mr. Galsworthy and the Labor Problem," OUTLOOK (NY), CI (20 July 1912), 607.
JG remarks on the causes of labor unrest in two recent articles in the London DAILY MAIL. Companies are run by directors whose responsibilities are to produce maximum profit for the shareholders without regard for "the good of society as a whole." JG's solution is an educational process that would awaken among the prosperous a sense of "the fundamental unity and interdependence of society," but in England the British public schools or " 'caste factories' " perpetuate the class split. The influence of the churches is inadequate for the task because there are many whom the churches do not affect, and the churches lack the strength to generate "a great national change towards the essence of Christianity." JG feels that both in America and in England education teaches one how to run a business but not how to develop spiritually.

316 West, Magda Frances. "Little Stories of the New Plays," GREEN BOOK ALBUM (Chicago), VII (June 1912), 1198–1200.
[Plot summary of *The Pigeon.*]

317 White, Matthew, Jr. "The Stage," MUNSEY'S MAGAZINE (NY), XLVII (May 1912), 273–85.
The Pigeon is caviar for the average theatergoer, actually noncommercial in intent. It has no definite dénouement and offers no solution to the problems presented. [Review of production at NY's New Theatre.]

318 "Youth Knocking at the Door: *The Eldest Son* and THE YOUNGER GENERATION," GRAPHIC (Lond), LXXXVI (7 Dec 1912), 897.
[Three stills from *The Eldest Son* at the Kingsway Theatre are reproduced.]

1913

319 Andrews, Charlton. THE DRAMA TO-DAY (Phila & Lond: J. B. Lippincott, 1913), pp. 72, 106, 125–32, 137, 144, 145, 205, 219.
JG insists that story must evolve from character, not vice versa. *Justice* wrestles with the paradox of human justice driving one to suicide—actually the predicament of a woman does it. The second act of *Justice* is pessimistic, unjustifiably long, and repetitive. In *The Silver Box* pessimism evolves from hopeless environment; in *Strife,* two obstinate wills struggle. *The Pigeon,* a well-constructed play, illustrates the futility of charity and society's illogical attitudes. *The Eldest Son,* exemplifying respectability as opposed to morality, lacks "high indignation" and "fanciful charm." JG the realist works with vital problems but often neglects effective use of dramatic technique. [Andrews hints several times at JG's naturalism but discusses realism without differentiating between the two.]

320 [Anthony, Luther B.] *"The Eldest Son,"* DRAMATIST (Easton, Pa), IV (Jan 1913), 327–28.
Structurally, *The Eldest Son* is JG's best play, but there is no conclusion. The two-hour treatment of unlicensed lechery is a "drab mess at its merriest." [Moralistic review.]

321 Aynard, Joseph. "L'Auberge de la Tranquillité" (The Inn of Tranquillity), LE JOURNAL DES DÉBATS (Paris), (15 Jan 1913), p. 1 [Édition quotidienne?].
As a reading of *The Inn of Tranquillity* shows, JG is, like Wells and Bennett, an apostle of the rationalist development of the human mind; he believes in determinism and follows the ideas of Spencer, Huxley, and Darwin, but his sentimental and artistic determinism is something new in England. It testifies to a deep change in English society. [In French.]

322 Bab, J. "Shaw und Galsworthy," GEGENWART, No. 46 (1913) [not seen]. [Listed in BIBLIOGRAPHIE DER DEUTSCHEN ZEITSCHRIFTEN LITERATUR, 1913 (Leipzig: Felix Dietrich, 1914).]
[In German.]

323 "A Book a Week," OUTLOOK (NY), CIII (25 Jan 1913), 231–32.
Essays and glimpses in *The Inn of Tranquillity* "are infused with . . . sympathy for human needs," gently expressed with "fine literary artistry." JG sees "hope and

seriousness in all human effort"; he is graceful in his transition from one essay to the next.

324 Bredvold, Louis I. "A Philosophy of Fiction," DIAL (Chicago), LIV (16 June 1913), 503–4.

In *The Inn of Tranquillity*, "Concerning Life" gives thoughtful and delicately sensitive distinction to seeming trifles, which come to have profound significance under JG's handling. "Concerning Letters" tells of the writer's pursuit of truth by "bringing the light into the street that people may see things as they are. . . . If the story is true it has a moral." Detachment is essential to the artist so that he may worship Truth impersonally, without any immediate practical purpose. JG's primary qualities are disciplinary and critical rather than inspirational, the last of which is perhaps the most important.

325 Bullis, Helen. "Galsworthy. An Allegory of Youth, Age and Passion in *The Dark Flower*," NEW YORK TIMES SUNDAY REVIEW OF BOOKS, 19 Oct 1913, p. 560; rptd in excerpt in NEW YORK TIMES SUNDAY REVIEW OF BOOKS, 30 Nov 1913, p. 664.

The beautifully written *Dark Flower*, with its emphasis on ill-starred love and the longing of youth, can be read either as argument or as allegory. JG is both a great English novelist and a great moralist, the latter because he teaches that the "dark flower of passion" has the breath of death, not life.

326 C., R. *"The Fugitive:* Fine Realism in Mr. Galsworthy's New Play," DAILY GRAPHIC (Lond), 17 Sept 1913, p. 3.

The Fugitive, the latest of a series dealing with women running away from their husbands that began with Meredith's DIANA OF THE CROSSWAYS, triumphs because of the acting of Irene Rooke as Clare Dedmond. The people are natural; the last act has especially fine realism; but as usual the stage propagandist JG is lost in the shadow and uncertainty of theme.

327 Cary, Lucian. "Fathers and Sons," NEW YORK TIMES SUNDAY REVIEW OF BOOKS, 2 Feb 1913, p. 47.

"Gentlemanliness" in *The Eldest Son* is both JG's "distinction and his limitation": his knowledge, sympathy, and skill allow him to portray the weakness of the gentility.

328 Cazamian, Madeleine. "La pensée de John Galsworthy" (The Thought of John Galsworthy), REVUE DU MOIS, XV (1913), 449–67 [not seen].

[In French.]

329 Clark, Barrett H. "Early London Season," DRAMA (Chicago), IX (Nov 1913), 187–93.

JG gets to the "root of humanity" in *The Fugitive*. [Plot-summary review that emphasizes JG's "sureness of touch."]

330 Clark, J. M. "The English Novel, 1870–1910," GERMANISCH-ROMANISCHE MONATSSCHRIFT (Heidelberg), V (1913), 667–76.

As "physician of the age" JG modeled his satire and various scenes in his works after Meredith.

331 Cooper, Frederic Taber. *"The Dark Flower,"* BOOKMAN (NY), XXXVIII (Dec 1913), 414.

The Dark Flower, "a curiously interesting and probing study of man's passions and woman's weaknesses," sacrifices JG's personality and individualized characterization as he strives for technique, condensation, and economy. Its beauty lies in its symmetry of structure and symbolism.

332 Courtney, W. L. "Realistic Drama. III, " FORTNIGHTLY REVIEW (Lond), C (1913), 103–10; rptd in LIVING AGE, CCLXXVIII (27 Sept 1913), 779–86.

The tone of *Strife,* hinted at in *The Silver Box,* has a touch of real cynicism, for the forces are so balanced that the individual is the one who suffers. [There is nothing about JG in parts 1 and 2.]

333 Curle, Richard. "John Galsworthy," BOOKMAN (Lond), XLV (Nov 1913), 91–97.

JG "has the instinct of the social reformer joined to the instinct of the artist." His method of impartiality is, as a writer in THE NATION said, " 'an artistic device, not a matter of divine indifference.' " In spite of his balancing, JG "loses in a double sense that aloofness without which it seems so impossible to create real people": his choice of subject must be arbitrary, and his stance as a reformer makes it obvious which side he is on. Generally, he does not have "sufficient creative power to force us to see his people apart from a background of pronounced but rather general characteristics." Another important aspect of his work is to be found in the way he enwraps his novels in an atmosphere "severe and soft."

In drama "art is legitimately wedded to preaching." Purely literary drama cannot now exist in England: witness the failures of James and Conrad. Of the moralizing playwrights—Shaw, Barker, and JG—JG is "the most impressive because he is the most natural and the most impersonal." *Strife* is his greatest achievement in dramatic form. Of his novels "one must imagine that to a considerable extent they are plays in the form of narrative." *The Island Pharisees* and *The Patrician* are poor as novels; as plays they might have been capital. Even in his best novels—*The Country House, The Man of Property,* and *Fraternity*—one notes that JG's insight into character is "dramatic rather than illuminating." He shows an "incapacity for dialogue" in his novels. As a novelist his chief drawbacks are that he "is not original in a great sense" and that "he is not sufficiently an artist." He "is a man of great talent, great depth of feeling, great comprehension, but he is not a great genius." He is not at heart a novelist; his novels, although excellent and unusual, "are always somewhat stilted." It is as a dramatist that his reputation is most secure.

334 Curle, Richard. "New Books: *The Dark Flower,*" BOOKMAN (Lond), XLV (Nov 1913), 107–8.

The Dark Flower is "a genuine, able, and eloquent novel." Part one is the poorest. "Mark Lennan is good in so far as he is typical, but poor in so far as he is meant to be a real creation." Olive Cramier and Nell Dromore are the best characters; most of the others are conventional. Such "is the inherent weakness of a novel in which the theme is the most important thing." Much of the humor is crude, but the novel is "an arresting and curious work of art."

335 *"The Dark Flower,"* A.L.A. BOOKLIST, X (Dec 1913), 156.

The Dark Flower presents with insight the "sympathetic . . . exquisite feelings" of love in the three stages of the protagonist's life. Especially effective is the part about youth. [Brief review.]

336 *"The Dark Flower,"* NATION (NY), XCVII (27 Nov 1913), 508.

The Dark Flower, a disagreeable and morbid chronicle, has "neither mawkishness nor fruitless eroticism." The three episodes in Mark Lennan's love life are developed to the exclusion of almost everything else.

337 *"The Dark Flower,"* OUTLOOK (NY), CV (8 Nov 1913), 548.

The Dark Flower, the "symbol of unregulated passion," is treated with restraint and good taste. [Moralistic plot summary.]

338 *"The Dark Flower,"* SATURDAY REVIEW (Lond), CXVI (11 Oct 1913), 464–65.

Life in *The Dark Flower* is "a queer vivid aching business." The reader is an interested spectator rather than a participator in JG's portrayal of the life of passion. His style is occasionally poetic.

339 "The Dark Flower on Several Occasions," NEW YORK SUN, 15 Nov 1913, p. 9.

[Plot-summary review of *The Dark Flower.*]

340 Edgett, Edwin Francis. "John Galsworthy—Mind Reader: His Latest Novel a Study of Three Epochs in the Love Life of a Man," BOSTON EVENING TRANSCRIPT, 11 Oct 1913, Sec. 3, p. 10.

The Dark Flower proves JG "a master analyst of the soul of man." A "franker and a finer discussion of certain aspects of life" than "Meredith or Hardy or Ibsen or Sudermann ever dreamed of writing," *Dark Flower* "discards all the old conventions . . . upsets some of the most sacred moral traditions . . . [and] throws aside all commonplaces of fiction."

341 *"The Eldest Son,"* NORTH AMERICAN REVIEW, CXCVII (Jan 1913), 142–43.

[Plot-summary review of the "artistically done" problem-play *The Eldest Son.*]

342 *"The Eldest Son; A Domestic Drama in Three Acts,"* A.L.A. BOOKLIST, IX (Jan 1913), 188–89.

JG's irony attacks convention in *The Eldest Son,* emphasizing the difference between the unwritten law as applied to an under-keeper and to a member of the gentry. Dialogue is natural without being vulgar. [Brief review.]

343 *"The Fugitive* at the Court,"* ILLUSTRATED LONDON NEWS, CXLIII (20 Sept 1913), 422.

The Fugitive has somberness and pity but lacks "the inevitability of true tragedy." [Primarily a plot-summary review.]

344 *"The Fugitive* at the Court Theatre,"* ACADEMY (Lond), LXXXV (27 Sept 1913), 400–401.

JG is artistically at fault in *The Fugitive* for making Clare unnecessarily unhappy. The psychological romance is "finely imagined and admirably played."

345 "Galsworthy's Dramatic Writings," REVIEW OF REVIEWS (NY), XLVII (May 1913), 632–33.

[Plot-summary review of *Plays: The Eldest Son, The Little Dream,* and *Justice.*]

346 Gibson, Wilfrid Wilson. "Mr. Galsworthy's Plays," BOOKMAN (Lond), XLIII (Jan 1913), 216–17.

The Little Dream illustrates that JG has no sense of poetry, genius, or fantasy. *The Eldest Son* is a well-made play, but characterization is shadowy and sketchy; it is workmanlike but undistinguished. *Justice* has "vitality of characterization" but "no clash of character." JG needs to lift dramatic crisis above the "clash of contemporary circumstances" in his drama. [Review of *Plays: The Eldest Son, The Little Dream, Justice.*]

347 Grossmann, Stefan. "Galsworthy," MAERZ (Munich), VII, pt. 2 (1913), 358–60.

[Grossmann, who was responsible for a Viennese production of *Strife,* ironically warns against considering JG as the strongest hope of the modern theater, for after all JG is a propagandist, a gentleman-revolutionary for whom the bourgeois theater is not yet ready. *The Silver Box* and *Justice* are exercises in mathematics, though they contain effective scenes; *Strife* is more than a chess game.] [In German.]

348 Handl, Willi. "Der Menschenfreund" (The Philanthropist), DIE SCHAUBUEHNE [Berlin], IX (1913), 920–22.

The Pigeon, a mild comedy striving too hard for serious effects, was disastrously produced at Prague. Shaw is a much better playwright and social critic than JG. [In German.]

349 Hangest, G. d'. "La Nature dans l'oeuvre de John Galsworthy" (Nature in the Work of John Galsworthy), REVUE GERMANIQUE, IX (1913), 172–94.

JG handles nature more effectively than Hardy did. In JG the psychological moment unites with itself as its opposite; the way that JG delineates nature gives the reader a chance to perceive more exactly the symbols of nature. He is remarkably faithful to nature. The anguish of the stricken bird in Mrs. Pendyce's garden evokes for the reader a universe that is very close to ours with its tragedies and loves; as this world reveals itself, the reader loses his ignorance of it and is brought almost to a remorse like that of the bird's.

Ethics are never separate from aesthetics for JG, and they emanate from nature. The intimate union of sensations and of subtle intellectual atmosphere is one of the constant traits of Galsworthian genius. As seen in *Jocelyn* love is the route designed by nature through which intelligence works on a universal plane. Jocelyn is the first of JG's women in whom passson is sharpened without being overintellectualized. Although women illustrate better than men JG's point of view, he seems more sympathetic to men like Hilary, Stone, and Courtier; they are intellectuals who do not resist human temptations by formulae. One sees in them the workings of the introspective conscience.

JG's sense of psychology is the key to his universe. Whether in high-class areas like Hampstead or elsewhere, nature plays the same role and remains indifferent to humanity; at moments of high tragedy the terrible presence of nature is affirmed. Because nature is indifferent to human tragedy and probably because the characters themselves are not serious enough, they cannot grasp the true meaning of the tragedy that befalls them.

For JG the realities of life are found in the fleeting tints of color; art represents the line which is frequently mutilated by truth. The purpose of art is not egoistic glory but the relevation to men of a pantheistic brotherhood. JG as poet loves to paint souls, places, and moments where the conflict is manifested between the impassible flowing of things and the love for that which one will never see twice. Men take precautions against nature and are therefore isolated in solitude. All the Forsytes are menaced by death as they gather around Aunt Ann's bier. As far as nature is concerned, death and birth are two equal gestures. Nature may be indifferent, or as with the death of the Hughes baby the parents accepted the reality without horror; for them the harmony with nature was automatic. Modern society rejects a relationship with nature; therefore, one must struggle against it. One struggles against nature in order to dominate it economically and thereby loses a sense of harmony; one struggles against an overwhelming grandness which is nature. Nature becomes a provisional enemy rather than an ally of man. Because of this struggle JG's sympathy goes towards humanity; his pity goes to the suffering of those who do not know either how to foresee or how to accomplish. For JG old age would never truly be a messenger of sadness; even if the power of the artist weakened, one would be rewarded by the discerning meditation (nobly intellectual), the rich memories of discovered aesthetics in a universal setting, and the subtle pleasures to be found in his work—the peace and the beauty of JG's magic visions. [In French.]

350 H[apgood], N. "Galsworthy's Latest," HARPER'S WEEKLY, LVIII (22 Nov 1913), 28.

The Dark Flower treats the topic of sex in a mature and decorous way, pointing a judicious path away from the squeamishness that often accompanies such a topic.

351 Henry, Albert S. "New Plays," BOOK NEWS MONTHLY (Phila), XXXII (Sept 1913), 71–73.

The Eldest Son is less effective than *Strife* and *The Pigeon;* but it is full of subtle interpretations of human nature and is praiseworthy as an indictment of dual standards of society.

352 Howe, P. P. "Mr. Galsworthy as Dramatist," FORTNIGHTLY REVIEW, XCIV (1913), 739–51; rptd in LIVING AGE, 7th Ser, LXI (1913), 331–40 [not seen]; rptd [?] in DRAMATIC PORTRAITS (NY: Mitchell Kennerley, 1913), 231–54.

JG's drama is a "drama of social contrasts." *Strife* is not about Anthony and Roberts; it is about "Anthony and his kind and . . . Roberts and his kind" when faced with strife. *Justice* is not about Falder; it is about the way those who are strong treat the weak. "The defect of Mr. Galsworthy's virtue of impartiality is that it has become self-conscious."

353 Hueffer, Ford Madox [Ford Madox Ford]. "Literary Portraits—VI: Mr. Galsworthy and the *Dark Flower,*" OUTLOOK (Lond), XXXII (18 Oct 1913), 527–28.

Satirical characters destroy the virtuous protagonists of a novel, and the virtuous protagonists destroy the effect of the book: e.g., Becky Sharp, Amelia, and Dobbin in VANITY FAIR. JG is the best—the only—satirist in England, but having a heart of gold and being a finished satirist "is a very ticklish affair." Frequently the power of his work is diluted by doctrinaire humanitarianism. JG is a fine dramatist—witness *The Silver Box* and *Joy; The Fugitive* is "almost always . . . a fine play," but today we cannot afford the sentimentality of Malise (the literary gentleman) as he chatters about leaving one's husband in such terms as "clouds and the growth of wings." Satire is not only negative; it "is in itself constructive." [Ford had planned to review *The Dark Flower* but had not received a copy of the novel in time.]

354 Kellner, Leon. "John Galsworthy," DAS LITERARISCHE ECHO (Berlin), XV (1913), 815–19.

JG is not a member of the avant-garde; he is an honest realist and reformer, who sympathizes with his characters in the manner of Tolstoy. *Strife* and *The Silver Box* owe much to Hauptmann's plays DIE WEBER [The Weavers] and DER BIBERPELZ [The Beaverskin], respectively. [In German.]

355 Korsch, Karl. "John Galsworthy," DIE TAT (Leipzig), V (1913), 961–64.

From an aesthetic point of view, *Justice, The Silver Box, The Man of Property, Fraternity,* and *The Country House* are average contributions to literature. If read in chronological order, the novels, which are superior to the plays, reveal JG's development from the social reformer to the objective but sympathizing observer of social events. [In German.]

356 L., S. R. "New Galsworthy Play. *The Fugitive* at the Court Theatre," DAILY CHRONICLE (Lond), 17 Sept 1913, p. 5.

The Fugitive shows care and sincerity but lacks the sense of humor that is the "salvation of seriousness." Yet Clare Dedmond is much superior to others of her type—a potentially good woman, but a fugitive. JG takes the study of an erring lady a step farther than either Arthur Wing Pinero in IRIS or Eugene Walter in THE EASIEST WAY.

357 Lawrence, Boyle. "A Tragedy of Discontent: Mr. Galsworthy's Play at the Court Theatre," DAILY EXPRESS (Lond), 17 Sept 1913, p. 4.

"If art means beauty," JG is a vivisectionist rather than an artist. JG continues to become more grim as he develops as a playwright, but he maintains his rigid impartiality. *The Fugitive* uses "austere restraint" to condense a "lifetime into an essence." The last act is "wonderful in its reserve, splendid in its suggestion of great tragedy, fine in its simplicity"—but "hateful."

358 MacCarthy, Desmond. *"The Fugitive,"* NEW STATESMAN, 27 Sept 1913 [not seen]; rptd in DRAMA (Lond & NY: Putnam, 1940), pp. 194–99.

JG's dramatic characters in general lack "personality"; this is especially true in *The Fugitive,* where JG is more interested in the case of the "runaway wife's battle with a hypocrite world" than in the individual. Such commonplaceness is the "category of the generalizing not the artistic mind." If Clare Dedmond were taken out of her predicament, she would be dull: the play fails because it is not an interesting character study. Clare's suicide gives JG an easy way out, because it solves nothing.

359 McGirr, Alice Thurston. "Reading List on John Galsworthy," BULLETIN OF BIBLIOGRAPHY, VII:5 (April 1913), 113.

[Lists reviews of *The Silver Box, Joy, Strife, The Eldest Son, Justice, The Little Dream,* and *The Pigeon* and nine general critical articles.]

360 "Mr. John Galsworthy's New Play. *The Fugitive* at the Court Theatre," TIMES (Lond), 17 Sept 1913, p. 9.

Most of JG's plays could be labelled "General cussedness of things: Exhibit No. ——." In *The Fugitive* it is "wife on strike." The play is well written but tedious because of lack of cheerfulness.

361 "The New Books: Galsworthy at His Best—A Piece of Him," INDEPENDENT (NY), LXXVI (30 Oct 1913), 218.
JG the "creator of beauty" is paramount in *Dark Flower.*

362 O., S. *"The Fugitive,"* ENGLISH REVIEW (Lond), XV (Nov 1913), 625–27.
The great merit of *The Fugitive* is its objectivity—no caricature, no compromise, no propaganda, just life. Characterization is subtle, the "work of an artist." The play fails because "after dinner the public wants entertainment." [An often flippant review of performance.]

363 O., S. "Play of the Month: *The Eldest Son,"* ENGLISH REVIEW (Lond), XIII (Jan 1913), 318–20.
The Eldest Son typifies the English tradition of "primogeniture, class tradition and snobbery" that is unable to see beyond horsemanship and tradition; only the son has "certain blurred moments of honour." One can laugh at *Son* because "the deeper emotions are not touched, because we English don't believe in misalliances."

364 Palmer, John. *"The Fugitive.* The Royal Court Theatre," SATURDAY REVIEW (Lond), CXVI (20 Sept 1913), 359.
The Fugitive is "honest work," but the characters illustrate JG's scheme and theme rather than develop an inner sense of direction. The occasionally unbelievable heroine has a "sullen and sombre glow of passion" that appeals.

365 Palmer, John. THE FUTURE OF THE THEATRE (Lond: G. Bell & Sons, 1913), pp. 39, 71, 83, 113–14, 132, 144, 149–52, 158, 176, 183.
JG's dramatic naturalism is the method of "protest and revolt"; it will most likely not lead to "revival and reconstruction" of English drama. The merit of JG's plays is "negative," showing distrust of, and rejecting, devices and dramatic clichés that might be considered "theatrical." He presents situations rather than writes plays; his "dramatic virtues" consist almost wholly in avoiding "dramatic vices." *The Eldest Son* is a case in point. JG's plays, like those of his contemporaries, are primarily naturalistic, protesting against the "exhausted and mechanical theatre of the Lord Chamberlain's period of undisputed supremacy."

366 *"Plays,"* OUTLOOK (NY), CIV (3 May 1913), 38.
JG's *Plays: The Eldest Son, The Little Dream,* and *Justice,* unlike Hauptmann's BEFORE DAWN and Strindberg's DANCE OF DEATH, are "written with the touch and spirit of a great surgeon rather than the gesture of a man flinging an . . . egg against a stone wall."

367 *"Plays. Second Series,"* NATION (NY), XCVI (15 May 1913), 505–6.
[Brief, conventional review of *The Eldest Son, The Little Dream,* and *Justice.*]

368 *"Plays. Second Series: The Eldest Son; The Little Dream; Justice,"*
A.L.A. BOOKLIST, IX (May 1913), 369.
[Brief announcement of publication.]

369 Polgar, Alfred. "Galsworthy und Wedekind" (Galsworthy and
Wedekind) DIE SCHAUBUEHNE (Berlin), IX (1913), 1025–27.
JG's *Justice,* which was well produced by the Viennese Volksbuehne, is a simple
and, in spite of its understatements, a sentimental play for members of Parlia-
ment. To move MP's is, however, more important than to move the critics. [In
German.]

370 Prilipp, Beda. "John Galsworthy, der Epiker und Dramatiker"
(John Galsworthy, the Epic Writer and Dramatist), GRENZBOTEN,
LXXII (1913), 501–6 [not seen].
[In German.]

371 "The Repertory Season at the St. James's Theatre," ACADEMY
(Lond), LXXXV (27 Dec 1913), 821–22.
[Brief, favorable review of performance of *The Silver Box*.]

372 "The Revival of *Strife* at the Comedy," DAILY GRAPHIC (Lond),
LXXXVII (10 May 1913), 774.
[Brief plot summary.]

373 "Rule That Proves the Exception," NATION (NY), XCVII (23 Oct
1913), 380.
In *The Pigeon,* the flower girl's reaction to being saved from suicide places JG as
a spokesman for the popular radical school that, led by Shaw, is conducting
guerilla warfare against things as they are. JG's play is epigrammatic with some
malice and some popular truth; but it lacks the robustness of real conviction.
[The reviewer qualifies the charge of radicalism by asserting that the whole play
is not radical—JG is a sane enough man after all.]

374 "Shaw, Galsworthy, und Strindberg" (Shaw, Galsworthy, and
Strindberg), DIE SCHAUBUEHNE (Berlin), IX (1913), 1107–10.
It is surprising that the Deutsche Kuenstlertheater produced *Strife* at all. The fact
that JG's works have effected social reforms is no reason for staging his well-
meant but boring social treatises. [In German.]

375 Skemp, A. R. "The Plays of Mr. John Galsworthy," ENGLISH
ASSOCIATION: ESSAYS AND STUDIES, IV (Oxford: Clarendon P, 1913),
151–71.
JG's basic ideas, very close to Shelley's, are obscured by his determined artistic
naturalism. Unlike Shaw, JG is content with the dramatic possibilities of the
commonplace. JG refuses to emphasize the "inner tendencies" of character even
though he sees them, thus losing the chance to heighten dramatic tension. JG is
limited by his desire to portray life as he sees it; the best artists, however,

"preserve the truth of a wider vision." The heroic rarely finds a place; neither does the romantic—even in *Joy,* "which cries aloud for romance." He constantly tones down the romantic element when revising the novels as well. In the spirit of comedy, his "sensitive sympathy gives his smile an ironic twist." Comedy in the plays is confined to "character, dialogue, and incidental situations," not the main action. Irony in fact makes life bearable.

JG has the power of the poet in his "unfailing recognition of the permanent and universal elements in his material"—by generalizing the significance of the action even though he might sacrifice individuality. From the "lack of sympathy and imagination" comes evil, for "without imagination true sympathy is impossible, and pity is a poor substitute."

JG's chief weakness as a dramatist lies in the lack of definite progress of character and action; but his "plot-worksmanship" is excellent. In stagecraft and in literary quality, JG is "characterized by unforced naturalism and reserve of emphasis." Stage directions reveal his "fine economy . . . concentration of effect," and alertness to the effects of the senses. [Skemp's critical and sympathetic essay is one of the best assessments of JG's dramatic ability.]

376 Storer, Edward. "Dramatists of Today: H. Granville Barker. John Galsworthy," BRITISH REVIEW (Lond), IV (Nov 1913), 248–62.
JG's success and failure lie in the fact that he "humanizes social contradictions . . . till they become real and poignant . . . and he dehumanizes his . . . characters by making them the servants of a theory . . . or a social anomaly." [Storer repeats general critical comments about *Justice, The Pigeon,* and *Joy;* other plays are mentioned in passing.]

377 *"Strife* Revived at the Comedy," ILLUSTRATED LONDON NEWS, CXLII (10 May 1913), 638.
[A brief notice, commenting on the pleasant fact that the leading original performers starred again in the revival.]

378 Terry, J. E. Harold. *"The Eldest Son,"* BRITISH REVIEW I (Jan 1913), 154–60.
The Eldest Son presents problems without solutions, emphasizing conflicts between parent and child, British social classes, and tradition and modernity. [Review of production at the Kingsway Theatre.]

379 W., H. M. [Massingham, H. W.?]. "Mr. Galsworthy's New Play: *The Fugitive* at the Court Theatre," PALL MALL GAZETTE (Lond), 17 Sept 1913, p. 7.
[A plot summary serves as a review of performance.]

1914

380 Anderson, Margaret C. *"The Dark Flower* and the 'Moralists,' "
LITTLE REVIEW, I (March 1914), 5–7.
The Dark Flower has aroused "more ignorant, naïve, and stupid condemnation
than [has] anything published for a long time." There is a beauty about this book
that few books achieve. The "handling of the episodes is so unepisodic that you
feel you've been given the man's whole life"; the "remarkable intensity of the
writing" helps give the book this "effect of completeness." JG's style creates
"an inevitability about its choice of beautiful and simple words that makes them
seem a part of the nature they describe." His "psychology is profound—
impregnable." In sum, *The Dark Flower* possesses a "noble simplicity" and a
"noble beauty."

381 [Anthony, Luther B.] *"The Fugitive,"* DRAMATIST (Easton, Pa),
V (April 1914), 459–61.
JG dismisses the concept of structure in his dramas. He "slightly modifies his
fiction form by making his chapters in acts and forcing his characters to tell the
story in the first person." Character is delineated in the novelist's manner rather
than through contact with his fellow man, which is necessary for viable drama.
Consequently, his plays are meaningless for the masses: *The Fugitive* is a case in
point.

382 [Anthony, Luther B.] *"The Mob,"* DRAMATIST (Easton, Pa), VI
(Oct 1914), 510–12.
JG is too much the propagandist, dismissing good dramatic technique to present
moral theses. The protagonist's self-sacrifice is not justified; the domestic complication of Act III is not warranted by earlier actions in *The Mob.*

383 Archer, William. "Recent London Productions," NATION (NY),
XCVIII (14 May 1914), 582–83.
The Mob is distinguished drama but less good than *The Silver Box* or *Strife.*
Because the humanitarian gets the better of the artist, the play is not life-like.
[Review of performance at the Coronet Theatre.]

384 Bascom, Elva L. *"The Mob,"* WISCONSIN LIBRARY BULLETIN
(Madison), X (Nov 1914), 260.
[Brief plot-summary review of *The Mob.*]

385 Bascom, Elva L. *"Plays, Third Series,"* WISCONSIN LIBRARY
BULLETIN (Madison), X (Dec 1914), 303.
[Brief review of *Plays. Third Series,* emphasizing JG's artistic technique.]

386 C., P. *"The Mob* in London," MANCHESTER GUARDIAN, 21 April 1914, p. 5.

The Mob at the Coronet Theatre marches forward with "grimly set teeth," with compassion for truth and justice, and with disinterested sympathy. The play lacks the touch of the artist because there is no real character development: JG addresses the audience as if it were a public meeting.

387 Carneades, Junior. "Letters to Certain Eminent Authors. XX. To Mr. John Galsworthy," ACADEMY (Lond), LXXXVII (22 Aug 1914), 230–31.

JG's progressive humanization can be traced from *The Country House* through *The Dark Flower. House*, filled with satirical humor, is glib and too polished, lacking in movement, in clash of temperament, and in genuine emotion. In *Strife* JG ceases to be a "university don" and becomes human. *The Patrician*— essentially true, alive, and appealing—is a perfect novel, not driven by JG's Fabian sentiments. *Flower* is "painful in its truth" and alive with emotion and passion; the subject is treated with delicacy, exactness of observation, and poetic justice. [Carneades does not mention *The Man of Property.*]

388 Chandler, Frank Wadleigh. ASPECTS OF MODERN DRAMA (NY: Macmillan, 1914); rptd (1939); rptd (St. Clair Shores, Mich: Scholarly P, 1971), pp. 84, 86, 126, 127, 223, 225, 324–25, 336, 340–42, 344, 345–46, 349, 352–54, 396, 427, 457–58.

In JG's symbolic drama *The Little Dream* the poetic prose is better than the verse, but "neither . . . is particularly distinguished." *The Fugitive* and *The Eldest Son* treat the "new freedom for women": Clare (*Fugitive*) is strong in honor and weak in self-control and reason; the fault lies in the fact that whereas Clare desires self-assertion, "the harsh world" is blamed for her failure. When the pregnant Freda (*Son*) rejects Honorable Bill's offer of marriage, JG introduces the new note of protest that a woman's honor is not vindicated merely by marriage to her seducer. The humor of *Joy* lies in the fact that each member of the family is an egotist; though following the unities, the acts are "queerly choppy" because people often come and go, talking with little apparent reason. *The Silver Box* and *Justice* assail the "undiscriminating interference of the law with private concerns." *Justice* is especially effective in its matter-of-factness. The fantasy *The Pigeon* reproaches "professional charity" for not truly helping "the irresponsible giver and the irresponsible vagabond." *Pigeon* is JG's "most agreeable play, artistic and genial," comic in its criticism, and apologetic for "old-fashioned loving kindness." In *Strife* JG "emphasizes the futility of conflict between capital and labor" but admits its contemporary inevitability. *Strife* has "more fire, more intensity" than other JG plays. [The discussion largely consists of plot summaries, with the various plays entered under chapter headings such as "The Drama of Symbolism" (*Dream*), "Wayward Women" (*Fugitive*), "Family Studies" (*Joy*), "Ideals of Honor" (*Son*), and "Plays of Social Criticism" (*Pigeon, Justice, Strife*).]

389 Croom-Johnson, A. "The Drama Month by Month: Mr. Galsworthy Holds the Scales," REVIEW OF REVIEWS (Lond), XLIX (June 1914), 496–97.

JG's chief characteristics are impartiality, refusal to intensify a dramatic situation that does not evolve naturally from the plot, and an almost total concern with social evils. [Croom-Johnson comments generally on *Justice* and *Strife*.]

390 "Drama. *The Mob* at the Coronet," ATHENAEUM, No. 4513 (25 April 1914), 603–4.

The idea behind *The Mob* is not clear; because of its mawkish sentimentality, the play does not convince.

391 Eagle, Solomon [pseud of John Collings Squire]. "Depressed Philanthropist," NEW STATESMAN (1914) [not seen]; rptd John Collings Squire, BOOKS IN GENERAL, FIRST SERIES (Lond: Martin Secker, 1919; NY: Knopf, 1919; Freeport, NY: Books for Libraries P, 1971), pp. 96–101.

The Little Man shows JG's defects at their worst: because he is so one-sided, the audience reacts to his views, even though the "dull monotony" is occasionally refreshed by glimpses of humor. In addition, his realism is phony. At heart a humanitarian, JG has devolved into "a dismal and costive kind of literary method which makes him look like a fretful and dyspeptic man who curls his discontented nostrils at life as though it were an unpleasing smell."

392 *"The Fugitive,"* NATION (NY), XCVIII (26 March 1914), 342.

The Fugitive is clever, vigorous, and well written, but unsatisfactory. The play falters because the fugitive is a victim of weak will rather than fate or circumstance. The dramatic argument favors free love.

393 *"The Fugitive,"* OUTLOOK (NY), CVI (14 Feb 1914), 371.

JG's fine craftsmanship and conciseness in *The Fugitive* complement a "study of the dislocated human spirit."

394 *"The Fugitive,"* REVIEW OF REVIEWS (NY), XLIX (April 1914), 501–2.

JG uses hackneyed dramatic expedients in *The Fugitive* to detail how human instincts break through the crust of modern life. Clare is a parasitic woman "robbed by false education and stultifying environment" of all usefulness and power of self-expression.

395 "Galsworthy's Anti-War Play," CURRENT OPINION, LVII (Oct 1914), 268–69.

[Plot-summary review of *The Mob*.]

396 "Galsworthy's Latest Play: *The Fugitive,* A Drama of Unalleviated Tragedy," SPRINGFIELD REPUBLICAN (Mass), 16 June 1914, p. 17.

The Fugitive has more dramatic highlights than some other JG plays, resembling

Paul Hervieu's work in the "inexorable focus of attention on . . . inevitable tragedy, and in the paring away of all alleviating details."

397 "Galsworthy's New Play, *The Mob,*" NEW YORK DRAMATIC MIRROR, LXXI (22 April 1914), 7.
[Plot summary and an announcement that Otis Skinner will play the role of Stephen More in *The Mob* at Washington's National Theatre.]

398 George, W[alter] L[ionel]. DRAMATIC ACTUALITIES (Lond: Sidgwick & Jackson, 1914), pp. 5, 8, 9, 21–22, 24–25, 26, 33, 50, 91.
The public on the whole shuns JG. *Strife* is "gloomy & cruel." The "intellectual playwrights," and JG is one of them, are guilty of "ten crimes": (1) shadowy plot, (2) the play without a climax, (3) hypertrophy of atmosphere, (4) sentiment, (5) garrulousness, (6) the exaggerated type, (7) inveterate gloom, (8) obscurity, (9) length, (10) shapeless purpose. JG, the leading British dramatist, is full of bitterness and gloom; his "young people are old"; *The Eldest Son* is bitter; *Joy* has no joy, only "pale egoism"; but *Strife* and *The Silver Box* are "perfectly constructed works." [This study is filled with undeveloped generalizations.]

399 Goldman, Emma. "John Galsworthy," THE SOCIAL SIGNIFICANCE OF THE MODERN DRAMA (Bost: Richard G. Badger; Toronto: The Copp Clark Co., 1914), pp. 196–225.
JG and Hauptmann are the best living writers. JG is neither propagandist nor moralist but a realist who presents true stories with characters that give an "inherent moral" without lecturing. A "true picture of life" outlives a moral code. The moral lesson of *Strife* is that men must quit trying to reconcile "Capital and Labor" and learn that revolutionaries like David Roberts will lead the way to a "truer recognition of human values." *Justice* has "socio-revolutionary significance" in portraying the "inhuman system" that destroys the Falders and Honeywills and suggests the helplessness of society as Ruth in desperation sells herself and Falder destroys himself. *The Pigeon* shows humanity crushed in life's "fatal mechanism": charity is incapable of coping with poverty. Professors (Alfred Calway), judges (Sir Hoxton), and preachers (the Canon Bertley)—symbolizing education, law, and theology—cannot cope with social problems; the sympathetic Christopher Wellwyn tries but cannot. *Pigeon* is satiric, because the three learned men lose sight of the poor as they pursue their theories. Ironically, English society prosecutes Megan, who tries to commit suicide because of the way society has dictated that she live. [Plot summary and propaganda.]

400 Hamilton, Clayton. STUDIES IN STAGECRAFT (NY: Henry Holt, 1914), pp. 5, 10, 84, 95, 97, 99, 154, 199, 201.
The Pigeon has "no rise . . . climax . . . fall . . . [or] catastrophe," yet it is acclaimed even though it is "merely an exposition of a problem of society." [Fleeting references to JG.]

401 Henderson, Archibald. THE CHANGING DRAMA: CONTRIBUTIONS AND TENDENCIES (NY: Henry Holt, 1914), pp. 38, 69, 70, 101, 102, 137, 155, 157, 158, 170, 171, 175, 176, 177, 178, 179, 218, 223, 256.

JG, like Ibsen and Shaw, "expose[s] the tragic consequences of adherence to 'duties' . . . no longer obligatory" and enjoins us to break away from old customs. Unities of time (six hours) and place (one) in *Strife* demonstrate remarkable control; *The Fugitive* illustrates true pity and terror in its use of a breach of the contemporary social and legal code; JG's work belongs to the class of "drama of social implication" rather than to the class of "drama of sociological injunction"; and his dramas often fail to stir the emotions because of his "inflexible sense of rectitude and fairness": he is the "contemporary examplar" of "complete impartiality." [A broad discussion of theater, with general occasional references to JG, unsubstantiated by specific critical reading.]

402 Jacobs, Joseph. "Mr. Galsworthy. *The Fugitive,* His Latest Play, Among His Best," NEW YORK TIMES SUNDAY REVIEW OF BOOKS, 22 Feb 1914, p. 87.

JG's economy in *The Fugitive* resembles that of Aubrey Beardsley: especially effective is the fitting of conversation to character without sounding too booklike. Act IV elevates the play above the ordinary, but Clare's suicide indicates a "poverty of dramatic invention." *Fugitive* "reeks of sex."

403 James, Henry. "The Younger Generation," TIMES LITERARY SUPPLEMENT (Lond), 19 March and 2 April 1914, pp. 133–34, 137–58; rptd in HENRY JAMES AND H. G. WELLS: A RECORD OF THEIR FRIENDSHIP . . . , ed by Leon Edel and Gordon N. Ray (Urbana: University of Illinois P; Lond: Hart-Davis, 1958), 178–215.

JG, Conrad, Maurice, H. G. Wells, and Arnold Bennett are the not-quite-so-young writers of the younger generation. JG, Edith Wharton, and Maurice Hewlett remain "essentially votaries of selection and intention and . . . [are] embodiments thereby, in each case, of some state over and above that simple state of possession of much evidence, that confused conception of what the 'slice' of life must consist of, which forms the text of our remarks."

404 "John Galsworthy's Latest Play: *The Mob,* a Drama of a Man Who Dies for His Ideal," SPRINGFIELD REPUBLICAN (Mass), 23 Aug 1914, p. 15.

In some respects, *The Mob* is not convincing because of its melodrama. To make the plot more believable, JG could have presented the hero's case more fully.

405 MacCarthy, Desmond. "John Galsworthy. *The Mob,*" NEW STATESMAN, III (2 May 1914,) 116–17; rptd in DRAMA (Lond & NY: Putnam, 1940), pp. 200–205; rptd in THEATRE (Lond: MacGibbon & Kee, 1954; NY: Oxford UP, 1955), pp. 107–10.

The Mob is more suited for the Boer War era than 1914. It does not pass the test as a work of art; rather, it is more like a daydream, with Stephen More standing above the flag-waving world because he is "too lofty to retaliate." The two main characters, Stephen and his wife, are too languidly drawn to be effective on the stage, embodying as they do two opposing points of view: "Stephen is gentle, dignified, and depressed; [his wife] . . . is reproachful and depressed—consequently *we* are depressed." The big problem with the play is that More's sufferings are more decorative than inward. [MacCarthy's brief but penetrating study of *Mob* is the best extant.]

406 Mencken, H. L. "Galsworthy and Others," SMART SET (NY), XLIII (July 1914), 153–60.
[Citation by E. H. Mikhail, JOHN GALSWORTHY THE DRAMATIST: A BIBLIOGRAPHY OF CRITICISM (Troy, NY: Whitston, 1971), p. 53, is incorrect. On these pages is "The Anatomy of the Novel," and there is no reference to JG.]

407 Mew, Egan. "*The Mob:* Miss Horniman's Season at the Coronet Theatre," ACADEMY, LXXXVI (25 April 1914), 533.
The Mob is still-born, dull, and without topical force; Stephen More is priggish and unbelievable.

408 "Mr. Galsworthy's Eruption," SATURDAY REVIEW (Lond), CXVII (7 March 1914), 298–99; rptd in LIVING AGE, CCLXXXI (11 April 1914), 116–18.
JG, disgusted with politics, is benevolent towards all, favors liberty and happiness, and advocates full employment. Unfortunately, he does not explain how to accomplish all of this. An absolutist in politics, JG needs to become "an embarrassed man of affairs" so that he can learn about the way the world is run. [This is a severely cutting criticism of JG's criticisms of Parliament's "barbarities."]

409 "Mr. Galsworthy's New Play: *The Mob* at the Coronet," TIMES (Lond), 21 April 1914, p. 4.
The theme of *The Mob* is fidelity to conscience. The play fails because the man is passive, standing "like a monument," with no character development. Attempts to embellish and to give color are artistically irrelevant. Moral indignation is not translated into artistic imagination.

410 "Mr. Galsworthy's Protest," NATION (NY), XCVIII (19 March 1914), 285–86.
JG is wrong if he thinks parliamentary reforms by themselves will cure the ills of society. [Comments on JG's letters to the TIMES (Lond), 28 Feb and 9 March, on "The Heartlessness of Parliament."]

411 "*The Mob,*" DIAL (Chicago), LVII (16 July 1914), 55.
The irony permeating *The Mob* is that the "mob-spirit" dominates individuals as well as groups, often destroying those who are faithful to their ideals.

412 "*The Mob,*" OUTLOOK (NY), CVII (25 July 1914), 758.
[Plot-summary review.]

413 *"The Mob* at The Coronet," ILLUSTRATED LONDON NEWS, CXLIV (25 April 1914), 698.

The Mob, written and dramatized in a "grim and melancholy key," suffers from a "certain rigidity." The characters are perhaps too sharply delineated. The producer shows courage—and stretches political credulity—by staging the play so soon after the Boer War.

414 *"The Mob.* Crowd Influence and Crowd Conscience the Subject of Mr. Galsworthy's Latest Play," NEW YORK TIMES SUNDAY REVIEW OF BOOKS, 26 July 1914, p. 321.

The Mob, a study in emotion, is especially vital to the United States at this time because of the understanding it can give concerning the Mexican question. The play unfortunately falters dramatically because it is more a conflict of ideas than of people.

415 Moderwell, Hiram Kelly [Hiram Motherwell]. THE THEATRE OF TO-DAY (NY & Lond: Dodd, Mead, 1914); rptd (NY: Dodd, Mead, 1927), pp. 218–19.

JG, the best living creator of the "well made play," has a "keen sense of proportion and fitness." He states unsolved problems with reserved seriousness and bitter humor.

416 Morton, Elsie E. (ed). SOME SLINGS AND ARROWS FROM JOHN GALSWORTHY (Lond: Elkin Mathews, 1914).

[A series of snippets, usually no more than a sentence, from works by JG on various topics. The collection is included in this secondary bibliography because of the critical judgment involved in Morton's selection and because the title might be misleading.]

417 "The New Books: The Frailty of Woman," INDEPENDENT (NY), LXXIX (17 Aug 1914), 250.

[Brief review of *The Fugitive.*]

418 "The New Order of Men of Letters," LITERARY DIGEST, XLVIII (4 April 1914), 758–59.

[An excerpt of JG's letter to the TIMES (Lond), 28 Feb, castigating Parliament for its callous inaction is followed by excerpts of editorial reaction.]

419 "The Newest Books: *The Mob,"* INDEPENDENT (NY), LXXIX (13 July 1914), 72.

The Mob, like *Strife,* is a "masterful portrayal of mob psychology, pillorying the man who braves it, in order that later it may erect a monument to him."

420 Norwood, Gilbert. "The Present Renaissance of English Drama," WELSH OUTLOOK (Cardiff), I (March 1914), 122–27; (April 1914), 165–70; (May 1914), 212–17.

The Dark Age of English drama comprises the years from 1779 (Sheridan's THE

CRITIC produced) to 1889 (first English production of A DOLL'S HOUSE). Ibsen deserves the credit for the fact that England now has real dramatists. For England he is the father of the "drama of ideas." At the present time our dramatists fall into three classes: (1) Sir Arthur Pinero, H. A. Jones, Somerset Maugham, Arnold Bennett, Rudolf Besier, Oscar Wilde; (2) John Masefield; (3) G. B. Shaw, JG, Harley Granville-Barker, St. John Hankin. The writers in the third class are the English Ibsenists. Although there is an exaggeration of mere photography in most of their work, three features characterize their work: a photographic series of scenes from life, a construction of scenes into significance, and a mastery of language.

JG's sole aim is reform, and the stage for him is a platform. His doctrinaire manner is often quite inartistic, and he forgets that one aim of drama is to entertain. Artistically, *Justice* is the extreme case of photography and, therefore, ranks low, although it is effective as propaganda. At the moment his reputation rests on *The Silver Box* and *Justice,* but he is "far too much of a phamphleteer and too little of a poet." G. B. Shaw is the most brilliant of the English Ibsenists. Except for Shaw, England's present leading dramatists "are mostly but good second-rate writers." The rise of the repertory theatres in Manchester, Glasgow, Dublin, and elsewhere is an additional important aspect of the present renaissance of drama in England.

421 *"Plays. Third Series: The Fugitive; The Pigeon; The Mob,"* A.L.A. BOOKLIST, XI (Oct 1914), 68.
[One-sentence statements of the themes of the three plays comprise this brief review.]

422 "Politics and Irrelevance," SPECTATOR (Lond), CXII (7 March 1914), 381.
[Reaction to JG's "platitudinous" letter to the TIMES (Lond), of 28 Feb 1914, about Parliament's inactivity.]

423 "The Right to Believe," NEW REPUBLIC, I (7 Nov 1914), 27–28.
In *The Mob* JG finally takes a stand on a moral issue, with an occasional suggestion of moral preciosity. *Mob* dramatizes courage.

424 Roger-Cornaz, F. "Une galerie de portraits. Les romans de M. John Galsworthy" (A Gallery of Portraits: The Novels of John Galsworthy), BIBLIOTHÈQUE UNIVERSELLE ET REVUE SUISSE (Lausanne), 4th ser, LXXIII, No. 217 (Jan 1914), 129–64.
One may overlook *The Island Pharisees* because JG has made a better job of it in *The Patrician* and *The Country House.* In four novels—*Patrician, The Country House, Fraternity,* and *The Man of Property*—JG has created an almost complete *oeuvre;* each presents a profound study of a class of English society. There is a gallery of portraits to be found in these novels; each portrait is different from the others and is distinctive and essential. In *Patrician* Lord Denis Fitz Harold and

Lady Barbara Caradoc are examples of the supreme flowering of the English aristocracy. Miltoun with his grand moral beauty and deep feelings remains a little unclear and is less alive than Lady Barbara. Mr. and Mrs. Pendyce in *House* exemplify the landed gentry. *Fraternity* is a book full of delicate and profound poetic beauty. Hilary, its hero, has become so intellectualized, so cultivated that it is difficult for him either to have a precise opinion or to accomplish a decisive act. Although *Property* is considered JG's best work, it has less charm than either *Fraternity* or *House,* and it is less brilliant than *Patrician.* One may, nevertheless, see in *Property,* perhaps better than elsewhere, JG's abilities for observing characters and for making known their essence by means of a few words or reference to a few crucial gestures. The Forsytes are *nouveau riche;* they have the prejudices of the aristocracy without their education, traditions, and culture. Outsiders like Courtier and Bosinney are not important for themselves but for the reactions they evoke in, for instance, the Forsytes. And in the end Hilary has left without the little model and Irene has returned home; society has reasserted its rights and is strong again. [No French translations had appeared at the time the article was written.] [In French.]

425 "Roll of Drums in Galsworthy's Play," NEW YORK TIMES, 26 July 1914, Sec. 5, p. 8.
[The article about *The Mob* is devoted solely to discussing the effectiveness of bagpipes playing to focus the contrast between the peace-loving Stephen More and the mob.]

426 "A Run Around the Playhouses," GRAPHIC (Lond), LXXXIX (2 May 1914), 772.
[A still from *The Mob* at the Coronet Theatre is accompanied by a cursory and unfavorable comment.]

427 Schuetze, Martin. "A Reply to Mr. Galsworthy," NATION (NY), XCIX (3 Dec 1914), 657–58.
[A polemic attacking JG for comments made in a letter about Germany: The comment, printed in many papers in the United States, tortures "half-truths" until they yield "untruths."]

428 W., H. M. [Massingham, H. W.?]. "Mr. Galsworthy's Play: *The Mob* at the Coronet," PALL MALL GAZETTE (Lond), 21 April 1914, p. 7.
JG exhibits both "conscientiousness and fairness" in *The Mob.* The pace of the play is sustained, the dialogue is vivid, and the "delineation of life faithful."

429 Wells, H. G. "The Contemporary Novel," AN ENGLISHMAN LOOKS AT THE WORLD (Lond: Cassell, 1914), pp. 148–69 [not seen]; rptd in HENRY JAMES AND H. G. WELLS: A RECORD OF THEIR FRIENDSHIP . . . , ed by Leon Edel and Gordon N. Ray (Urbana: University of Illinois P; Lond: Hart-Davis, 1958), pp. 131–56.
Despite the fact that there are grave risks for a novelist to intervene in person

before his readers, such intervention is acceptable if it is done without affectations—e.g., Conrad in LORD JIM—but JG's "cold, almost affectedly ironical detachment" is less effective than Conrad's.

1915

430 [Archer, William?]. *"A Bit o' Love,"* NATION (NY), CI (2 Sept 1915), 298–99.
Typical of JG is the "genuine realism enriched by imagination, a definite purpose, and sterling literary skill" in *A Bit o' Love.* Stage success is limited because of its conventional and dramatically feeble ending. The main dramatic defect is that "improbable instances" cannot really settle moral and religious problems. The chief virtue is its felicitous dialogue in Devonshire dialect.

431 Archer, William. "The Repertory Theatre. Two Preposterous War Plays," NATION (NY), CI (1 July 1915), 25.
A Bit o' Love is a "painful episode" rather than a tragedy, compensating for the pain by its underlying beauty and by its picture of how misery can be brought on by stupidity. The gloomy play is lightened by its scenes of rustic life and some humor during the village meeting. [Review of London performance.]

432 B., E. "Mr. Galsworthy in Eclipse," NEW REPUBLIC (NY), IV (2 Oct 1915), 240–41.
JG's art has slipped in *The Freelands.* People are social types, "a summary of society," unlike the Forsytes and Pendyces. Felix illustrates JG's forte of the delightful "free play of the mind and the imaginativeness of indecision"; Nedda is the freshest and most complete character; Derek, the moral revolutionary, is disappointing because he gives up too soon. JG occasionally seems "slipshod in his social sympathies," especially with Kirsteen; and his phrasing is glib, insignificant, and on occasion vulgar.

433 *"Bit o' Love,"* A.L.A. BOOKLIST, XII (Nov 1915), 76–77.
The delicate but insistent *A Bit o' Love* shows the difference between the theory and practice of Christianity. The play is more interesting for local atmosphere than for plot. [Brief review.]

434 *"A Bit o' Love,"* GRAPHIC (Lond), XCI (5 June 1915), 734.
A Bit o' Love at the Kingway Theatre is "characteristic" JG.

435 *"A Bit o' Love,"* NEW YORK DRAMATIC MIRROR, LXXIII (23 June 1915), 5.
The best part of *A Bit o' Love* is the constant suggestion of paganism. [Plot-summary review of London performance.]

436 *"A Bit o' Love* at the Kingsway,"* ILLUSTRATED LONDON NEWS, CXLVI (5 June 1915), 740.
A Bit o' Love is humane; the protagonist, "gentle and good." With the variety of opinions surrounding the central incident, the village seems to be the "central character of the tale." JG is England's "most brilliant dramatist."

437 *"A Bit o' Love:* New Galsworthy Play at the Kingway," TIMES (Lond), 26 May 1915, p. 11.
The theme of the sublimity of forgiveness in *A Bit o' Love* is treated with simplicity and dignity, but the play lacks color. The saint is not "warm and palpitating" enough for drama; beauty is present, but not energetically.

438 Caro, J. "John Galsworthys Dramen" (John Galsworthy's Dramas), DIE NEUEREN SPRACHEN (Marburg), XXIII (Dec 1915), 481–93.
In light of the continental tradition, JG's social realism is old-fashioned. JG is, however, a better craftsman than the more original Shaw and lets social problems speak for themselves. While he seems to forget about the class antagonism in *Strife* too soon, *The Silver Box, Justice,* and *The Eldest Son* are simple but impressive plays. [In German.]

439 "The Charitable Satirist," SATURDAY REVIEW (Lond), CXIX (22 May 1915), 532–33.
In *The Little Man, and Other Satires,* satire is balanced by sympathy; moods change quickly from irony to pity. "The Little Man" balances irony and humor. "The Plain Man" and "The Superlative" read together give a composite view of JG's message. The book actually is a "satire against satire": the mockers are mocked.

440 Clark, Barrett H. THE BRITISH AND AMERICAN DRAMA OF TO-DAY: OUTLINES FOR THEIR STUDY (NY: Henry Holt, 1915); rptd (Cincinnati: Stewart & Kidd, 1921), pp. vi, 15, 74, 82, 90, 93, 128–39, 156, 159, 165.
[Pages 128–39 contain general outline information about *Strife* and *The Pigeon.*]

441 Cooper, Frederic Taber. "Some Novels of the Month: *The Freelands,*" BOOKMAN (NY), XLII (Oct 1915), 218–19.
The Freelands is a "triumph of masterly and close-fitted construction."

442 Crawford, J. R. *"The Mob,"* YALE REVIEW, nsIV (April 1915), 622–23.
The theme of true vs. false patriotism in *The Mob* is lost because the audience cannot understand why Mrs. More leaves Stephen. JG's stage women have too much logic and not enough humanity.

443 Dickinson, Thomas H. (ed). CHIEF CONTEMPORARY DRAMA-TISTS (Cambridge, Mass: Houghton Mifflin, 1915; 2nd ed, 1922), p. 661.
[Biographical note precedes text of *Strife*.]

444 "Drama and Music," NATION (NY), C (10 June 1915), 663.
In *Plays. Third Series*, *The Fugitive* is uncompromisingly direct and poignant, with some special pleading for the trapped married woman. *The Mob*, notable for "literary skill and emotional and dramatic power," is especially remarkable for its high morality and courage in presenting an unpopular theme. *The Pigeon* is a delightful modern comedy.

445 "Dramatic Gossip," ATHENAEUM, No. 4570 (29 May 1915), 490.
[Notice of the last performance of *A Bit o' Love* at the Kingsway Theatre by the Liverpool Commonwealth Company.]

446 E[dgett], E[dwin] F[rancis]. "Galsworthy the Dramatist: A Little Play of English Country Life," BOSTON EVENING TRANSCRIPT, 19 June 1915, Sec. 3, p. 8.
A Bit o' Love is not a play of crucial social problems but a play of morals and character. Copious stage directions are "exact without being unimaginative."

447 E[dgett], E[dwin] F[rancis]. "Galsworthy The Reformer: His Latest Novel a Study of the English Land Problem," BOSTON EVENING TRANSCRIPT, 25 Aug 1915, p. 20.
The Freelands is essentially comprised of sociological discussions that contrast the poor with the rich and, in so doing, cast "clear light on reform and the socialistic point of view." The novel is more believable as a study of human futilities than as a record of things as they exist.

448 E[dgett], E[dwin] F[rancis]. "*The Little Man and Other Satires*: A Collection of John Galsworthy's Stories and Sketches," BOSTON EVENING TRANSCRIPT, 12 May 1915, Sec. 3, p. 4.
The Little Man adds nothing to JG's reputation.

449 "Fiction. *The Freelands*," ATHENAEUM, No. 4584 (4 Sept 1915), 158.
The value of *The Freelands* lies in drawing of character (especially women), balance without sentimentality in presenting the case of land policy in England, and style that evolves from "jerkiness" to fluency.

450 "Forgiveness A Sin? Another Galsworthy Problem Play," DAILY EXPRESS (Lond), 26 May 1915, p. 5.
A Bit o' Love at the Kingsway Theatre has "tenderness, sympathy, beauty, charm of language and scene, exquisite imagery and symbolism," but not strength. JG's bucolics are as real as Hardy's. The viewer decides whether Strangway's forgiveness is sin or virtue—it is certainly unheroic.

451 Franken, C. "Drei Stukken van John Galsworthy" (Three Pieces by John Galsworthy), NEOPHILOLOGUS (Gronigen), II (1915), 62.
[Information doubtful; listed in BIBLIOGRAPHIE DER FREMDSPRACHIGEN ZEITSCHRIFTEN LITERATUR, NF 1916–1919 (Leipzig: Felix Dietrich, 1920).] [In Dutch.]

452 *"The Freelands,"* A.L.A. BOOKLIST, XII (Oct 1915), 34–35.
Derek's love for his cousin lightens the story of the three generations of *The Freelands,* who contrast conservatism with revolt. [Brief notice of publication.]

453 *"The Freelands,"* NATION (NY), CI (2 Sept 1915), 291–92.
The Freelands presents antebellum England "muddling through," content with the status quo. Overt satire is dominant.

454 *"The Freelands,"* REVIEW OF REVIEWS (NY), LII (Oct 1915), 635.
JG indicts the British land system as the main cause of unrest in England. Even though characters are types of classes and symbols of movements, the propagandistic novel is written with imagination. Frances Freeland (a masterful, magnificent woman who is England personified) dominates the book.

455 *"The Freelands,"* SATURDAY REVIEW (Lond), CXX (11 Sept 1915), 258–59.
The didactic JG writes "critical, acid, destructive sort of stuff" in *The Freelands.* A "fanatic with a very palpable axe to grind," he is basically revolutionary, with just enough sex to keep his propaganda meaningful. People at the top of society are arrogant, in need of reform, and responsible for the world's evil. *Freelands* at times is "Hyde Park tub-thumping."

456 *"The Freelands,"* SPECTATOR (Lond), CXV (21 Aug 1915), 248.
It is JG as usual in *The Freelands,* as he demonstrates his "ingrained pessimism" by having "ineffectual revolutionaries" try to assist the unfortunate. JG illustrates no "poetic justice," admitting only that the world changes. Humor exists only in the character of Felix.

457 "Galsworthy's *A Bit o' Love:* A Soft-Hearted Curate Whose Quixotic Conduct Offends His Parishioners," SPRINGFIELD REPUBLICAN (Mass), 19 July 1915, p. 11.
A Bit o' Love belongs in the category of *Joy* and *The Pigeon,* combining the dramatic intensity of the one with the delicate comedy of the other.

458 Hale, Edward E. "John Galsworthy," DIAL (Chicago), LIX (16 Sept 1915), 201–3.
In addition to presenting "the immense inertia of the current life," JG introduces into the world of conservatives and patricians "radicals, adventurers, [and] wanderers of the spirit." He sees not only what is wrong with the present state of

things but also what is beautiful. Consequently, his radicals are never effective people. In his later novels the struggle between radical and conservative becomes less important, and greater emphasis is given to such matters as love and marriage. JG's philosophy is perhaps that the struggles and counter-struggles are fulfilling the purpose of God; hence, one solution is "quite as good as another."

459 L., P. "John Galsworthy Satirizes," NEW REPUBLIC (NY), III (8 May 1915), 22–23.
The Little Man, and Other Satires is "unbitter, unwhimsical, unenergetic, unenjoying, rather unmalicious." Occasionally one finds some "bright color" in JG's "delicate grays." He is most sensitive to "insensitiveness to other people's suffering"; most frequent satiric thrusts are at egotism and callousness. One waits for JG's delicate and reasonably laid fire to burst into flame, but it doesn't: constraint keeps ardor at bay.

460 Lewisohn, Ludwig. THE MODERN DRAMA (NY: B. W. Huebsch, 1915); rptd (1916, 1921, 1923); rptd (NY: Viking, 1928), pp. 41, 101, 111, 121, 174, 175, 176, 177, 180, 202, 207–18, 266.
JG's six masterpieces (to 1914) are *The Silver Box, Strife, The Eldest Son, Justice, The Pigeon,* and *The Fugitive.* The keynote of JG's art is restraint: "keen . . . clear and sober," he does not "overstep the modesty of emotions and events." JG selects "living incidents [that] . . . have in themselves the inevitable structure of drama"—*Strife* and *Justice,* for example. Stage directions are often psychological, with a touch of generalization. Unlike Shaw he is never polemical; his dramatic dialogue is the best in the language: the illusion of reality is complete, the rhythm of "spiritual action." *Box* characteristically depicts society's "gross inequality" and "ends with a cry for justice." *Son* and *Fugitive* deal with "the more vivid moral dilemmas of the personal life." "The finest triumph of his art . . . lies in the creation of character."

461 *"The Little Man, and Other Satires,"* A.L.A. BOOKLIST, XI (June 1915), 459.
Themes in *The Little Man, and Other Satires* are the hypocrisies and foibles of daily life, unified only by a note of satire. The ten portraits of "Studies in Extravagance" are incisive and serio-comic. [Brief review.]

462 *"The Little Man, and Other Satires,"* CATHOLIC WORLD, CII (Oct 1915), 104–5.
The doctrine of humanity is the general theme of *The Little Man, and Other Satires.* JG's satire and wit seem to be in decline despite several instances such as "The Little Man," in which he shows his former ability. The portrait of the Christian is poorly justified [from the Catholic doctrinal viewpoint].

463 *"The Little Man, and Other Satires,"* DIAL (Chicago), LVIII (27 May 1915), 427–28.

The Little Man, and Other Satires has well-written, vivid portrayal of characters. In the title story JG suggests that there is as much heroism in helping a woman in distress on a railway platform as in other, more adventurous feats.

464 *"The Little Man, and Other Satires,"* NATION (NY), C (20 May 1915), 567.

Studies in *The Little Man, and Other Satires* are more bitter than similar ones in *A Motley.* The volume emphasizes moral pettiness and evil; the artistry is pervasive despite "anemic carping" at human nature. [Brief review.]

465 *"The Little Man, and Other Satires,"* NORTH AMERICAN REVIEW, CCII (Aug 1915), 284.

The Little Man volume is meager in outline and shallow in narrative technique. Nevertheless, the well-delineated impressions are amusing, sympathetic, and penetrating.

466 MacGowan, Kenneth. "Sequels to A DOLL'S HOUSE," HARPER'S WEEKLY, LXI (11 Sept 1915), 263.

[*The Fugitive,* a tragedy of character, is quite similar to Ibsen's A DOLL'S HOUSE and to Brieux's LA FEMME SEULE. Especially notable are likenesses between Clare Dedmond and Nora.]

467 Marsh, Richard. "How I 'Broke into Print,' " STRAND MAGAZINE (Lond), L (Nov 1915), 573–79.

[Comments on JG are conventional, but Marsh reprints a rumor from an unnamed New York newspaper that JG had spent six months in prison to assimilate the realism of *Justice.* Marsh discounts the rumor.]

468 "Mr. Galsworthy on a Problem of Today," NEW YORK TIMES SUNDAY REVIEW OF BOOKS, 22 Aug 1915, p. 1.

In *The Freelands* JG tells critically and sympathetically why the existing land system is a menace to England, concentrating on the rights and wrongs of farm labor. *The Freelands* begins too slowly. Scenes between Derek and Nedda suggest the love scenes of Meredith's THE ORDEAL OF RICHARD FEVEREL: while lacking Meredith's "literary brilliancy," they are similarly intense and more natural. JG's tone questions rather than asserts.

469 "Mr. Galsworthy's *Freelands:* A Novel of Austere Social and Literary Purpose," SPRINGFIELD REPUBLICAN (Mass), 29 Aug 1915, Sec. 2, p. 17.

The appearance of *The Freelands* is a literary "event" because of "grasp of detail, keen characterization," control, and clear exposition.

470 "Mr. Galsworthy's Satires," NEW YORK TIMES SUNDAY REVIEW OF BOOKS, 23 May 1915, p. 194.

Although "The Little Man" butchers American English, JG's style is "close to perfection"—sure, precise, calm, and witty in *The Little Man, and Other Satires.*

"Studies of Extravagance" are "deliciously clever and keen, exquisitely done, and full of sardonic humor."

471 "Mr. Galsworthy's Satires: *The Little Man* and Other Ironical Sketches—An Overdone American," SPRINGFIELD REPUBLICAN (Mass), 24 May 1915, p. 13.

Satire in *The Little Man, and Other Satires* is everywhere, but not always dominant; in such places as "A Simple Tale" it is the undertone to a strain of quiet humor and pathos.

472 "The New Books: Revolution and Young Love," INDEPENDENT (NY), LXXXIV (4 Oct 1915), 23–24.

Irony outweighs poetry in *The Freelands*. JG is a "discouraged radical" who has carefully analyzed his characters.

473 "A New Galsworthy Play," NEW REPUBLIC (NY), III (26 June 1915), 210.

A Bit o' Love, one of JG's "gentlest pictures of cruelty," is "thin, distinguished, rich in . . . contrasts, freshly felt, a little old-fashioned, a little too explicit and even, in its delicate way, insistent." Strangway has a "passionate desire to liberate and to heal."

474 "The New Novels," OUTLOOK (NY), CXI (6 Oct 1915), 332–35.

The Freelands lives in its "human interest . . . its elusive glimpses of the secret and inarticulate influences that play on the spirits of man, its brilliancy of line in portraying the . . . inheritance of privilege, its power of suggesting the unspoken thought of those who have never learned how to speak." JG's story of innocent young passion is the best since Meredith's THE ORDEAL OF RICHARD FEVEREL.

475 P., J. "New Galsworthy Play. The Liverpool Players in *A Bit o' Love,*" DAILY CHRONICLE (Lond), 26 May 1915, p. 9.

A Bit o' Love gives "all the sentiment and theatrical sense" JG had been suppressing in previous plays, showing a "hysterica passio" instead of the usual noncommittal attitude. JG is "too skillful" in the play as he piles up contrasts of "laughing children and lonely men" and adds woe upon woe to the curate Michael Strangway, as fate and the author "conspire to achieve a successful martyrdom."

476 P., P. P. "*A Bit o' Love*. Mr. John Galsworthy's New Play at the Kingsway Theatre," DAILY GRAPHIC (Lond), 26 May 1915, p. 9.

"Ecstatic remoteness" runs through the "rustic scenes" of *A Bit o' Love* in a way reminiscent of Hardy. Strangway, a "St. Francis of Assisi in the black coat of a country curate," is a "curious mixture of passion and asceticism."

477 Payne, William Morton. "Recent Fiction," DIAL (Chicago), LIX (16 Sept 1915), 219–21.

In *The Freelands* JG attacks the right of landed property, arousing pity for the dispossessed man whose private life is regulated by his landlord. JG's real power is stylistic rather than logical—as seen in his prose-poetry description of the passing seasons.

478 Pierce, John Alexander (ed). THE MASTERPIECES OF MODERN DRAMA (Garden City, NY: Doubleday, Page, 1915), pp. 3–21.
[An abridgment of *Justice*.]

479 Roberts, R. Ellis. "John Galsworthy's Satires," BOOKMAN (Lond), XLVIII (July 1915), 109.
In *The Little Man, and Other Satires* JG demonstrates "an inherent distaste for the positive character." This indecisiveness is typified in "The Little Man," who "just suffers." "Ultima Thule" depicts the "false vision of literary sentiment." JG lacks the "artistic temperament"; unable to control his theories, he is "mastered by the formulae of his profession." The characters are "attitudes, not persons."

480 "Studies in Neutral Tint," SPECTATOR (Lond), CXIV (8 May 1915), 653.
In *The Little Man, and Other Satires,* JG's writing is the "negation of extravagance"; his universe is "flat, colorless, rationalized," and "synthetic." JG misinterprets Dostoievsky in "The Superlative."

481 "Two Modern Satirists," ATHENAEUM, No. 4570 (29 May 1915), 480.
In *The Little Man, and Other Satires* JG is "an orderly and veracious demonstrator of the absurd." "The Little Man" shows the difference between the theory and practice of altruism; "Ultima Thule" is more poetry of love than of satire; "Studies of Extravagance," occasionally tedious and bare, are enlivened by "grotesque fancies about people we know."

482 W., H. M. [Massingham, H. W.?] "A Beautiful Play: Mr. Galsworthy's *A Bit o' Love*," PALL MALL GAZETTE (Lond), 26 May 1915, p. 8.
A Bit o' Love at the Kingsway Theatre is one of the most beautiful and impassioned plays of our time.

483 Willcox, Louise Collier. "John Galsworthy," NORTH AMERICAN REVIEW, CCII (Dec 1915), 889–98.
JG is "the greatest prose impressionist of our generation." Whereas Wells lacks moral or artistic tradition or prejudice and Bennett "cannot distinguish form from matter," JG is sufficiently of the old school that he has in mind from the beginning "the beauty of the final picture." He is a selective artist and a gentleman. The best novel of his first period is *The Man of Property:* its one flaw is Irene's character. She has no "definite creative personality." *The Patrician* begins JG's middle period. *The Dark Flower* is not a novel; it is one long lyric.

The Freelands harkens back to the pre-lyric phase, and again the weakness is JG's women characters. "His women are too traditional, too passive, too uniformly Victorian. . . ." There is a falling off in *The Little Man, and Other Satires;* "the Zola element is active in it."

484 Woodbridge, Homer E. "Recent Plays of War and Love," DIAL (Chicago), LIX (14 Oct 1915), 325–28.

A Bit o' Love "bears the mark of genius." Characters are real, "unconscious of the audience," never "stagey." Interest is sustained by the "vivid and charming" characterization of the unyielding Strangway.

485 Zhantieva, D. G. "Epopeia o Forsaitakh Golsuorsi, kak ot-razhenie sobstvennicheskoi Anglii kontsa XIX—nachala XX v" (Galsworthy's Epic on the Forsytes as a Reflection of Proprietary England at the End of the Nineteenth and the Beginning of the Twentieth Centuries). Dissertatsiia na soisk. uchenoi stepeni kand. filol. nauk. Unpublished dissertation, (Moscow: MGU im. M. V. Lomonosova, 1915) [not seen].

[In Russian.]

1916

486 [Anthony, Luther B.] *"Justice,"* DRAMATIST (Easton, Pa), VII (April 1916), 676.

The performance of *Justice* succeeds because of John Barrymore's acting, not because of JG's writing and imagination.

487 Broeck, Helen Ten. "From Comedy to Tragedy," THEATRE (NY), XXIV (July 1916), 23, 38.

[Feature article on John Barrymore, emphasizing his successful transition from comic to tragic role as Falder in *Justice.*]

488 Eaton, Walter Prichard. PLAYS AND PLAYERS: LEAVES FROM A CRITIC'S SCRAPBOOK (Cincinnati: Stewart & Kidd, 1916), pp. 155–64, 196–99, 202–7, 271, 293–96, 305, 313–14, 392–93.

The Pigeon was the first production in Winthrop Ames's Little Theatre. Irony cuts underneath its wit and comedy in showing that social institutions are incapable of coping with "so individual and wild a thing as the human soul." JG overlooks the fact that others, like the Salvation Army, have the same concern as the old artist-pigeon. *Strife's* naturalism perhaps begins a trend away from sex and "eternal personal narrative" in contemporary drama. In *Justice* JG's "still white flame of spiritual sympathy" has burst into "a blaze of passion." Unlike other of JG's dramas, *Justice* "takes sides," not following the JG trademark of restraint. He attacks society's actions—making the audience the villain—in his sympathetic portrayal of Falder. JG's plays might fail in popularity because of sober themes and an absence of sex. [Reprints of reviews and essays that have appeared elsewhere, but the current editors have not identified the source of the original appearances.]

489 E[dgett], E[dwin] F[rancis]. "John Galsworthy Hurls His Lance," BOSTON EVENING TRANSCRIPT, 4 Nov 1916, Sec. 3, p. 7.
JG's essays in *A Sheaf* are contributions to the literature of humanitarian reform rather than of documentary reform. The volume shows JG's skill as debater and as a commonsense literary man. [Review is accompanied by a photograph.]

490 "Famous Authors on War's Aftermath," NEW YORK TIMES SUNDAY REVIEW OF BOOKS, 22 Oct 1916, p. 437.
The keynote of *A Sheaf* is "let us resolve that these dead shall not have died in vain." Written in austere and concrete prose, the work contains some practical suggestions.

491 "The First Nighter," NEW YORK DRAMATIC MIRROR, LXXV (5 Feb 1916), 8.
[Brief notice of the performance of *The Eldest Son* at the NY Lyceum Theatre.]

492 Follett, Helen T., and Wilson Follett. "Contemporary Novelists: John Galsworthy," ATLANTIC MONTHLY, CXVIII (Dec 1916), 757–67; rptd in SOME MODERN NOVELISTS: APPRECIATIONS AND ESTIMATES (NY: Holt, 1918), pp. 264–88.
An important characteristic of JG's style is that it succeeds without calling attention to itself. In his best work his careful selection of each gesture or word reveals "the secret direction of a whole life." His double training—for the drama and for the novel—explains his special contribution to the novel: "his perfection of the separate chapter as a unit in mood, in episode, and usually in scene." His novels are dramatic rather than epic. Rather than present a continuous line of development, JG uses a "series of dramatic nuclei or kernels." He elaborates the central episode and omits the connections. H. G. Wells and Arnold Bennett are exponents of the belief that the whole is the equal to the sum of all its parts. JG, by contrast, "chooses details, not to be added up into the sum-total of his meaning, but to point in the direction of it." If JG has a rival in this respect it would be R. L. Stevenson. As a satirist JG is not vindictive. The dominant qualities of his art are impersonality, restraint, and austerity. His major limitation is a "slenderness of effect."

493 Garnet, E. "Gol'suorsi (Perevod s angl. rukopisi)" (Galsworthy: Translation from an English Manuscript), RUSSKAIA MYSL', No. 12 (1916), 18–23. Otd. XXI "V Rossii i zagranitsei" (Section XXI, In Russia and Abroad) [not seen].
[In Russian.]

494 "A Great Stage Speech," THEATRE (NY), XXIV (Aug 1916), 77.
[The article's subtitle, "The Defense's Plea for Falder in *Justice* One of the Longest Ever Delivered," precedes the reprinting of the speech.]

495 H., F. "After the Play," NEW REPUBLIC, VI (15 April 1916), 294.
Justice at NY's Candler Theatre attacks the philistinism of England, especially its law and public opinion: Falder's sin is against property. The beauty of *Justice* is that it tries to upset society's morality and desire to be comfortable.

496 H., F. "One Americanization," NEW REPUBLIC, IX (4 Nov 1916), 16–18.
[A review of Roi Cooper Megrue and Irwin Cobb, UNDER SENTENCE, commenting on the obvious indebtedness to JG's *Justice*. JG's play is much superior to Megrue and Cobb's.]

497 Hamilton, Clayton. "Dramatic Talent and Theatrical Talent," BOOKMAN (NY), XLIII (May 1916), 340–42.
JG's dramatic talent in *Justice* is so great "that he achieves more by leaving life alone than he could possibly achieve by arranging life in accordance with a technical pattern, however dexterous theatrically."

498 "Hits on the Stage: *Justice,*" HARPER'S WEEKLY, LXII (22 April 1916), 440.
JG is enough of the artist to be detached and enough of the man to write about his own time. *Justice* is the "strongest play" to be presented in New York in years. "Impersonal, plain, artistic," *Justice* unfortunately had to await the public interest shown in the Osborne prison case before it could be performed. *Justice* presents the "vital truth" that unless prisons reform convicts, the system is a failure. The play's one weakness is its bleak and discordant ending.

499 "John Barrymore Arrives—A Great Man," EVERYBODY'S MAGAZINE, (NY) XXXV (July 1916), 122–24.
[Article praising John Barrymore, who is playing Falder in *Justice*.]

500 Jones, Francis Arthur. "How I 'Broke Into Print,' " EDITOR (Ridgewood, NJ), XLIII (17 June 1916), 628.
[Brief, general comments and biographical information based on JG's remarks about beginning to write.]

501 *"Justice,"* OUTLOOK (NY), CXIII (31 May 1916), 246–48.
Justice, like a Greek tragedy, moves inexorably to an unavoidable conclusion. The gloomy mood, depicting the contrast between essential justice and the impersonal machine of law, is not relieved by the "kindly whimsicality" of Cokeson. The dialogue is real; the play is impressive in its artistic presentation of truth. The seriousness of the play, in which John Barrymore as Falder "rises . . . to a very high plane of dramatic art," prompted six New York theater managers to refuse booking it. Seeing the play will make one think of prisons in terms of

people rather than bars and walls. The play is an artistic and financial success. [Review of a production at NY's New Theatre.]

502 *"Justice,"* THEATRE (NY), XXIII (May 1916), 296–97, 306, 308. [Excerpts from *Justice* are reprinted, with nine photos from the NY production and one of JG.]

503 *"Justice* at Labor Forum," NEW YORK TRIBUNE, 1 May 1916, p. 6.
As part of the meeting of the Labor Forum to discuss prison reform six members from the cast of *Justice* presented a scene from the play. Spencer Miller, deputy warden of Sing Sing, urged the forum to use its influence to provide more than one and one-half cents a day as pay for convicts.

504 *"Justice*—Galsworthy's Intense Prison Drama Which Has Startled New York Playgoers," CURRENT OPINION (NY), LX (May 1916), 324–28.
[The article is devoted to summarizing and quoting parts of the play and reprinting some of the New York critics' comments on the Corey–Williams–Riter production of *Justice.*]

505 *"Justice* Makes Deep Impression," NEW YORK TRIBUNE, 4 April 1916, p. 11.
Justice is a stark, realistic, deeply impressive tragedy—a play that is always dramatic without ever being theatrical.

506 *"Justice.* The Play of the Month," HEARST'S MAGAZINE (NY), XXX (Sept 1916), 165–67, 179.
[Excerpts from *Justice,* with nine photos of the NY production starring John Barrymore as Falder.]

507 Kaufman, George S. *"Justice* Et Al.," NEW YORK TRIBUNE, 9 April 1916, p. 2.
Justice is a simple, sincere, and natural tragedy that achieves its effects by an utter disregard of theatrical expedients. JG made no deliberate effort to be untheatrical; he wrote, letting the chips fall where they may. If JG were a practical playwright telling a story and not developing a theme, there would be no place for the second and third acts. The first and last acts embody both story and theme; the second and third, the theme alone. The storyless second and third acts are the most powerful. *Justice* gets its power from JG's message.

508 Kaye-Smith, Sheila. JOHN GALSWORTHY (Lond: Hutchinson [Writers of the Day Series]; NY: Holt, 1916); rptd (NY: Haskell House, 1972).
JG will never be widely read because he alienates two sets of readers: (1) those who believe a book should teach, and (2) those who believe a book should not teach. He displeases the first group because although he has something to teach

he avoids the direct appeal. The second group reject his trying to teach anything. His place in modern literature is as a great playwright. That he "carries on his propaganda almost entirely by situation" raises his dramatic art above that of "Shaw and other missionary dramatists." Rather than using dialogue for his theories, he relies on his characters and their deeds to enforce his moral. "The drama is a lawful means of propaganda, the novel is not." In his novels, except *The Dark Flower*, his characters do not change. They are types, not individuals. They are never puppets, but "there is nothing creative about them." There is not enough diversity in his characters. "There are few novelists with a finer sense of form than Galsworthy, few with a finer sense of style." His finest novels are *The Man of Property* and *Fraternity*. "Irene is one of Galsworthy's most vivid creations." *Fraternity* "comes as near being a perfect work of art as any novel ever written." *The Freelands* reverts to an earlier JG. In works like "Ultima Thule," *A Motley,* and *A Commentary* JG is guilty of "misplaced pity" for his characters. His verse is slight. He is "an artist before he is a social reformer." Although he is a master of situation, there are times when instead of sounding the depths he puts us off "with a consummate skill of arrangement." His virtues are his sense of situation, his sense of atmosphere, his poet's craftsmanship with words, and his economy of words. He has anglicized foreign influences. "The Russian pity is shorn of its mysticism, the French irony of its gaiety." In utilizing the pity and irony, JG has asserted "both his personality and his race."

509 L., W. D. "Cells and Souls," SURVEY (NY), XXXVI (15 April 1916), 71–72.
Justice indicts prison cells, court psychology, and phobias about criminals in a moving human story of a weak man caught in the wheels of justice. [Reviewer of production at NY's New Theatre emphasizes that the American prison system is superior to the British.]

510 Madison, Roberta. "Six Books of the Month: John Galsworthy's *A Sheaf,*" BOOKMAN (NY), XLIV (Nov 1916), 304–6.
A Sheaf exemplifies a "prose of pure gold that issues from a burning heart" and a masterful "bitter irony."

511 Metcalfe, [J. S.]. "Drama: Driving at Man's Inhumanity to Man," LIFE (NY), LXVII (13 April 1916), 706.
Justice, a tract on penology, is not really worth seeing. JG takes the easy way out in the solitary confinement scene; yet the play is literate, thoughtful, and interesting. [Metcalfe takes issue with underlying sociological assumptions in his review of NY's Little Theatre production.]

512 M[orderwell], H. I. "Galsworthy's Masterpiece Now Produced," BOSTON EVENING TRANSCRIPT, 6 March 1916, p. 16.
The first production of *Justice* in the professional American theater took place in New Haven, Connecticut, on Thursday, 2 March. *Justice* is "one of the notable

plays of this generation." The commercial chances for success are very good because prison reform is topical as a result of Warden Osborne of Sing Sing prison and his efforts at improving prisoners rather than punishing them. The play moves so smoothly that it seems as though it has no plan; there are two movements within the play: the first is the march of outward events dealing with Falder's crime and capture; the second, the emotional scheme, which is submerged for the first two acts, comes to the fore in Act III in its powerful comments on the conditions of prison life. "The pity and terror of Greek tragedy have nowhere in modern drama been more superbly revealed than in this marvelous last act [Act IV]. The final arrest and suicide come as a relief. They are not tragedy, but release to the spectator's tortured soul."

> **513** Moses, Montrose J. "Galsworthy's *Justice*," BOOK NEWS MONTHLY (Phila), XXXIV (June 1916), 432–33.

Justice is an example of drama with a high mission: artistic treatment of a social problem (prison reform) that might lead to reform. The realistic method negates much use of imagination. Notoriety of problems at Sing Sing Prison was primarily responsible for bringing *Justice* to the NY stage.

> **514** "The New Books: Two Kinds of Satire," INDEPENDENT (NY), LXXXV (10 Jan 1916), 59–60.

"Humor is subordinated to analysis and a moral frequently allowed to make itself evident" in *The Little Man, and Other Satires*. JG's irony is at its best in "The Latest Thing." Unfortunately, *The Little Man* is marred by the "trite caricature" of the American.

> **515** Osborne, Thomas Mott. "Answer to Unanswered Question of *Justice* Can Be Found at Sing Sing, Says Thomas Mott Osborne [with excerpts]," NEW YORK TRIBUNE MAGAZINE, 9 April 1916, p. 3.

Justice is a masterpiece, not propaganda. The play is just as relevant to America because "whatever the superficial difference in treatment of prisoners in the two countries . . . the two systems are fundamentally the same." A man should come out of prison a better man, not a worse one. As a work of art *Justice* is remarkable, but "it suffers because the note of hope which should resolve the discord is omitted." [Mr. Osborne, former warden of Sing Sing, was asked by the TRIBUNE for his opinion of the play's value as literature and as an aid to prison reform.]

> **516** Phelps, William Lyon. "The Advance of the English Novel, Part VIII. Conrad, Galsworthy, and Others," BOOKMAN (NY), XLIII (May 1916), 297–308, espec pp. 304–5; rptd in THE ADVANCE OF THE ENGLISH NOVEL (NY: Dodd, Mead, 1916; St. Claire Shores, Mich: Scholarly P, 1971), pp. 217–23.

JG "looks upon the world with disapproval, and England with scorn." Distinctive as a novelist and dramatist and respectable as a versifier, he is above all a satirist. JG's obsession is the theme of marriage without love, seen especially in *The Man of Property*. *The Country House* is dull; and the characters in *The Dark Flower* and *The Freelands* are "all body, and no soul." *Dark Flower* is written as men in their forties often think: regretting the lost opportunities of youth. It appeals to prurient instinct and emotions rather than to ennobling ideals. "A German [reading *Freelands*] . . . might easily be pardoned for believing that the best thing that could happen to Great Britain would be its conquest by Germany." [Bunker Hillian, rather than Olympian, condescension.]

517 "A Play on Prison-Reform," LITERARY DIGEST, LII (29 April 1916), 1220–21.
[Quotes reviews of JG's *Justice* appearing elsewhere.]

518 Pollock, Channing. "A *Real* Play At Last," GREEN BOOK MAGAZINE (Chicago), XV (June 1916), 969–77.
Justice is "not a play; it is an emotional experience, a tragedy in which you participate." [Three photos of John Barrymore as Falder are reproduced. In this favorable review of the Corey–Williams–Riter NY Candler Theatre production, Pollock devotes more energy to name-dropping than to criticism.]

519 *"A Sheaf,"* A.L.A. BOOKLIST, XIII (Dec 1916), 112.
[Brief review.]

520 *"A Sheaf,"* SPECTATOR, (Lond), CXVII (9 Dec 1916), 738.
[Brief, noncommittal review.]

521 *"A Sheaf,"* TIMES LITERARY SUPPLEMENT (Lond), XV (12 Oct 1916), 491.
[Brief notice of publication.]

522 *"A Sheaf* by Galsworthy: Sketches and Arguments That Stimulate Thinking," SPRINGFIELD REPUBLICAN (Mass), 7 Nov 1916, p. 6.
JG backs up his direct arguments with statistics and personal investigations, creating in *A Sheaf* an "ethically significant" work.

523 W., S. *"Justice,"* NATION (NY), CII (13 April 1916), 419–20.
[A favorable review of the production of *Justice* at the Candler Theatre, commenting on its appropriateness in light of the reform movement.]

524 Wyatt, Edith. "Cruelty and Confidence," NEW REPUBLIC, IX (18 Nov 1916), [sup.], 5–6.
A major theme of *A Sheaf* is human suffering; the tone is that of inward freedom.

525 An X Convict. *"Justice* From the Inside," NEW YORK TRIBUNE MAGAZINE, 9 April 1916, pp. 3, 7.
Falder's trial, prison experiences, and return to society are a true, honest description of what occurs here daily. My own experiences are absolutely parallel. Eighteen months ago I was arrested for larceny committed because I

wanted to rescue the woman I loved from her drunken, brutal husband. I was arrested, tried, and given a one-year sentence. Actually, prison conditions are a trifle better than those in the play. I have been out of prison for four weeks; I got a job as a salesman; for two weeks all went well until two of my former colleagues informed my co-workers of my past; since then, my work has become unbearable. [TRIBUNE editor notes that this is an unedited review.]

1917

526 *"Beyond,"* OUTLOOK (NY), CXVII (12 Sept 1917), 64.
Literary texture and the strength of Winton, Gyp, and other characters in *Beyond* sustain interest, but it is difficult to see what social conclusion is suggested. [Paragraph review.]

527 *"Beyond,"* PITTSBURGH MONTHLY BULLETIN, XXII (Nov 1917), 749.
[Brief review.]

528 *"Beyond,"* SATURDAY REVIEW (Lond), CXXIV (15 Sept 1917), 208.
Beyond is devoted to the sexual act, omitting "plot, characterization, humor, incident" in defiance of social codes.

529 *"Beyond,"* SPECTATOR (Lond), CXIX (15 Sept 1917), 272.
Beyond is clever but depressing. JG should extend his scope of writing beyond man's brutality and ingratitude, woman's "capacity for suffering," and harsh marriage laws.

530 Boynton, H. W. "Outstanding Novels of the Year," NATION (NY), CV (29 Nov 1917), 600.
Beyond does nothing to enhance JG's reputation; the novel will be read primarily because JG wrote it.

531 Boynton, H. W. "A Stroll through the Fair of Fiction," BOOK-MAN (NY), XLVI (Nov 1917), 339.
In *Beyond* JG reveals his distrust of the institution of marriage. "Half concealed by his cold and reserved manner lurks . . . the sex obsession of the skeptical bachelor."

532 Brunius, August. "John Galsworthys romaner" (John Galsworthy's Novels), ANSIKTEN OCH MASKER (Faces and Masks), (Stockholm: P. A. Norstedt, 1917), pp. 46–50.
JG is mentioned with respect but also with a certain hostility in the English press; for some JG is "an intolerable idealist." His novels show that he is a capable

analyst of great power and an artist capable of the watercolorist's delicacy. A few ordinary words, a banal meeting, a glance—these are brought dramatically to life before one's eyes; "this is English phlegmatism, English reserve raised to an artistic principle." Although *The Man of Property* is about dull people, the book is not dull. Some of his later books—*The Country House, The Patrician,* and especially *Fraternity,* are more artistic. His latest novel, *The Freelands,* is poetic and detailed, but its climax is abrupt and unsatisfactory. JG still has much to say. [In Swedish.]

533 Cunliffe, John W. "John Galsworthy," MODERN ENGLISH PLAYWRIGHTS: A SHORT HISTORY OF THE ENGLISH DRAMA FROM 1825 (NY & Lond: Harper, 1917), pp. 11, 95–113, 114, 209, 210, 252.
JG brought to English drama when it needed it an intimate knowledge of the "upper half of English society and the detachment springing from a superior social position." He is saved from his view of the plight of the poor as pathetic by his "resolute insight and . . . artistic sense of balance and proportion." He is realistic, depicting no true villains and few heroes. He adhered to his statement of purpose in "Some Platitudes Concerning Drama." [These criteria are examined generally in paragraph discussions of JG's major dramas, *The Silver Box, Joy, Strife, Justice, The Pigeon, The Eldest Son, The Fugitive, The Mob,* and *A Bit o' Love.*]

534 Dickinson, Thomas H. THE CONTEMPORARY DRAMA OF ENGLAND (Bost: Little, Brown, 1917), pp. 99, 155, 165, 167, 208, 210, 212–16, 220, 226, 236; (rev ed, 1931), 134, 164, 168, 169, 170, 173, 201–19, 261, 266, 267, 268.
As a novelist in the Turgenev style, JG is an idealist and a "thorough artist"; in his drama, he adds the technical qualities of Brieux. He has the remarkable ability to find the dramatic in natural and unforced situations. Because his plays have the texture of carefully molded reality, they are too severely and nakedly "architectured." Dialogue is crisp and human, comparable to Pinero but without Pinero's "occasional gifts of the magician." Because JG attains only "mechanical and mental adequacy" in characterization, he ranks at the top of the second class of English playwrights. Realizing this, JG turned from the drama of men to the drama of impersonal forces. [Dickinson's perceptive general comments and paragraph treatments of several plays make this one of the best contemporary apprrasals of JG drama. The 1931 revision extends coverage of the same, emphasizing JG's reserve, insularity, and "inner integrity of spirit." His plays are essentially the dramas of "the middle-class intellectual mind." Dickinson comments briefly on *The Silver Box, Joy, Strife, Justice, The Pigeon, The Eldest Son, The Fugitive, The Mob,* and *A Bit o' Love.*]

535 E[dgett], E[dwin] F[rancis]. "The Strange Case of John Galsworthy: His Latest Novel a Well-Told Tale in Which Men and Women Are

Dominated by the Obsession of Sex," BOSTON EVENING TRANSCRIPT, 25 Aug 1917, Sec. 3, p. 6.

Beyond "is so persistently enshrouded in a blinding mist of the erotic that the reader can see little in it but a perverse and offensive attempt at the mastery of pornography. It is impossible, however, to resist the appeal of its delicate phrases, of its insights into the social and Bohemian world of England, or to overestimate its rare pictorial quality."

536 *"The Fugitive,"* NATION (NY), CIV (29 March 1917), 379–80.

The Fugitive, produced at NY's 39th Street Theatre, is only "a sketch of a vital subject," melodramatic and in no way distinguished.

537 "Galsworthy (John). *Beyond,"* ATHENAEUM, No. 4622 (Oct 1917), 527.

[Paragraph review emphasizing *Beyond's* readability and lack of depth.]

538 Garnett, Edward. "Mr. Galsworthy's Art," DAILY NEWS AND LEADER (Lond), 11 Jan 1917, p. 4.

[Garnett in this review of Sheila Kaye-Smith's JOHN GALSWORTHY takes playful but firm critical exception to her contention that JG will be remembered primarily as dramatist rather than novelist, quoting Kaye-Smith's assertion that "social or moral problems" greatly enhance the plays but "constrict or impede the development" of the novels. Kaye-Smith presents an example, says Garnett, of the young school of novelists knocking the old school. Garnett concludes, challenging Kaye-Smith: JG's "certain intellectual hardness balances and safeguards his extreme sensitiveness and indignant pity. The amalgam of the two elements, cunningly tempered by his sense of beauty, of irony and humour, make up his rich, many-sided appeal."]

539 Gilman, Lawrence. "The Book of the Month. Mr. Galsworthy's Latest," NORTH AMERICAN REVIEW, CCVI (Oct 1917), 628–32.

Gyp in *Beyond* is guilty of "human and spiritual malfeasance": actually Fiorsen is betrayed—he was candid from the start; Gyp was on an ill-conceived soul-saving mission. JG does not seem to recognize this aspect of their relationship and, when Gyp denies Fiorsen her "inspiration" as well as her love, JG is guilty of "the feeblest aesthetic romanticism." Thought and expression in *Beyond* are often mechanical and perfunctory; his intellectual tone is curiously naive.

540 H., F. "After the Play," NEW REPUBLIC, X (24 Feb 1917), 106.

JG's hopelessly inadequate ability to handle things American in *The Little Man*, now appearing on stage in NY, makes an otherwise telling satire of American "humanitarian guff" implausible.

541 H., F. "A Different Galsworthy," NEW REPUBLIC, XII (15 Sept 1917), 194.

JG loses perspective and artistic control in *Beyond:* an uncritical and conventional narrator exudes "absurd platitudes."

542 Hamilton, Clayton. "Galsworthy as a Playwright," BOOKMAN (NY), XLV (May 1917), 292–96.

JG's plays "have been persistently overpraised, both by popular dramatic critics . . . and by academic annotators who prefer to study the current drama in the library instead of in the theatre."

543 Hamilton, Clayton [Meeker]. PROBLEMS OF THE PLAYWRIGHT (NY: Henry Holt, 1917), pp. 4, 5, 9, 62, 117, 121, 125, 141, 159, 239, 244, 246, 270, 275, 305, 318.

JG perceives the dramatic in life with his "careful sense of form . . . keen sense of characterization," and lofty perception of the theatre as outlet for his work. But he is not innately interested in the stage. All his plays show craftsmanship; but with the exception of plays like *Justice* that are inherently dramatic, he has had mediocre results. JG has not developed the necessary theatrical talent because (1) he looks at life as God, not the average man, would look at it, not considering the spectators in the theatre; (2) he is more interested in subject matter than theatrical technique (as in *Justice* where acts II and III could be omitted); and (3) he disdains to care about actors (Cokeson, for example, in *Justice*). Yet his dramatic talent lets him get along without "theatrical efficiency." His plays are destitute of heroes and villains; his questions admittedly are incapable of answer (as in *The Pigeon*). JG is a patrician in the democratic world of the theatre. His main problem is his "disinclination" or inability to use his material in the most effective way, often lacking the instinct for the "*scène à faire*" and showing a tendency to "underdramatize his dramas," as in *The Fugitive*.

544 Hornblow, Arthur. "Mr. Hornblow Goes to the Play," THEATRE (NY), XXV (May 1917), 277–80, 320.

Technically, *The Fugitive* (at the 39th Street Theatre), is clumsy; but the dialogue is concise, direct, and interesting.

545 K., P. J. "A Decadent Galsworthy," NEW YORK CALL, 18 Nov 1917, p. 15.

JG's detachment removes Gyp and other characters from real life in *Beyond:* they are sordid and unlovable. In addition, the material is shop-worn and shoddy.

546 "Latest Works of Fiction. *Beyond,*" NEW YORK TIMES SUNDAY REVIEW OF BOOKS, 26 Aug 1917, p. 310.

Beyond's tale of Gyp's love uncannily evokes "the very soul of life." Principal characters are original creations, especially Fiorsen with his "thousand contradictions of character."

547 Macy, John. "English Sports and Foreign Temperaments," DIAL (Chicago), LXIII (27 Sept 1917), 272–73.

Beyond is a superb study of two "good sports" in a tragedy of sex, who stoically stake everything and "pocket . . . losses without whimpering." [Macy is bemused by British novelists' desire "to regard erotic vivacity and romance as extra-English, continental, even Scottish or Irish, but not English." Thus Gyp, who is really not English, is snared by a Swede.]

548 Metcalfe, [J. S.]. "Drama: Can Either Drama Teach a Lesson?" LIFE (NY), LXIX (29 March 1917), 526–27.
The Fugitive is commonplace, without anything to distinguish it as drama. The wife, portrayed by Emily Stevens, is a fool, not a tragic figure. [Review of NY performance.]

549 Moses, Montrose J. "The Problem of *The Fugitive*," BOOK NEWS MONTHLY (Philadelphia), XXXV (May 1917), 357.
The Fugitive, currently being produced in NY, is worth mentioning only because JG wrote it. Theme and characters are conventional and self-evident.

550 "New Attractions for New York Playgoers," NEW YORK DRAMATIC MIRROR, LXXVII (24 Feb 1917), 7.
The Mob regards universal brotherhood cynically. Humor and irony combine with an interesting but insignificant study of character in the performance at the NY Maxine Elliott's Theatre.

551 "New Attractions for New York Playgoers. *The Fugitive,*" NEW YORK DRAMATIC MIRROR, LXXVII (24 March 1917), 7.
The Fugitive at NY's 39th St. Theatre is unrealistic, melodramatic, and unworthy of JG. Clare's death is crass and unconvincing; the best scene is Clare's parting from Malise.

552 "The New Books: Beyond the Law," INDEPENDENT (NY), XCI (22 Sept 1917), 473.
The inconclusive *Beyond* "lacks the greatness that compels the reader's sympathy for the actors in the tragedy—for Galsworthy always makes life a tragedy."

553 "A Post-War Play. *The Foundations* at the Royalty," TIMES (Lond), 27 June 1917, p. 9.
The Foundations is a "gentle little rippling stream of talk, half irony, half tenderness" about postwar London; it is "a feast of whim and fun and good sense and good feeling."

554 Ratcliffe, S. K. "The English Intellectuals in War-time," CENTURY (NY), XCIV (Oct 1917), 826–33.
JG, by nature and art a detached agitator and reformer, has joined the majority of Englishmen in the war effort. In the process, his ideas reveal him as a part of the "typical Englishman" class he has been challenging. [A portrait of JG is reproduced in this general survey of the war-time activities of various writers.]

555 Schrey, Kurt. "John Galsworthy und die besitzenden Klassen Englands" (John Galsworthy and the Propertied Classes of England). Unpublished dissertation, University of Marburg, 1917; rptd with minor

changes in DIE NEUEREN SPRACHEN (Marburg), XXV (1917–1918), 335–58, 385–410, 491–502.
[Listed incorrectly in Lawrence F. McNamee, DISSERTATIONS IN ENGLISH AND AMERICAN LITERATURE (NY & Lond: Bowker, 1968), as having been accepted in 1918. A well-informed survey of JG's works and themes.] [In German.]

556 *"A Sheaf,"* NATION (NY), CIV (4 Jan 1917), 24.
[Brief review of *A Sheaf*. The essays and addresses are humanitarian; especially noteworthy are those devoted to animals.]

557 Thommen, E. "John Galsworthy, Ein Künstler und Wahrheitskünder" (John Galsworthy, an Artist and Truth-sayer), SCHWEIZERISCHE LEHRERZEITUNG (Zurich), LXII (1917), 234–35.
[A favorable review of JG's works in twelve volumes (Tauchnitz ed). Recommends beginning with his sketches like "A Motley" and "A Fisher of Men" before reading the full-length novels. (The article was to be continued.)] [In German.]

558 Trumbauer, Walter H. R. GERHART HAUMPTMANN AND JOHN GALSWORTHY, A PARALLEL (Phila: University of Pennsylvania P, 1917).
The study is not intended as "analysis or critical appraisal" of Hauptmann and JG; rather, it is "interpretative comparison" neither exhaustive nor complete. Both JG and Hauptmann write about ordinary life, often depicting inter-class relationships, but differing in that Hauptmann approaches the material "from below," JG "from above." They also write about authors and artists who are often only dilettantes. Both also like family studies and "have a keen sense of place," idealism, and sympathy for suffering. Major themes of both are man's struggle (1) with a hostile environment, (2) with social bondage, and (3) with himself. In this, heredity and natural environment are the bases for most of their works. The themes of love and "the unhappy marriage" with its inevitable consequences appear often, with JG usually taking the side of the woman. "If love redeems, it does so chiefly through sacrifice." Both also expose "selfishness, hypocrisy, narrow-minded self-complacency," frequently repeating similar situations and characters, all the while realistically creating intellectual concepts rather than romantic symbolism.

Artistically, both JG and Hauptmann are realists primarily interested in enlightenment and idealists primarily seeking spiritual and material truth. To both, art is "the expression of a personality" that sees the world objectively. Both are good psychologists, but whereas Hauptmann's primary interest in characters is with the characters themselves, JG is primarily interested in the relationships between characters. In dialogue, both like to suggest rather than to announce. Though often naturalistic, the plays are not formless: suspense builds from character and situation rather than action, with the climax usually coming about the middle of the play. Both follow the "principle of the unities," occasionally use the soliloquy realistically as an "impersonal exclamation," handle masses of men well, create "rich, natural dialog," and effectively incorporate contrast and irony in their works. [The preceding characteristics of subject matter and art are well illustrated in the discussion of parallel plays in Chapter 4: DIE WEBER and *Strife;* DER BIBERPELZ and *The Silver Box;* HANNELES HIMMELFAHRT and *The Little Dream;* and MICHAEL KRAMER and *A Bit o' Love.* This dated study needs redoing, using contemporary critical methods.]

559 W[alters], E. W. "Letters to Living Authors: To John Galsworthy," GREAT THOUGHTS (Lond), Feb 1917, pp. 239–40.

The critics complain about your partisan attitudes, especially in your early novels. Although "one cannot say which side you favour in *The Patrician* and various other works from your pen, it is still protested that you are either 'a social reformer turned literary man, or a literary man beguiled into social reform.' " The "art for art's sake" notion is foolish because a work of art clearly does teach or preach. There seems to be less quarrel with your plays as regards your preaching. One critic observes that while purely literary drama cannot exist in Egland (the failures of James and Conrad) the drama of literary moralizing is thriving (the successes of Shaw, Barker, and JG). " 'Of this last group, Mr. Galsworthy is, perhaps, the most impressive, because he is the most natural and the most impersonal. Although it is not difficult to perceive that his unbiased presentation of all sides of a question is largely a ruse to press home more directly his point, still one cannot avoid seeing that he does admit that there are other arguable positions besides his own.' "

560 [Woolf, Virginia.] "Mr. Galsworthy's Novel," TIMES LITERARY SUPPLEMENT (Lond), XVI (30 Aug 1917), 415; rptd in CONTEMPORARY WRITERS (Lond: Hogarth P, 1965), pp. 63–66.

In *Beyond,* Gyp acts conventionally, without thought and without a code of morality. The flaw in JG's style is that he presents Gyp and her conventional surroundings without a touch of redeeming satire: life in *Beyond* is colorless rather than vicious or beautiful, containing nothing coarse, boisterous, or even desirable.

1918

561 Beckmann, Emmy. "John Galsworthy: Ein Blick in die englische Volksseele" (John Galsworthy: A Glimpse into the Soul of the English People), DIE FRAU (Berlin), XXV (1918), 391–94.

JG portrays the national character of the English in a much more dependable way than Wilde, Shaw, and previous satirists. *The Man of Property,* especially, reveals why Great Britain is a world power and so strong in the present war. Germans should not overlook this, and also they should fight materialism in their own country. [In German.]

562 C., A. "Interior Fiction," NEW REPUBLIC, XVI (10 Aug 1918), 53–54.
[Ambivalent review of *Five Tales*. "Stoic" and "Indian Summer of a Forsyte" are the best.]

563 "Declined With, or Without, Thanks," LITERARY DIGEST, LVI (16 Feb 1918), 27–28.
[Records reactions—in the Detroit JOURNAL, the Pittsburgh SUN, and the London NEW STATESMAN—to JG's refusing a knighthood.]

564 Denisova, Vas. Iv. "Eskiz'i dekoraīs'i ris. *Bor'ba*" (Sketches, Decorations, and Drawings. *Strife*), trans by L. Pokrovshoi (Moscow: Dennitsa, 1918) [not seen].
[In Russian.]

565 E[dgett], E[dwin] F[rancis]. "John Galsworthy's Mastery of Life," BOSTON EVENING TRANSCRIPT, 10 April 1918, Sec. 2, p. 8.
Five Tales is a refreshing corrective to *Beyond*, because JG has given renewed evidence that he can master life without exaggerated erotic significance.

566 Ervine, St. John. "The Later Plays of Mr. John Galsworthy," FORTNIGHTLY REVIEW, CX (1 July 1918), 83–92.
Despite some critical opinion, JG is not impartial; rather, his sympathies seem to be degenerating into prejudice. *The Mob* shows JG seriously flirting with the "mob-instinct of unreasoning chivalry." Sentiment begins to degenerate into sentimentality. In fact, to be weak is not always to be right. In the later plays he is so interested in "colliding characters" that he has "lost sight of the nature of his characters." In *The Fugitive* his determinism becomes willful: Clare Dedmond would be the last to end the way she does. The execution rather than the ideal fails. *The Fugitive* does not create the illusion of life that Ibsen does in A DOLL'S HOUSE or that Synge does in THE SHADOW OF THE GLEN. While the "unreality of *The Fugitive* is more apparent," JG is guilty of the same "unreality" in *Mob, A Bit o' Love,* and *The Foundations*. [One of the few perceptive and detailed studies in JG's lifetime that considers JG's use of verisimilitude.]

567 "*Five Tales,*" CATHOLIC WORLD, CVIII (Oct 1918), 115.
Five Tales, perhaps excellent illustrations for the technique of story writing, cannot be recommended for "entertainment. . . . edification or . . . social inspiration." The tales are sordid and "disgustingly real," devoted to "extrinsic display."

568 "*Five Tales,*" NEW YORK TIMES SUNDAY REVIEW OF BOOKS, 7 April 1918, pp. 147, 153.

Five Tales is full of irony and human pity. "The Apple Tree" is a simple presentation of an "unanswerable and despairing complexity"; "The Juryman" tells of human frustration; "The Indian Summer of a Forsyte" is "sweet, tender and . . . beautiful."

569 *"Five Tales,"* OPEN SHELF (Cleveland), July 1918, p. 79.
[Brief notice of publication.]

570 *"Five Tales,"* SPECTATOR (Lond), CXXI (28 Sept 1918), 335–36.
[Plot-summary review of *Five Tales,* with the conventional comment that JG's sympathies are with the underdog.]

571 "Galsworthy Appeals to the New World to Save the Old," CURRENT OPINION, LXIV (May 1918), 340–41.
[Primarily a quotation of JG's remarks that appeared originally in HARPER'S WEEKLY.]

572 "Galsworthy (John). *Five Tales,"* ATHENAEUM, No. 4633 (Sept 1918), 405–6.
[Paragraph review of *Five Tales* comments that art controls JG's presentation of psychological analysis, ethics, and social philosophy.]

573 George, W. L. A NOVELIST ON NOVELS (Lond: Collins, 1918); as LITERARY CHAPTERS (Bost: Little, Brown, 1918), pp. 18, 19, 30, 32, 62–63, 113–14, 129.
[A brief, general, favorable view of JG as one of the older serious novelists.]

574 Jackson, Holbrook. "John Galsworthy as a Playwright," TODAY, II (Feb 1918), 209–14.
JG's outstanding characteristic is his normality. His strength is his "passionate sense of right, and the artistry to express it." A good example of JG's method of conveying his message through "simple and even blundering characters" is Cokeson in *Justice.* He is an ironist, and *Strife* "is his best-constructed and most finely characterized play." JG's "method combines the humane ardour of a Charles Reade with the intellectual serenity of a Matthew Arnold." The atmosphere of reality in his plays "startles by its inevitability."

575 "Literary Knights," NATION (NY), CVI (31 Jan 1918), 108–9.
[The writer praises JG for refusing to accept a literary knighthood offered by England.]

576 "Mr. Galsworthy's Old Men," SATURDAY REVIEW (Lond), CXXV (17 Aug 1918), 752.
In *Five Tales,* "A Stoic" and "The Indian Summer of a Forsyte" are pathetic and realistic portraits. JG has finally omitted "sexuality and . . . socialism" from his writing; the five "ironical comedies" are quite well written.

577 "Mr. Galsworthy's Tales," TIMES LITERARY SUPPLEMENT (Lond), XVII (8 Aug 1918), 371.

Five Tales is dignified, "largely planned and stately built." Reverencing life, JG continues to grow as man and artist. His ironic method camouflages his shyness: he seems afraid to admit his tenderness, his "passion for beauty and good will." Consequently, it is masked in "The Apple Tree" and "The First and the Last." But he is direct and powerful in "A Stoic" and "Indian Summer of a Forsyte." "The Juryman," his subtlest tale, combines sternness with tenderness and imagination with sound sense.

578 Moses, Montrose J. *"The Silver Box,"* REPRESENTATIVE BRITISH DRAMAS: VICTORIAN AND MODERN (Bost: Little, Brown, 1918; rev ed, 1931), pp. 495–502, 986–87.

The Silver Box is one of JG's best dramas from the point of view of technical construction. [This introductory essay precedes the text of *Box,* pp. 502–31. It is based on Moses's "Galsworthy-Dramatist," BOOK NEWS MONTHLY, XXX (July 1912), 771–74.]

579 "Tales by John Galsworthy: Tabloid Pictures of Character as Revealed by Tragedy and Passion," SPRINGFIELD REPUBLICAN (Mass), 9 June 1918, p. 15A.

The theme of *Five Tales* is "life calls the tune—we dance," While JG might not understand the depths of human nature, he does search fearlessly for understanding.

580 Ward, Mrs. Humphry [Mary Augusta (Arnold) Ward]. A WRITER'S RECOLLECTIONS. Two Volumes (Lond: Collins; NY: n.p., 1918), II, 249.

Although JG has recently written some moving pages about the war, hopefully he will rediscover the quality in his writing that has been missing since *The Country House.* [A passing reference in a series of passing references to various writers.]

1919

581 *"Addresses In America,"* A.L.A. BOOKLIST, XVI (Nov 1919), 51.

The seven *Addresses in America* express the "sympaahetic insight, mutual shortcomings, aspirations and duties" of England and America. [Brief review.]

582 *"Addresses in America,"* DIAL (Chicago), LXVII (6 Sept 1919), 220.

[Unsympathetic and brief dismissal of JG's "fragmentary collection" of essays,

Addresses in America. Ironically, the reviewer shows the "curious lack of proportion" that he accuses JG of in relation to ecology and education.]

583 *"Another Sheaf,"* A.L.A. BOOKLIST, XV (April 1919), 255.
An open-minded examination of topics primarily relating to World War I, *Another Sheaf* is used as the main source for JG's current lecture tour of the United States. [Brief review.]

584 *"Another Sheaf,"* DIAL (Chicago), LXVI (8 March 1919), 253–54.
The chief value of *Another Sheaf* lies in pleas for reconstruction, for national policies that will help human conditions during demobilization following World War I, for increased food production, and for recognition of the intertwined destinies of English-speaking nations.

585 *"Another Sheaf,"* NATION (NY), CVIII (1 March 1919), 331.
Another Sheaf is vivid and forceful, but not original. JG is once again the "unflinching assailant of unimaginative morality and stereotyped economics."

586 *"Another Sheaf,"* OPEN SHELF (Cleveland), Sept 1919, p. 91.
[Brief notice of publication.]

587 *"Another Sheaf,"* SPECTATOR (Lond), CXXII (22 March 1919), 366–67.
[Noncommittal review that briefly states some themes in *Another Sheaf.*]

588 Birge, Anna G. "A Selected List of Current Books: *Addresses in America,"* WISCONSIN LIBRARY BULLETIN (Madison), XV (Oct 1919), 211.
[Inconsequential review.]

589 "Books in Brief," NATION (NY), CIX (29 Nov 1919), 694.
[Brief summary of JG's themes that are "persuasively presented" in *Addresses in America.*]

590 Boynton, H. W. "All Over the Lot," BOOKMAN (NY), XLIX (Aug 1919), 732.
JG is preoccupied with sex in *A Saint's Progress.* His "politesse of style" ornaments the situation without refining it. The characters in themselves are vulgar, but, "as . . . [JG] honestly doesn't know it, why should his readers—subject, as they are, to the enchantment of his clear, drawling recitative?"

591 Cunliffe, J. W. ENGLISH LITERATURE DURING THE LAST HALF CENTURY (NY: Macmillan, 1919) [not seen]; rev and enlgd (1923), pp. 220–36; (1930), pp. 220–34.
JG's permanent place in literature is based on his sympathy for the lower classes and his "skill in analysis of character and emotion." His early works—*From the Four Winds* to *Villa Rubein*—are not successful. Although *The Island Pharisees*

lacks the balance of his later work, Shelton and Ferrand are "firmly drawn." JG showed a mastery of his material with *The Man of Property,* and *The Forsyte Saga* is JG's most substantial achievement as a novelist. His ability to analyze romantic passion is his strongest gift. By 1917 both public and critics had decided that JG was a better playwright than novelist. A besetting weakness of his is a certain flatness in his minor characters. Upon reading "Some Platitudes Concerning Drama," one is not surprised to "find that Galsworthy despises plot construction," and the result is two weaknesses: (1) his characters often do not develop; (2) instead of plot he uses symmetry—one character balancing another, and the result is often an increased artificiality. There is a thinness in his imaginative work; his work may be saved from oblivion by the "beauty of his prose and his artistic sincerity."

> **592** Dutton, George B. *"Saint's Progress* by Galsworthy: Expressing This Novelist's Rebellion against Restraint," SPRINGFIELD REPUBLICAN (Mass), 31 Aug 1919, Sec. A, p. 15.

Time and again *A Saint's Progress* asserts itself in favor of "rebellion against restraint, yearning for escape, demand for expansion, for self-realization." The book is a penetrating analysis of unrest in our time.

> **593** E[dgett], E[dwin] F[rancis]. "The Progress of John Galsworthy: His Latest Novel a Story of the Manner in Which an English Clergyman Faces Family Trouble," BOSTON EVENING TRANSCRIPT, 2 July 1919, Sec. 2, p. 8.

In *A Saint's Progress,* JG "does not forsake his study and analysis of the subject of sex, but he involves in it other serious problems of life and personality." He attempts to portray people as they are rather than, morally speaking, as they ought to be.

> **594** "England's Opportunity," TIMES LITERARY SUPPLEMENT (Lond), 6 Feb. 1919, p. 66.

The reader's pleasure in *Another Sheaf* will depend less on the writing than on JG's counsel. What is valuable in this book "is the insistence on our present opportunity, and the vision of the goal which Mr. Galsworthy . . . displays before us." The essay "Back to the Land" urges England to become self-sufficient in food production. JG is no crank. "If he touches NEWS FROM NOWHERE on one hand, he touches a Blue-book on the other. The combination may not make for the perfection of his essays; it will make . . . for the easy access of his vision to minds which would find NEWS FROM NOWHERE mere nonsense."

> **595** Eskey, Elizabeth. "Government by Rabble or by Caucus Is Not Democracy, Says John Galsworthy," NEW YORK WORLD, 16 Feb 1919, Editorial Sec., p. 1.

[Report of an interview with JG, emphasizing his hesitancy and obvious difficulty in speaking without notes and without Ada by his side to help him. Finally,

JG suggests that Eskey buy *Another Sheaf,* which contains his thoughts on questions that Eskey asked. She does, and quotes several passages from *Sheaf.*]

596 "Essays on Reconstruction and Literary Criticism," REVIEW OF REVIEWS (NY), LIX (March 1919), 330–31.

Another Sheaf is written in the spirit of reconstruction following World War I. JG as an "intellectual-emotional manner of dealing with practical subjects."

597 "Galsworthy and the New Hedonism," NATION (NY), CIX (12 July 1919, 47–48.

The human cry that has been suppressed in other JG novels emerges in *A Saint's Progress.* Noel, who has "flame in her soul," is contrasted to her staid father. Leila effectively states the theme of the younger generation when she laments that "the most dreadful thing in life is the way people express their natural instincts." JG has seen beyond moral gesture to moral fact. JG demonstrates no "technical pedantry"; narrative harmony is maintained even though the "personal angle of the narrative" shifts from Pierson, to Noel, to Leila, to Jimmy.

598 "Galsworthy in America: Addresses Delivered while Author Was Here to Attend Lowell Centenary; Importance of Restrained Speaking and Truthful Reporting Insisted on—Influence of the Press in the Modern World," SPRINGFIELD REPUBLICAN (Mass), 24 Aug 1919, Sec. A, p. 15.

Addresses in America, "pungent and suggestive" in giving JG's life wisdom, ineffectively generalizes about Anglo-American relations.

599 "Galsworthy (John). *Saint's Progress,*" ATHENAEUM, No. 4669 (24 Oct 1919), 1082.

[Paragraph plot-summary review of *A Saint's Progress.*]

600 Gerould, James Thayer. *"Another Sheaf,"* BELLMAN (Minneapolis), XXVI (17 May 1919), 552.

The occasional and hortatory *Another Sheaf* discusses unsolved contemporary problems.

601 H., F. "Bankrupt?" NEW REPUBLIC, XX (3 Sept 1919), 154.

JG, once a decorous, exceptionally sensitive, and Turgenev-like writer, is now "a facile, graceful, rather nerveless and distinctly complacent magazine storyteller who has practically ceased to be an artist but who still presents an accomplished imitation of the real thing." He knows the upper middle-class Englishman, commands his idiom "almost too easily," and is "touched with a poetic appreciation of nature." In *A Saint's Progress,* the elderly clergyman, "too intent on his ideals to be a humanistic parent, becomes a Saint drearily sentimentalized." JG exhibits Noel "as a guilty creature to whom he is sweetly indulgent." But he is no longer meticulous in expression, as seen in the vulgar attitude of expression when writing about the love scenes. In the Saint, JG "believes he has portrayed a pathetic outworn figure. The truth is, he has stuffed a traditional clerical shirt."

602 "John Galsworthy Talks on Art in America, Education and Happiness," TOUCHSTONE, V (April 1919), 3–6.

JG emphasizes the need for a sense of balance and proportion in life to be achieved through the artist, teacher, and newsman. English universities prepare people more for the business world than for the artistic life: universities would best prepare students by combining culture and opportunity. The English and Americans need to read more Continental literature. Happiness comes through absorption in work or play, resulting in loss of self-consciousness. Form in writing is more important than personal feeling. [Based on an interview with JG.]

603 "Literature. John Galsworthy. *Another Sheaf,*" WISCONSIN LIBRARY BULLETIN, XV (April 1919), 110.

[Paragraph review recommends *Another Sheaf* for large libraries. The twelve essays are unified by a British view of post-World War I reconstruction needs.]

604 M[ann], D[orothea] L[awrance]. "*Another Sheaf:* A Collection of John Galsworthy's Wartime Reflections," BOSTON EVENING TRANSCRIPT, 12 Feb 1919, Sec. 2, p. 8.

JG speaks frankly in *Another Sheaf,* questioning seriously the road England must take as she and her citizen-soldiers readjust to life after World War I.

605 Mansfield, Katherine. "A Standstill," ATHENAEUM, No. 4670 (31 Oct 1919), 1123; rptd in NOVELS AND NOVELISTS, ed by J. Middleton Murry (NY: Knopf; Lond: Constable, 1930), pp. 99–104; rptd (Bost: Beacon P, 1959).

Saint's Progress as a novel is "a standstill."

606 "Mr. Galsworthy's Addresses," TIMES LITERARY SUPPLEMENT (Lond), 4 Dec 1919, p. 705.

The speeches of *Addresses in America* "are perhaps the best expression, out of all the many which have been put forth" regarding the postwar world. "It would be difficult to praise the book too highly." The essential thesis is that civilization is at a turning point which will determine whether society will move forward or collapse into "revolutions and wars." The book is a "civilized book, full of those four qualities which Mr. Galsworthy singles out as distinguishing human beings from the beasts . . . the sense of proportion, the feeling for beauty, pity, and the sense of humour."

607 "Mr. John Galsworthy," WORLD'S WORK, XXXVII (April 1919), 601.

[Caption beneath an Underwood and Underwood photo comments that JG, in the

United States to celebrate the James Russell Lowell centenary, advocates strong Anglo-American relations.]

608 Mosher, Joseph. "Of Goodly Grain," PUBLISHER'S WEEKLY, XCV (15 Feb 1919), 486.

JG indicates in *Another Sheaf* that all is not well with postwar England; but he suggests that things might be improved. Americans should heed his advice.

609 "The New Books," INDEPENDENT (NY), XCVII (8 March 1919), 341–42.

JG combines "honest conviction with literary charm" in *Another Sheaf:* the essays command attention and incite "sober second thought."

610 "New Books and Reprints: Literary," TIMES LITERARY SUPPLE-MENT (Lond), 27 Nov 1919, p. 698.

[A brief, one-paragraph statement about *Addresses in America;* see also "Mr. Galsworthy's Addresses," ibid., 4 Dec 1919, p. 705.]

611 "New Books to Take Along When You Go on Your Vacation: The Spirit That Giveth Life," INDEPENDENT (NY), XCIX (12 July 1919), 60.

It is not true, as it has been frequently argued, that JG poses problems without giving solutions. The whole telling of the human story in *A Saint's Progress* is a solution. [A photo accompanies the review.]

612 Nicholl, Louise Townsend. "Mr. Galsworthy's Interpretation of Coming Events," BOOKMAN (NY), XLIX (April 1919), 213.

Much of *Another Sheaf* is exquisitely written, especially the little sketch of soldiers returning home in "The Road," and "France, 1916–1917, An Impression."

613 *"Saint's Progress,"* A.L.A. BOOKLIST, XVI (Nov 1919), 58.

A Saint's Progress is an interesting, strong, and artistic treatment of an idealized vicar and his family, in which happiness comes even to sinners. [Brief review.]

614 *"Saint's Progress,"* DIAL (Chicago), LXVI (28 June 1919), 666; LXVII (6 Sept 1919), 211.

A Saint's Progress is devoted to types who question (1) the role of God and the church in a time of war and (2) uncharitable churchgoers. In Noel Pierson JG works with his speciality: portrayal of a "young girl at her loveliest, a creature of intelligence, simplicity, and charm." [The entry in LXVI is a three-sentence plot summary anticipating the fuller review in LXVII.]

615 *"Saint's Progress,"* NEW YORK TIMES SUNDAY REVIEW OF BOOKS, 22 June 1919, p. 338.

A Saint's Progress, the story of a man unable both to meet his daughter's need and to draw close to common humanity, is intensely human, interesting, sympathetic—a work of "exquisite artistry."

616 *"Saint's Progress,"* OUTLOOK (NY), CXXII (16 July 1919), 444.
A Saint's Progress illustrates JG's ability to interest the reader, to maintain the main characters' "outline and reality," and to depict "passion, sorrow, disillusionment and perplexity."

617 "Shabby-Genteel," SATURDAY REVIEW (Lond), CXXVIII (8 Nov 1919), 443.
JG's works increasingly leave the impression of "faded hopes, and failing environment." *A Saint's Progress* lacks vitality: the Rev. Pierson, not fully realized, remains puzzled throughout by his quest; Noel goes from youth and vitality "into the grey shadow" of JG's soul. JG uses a "meaningless forumla."

618 "The War Baby," TIMES LITERARY SUPPLEMENT (Lond), 23 Oct 1919, p. 587.
As always, the reader can count on JG's good faith in *A Saint's Progress;* he does not resort to a cheap exploitation of his characters or of the situation. From an artistic standpoint JG does not handle the subject well; Noel's behavior is not convincing. In order to make her convincing JG, if necessary, should have either risked outraging the public or chosen a different theme. The character of the Saint redeems the book. The portrait is "moving and just, except intellectually"; this is not one of JG's best.

619 Waugh, Arthur. TRADITION AND CHANGE: STUDIES IN CONTEMPORARY LITERATURE (Lond: Chapman & Hall; NY: Dutton, 1919), pp. 285–91.
[This is primarily a favorable review of *A Sheaf,* which was possibly first published in OUTLOOK: JG is praised for his "sense of proportion" and his humaneness.]

620 "Welcome Visitors from England," REVIEW OF REVIEWS (NY), LIX (March 1919), 241–42.
[Portrait of JG, accompanied by an article praising him for work helping to rehabilitate men maimed during World War I.]

621 Williams, Harold. MODERN ENGLISH WRITERS: BEING A STUDY OF IMAGINATIVE LITERATURE, 1890–1914 (Lond: Sidgwick & Jackson, 1919), pp. 253–59 (as dramatist), 369–74 (as novelist); rptd (1925), pp. 273–75 (as dramatist), 387–92 (as novelist).
Although noteworthy as a dramatist, JG is never the great artist, "for he is never lost to himself." The importance of his dramatic work is "not in its artistic power, but in its moral implications" and the ethical force of the author. The moral is deduced by the individual or the audience "from a faithful and undistorted presentation of things as they are for their own sake—in a word, the ethical method of Shakespeare." JG lacks humor. As a novelist the artist is frequently overwhelmed by "cold ratiocination." In *The Island Pharisees* JG "delivered the truth that was in him. He has done little since save amplify, expand and

comment." His canvas is too narrow. He rarely sees people except through "the veil of social economy." He has been able to express himself more fully and with greater artistry as a playwright.

1920

---

622 "Another Chapter of Forsyte History: John Galsworthy Continues Fortunes of This Family in His Novel *In Chancery,*" SPRINGFIELD REPUBLICAN (Mass), 21 Nov 1920, Sec. 1, p. 7.
JG's characters are "oftener types than individuals," representing "British racial types, British morals, and British hypocrisies," portraying the altering social and political fabric of England. *In Chancery* is one of JG's most characteristic and finest works.

623 [Anthony, Luther B.] *"The Skin Game,"* DRAMATIST (Easton, Pa), XI (July 1920), 1011–12.
[Waspish review of the "utterly amateurish" *The Skin Game.*]

624 "The Arts and Letters," LIVING AGE, CCCV (22 May 1920), pp. 493–95.
JG's unpleasant and striking play *The Skin Game* moves swiftly with "almost brutal violence," and portrays human nature perhaps too crudely and primitively. [Review.]

625 *"Awakening,"* SPECTATOR (Lond), CXXV (11 Dec 1920), 784.
[A brief, noncommittal review of *Awakening* that finds some of R. H. Sauter's illustrations "very pleasing."]

626 B. "A Rare Week for the Ardent Playgoer," GRAPHIC (Lond), CI (1 May 1920), 702.
[Plot-summary review of *The Skin Game.*]

627 "Beauty and the Beast," NATION (NY), CX (17 April 1920), 522.
A central theme of *Tatterdemalion* is that war and hate fill the world because there is not enough love of beauty. JG's emotion is stronger than his reflection. Stylistically, *Tatterdemalion* has mellowness without softness, "a virile tenderness of tone, an unobtrusive ease," and effective and occasionally beautiful diction without monotony.

628 Benchley, Robert C. "Drama: Commonplaces and Commoners," LIFE (NY), LXXVI (11 Nov 1920), 872–73.
The Skin Game is superior to much appearing currently on Broadway, but JG occasionally stoops to Hornblowerish tactics in theatricality. To read the play as an anti-war tract is to stretch credibility: the theme of class hatred is sufficient.

629 Blurton, P. "The Drama in England," NEW WORLD (Lond), III (June 1920), 84–85.

The Skin Game at the St. Martin's Theatre continues JG's interest in the class struggle.

630 Boynton, H. W. "Ideas and Stories," BOOKMAN (NY), LII (Nov 1920), 251.

In Chancery, in its depiction of human passions, should rank among JG's best. He knows "nothing about persons, and little about about daughters and not a whole lot about married life. But he knows all about Forsytes as clan and caste and symbol."

631 Boynton, H. W. "Studies in Modern Life," WEEKLY REVIEW (NY), III (27 Oct 1920), 382–83.

Fleur's generation in *In Chancery* lacks the initiative of the earlier Forsytes; Soames has evolved from a brave to a solid and safe man.

632 C., S. C. "Mr. Galsworthy's Plays," NEW REPUBLIC, XXIV (13 Oct 1920), 172.

A Bit o' Love has "rather sickly sentiment"; *The Foundations,* forced comedy; and *The Skin Game,* grasp and virility. [Brief review of *Plays. Fourth Series.*]

633 C., S. C. *"Tatterdemalion,"* NEW REPUBLIC, XXII (26 May 1920), 427.

Tatterdemalion combines thought, emotion, and irony in its treatment of the injustices of wartime. JG's soft and modulated tone occasionally becomes emotional, as in "Spindleberries." Justice and beauty are recurrent themes.

634 Cannan, Gilbert. "The English Theatre during and after the War," THEATRE ARTS MAGAZINE (NY), IV (Jan 1920), 21–24.

A strong repertory theater movement following World War I will help to produce new dramatists, just as the Court Theatre was largely responsible for JG's success.

635 "A Child of 1901," NEW YORK EVENING POST LITERARY REVIEW, 20 Nov 1920, p. 5.

Awakening is a "very tender and very delicate little study of small boyhood. One would be tempted to call it an idyll" were it not for its "simple but carefree realism."

636 Courtney, W. L. "Lecture," MORNING POST (Lond), 29 Dec 1920.

[Faulty citation in H. V. Marot, A BIBLIOGRAPHY OF THE WORKS OF JOHN GALSWORTHY (Lond: Elkin Mathews & Marrot; NY: Scribner, 1928); rptd (NY: Burt Franklin, 1968); rptd (Folcroft, Pa: Folcroft Library Editions, 1973).]

637 Edgett, Edwin Francis. "The Erratic Course of John Galsworthy: His Latest Novel a Continuation of His Researches in the Strange

Marital Relations of the Forsyte Family," BOSTON EVENING TRAN-
SCRIPT, 6 Nov 1920, Sec. 4, p. 4.

The Forsytes of *In Chancery* are boring. JG overestimates our interest in them as
well as "the value of his own contribution to modern imaginative literature."

638 E[dgett], E[dwin] F[rancis]. "Writers and Books: The Literary
World of Today," BOSTON EVENING TRANSCRIPT, 10 Nov 1920, Sec. 3,
p. 7; rptd from LONDON OBSERVER [not seen].

JG's "charming but bodiless" women represent ideas rather than persons who
assert themselves as individuals. Despite this, *In Chancery* is fine and delicate
but not completely convincing. It stimulates thought and touches the imagination.

639 Field, Louise Maunsell. "Mr. Galsworthy in War and Peace,"
NEW YORK TIMES SUNDAY REVIEW OF BOOKS, 28 March 1920, p. 139.

"Beauty," perhaps more than any other word in *Tatterdemalion*, represents JG's
overpowering concern in his craft as in his life. "A Green Hill Far Away" and
"Buttercup Night" are "exquisite."

640 Firkins, O. W. "Drama. Galsworthy and Ibsen," WEEKLY RE-
VIEW (NY), III (3 Nov 1920), 426–28.

The faults of *The Mob* are: (1) substitution of chronicle in dialogue for plot; (2)
monotony of action and feeling; and (3) treatment of the theme of conflict of
individual and mob in terms too general for concerted stage action. The excellent
production at NY's Neighborhood Playhouse and the performance of Ian Macla-
ren as More combine with JG's sincerity to create a worthwhile theatrical
experience.

641 Firkins, O. W. "Drama. The New Plays of Galsworthy," WEEKLY
REVIEW (NY), III (27 Oct 1920), 396–98.

Plays. Fourth Series (*A Bit o' Love, The Foundations,* and *The Skin Game*) are
relatively plotless. The mawkish Strangway in *Love* causes readers to lose sight
of the manly themes of forbearance and endurance. *Foundations* is almost a
fantastic burlesque of "melancholic earnestness" with surface realism: it lacks
verisimilitude because of incongruous weaving of tragic and comic parts. Characters in *Game* are inadequately developed; the theme is dramatically handled,
even though the coloring is occasionally flamboyant and sickly.

642 Firkins, O. W. "Drama. *The Skin Game* at the Bijou Theatre,"
WEEKLY REVIEW (NY), III (10 Nov 1920), 454–55.

The Skin Game, nominally tragic and moral, is too melodramatic. Some flaws are
the lack of a protagonist to contrast to the frailities of the Hornblowers and
Hillcrists and the unnecessary scene (II, ii) in Chloe's boudoir. Strengths are a
vigorous Act I, an excellent auction scene (Act II), and a tense boudoir scene
(despite its uselessness). Acting transcends JG's characterization in the ugly and
imperiously moral tale.

643 *"The Forsyte Saga,"* TIMES LITERARY SUPPLEMENT (Lond), XIX (28 Oct 1920), 698.

The passing of an age, symbolized by the death of Queen Victoria, is the focal point of *In Chancery*. JG "lights up his sober fabric with the golden thread of beauty."

644 "Forsyteism," SATURDAY REVIEW (Lond), CXXX (4 Dec 1920), 458.

Soames is "spiritually arid . . . physically and mentally repellent" in *In Chancery*. JG's indictment of England's Forsytes is "shadowy, pervasive, indirect"; to JG life seems "an enormous ganglion upon which he executes one neurotomy after another."

645 "Galsworthy in Tabloid: *Tatterdemalion* Comprises Stories of War and Peace's Return," SPRINGFIELD REPUBLICAN (Mass), 25 April 1920, Sec. A, p. 13.

Tatterdemalion's varied moods will not comfort those "fervid patriots who saw the war only as a glorified crusade against a benighted enemy." The book shows clarity of vision, diligence in craftsmanship, and candor.

646 "Galsworthy Not at His Best in *The Mob;* Production Is Good," NEW YORK CLIPPER, LXVIII (27 Oct 1920), p. 29.

The Mob is "not . . . up to the Galsworthy standard." The play lacks humor, and JG's thesis errs by "implying that mob spirit is a cause rather than a consequence" of war. Although the play evidences "potent dramatic writing," it is finally "wishy-washy and, at times, incredibly clumsy." "The company . . . succeeded in making a hit with the material at hand despite its deficiencies."

647 "Galsworthy Unlimited," INDEPENDENT (NY), CIV (25 Dec 1920), 442.

[Brief review of *Awakening*.]

648 Glaenzer, Richard Butler. LITERARY SNAPSHOTS (NY: Brentano, 1920), p. 18.

[Fourteen-line poem giving an impression of JG.]

649 Grein, J. T. "Old Lamps for New. *The Skin Game,*" ILLUSTRATED LONDON NEWS, 8 May 1920 [not seen]; rptd in THE WORLD OF THE THEATRE: IMPRESSIONS AND MEMOIRS, MARCH 1920–1921 (Lond: Heinemann, 1921), pp. 30–31.

The Skin Game is splendid. Although it may seem that the material side overwhelms human nature, one discovers that the human element is always there, except for Mrs. Hillcrist. The play's depth of inwardness is the real attraction or achievement, for almost every character represents not only an individual but a principle.

650 Harris, Frank. "John Galsworthy: A Notable Englishman," CONTEMPORARY PORTRAITS (Third Series) (NY: The Author, 1920), pp. 31–43.

JG with his emphasis on "balance and sanity" is a "typical" Englishman in his conservatism. *Justice* is better than the novels, and "The Apple Tree" is to be preferred over *Justice*. If JG were not an Englishman, he would be able to write a masterpiece. [This notice is primarily an interview that followed JG's lecture on the subjects of democracy and the League of Nations at the Aeolian Hall in NY.]

651 [Hornblow, Arthur.] "Mr. Hornblow Goes to the Play," THEATRE MAGAZINE (NY), XXXII (Dec 1920), 369–71, 414, 422–24.

The Mob, produced at NY's Neighborhood Theatre, is a futile argument against the futility of war.

652 *"In Chancery,"* A.L.A. BOOKLIST, XVII (Dec 1920), 116.

In Chancery is a "keen study, of not very likeable persons," expressing JG's ideas on divorce and social laws. [Brief notice of publication.]

653 *"In Chancery,"* NEW YORK TIMES SUNDAY REVIEW OF BOOKS, 24 Oct 1920, p. 24.

"In Chancery has dexterity . . . subtlety, realism . . . and penetration." "Rich in character, incident and thought," it is perhaps JG's biggest work in its "union of the individual, the family, and the era."

654 *"In Chancery,"* SPECTATOR (Lond), CXXV (18 Dec 1920), 820. [Plot-summary review.]

655 Jameson, Storm. MODERN DRAMA IN EUROPE (Lond: Collins; NY: Harcourt, Brace & Howe, 1920), pp. 12, 13, 154–57.

The *type* of realist drama is *The Silver Box.* JG is not original; "he is merely faithful to his vision of life; not inspired, but thoughtful; not imaginative, but only truthful." Because Falder is too feeble an individual, *Justice* is not a great tragedy. Other realists have gone "to the hovel, the business office and the police court for life" and have found "only the sweepings of worn-out souls"; in these same places JG has found "some dim knowledge of the spirit of humanity, some sense of the need for a purpose in life," and it is that that gives the play artistic value. Falder's defense counsel "is the articulate spirit of art in the play." When this spirit is missing JG's work is without value and is superficial: e.g., *The Eldest Son* and *The Fugitive*. Without striving for effect or using non-dramatic interests JG has "produced plays of no mean power and no common insight in the heart and brain of the social system. And he has written one great play"—*Strife*.

656 "Josephine Victor Scores in Brady's *The Skin Game,"* NEW YORK CLIPPER, LXVIII (27 Oct 1920), 29.

[Plot-summary review of performance at NY's Bijou Theatre. *The Skin Game* will never be the success that *The Mob* and *Justice* were.]

657 Kenney, Rowland. "John Galsworthy as Dramatist," BOOKMAN (Lond), LIX (Oct 1920), 9–11.

The Skin Game illustrates how thin the veneer of civilization is. The tedious auction scene intrudes into an otherwise good play. JG's plays are a considerable achievement, because "English realism is rarely impressive." [Two photos of scenes from the play are reproduced.]

658 "Leading Spring Books," NEW YORK TIMES SUNDAY REVIEW OF BOOKS, 18 April 1920, p. 191.

[Brief notice of *Tatterdemalion*.]

659 Lewisohn, Ludwig. "Drama: Ripeness and Youth," NATION (NY), CXI (10 Nov 1920), 539.

In *The Skin Game* at the Bijou Theatre, JG writes delicately and precisely, merging "the symbolic with the plainly human." Bitterness and humiliation are the result of not being able to stand the fire of conflict.

660 Lewisohn, Ludwig. "The Quiet Truth," NATION (NY), CX (29 May 1920), 732–34; rptd in THE DRAMA AND THE STAGE (NY: Harcourt, Brace, 1922); rptd (Freeport, NY: Books for Libraries P, 1969; St. Clair Shores, Mich: Scholarly P, 1970), pp. 168–73.

In *A Bit o' Love,* Strangway, a "miniature St. Francis," weakens the play; in *The Foundations,* JG suggests that the foundations must be rebuilt; *The Skin Game* localizes the tragi-comedy of all human conflict—"each contestant is both right and wrong." *Game* illustrates clearly and exactly "the inner nature, stripped of the accretions of myth and tradition, of the tragic process itself." JG's inner control and mental discipline allow him to follow the "rhythm of life" more assiduously than other English playwrights. [Review of *Plays. Fourth Series.*]

661 Lynch, Bohun. *"The Skin Game* (St. Martin's Theatre)," LONDON MERCURY, II (June 1920), 222–24.

The Skin Game is one of the best plays in years, despite its "unfortunate" title. Through the characters of Hillcrist and Hornblower, JG shows that in an imperfect world, under special conditions, "one class of society is liable to err in similar directions to those commonly ascribed by it to another class." This is shown through Hillcrist's use of "refined . . . blackmail." Squire Hillcrist is remarkably complete; Mrs. Hillcrist is not.

662 MaCarthy, Desmond. *"The Skin Game,"* NEW STATESMAN, XV (8 May 1920), 134–35.

The Skin Game, like most JG plays, makes the audience feel that it is "thoroughly looked after and taken in hand." While he has power to raise indignation and pity, he lacks the power of tragic feeling and free comedy. The tone is flat because he seems obsessed to prove that we should focus rights and wrongs correctly. Like Brieux he is a sociologist. Involved as we are by the feud between squirearchy and self-made capitalism, we are unmoved by Chloe's tragedy because we are unprepared for it. [Review of performance.]

663 Mansfield, Katherine. "Family Portraits," ATHENAEUM, No. 4728 (10 Dec 1920), 810–11; rptd in NOVELS AND NOVELISTS, ed by J. Middleton Murry (NY: Knopf; Lond: Constable, 1930), pp. 316–20; rptd (Bost: Beacon P, 1959).

Compared to *The Man of Property, In Chancery* seems less solid because its use of irony is fainter. A great creative artist must be able to withdraw from his characters in order to survey what is happening, but JG "is so deeply engaged, immersed and engrossed in the Forsyte family that he loses this freedom." Soames is the hero in *In Chancery;* he "is as solid, as substantial as a mind [as opposed to the artist's creative energy] could make him, but he is never real." Although not a great novel, *In Chancery* is a "fascinating, brilliant book." [The review is also of Edith Wharton's THE AGE OF INNOCENCE.]

664 Mathesius, Vilem. "Romany Johna Galsworthyho" (The Novels of John Galsworthy), ZEMĚ, II (1920–21), 4n [not seen]. [Cited in Modern Humanities Research Association BIBLIOGRAPHY, I.] [In Czech.]

665 Maurice, Arthur B. "A New Golden Age in American Reading," WORLD'S WORK, XXXIX (March 1920), 488–506.

[Underwood and Underwood photo of JG is accompanied by comment that *A Saint's Progress* has sold three times the copies that any other JG novel has.]

666 "Mr. Galsworthy," ATHENAEUM, No. 4701 (4 June 1920), 733.

In *Plays. Fourth Series,* JG is unable to stimulate emotional interest that does not come from the relation of character to environment. In *The Skin Game* the social problem gets the better of human beings; in *The Foundations,* class antagonism is treated with unusual and ineffective extravagant comedy; and the pathos of *A Bit o' Love* is suspect and too picturesque in the last scene.

667 "Mr. Galsworthy's *Skin Game,*" MANCHESTER GUARDIAN, 23 April 1920, p. 14.

The Skin Game at St. Martin's Theatre is filled with "pity and reserves and compunctions." JG is impartial, the play has less beauty than usual, and the force driving the people seems "something . . . smaller than fate."

668 "Mr. Galsworthy's War Play: *Defeat,*" ILLUSTRATED LONDON NEWS, CLVI (20 March 1920), 484, 486.

[Plot summary of JG's one-act play at the Lyric Theatre.]

669 "More Dramas by Galsworthy: Amusement Is of Intellectual Kind," SPRINGFIELD REPUBLICAN (Mass), 11 July 1920, Sec. 1, p. 11.

A Bit o' Love and *The Foundations* are comparable through similar "fragmentary treatment," resulting in "confusion of aims" and shifts in focus. Before these plays, JG had been "a little too impartial, a little too obviously the social investigator." *The Skin Game,* the most typically JG in *Plays. Fourth Series,* is a well-developed study in "closely paralleled humanity."

670 Muir, Edwin. WE MODERNS: ENIGMAS AND GUESSES (The Free Lance Books, IV) (NY: Knopf, 1920), pp. 60, 150, 189, 193–200.

Realism in Arnold Bennett and JG is "a reaction from asceticism." Conrad more subtly analyzes the human mind and heart than does H. G. Wells or JG. Both JG and Oscar Wilde "are decadent" because they lack "Love." JG is a collectivist who "sympathizes with the people," and Wilde "sympathizes with himself." Primarily, JG is a reformer, not an artist. Unlike Hardy, both JG and George Moore err in treating of love "with the meaning left out."

671 O., S. "Skin Games, East and West," ENGLISH REVIEW (Lond), XXX (June 1920), 564–68.

The Skin Game is a "study in type . . . a problem play of satire." It is brilliant, alive, "brutal, thrilling . . . an artist's work." *Game's* chief merit is balance; its chief fault, the inadequate conception of the role of women.

672 "A Peace Play Accused of War," LITERARY DIGEST, LXVII (6 Nov 1920), 30.

[A derivative review of *The Skin Game* and *The Mob* that takes issue with critics who find a war theme in *Game; Mob,* written before World War I, is confessedly a war play. The review consists primarily of quotations from various newspapers, notably the MANCHESTER GUARDIAN (23 April 1920, p. 14) and the NEW YORK TRIBUNE (not seen).]

673 Pem. "Mr. Galsworthy Returns to His Muttons/ *In Chancery*—A Fine Novel," JOHN O'LONDON'S WEEKLY, IV: 84 (13 Nov 1920), 173.

JG is always reasonable; he is restrained, sincere, truthful, and hopeful for the future. *In Chancery* is a remarkable novel. [Mostly a plot summary.]

674 "Plays by Galsworthy," NEW YORK TIMES SUNDAY REVIEW OF BOOKS, 19 Sept 1920, p. 15.

The disappointing *Plays. Fourth Series* is overly concerned with ethical intent. *A Bit o' Love* is strained and lacks dignity; *The Foundations* has "dexterity of character and humor"; *The Skin Game's* "tragic significance" makes it the most actable of the three. JG seems to be marking time artistically.

675 *"Plays; Fourth Series,"* A.L.A. BOOKLIST, XVI (July 1920), 337.

Sincerity and dramatic intensity enliven the social themes of *A Bit o' Love, The Foundations,* and *The Skin Game.* [Brief review.]

676 Pollock, John. *"The Skin Game,"* FORTNIGHTLY REVIEW, CXIII (June 1920), 961–65.

JG has found himself as a dramatist in *The Skin Game,* having gotten away from the crude effects of class contrast of earlier plays. He both pleases and surprises.

One problem is the unexplained and unjustified spying by the maid when Hillcrist's agent approaches Chloe with evidence about her past. [Pollock takes the unusual position that the aristocracy wins rather than the new world of business—that Hillcrist's actions are justified.]

677 Pure, Simon [pseud of Frank Swinnerton]. "The Londoner," BOOKMAN (NY), LI (Aug 1920), 659.

The Skin Game is characteristically serious and sincere. It is not a great play because JG prefers types to humans.

678 Reely, Mary Katharine. "A Selected List of Current Books," WISCONSIN LIBRARY BULLETIN (Madison), XVI (Dec 1920), 238.

[Brief plot-summary review of *In Chancery.*]

679 "Ridden by Ideas," SATURDAY REVIEW (Lond), CXXIX (26 June 1920), 590–92.

JG is "ridden by his ideas . . . has no spaciousness, no ease, no geniality," in *Plays: Fourth Series. A Bit o' Love, The Foundations,* and *The Skin Game* are primarily vehicles to expound the latest liberal ideas on love. Characters are born from the ideas, not the ideas from the characters. JG is second-rate.

680 Rothenstein, William. TWENTY-FOUR PORTRAITS, WITH CRITICAL APPRECIATIONS BY VARIOUS HANDS (Lond: Allen & Unwin [1920]) [n. p.]; portrait rptd in CURRENT OPINION, LXXII (Feb 1922), 238.

[Drawing of JG, with a one-page appreciation emphasizing JG's good breeding, sense of balance and fair play, and intellectual quality. British literature owes much to JG for helping to preserve its "dignity and thoughtfulness."]

681 Rowland, Kenney. "John Galsworthy as Dramatist," BOOKMAN (Lond), LIX (Oct 1920), 9–10.

The Skin Game shows that man has only a "veneer of civilization," for "we scratch and bite like beasts if our interests are directly threatened." The excellent play and product at the St. Martin's Theatre is marred only by the lack of a crowd on stage during the auction scene and JG's tendency to stereotype characters. JG gives little pleasure, but he holds the audience's attention.

682 S., J. V. "Book Notes," DRAMA (Chicago), X (July 1920), 355.

A Bit o' Love and *The Foundations* are good JG—readable, well phrased and well made. In *The Skin Game,* JG is at his best. [Brief review of *Plays. Fourth Series.*]

683 Sampson, George. "John Galsworthy as Playwright," BOOKMAN (Lond), LVIII (June 1920), 110–11.

A Bit o' Love, a "study in cruelty," fails because of emphasis on "incidental detail" rather than the "two grand passions" that are barely presented. *The Foundations* is filled with credible Dickensian humor. The weak spot of the popular *Skin Game* is the character of Chloe because the two sides of her character are melodramatic and unbelievable when presented as JG presents them. Yet the volume is distinguished by style and nobility of outlook. [Review of *Plays. Fourth Series.*]

684 *"The Skin Game,"* ILLUSTRATED LONDON NEWS, CLVI (1 May 1920), 744.
[Photo of JG is accompanied by a brief announcement of a performance of *The Skin Game* at the St. Martin's Theatre.]

685 *"The Skin Game,"* MORNING POST, (Lond), 23 Nov 1920, p. 8.
At St. Martin's Theatre the part of Hillcrist is now taken by Dawson Milward instead of Athole Stewart. The drama is one of exceptional quality and interest and is admirably played.

686 *"The Skin Game*—Galsworthy's New Tragi-Comedy of Warring Social Forces,"* CURRENT OPINION, LXIX (Nov 1920), 649–56.
[The plot-summary review of *The Skin Game* quotes from the play and prints four photos—one of JG and three stills from the production.]

687 Swinnerton, Frank. "Mr. Galsworthy's Criticism of Life," NATION (Lond), XXVIII (6 Nov 1920), 190.
The Foundations "is a humane, but not a very human play"; it lacks spontaneity. JG holds up "compromise" as an ideal, and surely one must question and have doubts about such an ideal. [A review of the Everyman Theatre production of *The Foundations.*]

688 Swinnerton, Frank. *"The Skin Game,"* NATION (Lond), XXVII (1 May 1920), 137–38.
One gets argumentative about *The Skin Game* because the play and its theme— that "gentility is no good unless it can stand fire"—appeal to thinking processes rather than to the imagination. The play is moderate, scrupulous, and not propagandist despite its air of propaganda—carrying conviction "by means of the bare simplicity of its handling." The melodrama of the guilty woman is incongruous. The main problem of the play is the absence of love. Characters are recognizably human with "a definite theatrical relevance"; yet there is no reaction to them as human beings. Despite this, *Game* is much better than most of its contemporaries.

689 Tarn. *"The Skin Game,* by John Galsworthy, St. Martin's Theatre,"* SPECTATOR (Lond), CXXIV (15 May 1920), 651–52.
The Skin Game is "metallic," perhaps because of strict adherence to unity of theme.

690 *"Tatterdemalion,"* A.L.A. BOOKLIST, XVI (July 1920), 347.
JG's "usual finished style and subtle characterizations" typify *Tatterdemalion.* [Brief review.]

691 *"Tatterdemalion,"* Times Literary Supplement (Lond), 19 March 1920, p. 186.

JG is not afraid, in an age that denigrates such things, to have pity, to be an idealist, and to admire beauty. He does not merely say "this is life"—rather he sees possibilities of a more comprehensive human life if people will devote themselves to it. [The reviewer in part justifies the obvious haste in the structure of *Tatterdemalion* by emphasizing that the work was done while JG was performing World War I duties.]

692 "Theatre Arts Bookshelf. *Plays. Fourth Series,"* Theatre Arts Magazine (NY), IV (Oct 1920), 348.

JG is at his best in *The Skin Game* when presenting scenes of powerful dramatic conflict. *The Foundations,* remarkable in its demand for stylized acting, emphasizes deliberately "the grotesque artificialities of the caricaturist"—presently the stage inadequately copes with the type of production needed. The sentimental *A Bit o' Love* presents admirably the puritanical nature of an English village. [Review of publication of *Plays. Fourth Series.*]

693 "Theatre Notes: A Pessimistic Play," Morning Post (Lond), 2 Dec 1920, p. 5.

JG's plays are always thoughtful and disturbing. *The Skin Game,* now in its eighth month, is a real popular success. The "flood" part of the play—Hornblower's buying land to erect works—is sound, fine drama; the "ebb" part—Mrs. Hillcrist's coercing Hornblower into relinquishing his plans—is violently theatrical. While an optimist loves his fellow creatures, JG can but pity them.

694 Townsend, R. D. "Novels Not for a Day," Outlook (NY), CXXVI (8 Dec 1920), 653.

After the confusing genealogy of the opening pages, *In Chancery*—which is concerned primarily with the theme of possession—develops into a rewarding "fine . . . penetrating . . . dramatic, tense, and vivid" study of temperament and heredity.

695 "What Galsworthy Thinks," Independent (NY), CIV (9 Oct 1920), 70.

[General review of *Plays. Fourth Series* (*A Bit o' Love, Foundations, The Skin Game*) and *Tatterdemalion.*]

696 Woollcott, Alexander. "Importing Tears and Laughter," Everybody's Magazine (NY), XLIII (Dec 1920), 30–34.

The Skin Game is a "war play" without the theatergoing public realizing it: conflict between the Hillcrists and Hornblowers suggests that JG was thinking of a larger fight. [This general essay on the current London theatre is accompanied by a photo of JG.]

1921

697 B., I. "Mr. Galsworthy's New Play," MANCHESTER GUARDIAN, 3 June 1921, p. 14.

A Family Man at the Comedy Theatre lacks JG's usual "meticulous balancing." The "dismal" and "genial" moods are too sharply and distractingly contrasted.

698 "The Book of the Week—Mr. Galsworthy's New Novel," JOHN O'LONDON'S WEEKLY, VI: 133 (22 Oct 1921), 1–2.

To Let is an achievement worthy of its author. [Mostly a plot summary.]

699 Boyd, Ernest. "A Shelf of Recent Books: See American Fiction First," BOOKMAN (NY), LIV (Oct 1921), 160.

To Let is in fact nothing more than a retelling of the story of Romeo and Juliet. JG, Hugh Walpole, and W. L. George all attempt to say roughly the same thing, and each succeeds in saying nothing. [Unsubstantiated American literary chauvinism runs rampant here: "the roughest labor of some pioneering beginner . . . [in America] has more promise of vitality than this literary landscape gardening."]

700 "The Breaking-up of England," LITERARY DIGEST, LXXI (29 Aug 1921), 43, 46.

It is perhaps well that with *To Let* JG has ended the Forsyte family's story, although the Fleur–Michael Mont story will present great temptations to continue with other volumes. *Let* is the story of first love and of the changing order of things in England, symbolized by Timothy Forsyte's funeral and his will with its "last stand in favor of entailed property." In *Let* Soames sees the Forsyte age and way of life end—" 'when a man owned his soul, his investments, and his woman, without check or question. And now the State . . . would have his investments, his woman had herself, and God knew who had his soul.' "

701 Chevalley, Abel. LE ROMAN ANGLAIS DE NOTRE TEMPS (The English Novel of Our Time) (Lond: Humphrey Milford, 1921), pp. 75, 103, 111–15, 124–25, 155, 170–76, 202, 210; trans as THE MODERN ENGLISH NOVEL, by Ben Ray Redman (NY: Knopf, 1925).

Some of the fictional principles developed by James—*"le récit indirect, la prédominance du 'point de vue' "*—are utilized by JG. He is "the most complete, the most solid, the best-balanced, perhaps the best writer, in the classical sense of the word, that England has produced for thirty years." JG has probably best expressed his talent in his plays. [In French.]

702 Chevrillon, André. TROIS ÉTUDES DE LITERATURE ANGLAIS: LA POÉSIE DE RUDYARD KIPLING, JOHN GALSWORTHY, SHAKESPEARE ET

L'Âme Anglaise (Three Studies in English Literature: The Poetry of
Rudyard Kipling, John Galsworthy, Shakespeare and the English Soul)
(Paris: Plon-Nourrit, 1921); trans as Three Studies in English Liter-
ature: Kipling, Galsworthy, Shakespeare, by Florence Simmonds
(NY: Doubleday, Page, 1923), pp. 153–219.

JG's work is especially difficult for foreigners because he presents the essential
and "recondite moods of the English soul" by mere suggestions tinged with tacit
irony. The general tone of his work is one of calm, precise, and deliberate
serenity. "No great English novelist of our times has shown so little of himself in
his books." The real subject of *The Man of Property* is the Forsytes themselves.
JG allows his characters to reveal themselves gradually, and he uses "indirect
speech" to suggest the inner workings of them. He utilizes a "wealth of psychological detail" and minute descriptions of setting; he makes "use of two opposite
devices simultaneously; one consists in saying everything, the other in not saying
everything." JG does this because he is often dealing with a dual reality. He uses
fragments and hints, and the reader must fill in the gaps. The strength of this
method is that the reader must observe and interpret for himself. In exploring the
Forsytes, JG presents their reactions to Irene and Bosinney, and it is through the
distorted images of the Forsytes that the reader apprehends the love story. The
idea that governs JG's art "is that the inner life of a man is seen only in flashes,
that we never get a direct view of it." JG "excels in making mere silence, an
arrested movement, as significant as decisive action."

George Eliot, George Meredith, and Henry James developed new ways to render
the shifting life, the fleeting hints, and sudden changes of the interior world, and
JG continues in this tradition. The relative simplicity of the Forsytes makes it
possible to study them in detail, but with the more complex characters like
Shelton of *The Island Pharisees* and the Dallisons of *Fraternity* JG's art becomes
so complex "that it is impossible to study it in detail." "The strange thing in the
conjugal drama which forms the subject of *Fraternity* is that from beginning to
end it remains mute and invisible." JG achieves his effect by the "gradual
accumulation of minute circumstances." He uses "infinitesimal phenomena" to
enlarge the domain of art. The most original factor in his art is his refusal to say
everything. Unlike Meredith, who painted exceptional figures, JG studies average persons. [In French.]

703 Cohen, Helen Louise (ed.). One-Act Plays by Modern
Authors (NY: Harcourt Brace, 1921; rev ed, 1934), pp. 339–60.
[A brief biographical sketch and a record of performances accompany the text of
The Little Man.]

704 "The End of an Era," Times Literary Supplement (Lond), 6
Oct 1921, p. 641.
To Let is the "most moving" of JG's novels, supple, charming, and penetrating in

character without the loss of dramatic detachment. One of JG's achievements is in giving an artistic form to the "successes and failures of Forsyteism."

705 Evors, E. M. "Mr. Galsworthy's New Play," GRAPHIC (Lond), CIII (11 June 1921), 706.
[Evors's plot summary passes for a review of the performance of *A Family Man* at the Comedy Theatre.]

706 "*A Family Man:* Mr. Galsworthy's New Play at the Comedy Theatre," DAILY CHRONICLE (Lond), 3 June 1921, p. 6.
A Family Man, a "Galsworthy farce with some screaming scenes," is a delightful change of pace from usual JG theater fare. At times naturalistic comedy comes in, but on the whole the play is "full of good things."

707 Grein, J. T. " 'Daniel.' English Plays Abroad," ILLUSTRATED LONDON NEWS, 19 Feb 1921 [not seen]; rptd in THE WORLD OF THE THEATRE: IMPRESSIONS AND MEMOIRS, MARCH 1920–1921 (Lond: Heinemann, 1921), pp. 155–58.
Mr. van Kerckhoven is going to ask JG to let him play *The Skin Game* at the Royal Flemish Theatre so that our Belgian friends may become acquainted with "the master-builder among our playwrights."

708 Grein, J. T. "The Dramatic Works of John Galsworthy," NEW WORLD (Lond), V (July 1921), 141–45.
The constant figure in the Galsworthian carpet is love in its broadest sense. The argument that JG's later plays do not measure up to *The Silver Box* and *Strife* errs because it fails to recognize that the later plays possess a riper wisdom and a greater latitude of tolerance. A play like *Justice* is full of divine charity, and the work of the theater is "as sacred and great as that of the pulpit and the rostrum." His plays like *The Skin Game, The First and the Last,* and *A Family Man* are human documents of great value.

709 Grein, J. T. "The Second Effort of a Prize-winner. *The Skin Game* Once More. Amateurs," ILLUSTRATED LONDON NEWS, 12 Feb 1921 [not seen]; rptd in THE WORLD OF THE THEATRE: IMPRESSIONS AND MEMORIES, MARCH 1920–1921 (Lond: Heinemann, 1921), pp. 151–54.
After seeing *The Skin Game* again, one is still deeply impressed with the actors and with the play. As an ensemble the performance is a fine example of English histrionic art now. The play is a human document of rare value because we are sympathetic to both sides. An English acting company sent abroad to present JG's plays "would do more for amity towards this Empire than all political efforts."

710 Herrick, Robert. "After The War," NEW YORK EVENING POST LITERARY REVIEW, 8 Oct 1921, p. 65.

To Let is not JG's best Forsyte novel because he seems unsure of the contemporary state of affairs he tries to portray.

711 Hind, Charles Lewis. "John Galsworthy," AUTHORS AND I (NY: John Lane; Lond: Bodley Head, 1921); rptd (Freeport, NY: Books for Libraries P, 1968), pp. 95–98.

The "two dark voices" of "abysmal cynicism" and "soaring sentiment" war in JG. Contemporary reviews mention JG as an artist "with a heart and a conscience" and thus, perhaps, a propagandist of "the very right kind." [Lewis reminisces about his reactions to JG, lamenting that the author of *Justice, The Silver Box,* and *The Man of Property* should have written *Tatterdemalion* and *A Sheaf.*]

712 [Hornblow, Arthur.] "Mr. Hornblow Goes to the Play," THEATRE MAGAZINE (NY), XXXIII (Jan 1921), 29.

Even though JG's dramatic style is slipping, *The Skin Game* is a pleasant departure from the run of comic trivialities current in NY theaters. Dialogue is trenchant and timely; characters are clearly delineated; and presentation of opposing sides is balanced. [Review of performance at the Bijou Theatre.]

713 Krutch, Joseph Wood. "New Plays and Old," BOOKMAN (NY), LIII (May 1921), 274.

JG is an "exponent of ideas . . . constantly struggling with and failing to conquer the difficulties of the dramatic form." *The Skin Game* and *The Mob* discuss important topics, but "intellectual discussion, however keen and impartial, does not constitute drama." JG, a sincere preacher but a perfunctory dramatist, neither charms nor delights, and an artist must do both.

714 L., L. [Lewisohn, Ludwig?]. "The Forsytes," NATION (NY), CXII (19 Jan 1921), 88–89.

[Plot-summary review of *In Chancery* and *Awakening.*]

715 L., S. R. "*A Family Man:* Mr. Galsworthy's Play at the Comedy," PALL MALL AND GLOBE (Lond), 3 June 1921, p. 9.

A Family Man is humorous; and observations of character are delightful.

716 L., S. R. "*The First and the Last:* Galsworthy and Chapin at Aldwych," PALL MALL AND GLOBE (Lond), 31 May 1921, p. 9.

The First and the Last, a "thriller," is a "mere piece of concocted irony," "well written, wonderfully well produced, well acted, and effective," but ethically unsound. [S. R. L. does not elaborate.]

717 Leonhard, Sterling Andrus. THE ATLANTIC BOOK OF MODERN PLAYS (Bost: Atlantic Monthly P, 1921; rev ed, Bost: Little, Brown, 1934), pp. 357–58, 379.

[Biographical note and snippets of criticism accompany the text of JG's one-act play *The Sun.*]

718 M., D. L. "Mr. Galsworthy S'Amuse," NATION AND ATHE-
NAEUM, XXIX (18 June 1921), 446–48.

A Family Man at the Comedy Theatre is best enjoyed "as the gorgeous intellectual farce that it really is" rather than as a "naturalistic study": unfortunately JG
keeps the audience fidgeting between these two extremes. On the whole, however, the play is delightful.

719 Mathesius, Vilem. "Galsworthy ův 'Zápas' " (Galsworthy's
Strife), ZEMĚ, III (1921–22), 109 [not seen]. [Cited in Modern
Humanities Research Association BIBLIOGRAPHY, III.]
[In Czech.]

720 "Murder and Suicide Seance. Mr. John Galsworthy's New Play at
the Aldwych," DAILY CHRONICLE (Lond), 31 May 1921, p. 6.

The production of *The First and the Last* is better than the play, which is unsound
dramatically and strains at irony.

721 N., E. W. *"In Chancery,"* FREEMAN, II (19 Jan 1921), 454.

JG's delicate cynicism is touched with good-natured humor and "careful ac-
rimony," with a consciousness of beauty. Too many Forsyte relations tend to
clutter *In Chancery.*

722 Norwood, Gilbert. EURIPIDES AND SHAW, WITH OTHER ESSAYS
(Bost: John W. Luce; Lond: Methuen, 1921), pp. 60, 71, 74, 80–86,
105, 205.

JG's sole aim is reform; he seeks "neither grace nor sublimity"; his "doctrinaire
manner is often . . . inartistic." JG forgets that a dramatist's aim should be to
"entertain" (defined as "a quiet possession of one's soul, a refreshment of the
emotions") and not simply to amuse. *The Eldest Son* has a "grace of background"; *The Pigeon* is halfway between the emotional drama of *Son* and the
"nagging admonitions" of *Justice;* the dramatic tone of *The Skin Game* is
"diluted melodrama." JG is more the pamphleteer than the poet.

723 "Old and New Forsytes," SATURDAY REVIEW (Lond), CXXXII
(15 Oct 1921), 465–66.

To Let, interesting as a study in the "science of society," is also intriguing as a
story of the "struggle of living passion against the grip of the past." Expression
of feeling and tenderness is more evident in *Let* than in *The Man of Property,* but it
has lost some of *Property's* gusto, boldness, and irony.

724 Phelps, William Lyon. ESSAYS ON MODERN DRAMATISTS (NY:
Macmillan, 1921), 99–141.

JG's reputation was made by a "rapid succession of masterpieces." In all his
plays "the Audience is the Villain. The unpardonable sin is indifference." One
of his contributions to modern drama is his impartiality; the reserve found in his
scenes and the dialogue is magnificent. He aims "directly at the intelligence of

the spectators." His four best plays are *The Silver Box, Strife, Justice,* and *The Pigeon. Justice* is a great play despite the fact that it is propaganda. The final curtain speech of the old clerk—"No one'll touch him [Falder] now. Never again! He's safe with gentle Jesus!"—constitutes the only artistic blot in the play, for the audience found the speech distracting and something like a bad joke. *The Pigeon* is in many respects JG's greatest play. It possesses "superb construction, continuous movement . . . economy of gesture"; and "it is filled with the atmosphere of poetry, mystery, and imagination." *The Fugitive* is a failure. Despite his achievements JG has "not added Personalities [like Candida, Peter Pan, or Cyrano] to modern drama" because "his persons are the embodiment of ideas—they are flesh and blood, they are real, but we are more interested in what they represent than in their own idiosyncrasies." Thus "our attention is not primarily drawn to the fortunes of a little group on the other side of the footlights, but rather to Humanity."

725 Pure, Simon [pseud of Frank Swinnerton]. "The Londoner," BOOKMAN (NY), LIV (Oct 1921), 371–72.
To Let, a simple, poignant love story, is popular in London.

726 Reely, Mary Katharine. "A Selected List of Current Books," WISCONSIN LIBRARY BULLETIN (Madison), XVII (Oct 1921), 156.
To Let interests only those who have read the earlier Forsyte novels.

727 Reely, Mary Katharine. "A Selected List of Current Books," WISCONSIN LIBRARY BULLETIN (Madison), XVII (Dec 1921), 210.
Six Short Plays is mediocre JG. [Brief review.]

728 Tarn. "The Theatre. *A Family Man* by John Galsworthy, at the Comedy Theatre," SPECTATOR (Lond), CXXVI (18 June 1921), 780.
JG is flogging a dead horse in *A Family Man,* but there is one good humorous scene—and a "good-tempered distrust" of British justice in the appearance of Builder before the bench. JG demonstrates his usual technical proficiency.

729 Tarn. "The Theatre and Its Critics," SPECTATOR (Lond), CXXVII (8 Oct 1921), 468–69.
On the whole, the dialogue of *Six Short Plays* is awkward, and *The Little Man* is tiresome. [Brief review.]

730 "Theatre Notes: The Drama of 1920," MORNING POST (Lond), 6 Jan 1921, p. 4.
Among the best plays for 1920 was *The Skin Game.*

731 *"To Let,"* A.L.A. BOOKLIST, XVIII (Nov 1921), 50.
Many will find *To Let* the most interesting of the volumes in *The Forsyte Saga.* [Brief review.]

732 Townsend, R. D. "Among the Fall Novels," OUTLOOK (NY), CXXIX (5 Oct 1921), 186–88.

To Let is a triumph of technical art in managing family complications. [Paul Thompson's portrait of JG is reproduced.]

733 "Two Matinee Plays," MANCHESTER GUARDIAN, 31 May 1921, p. 14.

The First and the Last at the Aldwych Theatre is "too simple in its sensationalism": the protagonist is too weak to make the play viable. The fact that JG always paints the successful person as the blackguard chills sympathy for dramatist and drama.

734 Vodák, J. "John Galsworthy a jeho názor na drama" (John Galsworthy and His Views on the Drama), JEVIŠTĚ (Prague), II (1921), 732–33.

JG is like Ibsen in his stern austerity, as can be seen in his definition of the optimist as one who cannot bear the world as it is and of the pessimist as one who not only takes the world as it is but even depicts it truthfully. JG's belief in seeing and depicting clearly and fearlessly can serve other dramatists who have no artistic doctrine of their own. [This article essentially recapitulates JG's "Some Platitudes Concerning Drama."] [In Czech.]

735 Walkley, Arthur Bingham. "Plays of Talk," PASTICHE AND PREJUDICE (Lond: Heinemann, 1921); rptd (Freeport, NY: Books for Libraries P, 1970), pp. 122–26, 288.

The Skin Game's "will-conflict" has an "intense reality"—with everyone speaking briefly and plainly: any "irrelevant talk" would ruin the play. [Walkley contrasts Harwood's "play of talk" GRAIN OF MUSTARD SEED to JG's "play of action" *Skin Game* to begin a peroration on the importance of the "play of talk."]

736 West, Rebecca. "Notes on Novels," NEW STATESMAN, XVIII (15 Oct 1921), 50–52.

To Let is especially welcome because it gives the public respite from JG's plays and because JG's soul is with him when he writes of the Forsytes. The novel is confusing despite "exquisite writing."

1922

737 Anderson, Graham. [Article on John Galsworthy], COUNTRY LIFE (Lond), XLIX (Spring 1922).

[Citation by Harold V. Marrot, A BIBLIOGRAPHY OF THE WORKS OF JOHN GALSWORTHY (Lond: Elkin Mathews & Marrot; NY: Scribner, 1928); rptd (NY:

Burt Franklin, 1968), rptd (Folcroft, Pa: Folcroft Library Editions, 1973), p. 203, is incorrect.]

738 Andrews, Kenneth. "Broadway, Our Literary Signpost," BOOK-MAN (NY), LVI (Dec 1922), 476–78.

Although unmatched in its "technical mastery," the end of *Loyalties* is "a cheap and fortuitous way of bringing the story to a halt." The always didactic JG cannot overcome the temptation of making his plays parables. He is, like Owen Davis, a manipulator of tricks.

739 B., I. "Mr. Galsworthy's New Play," MANCHESTER GUARDIAN, 26 April 1922, p. 14.

Windows at the Court Theatre is "tenderly done" with JG's typical scrupulous balance and detachment; yet it lacks narrative power. The window cleaner is not organically related to the play; one feels that JG forced a play from a newspaper clipping rather than developed a play with artistic worth in mind.

740 Bateman, May. "John Galsworthy," CATHOLIC WORLD, CXIV (March 1922), 732–47.

Irene of *The Forsyte Saga* is a "triumph of faithful literary portraiture." JG falls short in his works because he glorifies present pleasures rather than spiritual endurance and triumph. The central theme of *Saga* is "the failure of Irene's marriage." Her crowning tragedy occurs when Jon wants to marry Fleur. The least worthy of his books is *A Saint's Progress* because the story is not told from a spiritual point of view. How is it that a writer like JG, whose sensitiveness is at times even quixotic, can have so little reverence for God? Although JG has yet to reach the height of "austere beauty," the sincerity of his best dramas—*The Silver Box, Strife,* and *The Mob*—may yet lead him to it.

741 Bellesort, André. "Les Littératures Etrangères: La passion chez Galsworthy" (Foreign Literature: Love in Galsworthy), REVUE BLEUE, LX (4 March 1922), 150–54.

That JG is little known in France can in part be explained by the fact that minor works of his (like this present translation of *The Dark Flower* [trans by M. de Coppet]) are being published, while his major novels—*The Man of Property, The Country House, Fraternity,* and *The Patrician*—though already translated have yet to be published. Nevertheless, JG's fame is secure; he stands beside George Eliot and Thomas Hardy. [In French.]

742 Birch, F. L. "*Plays. Fifth Series,*" NEW STATESMAN, XX (23 Dec 1922), 360.

JG is a stage craftsman, not an artist. The old-fashioned *A Family Man* is filled with consistently irritating characters. *Windows,* illustrating that the windows through which we look distort life, is replete with sententious dialogue and improbable action. Overemphasis on theme in *Loyalties,* JG's best drama, is compensated for by admirable stage-craft, effective dialogue, and restraint. Characters in all three dramas are types.

743 Bullett, Gerald. "John Galsworthy: A Diagnosis," NEW STATESMAN, XIX (10 June 1922), 265–66.

There are two qualities in JG's writings that tend to irritate the sensitive reader, and these are his practice of referring to a young woman in her twenties as "the little lady," and his use of heavy overemphasis, a habit which is quite possibly due to his work in drama. [This is a review of the one-volume edition of *The Forsyte Saga.*]

744 Butt, G. Baseden. "Tragedy and Mr. Galsworthy," TODAY, IX (Sept 1922), 19–22; rptd in LIVING AGE, CCCXV (4 Nov 1922), 287–89.

There are two kinds of tragedy: Grand Tragedy and Tragedy. In Grand Tragedy powerful characters are overwhelmed by more powerful forces. This kind of tragedy is rare. Tragedy depicts pitiable people who go under, and with the possible exception of *Strife* JG's plays fit in this second category. It is a tendency of the times, and it is found especially in JG's earlier work, to use tragedy as social criticism. Particularly in his early plays JG carries destructive criticism to excess. "Real tragedy is the transmutation of defeat into victory."

745 Clifford's Inn. "*Loyalties* and Legal Etiquette," SPECTATOR, CXXIX (22 July 1922), 109–10.

The "Osborne pearl trial" is not proper precedent for the actions of JG's lawyers in *Loyalties* because nothing is known of the circumstances preceding the retirement of the lawyers from the defendant's case in the Osborne trial. There are no circumstances in which "counsel is justified in publicly retiring from a case and publicly disclosing facts learnt by him in the course of his conduct of the case, and therefore under the seal of professional secrecy, without any intimations whatever to his client." [See also Clifford's Inn, "Mr. Galsworthy and Legal Etiquette," ibid., 8 July 1922, pp. 44–45; Malcolm McIlwraith, "Mr. Galsworthy and Legal Etiquette," ibid., 15 July 1922, p. 76; H. L. Sanderson, "*Loyalties,*" ibid., 5 Aug 1922, p. 175.]

746 Clifford's Inn. "Mr. Galsworthy and Legal Etiquette," SPECTATOR, CXXIX (8 July 1922), 44–45.

Because *Loyalties* is a fine play, I regret that as a practicing solicitor I must object to the unprofessional behavior of Mr. Jacob Twisden and "Sir Frederic." My objections are two: (1) counsel, normally, must notify his client before publicly withdrawing from the case; (2) when withdrawing, counsel must not betray the "seal of professional secrecy." [See also Malcolm McIlwraith, "Mr. Galsworthy and Legal Etiquette," ibid., 15 July 1922, p. 76; Clifford's Inn, "*Loyalties* and Legal Etiquette," ibid., 22 July 1922, pp. 109–10; H. L. Sanderson, "*Loyalties,*" ibid., 5 Aug 1922, p. 175.]

747 "Court Theatre: Mr. Galsworthy Again," MORNING POST (Lond), 26 April 1922, p. 10.

Shaw and JG know how to write dialogue, but Shaw has never been guilty of JG's mistake of having his heroes in *Windows* "talk rubbish about the 'horrors out there,' and 'passing through three years of hell' in the late war." The cast is splendid. JG solves nothing. Except for one or two slow moments and one or two objectionable incidents, JG provided "brilliant entertainment" in last night's performance.

748 "Court Theatre: The Galsworthy Cycle," MORNING POST (Lond), 21 March 1922, p. 8.

Last night Messrs. Lion and Grein followed their revivals of *Justice* and *The Pigeon* with a revival of *The Silver Box*. Like many of JG's plays *Box* is depressing, and "not everybody will be reconciled thereto by the author's sincerity and great skill." The original production of the *Box* was a "landmark" in the history of the modern stage. The improvement in the stage has come from men who have made their reputations outside the theatre, and "of these Mr. Galsworthy is perhaps the most notable." The present production has been modified to keep it abreast of the times: e.g., Old Barthwick restores to the Unknown Lady the money stolen from her by his son in one-pound notes.

749 Courtney, W. L. "John Galsworthy as Dramatist," FORTNIGHTLY REVIEW, nsIII (March 1922), 441–56.

JG is "nearly in the first rank" of dramatists because of his individuality, which consists mainly of his sometimes annoying partiality and his emphasis on morality at a time when it is not popular to do so on the stage—to the extent that sometimes the characters lose vitality. JG sees clearly the dichotomy of life when one is given a choice of action by those who have something to gain and, conversely, by those who have something to lose. JG's plays often defend the idealist and favor those who suffer in life for whatever reason (Strangway, for example, in *A Bit o' Love*). JG is not in the first rank of dramatists because he lacks the "element of grandeur, of elemental bigness, of calm and philosophic outlook" and because his characters are not always alive.

750 "Domestic Tyranny and Revolution in Galsworthy's Play," SPRINGFIELD REPUBLICAN (Mass), 27 Aug 1922, Sec. A, p. 7.

A Family Man represents the "comedy of family life at its worst, painted in a vein of rollicking rather than sedate irony." JG like Shaw depicts characters who are either Dickensian caricatures or points of view. The "wit of the dialogue seldom falters," but irony is often too heavy.

751 Downs, Harold. "Modern Influences. CLXX. John Galsworthy. The Dramatist of the Day," MILLGATE MONTHLY, XVII (Aug 1922), 635–39.

JG will probably frighten more than he attracts because of his impartiality, which he explains in "Some Platitudes Concerning Drama." His abiding interest is in human nature rather than in a particular natural setting. JG's controlling dramatic devices are contrast and austerity (except in plays such as *The Pigeon*). His "width of outlook and health of vision" enhance his main role as dramatist, which is "to make us understand." [A full-page photograph precedes the article.]

752 Eaton, Walter Prichard. "New Wine in Old Bottles," FREEMAN (NY), VI (29 Nov 1922), 281–82.

JG follows Pinero rather than Shaw or Ibsen in creating *Loyalties* in the well-made play tradition to give maximum "inevitability and suspense." The characters of the play now appearing at NY's Gaiety Theatre are "deftly drawn," the story "carefully calculated." A well-made play like *Loyalties* has things to recommend it to large contemporary audiences that the voguish expressionistic dramas do not have.

753 "End of *The Forsyte Saga*," NATION (NY), CXIV (18 Jan 1922), 75–76.

To Let, continuing to demonstrate JG's theme of love for beauty and a noticeable nostalgia for the old order, creates an occasional "elegiac tone." *The Forsyte Saga* might have less "intellectual mobility," less sparkle, and "less immediacy" than its contemporaries, but its "beautiful literature . . . absorbs the troubled lives of men into the serenity of art."

754 Ervine, St. John. "The Realistic Test in Drama," YALE REVIEW, nsXI (Jan 1922), 285–303.

[Ervine strives for a working definition of realism, using Shakespeare's MERCHANT OF VENICE and JG's *The Fugitive* as cases in point. The critically acclaimed *Fugitive* fails Ervine's realistic test ("a play . . . should in its own plane be in accord with the facts of life") because Clare's original action in marrying George Dedmond and her later attempt at love with Malise are inconsistent with her character as JG inadequately presents it. In addition, stage directions for Clare's death scene do not record the behavior of real people.]

755 Ervine, St. John. SOME IMPRESSIONS OF MY ELDERS (Lond: Allen & Unwin; NY: Macmillan, 1922), pp. 113–60; [originally pub in NORTH AMERICAN REVIEW at intervals during 1920–21].

The Fugitive illustrates several of JG's faults: (1) a failure in execution, not idea; (2) obvious manipulation of characters; (3) over-theatricality. JG is "entirely excessive" in his attribution of a sense of property to his characters in *The Forsyte Saga*. *Saga* is, of course, his best work. JG's characters are not "humanly expressed." To be sure, he pities mankind; he does not love it.

756 "*A Family Man*," A.L.A. BOOKLIST, XVIII (July 1922), 356.

Thematically, *A Family Man* is similar to J. M. Barrie's THE TWELVE POUND BOOK. [Brief notice of publication.]

757 *"A Family Man,"* NEW YORK EVENING POST LITERARY REVIEW, 12 Aug 1922, p. 874.

A Family Man is better acted than read. JG has "sincerity of purpose," sharply defined characters, and some good dialogue; he demonstrates some theatrical skill, but the work falls short of other JG plays because of inconsistency in the presentation of the older sister, some improbability in incidents, and a sense of anachronism in the generation-gap theme.

758 *"Family Man,"* ST. LOUIS LIBRARY BULLETIN, XX (Oct 1922), 248.

[Brief review.]

759 *"A Family Man,"* THEATRE ARTS MAGAZINE, VI (Oct 1922), 350.

[Negative, brief notice of publication.]

760 *"Forsyte Saga,"* NATION (NY), CXIV (19 April 1922), 473.

[Brief, favorable notice of the appearance of *The Forsyte Saga* bound in one volume.]

761 *"Forsyte Saga,"* PITTSBURGH MONTHLY BULLETIN, XXVII (July 1922), 321.

[Brief review.]

762 *"The Forsyte Saga,"* TIMES LITERARY SUPPLEMENT (Lond), XXI (22 June 1922), 411.

To combine the three novels and two interludes into *The Forsyte Saga* is unfortunate, since the term *saga* is improper and inappropriate. The genealogical table is unnecessary, because all of us are Forsytes. JG's vision of beauty is conveyed more clearly by the shades of "dry, cool, and yet golden light" he uses when describing Old or Young Jolyon or Swithin than by his obvious infatuation with Irene's beauty.

763 Frias, Alberto Nin. "La Novela Contemporánea en Inglaterra: IV—John Galsworthy" (The Contemporary Novel in England: IV—John Galsworthy), REVISTA CHILENA (Santiago), (2) XV (1922), 494–96.

JG holds first place among contemporary English novelists, and he is the most appreciated English novelist abroad. JG has applied James's principles of "point of view" and "indirect narration" with great effectiveness. *The Island Pharisees,* in its combination of paradoxes and splendid truths, exhibits something of Shaw's flagellating spirit. *The Man of Property, The Country House, Fraternity,* and *The Patrician* "are the marrow of Galsworthy's satiric thought." In their varied aspects he makes obvious the tyranny of property and propriety that imbues England. His work will survive as classic. [In Spanish.]

764 "Galsworthy's Epic of a Passing Age: Notable Series of Novels Showing the Sense of Property at War with Love and Beauty," SPRINGFIELD REPUBLICAN (Mass), 28 May 1922, Sec. A, p. 7.

The absorbing *Forsyte Saga* is intense, genuine, and richly human; it depicts middle-class England with authenticity and relevance.

765 Goldie, Valentine. *"Windows,"* SATURDAY REVIEW (Lond), CXXXIII (13 May 1922), 490–91.

Windows at the Court Theatre is "fine and stimulating," but occasionally a little silly: the scene with the "tipsy Mrs. March" is "false and distasteful." The play discusses the truth that "there is no essential shame in possessing strong passions"—and that not all (Faith, in this case) repent and reform after a term in prison.

766 Hookham, Paul. "The Case of John Galsworthy," NEW STATESMAN, XIX (1 July 1922), 356.

[Reply to S. K. Ratcliffe's reply to Paul Hookham's comment on Gerald Bullett in NEW STATESMAN (XIX [17 June 1922], 265–66, 292, 321–33), all of which see.] JG is a propagandist.

767 Hookham, Paul. "John Galsworthy: A Diagnosis," NEW STATESMAN, XIX (17 June 1922), 292.

There is really nothing admirable about June and young Jolyon in *The Forsyte Saga*. There is "a certain attraction" in JG's straightforward style. JG's greatest problem is that he is a propagandist: no great writer has ever been one. Concerned with the curses rather than the blessings of life, he is sincere, the "least unpleasant of the modern propagandists"; but he needs a "love for what is good in life." JG is overrated, even though his style has a certain attraction. [A reply to Gerald Bullett, "John Galsworthy: A Diagnosis," NEW STATESMAN, XIX (10 June 1922), 265–66.]

768 Jameson, Storm. "New English Plays," YALE REVIEW, nsXI (Jan 1922), 425–30.

JG's nobility of purpose, sincerity, tolerance, humor, undying faith in humanity, and sanity in *A Family Man* are insufficient for great drama: he lacks the flame of intense vision to become the true artist.

769 JOHN GALSWORTHY: A SKETCH OF HIS LIFE AND WORKS (NY: Charles Scribner's Sons, 1922).

[A publishers's puff, blending biographical information with plot summaries and commonplace critical statements about various works.]

770 *"Justice:* Revival at the Court Theatre," TIMES (Lond), 8 Feb 1922, p. 8.

JG's purpose in *Justice* is that of "Counsel for the Defence—to indicate an unusual line of vision and to compel you to choose it by his emotional force." It is a "good play, brilliantly acted and faultlessly produced." The Assizes scene, however, is improbable.

771 L., S. R. "Mr. Galsworthy below Par: *Windows* Not Up to His Standard," PALL MALL GAZETTE (Lond), 26 April 1922, p. 7.
Windows is labored; the characters are only a "collection of personified points of view." Bly's comment—follow instinct but maintain balance—is the theme.

772 Lewisohn, Ludwig. "Concerning Faith," NATION (NY), CXV (18 Oct 1922), 420.
JG is in the "highest sense a moralist"; *Loyalties* is quiet, serene, and noble, attacking the concept of "mere solidarity" through the person of DeLevis the Jew. More important than faith is the object of one's faith. JG follows Hebbel's theory of art by visually embodying "the infinite through the individual." [Review of performance at NY's Gaiety Theatre.]

773 Lewisohn, Ludwig. "The Generations," NATION (NY), CXIV (31 May 1922), 654.
A Family Man continues the convention in modern drama that emphasizes the conflict between parents and children.

774 Lewisohn, Ludwig. "*Six Short Plays*. By John Galsworthy," NATION (NY), CXIV (14 Jan 1922), 21.
[Brief notice of the publication of the "beautifully tempered and true" *Six Short Plays.*]

775 Lockert, Lacy. "Some of Mr. Galsworthy's Heroines," NORTH AMERICAN REVIEW, CCXV (1922), 255–66.
Despite the fact that JG's art exhibits "restraint, a sense of form, command of language, capacity to analyze and depict familiar human types," there is "something of the meretricious in it," and "his moral philosophy is an immoral philosophy." Both *A Saint's Progress* and *The Dark Flower* display a "total incomprehension of decent standards." They "encourage free love and make marriage seem unnecessary." Mere desire does not make a thing right. We need to emphasize the fact "that marriage is *fundamentally a social institution.* . . . The theory of 'mated souls'—altogether recent—is inevitably productive of moral dissolution." Actually JG glorifies lust, not genuine love.

776 "*Loyalties,*" A.L.A. BOOKLIST, XIX (Dec 1922), 75.
Family, class, race, and professional loyalties are treated in a "tragic and absorbing" drama. [Brief review of publication of *Loyalties.*]

777 "*Loyalties*. Contrasting a Merchant of London and a Merchant of Venice," CURRENT OPINION, LXXIII (Dec 1922), 750–62.
[Review of performance at NY's Gaiety Theatre. Quotations from several critics are followed by extensive passages from *Loyalties,* a photo of JG, and six stills from the performance.]

778 *"Loyalties:* Galsworthy and Barrie at St. Martin's,*"* PALL MALL GAZETTE (Lond), 9 March 1922, p. 7.

If "loyalties" can be viewed as a thread binding scenes of *Loyalties* together rather than as a "profoundly considered theme," the play is a success with JG's bright and racy dialogue.

779 Lugli, Vittorio. "John Galsworthy," NUOVA ANTOLOGIA DI LETTERE, SCIENZE ED ARTI (Rome), 6th Ser, CCXVIII: 1203 (1 May 1922), 43–53.

JG has not become widely known outside the English-speaking world because, in contrast to writers such as Kipling, Shaw, and the later Wells, his subjects do not focus directly on contemporary interests, and they possess a markedly insular English quality. But the great literary merits of JG's writings rather than extrinsic points of interests will and ought to lead to a wider diffusion of his works. Although the strong reformist current in his work has led to the charge of tendentiousness, JG is really a moderate and balanced critic of Victorian institutions. The novels are praiseworthy for their understanding of humanity; JG exhibits a profound sense of reality and a mental subtlety which, despite his reformist stance, has permitted him to pose a problem but not to present facile solutions, in obedience to the dictum "life calls the tune, we dance." JG has been a worthy contributor to the revival of English drama during his generation, although his plays seem less important than the novels (their intensely English setting is a limitation which would not permit them to survive in an alien environment). JG has achieved in his novels a quality of universality through full expression of his artistic ideals; they are works of truth and reality marked by his own spirit. [This article is a highly laudatory essay (focused primarily on the novels and plays) introducing JG's works to the Italian public. The translation of JG's works into Italian first began in 1920, and the first Italian translation of a Galsworthy novel (*The Country House*) was being published at the time of this essay.] [In Italian.]

780 MacCarthy, Desmond. "The Galsworthy Cycle," NEW STATESMAN, XVIII (25 Feb 1922), 591–92.

A performance of the moving and pathetic *Justice* depends on the emotional intensity of the actor (Leon Lion) playing Falder. JG's strong suits are his undemonstrative yet sentimental handling of tragic themes and his presentation of a scene that allows for a poignant glance or gesture to have full effect. In *The Pigeon* JG errs by making character development succumb to type; his imaginative strength is in his sensitive understanding of character and motive. *The Pigeon* is excellent because it expresses JG's temperament without overemphasizing theme. [Review of the Court Theatre's revival of *Justice, The Pigeon,* and *The Silver Box.*]

781 MacCarthy, Desmond. *"Windows,"* NEW STATESMAN, XIX (29 April 1922), 94–95.

JG's drama seems deep, but it actually is quite near the surface; he fails to allow for the self-creative, ever-new element in human nature. *Windows* is, among other things, "thoughtful, inconclusive, amusing, wise, commonplace, mild—very mild." [Primarily a plot summary of performance at the Court Theatre.]

782 McIlwraith, Malcolm. "Mr. Galsworthy and Legal Etiquette," SPECTATOR, CXXIX (15 July 1922), 76.
In reply to the letter signed "Clifford's Inn," it is quite likely that the situation in *Loyalties* is based on the famous "Osborne Pearl case." The fact that Sir Charles Russell and his two juniors publicly withdrew from the case when new, conclusive evidence became known to them suggests that the lawyers' behavior in this play is not indefensible or unprecedented. [See also Clifford's Inn, "Mr. Galsworthy and Legal Etiquette," ibid., 8 July 1922, pp. 44–45; Clifford's Inn, *"Loyalties* and Legal Etiquette," ibid., 22 July 1922, pp. 109–10; H. L. Sanderson, *"Loyalties,"* ibid., 5 Aug 1922, p. 175.]

783 Manly, John Matthews, and Edith Rickert. CONTEMPORARY BRITISH LITERATURE: BIBLIOGRAPHIES AND STUDY OUTLINES (Lond: George G. Harrap, 1922; rev eds, 1928, 1935), pp. 63–66.
[A brief study guide containing bibliography and suggestions for reading JG.]

784 Massingham, H[enry] W[illiam]. *"Justice* and Mr. Galsworthy," NATION AND ATHENAEUM (Lond), XXX (18 Feb 1922), 768–70; rptd in H. J. Massingham (ed), H. W. M.: A SELECTION FROM THE WRITINGS OF H. W. MASSINGHAM (Lond: Jonathan Cape, 1925; NY: Harcourt Brace [n.d.]), pp. 266–88.
JG's mind is orderly, prudently observing, and graced with spiritual discernment; yet he is quite reserved: "he criticizes . . . protests, but he also qualifies." *Justice,* presently being performed at the Court Theatre, is "an impressive, poignant, and deeply religious work . . . [that] falls short of a masterpiece because the action is too formal . . . the powerful impulse of the play is not carried far enough, and Falder's tragedy is too minor." JG believes that the mind of the state is carnal, "at emnity not only with God but [also] with human nature."

785 Massingham, H[enry] W[illiam]. "Little Ironies: Mr. Galsworthy's *Windows.* Produced at the Court Theatre," NATION AND ATHENAEUM, XXXI (6 May 1922), 202, 204.
JG pales in significance beside Hauptmann. *Windows* is a "slight, evanescent affair," a "skilful piece of work." JG is becoming "less indignant and more impersonally judicial, more photographic and less of the sympathetic artist." JG takes and records too many notes—a true artist should do more than this.

786 Miles, Carlton. "Jaunts into Brightest England. The Second of a Series of Adventures in the Homes of Britain's Literary Great: John

Galsworthy," THEATRE MAGAZINE (NY), XXXVI (Dec 1922), 364, 410.

JG is warm, gracious, courteous, and slightly remote. His favorite plays are *Strife, The Silver Box,* and *The Pigeon.* To JG, postwar London theaters seem helter-skelter. American producers need to hire good British actors to do his (JG's) plays. Good contemporary American novelists are Lewis, Fitzgerald, Anderson, Cather, and Gale; the best American critics, Heywood Broun and H. T. Parker. Writing for the theater requires a distinct style because it is a "curiously artificial medium." [Record of an interview.]

787 "Mr. Galsworthy's New Play," MANCHESTER GUARDIAN, 9 March 1922, p. 9.

The realistic *Loyalties* at the St. Martin's Theatre is one of JG's "most finished and gripping plays," with concentrated interest and "tight economy of dialogue."

788 "Mr. Galsworthy's New Play: *Loyalties,*" MORNING POST (Lond), 9 March 1922, p. 8.

There are too many "loyalties" in this play: DeLevis to his race; Dancy to his country; Mrs. Dancy, to her husband; Twisden, to the law. Dancy and DeLevis are both cads. As a mystery play it is not very good. The play itself is well acted, but less loyalty and more life would have improved the play.

789 Moses, Montrose J. "The Art of Reading Plays," OUTLOOK (NY), CXXXII (6 Dec 1922), 619–22.

JG's dramatic types are always clear-cut, and his purposes always well defined. *Loyalties* has more "external action" than usual for him—but it is good and artistically successful.

790 "New Play by Galsworthy: Thrilling Crook Drama at St. Martin's Theatre," DAILY CHRONICLE (Lond), 9 March 1922, p. 5.

Loyalties is a good "crook drama" that sustains suspense until the last half-minute. Skill in construction compensates for slightly overdrawn characters.

791 O., S. "*Loyalties,*" ENGLISH REVIEW (Lond), XXXIV (April 1922), 386.

Loyalties is a hit at the St. Martin's Theatre because it is "crisp, simple, and progressive." The gentleman's suicide, however, does not really convince.

792 P., R. A. "*A Family Man,*" FREEMAN (NY), V (16 Aug 1922), 550.

A Family Man lacks the "serene reticence" of JG's earlier plays; he is intolerant of both sides; the play is drab, garish, and theatrical in a derogatory way.

793 Phelps, William Lyon. "English Family History," NEW YORK EVENING POST LITERARY REVIEW, 8 April 1922, p. 559.

The Forsyte Saga is as close to a work of genius as any contemporary fiction. The fifty or so characters, "nearly every one of whom is sharply delineated as a separate personality," nevertheless have a "family likeness" that is remarkably well presented. Vividness of character in part is owing to JG's own lack of snobbishness and his concern for humanity. The beauty of Irene, like that of Homer's Helen, is presented by showing the effects of her face on "the eyes and hearts of men." Profond (*To Let*) seems to be put in to show the "future type" of man as he is currently progressing. Soames invites comparison with Richardson's Solmes (CLARISSA). The moral of the saga: Women should not marry incompatible men; men should cultivate their hearts and minds to get away from the pride of possession. [Review of the three novels and two interludes of *The Forsyte Saga*.]

794 Phelps, William Lyon. "Galsworthy among the Works," NEW YORK TIMES BOOK REVIEW AND MAGAZINE, 10 Sept 1922, pp. 3, 19.
JG's reputation as a novelist rests on *The Forsyte Saga;* "that is his contribution to twentieth-century fiction." His work was under a shadow from the time of *The Dark Flower* until he returned to the Forsytes. [Review of the Manaton ed.]

795 Phelps, William Lyon. "Putting Galsworthy to the Vote," NEW YORK TIMES SUNDAY REVIEW OF BOOKS, 9 April 1922, p. 3.
The Forsyte Saga shows a mellowing JG. Sympathy is the keynote to his writing; a "virile modesty," the keynote to his character. *Saga* is a "powerful and permanent contribution" to social history and to literature—a refreshing change after the unfortunate *Dark Flower, Beyond,* and *A Saint's Progress.*

796 "*The Pigeon.* Revival at the Court Theatre," TIMES (Lond), 28 Feb 1922, p. 10.
The problem in *The Pigeon* is that the birds, "wild birds" and "pigeon" alike, are too conspicuously labelled. The actors "talk at" the audience rather than to each other.

797 Playgoer. "The Theatre: Mr. Galsworthy's Day," MORNING POST (Lond), 27 April 1922, p. 7.
At the moment JG is the supreme exponent of drawing-room drama; his work is always close to melodrama. A reason for his success is that he is "extraordinarily topical." JG, like Dickens, "conveys, with great skill, the profession and the status of his characters." His later plays are without some of the blemishes of his earlier work; JG had a special weakness for weak people. His later plays seem less thesis-ridden.

798 Pollock, John. "Four Plays of the Season: *Loyalties,* " FORT-NIGHTLY REVIEW, nsCXII (July–Dec 1922), 349–52.
Loyalties is, perhaps, on a larger scale than *The Skin Game* and may lack its driving force; nevertheless, *Loyalties* is "a fine, serious play of constant move-

ment and varied pleasantry." The production has several faults: (1) it is too restrained; (2) the bed in Act I is not made for the night; (3) the lighting is chiefly from above; (4) several accents are wrong. The professional behavior of Dancy's solicitors is questionable. On balance, however, JG "has achieved a fine work; it is crowned with success, and success is merited." [Review of performance at St. Martin's Theatre.]

799 Ratcliffe, S. K. "The Case of John Galsworthy," NEW STATESMAN, XIX (24 June 1922), 321–22.
[In a letter to the editor, Ratcliffe takes issue with a letter by Paul Hookham (NEW STATESMAN, XIX [1 July 1922], 292).] At least half of England's novelists have been propagandists. The central catastrophe in *The Forsyte Saga* is developed by the "writer's powers of intelligence and imagination" and has nothing to do with propaganda as propaganda.

800 Ratcliffe, S. K. "The Case of John Galsworthy," NEW STATESMAN, XIX (8 July 1922), 384.
[Letter to the editor in which Ratcliffe responds to Paul Hookham, who responded to Ratcliffe, who responded to Hookham, who responded to Gerald Bullett (NEW STATESMAN, XIX [10 June 1922], 265–66, 292, 321–22, 356)—all of whom see to decide which was the house that JG unwittingly built.]

801 Raymond, E. T. "John Galsworthy," JOHN O'LONDON'S WEEKLY, VI:150 (18 Feb 1922), 640.
One of the greatest charms of much of the greatest of English literature from Shakespeare and Fielding to Dickens and Wells is irrelevancy. The lack of irrelevancy is "a serious drawback" in JG's work. Irrelevancy is very English, and JG was intended by nature to be genial and happy-go-lucky after the true English manner; instead, he is a bit monotonous, and his philosophic wares suggest Ibsen, Tolstoy, M. Brieux, and perhaps a German or two. There is not a suspicion of genius in JG's work, but his talent has been "cultivated assiduously." His plays "are skillfully drawn indictments. His novels are eloquent pleadings."

802 Reely, Mary Katharine. "A Selected List of Current Books," WISCONSIN LIBRARY BULLETIN (Madison), XVIII (May 1922), 133.
[Inconsequential review—merely lists the works included in *The Forsyte Saga*.]

803 Reely, Mary Katharine. "A Selected List of Current Books," WISCONSIN LIBRARY BULLETIN (Madison), XVIII (July 1922), 182.
[Inconsequential review of *A Family Man*.]

804 Reely, Mary Katharine. "A Selected List of Current Books," WISCONSIN LIBRARY BULLETIN (Madison), XVIII (Dec 1922), 272.
Loyalties is comparable to *The Skin Game* in subject and manner of treatment.

805 S., E. G. *"Loyalties,"* BOOKMAN (Lond), LXII (July 1922), 192.
Loyalties is impartial, well constructed, and filled with characters who are able to hold their own against the onslaught of JG's ideas.

806 "St. Martin's Theatre. *Loyalties,* " TIMES (Lond), 9 March 1922, p. 10.
Loyalties is about loyalties, but not obtrusively so. It is a drama of incident, not of ideas, presented "slickly, naturally, truthfully, and dramatically."

807 Sanderson, H. L. *"Loyalties,"* SPECTATOR, CXXIX (5 Aug 1922), 175.
In his legal objection to the conduct of JG's lawyers in *Loyalties,* "Clifford's Inn" seems to have overlooked the interview between Mr. Twisden and Captain Dancy in scene 2, Act III, in which Captain Dancy is confronted with the stolen notes and admits his guilt. [See also Clifford's Inn, "Mr. Galsworthy and Legal Etiquette," ibid., 8 July 1922, pp. 44–45; Malcolm McIlwraith, "Mr. Galsworthy and Legal Etiquette," ibid., 15 July 1922, p. 76; Clifford's Inn, *"Loyalties* and Legal Etiquette," ibid., 22 July 1922, pp. 109–10.]

808 *"Six Short Plays,"* THEATRE ARTS MAGAZINE, VI (Jan 1922), 81.
The Defeat and *The First and the Last* are "bitingly true in their realism"; *The Sun* is mediocre; *The Little Man* is ironic and sympathetic; and *Hall-Marked* and *Punch and Go* are "puerile light comedies."

809 "Some Modern Plays," TIMES LITERARY SUPPLEMENT (Lond), XXI (7 Dec 1922), 809.
Windows suggests that JG is becoming increasingly mellow. He leaves unresolved the problems of what will happen to Faith, whose youthful rebelliousness has been tempered by the experience of war.

810 "Some Recent Additions: *A Family Man,* " OPEN SHELF (Cleveland), Sept–Oct 1922, p. 66.
[Inconsequential review.]

811 Sutton, Graham. "Galsworthy and the Producer," BOOKMAN (Lond), LXII (April 1922), 44–46.
Justice, revived at the Court Theatre, depends greatly on the producer because there is almost no personal element, no "old-fashioned star-lead." Realism and restraint are the strengths of the production, but the latter causes a "certain flatness" in the emotional appeal. *The Pigeon* (also at the Court) is filled with platitudes and tests the producer's equilibrium. *Loyalties* at the St. Martin's Theatre is a masterpiece of the fusion of ideas and humanity.

812 [Sutton, Graham?]. "Galsworthy's Plays," BOOKMAN (Lond), LXIII (Dec 1922), 180.
[Review of *Plays. Fifth Series.* John Builder in *A Family Man* lives by "respectability, not righteousness." *Windows* and *Loyalties* are mentioned briefly.]

813 Tarn. "The Theatre. *The Silver Box*. By John Galsworthy. At the Court Theatre. *Loyalties*. By John Galsworthy at St. Martin's Theatre," SPECTATOR (Lond), CXXVIII (1 April 1922), 398.

Whereas *The Silver Box* is crudely didactic, the technically perfect *Loyalties* is filled with "subtleties of characterization, of turns of phrase, of observations of manners." *Box* is "largely a woman's play"; in *Loyalties* women are sketched only in outline.

814 "*To Let*," DIAL (Chicago), LXXII (Jan 1922), 103.

Perspective in *To Let* might have been better if everything were observed through Soames's eyes; but the "shifting of centers" does allow the Romeo and Juliet theme to develop more fluently than otherwise would have been possible.

815 Townsend, R. D. "A Group of Some Novelists," OUTLOOK (NY), CXXXI (10 May 1922), 74, 76.

The Forsyte Saga is "constantly more and more engrossing" because it "deals with fundamental things—the longings, passions, aversions, foibles, fatal misconceptions of men and women." [Quoting Carl Van Doren's opinion that *Saga* "absorbs the troubled lives of men into the serenity of art," Townsend comments on the first appearance of the *Saga* trilogy.]

816 Towse, J. Ranken. "Bonds That Bind," NEW YORK EVENING POST LITERARY REVIEW, 2 Dec 1922, p. 260.

The success of *Loyalties* is due largely to JG's "dramatic workmanship," ingenious plotting, "variety and veracity" of characterization, and moral that is presented without preachment. Dialogue is crisp and "talkable." Because loyalties have been "offended, have been proved in the wrong," no one forgives. The play is "a first-class achievement in every way."

817 Towse, J. Ranken. "Characteristic Plays," NEW YORK EVENING POST LITERARY REVIEW, 14 Jan 1922, p. 347.

In *Six Short Plays* JG is occasionally guilty of special pleadings in his presentation of theme, and his idealism is not always in accord with his naturalism. *The Little Man* is full of "playful morality"; *The First and the Last* is moving melodrama, told with dramatic skill and distinct characterization; *The Defeat* is full of understanding of human nature; *Hall-Marked* is humorous social satire; and *Punch and Go,* an amusing satiric skit.

818 Turner, W. J. "*Justice. Pigeon*. Court Theatre," LONDON MERCURY, V (April 1922), 647–49.

[Turner's negative, condescending, and flippant comments presumably pass for dramatic criticism of *Justice* and *The Pigeon*.]

819 Turner, W. J. "*Loyalties*. St. Martin's," LONDON MERCURY, VI (May 1922), 90.

Loyalties is a "complete success," exhibiting all of JG's good qualities of "craftsmanship, his power of writing natural dramatic dialogue, his wide social knowledge and his sense of characterisation." The twenty characters are well thought out, each representing an "individual social type." JG's "complete illusion of everyday reality" reveals his deficiency as a dramatist, because "the greatest drama does not do this." [This latter point is not developed.]

820 Turner, W. J. "The Theatre. *Justice*. By John Galsworthy, at the Court Theatre," SPECTATOR (Lond), CXXVIII (18 Feb 1922), 207.

Justice is not even first-rate propaganda, much less art. JG simply "harrow[s] our humanitarian feelings," giving no sense of revelation. [Turner tries unsuccessfully to distinguish between artist and propagandist; he also tries to rewrite *Justice* from the proper (i.e., Turner's) perspective.]

821 Turner, W. J. "The Theatre. *Windows: A Comedy* (For Idealists and Others). By John Galsworthy. At the Court Theatre," SPECTATOR (Lond), CXXVIII (6 May 1922), 559.

JG has ability neither as a deep thinker nor as a comic genius: rather, he is "one mass of grievances and complexes." *Windows* is "a tissue of absurdities" because of the hodgepodge of artificial and unconvincing events injudiciously presented.

822 Wilson, A. C. "The Forsyte Family," MANCHESTER QUARTERLY, XLI (1922), 106–13.

JG is too good an artist to resort to caricature. He presents a typical Victorian family with its Victorian virtues of tenacity, self-control, and foresight. The motif of *The Forsyte Saga* is "that there are limits to property which were not generally recognised by the Victorian age," and the moral of *Saga* is " 'What shall it profit a man if he gain the whole world and lose his own soul?' " [The essay is primarily a plot summary of *Saga*.]

823 Wyse, Aileen. " 'Mrs. Hillcrist' and the Press Agent," DRAMA (Chicago), XII (Jan 1922), 122, 137.

The Skin Game initially worried the Chicago producer because some character types in the play are unknown in America. Mrs. Hillcrist is played unsympathetically because otherwise JG's theme—"start a fight, and you will go on and on purely from the primitive instinct to down your opponent, and will in all likelihood entirely lose sight of the original cause of the quarrel"—would be confused. Mrs. Hillcrist's actions are justified because (1) she has indicated in good British fashion that she wants nothing to do socially with the Hornblowers; (2) she doesn't want her sixteen-year-old daughter to become mixed up with the Hornblowers; and (3) Dawker, not Mrs. Hillcrist, leaks the news about Chloe (Mrs. Hillcrist only wanted Hornblower informed). [Wyse, who played Mrs. Hillcrist in the Chicago production, criticizes the Chicago news reporters for failing to cover the performance with any sense of sophistication or aesthetic responsibility.]

824 "Year's English Fiction in the Newer Modes: Galsworthy's *To Let* Portrays the 'Will to Have' Clashing With Love," SPRINGFIELD REPUB-LICAN (Mass), 1 Jan 1922, Sec. A, p. 11.

The intense analysis of our times in *To Let* penetrates and illuminates human conduct. The novel is pure in expression, symmetrical in structure, and unified in theme.

825 Y[oung], S[tark]. "Five Books of Plays," NEW REPUBLIC, XXX (15 March 1922), 83–84.

[Brief notice of the "unequal . . . well-intentioned and . . . thin" *Six Short Plays*.]

826 Young, Stark. *"Loyalties,"* NEW REPUBLIC, XXXII (8 Nov 1922), 277–78.

Loyalties at NY's Gaiety Theatre is held together by the "logics" of melodrama (depending on "the story, on the thrill and suspense of tangled incidents"), social idea (the Jewish motif), and the theme of loyalty. Good popular theater, *Loyalties* singularly lacks "creative power," as seen in the inane way in which JG handles the climax of the struggle between the opposing sides.

827 Y[oung], S[tark]. "A Page of the Drama," NEW REPUBLIC, XXXI (2 Aug 1922), 284.

"Facile patter" in *A Family Man* is no substitute for satire. [Brief review.]

828 Zachrisson, R[obert] E[ugen]. "John Galsworthys Romandiktn-ing: Forsytesagan" (John Galsworthy's Poetic Novel: *The Forsyte Saga*), VAR TID (Stockholm: Arsbok Atgiven av Samfundet De Niv, 1922), pp. 131–54; rptd with addition of a few anecdotes about JG's lecture tour to Stockholm and an updating that includes comments about *The White Monkey* and *The Silver Spoon* as MODERN ENGELSK VÄRLD-SÅSKÅDNING: I LITTERATURENS SPEGEL (Modern English Points of View: In a Critic's Looking Glass) (Stockholm: Hugo Gebers, 1928), pp. 81–118.

By the end of *The Forsyte Saga* Young Jolyon is the only truly appealing character; Soames is no longer totally pragmatic, and Irene is not purely noble and beautiful; in fact, she seems just as materialistic as Soames. Possibly this ambiguous conclusion is an aspect of JG's irony. The Forsyte novels do not give a true picture of the evolution of English society because their basis is too narrow. Although JG is one of the great modern masters, it is difficult to say precisely what his mastery consists of. Like Shaw, JG relies too heavily upon irony. Another limitation of his work is its restriction to the world of the gentleman; his work does not include the mob, and he closes his eyes to the genuine evil in the world. His art is not pleasing because it contains too much that is gray and ordinary, too many dull complaints, and an overabundance of gloomy melan-choly. And yet one must not conclude that JG is not a great artist; he is more French than English in his work. His language possesses a poetic and visionary quality, and in his use of dialogue he has few equals and no masters. He is what the English call "a man with a grievance." JG is an artist, a lover of beauty, and a cultivated man with a sense of form. [This survey is based on *The Forsyte Saga, The White Monkey, The Silver Spoon, Fraternity,* and several shorter works.] [In Swedish.]

829 Zangwill, Israel. "Mr. Galsworthy and Melodrama," MORNING POST (Lond), 1 May 1922, p. 6.
[Takes issue with "Playgoer's" 29 April comment about JG and melodrama, arguing that the true definition of melodrama has been lost. JG, at any rate, should continue to write drama.]

1923

830 Adcock, A. St. John. "John Galsworthy," GODS OF MODERN GRUB STREET (NY: Frederick A. Stokes, 1923), pp. 113–19.
JG's lawyer's concern for fact gives his stories a certain aridity and hardness. He is not an impressionist. JG is the successor to Trollope as the historian of the upper middle classes. Because JG takes life too seriously, he writes as a social critic and reformer rather than as a storyteller.

831 Agate, James. AT HALF-PAST EIGHT: ESSAYS OF THE THEATRE 1921–1922 (Lond: Cape, 1923), pp. 75–79, 134–38.
Shaw and JG, unlike most West End playwrights, "care enormously" for real people. JG's characters (*Justice*) are true to their identity; Shaw's reflect Shaw's "cast of mind." To the sentimental JG, "proneness to self-deception is both material and human"; to Shaw it is "unnatural and inhuman." JG has no humor. Shaw "gives you something to break your mind upon"; JG, something to "break your heart" upon. *Loyalties,* where the "right versus wrong" idea inverts the usual JG themes, gives "one the impression of a brain-storm recollected in convalescence." DeLevis is a "fussy . . . cad, a toady yet aggressive, a snob hankering after alien advancement yet aflame with the pride of his own race." General Canynge is "socially magnificent, intellectually contemptible." [Agate gives refreshing impressions rather than reasoned criticism.]

832 [Anthony, Luther B.] *"Windows,"* DRAMATIST (Easton, Pa), XIV (July 1923), 1167–68.
JG gets lost in his own psychology. Characters are not dramatized—they "all cackle in the same key." The shallow theme and development do not sustain emotional credibility.

833 Archer, William. THE OLD DRAMA AND THE NEW: AN ESSAY IN REVALUATION (Bost: Small, Maynard, 1923), pp. 22–24, 127–29, 226, 340, 341, 364–65, 383.

In intellectual stature JG is superior to the lesser Elizabethan dramatists. He has written some of the finest plays of our time: e.g., *The Silver Box, Strife, Justice,* and *Loyalties.* Unfortunately, some of his other dramatic efforts fail to arouse one's imagination or hold one's memory. [This essay is a partisan defense of the modern theater against those who praise the old because it is old.]

834 B[akelmans]., L. "John Galsworthy," DE BIBLIOTHEEKGIDS, II (Jan 1923), 1–4.

It is remarkable and even disappointing for JG's admirers that his name is rarely mentioned with the names of other great men of modern literature like Shaw, Ibsen, Turgenev, Anatole France. JG's works include thirteen novels, seven volumes of short stories, fourteen plays, and seven short plays. Edward Garnett observes that JG's mind is typically English. As a writer JG possesses a rich knowledge of life and people, of irony and love. He began writing under the influence of Turgenev and de Maupassant; recently in Amsterdam JG said of Turgenev that he made the novel into a piece of art by omitting all that is unnecessary and doing it with a sense of measure. JG is as much a dramatist as Shaw, and in the widest sense of the term JG is a humanist. *The Forsyte Saga* is a distinctive study of the propertied class, and his work deserves a place in libraries. [A list of Dutch translations of JG's works follows this brief essay.] [In Dutch.]

835 Benchley, Robert C. "Drama: Quite a Lot of Talk," LIFE (NY), LXXXII (25 Oct 1923), 18.

Windows is tiresome. The theatergoing public is weary of philosophizing menials (the window washer in JG's play).

836 Black, Alexander. "Galsworthy and May Sinclair in Friendly Rivalry," LITERARY DIGEST INTERNATIONAL BOOK REVIEW, I (Nov 1923), 21, 88–89.

JG never leaves the world in *Captures.* "A Feud" is "a finely co-ordinated dramatization of human motives." While often seeming fatalistic, JG always gives a "glint . . . of a British faith in favor of blundering through to the light." A romantic revolting against the injustices and hypocrisies of the world, JG goes beyond mere class consciousness. "Late-299," the best "study" in *Captures,* typifies JG's method of leaving the reader "with pities multiplied . . . bigotries chastened, social vision . . . cleared."

837 Boynton, H. W. "Book Reviews: Some British Headliners," INDEPENDENT (NY), CXI (10 Nov 1923), 228.

Captures expresses neither the humanitarianism of *Justice* nor the sex-conscious orientation of *The Dark Flower;* rather it presents the wistful JG.

838 Boynton, H. W. "Plain People, and People of Fancy," INDEPENDENT (NY), CX (26 May 1923), 352–53.

The Burning Spear is atypical of JG in mood and manner. The "picaresque farce" is comparable to the American wartime satire, Simon Strunsky's PROFESSOR LATIMER'S PROGRESS.

839 Bradley, Robert N. DUALITY: A STUDY IN THE PSYCHO-ANALYSIS OF RACE (Lond: George Routledge, 1923), pp. x, 73, 77–82.
JG is the greatest literary exponent of the "eternal duality": *The Man of Property* is a "book for all time" because more than any writer JG has developed the threefold conflicts of "male and female, Asiatic and Mediterranean, conscious and unconscious." [This muddle-headed attempt to explain *Property* in racial terms fails because Bradley is caught in his own confusing and ill-thought-out dualities.]

840 "Burning Spear," A.L.A. BOOKLIST, XIX (July 1923), 318.
[Brief review emphasizing that *The Burning Spear* ridicules flag waving.]

841 "The Burning Spear," DIAL, LXXV (Aug 1923), 201.
In *The Burning Spear* JG is a "master of pointed, fantastic caricature." [Brief notice of publication.]

842 "The Burning Spear," OUTLOOK (NY), CXXXIII (9 May 1923), 854.
The Burning Spear burlesques both the conscientious objector and the foolish people who try to help the war effort.

843 "The Burning Spear: Mr. Galsworthy's Satire Confessed and Revealed to American Readers," NEW YORK WORLD, 15 April 1923, Sec. E, p. 11.
The Burning Spear is written with smiling rather than stinging satire.

844 "Captures," DIAL (Chicago), LXXV (Nov 1923), 506.
Captures focuses on JG's mastery of a certain "artificiality" of form. "A Feud" is perhaps the best in the collection, balanced and full of the atmosphere of the English countryside.

845 "Captures," NEW YORK TIMES SUNDAY REVIEW OF BOOKS, 26 Oct 1923, p. 9.
The theme of *Captures*, a sensitive, questioning criticism of life, is that the world is hardly worth the effort. Psychologically viable characters play gallantly at the game of life with no prospect of winning and usually "without the satisfaction of being defeated" according to the rules of the game. This is emphasized by the references to World War I. Another theme is the war between the ascetic ideal and wild passion.

846 "Closeting Spoken Drama," NEW YORK TIMES SUNDAY REVIEW OF BOOKS, 14 Jan 1923, p. 4.
Loyalties, better on the stage than in the closet, is a "swift moving imbroglio" that reads "easily but sketchily." Thematically, JG argues for courage and impartiality rather than loyalties to "little shibboleths."

847 Cobley, W. D. "John Galsworthy: The Novels," MANCHESTER QUARTERLY, XLII (1923), 187–211.

JG is not a romantic who presents life through "the coloured glasses of the imagination"; he is not a realist who gives a clear presentation of everyday life; he is, instead, a classicist, as his subject is "man's relationships with his fellows, judged by a standard, a perfection to which mankind approaches or from which it recedes." He is a "Pagan monk" who sees that the world of men and women, rather than being bound in "bonds of brotherhood," is divided by selfishness, ignorance, folly, and vice. All his works, therefore, are tragedies.

As an artist it is JG's peculiar quality that he stirs the emotions through an intellectual presentation of life. His novels are lay sermons. His principal characters do not number more than a half-dozen: "a typical upholder of things as they are, whether as landlord, captain in big business, aristocrat or parson; then the dreamer of dreams, artist, journalist, essayist, idealist; then the submerged sufferer from his own folly, or man's inhumanity. His principal woman, the Irene Forsyte, Audrey Noel or Olive Cramier, is slow, seductive, beautiful, with passion haunted eyes. . . . rather too frequently she is the wife of somebody else. Next the capable managing woman of the June Forsyte type, with whom Galsworthy has no real sympathy; then the cowed and submissive drudges, the Mrs. Hughes and Mrs. Jones . . . whose unconscious heroism is surely the most powerful argument for some re-adjustment elsewhere. And . . . the young hoyden just bursting into flower, who is rather too frequently somebody else's daughter." JG's genius just falls short of creating great characters, his most satisfactory being Margaret Pendyce (*The Country House*).

His use of irony and his restraint give his work an air of "almost workhouse austerity," and "his style is a constant delight." Although his aloofness has been attributed to his irony, a better explanation is that he lacks any humor other than the ironical. He also lacks that "finer humour which sees the incongruities of life, the discrepancies between our intentions and our performances" and sees them "with the kindly tolerance of a fellow-culprit." *The Island Pharisees* is of little value as a piece of art. *Fraternity* shows JG's methods at their best and is his "best-balanced and most perfectly designed" novel. JG idealizes neither the poor nor the rich. Although Audrey Noel, "one of Galsworthy's two finest mature heroines," makes *The Patrician* memorable, the novel is "spoiled by the bitterness of the irony." A forerunner of *The Forsyte Saga* is *House*, except that importance and dignity play the role that money plays in *Saga*. Moreover, *House* contains JG's most successful attempt at humor in the character of the Rev. Hussell Barter; it also contains the superb characterization of Mrs. Pendyce and the "clever study in dog psychology, the spaniel John." *The Freelands* treats of the intangible but real powers of interference that estate owners possess and the powerlessness of the agricultural laborers. In *Beyond* the "possibilities of the theme, as tragedy, are sacrificed upon the altar of propaganda." *The Dark Flower* is remarkable for being JG's one attempt at character development (in Mark

Lennan). The first and last episodes leave an unpleasant aftertaste, and JG's definition of love seems without spiritual significance and can hardly be differentiated from animal passion. His masterpiece is the five novels of *Saga,* and Irene is his greatest woman. "The Man of Devon" "is a notable instance of Galsworthy's power to achieve pathos by an apparently plain statement—in this case of the truth that life breaks those who will not obey." JG's short stories are of the English type, "which is rather too long, too apt to suggest the condensed novel rather than an incident, an emotion, a phase."

JG is a baffling problem for the critic. "What is one to do with a writer who has no development of character; whose themes are faults of social government, things of a day, not eternal; whose puppets do not defy fate but laws and conventions, and are mostly failures without any real vital energy and spiritual strength. . . . whose humour is trivial when it is not an irony which makes his characters give not themselves away, but their causes; whose artistry leaves exposed many a wire and creaking joint; whose tragedy lies in the situation as first conceived rather than in any superstructure he raises upon it; whose appeal is primarily at least logical rather than emotional? What is one to do with such a man who nevertheless touches the fringe of greatness, can rob us of a heart-beat, can relate us to the universal by making us realise the kinship of all men?" Although there is fine intention behind his work, his art is limiting in that it reveals "life's failure to achieve an ideal," and "art is the revelation of the ideal in human life."

848 Cumberland, Gerald [Charles F. Kenyon]. WRITTEN IN FRIEND-SHIP: A BOOK OF REMINISCENCES (Lond: Grant Richards, 1923), pp. 263–69.

JG is a baffling problem for the critic. "What is one to do with a writer who has no development of character; whose themes are faults of social government, things if in order to do so he has to flay his hero alive." But in *The Forsyte Saga* his indictments are more indirect, pervasive, and shadowy. "Defending, he is a chevalier in hysterics; attacking, he is a Machiavelli *in petto.*" JG is always the "desiccated artist" in his work.

849 Dawson-Scott, (Mrs.) C. A. "As I Know Them: Some Famous Authors of To-day; John Galsworthy, Israel Zangwill," STRAND MAG-AZINE (Lond), Nov 1923, pp. 520–25.

The Man of Property, written in the Thackeray tradition, gives a history of the period seen from a carefully observed social perspective. The style has "limpid simplicity," except for the "inner preservative of fire" of the last few pages. JG is humble, has a "sensitive soul," and is willing to listen to others. His plays about social injustice are having the same effect that Dickens's novels did. A multifaceted man with "personal magnetism," his works have "spiritual importance." His chairmanship of the P. E. N. Club demonstrates an eye for business; and he is very much an internationalist.

850 Dean, Charlotte. "Galsworthy *Plays: Fifth Series—A Family*

Man—Loyalties—Windows By John Galsworthy," NEW YORK TRIB-UNE, 18 Feb 1923, p. 27.
Once again JG makes his readers aware of injustice to encourage intellectual and emotional involvement. He is convinced that justice does exist—even in a world of futility. The "clearly and beautifully written" plays cover familiar ground.

851 De Gruyter, J. "Een Geslacht dat Voorbijging" (A Generation That Passed Away), DE GIDS (Amsterdam), June 1923, pp. 455–75; July 1923, pp. 78–92 [not seen].
[In Dutch.]

852 Dukes, Ashley. THE YOUNGEST DRAMA: STUDIES OF FIFTY DRAMATISTS (Lond: Ernest Benn, 1923), pp. 121–23.
Only the quality of pity in JG's dramas elevates it above its usual plane of "banal emotion." A "realistic veil" conceals the "moral perversion of reality." [Dukes mentions briefly *Loyalties, The Silver Box, The Mob, The Fugitive,* and *Justice* in brief comments of dismissal and disdain.]

853 Edgett, Edwin Frances. "Twenty Years of John Galsworthy," BOSTON EVENING TRANSCRIPT, 6 Oct 1923, p. 4.
[An appreciative review of *Captures* and the first fourteen volumes of the Manaton ed.]

854 Evans, Powys. "John Galsworthy," LONDON MERCURY, VIII (June 1923), 119.
[Pen and ink portrait of JG.]

855 Farrar, John. "To See or Not to See," BOOKMAN (NY), LVIII (Dec 1923), 441.
Windows, "a genial, mellow, wise little comedy," is a "strangely inconclusive . . . mediocre play."

856 Fehr, Bernhard. DIE ENGLISCHE LITERATUR DES 19. UND 20. JAHRHUNDERTS (English Literature of the 19th and 20th Centuries) (Berlin-Neubabelsberg: [n.p.], 1923); rptd, (Potsdam: Akademische Verlagsgesellschaft Athenaion M. B. H., 1927, 1931), pp. 397–402.
[Nothing worth noting.] [In German.]

857 Field, Louise Maunsell. "The World Reappears in Fiction," LITERARY DIGEST INTERNATIONAL BOOK REVIEW, I (Aug 1923), 38–39.
The Burning Spear is a "mildly funny" treatment of the Don Quixote theme. Lavender's mind is unbalanced by wartime propaganda.

858 "Galsworthy, John. *Loyalties,*" PRATT INSTITUTE QUARTERLY BOOKLIST, Winter 1923, p. 28.
[Brief notice of the publication of the "successful and interesting" *Loyalties.*]

859 "A Galsworthy Satire: Frame of Mind That Works Up Patriotism for War Purposes," SPRINGFIELD REPUBLICAN (Mass), 6 May 1923, Sec. A, p. 7.

JG's Cervantic ridicule of popular extravagances in *The Burning Spear* are Pickwickian in situation and Shavian in satiric intent: The character development suggests J. M. Barrie's work.

860 "Galsworthy's *Captures:* Short Stories and Sketches Presenting Ironical Contrasts," SPRINGFIELD REPUBLICAN (Mass), 23 Sept 1923, Sec. A, p. 5.

JG seems to compress materials in *Captures* in a sometimes arbitrary manner; authorial stimulation appears to be a series of reactions to articles read in newspapers.

861 Gould, Gerald. "John Galsworthy as a Novelist," BOOKMAN, (Lond), LXV (Dec 1923), 133–35.

While *The Country House* and *The Freelands* use detail better, *The Forsyte Saga* has grandeur, a "moving picture of a moving time—and of a class which used to consider itself immovable." The story "discards neatness" in favor of more romantic qualities. JG also brings moral and intellectual seriousness to his works. Though less mannered in style, JG easily ranks with Wells, Bennett, and Conrad despite his lack of epigram and verbal acrobatics. Openly ironical, he focuses on hypocritical conventions but respects their strength. Conflict rather than solution is central to his thought and work: whereas the "supremely great" works (LEAR, CANDIDE) at the end answer the questions raised, JG does not, except partially in *Freelands*. The Pendyces (*House*) are types, yet human. In *Saga,* the struggle between Soames and Irene is "conflict at its purest"; JG is openly partisan when he calls Irene's cruelty (however justified) "wise realism." Soames elevates the plot to the heroic level of a saga: in essence Soames's story touches immortality because it is "in essence the story of the pilgrimage of a suffering human soul." [The essay is illustrated by R. H. Sauter's 1923 portrait of JG; Sauter's sketch of Wingstone, Manaton; and a full-page reproduction of the Walter Tittle drawing of JG.]

862 [Hornblow, Arthur.] "Mr. Hornblow Goes to the Play," THEATRE MAGAZINE (NY), XXXVIII (Dec 1923), 16.

In the Theatre Guild production of *Windows* at NY's Garrick Theatre, the story of the young unmarried mother is treated delicately and eloquently. As usual JG argues for more tolerance, understanding, and generosity; but the play does not have the universal appeal of earlier ones.

863 Hutchison, Percy A. "Plays Tragical-Comical and Historical-Pastoral," NEW YORK TIMES SUNDAY REVIEW OF BOOKS, 11 March 1923, p. 9.

Influence of World War I is evident in *Plays. Fifth Series,* illustrating JG's interest in spiritual forces. The themes of *A Family Man, Loyalties,* and *Windows* are the need to understand the loyalties of others and to reconcile oneself to them. Bly (*Windows*) ranks with Shaw's best comic characters. *Windows* is really more tragic than *Loyalties,* but "perfect . . . construction" makes the latter a more complete play.

864 J., G. W. "Don Quixote Rides," GREENSBORO DAILY NEWS (NC), 24 June 1923, Sec. M, p. 8.
The Burning Spear is a sparkling burlesque of the bombast and rodomontade of the period.

865 Kellock, Harold. "A Play—Pleasant and Unpleasant," FREEMAN (NY), VIII (31 Oct 1923), 186.
Windows contains some upper-class conventionalities that are, as usual with JG, brilliant in surface workmanship. The comedy is fast-paced and has a "well-tempered moral climax," but the plot is tenuous. The "idealistic negativeness" of the Marches keeps them in "a dead center of futile irritability." Faith's father serves as Greek chorus with his "decorous sagacities." Faith herself is the tenuous moral vehicle for the shopworn British theme: the wages of sin for a woman is unemployment. "If the world . . . has passed [JG] . . . he still has the power to breathe a semblance of life into his illusions." [Review of the Theatre Guild production.]

866 Lemonnier, Léon. "John Galsworthy et quelques auteurs francais" (John Galsworthy and Some French Authors), MERCURE DE FRANCE, CLXI (1 Jan 1923), 112–19.
Although English by birth and education, JG was French in his talent and in his critical spirit. He composed his novels logically; for him and for the French the novel is a rigorous development of an abstract idea. As can be seen in *The Man of Property,* JG champions art and passion and is critical of the bourgeois spirit of practicality and property. [In French.]

867 Lewisohn, Ludwig. "Drama: Muted Strings," NATION (NY), CXVII (24 Oct 1923), 469–70.
JG's "intellectual fineness" is coupled with a condescending and rigid conclusion in *Windows,* now playing at the Garrick Theatre. Dismissal of Faith with a "gesture of elegant despair" is troubling: JG needs to be firmer in his judgment of the world as he believes it to exist.

868 *"Loyalties,"* EVERYBODY'S MAGAZINE, (NY), XLVIII (Feb 1923), 96–103.
[Short introduction emphasizing *Loyalties'* theme of loyalty is accompanied by four photos from a production and excerpts from the drama.]

869 *"Loyalties,"* PITTSBURGH MONTHLY BULLETIN, XXVIII (Jan 1923), 28.
[Brief review.]

870 *"Loyalties,"* ST. LOUIS LIBRARY BULLETIN, XXI (Jan 1923), 12. [Brief review.]

871 MacGowan, Kenneth. "Diadems and Fagots on Broadway," THEATRE ARTS MAGAZINE (NY), VII (Jan 1923), 3–12.

Loyalties is excellent theater with subtle characterization, JG's best. The play is about war as well as social groupings: one senses JG's "liberal" reaction to the "sham failure" of World War I.

872 Mais, S. P. B. SOME MODERN AUTHORS (Lond: Grant Richards, 1923), pp. 57–62 (the novels), 280–87 (the dramas).

Soames's sense of property is not nearly so evil as "Irene's self-centredness." She is "almost grotesquely selfish." Her coercion of Jon in *To Let* is a serious blot on a fine novel. "A stronger man than Soames would have whipped her into satisfied docility"; she lacked the strength to make the best of things. JG avoided the real problem in *Loyalties:* whether DeLevis would follow the lure of money or the lure of caste; as a result, much of the play was irrelevant. JG has never written a bad novel, but he has written some "indifferent plays." *Windows,* however, is one of his best because of its sincerity.

873 Mortimer, Raymond. *"Captures,"* NEW STATESMAN, XXII (13 Oct 1923), 18.

Captures has a "flatter" style than usual for JG, but his aims are noble, and some reform might result.

874 "New Novels," TIMES LITERARY SUPPLEMENT (Lond), 13 Sept 1923, p. 602.

The stories in *Captures* "are neither unworthy of him nor yet on a level with his best work. They are characteristic. . . . they are deficient not in truth but in intensity."

875 O'Brien, Edward J., and John Cournos. "The Best British and Irish Short Stories: A Year's Survey," BOOKMAN (Lond), LXIII (Jan 1923), 199–203.

JG's "A Feud," "A Hedonist," "The Man Who Kept His Form," and "Santa Lucia" are among the best stories appearing in periodical literature.

876 Overton, Grant. "Mr. Galsworthy's Secret Loyalties," BOOK-MAN (NY), LVII (March–Aug 1923), 153–59; rptd in AMERICAN NIGHTS ENTERTAINMENT (NY: Appleton, George H. Doran, Doubleday Page, & Scribner's, 1923); rptd in AUTHORS OF THE DAY (NY: George H. Doran, 1924), pp. 13–21.

JG is "the kind of man who, if he were in some other station of life, would be a splendid subject for Joseph Conrad." In *Loyalties,* as in all of his novels and dramas, JG portrays how conflicting loyalties can both be right: he presents two sides and takes none. JG is "transparent without being . . . luminous"; he "refracts but he does not magnify." [Largely devoted to quotations from others' comments, particularly those of St. John Ervine, Carlton Miles, and Joseph Conrad.]

877 P., R. A. *"Windows,"* FREEMAN (NY), VII (28 March 1923), 70.
Windows, developed as usual in JG by placing different strata of society in opposition, has a strong current of humor.

878 Parker, Robert Allerton. "Loyalties Ltd.," INDEPENDENT (NY), CX (6 Jan 1923), 32–34.
Loyalties seems to have it all—"suspense, surprise, [and] characterization"; yet JG's characters fail to release "great" emotion. Dostoievsky breathes vitality into his characters and they exhale emotion, thus leaving the reader intensely satisfied; JG's writing, on the other hand, is like newspaper reporting, uncreative but "more masterful . . . artistic . . . [and] skillful."

879 Pearson, Hesketh. "Thackeray and John Galsworthy," THE PERSIAN CRITIC (Lond: Chapman & Dodd, 1923), pp. 45–49.
[The "Persian Critic" comments that if Thackeray were alive today he would be a "greater" JG—he would "whip the folly with his satire and move the heart to pity with his realism."]

880 Pendragon. "Books of Plays Old and New," NEW YORK WORLD, 22 July 1923, Sec. E, p. 8.
Windows is a delicate criticism of after-war conditions in England.

881 Phelps, William Lyon. "As I Like It," SCRIBNER'S MAGAZINE, LXXIII (Jan 1923), 117.
In *The Skin Game* JG has emphasized the "real danger of fighting."

882 Phelps, William Lyon. "As I Like It," SCRIBNER'S MAGAZINE, LXXIII (March 1923), 374.
While St. John Ervine unjustly underestimates JG in SOME IMPRESSIONS OF MY ELDERS, he is sound in all that he says "against that futile play, *The Fugitive.*"

883 Phelps, William Lyon. "The Novelist Who Never Wrote a Potboiler," LITERARY DIGEST INTERNATIONAL BOOK REVIEW, I (Sept 1923), 36–37, 53.
The Patrician ranks just below *The Forsyte Saga.* As JG continued the story of the Forsytes his attitude toward Soames changed; his irony became "suitable." *Saga* is an epic because it portrays the struggle between property and beauty on a vast scale. His use of "suitable irony" gives to his works "a saline preservative." [Review of the Manaton ed.]

884 *"Plays; Fifth Series,"* A.L.A. BOOKLIST, XIX (April 1923), 215–16.
[Notice of appearance in collected form of *A Family Man, Loyalties,* and *Windows.*]

885 [Quinn, John.] LIBRARY OF JOHN QUINN: PART TWO [D–H] (NY: Anderson Galleries [Sale 1783], 1923), pp. 321–26.
[A brief, one-paragraph biographical sketch; the Galsworthy items are numbered 3170–3249.]

886 Schirmer, Walter F. DER ENGLISHCHE ROMAN DER NEUESTEN ZEIT (Recent British Fiction) (Heidelberg: Carl Winter, 1923), pp. 1, 4, 12–17, 21, 25, 31, 33–34, 55, 60, 67.
JG, an important critic of Victorian society, concentrates on types and describes them accurately but frequently coldly. He is rather a moralist and propagandist than a creative artist, but he is one of the major prewar writers. [In German.]

887 Shanks, Edward Buxton. "Mr. John Galsworthy," LONDON MERCURY, VIII (1928), 393–404; rptd in LIVING AGE, CCCXIX (29 Dec 1923), 604–8; rptd in SECOND ESSAYS ON ENGLISH LITERATURE (Lond: Collins, 1927; Freeport, NY: Books for Libraries P, 1968), pp. 41–61.
JG is among other things a definite and practical critic of modern institutions. He views most things through the polarities of the haves and the have-nots, addressing himself to such problems as the inequity of justice (*The Silver Box*), the cohesive caste system (*Loyalties*), land (*The Freelands*), industry (*Strife*), and marriage and divorce (*The Forsyte Saga, The Dark Flower, The Fugitive, The Patrician*). The last category is predominant.

Stylistically, JG has the reputation of being a realist, but in *Box* and *Justice* JG loads the dice and consequently loses his touch as realist. In *Loyalties* the "intellectual structure" is flimsy because in life the drama would not have ended with a suicide; here as elsewhere JG fills his work with special pleading.

In his characterization, Irene (*Saga*) is the best example of one who rebels against the institutions of society: she is a "form of life," the embodiment of transcendent sexual attraction. Sylvanus Heythorp (*The Stoic*) and Swithin (*Saga*) are among those who, like JG, enjoy life most: Sylvanus in his love of good eating, and Swithin in his love of the good life in general. JG lavishes more care on the characters he does not approve of than on those he champions.

Saga, especially notable in its gradual revelation of JG's love for Soames, will endure because it fulfills the conditions of great art: "the persons in it are recognisable human beings, true to the requirements of time and place, but they are also symbols of forces which will continue in battle until human nature has evolved into some form" that we would probably not be able to recognize.

888 "Some Recent Additions: *The Burning Spear,*" OPEN SHELF (Cleveland), Sept–Oct 1923, p. 66.
[Inconsequential review.]

889 Starkloff, Edmund. "John Galsworthy als Romanschriftsteller.

Eine Stiluntersuchung Seiner Hauptromane" (John Galsworthy as Novelist. An Examination of the Style of His Chief Novels). Unpublished dissertation, Jena University, 1923.
[Listed in Lawrence F. McNamee, DISSERTATIONS IN ENGLISH AND AMERICAN LITERATURE (NY & Lond: Bowker, 1968).] [In German.]

890 Stocker, R. Dimsdale. "John Galsworthy's Play—*Loyalties,*" STANDARD, X:2 (Oct 1923), 57–61.
Loyalties "is no mere piece of stage-craft. It is, in all essential respects, true to life." [The play is used as a springboard for discussing the significance and ethical importance of loyalty in terms of society and the individual.]

891 Sutton, Graham. "A Note on Galsworthy's Plays," BOOKMAN (Lond), LXV (Dec 1923), 135–38.
JG will become a classic primarily because he mirrors English life so well. His general popularity has come with *The Skin Game* and *Loyalties*. Sheila Kaye-Smith's dictum that JG will never be widely read, for he "alienates two important sets of readers—those who insist that a book shall teach him something, and those who with equal force insist that it shall teach them nothing"—is true to the extent that the dichotomy Kaye-Smith refers to is that between "melodramatists" and "entertainment seekers." *The Pigeon* is perhaps JG's greatest play in its self-containment, its "lack of reforming zeal and moral bias," and its emphasis that in some cases "indignation is futile; social reform may alter circumstances [but] it cannot alter temperament; and there are certain temperaments outside the reformer's range." JG recognizes his biases and, in the dramas, weighs the scale against his side (especially in *Justice* and *Loyalties*). Unlike melodrama, his plays are "compact of pure thought," the most predominant thought being class consciousness. JG is the "apologist of the misfit."

892 Thomas, Bert. "Curiosities of Literature," PUNCH, CLXIV (14 Feb 1923), 152.
This satiric cartoon depicting JG as a ventriloquist with a puppet on each knee bears the caption, "Professor Galsworthy, The Country House Entertainer." [The two puppets suggest Hillcrist and Hornblower, *The Skin Game*.]

893 Tomlinson, H. M. "John Galsworthy," NATION AND ATHE-NAEUM, XXXIV (8 Dec 1923), 404; rptd in NEW REPUBLIC, XXXVII (13 Feb 1924), 317–18.
JG's work is too close for proper appreciation by the present generation; future generations will be able to return with gratitude to his work. [A review of the first four volumes of the Manaton ed. See also Robert Nichols, "Letters to the Editor," NATION AND ATHENAEUM (1924).]

894 Towse, J. Ranken. "Galsworthy Plays," NEW YORK EVENING POST LITERARY REVIEW, 25 Aug 1923, p. 928.
A Family Man, Loyalties, and *Windows* are sincere and ethical, filled with moral

purpose. *Loyalties* is most notable because of its veracity of characterization and its "constructive ingenuity and theatrical values." [This review of *Plays. Fifth Series* is primarily a plot summary with statements of the main theme—without interpretation.]

895 Wertheimer, Paul. "John Galsworthy," BRUEDER IM GEISTE: EIN KULTURBILDERBUCH (Brothers in Spirit: A Cultural Picture Book) (Vienna, Leipzig: Deutsch-Oesterreichischer Verlag, 1923), pp. 171–77.

[This expressionistic essay calls JG the poet of the workers and the critic of a denatured society and praises *The Dark Flower* for revealing the passionate soul of England.] [In German.]

896 *"Windows,"* DIAL, LXXV (Oct 1923), 401.

Windows shows JG's "technical expertness" and a "subtle and skilfully woven strand of comedy." [Brief notice of publication.]

897 Woodbridge, Homer E. "The Ascendant Galsworthy," NEW YORK EVENING POST LITERARY REVIEW, 6 Oct 1923, p. 103.

Captures is one of JG's most objective works and proves his mastery of the short-story form. Among the best are "A Stroke of Lightning," "The Feud," the humorous "Acme," and "The Broken Boot." JG sees life "more steadily than usual" in *Captures,* without his former emphasis on social class. Style shows improvement, too, in its "economy of diction" and "compactness of phrase."

898 Woodbridge, Homer E. "Belated Satire," NEW YORK EVENING POST LITERARY REVIEW, 9 June 1923, p. 747.

In *The Burning Spear* Mr. Lavender's attempts to propagandize the war are undermined by his naturally kind heart and his "instinctive English love of fair play." JG errs in assuming that war should be played as cricket is—"without rancor and lies, and by the rules." [Review of the republication of *Spear.*]

899 Woodbridge, Homer E. "Galsworthy," NEW YORK EVENING POST LITERARY REVIEW, 21 April 1923, pp. 617–18.

JG ranks with the best of his age both as novelist and as dramatist, and although he has attained great popularity, he has remained true to his own conception of truth. Each novel and play is a "finished unit, with its own plan and rhythm of action." His prose is sensitive and appropriate, free from pedantry, mannerisms, and vulgarity. By admission a realist, JG is a naturalist in "method and rhythm" but "sees too clearly and too deeply to be deceived by the simple formula of the Dreisers." Unfortunately, JG is too sentimental, as is especially evident in his treatment of the theme of love. JG is "hostile in spirit and purpose" in studying social groups, such as in *The Man of Property.* JG's formula for writing seems to be in playing "between the positive pole of a worship of passion and the negative one of a detailed and ironic analysis of social groups." His best characters are his old men who have passed the age of passionate love, when JG "undazzled, can regard them curiously"; and "frank young girls," not yet touched by passion. The plays generally are less sentimental than the novels. "The trouble with much of Mr. Galsworthy is that he has given his emotional power free play in the exaltation of passion and has limited his critical power to the conventions of society and their representatives." [A perceptive general essay inspired by the appearance of some volumes of the Manaton ed, and *Plays. Fifth Series*. Woodbridge overemphasizes JG's sentimentality.]

900 Wyatt, Euphemia Van Rensselaer. "It's a Play," CATHOLIC WORLD, CXVI (Jan 1923), 507–9.
The current performance of *Loyalties* is dramatically and technically the best of the season. Villain and hero are "hopelessly commingled" as JG presents both sides of the theme of loyalty. The "reactions of the human soul" are intriguing. DeLevis becomes the "exiled child of Israel"; when Dancy commits suicide, "Shylock [DeLevis] has exacted his pound of flesh."

1924

901 "Artist and Teacher: The Works of John Galsworthy," NATION AND ATHENAEUM, XXXV (5 April 1924), 18–20.
JG's artistic problem is two-fold: (1) he rarely forgets his moral message; and (2) he never quite decides what the moral message should be. [This review of the Manation ed's *Fraternity, The Island Pharisees, The Patrician*, and *The Country House* turns into a scathing general attack on JG's critical reputation, questioning whether JG is really the pundit he thinks he is and whether he is really an impartial thinker. The review is characterized more by its vicious temper than by balanced critical comment.]

902 B., I. "Portrait of an Old Man," MANCHESTER GUARDIAN, 22 Oct 1924, p. 8.
The Haymarket Theatre production of *Old English* is a portrait "firm in composition, rich in color." The focus is gloriously on Old English, but otherwise the play is "not well-orchestrated."

903 Baker, George P. "Introduction," *Representative Plays by John Galsworthy* (NY: Charles Scribner's Sons, 1924), pp. v–xxi.
"Art for man's sake" is the essence of JG's works, but he believes in focusing attention and stimulating thought rather than in preaching definite reforms. His work "rests on questioning 'Society' as 'Society' accepts itself." JG observes the injustices of life in *The Silver Box* and *Justice;* records the confusions and contradictions of love in *The Eldest Son, The Fugitive*, and *A Bit o' Love;*

becomes a seer of sorts with *The Mob;* misses with satire in *The Foundations* while giving admirable touches of humor and characterization; and presents the clash of social groups in *Loyalties.* JG's method is to "set before the public no cut and dried codes, but the phenomena of life and character, selected and combined, *but not distorted,* by the dramatist's outlook . . . leaving the public to draw such poor moral as nature may afford." Finally, JG is a naturalist. [In this introduction to *The Silver Box, Strife, Justice, The Pigeon, A Bit o' Love,* and *Loyalties,* Baker relies extensively on JG's "Some Platitudes Concerning Drama" and his prefaces to *Beyond* and *Villa Rubein* in the Manaton ed.]

904 Brickell, Herschel. "Again the Forsytes," NEW YORK EVENING POST LITERARY REVIEW, 25 Oct 1924, p. 3.

Any of the three plots of *The White Monkey* might have served for a full novel. The novel is lively and readable, full of "sprightly" language and effective use of slang and cockney idiom. JG's "technically perfect" characters are "beautifully executed portraits."

905 Brown, Ivor. "Mr. Galsworthy Goes on Tour," SATURDAY REVIEW (Lond), CXXXVII (15 March 1924), 258–59.

JG's early dramatic "essays in compassionate realism" brought fresh air to the theater; in *The Forest* at the St. Martin's Theatre JG has changed his style and mood: JG is no longer impartial. The weakness is that four acts are devoted to proving "self-evident propositions." Bastaple is "too gross . . . to be dramatically attractive." JG has also turned to melodrama. Conflicts of decency with knavery are interlaced with the conflict of human against natural forces.

906 Brown, Ivor. "The Old and the Bold," SATURDAY REVIEW (Lond), CXXXVIII (1 Nov 1924), 444–46.

The somewhat "meandering" *Old English* at the Theatre Royal must be seen for the sake of the roguish Old English, who is "defiance incarnate, sardonic in humour, metallic in resolution," yet warm-blooded.

907 Bullock, J. M. "Galsworthy Lost in *The Forest,*" GRAPHIC (Lond), CIX (15 March 1924), 364.

JG seems to be arguing for the validity of imperialistic expansion in the St. Martin's Theatre presentation of *The Forest;* but the point is obscured by the play's melodrama. [Four stills accompany the review.]

908 Cansinos-Assens, R. "Prólogo," *Flor Sombría (The Dark Flower)* (Madrid, 1924) [not seen].

[Introduction to a Spanish translation, also by Cansinos-Assens, of *The Dark Flower.*] [In Spanish.]

909 *"Captures,"* A.L.A. BOOKLIST, XX (Jan 1924), 139.

The short stories of *Captures* are not JG's best work because some are "slight and hurried" in execution. [Brief notice of publication.]

910 Douglas, A. Donald. "Galsworthy's World," NATION (NY), CXIX (3 Dec 1924), 603–4.

Soames in defeat is more admirable than the young people who practice the disintegration of the technique of painting and poetry in *The White Monkey*. Limited by his "fineness and his own pain at the harsh discords" of the modern world, JG is at his best when he is remembering things past.

911 "Drama as a Study: Prof. George P. Baker as an Interpreter of Galsworthy," SPRINGFIELD REPUBLICAN (Mass), 14 Nov 1924, p. 14.

Representative Plays by John Galsworthy has some significant works. JG uses irony in his plays to suggest the "illuminating quality that Aristotle gave to pity and terror in the tragedy"; he believes that the dramatist should arrest attention and stimulate thinking rather than preach definite reforms. [A review of George P. Baker's ed of *Plays*.]

912 Dutton, G[eorge] B. "From a High Place," INDEPENDENT (Bost), CXIII (20 Dec 1924), 549.

In *The White Monkey*, JG has created characters as alive and identifiable as Dickens's. The novel can stand independently from the rest of *The Forsyte Saga*. *Monkey* is a very readable "luminous crystallization of truth."

913 E., W. H. "Der Kampf um Afrika: Galsworthys Urwalddrama" (The Struggle for Africa: Galsworthy's *The Forest*), VOSSISCHE ZEITUNG (Berlin), No. 129, 15 March 1924, p. 3.

[Brief review of the London production of *The Forest*.] [In German.]

914 Ervine, St. John. THE ORGANIZED THEATRE: A PLEA IN CIVICS (Lond: Allen & Unwin; NY: Macmillan, 1924), pp. 146, 164.

[Passing references to JG which have no critical importance.]

915 F[arrar], J[ohn]. "The Editor Recommends: Mr. Galsworthy's Gentle Ironies," BOOKMAN (NY), LX (Dec 1924), 490–91.

In *The White Monkey*, JG "writes with tolerance, wisdom, and genial fun-poking at the foibles of the younger generation."

916 Field, Louise Maunsell. "John Galsworthy Vivisects Modern Youth," LITERARY DIGEST INTERNATIONAL BOOK REVIEW, III (Dec 1924), 35–36.

The White Monkey affirms throughout the "supposedly out-of-date values" such as common honesty, dependability, loyalty, pity, courage, and faith. Soames emerges as hero in a novel in which Fleur and Michael Mont grow away from shallow indifference because experience teaches them that old values do not die. *Monkey* is a good vivisection of the younger generation.

917 *"The Forest,"* A.L.A. BOOKLIST, XXI (Oct 1924), 15.

The Forest attacks satirically the "methods of modern business financiers." [Brief review.]

918 *"The Forest,"* OUTLOOK (NY), CXXXVII (27 Aug 1924), 642.
[Plot-summary review.]

919 *"The Forest* at the St. Martin's,"* ILLUSTRATED LONDON NEWS, CLXIV (15 March 1924), 480.
[Plot-summary review laments that the two plots of *The Forest* are not interwoven.]

920 Franklin, John. "New Novels," NEW STATESMAN, XXIV (8 Nov 1924), 140–42.
JG lacks the "grasp of human relations that make up the stuff of reality." *The White Monkey* has the unreality of a photograph, lacking conviction of anything solid. Except for the scene where Bicket sells balloons, almost any sensitive person could have written the novel.

921 "A Galsworthy Portrait at the Haymarket," ILLUSTRATED LONDON NEWS, CLXV (1 Nov 1924), 844.
Sylvanus Heythorp (*Old English*) is "superbly realized," but the characterization needs a better setting.

922 "Gentle and Good Mr. Galsworthy," SPECTATOR (Lond), CXXXIII (15 Nov 1924), 748.
The White Monkey has little strength because JG in his "pale charity" so assiduously tries to see both sides of a question or character. Yet the novel is full of "small competencies." The Bicket episode is the best.

923 Gould, Gerald. *"The White Monkey,"* SATURDAY REVIEW (Lond), CXXXVIII (8 Nov 1924), 476.
The White Monkey is the most amusing and most daring of JG's works. Soames emerges as the hero despite the central figure of Fleur. There are three problems: (1) love is treated as if it were either a disease or a "craziness"; (2) treatment of the Bickets is, while sympathetic, too abstract; (3) the main plot is too slick—and the apparent Galsworthian irony is not really discernible. Yet the "creative gusto" and the ability to spin a tale allows JG to create a masterpiece.

924 Graves, Robert. "Eleven Plays," NATION AND ATHENAEUM, XXXV (24 May 1924), 250–52.
[Plot-summary review of *The Forest* praises Bastaple, the "business-Machiavelli."]

925 Grein, James Thomas. THE NEW WORLD OF THE THEATRE, 1923–1924 (Lond: Martin Hopkinson, 1924), pp. 24, 97.
JG's plays *The Skin Game* and *Loyalties* have each run longer than a year at St. Martin's Theatre. Their depth and seriousness of subject matter, combined with long runs, prove that the London public is not so frivolous as is often charged.

926 Guedalla, Philip. "Mr. John Galsworthy," A GALLERY (Lond: Constable; NY: Putnam, 1924), pp. 101–14.

JG specializes in people to whom life is cruel: *Strife* is a "singularly faultless" drama because JG does not follow his penchant for wasting pity on weaklings. In the novel JG has not—as he has claimed he wanted to do in *The Forsyte Saga*—truly given a "social history" of the time. [A condescending discussion of the origins of the Court Theatre and the rise of the new "Drama of Ideas" as generated at the Court Theatre by Shaw, Granville-Barker, and JG; and of JG's gifts as a novelist. The opinionated essay has little specific substance.]

927 Hamilton, Clayton Meeker. CONVERSATIONS ON CONTEMPORARY DRAMA (NY: Macmillan, 1924); rtpd (Freeport, NY: Books for Libraries P, 1969), pp. 124–49.

JG deserves all but the highest respect as a man of letters, the highest being reserved for Kipling. Unlike others of the period who, in writing "cacophonous jargon," are writing with manner rather than with style, JG writes English prose for the educated ear. JG's biggest problem as a dramatist is that "he does not really like to write plays"; rather, he writes them out of a sense of duty, as in the case of *Justice*. [The subjective, conversational lecture begins with the assumption that novelists cannot write plays: consequently JG cannot be a good playwright. There is little, if any, critical insight.]

928 Hutchison, Percy A. "Mr. Galsworthy Continues *The Forsyte Saga,* and in *The White Monkey,* Points a Moral for the Day," NEW YORK TIMES SUNDAY REVIEW OF BOOKS, 26 Oct 1924, p. 9.

Old values win out in *The White Monkey* as Fleur returns to Michael: the white monkey's rind is not really squeezed out and eaten nor the eater "copped." JG emerges more the inductive social philosopher than the satirist and ironist, fastidious in pursuit of art by bringing many disparate elements into a single effective work.

929 Hutchison, Percy A. "Mr. Galsworthy Writes a Novel in the Form of Drama," NEW YORK TIMES SUNDAY REVIEW OF BOOKS, 25 May 1924, p. 14.

The Forest's theme of lust for power is developed by the play-within-a-play device. A "document in social and moral philosophy," *Forest* is a work "broad in conception, of ironic force" written with succinct stage dialogue. A stage defect is the presence of only one woman; but the main problem is that the appeal of Acts I and IV is intellectual, while the appeal of II and III is emotional. *Forest* should have been a novel.

930 "J'Accuse: The Dramatists v. Civilization," ENGLISH REVIEW (Lond), XXXVIII (April 1924), 599–602.

The Forest examines "competitive society" by putting a city group in an African forest "where nature and cannibal man supplement and symbolise his theme."

JG expects his audience to be concerned with the "constitution of society of which they form part." JG's mastery of "literary counterpoint" is often missed because the audiences primarily want "only a story" and fail to see the basic unity through counterpoint.

931 Legouis, Emile [Hyacinthe], and Louis Cazamian. HISTOIRE DE LA LITTÉRATURE ANGLAISE (History of English Literature) (Paris: Hachette, 1924); trans by W. D. MacInnis and Emile Legouis (Lond: J. M. Dent, 1926–27; NY: Macmillan, 1927); rev eds (1930, 1933, 1935, 1937, 1954, 1957, 1964, 1971), pp. 692–93, 1258–62, 1268–69 (1924 ed; pagination varies).

France and Russia have had a share in the formation of JG's realism, but he has fully assimilated these influences. His social criticism moves on lines parallel to those of Arnold, Meredith, and Butler. His fundamental moderation does not spring from the need of compromise but from a many-sided perception of things. His pity continues a thoroughly English tradition and reminds us of Dickens; his realism is of a delicate and scrupulous quality. As a painter of the physical universe and of the soul, JG is a poet. He is an able plot-builder and has a flexible style, at once impassioned and ironical. [In French.]

932 Leonhard-Schalit, L. "John Galsworthy," DER KAMPF (Vienna), XVII (1924), 156–61.

JG, who is not yet well known in Austria, is not simply a critic of society. In spite of his ironic bent he has pity on the underprivileged and is great both as a writer and as a man. *A Commentary, The Dark Flower,* and the saddening social novel *Fraternity* are among his best works. [A general survey.] [In German.]

933 M., S. P. B. "Galsworthy in the Conrad Vein. Drama of Tropical Africa at the St. Martin's: *The Forest,*" DAILY GRAPHIC (Lond), 7 March 1924, p. 2.

The beginning and end of *The Forest* are rather like *Strife,* but the middle of the play reminds one of Conrad's "more lurid" short stories.

934 MacCarthy, Desmond. "A Short Story with an Abrupt Ending," NEW STATESMAN, XXIV (1 Nov 1924), 109–10.

Old English disappoints on the stage because of comparison with the short story. The climax of the old man's struggle that was prepared for does not materialize. [Review of performance at the Haymarket Theatre.]

935 Mann, Dorothea Lawrance. "John Galsworthy and *The White Monkey,*" BOSTON EVENING TRANSCRIPT BOOK SECTION, 8 Nov 1924, p. 5.

The White Monkey motif is that of the younger generation's interest in the strange and new. The photographic study of this generation is important in demonstrating how, with "its longings, its struggles, its failures and its faiths," it "looks to the older generation."

936 Marriott, James William (ed). ONE-ACT PLAYS OF TODAY (Lond: George G. Harrap, 1924).
[Marriott's foreword comments on the acceptance of the one-act play as a legitimate art form. The volume includes JG's *The Little Man.*]

937 Martin, Dorothy. "Mr. Galsworthy as Artist and Reformer," YALE REVIEW, XIV (1924), 126–39.
Although the greater portion of JG's work is concerned with social reform, it is his work as an imaginative artist that will live. Too frequently he allowed his imagination to be inhibited by reason. In *The Silver Box* he seriously weakened his case by suppressing Jones's story. *Loyalties* is in JG's best tradition. His greatest weakness is found in his dramatic characterizations; they are unconvincing. His novels are less obviously reformist. His characters are "afflicted with a strange passivity" when confronted by opposing forces. They do not rebel; they run. JG succeeds in "Indian Summer of a Forsyte" and in "Awakening" in letting the gusto of life triumph. Soames (*The Forsyte Saga*), above all, is the figure that stands out as "he moves tragically forward to his doom of empty-handed maturity and age."

938 Miller, Nellie Burget. THE LIVING DRAMA: HISTORICAL DEVELOPMENT AND MODERN MOVEMENTS VISUALIZED. A DRAMA OF THE DRAMA (NY & Lond: Century, 1924), pp. 304–10.
In JG's dramas of social injustice the crises "creep upon us" naturally, whereas in Shaw they are presented with "noise and violence." JG presents both sides; Shaw gives us polemics. Henry Arthur Jones's characters "speak with an eye upon the audience"; JG's "are caught in the act of speaking." JG gives "the largest range of convincing characters" of any modern English dramatist. The basis of most of JG's plays is a passionate love of justice. [A series of one-sentence comments on several plays, followed by directions and questions for a discussion of *Strife.*]

939 "Mr. Galsworthy's New Play," MANCHESTER GUARDIAN, 7 March 1924, p. 16.
In *The Forest,* at the St. Martin's Theatre, JG drops his usual practice of finding a judicial balance, thus losing his strong point as dramatist. His forceful treatment of negative aspects of personal character becomes almost melodramatic.

940 Morgan, A[lbert] E[ustace]. "Galsworthy," TENDENCIES OF MODERN ENGLISH DRAMA (Lond: Constable, 1924), pp. 121–38.
JG's dominant dramatic quality is his use of realistic detail, especially in *Strife, Justice, The Silver Box,* and *Loyalties;* but this is menaced by his tendency to be didactic. Occasionally he lapses into "staginess," as when Freda reveals to Bill that she is pregnant in *The Eldest Son,* or when Rolf and Jill shake hands innocently and with ironic symbolism at the curtain of Act I in *The Skin Game.* Deep pity and regret about the injustices of life force him to take up various social causes: the penal system (*Box* and *Justice*); the struggle between capital and

labor (*Strife*); jingoism (*The Mob*); poverty (*The Pigeon*); the woman in society (*The Fugitive, Son, Family Man*); business efficiency vs. the aristocratic ideal (*Skin Game*); and caste (*Loyalties*). Doctrines are presented subtly and effectively; irony is often bitter and inconclusive; and artistic ideals are maintained at a high level, even though the reformer often gets the better of the artist.

941 Moses, Montrose J. "Our Drama Heritage," OUTLOOK (NY), CXXXVIII (26 Nov 1924), 508–11.
Within the context of other dramatists who write about social problems, JG is an artist and quite adequate in his method. [Omnibus review of seventeen volumes of plays, including *Representative Plays by John Galsworthy* and *The Forest*.]

942 Muir, Edwin. "Varieties of Realism," NATION AND ATHENAEUM, XXXVI (22 Nov 1924), 302.
JG's art is impartial and suggestive. The model and realistic characters in *The White Monkey* are wrong on the surface but in reality are justified by circumstance. *Monkey* is frank and sincere but "very mannered."

943 Nichols, Robert. "Letters to the Editor," NATION AND ATHENAEUM, XXXIV (22 March 1924), 884–85.
JG's *The Forsyte Saga* is greater than H. M. Tomlinson indicated [NATION AND ATHENAEUM, XXXIV (8 Dec 1923), 404]. *Saga* has affinities with another neglected novel of the country house—E. M. Forster's HOWARD'S END. By the end of *Saga* Soames "is bankrupt of all but property."

944 Nusinov, I. "Chelovek sobstvennik" (*The Man of Property*), KNIGONOSHA, No. 50 (1924), 17 [not seen].
[Review of the 1924 Russian translation of *The Man of Property*.] [In Russian.]

945 "*Old English*. New Play at the Haymarket," TIMES (Lond), 22 Oct 1924, p. 15.
Old Engllih is more a portrait than a play, presenting the courage and will with which an active person can approach old age.

946 Omicron. "From Alpha to Omega," NATION AND ATHENAEUM, XXXVI (1 Nov 1924), 186.
JG's characters in *Old English* are puppets whose lines are theatrical clichés; his hypotheses are inadmissible; his moral is banal. Given JG's views of life and art, the play is technically perfect. [Review of performance at the Haymarket Theatre lacks specific comment.]

947 Paterson, Isabel. "Butterflies in Amber: *The White Monkey,*" NEW YORK HERALD TRIBUNE BOOKS, 2 Nov 1924, p. 3.
The White Monkey, like other novels in *The Forsyte Saga,* is not great considered individually; but *Saga* will endure because JG has created a world capable of life itself.

948 Phelps, William Lyon. As I LIKE IT. 2nd ser (NY: Scribner, 1924), pp. 37, 80, 84, 118, 154, 174.
[Passing references to JG's work by a man who knew and admired JG.]

949 "Plays for the Stage and for the Study," NEW STATESMAN, XXIII (21 June 1924), 326–28.
Characters in *The Forest,* like those in *The Skin Game,* are placed in a significant setting to symbolize modern tendencies and institutions. *Forest* lacks subtlety of characterization; its exciting plot attacks empire-building.

950 "Post War Society: Mr. Galsworthy Contrasts New Freedom With Smug Traditionalism," SPRINGFIELD REPUBLICAN (Mass), 2 Nov 1924, Sec. A, p. 5.
The White Monkey presents a problem and paints a picture: it raises questions rather than answers them. The question of what comes after the fruit of life is asked not only by the younger generation but by "eternal humanity."

951 "The Prefaces of Mr. Galsworthy," TIMES LITERARY SUPPLE-MENT (Lond), XXIII (28 Aug 1924), 522.
As JG suggests in the prefaces to various volumes of the Manaton ed, art fuses "deep sensibility and creative expression." In JG's art, manner adapts to matter as in Irene (*The Forsyte Saga*), one of the "most attractive and vital creations of contemporary fiction." Some attribute JG's lack of relative popularity in England (contrasted to his great popularity on the Continent) to his purported "unpartiality" in the classical Greek pattern; perhaps his "cardinal sin" is that he does write with a conscious moral purpose (as in *A Saint's Progress* and *The Man of Property*), exposing English society sympathetically. JG errs in British eyes by going one step further than Meredith "by substituting for objective analyses of mental processes a sort of concretion and dramatization of those processes," resulting in a "clarity of exposition" and a "stereoscopic effect of circumstance which presents his characters to us as we might come to know them in . . . real life"—for example, in the first chapter of *Fraternity.* He turns his "gently ironic eye" on everyone.

952 R[oberts], R. E[llis]. "*The Forest.* By John Galsworthy, At the St. Martin's Theatre," BOOKMAN (Lond), LXVI (April 1924), 68.
JG's greatest weakness as a dramatist is his "inability to subdue the propagandist, and his unconscious tendency to identify with the evil in the world anything that shocks his sensibilities." Characters are types, and Strood is unbelievable; yet the play is exciting, and Acts II and III are moving.

953 Sackville-West, V. "John Galsworthy," NATION AND ATHE-NAEUM, XXXVI (8 Nov 1924), 236–38.
[A general review-essay based on the publication of the Manaton ed, volumes IX–XVIII, of JG's works. Sackville-West takes issue with the legend of JG's

greatness but adds nothing either to the controversy about JG's stature or to the critical canon of comment about his work.]

954 Shanks, Edward. "The Drama: *Old English,* " OUTLOOK (Lond), LIV (1 Nov 1924), 313.

Sylvanus Heythorp is more sentimentalized in the dramatic production of *Old English* than he was in short story "The Stoic."

955 Shanks, Edward. "The Drama: *The Forest,* " OUTLOOK (Lond), LIII (15 March 1924), 176.

In *The Forest* at the St. Martin's Theatre, the moral is trite, based on "shoddy illustrations." John Strood fails to convince because his shallowness and meanness belie what it normally would take to survive in the jungle. JG's drama, here as in other plays, does not display the subtlety of spirit evident in his novels. Yet the play is one of the three or four best going in London at the time.

956 Sharp, Evelyn. "The Youngest of the Forsytes," WEEKLY WESTMINSTER (Lond), nsIII:2 (8 Nov 1924), 60.

Every JG novel gets better and better. The remorseless truth of his picture of postwar youth in *The White Monkey* would be too ugly "but for his peculiar gift of making it beautiful because he convinces us of its truth." Fleur Mont is completely satisfying. The success of the novel rests finally on the "note of irrepressible hope." JG has never written a gayer or wittier novel.

957 Shipley, Joseph T. "A Galsworthy Play," NEW YORK EVENING POST LITERARY REVIEW, 5 July 1924, p. 878.

The melodramatic *The Forest* is a tale of imperialism destroying human lives; the "impartial" JG gives his villains certain saving characteristics.

958 Shipp, Horace. "England in the Theatre," ENGLISH REVIEW (Lond), XXXIX (Dec 1924), 861–63.

Despite editorial reactions to *The Forest* as "un-English," JG is typically English; and on the Continent he is "pre-eminently the interpreter . . . of Englishmen and the English spirit." *Old English* at the Haymarket Theatre only adds quantity to JG's work: there is good characterization and atmosphere, but the author seems to have taken an untypical "moral moratorium" in emphasizing the "very English virtue of doggedness."

959 "Some Recent Additions: *The Forest,* " OPEN SHELF (Cleveland), Nov 1924, p. 86.

[Brief review.]

960 "Some Recent Additions: *The White Monkey,* " OPEN SHELF (Cleveland), Dec 1924, p. 91.

[Inconsequential review.]

961 Spicer-Simson, Theodore. MEN OF LETTERS OF THE BRITISH

ISLES. . . . WITH CRITICAL ESSAYS BY STUART P. SHERMAN AND A
PREFACE BY G. F. HILL (NY: William E. Rudge, 1924), pp. 69–72.
JG is primarily a man of feeling, and the articles of his creed are the following: (1)
"I feel; therefore I am"; (2) "The more I feel the more I am"; (3) "The successful
life is measured by its moments of ecstasy." To provide an appropriate setting for
one of JG's "world-sacrificing passions" would require at least £100,000, and as
things develop, this lavish, "lawless splendour" dwindles down to a conservative conclusion.

> **962** Strachey, Evelyn. "*The Forest* at St. Martin's Theatre," SPEC-
> TATOR (Lond), CXXXII (15 March 1924), 406–7.

Interest in *The Forest* fails because the two halves of the play are not connected
enough for real effect.

> **963** Townsend, R. D. "A Symbolic Monkey," OUTLOOK (NY),
> CXXXVIII (19 Nov 1924), 460–61.

The painting of the monkey and the Pekingese pup symbolize the loss of value,
but *The White Monkey* is not cynical because those who have "fortitude, kindliness, and honesty of heart fare well and win satisfaction." *Monkey* can stand
alone as a novel, with its presentation of Fleur's problem, the creation of Michael
Mont, Soames's interesting "business complications," and even the "tensely
dramatic" director's meeting. The slightly ironic novel has a "sub-current of
humor."

> **964** Vernon, Frank. THE TWENTIETH-CENTURY THEATRE (Lond:
> George G. Harrap, 1924), pp. 40, 48–50, 55, 61, 63–65, 68–69, 101,
> 152.

JG's best plays are *The Silver Box* and *Strife*. He was both successful and
unconventional in making serious plays out of a police-court case and a strike—
both of which are without sex appeal. [Primarily passing references to JG in the
history of early twentieth-century drama, especially his relationship to the Court
Theatre.]

> **965** "*The White Monkey*," A.L.A. BOOKLIST, XXI (Dec 1924), 111.

[Brief notice of publication.]

> **966** "Who Are the 'Classic Authors' of To-day?" LITERARY DIGEST,
> LXXX (15 March 1924), 46–54.

[A report on the LITERARY DIGEST INTERNATIONAL BOOK REVIEW'S survey of
the best contemporary writers. JG, whose photo accompanies nine others, ranks
ninth.]

> **967** Williams-Ellis, A. "*Old English* at the Haymarket," SPECTATOR
> (Lond), CXXXIII (15 Nov 1924), 734.

In *Old English*, JG is competent but dreary.

968 Woolf, Virginia. MR. BENNETT AND MRS. BROWN (Lond: Hogarth, 1924); rptd in THE CAPTAIN'S DEATH BED AND OTHER ESSAYS (NY: Harcourt, Brace, 1950), pp. 94–119.

The Edwardian novelists—Arnold Bennett, H. G. Wells, and JG—are unsatisfactory because they rely on surface detail and matter-of-factness for the realities of life; as a consequence, life itself (the spirit by which we live) escapes them. Their novels are incomplete. "In order to complete them it seems necessary to do something—to join a society, or more desperately, to write a cheque." The Edwardians are interested in the externals of life—in social forces, progress, and science.

969 Wright, Ralph. "Webster and Galsworthy," NEW STATESMAN, XXII (15 March 1924), 667.

Characters in *The Forest* look and act like people, but one really does not get to know them because they are only stock characters. *Forest* is bad JG.

1925

---

970 Agate, Evershed. THE CONTEMPORARY THEATRE, 1924 (Lond: Chapman & Hall, 1925); rptd (NY & Lond: Benjamin Blom, 1969), pp. 20, 147, 161–64, 199–203.

The Forest is indebted to C. K. Munro, and most likely to deVere Stacpoole and THE BOY'S OWN PAPER. JG's "gentle lamp" is not so "scathing a beam" as Munro's. The middle acts set in Africa are too long. *Forest* leaves much to be desired, but the production at the St. Martin's Theatre is excellent. In *Old English*, performed at the Haymarket Theatre, Heythorp (Old English) represents the "dominating spirit of our race." *Old English* has two parts: (1) an act of malfeasance, and (2) escape from retribution. JG fails in his attempt at "minor pleasantries" in the scene at Millicent Villas. [The two reviews of performances also comment on the abilities of the various actors.]

971 Aiyar, R. Sadasiva. INTRODUCTION TO GALSWORTHY'S PLAYS ([Poona: Aṙyabhushan P], 1925); rptd (Folcroft, Pa: Folcroft Library Editions, 1973).

"JG is an artist first and a propagandist second," because he wants to see life steadily and wholly. His sympathy does not blind him to faults in his characters. [Most of the plays discussed by Aiyar have several pages devoted to them, a significant portion being given to quotations from the text to illustrate theme and character traits. Discussions are broken down rather artificially into chapters entitled: "Plays based on some social idea or problem" (*Strife, The Pigeon, The Foundations, The Fugitive, The Skin Game, Windows*); "The Forsyte World"

(*The Silver Box, The Eldest Son, A Family Man, Old English, The Forest*); "Plays glancing at international and racial justice" (*The Mob, Loyalties*); "Character plays" (*Joy, A Bit o' Love*); and "An allegorical dream-fantasy" (*The Little Dream*). As Aiyar's chapter headings indicate, he emphasizes theme at the expense of other aspects of drama. The book was written in part as a guide for students who were studying *Joy, The Silver Box,* and *Strife* for the B.A. examination at Bombay University, and that unfortunately shows in the writing, especially in the survey chapters on "Ibsen and the Modern Drama," "A Chapter of Names," and the perfunctory concluding chapter "Characteristics." V. Dupont's JOHN GALSWORTHY: THE DRAMATIC ARTIST, rptd like Aiyar's work by the Folcroft P (Folcroft, Pa, 1970), contains a much more thorough discussion of JG's work as a dramatist.]

972 [Anthony, Luther B.] *"Old English,"* DRAMATIST (Easton, Pa), XVI (Jan 1925), 1249–50.

JG continues to "swamp the stage with the irrelevant notions of the novelists"; he can "paint a patch of personality" in the novel, but cannot dramatize it in a play. A case in point is *Old English*.

973 "Assembled Tales," TIMES LITERARY SUPPLEMENT (Lond), XXIV (16 April 1925), 264.

The yoking of tales in *Caravan* works to JG's disadvantage, because there is little evidence of maturing, perhaps understandably since to JG short stories are diversions from his novels, where his forte is his "steady, penetrating and tolerant vision of life." In the shorter tales, like "Ultima Thule," JG tends to preach. Longer tales like "A Stoic" and "The Apple Tree" are much better. "The Apple Tree," poignantly "aching" for beauty, focuses on the "sense of exile from a passionate paradise."

974 Aynard, Joseph. "Le propriétaire" (*The Man of Property*), LE JOURNAL DES DEBATS (Paris), XXXII (7 Aug 1925), 227–29.

[Review of Camille Mayran's translations into French of *The Man of Property*.] [In French.]

975 Balmforth, Ramsden. "Galsworthy's *The Forest* and *Justice,"* THE ETHICAL AND RELIGIOUS VALUE OF THE DRAMA (Lond: Allen & Unwin, 1925), pp. 197–208.

JG satirically and impartially points to what is wrong in life and sides with the underdog. [Primarily plot summaries of *The Forest* and *Justice,* with little reference either to ethical or to religious value.]

976 Benét, William Rose. "A Shelf of Recent Books: Galsworthy's *Understanding,"* BOOKMAN (NY), LXI (Aug 1925), 698–99.

Caravan is filled with the "irony of life . . . the trickery of fate, the defeat of nobility, faithfulness and courage, the cowardice of average humanity."

977 Blake, George. "Mr. Galsworthy's Secret: 'The Apple-Tree, the Singing, and the Gold,' " JOHN O'LONDON'S WEEKLY, XIII (25 April 1925), 106.

The secret to the success of *Caravan* can be seen in "The Apple Tree": the ability to "bring home . . . the sad, wistful beauty of young love, the vagrant loveliness of passion . . . the gift of poetry that transcends the hardness of the social world he depicts." For this reason *The Dark Flower* is perhaps JG's best novel. [Review of *Caravan*.]

978 Brickell, Herschel. "Fifty-Six Galsworthy Short Stories Included in One Admirable Volume," NEW YORK EVENING POST LITERARY REVIEW, 8 Aug 1925, p. 2.

The short stories of *Caravan* are masterful, not written according to formula. The theme of pity often appears, with an occasional touch of sentimentality.

979 Brown, Ivor. "Two Kinds of Show," SATURDAY REVIEW (Lond), CXL (11 July 1925), 38–39.

The Show at the St. Martin's Theatre is a "drab study of decent people involved in humiliations and reacting to distress in unrhetorical ways." Yet it has a "quiet honesty of purpose," illustrating that "guilty parties in social crimes are hard to locate." [Brown defends JG against critics who accuse him of "libelling the Press, the police, and the world in general."]

980 Camerlynck, G. "Notes et Documents: Mr. Galsworthy à Paris" (Notes and Documents: Mr. Galsworthy in Paris), REVUE DE L'EN-SEIGNEMENT DES LANGUES VIVANTES, XLII (June 1925), 262–64.

[Gives an account of the ceremony honoring JG at the Sorbonne. See also Emile Legouis and Louis Cazamian, "L'hommage . . . ," ibid., (June 1925), 241–45.] [In French.]

981 *"Caravan,"* A.L.A. BOOKLIST, XXII (Oct 1925), 33.

The fifty-six short stories (appearing 1920–1923 in different periodicals) of *Caravan* have mixed quality and are grouped in pairs by theme or mood—even though having been written some years apart. [Brief review.]

982 Cazamian, Madeleine L. "John Galsworthy: Hier et aujourd'hui" (John Galsworthy: Yesterday and Today), REVUE ANGLO-AMÉRICAINE, III (Dec 1925), 97–104.

Because JG's art is directed equally to the imagination, the intelligence, and the heart, his art has achieved a "balance, perfection, richness, variety, and finally the quality which is, perhaps, without equal." [Review of *The Forsyte Saga*, *Caravan*, and *The White Monkey*.] [In French.]

983 Clark, Barrett H. A STUDY OF THE MODERN DRAMA (NY: D. Appleton, 1925, 1928; 2nd ed rev, 1938), pp. 9, 49, 80, 125, 126, 180, 225, 226, 239, 245, 261, 272–80, 281, 282, 302, 309, 368.

Strife is an "austere and just arrangement of acts, facts, motives, and opinions" that well emphasize a "certain detachment" of author from the text. In *The Pigeon* emphasis on human charity is less cold in presentation than the theme of *Strife*. Act I of *Pigeon* is JG's best. He avoids "theatrical" effects, the "big scene," and "hackneyed dialogue and situations." [Clark's book is designed primarily as a study guide, with pp. 272–80 presenting a biographical sketch, selected bibliography, and study notes for *Strife* and *The Pigeon*. Clark emphasizes JG's austerity, spire of meaning, detachment, realism, and lack of theatrical gimmicks.]

984 Conrad, Joseph. "A Glance at Two Books," FORUM, LXXIV (Aug 1925), 308–10.

The Island Pharisees has for "its only serious defect that of not being long enough; and for its greatest quality that of a sincere feeling of compassionate regard for mankind expressed . . . through a fine imagination." [This essay was written in March 1904, and concerns JG's *The Island Pharisees* and W. H. Hudson's GREEN MANSIONS.]

985 Cruewell, G. A. "Galsworthy als Erzaehler" (Galsworthy as a Storyteller), NEUE FREIE PRESSE (Vienna), 13 Sept 1925, pp. 28–29.

JG is a late Victorian, not a modern writer. While his tales (*Caravan*) are often too long, the faulty German translation of *The Patrician* reveals JG's humanity, even though the handling of the plot is mechanical. [In German.]

986 Dinamov, S. "Momental'nys snimki i Liubox' khudozhnika" ("A Portrait" and *Villa Rubein*), KNIGONOSHA, Nos. 31–32 (1925), 17 [not seen].

[Review of Russian translations of "A Portrait" and *Villa Rubein*.] [In Russian.]

987 Dobrée, Bonamy. "A Batch of Plays," NATION AND ATHENAEUM, XXXVIII (14 Nov 1925), 246.

The Show is a "socio-morality" document. JG writes with his "usual skill . . . scrupulous fairness and bitter generosity" to no purpose. Plot and development are conventional; the satiric effect is blunted because of wrong focus.

988 Eaton, Walter Prichard. "Come One, Come All," NEW YORK HERALD TRIBUNE BOOKS, 18 Oct 1925, p. 15.

The Show is one of JG's weaker dramas. The theme that unfavorable publicity is "cruel torture to a man's relatives and loved ones" does not really need elaboration.

989 Eaton, Walter Prichard. "For the Stage," NEW YORK HERALD TRIBUNE BOOKS, 8 March 1925, p. 9.

Old English is a "commonplace and crudely jointed frame for a 'character part'—and even that part . . . is chiefly a collection of old traits and tricks."

990 Engel, Fritz. "Galsworthys 'Gesellschaft'" (Galsworthy's *Loyalties*), BERLINER TAGEBLATT, XXVI (27 Sept 1925), 9.

Loyalties, a work by the English Brieux, was well produced by Max Reinhardt, but it is a weak play that is not saved by its praiseworthy case against anti-Semitism. [In German.]

991 Fannière, Edouard. "Lorsq'un Francais Lit Galsworthy" (When a Frenchman Reads Galsworthy), BULLETIN DE L'ASSOCIATION "FRANCE-GRANDE BRETAGNE," (15 April 1925) [not seen]; rptd in REVUE DE L'ENSEIGNEMENT DES LANGUES VIVANTES, XLII (May 1925), 202–7.

JG is not as popular in France as Wells or Kipling. JG learned the art of writing from Flaubert and de Maupassant. JG's concise, harmonious style reminds one of Flaubert. An analysis of *The Man of Property* shows its classic qualities. Above all, JG is a stylist. Moreover, JG the philosopher and moralist should also please the French temperament. *Strife* shows that he can be impartial. His work is lifelike and like life has no conclusion. Like Meredith JG reconstructs the world through the minds of his characters and lets the reader deduce their feelings from the dialogue. He is the epic poet of contemporary society; as a conservative he wishes for the adaptation, not the destruction, of the Forsytes. JG exhibits his faith in the English middle classes. A French reader can thus appreciate both the French and the English aspects of JG and his work. [In French.]

992 F[arrar], J[ohn]. "Editor's Column," BOOKMAN (NY), LXI (July 1925), 583.

[The editor of BOOKMAN strongly recommends *The White Monkey*, as the Forsyte family "in younger phases marches on."]

993 G., H. "Shout from Pit at First Night; Mr. Galsworthy's Worst Play: *The Show*," DAILY CHRONICLE (Lond), 2 July 1925, p. 5.

The Show is JG's worst play: characters are dull, their tragedy unreal. Most of the audience agreed with a heckler who said during the play: "He might have given us something better"—but all agreed the heckler was rude.

994 "Galsworthy at Home and Abroad," LIVING AGE, CCCXXVII (28 Nov 1925), 470–71.

[Using some trivial comments by JG on the detrimental nature of an affected Oxford accent as a point of departure, the writer quotes Edmund Jaloux's comments in NOUVELLES LITTÉRAIRES that JG's place in literature is based on the Taine-like principles of race, environment, and moment rather than any exceptional artistic merit. JG usually appears in his work as a "pitiless and discreetly indignant witness." His great power to invent incident (continues Jaloux) complements his power to suggest the "state of mind of his characters from the outside; a landscape, a broken word, an unfinished gesture . . . the observation of a servant, two glances which cross each other." The article is accompanied by Raphael Nelson's caricature of JG.]

995 "Galsworthy, John. *Caravan,*" PRATT INSTITUTE QUARTERLY BOOKLIST, Autumn 1925, p. 39.
[Brief notice of publication of *Caravan.*]

996 "Galsworthy's New Play," LIVING AGE, CCCXXVI (8 Aug 1925), 337.
[Short plot-summary review of *The Show* that emphasizes the harm that ferreting newsmen and over-zealous detectives can do.]

997 Gillet, Louis. "Dernières nouvelles des Forsyte" (Latest News of the Forsytes), REVUE DES DEUX MONDES, 7ième période, XXVIII (1 July 1925), 198–210.
A long, descriptive review of *The White Monkey* seen through the main characters and some episodes in the story. The review stresses the characteristics of the Forsytes of the inter-war period as described by JG. [In French.]

998 Gould, Gerald. *"Caravan,"* SATURDAY REVIEW (Lond), CXXXIX (25 April 1925), 437.
Caravan presents wordly knowledge (as in "A Stoic") with an "air of unostentatious thoroughness." The attempt to write about and with romantic beauty in "The Apple Tree" falls short of greatness because JG's "good writing" has little "lyric rapture."

999 Grein, J. T. "Galsworthy's *The Show:* Superb Acting," ILLUSTRATED LONDON NEWS, CLXVII (25 July 1925), 176.
[Grein emphasizes the excellent acting rather than the play itself.]

1000 Grein, J. T. "The World of the Theatre. Basil Dean Speaks Out.—A Young Producer," ILLUSTRATED LONDON NEWS, CLXVII (11 July 1925), 84.
[Three stills from *The Show* are reproduced on the same page with an article that has nothing to do with JG.]

1001 Hartley, L. P. *"Caravan,"* BOOKMAN (Lond), LXVIII (May 1925), 114–15.
The fifty-six stories of *Caravan* are characterized by pathos rather than tragedy and by a lack of happiness. Many stories, especially the long ones, "are models of what stories ought to be: delicately written, conscientious, well worked out, amusing . . . moving." Characters seldom attain tragic proportions because JG will not accept the concept of "personal responsibility." JG is best when his emotions are restrained.

1002 [Hornblow, Arthur.] "Mr. Hornblow Goes to the Play," THEATRE MAGAZINE (NY), XLII (March 1925), 15–19, 62, 64.
Old English, produced in NY at Winthrop Ames's Ritz Theatre, is a distinctive treat for serious playgoers. The crisp dialogue, the quick changes of mood, and

the subtle character revelations of Sylvanus Heythorp give actor George Arliss a masterful chance to perform.

1003 Hutchison, Percy A. "Galsworthy Sends Out a *Caravan,* " NEW
YORK TIMES SUNDAY REVIEW OF BOOKS, 2 Aug 1925, pp. 1, 19.
JG strives for complete unity, especially of mood, in his short stories. In "The Apple Tree," the best short story in *Caravan,* the perennial mood of spring is captured in Megan's "pagan purity" and "Botticelli wistfulness." "Philanthropy" and a few other tales only incidentally detract from an otherwise excellent collection.

1004 Hutchison, Percy A. "Sophisticated Comedy and Elemental
Drama," NEW YORK TIMES SUNDAY REVIEW OF BOOKS, 20 Dec 1925,
p. 13.
JG's curiosity penetrates to the inner recesses of life in *The Show.* The technique of seeing the suicide from varying points of view is indebted to Browning's RING AND THE BOOK. The theme of respectability at any cost becomes a comedy of a "searingly bitter sort." *The tour de force* lacks vitality in characterization; consequently, JG needs all his customary dramatic artistry to allow the play with its sometimes brittle dialogue to succeed.

1005 J., R. "The Theatre. Unreal Realism. Mr. Galsworthy and Mr.
Zangwill," SPECTATOR, CXXXV (18 July 1925), 100–101.
The Show at the St. Martin's Theatre does not convince because JG has not given "a sufficiently plausible set of facts" to justify his indignation at idle curiosity. The technique of the letter is implausible and inartistic.

1006 "John Galsworthy," DIE LITERATUR (Stuttgart), XXVII (1925),
226.
[Quotes from Max Meyerfeld's "Englische Menschen" (English People), DIE NEUE RUNDSCHAU, XXXV:11]. [In German.]

1007 Kennedy, P. C. "New Novels," NEW STATESMAN (Lond), XXV
(9 May 1925), 106–7.
Although a "golden mediocrity honeys and mitigates . . . his achievement," *Caravan* has some artistic successes in JG's "A Stoic," "Had a Horse," and "Salvation of a Forsyte."

1008 Kolars, Mary. "We Sat Smoking After Dinner," NEW YORK
HERALD TRIBUNE BOOKS, 6 Sept 1925, p. 4.
The noteworthy *Caravan* is "unconsciously addressed to a group of . . . gentlemen with the leisure for after-dinner smoking."

1009 Krutch, Joseph Wood. "Galsworthy Escapes Drama," NATION
(NY), CXX (3 June 1925), 635–36.
A Bit o' Love is unusually consistent because JG "makes no compromise between the impulse of human nature and the Christianity which it preaches." One

respects JG more as a moralist than as a dramatist because of the lack of action; in addition, JG fails to develop the contrast of the Christian strength of Strangway with the other forces because no one in the village comes close to the stature of Strangway: had his wife embodied the truly pagan philosophy of life, there could have been a dramatic scene in the confrontation of Strangway and his wife. [Review of performance at NY's 48th Street Theatre.]

1010 Krutch, Joseph Wood. "The Giant Race," NATION (NY), CXX (14 Jan 1925), 49–50.
Sylvanus Heythorp in *Old English,* separated from the present by a lifestyle modern thought cannot understand, "gives the unmistakably heroic ring to prejudices and to passions which all the teachings" of JG "would lead us to believe disreputable and contemptible." [Review of performance at the Ritz Theatre.]

1011 Lacon [pseud of Edmund Henry Lacon Watson]. "Mr. John Galsworthy," LECTURES TO LIVING AUTHORS (Lond: Geoffrey Bles, 1925); rptd (Freeport, NY: Books for Libraries P, 1968), pp. 41–50.
[A series of commonplace critical comments, presented as if spoken to JG, is accompanied by a portrait by "Quiz."]

1012 Legouis, E[mile], and L[ouis] Cazamian. "L'hommage de la Sorbonne à Mr. Galsworthy" (Homage of the Sorbonne for Mr. Galsworthy), REVUE DE L'ENSEIGNEMENT DES LANGUES VIVANTES, XLII (June 1925), 241–45.
[Contains the texts of the papers read at the Sorbonne during the ceremony held on 22 May 1925 in honor of JG. Emile Legouis introduced JG to the audience and paid homage to him both as novelist and as playwright. JG already was considered a classic in the French universities; Legouis expressed regret that JG's plays had not yet found their way to France. Louis Cazamian thanked JG for his lecture on the novelists—Dickens, Turgenev, de Maupassant, Tolstoy, Conrad, and A. France.] [In French.]

1013 Maurice, Arthur B. "Speaking of John Galsworthy," MENTOR (NY), XIII:9 (Oct 1925), 19–21.
JG's wealth enabled him to devote himself to his writing. His earnestness and his tenacity have always been his salient characteristics.

1014 "Mr. Galsworthy's New Play: *The Show,"* MANCHESTER GUARDIAN, 2 July 1925, p. 8.
The Show at St. Martin's Theatre is a "somber, clear-cut picture of the law in action." JG takes dramatic risks because there is really no visible dramatic conflict.

1015 "Mr. Galsworthy's *Show,* at St. Martin's," ILLUSTRATED LONDON NEWS, CLXVII (11 July 1925), 94.

The Shows "harrows on insufficient grounds": JG's humanitarianism dominates his artistry.

1016 Moses, Montrose J. "Three Plays of the Season," OUTLOOK (NY), CXXXIX (25 March 1925), 458–59.

Old English illustrates the belief that JG is "fundamentally a novelist interested in those finer details which cannot be allowed to clog drama." The slim plot is amusing, with touches of sentimentality and pathos.

1017 Muir, Edwin. "Fiction," NATION AND ATHENAEUM, XXXVII (18 April 1925), 78–79.

Caravan is written according to formula; JG is thus a "careful rather than a creative artist." If he had been less strict in his deliberate objectivity, his "propagandist appeals to our hearts" would have been fewer and would consequently have enhanced his art.

1018 Muir, Edwin. "The Plays of Mr. Galsworthy," NATION AND ATHENAEUM, XXXVI (31 Jan 1925), 616.

JG, who is not really an objective observer of life, is preoccupied with the evils of society without understanding them. His sense of drama is confused by the desire "to prove that all drama is a by-product of social wrongs": beginning as propaganda, the dramas are modified to give an appearance of art. One surviving quality is conscientious craftmanship. He stops short of dramatic expression, not making us more conscious of our lives. [General review of the Manaton ed, volumes XIX, XX, XXI, containing plays from *Justice* to *Windows*, and *Six Short Plays*.]

1019 Nathan, George Jean. "The Theatre," AMERICAN MERCURY, IV (Feb 1925), 244.

Old English is a "singularly hashy play" written simply for a "ham actor of the old school." Old English is less the "old Englishman of affairs" than he is the old actor, filled with the clichés of many performances.

1020 Nathan, George Jean. "The Theatre," AMERICAN MERCURY, V (Nov 1925), 373–78.

When the public listens to JG, it believes only half of what it is told.

1021 "New Books in Brief Review: *Caravan*," INDEPENDENT (Bost), CXV (15 Aug 1925), 192.

[General review.]

1022 Nicoll, Allardyce. BRITISH DRAMA: AN HISTORICAL SURVEY (Lond: G. G. Harrap, 1925; 2nd ed, NY: Thomas Y. Crowell, 1925; 3rd ed, Lond: Harrap, 1932; 4th ed, Lond: Harrap, 1949; Lond: Harrap, 1958; 5th ed, NY: Barnes & Noble, 1963), pp. 254–58, 260, 261, 263, 276, 290, 324.

JG and Harley Granville-Barker are the most important dramatists of domestic and social problems. JG, to the consternation of some critics, "has adopted the faiths, ideals, and forces of modern social life" focusing on ordinary and less-than-ordinary characters rather than on traditional tragic types. His plays (the best are *The Silver Box, Strife, Justice, The Pigeon, The Eldest Son, The Fugitive, The Mob, The Skin Game,* and *Loyalties*) have the same features: (1) a social comment presented in a natural way, (2) naturalism (sometimes ordinary) in dialogue, (3) "native kindliness of heart" added to the "sternness of the true tragic artist," (4) absence of sentimentalism. The "omnipresent force of civilization" takes the place of the ancient tyrant. JG's plays underscore the sense of tragic waste of human potential. The plays have no "true hero," yet are full of heroes; the "tragic impression is sure" because of the "sense of superhuman forces and of the waste involved in their clash and conflict." Changing times dictate changes in tragic drama, and JG reflects this change. [The preceding is an annotation of the 1925 ed.]

JG became a dramatic force as a major British developer of social drama. *Box* gets theatrical effect "from social situation rather than from character." Roberts and Anthony in *Strife* are men of iron will but are not presented in "individualistic heroic terms." *Justice* impresses with its emphasis on the tragic waste caused by the judicial process. In other plays the faiths of men are their masters. JG's qualities as a craftsman are as follows: (1) a profound humanitarianism, (2) a general lack of sentimentality, (3) "an excellent sense of dramatic architecture," and (4) an ability to give life to some of his characters. Faults derive from his selection of ordinary subject matter and character, not enabling him to rise to dramatic heights of creativity or to the metaphysical vision necessary for tragedy. His realistic prose dialogue does not really allow the heights of emotion needed for great drama: thus his plays often close with stage directions. [This annotation is based on the 1963 ed.]

1023 *"Old English,"* A.L.A. BOOKLIST, XXI (April 1925), 269.
Old English's life of gallant and often intemperate self-indulgence does not destroy his mental and spiritual alertness. [Brief review.]

1024 *"Old English,"* ST. LOUIS LIBRARY BULLETIN, XXIII (Sept 1925), 351.
[Brief review.]

1025 *"Old English,"* THEATRE ARTS MONTHLY, IX (July 1925), 490.
The character of Old English (Heythorp) is better than the play *Old English* itself. [Heythorp on the page as well as on the stage is of "almost epic grandeur."]

1026 *"Old English,* A Play in Which a Great Stage Rascal Has No Rival,"* CURRENT OPINION, LXXVIII (March 1925), 316–23.
[Review quotes passages from other reviewers and prints a segment of *Old English,* a photo of JG, and three stills from the play.]

1027 *"Old English*. By John Galsworthy," SATURDAY REVIEW OF LITERATURE, I (7 March 1925), 585.
Only Sylvanus Heythorp, the embodiment of "unscrupulous egotism," is good JG. Delineation is ironic and satiric, but the dramatic aspect is conventional and insignificant. [Review of *Old English*.]

1028 Omicron. "From Alpha to Omega," NATION AND ATHENAEUM, XXXVII (18 July 1925), 488.
JG exhausts our patience because of his tediousness and lack of subtlety in *The Show*. Pomposity denigrates his "intense humanity."

1029 Phelps, William Lyon. "As I Like It," SCRIBNER'S MAGAZINE, LXXVII:3 (March 1925), 321–22; rptd with slight variations in As I LIKE IT, Third Ser (NY: Scribner's, 1926), 94–97.
One of the most interesting features of *The Forsyte Saga* is JG's treatment of Soames as he changes from being unlikable to being admired. Other instances of characters who change from being disliked are Mr. Pickwick and Dick Swiveller. JG "seems to have no theoretical philosophy, because life is to him an insoluble riddle."

1030 Phelps, William Lyon. "As I Like It," SCRIBNER'S MAGAZINE, LXXVII:6 (June 1925), 155.
The success of *Old English* is owing chiefly to the acting, "for I found it unreadable."

1031 "Play About the Press and Public Curiosity: Galsworthy's *The Show* Deals with Legal and Journalistic Inquiry into Personal Troubles," SPRINGFIELD REPUBLICAN (Mass), 11 Oct 1925, Sec. A, p. 5.
The "clean-cut and judicial" *Show* illuminates "human motives and the organized processes of society." Suspense is maintained despite the shallow development of characters selected obviously to fit the scheme of the drama.

1032 "The Play That Is Talked About," THEATRE MAGAZINE (NY), XLII (July 1925), 26, 28, 52, 54.
[Excerpts from the "humorously philosophical" but "soundly conventional" *Old English* are reprinted, along with two photos from the Winthrop Ames-Ritz Theatre (NY) production.]

1033 Pocock, Guy N. "The Greatest Dramatic Achievement of John Galsworthy," PEN AND INK (Lond: J. M. Dent, 1925), pp. 215–20.
Justice, the "tragedy of the weak," is pitiable and moving, and the atmosphere is "masterly." But *Strife,* JG's greatest play, is a "tragedy of strength," an "almost perfect play," with artistic "economy . . . and compression in the dialogue." *Strife* has the "full dignity of tragedy."

1034 Priestley, J. B. "Modern English Novelists: John Galsworthy," ENGLISH JOURNAL, XIV (1925), 347–55.

JG's art "is fundamentally a criticism of success framed in the light of what success has failed to take into account, criticism of the heritage of civilization by one civilized man who has unusual sympathy with the disinherited, of the strong by the weak, of the proud by the humble." Although he is a competent novelist and a competent playwright, he is essentially "the critic and historian of contemporary social developments." He uses irony as a corrective for sentimentality. There is no sentimentality in *The Forsyte Saga* and its sequels, and these are the novels by which he should be judged. His characters tend to be social types. His reputation has declined in the last dozen years primarily because of changing social conditions. As social history, *Saga* will rank along with the novels of Balzac.

1035 Reely, Mary Katharine. "A Selected List of Current Books: *Caravan,*" WISCONSIN LIBRARY BULLETIN (Madison), XXI (Oct 1925), 231.
Caravan is "artistic and invariably gloomy." [Brief review.]

1036 Reely, Mary Katharine. "A Selected List of Current Books: *Old English,*" WISCONSIN LIBRARY BULLETIN (Madison), XXI (March 1925), 87.
[Inconsequential review.]

1037 Root, Wells. "Plays by Three Dramatists," NEW YORK WORLD, 20 Dec 1925, Sec. M, p. 7.
JG once again concerns himself with the "ills and perversities" of the world in *The Show,* which strives to "castigate curiosity"—but manages to conclude "with very little conclusion."

1038 Royde-Smith, N. G. "The Drama: Ibsen, Galsworthy, and a New Playwright," OUTLOOK (Lond), LVI (11 July 1925), 25.
The Show at the St. Martin's Theatre does not rise to tragedy; the most appealing character is the "bustling and competent" detective.

1039 "St. Martin's Theatre. *The Show,* " TIMES (Lond), 2 July 1925, p. 14.
The Show, strictly realistic and without dramatic excitement, presents the theme of public exposure. It is dull because the prime characteristic of "moral indignation" is not enough to sustain dramatic interest. Art is present negatively in simplicity and economy of statement.

1040 Salpeter, Harry. "*Caravan,*" LITERARY DIGEST INTERNATIONAL BOOK REVIEW, III (Sept 1925), 678–79.
[Effusive and laudatory general essay on *Caravan*. JG apparently can do no wrong.]

1041 Salten, Felix. "*Gesellschaft*" (*Loyalties*), NEUE FREIE PRESSE (Vienna), 10 April 1925, pp. 1–3.

Loyalties is Brieux modified by JG's tact and sense for understatement. The moving and thoughtful play was well produced by the Theater in der Josefstadt. [In German.]

> **1042** Salten, Felix. "John Galsworthy: Zur deutschen Ausgabe des Romans *Die Forsyte Saga*" (John Galsworthy: The German Edition of *The Forsyte Saga*), NEUE FREIE PRESSE (Vienna), 8 Dec 1925, pp. 1–4.

JG is one of the few that have remained faithful to the middle classes without betraying human values. [In German.]

> **1043** Scribner [publisher]. JOHN GALSWORTHY: A SKETCH OF HIS LIFE AND WORKS (NY: Scribner, 1925), 16 pp.

[This brochure is a generally favorable sketch with some critical comments.]

> **1044** "A Selection From Recent Additions: *Old English,*" OPEN SHELF (Cleveland), Sept–Oct 1925, p. 88.

"Another dull play."

> **1045** Shipp, Horace. "Upon Being Shown Up," ENGLISH REVIEW (Lond), XLI (Aug 1925), 288–90.

The Show at the St. Martin's Theatre castigates society, especially the police and the press, for prying into the private lives of other people. Unfortunately the play is overstated, it has a "devastating anti-climax," and the comedy scene with the jury is not true to the play. The basic weakness, however, is that the play is "an incident," not a tragedy. Yet the "human vivisection" that JG presents is true to life and enjoyable.

> **1046** *"The Show,"* A.L.A. BOOKLIST, XXII (Dec 1925), 109.

[Brief plot summary.]

> **1047** Sloan, J. Vandervoort. "Mr. Galsworthy and Others in the Loop," DRAMA (Chicago), XVI (Dec 1925), 96, 116.

[The paragraph review of the production of *The Forest* at the Goodman Memorial Theatre damns the play and the actors.]

> **1048** "Some Modern Plays," TIMES LITERARY SUPPLEMENT (Lond), XXIV (24 Dec 1925), 894.

Plays. Sixth Series is disappointing. *The Forest* and *The Show* do not successfully combine moral feeling with artistic rectitude. *Old English* succeeds as art largely because JG is not overly concerned with morality.

> **1049** "Some Writers of Today," TEACHERS WORLD (Lond), 24 July 1925 (August Extra Number: Modern Literature), p. 857.

[Brief biographical sketch with list of works.]

> **1050** S[utton], G[raham]. *"The Show.* By John Galsworthy," BOOK-MAN (Lond), LXVIII (Sept 1925), 320.

The idea of human privacy is persecuted rather than presented in *The Show*. The "bare incident-plot" "owes much to [JG's] . . . command of realistic detail and to his knowledge of law."

1051 Tilby, A. Wyatt. "The Epic of Property," EDINBURGH REVIEW, CCXLI (April 1925), 271–85.

Balzac and JG are the only two "novelists who take the business of property . . . seriously enough to describe it correctly." The main difficulty for JG is that he hates "the idea that life is a conflict and a struggle." Those who are failures in JG's fictional world still seek the same kind of success as enjoyed by the Forsytes. "It is not the mystic but the drudge who envies the millionaire." JG succeeds better with his men than with his women. Irene leaves one cold. [A review of *The Forsyte Saga* and *The White Monkey*.]

1052 Townsend, R. D. "Stories Well Worth Reading," OUTLOOK (NY), CXLI (16 Sept 1925), 98–99.

Caravan reveals how little development there has been in JG's "ripeness" and social purview through the years, although there may be a difference in manner and technique. JG can write "short bits" of character-work as well as novels.

1053 Towse, J. Ranken. "Plays by St. John Irvine, Galsworthy and Philpotts," NEW YORK EVENING POST LITERARY REVIEW, 24 Oct 1925, p. 3.

"The motive, aim and moral" of *The Show* are "sound, vital and timely." JG successfully blends varied action and emotion to illustrate the effects of scandal-mongering by newspapermen and over-zealous activity by police.

1054 Trebitsch-Stein, M. "Neue Galsworthy-Buecher" (New Books by Galsworthy), NEUE FREIE PRESSE (Vienna), 15 Feb 1925, pp. 32–34.

[Favorable reviews of the English ed of *The White Monkey* and "*Der Menschenfischer*" *(Caravan)*, a collection of tales.] [In German.]

1055 Van Doren, Mark. "First Glance," NATION (NY), CXXI (2 Sept 1925), 258.

JG's predilection for death in *Caravan* results in seventeen of the fifty-six tales closing with death. His vision is limited to three phenomena: (1) the despairing man who must witness the anomalies, discrepancies, and injustices of life that he can never resolve; (2) the woman who solves the riddle by "ignoring it and being only beautiful, soft, and darkly, inexplicably passionate"; and (3) "the fleshly old gentleman" who "asks no questions and offers no answers but eats or drinks or loves his life to a positive, if sometimes brutal, conclusion." JG has treated these themes too often.

1056 Vol'kenshtein, V. "*Serebrianaia korobka*" *(The Silver Box)*, KNIGONOSHA, No. 24 (1925), 15 [not seen].

[Review of a translation of *The Silver Box*.] [In Russian.]

1057 Weygandt, Cornelius. "John Galsworthy, Gentleman," A CENTURY OF THE ENGLISH NOVEL (NY: Century, 1925); rptd (Freeport, NY: Books for Libraries P, 1968), pp. 21, 71, 221, 343, 389–90, 428, 430, 437, 438, 478, 479.

JG's personality, character, and sympathies influence readers. "If [only his] artistry and seership . . . were as his humanity and his knowledge of life!" Artistry and seership, unfortunately, are reached only in *The Man of Property* and *The Country House*. JG is indebted to few writers, but his work occasionally suggests George Meredith. *The Forsyte Saga* impresses with its scope, but JG should have stopped with *Property*. Soames is able, tenacious, and unscrupulous outside his narrow code, but is baffled and driven to brutality by Irene—a universal, yet individual, inscrutable "more than . . . woman." English businessmen are satirized in *Property*, English squires in *House;* unfortunately both novels suffer from an excess of satire and propaganda. *House* has a mellowness not evident in other JG works.

A better novelist than playwright, JG is relatively more important as a dramatist because of the absence of contemporary dramatic talent. As a satirist, JG has revived the use of charactonym; he also works with allegory (*The Little Dream,* "A Novelist's Allegory" in *The Inn of Tranquillity,* and *The Little Man*). The love of Felix and Nedda in *The Freelands* departs from JG's usual treatment of love as an "irresistible and obsessing, even destroying . . . passion"—the latter of which receives good treatment in *The Dark Flower*. Though he tries to make it better, JG views life as a muddle, keenly observing and using the theme of time passing. Emotional intensity, love of animals, and the appreciation of nature's beauty are characteristic, even though JG seldom develops descriptive passages. Art often serves morality rather than morality, art. As a novelist, JG ranks below Hardy and Conrad, but perhaps above George Moore and Arnold Bennett.

1058 "White Monkey and Errant Sailor," CURRENT OPINION, LXXVIII (Jan 1925), 37–38.
[A plot-summary review of *The White Monkey* is accompanied by a portrait of JG.]

1059 Wittko, P. "Galsworthy[?]," DIE RAMPE (Hamburg: Deutsches Schauspielhaus, 1925–1926), pp. 141–49 [not seen].
[Listed in BIBLIOGRAPHIE DER DEUTSCHEN ZEITSCHRIFTEN LITERATUR (Leipzig: Felix Dietrich, 1927).] [In German.]

1060 Woodbridge, Homer E. "Sands of Life," SATURDAY REVIEW OF LITERATURE (NY), II (3 Oct 1925), 171.
The short stories in *Caravan* are full of well-turned narrative technique; JG works with greater freedom than he does in novels and plays. [Laudatory review of *Caravan,* with a dozen pieces singled out for half-sentence commentary.]

1061 Woolf, Virginia. "Modern Fiction," in THE COMMON READER, First Series (Lond: Hogarth, 1925; NY: Harcourt, Brace, 1925); rptd in THE COMMON READER. First and Second Series (NY: Harcourt, Brace, 1948); rptd in THE COMMON READER, First Series (NY: Harcourt, Brace & World, n.d.), pp. 150–58.

One quarrels with Wells, Bennett, and JG because they are materialists; "they are concerned not with the spirit but with the body" and have, as a consequence, disappointed the reader. One is grateful to Hardy, Conrad, and to a lesser degree, W. H. Hudson.

1926

1062 Agate, James [Evershed]. THE CONTEMPORARY THEATRE, 1925 (Lond: Chapman & Hall, 1926); rptd (NY & Lond: Benjamin Blom, 1969), pp. 259–64.

In *The Show,* performed at St. Martin's Theatre, JG "has a passion for the ill-used." The melodrama is ill-conceived: the first act suggests a drama of remorse and guilty passion; the second act, a possible justification for the remorse. This sequence is followed by events that make the play "unaccountably fritter itself away" in the "red herring" of a third act. JG's interest is "not so much the dirtiness of the linen as the insistent way in which those who must wash it in public demand to be screened." *Show* fails because the story does not keep interest, and JG erred in attacking "reasonable publicity." [Agate takes issue with JG's penchant for making all those who are "worth more than 3 pounds a week . . . objectionable from every point of view."]

1063 "Ambassadors Theatre. *Escape,*" TIMES (Lond), 13 Aug 1926, p. 8.

JG's primary interests in *Escape* are in the hunt and the quality of mercy. Characters are ingeniously sketched, especially Matt Denant.

1064 "Among the New Spring Books," INDEPENDENT (Bost), CXVI (27 March 1926), 368.

Of *Plays. Sixth Series,* JG fans will probably appreciate *The Forest* more than *Old English* and *The Show* because it is one of the few works set outside of England.

1065 Arns, Karl. "Ein Streifzug durch das neuste englische Schrifttum" (A Promenade through the Latest English Literature), LITERARISCHER HANDWEISER (Munich, Freiburg), LXIII (1926–27), 575–82.

The Forsyte Saga belongs to the genre of the life-novel. It is unfortunate that JG added sequels to his main work. He uses the point-of-view technique of Henry

James. Rather than using elaborate descriptions, JG relies on photographic depiction of gesture and accuracy of dialogue to suggest or evoke feelings or emotions. [In German.]

1066 "Ausländisches" (Books Abroad), ORPLID (Augsburg), III:9 (1926), 72–75.
[Commenting on the German translation of *The White Monkey,* the author praises the fact that the will to live emerges out of the various passing fads and confusions presented therein.] [In German.]

1067 B., I. "*Escape.* Mr. Galsworthy's New Play," MANCHESTER GUARDIAN, 13 Aug 1926, p. 8.
Escape at the Ambassadors Theatre touches the "completeness of life," not the "gaudy fringe." Matt Denant's personality holds the episodic play together.

1068 Bab, Julius. "Galsworthys *Gesellschaft* und die Judenfrage" (Galsworthy's *Loyalties* and the Jewish Question), CV-ZEITUNG (Berlin), V:10 (1926), 138–41.
Jews ought to appreciate JG's play as a work that is neither anti-Semitic nor philo-Semitic but that describes the Jew as a human being with good and bad qualities. Apart from the theatrical suicide of the captain, the play is a successful study of the idea of justice. [In German.]

1069 Barry, Iris. "Mr. Galsworthy's Gloomy Novel and Some Others," SPECTATOR (Lond), CXXXVII (28 Aug 1926), 314.
JG's characters are "intensely individual creatures isolated from the . . . rest of humanity." The "disintegrated generation" of Marjorie Ferrar does not hold the reader's interest in *The Silver Spoon* because JG can write well only about what invigorates him, such as the older generation of Forsytes. *Spoon* is the novel of the loss of heart. JG despises "the poor because they are weak" and the aristocrats because they are shackled by an aristocratic code. [Barry gives no evidence to substantiate the peculiar comment about JG's contempt for the poor.]

1070 Bennett, Charles A. "Life Through Fiction: *Loyalties,*" BOOKMAN (NY), LXIII (April 1926), 161–65.
Loyalties attacks "the disastrous doctrine that loyalty comes before everything."

1071 Binz, Arthur Friedrich. "Galsworthy, John; *Der Weisse Affe*" (Galsworthy, John; *The White Monkey*), LITERARISCHER HANDWEISER (Munich, Freiburg), LXIII (1926–27), 450–51.
The White Monkey is typical JG. The frenzies of modern living do not succeed in suppressing the longings of the soul for higher values. [In German.]

1072 Binz, Arthur Friedrich. "John Galsworthy," LITERARISCHER HANDWEISER (Munich, Freiburg), LXIII (1926–27), 95–100; enlgd and rptd, ORPLID, III:8 (1926), 53–63; revised as "Roman der Gesellschaft" (A Novel of Family Gatherings), VON AUFBRUCH UND UNTERGANG:

AUFSÄTZE ÜBER DICHTER UND DICHTUNGEN (Heidelberg: Hermann Meister, 1927), 71–86.

JG is more natural and has a larger scope than Thomas Mann. Too much has been made of JG as a social critic and of his moral attitude. He is not biased. Although he is aware of the weaknesses of society, he affirms its values, since he belongs, both intellectually and artistically, to the cultural groups whose decline he chronicles. He has a deep sense of the melancholy and transience of human existence. His works gain their dimension from his observation of reality, his spiritual awareness, and his fusion of individual lives with the fate of the nation. He portrays the Victorian age and seeks beauty amidst death and decline. [Review-article on the German trans of *The Forsyte Saga*.] [In German.]

1073 "The Bookman's Guide to Fiction," BOOKMAN (NY), LXIV (1926), 90.

The Silver Spoon is more entertaining than *The White Monkey*.

1074 Bott, Alan. "John Galsworthy's New Play: Convict's Adventures in *Escape*," DAILY CHRONICLE (Lond), 13 Aug 1926, p. 5.

Suspense is maintained, but dramatic conviction falters in the "disjointed, almost film-like action" of *Escape* at the Ambassadors Theatre.

1075 Brown, Ivor. "Less Than Justice," SATURDAY REVIEW (Lond), CXLII (21 Aug 1926), 200–201.

In *Escape* at the Ambassadors Theatre, "philosophic interest" in the "one versus the many" theme increases as "narrative allurement" begins to fail about halfway through. Denant gets "less than justice because [justice] gets less than normal work." JG raises questions, "sets them tingling in the mind," but does not answer them; thus *Escape* becomes a "vehicle of suggestion about . . . universal things."

1076 Bullett, Gerald. MODERN ENGLISH FICTION (Lond: Herbert Jenkins, 1926), 46–53.

JG's "Ironic Muse wears hobnailed boots." What is valuable in his work is "its fidelity to a steady, penetrating, and tolerant vision of life. The minuteness of his observation, his imperious sense of justice, the sanity and sincerity of his writing" enable JG to attain some of his most valuable effects. *The Forsyte Saga* is a triumph of craftsmanship and "industrious imagination." His bias against Soames is a flaw, but as *Saga* continues, JG's sympathy for Soames becomes more evident. Irene is marvelous; she "is a subtle and fragrant presence, seductive mystery, embodied charm."

1077 Canfield, Mary Cass. "Galsworthian Drama. *The Show,*" SATURDAY REVIEW OF LITERATURE (NY), II (1 May 1926), 754–55.

The "surface of life" in *The Show* is "so meticulously reported that inner reality finds no voice." Characters in the *pièce à thèse* are conventional, the action stiff, and the tone homiletic.

1078 Cano, B. Sanin. "John Galsworthy," INDAGACIONES E IMAGENES (Inquest and Images) (Bogota: Ediciones Colombia, 1926); rptd in REPERTORIO AMERICANO (San José, Costa Rica), XXVII:1 (July 1933), 24, 27.

[Comments on the plots of various works such as *The Country House, Fraternity, The Patrician, Justice, The Silver Box,* and *The Fugitive;* JG is compared with Cervantes, Swift, Sterne, and Bernard Shaw.] [In Spanish.]

1079 Carlton, W. N. C. "Novels by Galsworthy and Barrington," NEW YORK EVENING POST LITERARY REVIEW, 17 July 1926, p. 3.

In *The Silver Spoon* JG lavishes care on Marjorie, hoping to be fair to the "postwar ultra amoral set." The development of the older Soames is masterful. *Spoon* is a "chip from his workshop rather than a broadly planned, fully modeled creation."

1080 Chubb, Edwin Watts. "The Sensitiveness of John Galsworthy," STORIES OF AUTHORS (NY: MacMillan, 1926), pp. 401–4.

[Reprint of some comments by St. John Irvine from an unidentified source, and a page of general biographical information.]

1081 Coats, R. H. JOHN GALSWORTHY AS A DRAMATIC ARTIST (NY: Scribner, 1926).

[Uses six categories—sincerity, sympathy, impartiality, irony, pity and indignation, and artistry—to analyze the ideas, kinds of characters, and plot situations in JG's plays. Some consideration of JG's dramatic technique and his use of recurrent devices is given.]

1082 Cosulich, Bernice. "Life's Ironies Inspire John Galsworthy," LITERARY DIGEST INTERNATIONAL BOOK REVIEW, IV:5 (April 1926), 297–98.

[An interview in which JG describes how he works as a writer.]

1083 Cox, Emily. "Mr. Galsworthy and the Humane Standpoint," NATION AND ATHENAEUM, XL (9 Oct 1926), 20–21.

In both novels and dramas, JG records better than any contemporary writer the "reaction of the modern mind confused by the suffering of the feeble and the disabled." JG should be recognized as a leader of "modern humanitarianism." [Moralistic general commentary takes issue with Bonamy Dobrée (NATION AND ATHENAEUM, XXXIX [21 Aug 1926], 584–85), who argues that JG cannot escape in his writings from his sense of decency.]

1084 Demmig, Ch. "John Galsworthy," DER GRAL (Ravensburg), XX (1926), 493–500.

JG, writer and gentleman, excels in his descriptions of classes that resist social change. Like Thomas Mann he is skeptical about emotional involvement and does not offer pat solutions for social problems. Though disillusioned, he longs for a new religion with which to oppose the materialism of his age. As a playwright he is of importance only for England. The extraordinary success of *Loyalties* in Berlin is owing to Reinhardt's reinterpretation of the play. [In German.]

1085 Dinamov, S. *"Chlen palaty Mil'toun* i *Pervye i poslednie"* (*Member of Parliament Miltoun* and *The First and the Last*), KNIGONOSHA, Nos. 3–4 (1926), 41–42 [not seen].
[Review of a Russian translation of *The Patrician* and *The First and the Last.*] [In Russian.]

1086 Dobrée, Bonamy. "Mr. Galsworthy's Play," NATION AND ATHENAEUM, XXXIX (21 Aug 1926), 584–85.
JG's dramatic intuitions and human observations are believable in *Escape* at the Ambassadors Theatre, but it is difficult to believe that society is as bad as he would have us believe. The fault of the drama lies in the fact that the characters are "too much like life" when they ought to be, in addition, "symbols of the author's intuitions, not just the results of his observation." The play is not properly paced. *Escape* is not a great play because the "question raised by a great play is . . . a metaphysical one, not a moral one"—and JG's questions are moral.

1087 Drew, Elizabeth. THE MODERN NOVEL: SOME ASPECTS OF CONTEMPORARY FICTION (NY: Harcourt, Brace, 1926), pp. 7, 18, 19, 44, 57, 59, 153–73, 234.
Despite JG's many strengths—his sound, sincere thinking, his workmanship and exquisite sense of form, his profound sympathy—one has a feeling, if not of narrowness, of smallness and sparseness of effect. A good illustration of the lack of robustness and vitality in his work is the moment of silence on which *Strife* closes. JG is an ironist, and he has written the epic of the upper middle classes, *The Forsyte Saga.* In all his works one finds "a situation where the instinct for conformity finds itself at odds with some powerful disintegrating force." From his works one gets a sense of "the inexorable sadness of things."

1088 Ervine, St. John. "At the Play, Mr. Galsworthy Takes Leave of the Theatre," OBSERVER (Lond), 15 Aug 1926, p. 9; rptd as "Galsworthy's New Play," LIVING AGE, CCCXXX (25 Sept 1926), 673–76.
In *Escape* at the Ambassadors Theatre JG presents the theme of escape but does not comment. His mastery of stage craft is excellent in the fluent manipulation of theme. The weak point is the picnic scene, where JG arbitrarily subordinates fact to theme. JG is one of the least impartial men of letters, current opinion to the contrary.

1089 Ervine, St. John, and John Galsworthy. "Dramatist and Critic," LIVING AGE, CCCXXXI (15 Nov 1926), 340–45; rptd from the OBSERVER (Lond), 25 Sept and 30 Oct 1926 [not seen].
[JG and Ervine debate points made by Ervine in his review of JG's *Escape.*]

1090 Farrar, John. "The Editor Recommends," BOOKMAN (NY), LXIV (1926), 92.

The Silver Spoon should "be read by all cultivated people everywhere, for it is charming, urbane, witty."

1091 Field, Louise Maunsell. "Mr. Galsworthy Presents Modern England," LITERARY DIGEST INTERNATIONAL BOOK REVIEW, IV (Aug 1926), 550, 552.

The Silver Spoon depicts and criticizes the social and political condition of modern England, especially artistic and literary aspects of modernity. Fleur's silver spoon is her selfishness; Michael's, his "tradition of accepted responsibilities"—as seen in his espousal of a future-oriented Foggartism. Soames, a central figure with abundant life and energy, espouses the old-fashioned values that are the essence of British vitality.

1092 "Galsworthy's Plays: *The Forest, Old English,* and *The Show,*" SPRINGFIELD REPUBLICAN (Mass), 7 April 1926, p. 20.

The pervasive spirit of *The Forest* is that of "indignation repressed and poised"; of *Old English,* "admiration critical and without sentiment"; of *The Show,* "reproof tempered by understanding of a complex social system." [Review of *Plays. Sixth Series.*]

1093 H., G. F. "On John Galsworthy the Dramatist—*Escape,* at the Ambassadors," ILLUSTRATED LONDON NEWS, CLXIX (28 Aug 1926), 372–73.

JG is essentially a critic of contemporary social institutions, a man of "feeling" who uses his "imagination in the service of his generation"; his argument is always for the "humane and generous view." *Escape* presents on the stage "a representative world of men and women." The propagandist dominates *Justice;* the artist dominates *Escape.* [Five stills of scenes in *Escape* are rptd.]

1094 Hartley, L. P. *"The Silver Spoon,"* SATURDAY REVIEW (Lond), CXLII (28 Aug 1926), 236.

JG's propaganda in *The Silver Spoon* is "essentially defeatist." The Forsyte world, "a little unimaginative, a little inelastic, a little lacking in humour, a little too dynastic," nevertheless suggests the real world. The conclusion, that England lacks an instructed public opinion that has Britain's best interests at heart, is presented in a clash of new and old.

1095 Henderson, Archibald. EUROPEAN DRAMATISTS (NY & Lond: Appleton, 1926), pp. 469–79.

JG is a dramatist *manqué;* his theatre is interesting but unreal. His genius appears only in his fiction, and even there it is sporadic. [The chapter on JG is not in the first ed (1913).]

1096 Hübner, Walter. "Galsworthys Dramen und die neuere politische Theorie: Ein Beitrag zur schulmässigen Interpretation des Dichters" (Galsworthy's Dramas and Modern Political Theory: An Essay on Scholastic Interpretation of Creative Writers), SCHULE UND WISSENSCHAFT (Berlin, Hamburg), I (1926–27), 17–31.

Because JG is a sober and impartial critic of life, his plays provide a suitable introduction to the political situation in present-day Britain. In his efforts to discover "the essential meaning of things" JG shows the contradictory forces that are at work in society, but he does not advocate reforms. In his best play, *Strife*, the basic conflict is that between two classes. The problems he discusses in all his plays are so basic to society that his works, as L. Rockow [CONTEMPORARY POLITICAL THOUGHT IN ENGLAND (Lond, 1925), p. 261] said, may serve as a source for the political historian. [After surveying the development of British political thought in the nineteenth century, Hübner concludes that JG's time is characterized by conflicting group interests and the increasing but questionable power of the state over the individual.] [In German.]

1097 Hutchison, Percy A. "Galsworthy Sounds a Warning," NEW YORK TIMES SUNDAY REVIEW OF BOOKS, 11 July 1926, p. 1.

The plot of *The Silver Spoon* is almost without complication—almost trivial; thus the whole *Forsyte Saga* background is needed. Then the novel becomes vibrant in its emphasis on the inward feelings of Michael and Fleur. The Marjorie Farrar episode suggests that the world is headed for a debacle unless it shapes up.

1098 J., E. M. "Galsworthy Goes on with Forsyte Group: Ambitious Woman and Cynically Hard-headed Girl Are Prominent in *The Silver Spoon,*" SPRINGFIELD REPUBLICAN (Mass), 8 Aug 1926, Sec. F, p. 7.

The Silver Spoon, read without knowledge of other works in *The Forsyte Saga,* is an interesting study of contemporary English life with characters developed well enough to compensate for a trivial plot.

1099 J., R. "The Hero as Convict," SPECTATOR (Lond), CXXXVII (21 Aug 1926), 275.

JG presents "a dramatic tale swiftly narrated" with incidents selected to illustrate social types and conventions in *Escape,* playing at the Ambassadors Theatre. "Dexterously touched episodes . . . [try] to convey the impression of an impartiality that doesn't . . . exist in art." Many critics belabor JG's presumed impartiality and moral presentations.

1100 Jedlička, Jaromir. "Galsworthyho realismus v románě" (Galsworthy's Realism in the Novel), PRITOMNOST (Prague), III (3 June 1926), 328–31.

JG, a strict realist, rejects the concept of beauty and replaces it with the concept of rhythm or harmony, which for him includes an internal harmony he identifies with truth. The artist should make discoveries in the service of mankind. The division of art into realism and romanticism is important for JG: the realist writes from a specific moral standpoint and with a specific "tendency." JG demands, however, that the literary work be an impartial depiction of reality, the artist's moral convictions being apparent only in his selection and combination of phenomena. He admires the Russian novelists, especially Turgenev, for their ability to write with a moral purpose without moralizing. JG's theory of realism is an attempt (best seen in *The Man of Property*) at a compromise between Russian "tendency" and English moralizing. Because JG is a social critic as well as an artist, his works depict the problems of social classes rather than those of individuals; his characters are social types.

In investigating the English intellectual, JG discovered the conflict between passion and intellect; passion became the theme of his two purely artistic works, *The Dark Flower* and *Beyond*. For JG, humanity is divided into three types: the representatives of society who cannot see beyond its prejudices and are incapable of passion; those who ignore the demands of society and follow their hearts; and those who, although within society, can see beyond its boundaries. The major characters of the novels of passion are artists and women; the conflicts are between those who unhesitatingly follow their emotions and those who do not. In the social novels JG uses extramarital love as a symbol of freedom and the struggle against society for freedom. In the novels of passion, it is no longer a question of society's guilt: here following the dictates of one's heart leads to renunciation. JG the artist is a pessimist; JG the thinker, who identifies beauty with truth, is an idealistic optimist. In the novels of passion the conflict becomes apparent: the allure of beauty is seen to be deceptive; when the heroes realize that beauty and truth are not the same thing, they surrender to renunciation.

In the character of Fiorsen (*Beyond*) JG went furthest from his theoretical optimism. This representative of freedom is not burdened with social goals. But the author "defends" himself against the character by making him disappear in the second half of the novel. As in *Dark Flower,* the idea supports the structure of the novel, which collapses where there is no "tendency." In the depiction of the relationship between Gyp and Fiorsen the failure of JG's morality (that represented by his third type of men) becomes apparent. The lack of that sympathy and love for the social outcast that his theory demands prevents JG from depicting the individual lives which have their own truths, different from those of society, which have to be felt.

It is only outside the social theme that JG the artist and JG the thinker merge. Here the different demands of the two halves of his being, each with its own demands on realism, are incompatible. "Realism, which should be true to reality, cannot serve essentially moral ideas." [In Czech.]

1101 JOHN GALSWORTHY: AN APPRECIATION TOGETHER WITH A BIB-LIOGRAPHY (Lond: Heinemann, 1926), p. 22.

JG's outstanding features in novels and dramas are balance, form, penetration, and a keen sense of situation. JG reveals character well through his portrayal of family relationships, especially in *Fraternity, The Freelands,* and *The Forsyte Saga.* JG, like Turgenev and Maupassant, "seeks to penetrate to the essentials," to "interpret life," thus eliminating distracting details. JG has gradually evolved as an artist. *The Man of Property* is great because of JG's restraint and "pervading subtle sense of 'personality.' " [Comments briefly, in one or two sentences, on JG's prose works—a puff by his publisher to promote the sale of *Caravan* and *The Silver Spoon.*]

1102 "Joseph Conrad's Intimate Letters to John Galsworthy and H. G. Wells," WORLD'S WORK, LIII (Nov 1926), 16–24.

[Includes thirteen letters of Conrad to JG written from 28 Oct 1898 to 17 May 1910; the main thrust of the correspondence is Conrad's expression of his gratitude to JG for JG's help and encouragement.]

1103 Joseph, Michael. "The Seven Seas," BOOKMAN (NY), LXIV (Oct 1926), 244–45.

From central Europe there are glowing accounts of JG's popularity. During his recent tour of Czechoslovakia, Hungary, and Austria on behalf of P.E.N., JG was struck by the appalling poverty of the middle classes and has ordered that all future royalties from performances of his plays in Hungary are to be devoted to funds for the relief of the Hungarian intelligentsia.

1104 Kennedy, P. C. "New Novels," NEW STATESMAN, XXVII (11 Sept 1926), 612–13.

The Silver Spoon is faithful to JG's old theme of rich and poor, but the contrast is presented with too brisk an irony, and he tends to forget the facts of human experience. Fleur—destitute of "brains, character, charm, and even identity"—is psychologically false. The solidity of the original Forsyte trilogy is gone; but the court case between Fleur and Marjorie effectively exposes "social fatuities and legal futilities."

1105 Klaeger, Emil. "Galsworthys *Urwald*" (Galsworthy's *The Forest*), NEUE FREIE PRESSE (Vienna), 14 May 1926, p. 13.

The Forest, which is directed against British imperialism, contains a few truths but is trash produced by a skilled writer. The Moderne Theater did its best with this uninteresting play. [In German.]

1106 Lalou, René. PANORAMA DE LA LITTÉRATURE ANGLAISE CONTEMPORAINE (Panorama of Contemporary English Literature) (Paris: Simon Kra, 1926–27), pp. 217–24, 229–30.

JG's work merits respect because of its courageous dignity and artistry. In *The Island Pharisees* the satire is superficial, and even in his better books the satire is often mechanical and conventional, permitting interruptions that are often sociological and dogmatic. Many of his novels are thesis-ridden. To be sure, his chief work is *The Forsyte Saga,* but *Fraternity* is his most human novel. Of particular merit is his use of psychology. He is an impressionist who lies in wait for the revealing details, the symbolic associations, and the significant images; and he has enriched the English novel with his gallery of characters, especially the Forsytes, despite the fact that many of his characters are never more than marionettes. His weaknesses include a misuse of leitmotifs, a choice of details that are inappropriately made into symbols, and a reliance on images that are forced for their sentimental effect. In *The Patrician,* for example, he tries to present every point of view, but the result is that there are many beginnings but no decisive destination. As a novelist JG is too scrupulous to pander to the mob, but as a thinker he is too vague to influence seriously an elite. Nevertheless, he succeeds in touching the soul when he evokes the feverish soirées or the swooning heart or the night containing the swarming stars. As a dramatist JG's masters are Ibsen and the Russians. His best works are social tragedies drawn by a jurist who carefully delineates all the elements in the eternal trial between society and the individual. [In French.]

1107 Landa, Myer Jack. THE JEW IN DRAMA (Lond: P. S. King, 1926); rptd (NY: KTAV Publishing House, 1969), pp. 202, 236–40.
Loyalties is "in a class by itself" in its serious attempt to grasp the English Jewish problem. The true-to-life play has the "relentlessness of Greek tragedy" as JG arbitrates between the clashes of loyalties. [Primarily plot summary.]

1108 "Leon M. Lion Presents *Escape, an Episodic Play in a Prologue and Nine Episodes,* by John Galsworthy," PLAY PICTORIAL (Lond), XLIX (1926), 50–68.
[A one-page summary of *Escape,* being performed at the Ambassadors Theatre, is followed by seventeen pages (twenty-two photos) of scenes from the production. The summary emphasizes the role of World War I in shaping Matt Denant's actions.]

1109 Loks, K. *"Pervye i poslednie* i *Chlen palaty Mil'toun"* (*The First and the Last* and *Member of Parliament Miltoun*), PECHAT I REVO-LUTSIIA, III (April–May 1926), 225–26 [not seen].
[Review of a Russian translation of *The First and the Last* and *The Patrician.*] [In Russian.]

1110 "London Notes," WORLD (NY), 31 Jan 1926, Sec. 3, p. 2M.
The revival of JG's brilliant and bitter tragedy, *The Silver Box,* a fortnight ago in London was, according to a commentator from the London TIMES, treated as a farce because the "most tragic figure in it is a charwoman."

1111 Lovett, Robert Morss. "Review: *The Silver Spoon,*" NEW RE-PUBLIC, XLVIII (1926), 25.
Many of JG's works have the pattern of a situation in which an individual sacrifices or is tempted to sacrifice the family mores to personal desires. If JG

were a Victorian, the problem would be solved by renunciation, but as a modernist JG's concern is how far the family will compromise with the individual and "mediate with society to save face."

1112 MacCarthy, Desmond. *"Escape,"* NEW STATESMAN, XXVII (18 Sept 1926), 642.

Escape is "slow and daggle-tailed." The concluding scene sheds no light on the moral question: When does one's sense of pity take precedence over one's sense of duty? The slow, humanitarian, and "pensive naturalism" scarcely "befits a play about a dash for freedom." [Review of performance.]

1113 Member of the European Press. "Gespraech mit John Galsworthy" (Conversation with John Galsworthy), NEUE ZUERCHER ZEITUNG (Zurich), 29 Aug 1926, p. 2.

JG, who likes to travel, does not believe in the decadence of European culture and wishes to solve the economic crisis by advocating emigration and support of agriculture. [In German.]

1114 "A New Galsworthy at The Ambassadors," ILLUSTRATED LONDON NEWS, CLXIX (4 Sept 1926), 436.

Escape, a drama "panoramic, full of excitement and pace, lavish in the variety of character sketches," is one of JG's best—he even says a "good word for the public."

1115 Paterson, Isabel. "The Flower of the Forsytes," NEW YORK HERALD TRIBUNE BOOKS, 11 July 1926, p. 1.

The Silver Spoon is unified and artistic enough to survive alone, but it is properly judged with the whole *Forsyte Saga.* Later volumes unfold and refine earlier ones, frequently substituting grace and delicacy for the sturdiness of earlier volumes. Incidents in *Spoon* provide focal points to allow JG to observe and record life with artistic dexterity and technical competence. One flaw: the American Wilmot is unbelievable.

1116 Phillips, Henry Albert. "Three More Authors Consider the Films," MOTION PICTURE CLASSIC (NY), XXIV (Oct 1926), 26, 77.

The Skin Game was a failure in the cinema because JG believes that a photoplay should be a stage play, which it is not. [Report of an interview with JG.]

1117 Platnauer, J. B. "A Playgoer's Notebook," GRAPHIC (Lond), CXIV (21 Aug 1926), 307.

[A brief summary serves as criticism of appearance of *Escape* at the Ambassadors Theatre.]

1118 *"Plays. Sixth Series,"* NEW YORK EVENING POST LITERARY REVIEW, 6 March 1926, p. 8.

[Brief notice of publication.]

1119 Rascoe, Burton. "Contemporary Reminiscences; John Galsworthy Contrasts Manners of Today and Yesterday," ARTS AND DECORATION, XXV (Sept 1926), 54, 80.

[Inconsequential reminiscences about an early interview with JG, commenting especially on his courtesy, his charm, his willingness to please, and his slowness in answering questions. Rascoe's comments trail off into a plot summary of *The Silver Spoon*.]

1120 Reely, Mary Katharine. "A Selected List of Current Books: *The Silver Spoon*," WISCONSIN LIBRARY BULLETIN (Madison), XXII (Oct 1926), 274–75.

The young southern American in *The Silver Spoon* is unreal. [Brief review.]

1121 Reilly, Joseph John. "John Galsworthy and His Short Stories," CATHOLIC WORLD, CXXIII (1926), 754–62; rptd in DEAR PRUE'S HUSBAND (NY: Macmillan, 1932; Freeport, NY: Books for Libraries P, 1971), pp. 45–67.

JG's humorless and ironic style in *Caravan* frequently flows with "unfaltering felicity and grace." Faults demonstrated are the following: (1) JG's tendency to sympathize with underdogs far beyond their merits; (2) his desire to place responsibility for individual faults at society's door; (3) his sentimentality that occasionally borders on decadence; and (4) his emotions that cloy his rational processes. Yet JG is an "artist [,] a . . . careful craftsman, and the greatest living master of prose style in English fiction," whose chief strong point is his portrayal of contemporary life. Especially praiseworthy are "The First and the Last," "A Stoic," and "The Apple Tree." [Reilly's review is the most comprehensive available on *Caravan*.]

1122 Root, Wells. "*Plays; 6th Series*," WORLD (NY), 14 March 1926, p. 6M.

[The above citation is that given by the BOOK REVIEW DIGEST (1926), p. 256; and the following observation is made: Most of JG's characters are lean personalities. JG always has something to say, but it would be preferable if he had less and his puppets more. The citation appears to be faulty, for the original article could not be located.]

1123 Royde-Smith, N. G. "The Drama: A Triple Bill," OUTLOOK (Lond), LVII (5 June 1926), 393.

The one-act drama *Punch and Go* is pre-expressionistic, filled with realism and disillusionment tempered by JG's humor. [Review of performance.]

1124 Royde-Smith, N. G. "The Drama: The Quality of Mercy," OUTLOOK (Lond), LVIII (21 Aug 1926), 177.

In JG's plays the "hero" is always a "victim" who never triumphs, "even in spirit." [Royde-Smith in this review of *Escape* at the Ambassadors Theatre takes issue with the prevailing opinion that JG is "god-like" in his "compassion for his fellow creatures," because JG's "will to punish" gets the better of him: the protagonists usually end unfortunately, occasionally with suicide as a factor. Royde-Smith does not distinguish between JG as humanist and JG as dramatist.]

1125 Sch. "Romane von Galsworthy" (Novels by Galsworthy), DER KUNSTWART (Dresden, Munich), XXXIX (1926), 317–19.
About two hundred pages of *The Forsyte Saga* reveal JG as a *dichter* (poet, creative artist); the rest is the work of a craftsman who is not much of a thinker and does not clarify his attitude towards the present age. The translations by the Schalits are extremely bad. [In German.]

1126 Schriftgiesser, Karl. "Mr. Galsworthy Muddles Through," BOSTON EVENING TRANSCRIPT BOOK SECTION, 10 July 1926, p. 4.
JG's latest, *The Silver Spoon*, "makes us wonder whether . . . [JG] is any longer equal to the task of being the commentator of the Forsytes." JG, as much a realist as Dreiser, unfortunately allows his satire and perception to fall below the level found in his earlier works. Despite the good plot, JG can only "muddle through."

1127 Selver, P. "Englischer Brief" (Letter from England), DIE LITERATUR (Stuttgart), XXIX (1926–27), 417–18.
The younger generation in England regards JG's works as well-intentioned products of little value. *The Silver Spoon* is better than the faulty and often absurd *White Monkey.* [In German.]

1128 Shipp, Horace. "The Novel and the Play," ENGLISH REVIEW (Lond), XLIII (Oct 1926), 469–71.
Escape at the Ambassadors Theatre employs many scenes with "no lurking sense of some missing element." *Escape* succeeds as art because of the "impress of the author's individuality" and the "dramatic situation . . . humor and characterization" of the play.

1129 "Silver Spoon," A.L.A. BOOKLIST, XXIII (Nov 1926), 80.
[Brief plot summary.]

1130 "The Silver Spoon," DIAL (Chicago), LXXXI (Nov 1926), 443.
The Forsyte Saga, a "never altogether living organism," is perhaps incapable of sustaining further appendages. [The reviewer's judgment is underscored by relegating the review of *The Silver Spoon* to the "Briefer Mention" section of DIAL, whereas other volumes in the *Saga* had been given a full-length review.]

1131 "The Silver Spoon," TIMES LITERARY SUPPLEMENT (Lond), XXV (26 Aug 1926), 562.
The Silver Spoon is thin, empty, spun out, and labored. JG's style has slipped into an occasional "cheap smartness." Except for a few stimulating parts, such as Michael Mont's visit to Sir James Foggart, the novel is generally a series of shallow illustrations in a social study rather than a development of character.

1132 Steinermayr, F. C. "Der Werdegang von John Galsworthys Welt—und Kunstanschauung" (The Development of John Galsworthy's World View and Art). ANGLIA, XLIX, nsXXXVII (1926), 97–152; ibid., L, nsXXXVIII (1926), 153–78, 244–86.

[This positivistic survey of JG's work up to 1914 deals with the plays, novels, stories, and essays in chronological order; comments on the themes, characters, and techniques; and, in passing, makes a few valuable observations.] [In German.]

1133 Sydenham, John. "The Fiction Shelf," EMPIRE REVIEW, XLIII (Feb 1926), 175–78.

[A brief, minor review of *The Burning Spear,* a work which was first published in 1919 as written by A. R. P-M and which was now being reissued under JG's name.]

1134 Waldman, Milton. "Chronicles: The Drama. *Escape.* By John Galsworthy. Ambassadors Theatre," LONDON MERCURY, XV (Nov 1926), 83–84.

In *Escape,* the emotions that Matt Denant arouses in those who help him "have little to do with the feelings of the human heart to the hunted man"—rather, they are moved because they believe him innocent or because of similar breeding.

1135 Windscheid, K. "Galsworthy als sozial. Dichter," (Galsworthy as Writer about Society) LEIPZIGER NEUESTE NACHRICHTEN, No. 26 (1926), 1 [not seen].

[Listed in BIBLIOGRAPHIE DER DEUTSCHEN ZEITSCHRIFTEN LITERATUR, 1926 (Leipzig: Felix Dietrich, 1927).] [In German.]

1136 Woodbridge, Homer E. "Altruism and a Skin Game," SATURDAY REVIEW OF LITERATURE (NY), III (7 Aug 1926), 22.

JG continues the treatment of familiar themes in *The Silver Spoon.* The main interest is the "delicately shaded" interaction between Soames, Michael and Fleur Mont, and Marjorie Ferrar. Characters are not so deeply drawn as in earlier novels: Francis Wilmot makes a wretched American in his use of idiom; Michael Mont (and JG) seems not to realize the inhumanity of the Foggartist's proposal of shipping children abroad—unless JG is satirizing futile humanitarianism.

1137 Woolf, Leonard. "Mr. Galsworthy," NATION AND ATHENAEUM, XXXIX (11 Sept 1926), 674.

JG must be reviewed with especial consideration because of his stature. *The Silver Spoon* stands on its own merely as a story, but it fades away when the critical criteria of art are applied. The writing is slipshod and undistinguished. JG habitually begins "chapters on a low note of humour or smartness" and ends them "on a high note of emotion or sentiment." It is better to judge the novel as a "social document" than as art, especially since his characters are "sociological types." [A disorganized and negative essay with undeveloped glimpses of insight.]

1927

1138 Agate, James [Evershed]. THE CONTEMPORARY THEATRE, 1926 (Lond: Chapman & Hall, 1927); rptd (NY & Lond: Benjamin Blom, 1969), pp. 142, 220–23, 342.

The episodic *Escape* is inferior to JG's great plays (*The Silver Box, Strife, Justice*) because JG "muddles" things by "so obviously making his convict the victim of mistaken justice." The conclusion—the convict surrendering to save the parson's conscience—is "Galsworthian bosh." In his attempt to "photograph life," JG occasionally is wrong (i.e., "What modern man ever said to a constable, 'I *smote* him on the jaw'!") [Nicholas Hannen played the role of Captain Matt Denant.]

1139 Atkinson, J. Brooks. "Mr. Galsworthy's Last Play," NEW YORK TIMES SUNDAY REVIEW OF BOOKS, 27 Oct 1927, p. 33.

JG studies human character seriously in a "brief and gentle evening of sincerity and truth," continuing to raise questions rather than to solve problems. *Escape* at New York's Booth Theatre lacks the vigor and stature necessary for survival on Broadway.

1140 B., F. R. "John Galsworthy's *Escape*," OUTLOOK (NY), CXLVII (9 Nov 1927), 308–9.

JG emphasizes in Captain Denant's escape and subsequent capture the concept of "the Englishman to whom life is a sporting event" and to whom observing the rules of the game is of more value than success or failure. *Escape* is a "romantic version of *Justice*, done technically in the EMPEROR JONES manner." [Review of NY performance.]

1141 Bailey, Ralph Sargent. "The Curtain Rises," INDEPENDENT (NY), CXIX (Dec 1927), 606.

Escape is magnificent drama. "Perhaps in no play heretofore has Galsworthy written with such a light and gracious hand; yet in none of them has he commented more keenly on the workings of man's social mind or the vagaries of communal ethics."

1142 Banks, Paul. "Galsworthy," NEW AGE, nsXLI (21 July 1927), 138.

JG as a dramatist has too much pity, too much irony, too much impartiality. "With [JG] the audience must feel that it has been sent back to a social school, whereas with Shaw it feels engaged in social life." His themes were established by tract writers who preceded him; and because his characters are caught in the theme, they do not grow. His contribution to drama is in introducing new subject matter to the stage rather than in contributing to dramatic technique. [Pejorative comments are made in a nominal review of R. H. Coats's JOHN GALSWORTHY AS A DRAMATIC ARTIST (NY: Scribner's, 1926).]

1143 Barnes, H. S. "John Galsworthy," OXFORD MAGAZINE, XLV (24 Feb 1927), 242–43.

JG brought the technique of naturalism "to such perfection that . . . he exhausted its possibilities as a mode of dramatic expression and thus hastened its decay." The social side of JG's works makes them continuingly relevant. His aesthetic qualities often are not understood by the theatergoing public, and he is unique as a "moral philosopher and satirist of social abuses." Shaw never attains JG's depth of feeling for humanity; and JG is perhaps the "greatest propagandist" ever to use the stage as a vehicle of expression. He is also excellent as a technician, creating scenes with verisimilitude and with the absence of falseness. His later plays (beginning with *The Forest*) show JG in decline because he is trying to adapt to more modern methods, losing his sure touch in the process. JG culminates the dramatic revival of the early twentieth century. [A review essay of R. H. Coats, JOHN GALSWORTHY AS DRAMATIC ARTIST (NY: Scribner's, 1926).]

1144 Benchley, Robert [C.]. "Drama: Six of One, Etc.," LIFE (NY), XC (17 Nov 1927), 25.

Escape is a moving, thrilling, and suspenseful series of seven glowing episodes. [Review of NY performance.]

1145 Binz, Arthur Friedrich. "John Galsworthy," DER BUECHER-WURM, (Dachau, Munich, Leipzig), XII:5 (1927), 134–35.

JG's readers are to be found in the propertied classes he describes. He is not so much a social reformer as an analyst who, while accepting social change, describes the effects of time nostalgically. [In German.]

1146 Blunden, Edmund. "The Language Test," NATION AND ATHENAEUM, XLII (3 Dec 1927), 368.

JG is primarily concerned in *Castles in Spain* with the present age's "struggles to escape"; but his essays and addresses are tame, lacking brilliance of language that might enhance the "glowing light" of his philosophy.

1147 Bodelsen, C. A. "John Galsworthy," NATIONALTIDENDE (Copenhagen), 14 Aug 1927, pp. 9–10.

After Shaw and Wells, probably JG is the modern English author most read in other countries. JG is more typical of his country and his times than either Shaw or Wells. Criticism of society and the social order is found throughout his work, but unlike Wells JG is no politician, no spokesman for a particular political or social reform; moreover, there is no trace of fanaticism in his criticism of the brutality and injustice of modern society. Usually there is more sympathy than anger in the way JG regards the pettiness and cruelty of human beings. *The Forsyte Saga* (not yet completed) is his most important work. *The Man of Property* attacked the Victorian spirit, while the marital conflict is reminiscent of Ibsen. JG failed to make Irene more than a symbolic figure. As *Saga* continues it becomes less of an Ibsenian revolt and more and more an objective portrayal of the period. Fleur and Michael Mont are representatives of the postwar era.

Fleur's Forsyteism is even more unpleasant than that of the preceding generation; Michael is a skeptic and melancholy humorist who tries to be helpful to others. JG's plays are less interesting than his novels because there is something dry and mechanical about them, and they are all propagandistic. Unfortunately the bitter satire of *The Silver Box* was turned into low comedy in the Copenhagen production. [In Danish.]

1148 Brickell, Herschel. "The Literary Landscape," NORTH AMERICAN REVIEW, CCXXIV (Dec 1927), [n.p.].
[Brief notice of *Castles in Spain*.]

1149 Carb, David. "Seen on the Stage," VOGUE (NY), LXX (15 Dec 1927), 66–67.
Escape, as firm and polished as any JG play, is perhaps more logical and measured because of its picaresque nature. [Plot-summary review of Winthrop Ames's NY production.]

1150 *"Castles in Spain,"* BOSTON EVENING TRANSCRIPT BOOK SECTION, 17 Dec 1927, p. 3.
Castles in Spain is interesting, "calculated to do much for the reader who would seek more keenly the bright spots of literature."

1151 *"Castles In Spain,"* SPECTATOR (Lond), CXXXIX (19 Nov 1927), 897.
[Brief notice of the "tolerant, thoughtful" *Castles in Spain*.]

1152 Cazamian, Madeleine L. "L'Angleterre nouvelle jugée par Galsworthy" (Contemporary England as Judged by Galsworthy), REVUE ANGLO-AMÉRICAINE, IV (June 1927), 398–402.
Fiction has nothing to prove; therefore, it should be without conclusion. [This review of *The Silver Spoon* summarizes the novel and praises JG because *Spoon* lacks a conclusion.] [In French.]

1153 Cunliffe, J. W. MODERN ENGLISH PLAYWRIGHTS: A SHORT HISTORY OF THE ENGLISH DRAMA FROM 1825 (NY: Harper, 1927), pp. 95–113.
JG gave greater recognition to action in *The Skin Game* and *Loyalties* than he did in earlier dramas. To suggest that *Loyalties* is anti-Semitic is absurd. JG's meaning is at times obscure, as can be seen by the fact that the critics are at a loss with *Windows*. JG lacks Shaw's originality and puritanic zeal, but he possesses a greater balance and artistic power. [For Cunliffe's criticism of earlier plays, see MODERN ENGLISH PLAYWRIGHTS: A SHORT HISTORY OF THE ENGLISH DRAMA FROM 1825 (Lond & NY: Harper, 1917), pp. 95–113.]

1154 D., H. E. "The Galsworthy Play," NEW YORK EVENING POST, 12 Nov 1927, Sec. 3, p. 11.
Escape at NY's Booth Theatre might be JG's best because of its "ensnaring story" and "breathlessly anxious" action.

1155 Elster, Hanns Martin. "John Galsworthy: Zu seinem 60. Geburtstage" (John Galsworthy, on His Sixtieth Birthday), LEIPZIGER NEUESTE NACHRICHTEN, XIV (1927), 8.
JG is the mildly melancholic chronicler of an age of transition. His worldwide reputation is justified by his attempt to synthesize materialism and idealism. [In German.]

1156 Engel, F. "Galsworthy's *Fenster*" (Galsworthy's *Windows*), BERLINER TAGEBLATT, No. 3 (1927), 6 [not seen].
[Listed in BIBLIOGRAPHIE DER DEUTSCHEN ZEITSCHRIFTEN LITERATUR (Leipzig: Felix Dietrich, 1928).] [In German.]

1157 F[arrar], J[ohn]. "This Stream of Poets," BOOKMAN (NY), LXV (March 1927), 80.
Verses, New and Old are pleasant enough but "offer no great vistas of imagination or peaks of poesy."

1158 Fischer, Otokar. "Galsworthy Dramatik" (Galsworthy as a Dramatist), LITERÁRNÍ SVET (Prague), 1927–1928 [n.p.] [not seen].
[Listed in MODERN HUMANITIES RESEARCH ASSOCIATION BIBLIOGRAPHY, VIII (Cambridge: Cambridge UP, 1928).] [In Czech.]

1159 Gillet, Louis. "Un roman de l'inquiétude anglaise" (A Novel of English Restlessness), REVUE DES DEUX MONDES, 7ième période, XXXIX (1 June 1927), 687–98.
Although the action drags a little, *The Silver Spoon* contains two or three unforgettable scenes. It is an admirable rendering of the postwar atmosphere and a powerful study of the British temperament; there is, however, a curious lack of interest in spiritual things on the part of JG. [In French.]

1160 Guiterman, Edmund. "Poems, Opaque, Translucent, and Clear," OUTLOOK (NY), CXLVI (6 July 1927), 319–21.
[Guiterman quotes one stanza from *Verses, New and Old* in an omnibus review of fifteen volumes of poetry.]

1161 Hutchison, Percy. "Two Novelists Turn to the Essay," NEW YORK TIMES SUNDAY REVIEW OF BOOKS, 30 Oct 1927, p. 5.
Castles in Spain and Other Screeds might readily be called "The Faith of a Novelist." JG's essay style reminds one of R. L. Stevenson.

1162 "Interviews with Famous Authors: John Galsworthy," BOOK WINDOW (Lond), I (July 1927), 47–50.
An interview with JG produced the following observations: (1) great art is incompatible with deliberate propaganda; (2) the advantage of the trilogy is that, once background is given, there is more room for character development; (3) *A Modern Comedy* is forthcoming; (4) JG's favorite works are DON QUIXOTE, PICKWICK PAPERS, HUCKLEBERRY FINN, VANITY FAIR, and novels by Dos-

toyevsky, Tolstoy, and Turgenev. [The interview is followed by JG's poem "Picardy" and a bibliography of his works.]

1163 Jean-Aubry, G[eorges]. JOSEPH CONRAD: LIFE AND LETTERS. Two Volumes (Lond: Heinemann; NY: Doubleday, Page, 1927). [Letters of Conrad to JG are reprinted.]

1164 "John Galsworthy," DAS NEUE REICH (Vienna), X (1927–28), 888–89.
The Forsyte Saga, which resembles Mann's BUDDENBROOKS, is the English *comédie humaine*. With the exception of *Loyalties*, his plays are inferior to his novels but better than Shaw's conversation pieces. [Review of the article by Erwin Stranik in NEUE SCHWEIZER RUNDSCHAU (June 1927).] [In German.]

1165 "John Galsworthy: Zum 60. Geburtstag (14. August)" (John Galsworthy: On His Sixtieth Birthday), DIE LITERATUR (Stuttgart), XXX (1927), 29.
[Quotes from remarks about JG in the daily press.] [In German.]

1166 Jones, Howard Mumford. "Galsworthy and Saltus as Poets," NEW YORK WORLD, 6 Feb 1927, Sec. M, p. 9.
JG's novels contain more authentic poetry than *Verses, New and Old*. His precision as a writer prevents him from doing anything too badly, and although *Verses* is often sentimental, one still finds it "finely carved and reticent."

1167 Kirchner, Rudolf. "Die Welt des [*sic*] Forsytes" (The World of the Forsytes), EUROPÄISCHE REVUE (Leipzig), II (Feb 1927), 303–11.
Contemporary British writers are dealing with a period of transition, and instead of portraying the deep inner constancy of the people, they emphasize the decline of the old external order. JG, unlike Shaw, brings a sympathetic humanity to bear upon his criticism of the upper middle class; even so JG fails to portray fully the enduring spirit of the British bourgeoisie because he does not look beyond its present deplorable state to a more promising future based on its now-hidden qualities and strengths. Even after the introduction of Michael Mont as a social hero who faces the problems of society, the picture of the decline of the Forsytes remains one-sided because JG forgets that the sense of property was never the sole reason for the rise of the upper classes during the Victorian age. For example, JG disregards their religious motives. Society reaches the nadir of disintegration in *The Silver Spoon*. JG suggests that there will be new men, new hopes, but he does not say so clearly enough. His contemporaries have begun to recognize their duties, while the Forsytes still seem to be in the dark. [This appreciation is based on the German translation of the Forsyte materials.] [In German.]

1168 Korda, T. "Galsworthy in seinem Heim" (Galsworthy at Home), WESER-ZEITUNG (Bremen), XIV (14 Aug 1927), 8.
[In this interview JG calls Conrad his only good friend, expresses misgivings

about journalism, industrialization, the vote for women, and the state of the theater, and is described as a gentleman who, like his home, seems to belong to the Victorian age.] [In German.]

1169 Krutch, Joseph Wood. "Hare and Hounds," NATION (NY), CXXV (16 Nov 1927), 553–54.

Escape makes a "typically Galsworthian" comment on society: "The most generous impulses of his characters arise in those parts of their souls least likely to be reached by any formal . . . agencies for moral cultivation." The "sporting instinct" causes the characters to aid the convict. Compassion seems to arise from a sense of guilt. [Review of performance at Booth Theatre.]

1170 Ludwig, Albert. "*Jenseits*. Roman" (*Beyond*. A Novel), DIE LITERATUR (Stuttgart), XXX (1927–28), 294.

JG is quite popular in Germany, but it is doubtful whether all his works should be translated. Because of its description of divorce procedures, *Beyond* will be incomprehensible to ninety-nine percent of the German reading public. [In German.]

1171 M., D. L. "Galsworthy the Poet: A Group of Verses, New and Old," BOSTON EVENING TRANSCRIPT BOOK SECTION, 26 Feb 1927, p. 7.

Verses, New and Old is "so gentlemanly that it almost seems emasculate." Exquisite notes, refinements of emotion, and chiselled phrases do not enliven the "cold beauty" of the works.

1172 M., H. "The Music of Words," SPECTATOR, CXXXVIII (19 Feb 1927), 296–97.

Verses, New and Old, pleasantly capturing days and moods of old, is "sentimental . . . at worst," and "pleasantly epigrammatic" at best. [Brief review.]

1173 MacCarthy, Desmond. "Family Unhappiness," NEW STATESMAN, XXIX (17 Sept 1927), 711.

Builder, whose character and views are central to *A Family Man,* must be in a "towering passion" most of the time. JG characteristically leaves to the viewer the task of interpreting Builder's climax of emotion at the conclusion of the drama. JG's dramatic naturalism is based on using everyday speech, failing when the dramatic emphasis calls for the sudden release of emotions; he is more successful when the "point of his dramatic situation lies in the contrast between the humdrum tone of proceedings and the concealed or suppressed agonies and embarrassments of those concerned in them." The scene before the bench presents JG's matter-of-fact irony at its best. JG's "good" characters do not really succeed because he often dips too much into the sentimental. [Review of revival of *Man* at the Everyman Theatre.]

1174 March, Joseph Monclure. "John Galsworthy as a Poet, By Request," NEW YORK EVENING POST LITERARY REVIEW, 29 Jan 1927, p. 6.
[Brief, general, and flippant review of *Verses, New and Old.*]

1175 Marshall, Lenore G. "John Galsworthy, Poet," NEW YORK HERALD TRIBUNE BOOKS, 20 March 1927, p. 17.
JG's poetry is evident in his novels, dramas, and essays; and in fact they may be preferable to *Verses, New and Old,* which, although "often moving and often lovely," are nonetheless "dimmed by an intellectual precision."

1176 Maurois, André. ÉTUDES ANGLAISES (ENGLISH STUDIES) (Paris: Grasset, 1927), pp. 258–59, 267–70, 281.
The Edwardians—Bennett, Wells, Galsworthy, and Shaw—attacked traditions and values with seriousness and in the name of other absolute values: Bennett in the name of strenuous energy, Wells in a kind of diffuse, noble pantheism, Galsworthy in the name of an obscure fraternity, and Shaw in the name of Fabian socialism. But these abstractions served to irritate the younger postwar generation of writers like Virginia Woolf in, for example, "Mr. Bennett and Mrs. Brown" (1925). [In French.]

1177 "Mr. Galsworthy's Humanism," TIMES LITERARY SUPPLEMENT (Lond), 17 Nov 1927, p. 835.
The papers in *Castles in Spain and Other Screeds* "make up together something like a *confessio fidei* from a writer who in novel or play . . . has never really had any narrower subject than the ultimate meaning of life." He "blends a Morrisian preference for the craftsman with a more immediately realistic sense of the need for 'life on the land' " in order to make England strong and safe. The book contains the substance of JG's philosophy expressed in "plainer statements than plays or stories permit."

1178 "Mr. Galsworthy's Verses," TIMES LITERARY SUPPLEMENT (Lond), 24 March 1927, p. 211.
Most of the poems in *Verses, New and Old* are occasional; many are about nature. "It is tempting to call the poems about nature sentimental, not in order to describe them definitely, but to limit the field of description. Thus, if they are sentimental they cannot be classical—that is to say, they are emotional rather than reasonable, or inspired by reason." "He is not a phrase maker nor has he a great mastery of rhythm. He does not use conceits or metaphors and his figures and images are as often as not overladen with too much poetical association."

1179 Muir, Edwin. "Verse," NATION AND ATHENAEUM, XL (22 Jan 1927), 568.
Verses, New and Old is sentimental at worst, "pleasantly epigrammatic" at best.

1180 Myers, Walter L. THE LATER REALISM (Chicago: University of Chicago P, 1927), pp. 4, 5, 83, 97, 107, 114–18, 131–34, 146–47.

JG is to be praised for his ability to individualize his characters and for his ability to establish identity by visual means. JG's characters compare favorably to D. H. Lawrence's; Lawrence's characters frequently exhibit a "lack of center" or typicality.

1181 "New Books in Brief Review," INDEPENDENT, CXIX (19 Nov 1927), 509.
[A favorable one-paragraph notice of the publication of *Escape*.]

1182 Omicron. "Plays and Pictures," NATION AND ATHENAEUM, XLI (23 July 1927), 547–48.
Some of the dialogue and the two drunken scenes in *Windows* seem superfluous, but there is fine discourse between mother and son in act two. [Review of performance at the Everyman Theatre.]

1183 Pence, Raymond Woodbury (ed). DRAMAS BY PRESENT-DAY WRITERS (NY: Charles Scribner's Sons, 1927), p. 61.
[Brief biographical note, followed by the text of *Loyalties*.]

1184 "Poetry. *Verses New and Old*," SATURDAY REVIEW OF LITERATURE (NY), III (5 Feb 1927), 569.
[Brief, negative review of the "sentimentalized and trite" poetry that appears in *Verses, New and Old*.]

1185 Reely, Mary Katharine. "A Selected List of Current Books: *Verses New and Old*," WISCONSIN LIBRARY BULLETIN (Madison), XXIII (March 1927), 77.
[Inconsequential review.]

1186 Ross, Betty. "Galsworthy on Love," NEW YORK HERALD TRIBUNE MAGAZINE, 6 Feb 1927, pp. 1–2.
JG believes women should have careers if they want them. Equal opportunity is the main point, just as self-respect was the real value in the struggle for woman's suffrage. Beauty is not the key to the enjoyment of life; unself-consciousness is. One avoids self-consciousness by losing oneself completely in what one is doing and feeling. [An interview.]

1187 Ross, Hugh. "The Prophets II.—John Galsworthy," NEW AGE, 25 Aug 1927, p. 198.
JG, "born a moralist," is serene and fair; he blames no one. His plays have no catharsis; consequently he irritates rather than satisfies his audience. JG is "a moralist troubled by an artistic conscience . . . a prophet cursed with a logical mind." His dice are always loaded, despite his reputation for impartiality: he "enlists the sympathy of the spectator and then betrays it." *The Show* is a case in point: the people with whom he is infuriated are the ones he is "bound in fairness to exonerate." JG's tragedy is the "tragedy of weakness and misunderstanding and unimaginative selfishness," neither romantic nor classical. Technically, JG

is excellent in his presentation of "natural dialogue" and flawless construction—but to JG the message is the important thing. He "in part has allowed art to subdue him. Thus he . . . has mistaken his vocation. For he was born a moralist." [A short but penetrating argument.]

1188 Rüegg, August. "Galsworthy im Zenith" (Galsworthy at the Zenith), SCHWEIZERISCHE RUNDSCHAU, (Stans, Switzerland), XXVII (1927), 334–42.

The White Monkey gives a picture of family emancipation and disintegration. The main action interlaces the vulgar social stratum and its contrasting views contrapuntally. *Monkey* exhibits a mastery of the social-ethical idea. *The Silver Spoon,* however, is not as well balanced. It is clear that JG scorns Fleur and Mont. From his merciless acidity regarding them, it seems as though he were angered by their scandalous and dilletante ways. The Mephistophelian spirit of Negation rules in *Spoon.* JG's critical spirit is not balanced by a joy in life. Although it is possible that England may be in a period of moral depression, it is more likely that England is in a transitional situation. [In German.]

1189 Sampson, George. "The Audit of Mr. Galsworthy," BOOKMAN (Lond), LXXII (April 1927), 30–31.

R. H. Coats "audits" rather than "criticizes" JG, with clarity, balance, and imperturbability. But Coats incorrectly argues that JG is impartial, for JG tampers with the scales. JG's gift to the stage is not that he is "impartial or pitiful or sympathetic" but that he knows how to make "a strong, squarely-built stage play "that sustains audience interest and "wins most of their feelings and some of their judgments." *A Bit o' Love* shows JG's vital weakness—an "indeterminate pity—a sympathy with the feeble for their very feebleness, and with the characterless for their lack of character. Real pity has a firmer outline than [JG] . . . gives it." JG lacks the faith necessary for real tragedy, which has its roots in religion or in poetry. That JG does not have the creative spirit of poetry makes him a good playwright rather than a great dramatist. [Review of R. H. Coats, JOHN GALSWORTHY AS A DRAMATIC ARTIST (NY: Scribners, 1926), with a photo of JG by Henry B. Goodman.]

1190 Sayler, Oliver M. "The Play of the Week. *Escape,* " SATURDAY REVIEW OF LITERATURE (NY), IV (12 Nov 1927), 299–300.

Escape, at NY's Booth Theatre, is one of JG's best, fitting R. H. Coats's six categories of sincerity, sympathy, impartiality, irony, pity and indignation, and artistry. Especially artistic is JG's handling of quick entrances and exits of characters.

1191 Selver, P. "Englischer Brief" (Letter from England), DIE LITERATUR (Stuttgart), XXX (1927–28), 721–23.

Lawrence's criticism of JG in Rickword's SCRUTINIES is hardly convincing. [In German.]

1192 Shore, W. Teignmouth. "An Intimate Chat with Galsworthy," WORLD REVIEW (Mount Morris, Ill), IV (28 March 1927), 124.
[Commonplace literary chitchat, rptd from the DEARBORN INDEPENDENT (no other information about the INDEPENDENT is given).]

1193 Simrell, V. I. "John Galsworthy: The Artist as Propagandist," QUARTERLY JOURNAL OF SPEECH EDUCATION, XIII (June 1927), 225–36.
Propaganda is not rightly opposed to art. "An exaggerated opinion has as little power to persuade the mind as a disproportioned statue has to attract the eye." The view that in JG's plays the audience is the villain has arisen not because JG doubts "our impulses" but rather because he is convinced "of our lack of understanding." The Greeks relied on pity and fear, whereas the appeal in the modern theater is aimed at understanding. The propagandist who appeals to the intelligence of his audience must do so effectively and intelligently. An important principle of JG's work which makes his art and propaganda ring true is his sense of proportion in conception, in portrayal, and in the moods which color the portrayal. Although JG uses specific problems, he does not lose universality. In *Strife* the real point is not between capital and labor; "it is between understanding and strife, between means and extremes."

1194 Trueblood, Charles K. "The Art of Revelation," DIAL (NY), LXXXIII (Aug 1927), 165–67.
Only occasionally in his works does JG go beyond the criticism of life to the higher calling of art that is the creation of life. His novels are pervaded by the sense of "what ought to be," frequently neglecting character development (the "real business of the novelist") to develop situations that show a character's weakness. [Review of the Grove ed: *Beyond, A Saint's Progress, The Dark Flower, The Freelands, The Island Pharisees, The Patrician, Fraternity,* and *The Country House,* directing attention to JG's prefaces.]

1195 *"Verses New and Old,"* A.L.A. BOOKLIST, XXIII (April 1927), 304.
[Brief notice of publication.]

1196 *"Verses New and Old,"* DIAL (Chicago), LXXXIII (Aug 1927), 174.
[Pejorative review of *Verses, New and Old,* concluding that JG lacks everything a great poet has except "integrity and gravity"—and the latter is sometimes in short supply.]

1197 Wells, H. G. MEANWHILE (NY: George H. Doran, 1927), p. 250; 2nd ed (Lond: Ernest Benn, 1962), p. 175.
In Soames Forsyte (*The Forsyte Saga*), JG has described accurately the type of men who run the English government.

1198 Wertheimer, Paul. "Das neue Drama John Galsworthy" (John Galsworthy's New Play), NEUE FREIE PRESSE (Vienna), 15 Feb 1927, pp. 10–11.

Though not tightly structured and occasionally boring, *Escape* is even more humane than *Justice*. Its production by Deutsches Volkstheater was a great success. [In German.]

1199 Wilson, Edmund. "The Social Dramatist," NEW REPUBLIC, XLIX (9 Feb 1927), 335–36.

Humor, flavor, and spirit compensate for lack of structure in *Old English. The Forest* and *The Show* lack these saving qualities, where the characters primarily are contrasting types. JG has no deep criticism, and some of his plays give the reader the old-fashioned social problem play at its least desirable. [Review of *Plays. Sixth Series*; *Representative Plays*; *Verses, New and Old*; and R. H. Coats's JOHN GALSWORTHY AS A DRAMATIC ARTIST (1926).]

1200 Wolff, E. "Galsworthy," HAMBURGER FREMDENBLATT, No. 14 (1927), 8 [not seen].

[Listed in BIBLIOGRAPHIE DER DEUTSCHEN ZEITSCHRIFTEN LITERATUR, 1927 (Leipzig: Felix Dietrich, 1928).] [In German.]

1201 Wolff, Lucien. "M. Galsworthy Conteur" (Mr. Galsworthy, Storyteller), REVUE ANGLO-AMÉRICAINE, V (Oct 1927), 10–28.

In all his work JG satirizes by implication or opposition; direct satire is rare. "It is always as a poet that JG handles the indifference of Nature to its creation." The short story "Timber" (*"Futaies à vendre"*) is one of the really impressive stories that depict JG's mysticism. The secret of his art is found in the contrast between JG as the mystic poet of life and human psychology and JG the exacting realist. The weaknesses that can sometimes be seen in his work are as follows: (1) he tries too hard for certain effects; (2) at times he is too puritanical; (3) his righteous hate against property has a romantic allure which is plainly passé; (4) he idealizes the lower classes; (5) his deep pity occasionally becomes sentimentality; (6) his efforts at direct ridicule usually fail. Of the great contemporary English writers JG best satisfies French taste. His sense of proportion and his conciseness recall Flaubert and Maupassant. *Caravan* is an excellent introduction to JG's work because it is concise, it offers a harmonization of his thought, it gives a clearer picture of the balance of artistic values than do the novels, and it shows the most recent manner of JG. [In French.]

1202 Wyatt, Euphemia van Rensselaer. "The Drama. *Escape*," CATHOLIC WORLD, CXXVI (Dec 1927), 379–80.

Escape at the Booth Theatre is JG's finest play, economical in words and rich in ideas. The fugitive thematically unites otherwise unrelated scenes. Denant finds freedom in surrender within a Christian framework. [Wyatt strains to find Christian salvation somewhere.]

1203 Young, Stark. "With Leslie Howard," NEW REPUBLIC, LII (9 Nov 1927), 311–12.
Escape at NY's Booth Theatre begins with "leisurely security," builds to a "delicious suspense" for a few scenes, "simmers down" to a series of one-act pieces that are variations on the theme of justice and human habits of mind, and ends "pleasantly" tragically. JG contrives scenes successfully, but the play does not develop beyond "talented facility and expert novelism."

1204 Z., Iu. *"Ostrov fariseev"* (*The Island Pharisees*), MOLODAIA GVARDIIA, No. 2 (1927), 207 [not seen].
[Review of a translation of *The Island Pharisees*.] [In Russian.]

1928

1205 Aiken, Conrad. "The Last of the Forsytes," NEW REPUBLIC, LVI (10 Oct 1928), 221–22; rptd in A REVIEWER'S ABC: COLLECTED CRITICISM FROM 1916 TO THE PRESENT (NY: Meridian Books, 1958), pp. 313–17.
Austen, Trollope, and JG combine to give a continuum of English social life, presenting the wholeness of the social picture with "something of the un-exaggerative detachment of the sociologist." But JG is more interested in the "thing said" than in the manner of saying it; he seems too often to describe his characters rather than let them live; and he uses coincidence too often.
In *Swan Song,* the focus throughout is on the approaching love scene of Jon and Fleur, but when it finally arrives, it is totally inadequate. This illustrates JG's gravest fault—the tendency to think his way "by sheer intelligence into situations which he has not sufficient psychological insight to feel."

1206 [Anthony, Luther B.] *"Escape,"* DRAMATIST (Easton, Pa), XIX (Jan 1928), 1363–64.
Escape fails because drama needs two combatants: *Escape* has only one on the stage. JG continues his record of being unable to write believable drama.

1207 B., R. "A Good Play Spoiled," NEW STATESMAN, XXXI (18 Aug 1928), 588–89.
The revival of *Loyalties* at Wyndham's Theatre presents JG's subtly accurate conflict between the standards of the practical and proud Jew and the "public school service-club class," but he leaves too much for the actors to do and, with the exception of Leon Lion as De Levis, very few are able to perform successfully. The meaning of *Loyalties'* last line is not clear.

1208 Benchley, Robert. "Bedtime Plays," LIFE (NY), XCI (2 Feb 1928), 21.

To revive *The Silver Box* now permits a reviewer to catch up on his sleep. A play about a lost fraternity pin would have "a first act as exciting as Mr. Galsworthy's." With some dialogue "about the Trusts having probably stolen it we could also approximate the social philosophy of *The Silver Box*." The play is "tepid."

1209 Bickley, Francis. "A Galsworthy Bibliography," BOOKMAN (Lond), LXXV (Dec 1928), 157–58.
Not only has H. V. Marrot supplied in his A BIBLIOGRAPHY OF THE WORKS OF JOHN GALSWORTHY the expected collation, but he has also noted such items as the date of publication, the description of the bindings, and the number of copies made.

1210 Birrell, Francis. "New Novels," NATION AND ATHENAEUM, XLIII (14 July 1928), 499–500.
Swan Song will probably bring to a close the Victorian novel as well as *The Forsyte Saga*. *Song* is "continually a comment, never a construction . . . like reading a series of leading articles." The Forsytes seldom really talk about anything; rather, they live in a grey limbo of understatement. *Saga* is filled with love, but JG lacks the artistic ability to make us suffer with the lovers. JG is popular despite the absence of beauty and form in his work. Americans like him primarily as an "annalist," just as the British prefer Dreiser. [Reviewer's enigmatic comments of dismissal about Soames's (and JG's) taste in art tell more about Birrell's tastes than JG's.]

1211 Brickell, Herschel. "The Literary Landscape," NORTH AMERICAN REVIEW, CCXXV (Jan 1928), [n.p.].
[Brief notice of publication of *Escape*.]

1212 Brickell, Herschel. "The Literary Landscape," NORTH AMERICAN REVIEW, CCXXVI (Sept 1928), [n.p.].
[Brief notice of publication of *Swan Song*.]

1213 Brother Leo. ENGLISH LITERATURE: A SURVEY AND A COMMENTARY (Bost: Ginn & Co., 1928), pp. 653–54, 668–71, 681.
In the twentieth century, drama in England is dominated by Shaw, Barrie, and JG. JG "is the most many-sided author of our generation." His ablest contribution to prose fiction is *The Forsyte Saga*. There are two strands in *Saga;* the one involves those who are practical and hard-hearded, and the other, those who are dreamers and lovers of beauty. Although the series of Forsyte novels is not yet complete, the series "is an extended allegory suggesting the softening and enriching function of art in modern life."

1214 Brown, Ivor. "Fancy Free and Fancy Freakish," SATURDAY REVIEW (Lond), CXLVI (10 Nov 1928), 604–5.
The "queer stuff" of 1905 now causes "undergraduates to yawn." Yet *The Silver Box* at the Everyman Theatre is a repertory classic.

1215 Brown, Ivor. "John Galsworthy, Dramatist," BOOKMAN (Lond), LXXV (Dec 1928), 151–56.
[JG's dramatic works and connections with the Barker-Vedrenne management are reviewed; six photographs of scenes from *Joy, The Skin Game, Strife,* and *Justice* are included. JG's dramatic method "has been a great source of strength to the new English theatre."]

1216 Brown, John Mason. "Tragedy, Comedy, Pastoral," THEATRE ARTS MONTHLY (NY), XII (Jan 1928), 7–20; rptd in THEATRE ARTS MONTHLY, ed by Rosamund Gilder et al. (NY: Theater Art Books, 1950), pp. 606–7.
Unlike in his other dramas, JG in *Escape* is not trying to "reform the statute book"; rather, he is interested in the "agony of the pursued," who is a victim of bad luck. Matt Denant's escape is followed by nine uneven scenes that evolve with "gnawing crescendo," fulfilling the JG dictum of the performance of the "spire of meaning." Winthrop Ames produced the play; Leslie Howard acted the role of Matt Denant.

1217 Cajumi, Arrigo. "Galsworthy Minore" (Lesser Works of Galsworthy), LA FIERA LETTERARIA (Milan, Rome), IV (26 Aug 1928), 4.
Increased opportunities for readers to know JG's works permit one to explore and define the characteristics of his art. His theater remains almost unknown in Italy. A work like "A Man of Devon" indicates the tenuousness of his themes, the lack of a strong central plot, and the predilection for character analysis. The influence of Maupassant and Turgenev are clear. To understand JG's lyricism, one should read "A Portrait," *Captures,* "A Feud," "The Man Who Kept His Form." Certain aspects of his art are difficult for the continental reader—the poetic tonality of his landscapes and the very Englishness of his work. The following characteristics of his art are especially significant: the seriousness and subtlety of many scenes; the very careful composition; the use of dialogue not as a means of furthering the action but rather as a means of revealing and delineating characters and events; the sobriety and inner dignity; and the reasons and motives for idealizing and satirizing the lost world of the Victorians. Frequently in his minor works JG theorizes about his experiences, his memories of his literary life, and his artistic beliefs: for example, *The Inn of Tranquillity, Castles in Spain,* "A Novelist's Allegory," and "On Expression." These revelations are interesting and helpful. [In Italian.]

1218 Carb, David. "Seen on the Stage," VOGUE (NY), LXXI (15 March 1928), 98–99, 146, 158.
The Silver Box, in its NY revival, still has appeal. JG's treatment of dual justice (for rich and poor) is more mature than most dramatists' because he insists on a balanced presentation.

1219 Connolly, Cyril. "New Novels," NEW STATESMAN, XXXI (18 Aug 1928), 591–92.

Swan Song fails because Soames has become "hopelessly overtired." Comments on current affairs take the place of "the continuous performance in an empty cinema," which is the thought process of real people. JG lacks a stream-of-consciousness technique to make the satire believable. *Swan Song* is unsatisfactory because of mediocrity of comment, woodenness of character, and equivocal attitudes toward modern society. JG erred in *The Forsyte Saga* by not continuing to satirize the Forsytes; instead he made the Forsytes—limited intellectually as they are—satirize others. *Swan Song* read without the rest of the *Saga* shows that "ossification" of character has aken place. [Connolly makes no attempt to distinguish between Soames and JG on ideas of the time.]

1220 Dounce, H. E. "Death of the Man of Property," NEW YORK EVENING POST, 21 July 1928, Sec. 3, p. 5.
Swan Song, likened by some to Thackeray's VANITY FAIR, is JG's "fullest expression of his remarkable catholic sympathy." The indiscriminate use of exclamation points in passages that ought not to need them, however, "suggests an effort to make the passages look more significant, and the writing more vivacious, than they are."

1221 Eaton, Walter Prichard. "New Plays for Old," NEW YORK HERALD TRIBUNE BOOKS, 1 Jan 1928, p. 10.
Escape, which abandons the well-made play technique handled so well in *Loyalties,* does not really show the usual JG desire to prove something.

1222 "The End of the Forsytes," LITERARY DIGEST, XCVIII (25 Aug 1928), 27–28.
[Excerpts from British reviewers' reactions to the greatness of *The Forsyte Saga,* on the publication of *Swan Song.*]

1223 "The End of the Forsytes," SATURDAY REVIEW OF LITERATURE (NY), IV (14 July 1928), 1029.
JG does not flirt in *Swan Song,* as young novelists do, with behaviorism and the unconscious: his fiction has "the texture and stability of nineteenth century England," very much like that of Thackeray. The unique Soames and Irene, the "late Victorian Helen," are the "sum total" of JG's contribution to the novel.

1224 *"Escape,"* A.L.A. BOOKLIST, XXIV (Jan 1928), 154.
Escape portrays various mental reactions to a convict in a "diverting and pleasant instead of tragic" drama.

1225 F., E. "Novyy roman Dzhona Golsuorsi *Lebedinaia pesn*" (A New Novel by John Galsworthy: *Swan Song*), VESNIK INOSTRANNOI LITERATURY, No. 9 (1928), 147–48 [not seen].
[Review of *Swan Song.*] [In Russian.]

1226 Fadiman, Clifton P. "The End of Soames," NATION (NY), CXXVII (29 Aug 1928), 204–5.

In *Swan Song,* JG attempts to do three things. (1) He tries to record and interpret current events, failing because characters are too familiar and too "simple-symbolic." The reader's interest is in what happens to the characters rather than in what they are. (2) He tries to portray postwar youth, faltering because he is unable to "abstract the passionately complex and essential from a contemporary world" as Proust does. (3) He tries an "artistic and symbolic conclusion" to *The Forsyte Saga,* failing because the symbolic conclusion is too slick. Soames loses tragic grandeur because of the pettiness of "piddling youngsters."

1227 Farjeon, Herbert. "The London Stage: *Loyalties,*" GRAPHIC (Lond), CXXI (18 Aug 1928), 262.
JG is "too much a gentleman" to be a really good artist, because he never lets himself go far enough emotionally or psychologically. In *Loyalties* at Wyndham's Theatre, the theft of £1000 from De Levis in the circumstances presented by JG strains credulity. JG could have developed better the irony that the loyalty of Captain Dancy's wife (to the ideal she has of him) leads to his destruction. On the whole, however, *Loyalties* is a bright spot in a drab season.

1228 Gabriel, Gilbert W. "How to Know a Good Play," MENTOR (Springfield, Ohio), XV (Jan 1928), 33–38.
[Caption under a Herbert photo of JG comments on the playwright's distinctive plays *Justice, Loyalties,* and *Escape.*]

1229 Gadalina, V. "S predisl, *Sdaetsia v naem*" (Foreword, *To Let*), trans by N. Bol'pin (Riga: Literatura, 1928) [not seen].
[In Russian.]

1230 "Galsworthy, John. *Swan Song,*" PRATT INSTITUTE QUARTERLY BOOKLIST, Autumn 1928, p. 43.
[Brief notice of publication.]

1231 "Galsworthy's *Plays:* Collected in Single Volume of 700 Pages," SPRINGFIELD REPUBLICAN (Mass), 28 Nov 1928, p. 10.
[Brief technical description of printing technique, type, content, etc., of *Plays.*]

1232 Grabo, Carl H. THE TECHNIQUE OF THE NOVEL (NY: Charles Scribner's Sons, 1928), pp. 60–64, 138, 263, 291.
JG is exasperating in "embroidering his human *leit motif* with a canine counterpart" and in "ostentatiously contrasting" his "lyrical descriptions of nature . . . with the pettiness of man." JG's characters primarily represent "types, classes, and intellectual points of view," but they are well-defined "types and mouthpieces." Both characters and social atmosphere are clearly and quickly drawn in the initial scene of *The Country House,* which has a neatly formed plot; but the "descriptive passages are too often things apart," not truly integrated into the novel as a whole. The major flaws of *House* are the discussion of English divorce law that is "too purely critical and expository to have narrative interest"

and the intrusiveness of the author. The "expressionist" JG is "the modern man of feeling brushing aside the furtive tear."

1233 Grein, J. T. "Galsworthy in a New Dramatic Form," ILLUS-TRATED LONDON NEWS, CLXXIII (15 Dec 1928), 1128.
Simplified presentations of drama have been increasing (e.g., play-readings); Ruth Draper and Elspeth Douglas-Reid write "dramalogues" and impersonate them; and now Miss Eva Saunderson has developed " 'mono-playing,' " a form of dramatization in which she acts the entire play herself. Having performed several of Shaw's plays in this manner, she recently with JG's approval performed *The Skin Game*. The performance was a great effort and success.

1234 Hansen, Harry. "The First Reader: Meditations on John Galsworthy's Soames Forsyte, Events Seen from the Desk of the Literary Editor," NEW YORK WORLD, 15 July 1928, Sec. M, p. 7.
Soames Forsyte is a part of England and a large part of JG in *Swan Song*.

1235 Hartley, L. P. *"Swan Song,"* SATURDAY REVIEW (Lond), CXLVI (14 July 1928), 54–56.
Swan Song brings *The Forstye Saga* to an adequate, but "not perhaps a glorious, conclusion." The best passages are outside the main purpose (Stainford, for example); JG continues his habit of using schoolboy slang. His work generally maintains a "high average," but there are few peaks.

1236 Hartley, L. P. *"Two Forsyte Interludes,"* SATURDAY REVIEW (Lond), CXLV (11 Feb 1928), 170–71.
[The review states briefly the theme and place of *Two Forsyte Interludes* in *The Forsyte Saga.*]

1237 Hutchison, Percy. "Galsworthy Closes an Account. *Swan Song* Brings to an End the Social Epic of the Forsytes," NEW YORK TIMES SUNDAY REVIEW OF BOOKS, 15 July 1928, pp. 1, 18.
That JG knows well the human heart, understands well the human mind, and is sensitive to human feeling and passion is especially evident in *Swan Song*, where Soames sees Irene in Washington. The novel's main contrast is in Michael the Georgian forgiving Fleur's transgressions, whereas Soames the Victorian could not forgive Irene's. *Swan Song*, "impressive in its maturity of artistic power . . . faithful in its development and consummation," is a crown for the earlier novels: *The Forsyte Saga* will endure. [Review of *Swan Song* and *Two Forsyte Interludes.*]

1238 "John Galsworthy," DAS NEUE REICH (Innsbruch, Vienna, Munich), X (14 July 1928), 888–89.
[Summarizes Erwin Stranik's essay in NEUE SCHWEIZER RUNDSCHAU (June 1928) and points out that JG, like Thomas Mann, is an ironic realist who tends to repeat himself. While *The Forsyte Saga* is JG's most important work, his plays

are not so bad as Stranik believes, especially if one compares them to Shaw's superficialities. Beside Dibelius's book on England, JG's works offer the best introduction to the spirit of the English.] [In German.]

1239 Kahn, H. "Galsworthy und Kein Ende" (Galsworthy and No End), SCHAU-INS-LAND, XXIV (1928?), 490 [not seen].
[Listed in BIBLIOGRAPHIE DER DEUTSCHEN ZEITSCHRIFTEN LITERATUR, 1928 (Leipzig: Felix Dietrich, 1929).] [In German.]

1240 Klavehn, Carl. "Galsworthy's Message on Education," DIE NEUEREN SPRACHEN (Marburg), XXXVI (Nov 1928), 481–90.
"It is by the personality behind his work, and because his books are not the products of his study, but the outcry of a heart in pain through the closest contact with the world, that JG exercises his strong and ennobling influence upon all who are ready to listen." [A lecture in English to a teachers' conference in Bavaria.]

1241 Knapp, Otto. "John Galsworthy," HOCHLAND (Munich, Kempten), XXVI (Oct 1928), 81–95.
As a realist JG is distinguished by his humanism, the finest flower of the aristocratic culture of his country. His social criticism is permeated by pity and characterized by his unfulfilled longing for love, passion, and beauty. *The Forsyte Saga* is the core of his *oeuvre*, whereas the plays are too calculated. JG's influence outside England is greater than that of Shaw and Wells. He lacks, however, the penetrating power of the truly original poet who sounds the mysteries of life. [A survey of JG's works and themes.] [In German.]

1242 Lann, E. "Dzhon Golsuorsi" (John Galsworthy), KRASNAIA PANORAMA, No. 49 (1928), p. 10 [not seen].
[In Russian.]

1243 Lawrence, D. H. "John Galsworthy," SCRUTINIES BY VARIOUS WRITERS, comp by Edgell Rickword (Lond: Wishart, 1928); rptd (1931; Lond: Heinemann Educational Books, 1956; Lond: Mercury Books, 1961; Lond: Heinemann Educational Paperbacks, 1967), pp. 118–31; rptd in PHOENIX: POSTHUMOUS PAPERS, ed by Edward D. McDonald (NY: Viking, 1936), pp. 539–50; rptd in SELECTED LITERARY CRITICISM, ed by Anthony Beal (NY: Viking, 1956), pp. 118–31.
None of the Forsytes is "a really vivid human being. They are social beings." One cannot escape a sense of dissatisfaction with them. A human being is one who has "the sense of being at one with the great universe-continuum," and the social being is one who has lost "his naïve at-oneness with the living universe"; "he falls into a state of fear and tries to insure himself with wealth." For social beings material salvation is the only salvation. The Forsytes who rebel against money are only "anti-materialists," and they are not different from the materialists. All of JG's characters are "social beings, positive and negative." *The Man of Property* has elements of a "very great novel, a very great satire," but JG

lacked the courage to carry it through. The sentimentalizing of Old Jolyon and the love affair of Irene and Bosinney are fatal blemishes. Today's tragedy "is that men are only materially and socially conscious. They are unconscious of their own manhood, and so they let it be destroyed."

There "is nothing but Forsyte in Galsworthy's books. . . . every character is determined by money." His treatment of passion is "nothing but a doggish amorousness and a sort of anti-Forsytism." His heroes are afflicted with "chronic narcissism" and know "just three types of women: the Pendyce mother [Mrs. Pendyce, *The Country House*], prostitute to property; the Irene [*Man of Property*], the essential *anti*-prostitute, the floating, flaunting female organ; and the social woman, the mere lady." "Bosinney and Irene are more dishonest and more indecent than Soames and Winifred." The promise of the early novels, *The Island Pharisees, The Man of Property,* and *Fraternity* fizzled out, and the later novels are "purely commercial." [This provocative and often impish essay touched the fancy of the younger generation of critics and has played a major role in influencing JG criticism.]

1244 Marble, Annie Russell. A STUDY OF THE MODERN NOVEL BRITISH AND AMERICAN SINCE 1900 (NY & Lond: D. Appleton, 1928), pp. 4, 7, 78–81, 302.

JG, read primarily for his character analysis, is a "sincere, restrained critic and photographer of society in upper middle-class England." As a novelist, he is both "observer and diagnostician," who holds the "mirror of fiction" before modern life. Unlike Moore and Joyce "he is not a surgeon"; unlike Wells "he is not a philosopher or propagandist." [Biographical sketch and half-sentence encapsulations of his works.]

1245 Marrot, H. V. A BIBLIOGRAPHY OF THE WORKS OF JOHN GALSWORTHY (Lond: Elkin Mathews & Marrot, 1928; NY: Scribner, 1928); rptd (NY: Burt Franklin, 1968; Folcroft, Pa: Folcroft Library Editions, 1973).

[The bibliography is an uncritical one. It includes first English and American eds to date, translations, and periodicals which contain work by or about JG.]

1246 Marrot, H. V. A NOTE ON JOHN GALSWORTHY, DRAMATIST (Lond: Elkin Mathews & Marrot, 1928) [not seen, but see item 1318 for possible duplication].

1247 Martin, W. G. "Mr. John Galsworthy," HUMBERSIDE (Hull, England), III (1928), 11–22 [not seen].

1248 Maurice, Arthur. "Scanning the New Books," MENTOR (Springfield, Ohio), XVI (Sept 1928), 60.

[Brief notice of publication of *Swan Song,* accompanied by Doris Ulmann's photograph of JG.]

1249 Mayer, Jacob. "Zur Situation des englischen Romans— Gelegentlich *The White Monkey* by John Galsworthy" (Concerning English Novels: *The White Monkey* by John Galsworthy), ZUR INTERPRETATION DES GEGENWÄRTIGEN MENSCHEN (On the Interpretation of Contemporary Men) (Berlin-Itzehoe: Gottfried Martin, 1928), pp. 79–85.

JG chooses to see in the constancy of human nature a guarantee for the solution to contemporary problems. [In German.]

1250 Muir, Edwin. THE STRUCTURE OF THE NOVEL (Lond: Hogarth, 1928; NY: Harcourt, Brace, 1929), pp. 116–25; new ed (1957); rptd (1961, 1963).

There are several categories of the novel: the novel of action, the novel of character, the picaresque novel, the dramatic novel, the chronicle, and the period novel. At the present time [1928] the chronicle is the "ruling convention," and novels like SONS AND LOVERS, A PORTRAIT OF THE ARTIST AS A YOUNG MAN, and JACOB'S ROOM are "perhaps the best chronicles that have appeared in recent years." The period novel, while superficially resembling the chronicle, does not try to show human truths as valid for all time; instead, it is concerned with showing a society at a particular time of transition. "The bondage of the novel to period has naturally degraded it." Representative period novels are Bennett's CLAYHANGER trilogy, JG's *The Forsyte Saga,* Wells's THE NEW MACHIAVELLI, and Dreiser's "records of American life." That *Saga* is historically true will not matter in twenty years. The period novel is already outmoded and dying out. It is not an aesthetic form; "drawing a picture of the contemporary changes in society . . . is not literature, but journalism."

1251 Nathan, George Jean. "Galsworthy's Swan Song," AMERICAN MERCURY, XIII (Jan 1928), 118–20; rptd in ART OF NIGHT (NY & Lond: Knopf, 1928; Rutherford, NJ: Fairleigh Dickinson UP, 1972) pp. 198– 203; rptd in THE MAGIC MIRROR: SELECTED WRITINGS ON THE THEATRE BY GEORGE JEAN NATHAN, ed by Thomas Quinn Curtiss (NY: Knopf, 1960), pp. 61, 188, 192–95.

Escape, a "valentine drama" dripping with sentimentality, is a poor choice for JG's swan song for the theater. He has never written a poorer play; all he does is "to ask sociological questions of the kindergarten class." JG's eminence in drama is due to the "dignity of his emotions" rather than to the dignity of his thought.

1252 Neumann, Henry. "Where Galsworthy and Governor Smith Would Agree," STANDARD (NY), XIV:6 (Feb 1928), 161–65.

JG and Governor Smith would agree that rehabilitation of criminals needs serious study. *Escape* dramatizes the question whether it is better for the offender and for society if the offender is turned over to the authorities. [The main purpose of this article is to support Governor Smith's recommendations for studying the treatment and rehabilitation of criminals.]

1253 "New Books in Brief Review: *Swan Song,*" INDEPENDENT (Bost), CXXI (18 Aug 1928), 165.

In *Swan Song* JG "has not been led afield by the postwar mania for spotlighting minutia, supporting life with the unstable props of bedroom farce." He portrays life "in the shifting perspective of actuality."

1254 "New Novels. *Swan Song,*" TIMES LITERARY SUPPLEMENT (Lond), 19 July 1928, p. 534.

Swan Song is primarily a mechanical commentary on contemporary events. Both JG's art and Soames's personality have lost vitality. *The Forsyte Saga* ends sentimentally; Michael Mont is not the appropriate person to mourn the passing of Forsyteism.

1255 O., A. B. "Galsworthy Ends His Forsyte Saga: The 'Sense of Property' Adjusted to a New Age—The Civic Conscience," SPRINGFIELD REPUBLICAN (Mass), 29 July 1928, Sec. F, p. 7.

Character portraits of *Swan Song* will survive the types themselves.

1256 Omicron. "Plays and Pictures," NATION AND ATHENAEUM, XLII (28 Jan 1928), 649–50.

[Brief, favorable review of *The Eldest Son* at the Everyman Theatre, emphasizing its excellent technical quality and JG's usual fairness.]

1257 Omicron. "Plays and Pictures," NATION AND ATHENAEUM, XLIII (14 July 1928), 495.

Justice is unfortunately a museum piece; characters are merely types; symbolism is expressed largely in terms of photographic realism. [Review of performance at Wyndham's Theatre.]

1258 Omicron. "Plays and Pictures," NATION AND ATHENAEUM, XLIII (18 Aug 1928), 648.

Leon Lion is valiant in trying to revive *Loyalties,* but the production and acting are mediocre. [Review of performance at Wyndham's Theatre.]

1259 Paterson, Isabel. "Heirs and Assigns," NEW YORK HERALD TRIBUNE BOOKS, 15 July 1928, pp. 1–2.

The theme of *The Forsyte Saga,* "so admirably sustained through half a dozen rounded tales and several generations," is not merely ended in *Swan Song:* everything develops "naturally from events already on record without depending on them for explanation."

1260 Raymond, E. T. [Edward Raymond Thompson]. "Literary Swashbucklers and Sentimentalists," in PORTRAITS OF THE NEW CENTURY: THE FIRST TEN YEARS (Lond: Ernest Benn, 1928), pp. 38–62.

JG's plays "are brilliantly drawn indictments; his novels eloquent pleadings." Although there is a tremendous amount of mere fact in his works, his characters are seldom alive. One feels sorry for him.

1261 Reely, Mary Katharine. "A Selected List of Current Books: *Plays*," WISCONSIN LIBRARY BULLETIN (Madison), XXIV (Dec 1928), 343.
[A one-paragraph notice of publication of *Plays*.]

1262 Reely, Mary Katharine. "A Selected List of Current Books: *Swan Song*," WISCONSIN LIBRARY BULLETIN (Madison), XXIV (Oct 1928), 253.
The character of Soames is the outstanding aspect of *Swan Song* specifically and *The Forsyte Saga* generally. [Brief review.]

1263 Robbins, Frances Lamont. "A Proper Champion," OUTLOOK (NY), CIL (1 Aug 1928), 552–53.
Swan Song and *Two Forsyte Interludes* add to the impression that JG's total work is the measure of his greatness, which shows his vast knowledge of the human heart. JG appears to be the last in the line of British novelists of manners in the tradition of Fielding, Austen, Thackeray, and Trollope. *Swan Song*, showing JG's detachment, "irony without bitterness or superiority," and "compassion without softness," can survive without the rest of *The Forsyte Saga*.

1264 Schaffner, Halle. "The End of an Era," SURVEY, LXI (1 Oct 1928), 43.
The younger Forsytes in *Swan Song* are "milder" than old Soames, lacking "edge." Soames emerges "admirable in restraint," human in his capacity to endure; but he remains tragically inarticulate. As the "tragically inarticulate" Forsytes parade before us, "our egoism . . . [becomes] their egoism; our sense of property no less confirmed." JG remains "pure crystal" in his style.

1265 Schalit, Leon. JOHN GALSWORTHY: DER MENSCH UND SEIN WERK (John Galsworthy: The Man and His Work) (Berlin: P. Zsolnay, 1928); trans as JOHN GALSWORTHY: A SURVEY (NY: Scribner's; Lond: Heinemann, 1929).
JG's whole technique is indirect; he is a "thorough, painfully exact, often grey realist" and at the same time "a mystic, a symbolist, a lyrist with a lofty conception of Art." In *The Country House*, for example, JG uses the lyric and poetic descriptions of the scenery to counterbalance the bigotry of the unimaginative, tradition-bound Pendyces. "The landscape is given a soul as it were, becomes alive, participates in the action." The main claim for his art lies in the blending of the lyric poet and the ironic satirist and social critic. JG was primarily influenced by Turgenev's technique and Maupassant's irony. [Detailed synopses and criticism of JG's work from *Villa Rubein* through *A Modern Comedy*, including the plays and short fiction, are given. Being the major translator of JG's

work into German, Schalit knew and corresponded with JG, and he provides a number of personal impressions and insights about JG.]

1266 Schriftgiesser, Karl. "John Galsworthy Ends the Forsyte Saga," BOSTON EVENING TRANSCRIPT BOOK SECTION, 14 July 1928, p. 4.
Swan Song, the best of the three postwar Forsyte novels, fails to equal the quality of the original volumes that comprise *The Forsyte Saga;* but it does surpass *The White Monkey* and *The Silver Spoon.* JG's manner of presenting the outward looks and inner feelings of people is excellent.

1267 Seldes, Gilbert. "The Theatre," DIAL, (Chicago), LXXXIV (Jan 1928), 78–83.
The boring *Escape* is six scenes too long. [Review of NY performance.]

1268 Shipp, Horace. "First Fruits of the Autumn Season," ENGLISH REVIEW, (Lond), XLVII (Oct 1928), 484–86.
Characters in *Loyalties* (at Wyndham's Theatre) are "fully revealed." It is fine drama, despite the "debatable" suicide.

1269 Stranik, Erwin. "John Galsworthy," NEUE SCHWEIZER RUNDSCHAU, XXI (1928), 459–68 [not seen].

1270 *"Swan Song,"* A.L.A. BOOKLIST, XXV (Oct 1928), 29.
In *Swan Song,* Fleur's "defeat is final, sealed by Soames's death." Strike-bound England and contemporary ideas of art and life are "reviewed . . . through Soames's mind."

1271 *"Swan Song,"* DIAL (Chicago), LXXXV (Oct 1928), 356.
The "well-contained" *Swan Song* has "eminent technique and sympathies" but does not really advance *The Forsyte Saga* much beyond *The Silver Spoon.* [Review fails to mention the evolution of Soames's character.]

1272 *"Swan Song,"* PITTSBURGH MONTHLY BULLETIN, XXXIII (Oct 1928), 428.
[Brief review.]

1273 Swinnerton, Frank. "John Galsworthy," BOOKMAN (Lond), LXXV (Dec 1928), 147–51.
Of the novelists of his generation JG "must be regarded . . . as one of the half-dozen outstanding figures."

1274 Thorogood, Horace. "Mr. Galsworthy's Englishman: The 'Beam, Beef, and Beer' Ideal," JOHN O'LONDON'S WEEKLY, XIX (18 Aug 1928), 600.
JG has no personal arrogance, but the "arrogance of race . . . of being . . . an Englishman" runs throughout his work. This is seen, for example, in Jon Forsyte's return to England after five years in America; and in Sir Lawrence

Mont's comment that the English always "hanker after beam, beef, and beer " in their leaders rather than brains. [There is much more Thorogood than JG here.]

1275 "Three Decker Novel Revived Or Omnipresent," SPRINGFIELD REPUBLICAN (Mass), 4 Aug 1928, p. 8.
[This review of *Swan Song* attempts to place JG in the long literary tradition of authors of voluminous works that includes Dreiser's AMERICAN TRAGEDY and Proust's REMEMBRANCE OF THINGS PAST.]

1276 *"Two Forsyte Interludes,"* BOSTON EVENING TRANSCRIPT BOOK SECTION, 25 Feb 1928, p. 4.
[Brief review, emphasizing the relationship of *Two Forsyte Interludes* to *The Forsyte Saga.*]

1277 *"Two Forsyte Interludes,"* LIVING AGE, CCCXXXIV (15 Feb 1928), 374.
[This brief review originally appeared in the MANCHESTER GUARDIAN (not seen).]

1278 *"Two Forsyte Interludes,"* NATION (NY), CXXVI (22 Feb 1928), 219.
[Brief notice of appearance of "Silent Wooing" and "Passers By."]

1279 *"Two Forsyte Interludes,"* PITTSBURGH MONTHLY BULLETIN, XXXIII (May 1928), 243.
[Brief review.]

1280 *"Two Forsyte Interludes,"* SATURDAY REVIEW OF LITERATURE (NY), IV (10 March 1928), 674.
[Brief mention.]

1281 Vidaković, A[leksandar]. "Umetnost Džona Golsvordija" (The Art of Galsworthy), TAMNI CVET (*The Dark Flower*), trans by A[leksandar] Vidaković, (Belgrad: Srpska knjievna madruga, 1928), pp. iii–xxx [not seen].
[In Serbo-Croatian.]

1282 Walpole, Hugh. "The End of the Forsytes," SPECTATOR (Lond), CXLI (14 July 1928), 56.
Swan Song successfully completes *The Forsyte Saga,* but it disappoints as an individual novel. JG is too obviously symbolic in having Soames lose his life trying to save his property from fire; and in having as the final tragedy Anne, Jon's wife, insisting on the same property rights that Soames had in *The Man of Property.* The novel and the saga naturally fade away "into an echo, a sigh." The beauty of *Swan Song* comes in its "restraint, economy, and pathos."

1283 Walton, Edith H. "The Elusive Novel," BOOKMAN (NY), LXVIII (Sept 1928), 97.

In *Swan Song,* JG has left the survivors in a "new, hard-paced England, less tenacious of property and seemly tranquility." Soames Forsyte dies as he lived in a way that befits a man of property: defending his art treasures and his daughter. [Brief review.]

1284 Ward, Alfred Charles. TWENTIETH CENTURY LITERATURE: THE AGE OF INTERROGATION 1901–1925 (Lond: Methuen, 1928; 2nd ed, 1940; 3rd ed, 1956; NY: Barnes & Noble, 1956), pp. 16, 26–33, 43, 71–76, 87, 88, 91, 205, 209.

While JG's subject matter sometimes suggests "a well-meaning but over-anxious aunt," his style has "cool assurance," "self-confident repose," and "persuasive charm." The "crisp . . . athletic" prose style is effective in his novels, but less effective in the dramas. Creations of beauty, sometimes of "*abstract* Beauty suspended in a clear, ethereal atmosphere" appear in such works as *The Country House, The Patrician, The Forsyte Saga.* JG's purpose as novelist is stated by Cethru in *The Inn of Tranquillity:* "to bring light to wayfarers and to compel them to take action against the evils of life." Despite his attempt at impartiality, emotions occasionally disturb his balance as he pursues the predominant theme of the "cult of the underdog." JG's world has two classes: fugitives and pursuers. The pursuers, like the fugitives, are to be pitied because they are often driven by fear. Sympathy defeats impartiality in his dramas in one of three ways: (1) choice of incident at the climax of the play—as in the death of David Roberts's wife in *Strife;* (2) an "alienating strain of blatancy" in a particular character—as in Hornblower in *The Skin Game;* and (3) "emotional weight of a 'third party' commentator"—like Cokeson in *Justice.* The opening scene of *The Silver Box* illustrates JG's control of language to get "fulness of effect" with economy of means. Economy of style and characterization go to extremes in *A Bit o' Love* and *Loyalties.* [Ward's opinions of JG remain unchanged in the second and third eds.]

1285 Wauer, Max. "John Galsworthy," DER KREIS, V (1928), 339–45.

[This brief survey of JG's work stresses his compassion, his sensibility, and his intense dislike of hypocrisy. JG is one of the few living writers worth reading.] [In German.]

1286 Weltzien, Erich. "Galsworthys Dramen als kulturkundliche Lesestoffe: I. *The Silver Box.* II. *Strife*" (The Structure of English Society as Seen in Galsworthy's Dramas: I. *The Silver Box.* II. *Strife*), ZEITSCHRIFT FUR FRANZOSISCHEN UND ENGLISCHEN UNTERRICHT, XXVII (1928), 32–47, 434–45, 570–85.

Plays like *The Silver Box* and *Strife* provide excellent opportunities for studying the structure of English society and the relationships among the English social classes. Both plays present the relationship between the prosperous middle class and the lower class as a social problem of great moment. In each, justice appears as the defender of the middle class. Anthony, in *Strife,* represents the leader who is ruthless in his opposition to the lower classes. His concern is for the broader victory—the preservation of middle-class authority rather than matters of mere profit and loss. Roberts, like Anthony, represents an extreme, and the end of *Strife* shows that victory goes to common sense, which is represented by Harness, the trade union official. [In German.]

1287 West, Rebecca. "Uncle Bennett," in THE STRANGE NECESSITY (NY: Doubleday, Doran, 1928), pp. 215–31.
In our youth the writers Wells, Shaw, JG, and Bennett "hung about the houses of our minds like Uncles." JG was "Uncle Phagocyte." Just as in the blood the phagocytes attack infection, so JG attacked the infections of the English middle class: materialism, self-righteousness, narrowness, and other "unjailable forms of hoggishness." There is a pallor in his work, but there is also the "grace of his pity, and those pages of his writing that are as lovely as the underwing of a butterfly where the message is most delicately written. . . . all in all, he is a very good uncle to have."

1288 Whyte, Frederic. WILLIAM HEINEMANN: A MEMOIR (Lond: Cape, 1928), pp. 138, 150, 213, 267.
[Brief references to JG in passing.]

1289 Wild, Friedrich. DIE ENGLISCHE LITERATUR DER GEGENWART SEIT 1870: DRAMA UND ROMAN (English Literature since 1870: The Drama and the Novel) (Wiesbaden: Dioskuren Verlag, 1928), pp. 63–69, 267–78, *et passim*.
JG's problem plays are inferior to his novels. [A sketchy survey.] [In German.]

1929

1290 Arns, Karl. "Der Abschluss der *Forsyte-Saga*. Galsworthy's Schwanengesang" (The Conclusion of *The Forsyte Saga*. Galsworthy's *Swan Song*), GERMANIA, WERK UND WERT, XXI (1929), [n.p.] [not seen].
[Listed in MODERN HUMANITIES RESEARCH ASSOCIATION BIBLIOGRAPHY, X (Cambridge: Cambridge UP, 1940).] [In German.]

1291 B., I. "New Play by Mr. Galsworthy," MANCHESTER GUARDIAN, 20 June 1929, p. 15.
JG returns to the familiar ground of favorite types and compassionate philosophy in *Exiled*. Largeness of vision is unfortunately accompanied by a "too emotional treatment" and "unabashed moralizing." [Review of a performance at Wyndham's Theatre.]

1292 B-W., J. "Mr. Galsworthy's Worst," NEW STATESMAN (Lond), XXXIII (6 July 1929), 402–3.
In *Exiled* at Wyndham's Theatre JG is sentimental despite his surface realism; Sir John and Sir Charles are "mere pasteboard figures." *Exiled* in part makes an impression on the audience because JG is "genuinely perturbed by social problems" and suffering.

1293 Bennett, Arnold. "The Progress of the Novel," REALIST, I (1 April 1929), 3–11; rptd in THE AUTHOR'S CRAFT AND OTHER CRITICAL WRITINGS OF ARNOLD BENNETT, ed by Samuel Hynes (Lincoln: University of Nebraska P, 1968), pp. 90–98.
[Bennett, who classifies the novel in various ways in this work, suggests in passing that JG is not content only to be destructive in his novels; rather, he is "full of compassion."]

1294 Birrell, Francis. "Love and Mr. Galsworthy," NATION AND ATHENAEUM, XLV (29 June 1929), 432.
Exiled offers a rather nebulous love as panacea. The play is terrible; but because JG is such a nice man, people will forgive him for being a "rather sentimental . . . trifle unreal" writer who seldom sees below the surface. [In the review of the production at Wyndham's Theatre, Birrell wonders why, with his emphasis on sex, JG has not run afoul of the censors.]

1295 Bodgener, J. H. "John Galsworthy Looks At Life," LONDON QUARTERLY REVIEW, CLII (July 1929), 73–81.
Keynotes to the JG approach to literature are clarity, conscientiousness, beauty, studious observation, and balance. These qualities are especially evident in *The Forsyte Saga,* where his main aim is to present the modern era and to demonstrate how rapidly the tide of reaction is sweeping against the Victorian era: against "an individualistic society . . . time-honoured institutions . . . moral codes and religious sanctions." In all of this JG is a spectator, not a combatant, even though his aristocratic sentiments are present. JG is not clear in presenting his concept of God—hints given by various characters in the works suggest that JG seeks some type of balanced view of God, but he presents no more than a "Pale Pantheism": Jolyon's "The Unknowable Creative Principle" (*The Forsyte Saga*); or Nedda's "O Darkness . . . out there" (*The Freelands*); or a "Great Underlying Mood or Principle" (*The Inn of Tranquillity*). JG's belief in God, "whatever [his] . . . faith may be . . . does not glow nor convict."

1296 Boyd, Ernest. "John Galsworthy: The Novelist as Dramatist," THEATRE ARTS MONTHLY, XIII (May 1929), 337–41.
The English repertory movement, and especially the Vedrenne–Granville–Barker Court Theatre group, is primarily responsible for JG's dramatic writings. His abstractness detracts from his dramatic prowess. The plays are too articulate;

the characters too eloquent. Pitying but never preaching, his interests are becoming dated. [General appreciation that serves as a review of *Plays*, from *The Silver Box* to *Escape*.]

1297 Boynton, H. W. "John Galsworthy [with selections]," in WRITERS OF MODERN ENGLAND, vol. XV of THE COLUMBIA UNIVERSITY COURSE IN LITERATURE, ed by John W. Cunliffe et al. (NY: Columbia UP, 1929), 444–48.

JG epitomizes things British. From *The Island Pharisees* on, his work is substantially protestant, satirical, and negative. *The Man of Property* is a better novel than *Pharisees*, which is episodic and a book of protest, because there is more story, less satire. In all his work he focuses on "the smugness of the civilized world, and the desperateness, almost the hopelessness of combating it." His treatment of marriage and sex may be narrow and negative, but it is never ignoble except in *The Dark Flower*, about which there is "something inherently unwholesome." His writing embodies a perfection of phrasing "with something very much like perfection of structure." His is a plain, simple, and distinguished style. In the later Forsyte novels Soames became "a person of rapidly waning dignity." As Professor Weygandt has observed, his novels are better than his plays, but his dramas take on a greater importance because so much of contemporary drama is mediocre. JG will be remembered as a prose writer of dignity and charm and as the prime interpreter of the English upper middle class for the period from 1875 to 1925.

1298 Braybrooke, Patrick. *"The Forsyte Saga,"* CURRENT LITERATURE AND THE PUBLISHER'S MISCELLANY (Lond), no. 252 (Dec 1929), 446–50.

[Descriptions of the various characters in *The Forsyte Saga* are given; Soames is seen as a tragic figure.]

1299 Brickell, Herschel. "The Literary Landscape," NORTH AMERICAN REVIEW, CCXXVII (Jan 1929), [n.p.].

[Brief mention of the publication of the collected *Plays*.]

1300 Brown, Ivor. "Building Notes. *The Roof,*" SATURDAY REVIEW (Lond), CXLVIII (2 Nov 1929), 508.

The Roof at the Vaudeville Theatre is a variation of the earlier *Escape* but weakened by the absence of a strong central figure.

1301 Brown, Ivor. "The Soft Spot," SATURDAY REVIEW (Lond), CXLVII (29 June 1929), 860–61.

JG's occasional penchant for "soft spots" surfaces in *Exiled* (at the Wyndham Theatre), such as the characterization of the "vexatious" Denbury. Still, the play is better than many being performed.

1302 Brulé, A. "John Galsworthy: *Swan Song,* London, Heinemann, 1928," REVUE ANGLO-AMÉRICAINE, VI (Aug 1929), 570–71.
Swan Song is clearly superior to most modern novels despite the fact that JG seems a little lost in the modern world, a world for which he has not been able to discover either a key or a unity. [In French.]

1303 Chandler, Frank W. "Twentieth-Century Drama in England," in WRITERS OF MODERN ENGLAND, vol. XV of THE COLUMBIA UNIVERSITY COURSE IN LITERATURE, ed by John W. Cunliffe et al. (NY: Columbia UP, 1929), 462–64.
As a naturalistic dramatist JG analyzes in his most typical work the anomalies of society. In his later plays JG turns to consideration of personal problems that "involve both love and woman's new freedom." *Loyalties* is the best of his late work. He reverts to his earlier manner in *The Show* and *Escape.*

1304 Edgett, Edwin Francis. "About Books and Authors," BOSTON EVENING TRANSCRIPT BOOK SECTION, 11 Oct 1929, p. 4.
The Forsyte Saga illustrates the fact that JG is one of the English novel's "most significant protagonists" of the first part of the twentieth century. Tenacity of purpose and an intense seriousness that occasionally borders on dullness keep JG from attaining the stature of Trollope, Balzac, and Zola. [Nominally a review of *A Modern Comedy.*]

1305 F., R. "Mr. Galsworthy's *Forsyte Chronicles,*" BRITISH MUSEUM QUARTERLY, IV (1929), 29–31.
[Records the gift of the holograph MSS of *The Forsyte Chronicles*—through *Swan Song*—to the British Museum, with the exception of the original and typed MSS of *The Man of Property.* JG complained at the time about the "chaotic and illegible condition" of the MSS. He also commented in a note that the "scheme of development" for continuing *Saga* beyond *Property* came on a Sunday in July 1918.]

1306 Fassbinder, Klara M. "Das Weltbild des Dramatikers John Galsworthy" (The Worldview of the Playwright John Galsworthy), MAEDCHENBILDUNG AUF CHRISTLICHER GRUNDLAGE (Paderborn), XXV (1929), 519–23.
[Traces the development of JG as a dramatist, singles out *Strife* for special praise, but favors those postwar plays that deal not so much with specific social problems as with general social and moral questions.] [In German.]

1307 Frisch, E. "John Galsworthy," BLÄTTER DER WÜRTTEMBERGISCHEN VOLKSBUHNE (Stuttgart: M. Beck, 1929), XI, 45 [not seen].
[Listed in BIBLIOGRAPHIE DER DEUTSCHEN ZEITSCHRIFTEN LITERATUR, 1929 (Leipzig: Felix Dietrich, 1930).] [In German.]

1308 Funke, Otto. "Zur 'Erlebten Rede' bei Galsworthy" (Concerning "Indirect Speech" in Galsworthy), ENGLISCHE STUDIEN, LXIV (1929), 450–74.

JG's use of "erlebte Rede" (indirect speech) developed as he developed. Its use is limited in such early works as "Salvation of a Forsyte," "The Silence," *The Island Pharisees*, and *The Country House*. His use of it in *The Man of Property* was more effective, but it was not until the later parts of *Saga* that he used it masterfully. "Indirect speech" serves a valuable purpose in *Saga* by setting up a contrast with the actual dialogue; this contrast permits subterranean attitudes to be observed. Another effective use of it is found in Jolly's delirium as he dies; "indirect speech" helps to emphasize the dramatic element in this scene. [In German.]

1309 "Galsworthy, John. *Plays,*" PRATT INSTITUTE QUARTERLY BOOKLIST, Spring 1929, p. 25.

[Brief notice of publication of JG's collected plays.]

1310 Hammond, Josephine. "Depending Mr. Galsworthy, Dramatist," PERSONALIST, X (Jan 1929), 21–35.

A catalogue of JG's faults includes the following: (1) failing to develop "fullborn creations"; (2) belaboring the effect of "faulty environment" on individuals despite protests to the contrary (*Justice, Escape*); (3) being preoccupied with the ephemeral; (4) evading psychological problems; (5) using obsessively the "theme of the woman hounded by society into sexual irregularity" (*The Fugitive, Windows*); and (6) filling the world more with "frailty" than with "courage." JG is capable of better. [Hammond's general essay capitalizes on the critical tide that is beginning to run strongly against JG the dramatist; what once were considered innovative and creative dramas in retrospect are banal performances. The title is not in error; it is "Depending," not "Defending."]

1311 Hutchison, Percy. "Galsworthy's Enduring Tale. *A Modern Comedy* Brings the Great Forsyte Chronicle to an End," NEW YORK TIMES SUNDAY REVIEW OF BOOKS, 8 Sept 1929, pp. 1, 31.

The Forsyte Saga and *A Modern Comedy* are without parallel in the study of manners and society. The younger Forsytes of *Comedy* suggest the change implied by a shift from the concept of "saga" (suggesting continuity and a certain stability) to that of comedy—or life as a merry-go-round. In *The White Monkey*, JG's most ironic work after *The Man of Property*, Michael Mont "of gay exterior, but of a solid core within" becomes JG's spokesman. No author treats the spiritual consequences of seduction so superbly. The two trilogies and connecting stories move with "conviction, with sprightliness and with compelling vigor." Scores of minor characters are properly subordinated, indicating a mastery of dramatic as well as narrative technique. The "prose epic," contrasting ideals of beauty and property, contributes positively to social history and literature.

1312 Jameson, Storm. THE GEORGIAN NOVEL AND MR. ROBINSON (Lond: Heinemann, 1929).
The Edwardian novel—the novels of Bennett, Wells, and JG—can be viewed as the midway point between the Victorian novel of Dickens and the Georgian novel of Virginia Woolf. [The JG references are to be found in passing.]

1313 Jennings, Richard. "The Theatre. *Exiled,*" SPECTATOR (Lond), CXLII (29 June 1929), 1005–6.
[Review of performance at Wyndham's Theatre.]

1314 Jennings, Richard. "The Theatre. *The Roof,*" SPECTATOR (Lond), CXLIII (16 Nov 1929), 711–12.
The Roof at the Vaudeville Theatre is a variety show as well as a morality play.

1315 Liebenfels, J. Lanz von. "John Galsworthy, ein englischer Ariosoph" (John Galsworthy, an English Ariosoph), ZEITSCHRIFT FÜR GEISTES—UND WISSENSCHAFTSREFORM (Duesseldorf), IV (1929), 50–53.
JG, who belongs with the greatest writers of the world (Strindberg, for example) is a representative of the heroic Aryan type, though he is forced by his environment to pose as a liberal and socialist reformer. [In German.]

1316 Maier, David. "Captain Kidd's Successor: The British Exchequer Withholding Three Hundred Millions from Rightful German Owners," AMERICAN MONTHLY, XXIII (Dec 1929), 8.
[Propagandistic article about the British government's refusal to return land to Germans in the aftermath of World War I. JG is opposed to this practice.]

1317 Marriott, James W. (ed). GREAT MODERN BRITISH PLAYS (Lond: George G. Harrap, 1929).
[Marriott's brief introduction mentions JG's popularity in Germany. The JG selection here is *Strife.*]

1318 Marrot, H. V. A NOTE ON JOHN GALSWORTHY, DRAMATIST (Lond: pvtly ptd at the Curwen P, 1929).
[This brief (14 pp.) and inconsequential biographical commentary concludes that JG "is essentially a believer in the attitude: 'there it is, take it or leave it.'"]

1319 "Mr. Galsworthy's Dramatic Method," TIMES LITERARY SUPPLEMENT (Lond), 11 July 1929, p. 554.
JG is an accomplished technician; his work suffers from two weaknesses: (1) a tendency to overuse comic relief, and (2) a habit of rubbing in his conclusions. The success or failure of his dramas depends on the suitability of his subject to naturalistic treatment. Naturalism for JG was a strait jacket. The subjects of his best plays (*Loyalties, The Skin Game, Justice*) either are concrete or are those "in which he has made a clear and definite movement away from naturalism towards a higher compression." His dramas are a link between the early photographic

naturalists and the writers of today "who seek freedom from photography in new conventions analogous to the poetic." His plays will be well remembered, though dated by humanitarianism. [A review of *Plays,* vols. XVIII–XXII, Manaton ed, and *Exiled.*]

1320 *"A Modern Comedy,"* SPECTATOR (Lond), CXLIII (30 Nov 1929), 827.
[Brief, favorable notice of the second Forsyte trilogy bound in one volume.]

1321 P., J. B. "Mr. Galsworthy's New Play: Smoke Fills Theatre in Fire Scene," DAILY CHRONICLE (Lond), 6 Nov 1929, p. 6.
The Roof at the Vaudeville Theatre consists of a series of scenes in which action is simultaneous rather than continuous. The first act needs drastic revision; the play generally is dull because it is too photographic and the conversations too real.

1322 P., J. B. "Mr. Galsworthy's New Play: The Ills of England in *Exiled,*" DAILY CHRONICLE (Lond), 20 June 1929, p. 7.
Exiled at Wyndham's Theatre had a mixed reception because it "roams sociologically and dispassionately over England's ills" without giving the action or characters a vital "humanistic spark."

1323 *"Plays,"* A.L.A. BOOKLIST, XXV (Jan 1929), 154.
[Brief notice announces the collection of nineteen long and six short plays.]

1324 *"Plays,"* DIAL (Chicago), LXXXVI (March 1929), 266.
[Condescending brief dismissal of the collected *Plays* as "already happily forgotten."]

1325 "Plays, by John Galsworthy," CHRISTIAN CENTURY, 17 Jan 1929, p. 82.
[Brief notice of publication of the complete ed of JG's plays. JG is a "social philosopher."]

1326 "Portrait," DELINEATOR, CXIV (Jan 1929), 4.
[Photograph of JG, advertising the appearance of some JG short stories in DELINEATOR.]

1327 Redman, Ben Ray. "Old Wine in New Bottles," NEW YORK HERALD TRIBUNE BOOKS, 28 April 1929, p. 10.
JG's prose narratives in *Plays* are "more successfully dramatic than his dramas."

1328 Rosenbach, E. "J. Galsworthy, *Swan Song,*" DIE NEUEREN SPRACHEN (Marburg), XXXVII (1929), 342–43.
Swan Song is not, as has been said, the world-weary work of an old writer but a novel which deserves its title and proves JG's incomparable artistry once again. [In German.]

1329 Rusev, R. "S predg" (Foreword), *Bialata Maimuna* (*The White Monkey*) (Sophia: Iv. T. Ignatov, 1929) [not seen].
[In Bulgarian.]

1330 Schalit, Leon. "John Galsworthy: Some Personal Notes," BOOKMAN (Lond), LXXVI (June 1929), 149–50.
[Snippets from Schalit's JOHN GALSWORTHY, A SURVEY (Lond: Heinemann, 1928), with Henry Goodman's photo of JG and a photo of David Evans's bust of JG.]

1331 Schriftgiesser, Karl. "John Galsworthy Completes the Chronicle of the Forsytes," BOSTON EVENING TRANSCRIPT BOOK SECTION, 28 Sept 1929, p. 2.
The publication of *A Modern Comedy* is important because it ends the Forsyte history. "Where else can so extended, so careful, so impressive, so ironic, a study of society be found" than in JG's novels? His history of manners cannot be equalled. "We may disagree with his sociology, but with his knowledge and understanding of humanity we cannot quarrel."

1332 Seidl, Florian. "John Galsworthy," DIE SCHOLLE (Ansbach), [V?] (1929), 624–28.
JG's mind and heart are in favor of social change, but by temperament he is still close to the irrecoverable prewar period. This ambivalence makes him a much better historian of his age than Shaw or any other of his contemporaries. [In German.]

1333 Shanks, Edward. "*A Modern Comedy,*" SATURDAY REVIEW (Lond), CXLVIII (17 Aug 1929), 189–90.
[This brief review praises the character of Soames and laments the title *A Modern Comedy.*]

1334 Shipp, Horace. "The Art of John Galsworthy," ENGLISH REVIEW (Lond), XLIX (1929), 764–66.
The Roof is good entertainment, but it suffers from conscious moralizing. JG's "philosophy tends to be sentimental in its all-embracing optimism." In his *Collected Plays* (all twenty-seven of them) JG is at his best when he writes of property. "Property, and Class, which is property in the soul, are his dual theme."

1335 Shipp, Horace. "*Exiled,*" ENGLISH REVIEW (Lond), XLIX (Aug 1929), 243–44.
In *Exiled,* at Wyndham's Theatre, JG "allows his social consciousness to run away with his logic." "Universal pity," so evident in JG's plays, has the seed of its undoing because that takes the reader or viewer nowhere. The play is undistinguished.

1336 Swaffer, Hannen. "John Galsworthy," in HANNEN SWAFFER'S WHO'S WHO (Lond: Hutchinson & Co. [1929]), pp. 131–32.
[Anecdotal comments about JG.]

1337 "Vaudeville Theatre. *The Roof,* " TIMES (Lond), 6 Nov 1929, p. 12.
Even though *The Roof* presents human behavior accurately, the seven scenes are not cohesive.

1338 Vonschott, Hedwig. "Die Frau und die Familie in Galsworthys Romanen" (Women and the Family in Galsworthy's Novels), DIE CHRISTLICHE FRAU (Cologne), XXVII (Feb 1929), 33–39.
[Discusses different types of women in JG's novels and the disintegration of the family in *The Forsyte Saga.*] [In German.]

1339 Ward, A. C. TWENTIETH CENTURY LITERATURE (Lond: Longmans, 1929); rptd (1940, 1956; Lond: Methuen, 1956, 1964).
[Contains no information about JG that is not covered in more detail in TWENTIETH CENTURY LITERATURE: THE AGE OF INTERROGATION, 1901–1925 (Lond: Methuen, 1928).]

1340 West, Rebecca. "A Letter From Abroad: John Galsworthy Receives the Order of Merit," BOOKMAN (NY), LXX (Sept 1929), 91; rptd as "O.M.," ENDING IN EARNEST: A LITERARY LOG (Garden City, NY: Doubleday, Doran, 1931; Freeport, NY: Books for Libraries P, 1967), pp. 129–33.
Awarding the Order of Merit to JG is an "affront to persons of culture." The award should have gone either to George Bernard Shaw or to H. G. Wells, both of whom are superior to JG. "It is infuriating when the Order of Merit is withheld from both the persons who deserved it." JG's heart is in the right place, "but his work is minor." JG is a fine man, but a minor author: he copies rather than interprets.

1341 Woodbridge, Homer E. "A Galsworthy Trilogy. *A Modern Comedy,* " SATURDAY REVIEW OF LITERATURE (NY), VI (7 Dec 1929), 509.
A Modern Comedy is less successful than *The Forsyte Saga* for two reasons: it lacks vividness of characterization, and the 1920s are too close for clear perspective. *Comedy* does have more organic unity, and Soames's presence gives it more symmetry. The young people are the "gilded fringe" of the present, dabbling in art and love-making; Fleur is not complex enough to be interesting. The evolution of Soames as he watches over Fleur provides the unifying interest—as his evolution from "villain into the tragic hero is complete . . . never whitewashed or sentimentalized."

1342 "Wyndham's Theatre. *Exiled,*" TIMES (Lond), 20 June 1929, p. 14.

In *Exiled,* Mr. East and the tramp come across well on the stage, and Sir Charles Denbury and Sir John Mazer are admirable. The final scene, however, belabors the moral of the good departed England; the love story is irrelevant, almost spoiling a play that is good despite its oddities.

1930

1343 Ament, William S. "Fiction and Naturalism," LECTURES ON SIGNIFICANT TENDENCIES IN CONTEMPORARY LETTERS: SCRIPPS COLLEGE PAPERS, No. 2 (Claremont, Calif, 1930), pp. 13–33.
Although a competent workman, JG is "more successful in embalming the Victorian generation than in castigating or interpreting ours."

1344 Anderson, Margaret. MY THIRTY YEARS' WAR (NY: Covici Friede, 1930), pp. 45–47, 48.
[Anderson prints a letter by JG and refers to an article she did on JG's *The Dark Flower* for the LITTLE REVIEW, (1917?).]

1345 Ault, Leslie. "Mr. Galsworthy Fills in the Gaps," NEW YORK EVENING POST, 22 Nov 1930, Sec. D, p. 4.
Magazine publication has affected *On Forsyte 'Change.* Readers "seem compelled to do an uncommon lot of peeking and grinning, and the author stands beside us and smiles in unison instead of being behind the scenes with his hand." While these stories can be read independently, they are much better when read with *The Forsyte Saga.*

1346 "Books to Give for Christmas: *On Forsyte 'Change,* " OPEN SHELF (Cleveland), Dec 1930, p. 150.
[Brief, inconsequential review.]

1347 Brewster, Dorothy, and Angus Burrell. ADVENTURE OR EXPERIENCE: FOUR ESSAYS ON CERTAIN WRITERS AND READERS OF NOVELS (NY: Columbia UP, 1930); rptd (Freeport, NY: Books for Libraries P, 1967), pp. 40, 138–39, 148.
As years pass after reading *The Forsyte Saga,* one remembers the "contemplation of life" rather than involvement in character conflict as in Lawrence's SONS AND LOVERS.

1348 Bryan, J[ohn] Ingran. THE PHILOSOPHY OF ENGLISH LITERATURE (Tokyo: Maruzen, 1930), pp. 267, 270–72.
In his novels and plays JG attacks the landed classes who live unto themselves and the power of the strong over the weak. JG says lucidly "what George

Meredith said obscurely: he has the same critical attitude to pharisaism and the national subordination of women."

1349 Butcher, Fanny. "These Authors Depict Nations in Their Books: Galsworthy, Edith Wharton Fill in Pictures," CHICAGO DAILY TRIBUNE, 1 Nov 1930, p. 13.
JG, like Edith Wharton, chronicles typical national groups. *On Forsyte 'Change* is written with JG's usual "beautiful and meticulous care."

1350 Chitil, Klaudius. "Der Schuster als Platoniker" (The Shoemaker as Platonist), WIENER BLAETTER FUER DIE FREUNDE DER ANTIKE, VII (June 1930), 18–19.
The younger shoemaker in "Quality" is a Platonist. [In German.]

1351 Clemens, Cyril. "Personal Visits to G. K. Chesterton, Anthony Hope, John Galsworthy, Walter de la Mare," OVERLAND MONTHLY, LXXXVIII (Dec 1930), 357–58, 373–74, 378.
JG's favorite novels are PICKWICK PAPERS and HUCKLEBERRY FINN; his favorite American writers are Harte, Poe, and Lewis. [Literary chitchat.]

1352 Cohn, Louis Henry. "Book Madness," SCRIBNER'S MAGAZINE, LXXXVII (May 1930), 545–53.
[Cohn reminisces wistfully about getting into the business of collecting JG first editions and about the mania of trying to win in the first editions collection game.]

1353 Cross, Wilbur L. "The Forsytes," YALE REVIEW, XIX (March 1930), 527–50; rptd in expanded form in FOUR CONTEMPORARY NOVELISTS (NY: Macmillan, 1930), pp. 101–53.
JG's novels have little direct propaganda except for what is "inherent in his naturalistic method which endeavors to transfer to fiction the social scene as it appears to a man who would look beneath the surface." The problems he deals with are for the reader to solve, and his theme is "the liberation of the mind." In form *The Man of Property* "is an expanded Greek tragedy," which depicts the antagonism between Forsyteism and art. JG's irony and silences often remind one of Sophocles. Bosinney is a failure because his character is forced to fit into the pattern of the book. Whereas *Property* is "an emotional study in the physiology of nerves," the rest of *Saga* except for "Indian Summer of a Forsyte" is more objective, and the drama is subdued to the narrative. JG is right in not letting Fleur and Jon marry, for such a development is "quite out of harmony with his general design."

1354 Curle, Richard. "The Story of a Remarkable Friendship," in John Galsworthy, *Two Essays on Conrad* (Freelands: pvtly ptd [Cincinnati: Ebbert & Richardson, 1930]).

[Biographical comments on the widely known facts about the JG-Conrad relationship. Only twenty-five copies were printed.]

1355 Duffin, Henry Charles. "The Rehabilitation of Soames Forsyte," CORNHILL MAGAZINE, nsLXVIII (April 1930), 397–406.

Soames's rehabilitation from the negative character presented in *The Man of Property* through the rest of *The Forsyte Saga* and *A Modern Comedy* "is involved with, and partly proceeds from, Irene's failure." The intrigue between Bosinney and Irene is "common" and "abominable"; her intrique to keep Jon and Fleur apart is "plainly culpable," whereas Soames's reaction is "right and decent." Irene transforms quickly from her unpleasant affair with Soames through "Indian Summer of a Forsyte"; it takes Soames longer. In *In Chancery,* JG is no longer caustic when writing about Soames; he becomes more respectable, showing "signs of being sensible to natural beauty." Irene fails terribly with Jon, because she is basically hypocritical; Soames, like Irene, has doubts about the Jon-Fleur relationship, but he loves Fleur unselfishly; and the key to the apotheosis of Soames is the entry of love into his life.

1356 "Fiction: *On Forsyte 'Change,*" BOOKMAN (NY), LXXII (Nov 1930), 310.

Stories in *On Forsyte 'Change,* written in JG's usual prose, "easy but strong, dignified but colloquial, are not of a piece." Some, light in tone, are slight in content; others treat seriously the force of unsuccessful love; some relate the Forsytes to the non-Forsyte world; and some relate the Forsytes to each other.

1357 "Galsworthy on the Talkies," LIVING AGE, CCCXXXVIII (15 May 1930), 349–50.

[Report of an interview with JG, made when *Escape* was filmed. JG hopes that with the advent of talking movies, the art of the silent film will not be lost.]

1358 Gary, Franklin. "Galsworthy and the POETICS," SYMPOSIUM, I (1930), 72–81.

The Silver Box may be evaluated on the basis of Aristotle's idea that "the power of tragedy . . . is felt even apart from the representation and actors": that is, the power of a play can be seen in its language and dialogue. Modern realistic plays function as collaborations among actors, directors, and set designers; without stage directions speech is "partly incomprehensible." From this perspective it can be said that JG's plays "remain on the surface and never penetrate to what lies beneath."

1359 Gerstenberg, Ernst. "Galsworthy im Unterricht" (Galsworthy in Class), ZEITSCHRIFT FUER FRANZOESISCHEN UND ENGLISHCHEN UNTERRICHT, XXIX:1 (1930), 36–44.

If high school students are to study England through its works of art, it is a good idea to start with JG's description of the funeral of Queen Victoria (*The Forsyte Saga*) and continue with his powerful play *Strife.* [In German.]

1360 Gillett, Eric W. BOOKS AND WRITERS (Singapore: Malaya Publishing, 1930), pp. 119–26.
[Passing, rambling comments on JG's dramas, some comments being unfavorable.]

1361 Hutchison, Percy. "New Tales of the Forsyte Clan," NEW YORK TIMES SUNDAY REVIEW OF BOOKS, 12 Oct 1930, p. 1.
The short stories of *On Forsyte 'Change* are "varied in mood and perfect in execution." JG delighted in allowing his mid-nineteenth century Forsyte women "a fling at rebellion." "The Peacock Cry" shows depths of Victorian passion that even *The Forsyte Saga* did not fully explore.

1362 Janvrin, F. "Experimental Analysis of a Record of Verse Spoken by John Galsworthy Himself," in BERICHT ÜBER DIE 1. TAGUNG DER INTERNATIONALEN GESELLSCHAFT FUER EXPERIMENTELLE PHONETIK IN BONN VOM 10. BIS 14. JUNI 1930 (Report of the First Conference of the International Society for Experimental Phonetics in Bonn, 10–14 June, 1930), ed by Paul Menzerath [1930], 39–41.
[This analysis of JG's reading of the first stanza of "Devon to Me!" praises the complexity and perfection of rhythmic action and quotes from a letter of JG to support the thesis that the poem was worked up in its finished form in the unconscious mind.]

1363 Laski, Harold. "Four Literary Portraits," DAILY HERALD (Lond), 1930 [not seen]; rptd in LIVING AGE, CCCXXXIX (Nov 1930), 285–93.
JG's reputation is built on his emotional insight into the English upper middle class. His best is in *The Forsyte Saga,* for JG can depict "man's search for security, his doubts of the bizarre, his contempt for the artist, his suspicion of the intellectual . . . as no one else has ever depicted them." But JG often becomes sentimental with the laboring class and the aristocracy because he is unable to understand them; yet all is done with great distinction and fine feeling. He is a "man of feeling" rather than of ideas. He does not see life in terms of cause and effect, and consequently he cannot communicate that. His art and life seem to be a series of brief visions, caught with the "exquisite sensitiveness of the artist." His poetry is lyric rather than philosophic, and his painting is of "mood rather than the expression of a faith." To be virtuous is to consider the feelings of others. JG is not excited by life; he is "grave, a little melancholy, tranquil" with a bit of the stoic in him. [Laski's essay, one of the best brief general comments on the essential JG, is accompanied by essays on Kipling, Wells, and Shaw.]

1364 Leimert, Erika. VIKTORIANISMUS BEI GALSWORTHY (VICTORIANISM IN GALSWORTHY). Published dissertation, University of Marburg (Marburg: Hermann Bauer, 1930).
JG's Forsyteism resembles Carlyle's Gigmanism and Arnold's Philistinism. JG

opposed Victorian materialism with a new faith in perfection and beauty and criticized such Victorian middle-class values as the belief in respectability, the sense of property, the longing for security, and the high esteem of restraint. When he became aware of the restlessness and insecurity of the postwar generation, he was willing to acknowledge the more positive aspects of Victorianism. This is why his evaluation of Soames changed in the course of *The Forsyte Saga*. [A survey of most of the novels.] [In German.]

1365 M., A. E. "Galsworthy the Dramatist," DUBLIN MAGAZINE, V (Jan–March 1930), 72–73.
[Brief note about the appearance of *Plays*.]

1366 Mann, Thomas. "An Impression of John Galsworthy," VIR-GINIA QUARTERLY REVIEW, VI (1930), 114–16.
The Dark Flower is "one of the most beautiful and fresh love romances in the English language." Middle-class authorship "is a tentative criticism of its own form of life which as a personal possession is yet naive and genuine but which in the spiritual realm is fragmentary and precarious. This is so because it wins the confidence of the millions, whose darkly-felt situation it expresses and ennobles insofar as objectification and representation do ennoble." JG can best be de-scribed by the word *gentleman* if the term connoted something more spiritual. [This brief account of JG is based on Mann's being a guest of the PEN Club in London a few years ago.]

1367 "New Novels," TIMES LITERARY SUPPLEMENT (Lond), 9 Oct 1930, p. 804.
The Forsyte world gives a unity to the stories of *On Forsyte 'Change*. As time has passed, JG's Forsytes, "who began by being very much of a joke, have acquired the dignity of history; they are no longer mere individuals or a mere family, they are a whole social order and a lost one."

1368 *"On Forsyte 'Change,"* BOSTON EVENING TRANSCRIPT, 22 Nov 1930, p. 2.
[A two-paragraph appreciation.]

1369 *"On Forsyte 'Change,"* PITTSBURGH MONTHLY BULLETIN, XXXV (Nov 1930), 79.
[Brief review.]

1370 *"On Forsyte 'Change,"* SATURDAY REVIEW (Lond), CL (11 Oct 1930), 453.
The stories included in *On Forsyte 'Change* bridge the gap between *The Forsyte Saga* and *A Modern Comedy*. In "Soames and the Flag, 1914-1918," JG deals with "the sensitive patriotism of a civilian to whom vicarious heroism seemed repugnant." [A brief two-paragraph review in an omnibus review of six novels.]

1371 Orage, Alfred Richard. THE ART OF READING (NY: Farrar & Rinehart, 1930), pp. 249–50.

JG "has not an ounce" of the dynamic in him. Falder in *Justice* irritates us with his weakness and submissiveness. In *The Mob,* JG has tried to make a hero of "a mere negative": his protagonists always tremble "lest Fate should overwhelm them." The audience in Hamburg rightfully hissed *Justice* off the stage.

1372 Pritchett, V. S. "Five Established Novelists," SPECTATOR (Lond), CXLV (18 Oct 1930), 554.

Episodes of *On Forsyte 'Change* are "amusing" but mere "shadows of shades" of the former JG.

1373 Proteus. "New Novels," NEW STATESMAN, XXXVI (22 Nov 1930), 207–8.

Stories in *On Forsyte 'Change* are "all skilful, some lovely, some merely intelligent"; but none is inspired by genius.

1374 R., F. L. "The Week's Reading," OUTLOOK AND INDEPENDENT (NY), CLVI (29 Oct 1930), 348.

[A paragraph review of the slight but delightful and pleasing *On Forsyte 'Change.*]

1375 Ross, Virgilia Peterson. "The Return of the Forsytes: *On Forsyte 'Change,*" NEW YORK HERALD TRIBUNE BOOKS, 12 Oct 1930, p. 5.

JG is "painstakingly tender" with the "picture gallery" of *On Forsyte 'Change.* In his crystal clear restraint JG has "sifted, filtered . . . [the] essence of life."

1376 Russell, Frances T. "Ironic John Galsworthy," UNIVERSITY OF CALIFORNIA CHRONICLE, XXXII (Jan 1930), 78–87.

Some of the elements of irony in JG's works are considered.

1377 Scott-James, R. A. "Mr. Galsworthy's Forsytes," CHRISTIAN SCIENCE MONITOR, 15 Nov 1930, p. 9.

The episodes in *On Forsyte 'Change* show JG at his best and worst. His reminiscent manner occasionally becomes sentimental.

1378 Semper, I[sidore] J[oseph]. "Saga of English Gentlemen," CATHOLIC WORLD, CXXXI (June 1930), 280–89; rptd as "Galsworthian Gentleman," RETURN OF THE PRODIGAL (NY: Edward O'Toole, 1932), pp. 112–34.

The Forsyte Saga and *A Modern Comedy* give a cross section of life, and illustrate the "Piccadilly parade of conventional virtues" constituting the duty of the gentleman. Soames's anxiety to become a gentleman suggests the "inferiority complex of a person who has not yet arrived"; his fear of scandal (with Annette and Prosper) rather than morality suggests the motif of money-respectability-gentility; Young Jolyon, who contrasts to Soames, has "true refinement" and a "striking horror of the moral attitude," and is "casual . . . self-conscious . . .

apologetic." Jon (who never goes back on his word), and Michael (the man without reproach) are further developments of the gentleman theme; but Michael is the epitome of the JG gentleman. [Semper concludes by objecting from "the Catholic standpoint" that JG parades "refinement" instead of "religion." The essay is largely plot summary.]

1379 Sutton, Graham. "Re-Enter Mr. Galsworthy," BOOKMAN (Lond), LXXVII (Feb 1930), 305–6.
[Brief reviews of the collected ed *The Plays of John Galsworthy* and *The Roof.*]

1380 Thurston, Herbert. "John Galsworthy, Dog-Lover," STUDIES: AN IRISH QUARTERLY REVIEW, XIX (Dec 1930), 595–606; rptd in STUDIER I MODERN SPRÅKVETENSKAP (Uppsala), XIX (1931), 595–606 [not seen].
No writer can equal JG in his "comprehension, sympathy . . . [and] minute observations" of dogs. Unlike JG's sometimes cynical and irritating comments about modern life, his references to dogs have a freshness of communication and brilliance convincing in "truth and vividness." [Quotes copiously from *The Forsyte Chronicles, Beyond,* and *The Country House.* Thurston, an S.J. priest, is admittedly displeased with themes in JG's works that are contrary to Roman Catholic teachings—the Soames-Irene estrangement, for example.]

1381 Van Doren, Dorothy. "Portrait of a Family," NATION (NY), CXXXI (22 Oct 1930), 447.
[Short, favorable notice of *On Forsyte 'Change.*]

1382 Weeks, Edward. *"On Forsyte 'Change,"* ATLANTIC BOOKSHELF, Dec 1930, p. 52.
On Forsyte 'Change is "looser in form" than *Caravan.* JG writes with animation, and draws his characters "roundly." [Brief review.]

1383 Wolff, Bruno. "Gegen Galsworthy und Salten" (Against Galsworthy and Salten), DIE VEGETARISCHE WARTE (Leipzig), LXIII (Dec 1930), 371–76.
[Criticizes JG's views on vivisection and vegetarians as presented in his article "Bekenntnis zum Tier" ("For Love of Beasts"?), HAMBURGER ANZEIGER.] [In German.]

1384 Woodbridge, Homer E. "The Forsyte Clan," SATURDAY REVIEW OF LITERATURE (NY), VII (1 Nov 1930), 285.
The short episodes of *On Forsyte 'Change* that help to fill in the Forsyte family history can stand by themselves as interesting and "capital stories." In the twenty-four years since *The Man of Property,* JG tends more to imply rather than to express his critical point of view; he even admires the solid virtues of the older generation. Meredith's Comic Spirit reigns supreme.

1931

1385 Arns, Karl. "John Galsworthy, der Erzaehler und Gesell-schaftskritiker" (John Galsworthy, the Novelist and Critic of Society), DAS NEUE REICH (Vienna), XIII (1931), 678–79.
Because of his honesty, JG is more important than Bennett, Conrad, and Wells. It is true that in his postwar novels he tends to sentimentalize Victorian values and to adopt a reactionary attitude, but it is worthwhile—keeping in mind his belief in the triumph of idealism over materialism. One should read him in a spirit of opposition against contemporary Anglo-Saxon crime and erotic literature. [In German.]

1386 "Aspects of England," NEW STATESMAN AND NATION, nsII (7 Nov 1931), 582.
JG's ironic form has slipped in *Maid In Waiting*. "Vivid incidents" complement JG's theme emphasizing the belief that every man has a right to certainty and security.

1387 Austin, Hugh P. "John Galsworthy," DUBLIN REVIEW (Lond), CLXXXIX (July–Sept 1931), 95–106.
JG will live as a master, once critical perspective becomes settled, because of his "fine humanity," his concern with giving a picture of a "whole class and a whole period," his preoccupation with "normal people" rather than "the exceptions of life," and his "historical mind." He will live in much the same way that Henry Fielding and Jane Austen will live. *The Forsyte Saga* represents all his work, except that his great gift of sympathy and pity for the underdog and the failure, and his sense of the "infinite sorrows for suffering man" comes out better in his plays and short stories, as in *Justice*. Irene leaves Soames in "a perfectly quiet and natural way." JG is at his best when he breaks away from the "strictly impartial view . . . with a natural philosophy" that borders on but does not definitely accept fatalism. *Saga* chronicles the decay of family authority as it was happening historically. Neither young Jolyon nor Winifred nor Soames could assume leadership of the family. The Forsytes are neither "more vicious nor more virtuous" than those about them. *Saga* also chronicles the rise of the acquisitive spirit, symbolized by Soames's attitude toward art. The key to the greatness of *Saga* is the authoritative, truthful, and masterful creation of Soames, "a portrait of a gentleman of a period and at the same time a portrait of a period in a gentleman. . . . Soames is typical, but . . . remote . . . from being a patchwork or a composite individual." JG appeals most to the reader whose interest lies in characterization, atmosphere that "melts into characterizations," history, and the appeal of everyday life rather than to those who want "brilliance of epigram . . . eroticism and cynicism."

1388 Bond, Richard P. *"Maid in Waiting,"* BOOKMAN (NY), LXXIV (Dec 1931), 470.

Maid in Waiting, a good rather than a great work, does little for JG's reputation. But JG at second best exceeds most writers at their best.

1389 Chatfield-Taylor, Otis. "The Latest Plays," OUTLOOK AND IN-DEPENDENT (NY), CLIX (11 Nov 1931), 343.

[Brief note of dismissal of *The Roof.* JG's chief fault is the failure to show the effect of crisis on his characters.]

1390 Eaton, Walter Prichard. "Recent Plays: *The Roof* by John Galsworthy," NEW YORK HERALD TRIBUNE BOOKS, 13 Dec 1931, p. 19.

One can quickly understand why JG's *The Roof* had such a quick demise on the stage. [Review of publication of the play.]

1391 Ellehange, Martin. STRIKING FIGURES AMONG MODERN EN-GLISH DRAMATISTS. . . . (Copenhagen: Levin & Munksgaard, 1931), pp. 30–46.

[The discussion of JG's plays is very general: sometimes his plays are related to various Continental movements.]

1392 Fadiman, Clifton. "The Men of Property," NATION (NY), CXXXIII (2 Dec 1931), 612.

"Galsworthy piddles while England burns." [Review of *Maid in Waiting.*]

1393 Guha-Thakurta, P. "John Galsworthy as a Dramatist," CAL-CUTTA REVIEW, 3rd ser, XXXVIII (March 1931), 423–29.

JG, a "master craftsman" in character construction, sets down the "phenomena of life and character" with prejudice, leaving the public "to draw such poor moral as nature may afford." Unlike Shaw, who proclaims his ideas "emphatically and aggressively," JG is a quieter, "mellower apostle" who does not let the moral get the better of his artistic sense. JG's plays are strong, vital, "free from dialectical fireworks," and economical in style without the "crackling smartness of Shaw" or the "paroxysmal cleverness" of Noel Coward. JG is the most "polished dramatic artist of the modern age."

1394 Harwood, H. C. *"Maid in Waiting,"* SATURDAY REVIEW (Lond), CLII (7 Nov 1931), 592–93.

The plot of *Maid in Waiting* turns on the "conflict between institutional and imaginative justice." It is not one of JG's best, because his always reserved humor sinks to "dim irony," and the characters' individuality is lost in types.

1395 Hawkins, Ethel Wallace. "The Man of the Month: John Galsworthy," ATLANTIC BOOKSHELF, Dec 1931, p. 20.

In *Maid in Waiting,* Dinny Cherrell is "the child of traditions" as opposed to the "frank individualist" Fleur Forsyte, who is married to Dinny's cousin Michael

Mont. The inner significance of Dinny is that she refuses "half-baked emotional experience." *Waiting* is rich in love of "English earth" and in the "sense of the divine continuity of beauty," but JG is not always accurate in his use of American idiom. [Brief review.]

1396 Hutchison, Percy. "Galsworthy's Studies of National Types," NEW YORK TIMES BOOK REVIEW, 1 Nov 1931, p. 7.
One wishes for the less than perfect Fleur Forsyte rather than the unselfish Dinny of *Maid in Waiting*. The novel studies contrasting civilizations by focusing on the types as individuals—Hubert (English) and Hallorsen (American). The Uncle Adrian and Diana portion of the story falls below JG's standard because it lacks proportion and firm treatment. Expert style and character delineation make even a second-best effort like *Waiting* welcome.

1397 "Incomparable Galsworthy," CHRISTIAN CENTURY, XLVIII (9 Dec 1931), 1560.
[Brief, favorable review of *Maid in Waiting*.]

1398 Inglis, Rewey Belle, Alice Cecilia Cooper, Marion A. Sturdevant, and William Rose Benét (eds). ADVENTURES IN ENGLISH LITERATURE (NY: Harcourt, Brace, 1931; rev eds, 1938, 1946, 1949, 1952, 1968), pp. 988–89, 1055–56.
[Biographical sketch and statement of the theme of *Strife* precede the text of the play, which is followed by questions designed for secondary school students. The same format (with different pagination) occurs in all eds.]

1399 Knight, Grant. THE NOVEL IN ENGLISH (NY: R. R. Smith, 1931), pp. 320–26.
Contrasts may be made between H. G. Wells and JG. Much is to be said for JG's balance between extremes of philosophical anarchism and Toryism; it is fortunate that JG's "ironically patrician mind . . . preserved him from becoming a doctrinaire and allowed him to remain an artist."

1400 Lovett, Robert Morss. PREFACE TO FICTION. A DISCUSSION OF GREAT MODERN NOVELS (Chicago: Thomas S. Rockwell, 1931), p. 81.
[Brief reference to JG, classifying *The Forsyte Saga* as a geneaological series of novels.]

1401 *"Maid in Waiting,"* A.L.A. BOOKLIST, XXVIII (Dec 1931), 151.
Characters in *Maid in Waiting* are "genuine, intelligent, and human" but uninteresting.

1402 *"Maid in Waiting,"* NEW REPUBLIC, LXIX (9 Dec 1931), 117.
[Paragraph review of *Maid in Waiting*, consisting primarily of a brief plot summary.]

1403 *"Maid in Waiting,"* PITTSBURGH MONTHLY BULLETIN, XXXVI (Dec 1931), 84.
[Brief review.]

1404 *"Maid in Waiting:* John Galsworthy in Lighter Type of Fiction,"
SPRINGFIELD REPUBLICAN (Mass), 22 Nov 1931, Sec. E, p. 7.
The characters of *Maid in Waiting* are "lively and plausible, if not profound." [A brief plot summary.]

1405 Miller, Anna Irene. THE INDEPENDENT THEATRE IN EUROPE: 1887 TO PRESENT (NY: Ray Long & Richard R. Smith, 1931), pp. 1, 5, 8, 157, 199, 230, 244, 296, 313, 382.
JG's drama, like Shaw's, is "the drama of social indignation" rather than "the drama of definite political purpose." [Passing references to JG in a study devoted primarily to independent European theaters of the Vedrenne-Barker Court Theatre variety, which gave JG his start.]

1406 "New Novels," TIMES LITERARY SUPPLEMENT (Lond), 5 Nov 1931, p. 862.
The humor in *Maid in Waiting* is at times somewhat mechanical. Although not up to the standards of the novels and interludes of *A Modern Comedy, Maid in Waiting* "will in no way derogate from Mr. Galsworthy's great and well-deserved reputation."

1407 Newman, Evelyn. THE INTERNATIONAL NOTE IN CONTEMPORARY DRAMA (NY: Kingsland P, 1931), pp. 4, 5, 7, 8, 24, 25–26, 28, 116, 133–34.
JG has kept his "humanitarian faith" and his sincerity in pre-World War I drama, and is one with Shaw and Hauptmann in attacking "militarized religion." *The Mob* (1914) is indicative of antiwar sentiment in English drama before World War I. [Attempts without much success to find antiwar sentiment in *The Foundations* and *Escape.*]

1408 Ockham, David. "People of Importance in Their Day: John Galsworthy," SATURDAY REVIEW (Lond), CLII (25 July 1931), 115.
It is JG's humanity that accounts for his appeal in Europe. Despite the fact that he was born into a wealthy family, he shows in his early novels a sympathy like Dostoevski's for the underdog and the dispossessed. Like Balzac, JG has given his readers "valuable contemporary documents" and universal characters. Unfortunately he carried *The Forsyte Saga* "beyond its legitimate conclusion." His sympathy with the contemporary generation is more on an emotional rather than an intellectual plane.

1409 Omicron. "Plays and Pictures," NATION AND ATHENAEUM, XLVIII (7 Feb 1931), 601–2.

Even though there is dramatic value in the interrelationship of characters, *The Silver Box* is dated. Act three is hardly necessary; the conclusion is banal. [Review of revival at the Fortune Theatre.]

1410 *"On Forsyte 'Change,"* A.L.A. BOOKLIST, XXVII (Jan 1931), 207.
[Brief notice announces the appearance of nineteen new and varied episodes that complement *The Forsyte Saga* and *A Modern Comedy,* with dates ranging from 1821 to 1918.]

1411 Reely, Mary Katharine. "A Selected List of Current Books," WISCONSIN LIBRARY BULLETIN (Madison), XXVII (Dec 1931), 313.
Maid in Waiting is not significant. [Plot-summary review.]

1412 Rhys, Ernest. EVERYMAN REMEMBERS (NY: Cosmopolitan Book Corp., 1931), pp. 230, 291, 303–6.
[Several passing references to JG and a discussion of JG as president of the P.E.N. Club.] JG believed that P.E.N. was a way of bringing about an international union of writers of the world.

1413 Ross, Virgilia Peterson. "Some Fall Novels," OUTLOOK AND INDEPENDENT (NY), CLIX (11 Nov 1931), 344.
Maid in Waiting lacks the vitality of earlier JG novels. Dinny is generous yet impersonal enough to keep the reader's sympathy in bounds. The American professor does not come alive.

1414 Schriftgiesser, Karl. "Galsworthy in an International Mood: His First Novel since He Gave Up the Forsytes Contrasts Various Types of Characters," BOSTON EVENING TRANSCRIPT BOOK SECTION, 7 Nov 1931, p. 3.
JG contrasts the British and American heritages in *Maid in Waiting,* drawing characters with acuteness and sureness of touch; yet the book is second-rate JG.

1415 Skinner, R. Dana. OUR CHANGING THEATRE (NY: Dial P, 1931), pp. 195, 220–24, 241.
Old English is a "sad effort" that oversentimentalizes a "perverse character" and owes its transitory success to the acting of George Arliss as Heythorp. The moral of the play is perverted; the portrait of Heythorp would have been good if JG had not tried so hard to make the viewer (or reader) sympathize with him. *Escape* is "garnished" with "false and cheap sentimentality"; it "sins against the integrity of characterization" and is dishonest because JG tries too hard to "engage the sympathy of his audience" for Matt Denant.

1416 "Suggestions for Christmas Gifts: *Maid in Waiting,*" OPEN SHELF (Cleveland), Dec. 1931, p. 145.
[Inconsequential review.]

1417 Todd, Barbara Euphan. "Portrait of a Lady," SPECTATOR, CXLVII (7 Nov 1931), supp, 607.
JG continues to be a "great novelist" and "contemporary historian" in *Maid in Waiting* as he captures with "autumnal melancholy" the passing of the old age. Dinny Cherrell will hang in JG's "great picture gallery of English types." *Waiting* is an excellent, "sane . . . study of insanity."

1418 Watson, Ernest Bradlee, and Benfield Pressey (eds.) CONTEMPORARY DRAMA: ENGLISH AND IRISH PLAYS (NY: Charles Scribner's Sons, 1931), pp. 347–53; rptd as CONTEMPORARY DRAMA. NINE PLAYS (NY: Charles Scribner's Sons, 1931), pp. 169–71.
The chief JG dramatic characteristics are balance, intellectual rather than inspirational qualities, social concern, realism in form, poise, irony, and sense of proportion. [Biographical note and introduction to *Justice*.]

1419 West, Rebecca. "Galsworthy's Popularity: *Maid in Waiting* by John Galsworthy," NEW YORK HERALD TRIBUNE BOOKS, 15 Nov 1931, p. 1.
Although *Maid in Waiting* is not one of JG's major works, it is characteristic. Not "life-like . . . it is like life": "the whole story has no relation to life"; however, it is like life in its vivacious characterizations. "Such work is not, of course, authentic art; for the purpose of art is to enlarge man's experience of the universe, and this, having nothing to do with experience, cannot enlarge it." JG's exciting characterizations add to his popularity, but the lack of verisimilitude removes it from the realm of art.

1420 Whitman, Charles Huntington (ed). "*Strife*," SEVEN CONTEMPORARY PLAYS (Bost: Houghton Mifflin, 1931), pp. 546–50; rptd as REPRESENTATIVE MODERN DRAMAS (NY: MacMillan 1936), pp. 607–10.
JG views dramas as an undistorted record of life and character. His pervasive irony is detached and dispassionate; and he is sane, moderate, tolerant, and sympathetic. Dialogue is flexible, and workmanship careful. Major characters are vital, while minor ones tend to woodenness. [Appendix to the text of *Strife*.]

1421 Wild, Friedrich. DIE ENGLISCHE LITERATUR DER GEGENWART SEIT 1870: VERSDICHTUNGEN (UNTER AUSSCHLUSS DES DRAMAS) (English Literature since 1870: Poetry, excluding Verse Dramas) (Leipzig: Dioskuren Verlag, 1931), pp. 189, 258.
[Brief mention of JG's poetry.] [In German.]

1422 Winters, Edna Spring. "A Modern Socrates—John Galsworthy," (Ithaca, NY: [pvtly ptd], Sept 1931), 8 pp.
[This abstract of a Ph.D. dissertation offers a "pertinent comparison" of the life and thought of Socrates and JG: both are original philosophers who question life

independently, often with indirect criticism. Both accept the precept that "Love is a condition of the soul."]

1423 Woodbridge, Homer E. "Still Experimenting," SATURDAY RE-VIEW OF LITERATURE (NY), VIII (12 Dec 1931), 366.
Dinny of *Maid in Waiting* is JG's most delightful heroine, revealed fully and intimately; JG fails in trying to make Hallorsen an American because he does not know the American idiom. *The Roof* is a "curious and skillfully executed stunt," not good drama: the time scheme confuses; the play does not focus.

1424 Wyatt, Euphemia Van Rensselaer. *"The Roof,"* CATHOLIC WORLD, CXXXIV (Dec 1931), 333.
The Roof at the Charles Hopkins Theatre is a "study of humanity confronted with sudden death."

1425 Zucker, Irving. LE "COURT THÉÂTRE" (1904–1914) ET L'EVOLUTION DU THÉÂTRE ANGLAIS CONTEMPORAIN (The Court Theatre 1904–1914 and the Evolution of Contemporary English Theatre), (Paris: Les Presses Modernes, 1931), pp. 112–13.
[Zucker's discussion of *The Silver Box* and *The Fugitive*, primarily restating ideas from JG's *Another Sheaf* and "Some Platitudes Concerning Drama," contains no insight not found in Leon Schalit, JOHN GALSWORTHY: A SURVEY (NY: Scribner's; Lond: Heinemann, 1929) and R. H. Coats, JOHN GALSWORTHY AS A DRAMATIC ARTIST (NY: Scribner's, 1926). JG wants to make the public aware of the plight of the poor and oppressed through his sincere, impartial, and realistic drama.] [In French.]

1932

[For abstracts of items concerned with JG's receipt of the Nobel Prize for Literature, 1932, see Gunnar Ahlström (1967) and Anders Österling (1967).]

1426 Armstrong, Anne. *"Flowering Wilderness,"* SATURDAY REVIEW (Lond), CLIV (5 Nov 1932), 480.
Flowering Wilderness has depth and understanding—both a "moral problem and a meaning." Dinny is one of the great heroines of fiction. [Armstrong waxes sentimental.]

1427 Beach, Joseph Warren. THE TWENTIETH CENTURY NOVEL (NY: Appleton-Century-Crofts, 1932), Chap XXI and passim.
JG's multiple novels in series—*The Forsyte Saga, A Modern Comedy*—can be considered sequence novels. His works lack the "force, depth, and solidity" that one finds in Fielding, George Eliot, Mann, and Proust. Not only are his chapters

short, but their shifting from one center of interest to another indicates a lack of steadiness. "He is a graceful swimmer near the shores of human feeling, but he never ventures into the deep waters." His characters suffer the "mild pains of the well-to-do." A well-developed scene in his work is impossible. In fact, his popularity may in part be due to "readers who wish to spare their sensibilities." In his work there is a kind of sentimentalism "which results from simple want of intellectual thoroughness"; the end result of his work is a "scrappiness of effect."

1428 Bennett, Arnold. THE JOURNAL OF ARNOLD BENNETT. Three volumes (NY: Viking, 1932–33; Lond: Cassell, 1932–33); rptd, three vols in one (NY: Literary Guild, 1933).

[There are many scattered references to JG under various dates. "I couldn't *stick* the Galsworthy" (i.e., *Fraternity,* 20 Feb 1909), which Bennett reviewed for NEW AGE (see JOURNAL, 26 Feb 1909). Bennett reports that he got on well with JG at their first meeting, 7 April 1909. He likes *The Man of Property* and believes that the erotic passages suggests the influence of Moore; he praises *The Skin Game* and thinks that some of the principal characters in *Old English* are effective.]

1429 "Books," CHRISTIAN CENTURY, XLIX (23 Nov 1932), 1443.

[Paragraph review of *The Flowering Wilderness* emphasizing that Wilfred Desert's gunpoint conversion to Islam is not really interesting to Americans. JG's stature will give the novel some appeal.]

1430 Brande, Dorothea. "Four Novels," BOOKMAN (NY), LXXV (Dec 1932), 870.

Flowering Wilderness is a "grotesque imitation of a serious book" because JG avoids "all discussion of Christianity as a living religion." If JG were intent on presenting as the focal point a character who renounced his religion, he ought to have shown his readers "that he is capable of comprehending what religion is." [She misses the point.]

1431 Brion, Marcel. "John Galsworthy, prix Nobel" (John Galsworthy, Nobel Prizewinner), REVUE HEBDOMADAIRE, XLI (1932), 99–104 [not seen].

[In French.]

1432 Brown, Ivor. "The Play: *Loyalties* by John Galsworthy," WEEK-END REVIEW (Lond), VI (27 Aug 1932), 232.

Loyalties at the Garrick Theatre is a "modern tragedy" in which "gents are gents and Jews are Jews, and the twain meet at some risk to social harmony."

1433 Chesne, A. Chesnier du. "M. John Galsworthy, prix Nobel" (Mr. John Galsworthy, Nobel Prizewinner), L'OPINION (Paris), 25th year, No. 24 (19 Nov 1932), pp. 11–12.

JG is less known than Kipling to French readers. His pity is limited by the fact that he is a gentleman; he is a lover of justice but remains objective; his work evinces a pantheistic tendency; he is a good craftsman as a novelist. [JG is criticized for implying, in connection with Irene and Fleur, that adultery is something typically French and for calling a dog Foch in *Flowering Wilderness*. This biographical sketch warmly approves the award of the Nobel Prize to JG.] [In French.]

1434 Collins, Norman. THE FACTS OF FICTION (Lond: Victor Gollancz, 1932; NY: Dutton, 1933), pp. 41, 128, 269–75.

JG's plays are concerned primarily with the heart rather than with causes. The characters in *The Forsyte Saga* really are actors in a "morality play" with Soames something of a Malvolio and Irene something of an Ophelia. JG, like the elderly Soames, stands "apart, sedate, superior, a little supercilious. And just a little anxious about himself." [This general subjective comment gives no evidence of critical analysis.]

1435 Cowley, Malcolm. "Nobel Prizeman," NEW REPUBLIC, LXXIII (14 Dec 1932), 133–34.

Flowering Wilderness is written by a class writer, a "proletarian . . . turned upside down." The days of the class writer, however, are gone; and JG is "all the Shakespeare" that the type has.

1436 Daniel-Rops. "Le prix Nobel: [John Galsworthy]" (The Nobel Prize), LA VIE INTELLECTUELLE, XVIII (25 Dec 1932), 507–11.

The awarding of the Nobel Prize provides an insight into the prevailing concerns in the world at large, and it is significant that JG, whose work bears witness to the present social unrest, is the latest recipient. Although he is well-known in France (Calmann-Lévy has published most of *The Forsyte Saga*), French readers are not familiar with his work. At times, in *To Let,* for example, JG seems to verge on the tedious twaddle of Arnold Bennett. Nevertheless, JG has great gifts. His characters are true to life; Soames is a great success. JG steers a middle course between the tragic and the comic; he has an inborn sense of nature and conveys to his readers the drama of creation and life from a pantheistic, not a Christian, point of view. Although JG possesses great talents, he is no genius. His true greatness lies in the discovery that the tragedy of our times lies in the conflict between material forces and moral truth. His work consists in the study of men of property, a class he has painted with great insight and irony. He can, unlike Zola, vary his portraits, and he never identifies the man with the caste. JG works to suggest a spiritual attitude; his models are Dickens, Balzac, Maupassant, and Chekhov. JG suggests as a solution the gift of oneself. Charles Péguy, like JG, saw the close relationship between the avarice of the hand and the avarice of the soul. Although JG's work has a high moral value, it fails to satisfy us completely because it lacks "the deep meditation" without which "true charity cannot possibly evolve." [In French.]

1437 Davey, Randall. "Portrait. John Galsworthy," SATURDAY REVIEW OF LITERATURE (NY), IX (26 Nov 1932), 269.
[Davey's portrait is reproduced with a brief comment about JG receiving the Nobel Prize.]

1438 De Bruyn, Jeanne. "John Galsworthy," DIETSCHE WARANDE EN BELFORT [Amsterdam], XXXII (1932), 83–92.
Whereas Hardy belongs to the moderns, JG doesn't; as an artist JG belongs to the period before World War I. He is a liberal in the philosophic, not political, sense, and there is within him a near pathetic urge to be fair. Books like *Fraternity, The Island Pharisees,* and *The First and the Last* do not indicate that JG is a member of the establishment. *The Freelands,* which is a story of good will, depicts a total inability of the characters to *do* something. His works as a dramatist are not among his most powerful, but a few of his short stories and novels are among the best to be found. Although he is sometimes careless in his writing, his descriptions are excellent. His best novels are *The Man of Property* and *Freelands.* Irene is one of the few truly poetic persons created by JG, and yet she does not fit into the environment he created for her. The novels of *A Modern Comedy* are weaker and do not belong with *The Forsyte Saga.* The morals, goals, and ambitions of the postwar youth are unknown to JG. Although he is not a born storyteller, JG is a born psychologist. His is a mild pessimism. He is not a great writer, but there are a few images one remembers—the man from the city, Irene, and the pair of farmer's girls in "A Man of Devon"; JG is a waiverer, one " 'who sees both sides of every question and so, of course, is not good at making up his mind.' " [In Flemish.]

1439 F., D. C. *"Loyalties,"* THEATRE WORLD (Lond), XVIII (Sept 1932), 120.
JG depicts the conflict between Dancy and De Levis with brilliant dramatic skill. Although the acting cannot be compared with that of the original 1922 production, the play is intensely gripping and perfectly constructed.

1440 Fabes, Gilbert H. "Introduction," JOHN GALSWORTHY. HIS FIRST EDITIONS: POINTS AND VALUES (Lond: W. & G. Foyle, 1932), pp. ix–xxiv.
[The introduction contains a brief record of the progress of JG items to 1932 and some general comments on book collecting. The bibliography itself contains bibliographical descriptions of the works and their current (i.e., 1932) value, ranging from the uncut *Island Pharisees* (£150) and *Captures,* first issue (£100) to *The Land, The Little Man,* and *The Roof* (5 s.).]

1441 Finn, R. Weldon (ed). A GALSWORTHY OCTAVE (Lond: Heinemann, 1932), pp. vii–xv.
JG is the most restrained of contemporary writers. From 1900 on in his development there are "two inseparable" JG's, the poet and the ironic satirist. In his

drama JG creates characters by emphasizing their essentially normal humanness; there is no exploitation of the abnormal. He is not fatalistic because his realistic criticism of life does not fail to suggest a way out, and he does not give in to the "national habit of compromise." He gives non-Englishmen insight into British life and culture. Soames, for example—while one has never met him, one can recognize his every foible in someone else. Unlike Dickens, he does not caricature. JG was a born rebel—against convention, stultifying mental environment, restriction of personal liberty, and sentimentality. JG deals with the humor in life without having to fabricate jokes. [The collection is a selection of short stories and excerpts, each one preceded by an explanatory but uncritical headnote and followed by a series of questions relating to the excerpt.]

1442 *"Flowering Wilderness,"* A.L.A. BOOKLIST, XXIX (Dec 1932), 114.
"A polished, richly detailed social study," *Flowering Wilderness* is more meaningful to British than to American readers. [Brief notice of publication.]

1443 *"Flowering Wilderness,"* CHRISTIAN SCIENCE MONITOR, 3 Dec 1932, p. 7.
The plot of *Flowering Wilderness* strains credulity, and Wilfred is not consistently drawn; yet JG's usual craftsmanlike style, especially in dialogue, is evident.

1444 *"Flowering Wilderness,"* FORUM (NY), LXXXVIII (Dec 1932), ix.
JG's skill allows the improbable plot—emanating from Wilfred Desert's turning Islamic at gunpoint—to be convincing in *Flowering Wilderness*.

1445 *"Flowering Wilderness,"* PITTSBURGH MONTHLY BULLETIN, XXXVII (Dec 1932), 76.
[Brief review.]

1446 Furman, Hazel Winslow. "The Ideas in Galsworthy's Plays and How He Conveys Them to the Audience," UNIVERSITY OF COLORADO STUDIES: ABSTRACTS OF THESES FOR HIGHER DEGREES, 1932, XX (1932), 34–35. Master's thesis.
Some of the devices JG uses to convey the ideas in his plays to his audiences are the following: (1) use of illustrative stories; (2) use of two parallel cases; (3) use of illustrative incidents; (4) use of group discussions. Other devices are "repetition, contrast, symbolism, special sound effects, and significant pantomime."

1447 "Galsworthy Awarded Nobel Prize," PUBLISHER'S WEEKLY (NY), CXXII (12 Nov 1932), 1860.
JG's idealism is a chief justification for being awarded the Nobel Prize for Literature. "*Strife* . . . first brought [JG] . . . to the attention of a wide audience in America and made him felt as a social force." [A brief, four-paragraph appreciation.]

1448 "Galsworthy—One of God's Fools," WORLD TOMORROW (NY), XV (23 Nov 1932), 483.

Although H. G. Wells is certainly as worthy of the honor, the award of the Nobel Prize to JG shows intelligent judgment.

1449 "Galsworthy's Latest: *Flowering Wilderness* and Upper-Class Tradition," SPRINGFIELD REPUBLICAN (Mass), 20 Nov 1932, Sec. E, p. 7.

The plot of *Flowering Wilderness* is tenuous; JG "has not made his people sufficiently aware of the social changes wrought by the war."

1450 Greene, Graham. "A Prisoner of the Forsytes," SPECTATOR (Lond), CXLIX (8 Oct 1932), 454.

Candelabra's chief value is the insight it gives into the thought of the creator of *The Forsyte Saga*.

1451 Guyot, Edouard. "John Galsworthy: De l'homme à l'écrivain" (John Galsworthy: From the Man to the Writer), REVUE DES VIVANTS; ORGANE DES GENERATIONS DE LA GUERRE, VI (1932), 758–74.

That JG is a Roman patrician can be readily seen from his portrait. His Englishness is a primary characteristic. Balzac's characters are driven by their lust for money; they are complete strangers to beauty, tenderness, or even a joy of living. JG is not a novelist like Balzac, but Balzac's characters are the ancestors of JG's characters. The avarice of JG's characters has become less savage and more decorous.

Such terms as "reward" and "punishment" are not appropriate to JG's work. His characters are rewarded or punished for what they have done and not for what they are. Although his characters suffer and are often anxiety-ridden, they remain masters of themselves (unlike Hardy's characters, who are often shattered). JG remains sufficiently impartial that he shuns any intervention that would deprive his characters of their autonomy.

Pity is an important force in his work; it makes him more than a simple painter of customs. His pity is completely human, and yet it seems to have its source not only in JG's temperament but also in a principle that one may call divine. (One is reminded of Sterne.) JG's pity is almost cosmic in nature. He came late to literature, and in his work there is no character that speaks directly for JG. [In French.]

1452 H., G. F. "Problems of Control over Character and Plot," ILLUSTRATED LONDON NEWS, CLXXXI (3 Sept 1932), 338.

A revival of *Loyalties* at the Garrick Theatre emphasizes the problem of "stress on design," the exercise of the "conscious deliberate mind at the expense of essential truth." [General remarks on the topic of the title have passing references to *Loyalties*, accompanied by a still of a scene from *Loyalties*.]

1453 Herrick, Marvin Theodore. "Current English Usage and the Dramas of Galsworthy," AMERICAN SPEECH, VII (Aug 1932), 412–19.
JG's "On Expression" provides a statement of his theory about language. From a study of the language of his plays one may conclude that JG "has never avoided the common speech of his fellow men; he has merely avoided the extremes" of the overstatement and the understatement. He "has deliberately cast his lot with current usage."

1454 Hutchens, John. "Greece to Broadway: Broadway in Review," THEATRE ARTS MONTHLY, XVI (Jan 1932), 13–24.
The Roof has "excellent dialogue" but "bad structure"; the play fails because the disparate schematic items are not fused; the conclusion prepared for does not materialize.

1455 Hutchison, Percy. "John Galsworthy in His Most Acidly Ironical Vein," NEW YORK TIMES BOOK REVIEW, 13 Nov 1932, p. 5.
Flowering Wilderness continues JG's "satirical description of the postwar, post-Forsyte world." *Wilderness* is better than *The Man of Property* in perception of artistry and the attempt to discipline the confused contemporary scene into terms of art. Not the lack of loyalty (the theme of *Wilderness*) but his own mental state drives Wilfred away from Dinny. JG is acidly ironic in his treatment of professing Christians. [Hutchison, a pro-Galsworthy reviewer, seems defensive about what he fears will be negative critical reaction to the later Galsworthy novels.]

1456 Leavis, J. D. FICTION AND THE READING PUBLIC (Lond: Chatto & Windus, 1932), pp. 36, 39, 46, 63, 71, 76.
A newspaper questionnaire in 1930 identified JG as the first favorite among living writers; he is a respected middlebrow novelist. The plays of Shaw and JG and the novels of writers like Philip Gibbs, Wells, and JG have helped in spreading the ideas and feelings of the intellectuals before 1914 among the masses.

1457 Lovett, Robert Morss, and Helen Sard Hughes. THE HISTORY OF THE NOVEL IN ENGLAND (Bost: Houghton Mifflin, 1932), pp. 382–88, 443.
JG "holds the most distinguished place in English fiction today," representing the "English tradition of realism directed by a belief in the significance of things" and uniting them through symbolism. His fundamental theme is social stratification. The Forsytes are the same as Arnold's Philistines haunted by scandal. The plays often emphasize struggles of different parts of society. JG's eclecticism suggests historical development. Documentation is as careful as Zola's, "with the added skill of the lawyer in weighing evidence," using "newer psychology." Analysis is "less rigid than Eliot's and less idiosyncratic than Meredith's"—without their sentimental attachment to characters and with a kindness shot through with irony. The consciousness of Soames is important in *The Man of Property*. Occasionally JG uses Meredith's "oblique method of writing," but without Meredith's whimsy. Technically he is indebted to Henry

James; and philosophically he suggests some of Hardy's pessimism. He senses the hopelessness of class separation, reflecting the "inadequacy of humanity . . . to meet its situation." JG's works are full of the suggestion of human kinship with animals, especially dogs.

1458 *"Maid In Waiting,"* FORUM (NY), LXXXVII (Jan 1932), vi.
[A plot summary suggesting some improbabilities serves as a short book review of *Maid In Waiting.*]

1459 "Mr. Galsworthy's Essays," TIMES LITERARY SUPPLEMENT (Lond), 29 Sept 1932, p. 685.
The essays in *Candelabra* express JG's philosophy of humanism, which holds that "men's fate is in their own hands, for better, for worse."

1460 "New Novels," TIMES LITERARY SUPPLEMENT (Lond), 3 Nov 1932, p. 810.
[A favorable summarizing review of *Flowering Wilderness.*]

1461 "Nobel Prize for Literature," NEW REPUBLIC, LXXIII (23 Nov 1932), 29–30.
[Brief notice about JG's receiving the Nobel prize, emphasizing its appropriateness because JG represents the "idealistic, humanitarian impulse" that the Nobel Foundation typifies.]

1462 "The Nobel Prize: Mr. Galsworthy," LONDON MERCURY, XXVII (Dec 1932), 99–100.
JG has been awarded the Nobel Prize for Literature, despite the fact that "to the best of our knowledge" the British Nobel Committee has not functioned for years because of the Swedish Academy's refusal to consider seriously the candidacy of Thomas Hardy. JG is to be congratulated as a "laborious craftsman" and a hard-working public servant who has promoted international understanding. While opinions differ about the permanence of his work, his life has been "devoted to the service of humanity; from the moral point of view he has never written a line that he need wish to blot."

1463 "Nobelova cena Galsworthymu" (Nobel Prize to Galsworthy), PESTRÝ TÝDEN (Prague), VII:47 (19 Nov 1932), 3.
[Photograph and brief notice of JG's works.] [In Czech.]

1464 P., V. S. "Mr. Galsworthy's Opinions," CHRISTIAN SCIENCE MONITOR, 15 Oct 1932, p. 5.
JG says "nothing very striking" with amiability and wit in *Candelabra*. A "judicial bleakness" of temper complements his belief that pessimism is realism.

1465 Paterson, Isabel. "New Scenes from Galsworthy's Rich Pageant," NEW YORK HERALD TRIBUNE BOOKS, 13 Nov 1932, p. 3.

[Plot-summary review of *Flowering Wilderness* emphasizing JG's gentleness, grace, and sympathy. Paterson questions whether or not the theme of *Wilderness* will appeal to Americans. Edmund Sullivan's 1930 etching of JG is reproduced, along with W. T. Benda's conception of what Dinny Cherrell looks like.]

1466 Reely, Mary Katharine. "A Selected List of Current Books: *Flowering Wilderness*," WISCONSIN LIBRARY BULLETIN (Madison), XXVIII (Dec 1932), 335.
[Inconsequential review.]

1467 Reilly, Joseph John. "John Galsworthy—An Appraisal," BOOKMAN (NY), LXXIV (Jan–Feb 1932), 483–93; rptd in OF BOOKS AND MEN (NY: Julian Messner, 1942), pp. 108–16.
JG's reputation is largely founded on the two *Forsyte Saga* trilogies. JG is a conscientious workman, with the kind of care one would expect of a solicitor; it is no accident that his "most completely realized" male character, Soames, is a "lawyer, meticulously attentive to every detail of his life; that he has, in a word, the Galsworthian conscience." Fleur also has a "similar sense of orderliness and efficiency" despite her postwar environment; so has Michael Mont. JG's orderliness is also evident in his style, which is "smooth, graceful, supple . . . competent . . . skilful." His principal concern is with social conditions affected by the injustice, selfishness, and lack of vision of the wealthy and aristocratic classes. Poverty and its attendant evils are not seen primarily as "superscientific questions" as in Wells, or as "merely personal conditions like Bennett," or as things to be "triumphed over by an imagination . . . but as objects of human sympathy and intolerable effects of a social and economic situation for which well-to-do Britons must be answerable."

Soames's defeat by Irene prefigures the downfall of his social order. In Fleur the "undying possessive passion of Soames" changes from "the acquisition of property" to "the gratification of merely social ambition, personal vanity, and even lust." In *Saga,* his irony and satire imply that society is polarizing. *A Modern Comedy* implies that things are drifting toward "moral chaos." JG's attitude seems to be that summed up in Young Jolyon's attitude "to be kind, and keep your end up—there's nothing else in it."

Stylistically, JG's characters, especially Annette, Bosinney, and Irene, lack the vitality of those in Bennett's OLD WIVES' TALES. The older Forsytes for the most part are "brought as near to a three dimensional existence as they ever get by the device of a pet interest or a pet phrase in the Dickens manner." Only in *The Man of Property* is Soames a "human creature, capable of thought and action"; he later becomes "less corporeal." Reasons for lack of character development can be attributed to JG's involvement in the contemporary English scene; and to the feminine strain that is "revealed in his style and in his eye for decorative, non-essentials of deportment, appearance, or *milieu*" and that prevent his men from taking form. JG fails as a great novelist because of lack of verisimilitude. [Good criticism, in which Reilly tries to counteract the critics who have praised JG without truly realizing the nature of the function of the novelist in creating the Jamesian "illusion of life."]

1468 Roberts, Kenneth. "For Authors Only," SATURDAY EVENING POST, CCV (24 Sept 1932), 14, 46, 48, 50.
[Roberts mentions in passing JG's struggles in presenting an American scientist and professor in *Maid in Waiting,* citing the scrambling of some Anglo-Americanisms. A photo of JG with his dog is reproduced.]

1469 Robertson, Stuart. "American Speech According to Galsworthy," AMERICAN SPEECH, VII:4 (April 1932), 297–301.
JG fails in his attempts to reproduce American speech in his works; his failure can be particularly noted in the speech of Professor Hallorsen (*Maid in Waiting*), Francis Wilmot (*The Silver Spoon*), and the American in "The Little Man."

1470 *"The Roof, A Play in Seven Scenes,"* A.L.A. BOOKLIST, XXVIII (Jan 1932), 190.
[Brief plot summary.]

1471 Schriftgiesser, Edward B. "John Galsworthy's *Flowering Wilderness:* His Latest Novel Seems to Suggest a Text Book Dealing with Ethical Problems," BOSTON EVENING TRANSCRIPT BOOK SECTION, 19 Nov 1932, p. 2.
Unlike most British authors, JG "still takes the trouble to give plot" to his writings, at the same time giving clear characterizations and remaining true to the distinctive "flavor" of the English dialogue. *Flowering Wilderness* is, in some respects, comparable to a textbook of ethical problems—a fault occasionally noticed in several of his other works.

1472 "A Selection from the More Recent Titles: *Flowering Wilderness,"* OPEN SHELF (Cleveland), July 1932, p. 16.
[Inconsequential review.]

1473 Strong, L. A. G. *"Flowering Wilderness,"* SPECTATOR (Lond), CXLIX (11 Nov 1932), 672.
Flowering Wilderness is excellent JG. The book, built around a special problem in conduct (Wilfrid's "pukka sahib" shortcomings), "speedily transcends its issues for something universal." The book is a triumph despite some minor flaws such as Dinny's wisecracks and occasional "ill-timed analysis and description."

1474 "A Touch of Fever," NEW STATESMAN AND NATION, IV (12 Nov 1932), 592, 594.
Flowering Wilderness is another of JG's "untiring tributes to beauty and despairing love" amid a realistic background of London society.

1475 Turynowa, Felicja. *"Saga rodu Forsyte'ow* Galsworthy'ego" (Galsworthy's *Forsyte Saga*), PRZEGLĄD WSPÓŁCZESNY, 1932, pp. 373–80 [not seen].
[In Polish.]

1476 Ulmann, Doris. "Portrait of John Galsworthy," BOOKMAN (NY), LXXV (Dec 1932), 777.
[Doris Ulmann's photo of JG and a caption announcing that he has received the Nobel Prize for Literature.]

1477 Walpole, Hugh. "Prelude to Adventure," THE APPLE TREES: FOUR REMINISCENCES (Waltham Saint Lawrence: Golder Cockerel P, 1932), pp. 21, 40.
[Literary chitchat in which JG's name is among dozens dropped.]

1478 Weeks, Edward. *"Flowering Wilderness,"* ATLANTIC BOOK-SHELF, Dec 1932, [n.p.].
The reaction to Wilfred Desert's pistol-point conversion to Mohammedanism in *Flowering Wilderness* is too theatrical for belief. [Brief review of *Wilderness*, lamenting JG's lack of humor and his waning power of sympathy.]

1479 Woodbridge, Homer E. "Pukka Sahib," SATURDAY REVIEW OF LITERATURE (NY), IX (26 Nov 1932), 269.
Dinny's dominant trait in *Flowering Wilderness* is "generous chivalry." Overindulgence in the "point of honor motif" will turn away many non-British readers: but JG does perform a "notable achievement" in satirizing this overindulgence. The story is a credible "modern and subtle variation" of the ancient conflict of love and honor—from the point of view of the heroine.

1480 "The World and the Theatre," THEATRE ARTS MONTHLY, XVI (March 1932), 261–68.
[General essay with subtitle "Playwrights Vs. Novelists," commenting that JG the novelist is better than JG the dramatist.]

1481 Z., I. "John Galsworthy. *Maid in Waiting,"* INOSTRANNAIA KNIGA, No. 2 (1932), 70–71 [not seen].
[Review of *Maid in Waiting.*] [In Russian.]

1933

1482 Abramov, A. "Poslednie iz Forsaetov" (The Last of the Forsytes), VECHERNAYA MOSKVA, 5 Feb 1933, p. 3, cols. 2–6.
JG was the "literary bard of the English conservative bourgeoisie." With his death one has come to the end of a vast sociological panorama of English history

covering the last half-century. His *Forsyte Saga,* written in the tradition of the English realistic novel as influenced by Meredith, Tolstoi, and Zola, provides a somewhat iconographic but undoubtedly sensible portrayal of the bourgeois milieu. (Rosa Luxemburg wrote a letter, 7 July 1916, to Sophie Liebknecht praising *The Man of Property.*) JG saw the doom of a society based on the sanctity of private property. "Unfortunately and ironically . . . with the change in the social makeup of the epoch the political makeup of the writer also changes. Irony disappears and increasingly the Man of Property acquires the author's sympathy." In *Swan Song* one sees JG's perplexity as an artist in dealing with the general strike of 1926 when he is faced with the appearance of a new force on the historic stage. In this sense one can contrast JG with Dreiser (AN AMERICAN TRAGEDY). The decline of JG's talent can be seen in his preoccupation with religion in *Flowering Wilderness,* written at the time of the general strike. Because JG was a Forsyte himself he "could not and did not want to understand the new England, whose voice he heard at the time of the general strike." [In Russian] [For another report on this essay see D., K. N. "Galsworthy's Works in the Soviet Union," ADELPHI (Lond), nsVI (Aug 1933), 364–66.]

1483 Alexander, Henry. "Galsworthy as Dramatist," QUEEN'S QUARTERLY, XL (May 1933), 177–88.

Whereas his later novels (except for the last three) show a steady advance in content and technique, JG's later plays decline. A social critic of human organizations and society rather than of cosmic flaws, JG diagnoses rather than prescribes a remedy. The themes of strife, of the harshness of the law, "of dangers of press publicity, persecution of the idealist," and family problems date the plays. His famed impartiality gives both positive and negative results, as in capital vs. labor in *Strife* and rich vs. poor in *The Silver Box. Strife* illustrates well JG's pervasive sympathy for human suffering; *Box* introduces a new colloquial speech suitable for the humble people, as well as the ironic humor as the underdog indulges in. The most moving scene of *Justice* is Falder's solitary confinement, "a masterly piece of realism": although not tragic in the Aristotelian sense, there is tragedy in the inability of a weak character to face the challenge of his environment. *The Skin Game* and *Loyalties* treat social acceptability impartially. The episodic *Escape* and *The Roof* suggest cinema rather than stage, lacking adequate plot construction. Typing of social classes in *Escape* is psychologically inadequate. *The Little Dream,* a symbolic poetic fantasy, and *Windows,* combining symbolism and realism, are out of JG's area of competence. *The Little Man, Pigeon,* and *Joy* have tragedy implicit even if the tragic motif is not so prominent as in other JG plays.

1484 Armstrong, Anne. *"Over the River,"* SATURDAY REVIEW (Lond), CLVI (7 Oct 1933), 372–73.

[The general, laudatory, and brief review champions JG's treatment of women.]

1485 Armstrong, Anne. "The Women of Galsworthy," SATURDAY REVIEW (Lond), CLV (4 Feb 1933), 115.

JG was right in making "his women no more than incidental music in the great male orchestra of property and business." But in later works, JG's women are "more effective than his men." [More follows, but note-taking stopped when general criticism gave way to specifics—and Fleur somehow became Irene's daughter.]

1486 Baillon de Wailly, L. "Les Littératures Etrangères: John Galsworthy," (Foreign Literatures: John Galsworthy), REVUE BLEUE, LXXI:13 (1 July 1933), 408–12.

JG is a keen and honest observer, a clear-headed though not pitiless critic, a realist who keeps his feelings in check, and a conscientious artist whose books conform to classic rules of precision and clarity. A national writer, JG shows by his mental unrest how deeply he cares for the values he criticizes, and his motto is the same as Jolyon's: to be good and to go courageously one's own way. There is a note of bitterness and disillusionment in JG's wisdom and also an element of pity for mankind. His work is similar to that of the writer Georges Duhamel and the painter Camille Corot. [This sketch of JG's career and personality recalls his lecture at the Sorbonne in 1925 and emphasizes his qualities as a writer and portrayer of society: his sense of justice, his generosity, and his artistic self-control.] [In French.]

1487 Bates, Ernest S. "John Galsworthy," ENGLISH JOURNAL, XXII (1933), 437–46.

[An appreciation.]

1488 Bellessort, André. "John Galsworthy, Prix Nobel" (John Galsworthy, Nobel Prize Winner), LE CORRESPONDANT, No. 1687 (10 Jan 1933), 123–31.

JG is a great novelist who would have been a very great novelist had he used a little more severity towards himself. The award of the Nobel Prize to JG is a judicious choice. Although his ideas are critical of the established order, JG was not constrained or restricted by them as he created his characters. Despite the fact that his radical ideas make him read like a "primer," his ability as a novelist allows him to rise above these limitations. His heroines are especially successful, and his greatest novel is *The Dark Flower*. [In French.]

1489 Birnbaum-Gohr, J. "John Galsworthy," DER TÜRMER (Stuttgart), XXXV, part 2 (1933), 271–72.

JG's worldwide fame rests on his novels. He was a member of the upper middle class, and he became its critical historian. He combined Ruskin's and Pater's doctrines of beauty with Carlyle's ethos of moral strictness, and Thackeray's realism with the lyrical softness of the neo-Romantics. His novels mark the end of a phase in the history of the English novel. *The Forsyte Saga* is his greatest achievement, showing his power of psychological analysis and his ability to evoke the phenomenal world through carefully observed details. His plays, the best of which is *Justice*, have suffered from neglect in Germany. [In German.]

1490 Brickell, Herschel. "The Literary Landscape," NORTH AMERICAN REVIEW, CCXXXV (Jan 1933), 87–96.
JG presents an exact and accurate picture in *Flowering Wilderness*, but he has difficulty with modern dialogue.

1491 Brickell, Herschel. "The Literary Landscape," NORTH AMERICAN REVIEW, CCXXXVI (Dec 1933), 567–76.
One More River is one of JG's best later novels—better because of reasonableness of plot and absence of Americans.

1492 Brown, Ivor. "The Play: *Strife* by John Galsworthy," WEEKEND REVIEW (Lond), 20 May 1933, p. 562.
Strife, revived in 1933 at the Little Theatre, reminds the theatergoer how much tastes have changed. An example of audacious realism in 1908, it still has valid theatrical qualities.

1493 Butcher, Fanny. "Critic Presents Intimate View of Galsworthy," CHICAGO DAILY TRIBUNE, 4 Feb 1933, p. 14.
[Obit essay emphasizing JG the gentleman.]

1494 Canby, Henry Seidel. "Galsworthy: An Estimate," SATURDAY REVIEW OF LITERATURE, IX (18 March 1933), 485–87; rptd in ESSAY ANNUAL: 1933, ed by E. A. Walter (Chicago: Scott, Foresman, 1933); and in Henry Seidel Canby, SEVEN YEARS' HARVEST: NOTES ON CONTEMPORARY LITERATURE (NY: Farrar & Rinehart, 1936), pp. 30–39.
JG cannot be categorized simply as idealist, romanticist, or sentimentalist. He was a great realist in the way realism mattered to the English in the early twentieth century. Personal experience with JG revealed him to be the "liberal, intellectual aristocrat, spiritual, sensitive, humanitarian, proud." JG presents the "bourgeois aristocracy" that "subtly modified" the old code of behavior, keeping responsibility to state, class, chivalry, and duty, but turning their backs on the "Cyprian Venus" and those gods whose "duty it is to see that the human heart stays human." Property made and chilled the Forsytes. Soames's story is that of the nineteenth-century Englishman "wrestling with property, and thrown by it at the moment of apparent victory." Soames "knows what he cannot have and gives it up—a stoic, not to be envied, not to be loved, but . . . to be respected and approved." *The Forsyte Saga* is "a tragi-comedy with a stoic ending." JG was respected on the Continent because in "him and his were to be found the living explanations of what England was in the period of her dominating greatness." Europeans saw that JG's work was epic in scope (despite faults of sentiment and diffuseness) and "had that broad stretch of significance, which, since Balzac and the Russians, we have expected of fiction that deals with mores

rather than manners." JG gives the "moral meaning of a generation": concern with fundamental morality is what gives novelists and dramatists magnitude. The theater did not give JG enough room; he was at his best "pageant-wise, not drama-wise," his strength being in the slow tenacity of descriptive narrative, not in quick symbols or isolated events; but JG ought to have left Americans alone in *Saga*. [Excellent overview of JG's contributions, written as a tribute shortly after his death.]

1495 *"Candelabra,"* CHRISTIAN CENTURY, L (15 March 1933), 362. [Brief, favorable notice of publication of *Candelabra*; JG is contemplative, penetrating, and serene.]

1496 *"Candelabra:* Posthumous Volume of John Galsworthy's Essays," SPRINGFIELD REPUBLICAN (Mass), 24 May 1933, p. 10. JG's light touch makes the heavy subject matter of *Candelabra* palatable. The collection is an excellent introduction to his voluminous works.

1497 *"Candelabra, Selected Essays and Addresses,"* A.L.A. BOOK-LIST, XXIX (April 1933), 235. [Brief notice announces the appearance of a collection of essays ranging in date from 1909 to 1931.]

1498 Č[apek], K[arel]. "Autor *Forsytu* zemřel" (The Author of *The Forsyte Saga* is Dead), LIDOVE NOVINY (Prague), XLI:57 (1933), 1 [not seen]. [Obit.] [In Czech.]

1499 Chassé, Ch. "John Galsworthy est mort" (John Galsworthy Is Dead), FIGARO, 1 Feb 1933, p. 5. JG's success was never comparable to that of Dickens, Wells, or Kipling. His plays—*Strife, Justice, The Silver Box*—were dramatic triumphs, and yet not long ago he had announced his intention of not writing for the theater. He refused the offer of a knighthood. His work was thought to be too socialistic by the aristocracy. Although he criticized middle-class ideals, he remained attached to them. Like Meredith he criticized egoism, but unlike Meredith he did not avoid intervening personally in his novels. His purpose was to rouse the reader's pity without advocating a political solution to social problems. He dreamed of a moral, not a social, revolution: he wanted to help his countrymen to see, to understand, and to love. He would have had the aristocracy resume its former role as revered guides of the masses, as undisputed masters of the nation. [Favorable evaluations of JG's work by Abel Chevalley, LE ROMAN ANGLAIS DE NOTRE TEMPS (Lond: Milford, 1921) and Madeleine L. Cazamian in REVUE ANGLO-AMÉRICAINE (1925) are referred to.] [In French.]

1500 "Chronicle and Comment: Mr. Galsworthy's England and Mr. Lewis's America," BOOKMAN (NY), LXXVI (Jan 1933), 48.

When JG received the Nobel Prize, the English press was curiously quiet. Apparently the rest of the world, especially America, appreciates his novels for having "built up a private picture of England and the English people; and this picture, representative or not, is unacceptable to the Englishman of 1932." This situation parallels that of Sinclair Lewis who, after receiving the Nobel Prize, was subjected to much hostile criticism for having presented "a distorted picture of his country to the rest of the world."

1501 Chudoba, František. "John Galsworthy zemřel" (John Galsworthy Is Dead), LIDOVE NOVINY (Prague), XLI:57 (1933), 5 [not seen]. [Obit.] [In Czech.]

1502 Chudoba F[rantišek]. "Pohled do dílny Johna Galsworthyho" (A Look into John Galsworthy's Workshop), NOVÉ ČECHY (Prague), XVI (1933), 124–32, 165–71, 240–45.
JG's early works reflect the Victorian optimism in humanity he inherited from his father and described in "Portrait." His experiences during the World War and his travels around the world destroyed his belief in a loving God and the perfectibility of mankind; a pessimism pervades his later works. Turgenev and Maupassant provided JG with models of literary realism. The *Forsyte Saga* gives a more lyrical expression of his views than is found in his earlier works. The mood of both Turgenev's and JG's works, passive dissatisfaction, was due to an inability to find in humanity, nature, art, or beauty a recompense for a lost faith in absolute existence. Neither was able, like Hardy, to accept the idea of a blind Will, and neither was able to accept the beliefs of the older or younger generations. This was the source of their spiritual melancholy. [In Czech.]

1503 Codman, Florence. *"One More River,"* NATION (NY), CXXXVII (22 Nov 1933), 601.
JG is repetitious in *One More River,* and he does not use material wisely. [Brief review.]

1504 Colton, Arthur. "A Variety of Essays. *Candelabra,"* SATURDAY REVIEW OF LITERATURE (NY), IX (22 April 1933), 547.
JG's chief asset as a writer is "a certain cleanness of workmanship." He was a good novelist and dramatist of his time because of his "extraordinary clearheadedness."

1505 Cortissoz, Royal. "Novelist on a Holiday Discusses His Art: Galsworthy Felt That Art Alone Could Destroy the Barriers Between Man and Man," NEW YORK HERALD TRIBUNE BOOKS, 5 March 1933, p. 6.
Candelabra has an infusion of "quiet . . . urbane . . . and persuasive" rationalism. Most interesting are the essays that explore JG's "mystery . . . tastes and convictions."

1506 Croman, Natalie. JOHN GALSWORTHY: A STUDY IN CONTINUITY AND CONTRAST (Cambridge: Harvard UP [Radcliffe Honors Thesis in English No. 3], 1933).

It is the motif of possession that links the novels and interludes of *The Forsyte Saga* and *A Modern Comedy*. The "dark texture" of Soames's character which JG developed in *The Man of Property* changes to the "comically pathetic" in the tranquil and mellow mood of *In Chancery*. The "terrible and grim spirit haunting the darkly turbulent *Man of Property*" is missing in JG's later Forsyte novels. *To Let* is, artistically and philosophically, the transition novel. The contrast between Soames and young Jolyon states "the large truth of *In Chancery*," just as the juxtaposition between Soames and Prosper Profond conveys the message of *To Let*. In *To Let* the drama of *Property* is reenacted, but instead of the bitterly ironic mood JG evokes an idyllic mood for the love story of Jon and Fleur. In *The White Monkey* JG's portrayal of Fleur is far removed from his initial manner of treating the possessive theme; Fleur in *The Silver Spoon* appears in a humorous light. Not until *Swan Song* does JG return to the original motif in his theme of possession. "*A Modern Comedy* is the most diffuse, the most superficial, of the novelist's studies of manners. Its characters, with the exception of Soames, and possibly Fleur, are the least vital."

1507 Cross, Wilbur. "Well and Fair," YALE REVIEW, nsXXII (Summer 1933), 816–17.

In *Candelabra* JG argues that novels are remembered primarily because of characters; his method is to enliven "realistic portraiture with quasi-satire."

1508 Cunliffe, J. W. ENGLISH LITERATURE IN THE TWENTIETH CENTURY (NY: Macmillan, 1933; 1934; 1935; 1939), pp. 163–84; rptd (Freeport, NY: Books for Libraries P, 1967), pp. 163–84.

The qualities that give JG a permanent place in the literature of the period are a real sympathy for the lowest working class and a skill in analysis of character and emotion. *From the Four Winds* shows immaturity and uncertainty and gives no promise of what is to come. Both *Jocelyn* and *Villa Rubein* fail in their attempts to "analyse overmastering passion." Although the women in *The Island Pharisees* are shadowy, Shelton and Louis Ferrand are "firmly drawn." His complete mastery of his material and art is first evident in *The Man of Property*. *The Patrician* is flawed by the "shift of central interest from Lord Miltoun in the first half to Lady Barbara in the second"; the novel lacks real suspense because it is obvious that both Miltoun and Barbara "will remain true to the traditions of their class." JG's strongest gift—the analysis of romantic passion—is the focus in *The Dark Flower*, and the book is "originally conceived and powerfully as well as delicately executed." When *The Forsyte Saga* was completed with the publication of *In Chancery* and *To Let*, "the bankruptcy of the Forsyte conception of life" became clear. *Saga* is JG's "most substantial claim for endurance as a writer of fiction" and is an important contribution to the social history of the English upper middle class during the period that ended with World War I. The sequel to

Saga, A Modern Comedy, is less massive in construction and is inferior in interest, "though it contains a great deal of artistic and conscientious work." JG was not sympathetic to the postwar younger generation, and his satire is rather malicious. *Maid in Waiting* and *Flowering Wilderness* exemplify "cases of conscience in conflict with love." The troubles of the characters in these novels are conventional, and JG failed to persuade the reader that what happens is either important or credible.

Perhaps one reason why some have held that JG was a better playwright than novelist is that good plays are rarer than good novels and that in dramas skillful actors can correct minor weaknesses; a besetting weakness of JG's dramas is the fact that his minor characters are rather flat. Of his postwar plays *The Skin Game* and *Loyalties* are remarkable successes. In *Skin Game* JG shows "unusually clever stagecraft"; both plays illustrate his belief that "a drama must be shaped so as to have a spire of meaning." Two weaknesses in his dramas (and both result from his disregard of plot construction) are as follows: (1) the failure of his characters to develop within the action of the play; (2) his reliance on symmetrical balance instead of plot, the result too frequently being an increase in the artificiality of the material.

Although there is a "thinness" in his imaginative work, "the beauty of his prose and his artistic sincerity may save much of his work" from being forgotten. There is sentimentality in those novels written after *Modern Comedy* and in such dramas as *Windows, The Show, Exiled,* and even *Escape.*

1509 Cunliffe, J. W. "Galsworthy the Man," SATURDAY REVIEW OF LITERATURE, IX (11 Feb 1933), 422–23.
At the time when Wells "was arguing energetically for the League of Nations and Arnold Bennett was no less busily engaged in the National Publicity Office," JG "had been working quietly and anonymously in a French military hospital as a masseur." JG was asked to deliver the address honoring James Russell Lowell (1919) before the American Academy of Arts and Letters. The argument that persuaded JG to accept was that by so doing "he could help cement the bonds between the United States and Great Britain." JG's address at Columbia University was "The Herd Spirit." Max Beerbohm's quip that JG had "sold his birthright for a pot of message" is only partially true, for JG never sacrificed his artistic integrity. [Cunliffe met JG frequently in the years 1918–1919.]

1510 Cunliffe, John W. "John Galsworthy," SATURDAY REVIEW OF LITERATURE, IX (11 Feb 1933), 420, 423.
The "strange and thrilling social conscience, which was more articulate and more persuasive in his novels than in the raucous shoutings of our own muckrakers, or the ironical disintegrations of Bernard Shaw" won popularity for JG between 1906 and 1909. *The Man of Property* is still JG's most impressive work,

and it is "worthy of comparison with Thackeray, and comparable in sincerity and scope, if not in variety, with Balzac." [An obit notice.]

1511 D., K. N. "John Galsworthy's Works in the Soviet Union," ADELPHI (Lond), nsVI (Aug 1933), 364–66.

Although JG is thought to be "ideologically harmful" because his art and realism might awaken sympathy for Soames and the bourgeoisie, he is probably the most popular modern British writer in the Soviet Union. JG's death ends the recording of the English sociological panorama; his sober account of the bourgeois was influenced by Meredith and Tolstoy. As *The Forsyte Saga* progressed, JG unfortunately began to lose his sense of irony, and the man of property becomes a more sympathetic figure. [This article summarizes A. Abramov, "Poslednie iz Forsaetov" (The Last of the Forsytes), VECHERNAYA MOSKVA, 5 Feb 1933, p. 3, cols. 2–6.]

1512 Davies, S. H. "Galsworthy the Craftsman," BOOKMAN (Lond), LXXXV (Oct 1933), 18–20; LXXXVI (April 1934), 12–16; and LXXXVII (Oct 1934), 27–31.

[A somewhat detailed description of the MSS of the Forsyte Chronicles, which are held by the British Museum. The first article includes detailed drawings of Robin Hill. The MSS are also briefly described in BRITISH MUSEUM QUARTERLY, IV (1929–30), 29–31 and V (1930–31), 118. See also S. H. Davies, STUDIES IN THE ORIGINAL MANUSCRIPTS . . . (1934).]

1513 Davis, H. J. "John Galsworthy," CANADIAN FORUM, XIII (March 1933), 221.

[Obit.]

1514 Dyboski, Roman. JOHN GALSWORTHY (1867–1933) (Cracow, 1933), 30 pp., rptd from PRZEGLĄD WSPÓŁCZESNY [not seen].

[In Polish.]

1515 Eckeren, Gerard van. *"De Kronieken der Forsytes"* (*The Forsyte Chronicles*), GROOT-NEDERLAND (Amsterdam), April 1933, pp. 338–55.

Grillparzer wrote that a masterpiece must be like nature: the most intense view cannot explain it, but a critical analysis will bring to light some understanding of it. In reading *The Forsyte Chronicles* (*The Forsyte Saga* and *A Modern Comedy*), we can recognize that they are a work of art. The books describe the human experience in its most vital and in its spiritual aspects; contained therein are the joy of life and the anxiety of death, and thus the chronicles possess an epic structure. The Forsytes are representatives of mankind in its most primary sense. The sacrifice of himself that Soames could not make for Irene he will make for Fleur, but even in his love of Fleur, Soames is kept a prisoner of his Forsyte nature. As regards Robin Hill, Soames is like Moses; he can only look on the promised land from a distance. Robin Hill remains a place where the Forsyte spirit cannot penetrate, or if it does it will die there. After Old Jolyon buys Robin Hill, he meets its magic on the path from the small woods, and the "old Forsyte" in him has already died before he closes his eyes on Robin Hill for the last time. Robin Hill is a fortress to protect Forsytes from themselves, and it is in a sense a paradise. Many years later when Soames visits Irene at Robin Hill on behalf of Fleur, the angel with the flaming sword sends him back. The love story between Irene and Bosinney would in itself have been banal, but it needs to be seen within the context of the concentrated effort to depict the family atmosphere of the Forsytes themselves. [In Dutch.]

1516 Ervine, St. John. THE THEATRE IN MY TIME (Lond: Rich & Cowan, 1933), pp. 102, 142, 146, 159, 160, 161, 162.
JG represents the "neo-democracy" of writing about unheroic characters, the most characteristic of whom in JG's "dramas of depressing people" is Falder in *Justice*. [Passing references in a book of reminiscences and casual observations about drama.]

1517 Field, Louise Maunsell. "The Modern Novelists," NORTH AMERICAN REVIEW, CCXXXV (Jan 1933), 63–68.
Flowering Wilderness shows the trend of novelists turning away from the problems of mass society to individual dilemmas. Dinny and Wilfred are concerned with "how far defiance may be carried" and "how far a person might go to save his life without losing . . . his soul." [Field's flattering review stretches the point in relating her comments to JG.]

1518 Ford, Ford Madox. "Contrasts: Memories of John Galsworthy and George Moore," ATLANTIC MONTHLY, CLI (May 1933), 559–69.
"In one January week the Western World lost its most skilled writer [Moore]— and its best man [Galsworthy]!" [Except for the profusion of anecdotal reminiscences several of the major points made here repeat what Ford [Hueffer] wrote about JG in "Literary Portraits: Mr. John Galsworthy," TRIBUNE (NY), 10 Aug 1907, p. 2, which see.]

1519 Ford, Ford Madox. "John Galsworthy and George Moore," ENGLISH REVIEW, LVII (1933), 130–42; rptd in IT WAS THE NIGHTINGALE (Phila & Lond: Lippincott, 1933,), pp. 30, 32, 33, 41–62, 129.
In one week "the Western World lost its greatest writer [Moore]—and its best man [JG]!" George Moore, the "lean, silent, infinitely swift and solitary" wolf, contrasts with JG, the "infinitely good . . . patient . . . tenacious" dog "that guards our sheepfolds and farmsteads from the George Moores. Only, there was only one George Moore." There was a quality of "grim persistence" about JG, and yet the main impression of him would be his smile and his softness. Whenever Conrad referred to JG in later years it was always to "Poor Jack," because JG always worried about his writing. JG was helpful with the ENGLISH REVIEW though perhaps not always approving. JG's grim persistence and tenac-

ity were probably better suited to his writing plays than novels. "It was curious and touching to hear" JG tell a group of French writers in Paris that if he had any skill in letters "it came from a long discipleship to Flaubert and Maupassant and Anatole France . . . and to Turgenev and Conrad. . . . "

1520 Frias, Alberto Nin. "John Galsworthy," LA NACIÓN (Buenos Aires) [not seen]; rptd in REPERTORIO AMERICANO (San José, Costa Rica), XXVI:16 (1933), 241–43.

JG, the creator of *The Forsyte Saga,* is the greatest novelist in thirty years, and few critics would deny him the first place among English writers. His form of narration can be compared to that of Jane Austen. He is a master who takes advantage of all the progress made in novel writing by predecessors like Henry James. One finds in his work "a model example of narration whose logic and beauty lie in half saying things, suggesting them, and permitting the reader to terminate them." Contact with people whose ideas and expressions were more liberal turned him into a complete historian of contemporary English life. [A brief survey and summary of his works is enthusiastically given in flowery Spanish.] [In Spanish.]

1521 Gallenga, Romeo. "John Galsworthy," NUOVA ANTOLOGIA DI LETTERE, SCIENZE ED ARTI (Rome), Series VII, CCCLXVII:1471 (1 July 1933), 82–92.

JG's translated works have struck "a responsive chord" in Italian readers despite the very English tone and settings. His works are noteworthy for their solidity and serenity, and they contrast favorably with the excessive emphasis on novelty that is characteristic of some of JG's later contemporaries. His success is due particularly to *The Forsyte Saga* in which he became the historian of that era as well as a novelist, and as such he evoked "tastes, beliefs, and prejudices still remembered with nostalgia." *Saga* is more the reconstruction of an epoch than the story of a group of people. Despite the great differences between them, JG is like Proust in his ability to frame in a few words the mood of a passing moment. There is a universality in JG's works, even though for him England was essentially London, and London for the most part was "the City," with its merchants, bankers, and lawyers. He was an artist who understood those elements of the universe which are "shadowy, unlimited, full of enchantment and poetic inspiration." These qualities, balanced by his psychological insights—revealed through gesture and fragments of dialogue rather than prolonged analysis—explain JG's success. [This appreciation (almost a eulogy) of JG places him in the context of modern, especially English, literature. Gallenga strongly defends JG against the criticism (Virginia Woolf is cited) of superficial character analysis.] [In Italian.]

1522 "Galsworthy," LITERATURARCHIV (Berlin), XXXVIII (1933), 116 [not seen].

[Listed in BIBLIOGRAPHIE DER DEUTSCHEN ZEITSCHRIFTEN LITERATUR, 1933 (Leipzig: Felix Dietrich, 1934).] [In German.]

1523 "Galsworthy on Life and Letters," NEW YORK TIMES BOOK REVIEW, 5 March 1933, p. 2.

Even though JG has never been a professional literary critic, some observations in *Candelabra* probe deeply into aesthetic truth. His works, like his life, are characterized by nobility of spirit. His chief artistic tool is irony; his chief characteristics are "love of beauty, gentleness, pity, and unwavering idealism." [Reprints Randall Davy's portrait of JG.]

1524 "A Galsworthy Triad: *Three Novels of Love* in Single Volume," SPRINGFIELD REPUBLICAN (Mass), 30 April 1933, Sec. E, p. 7.

Three Novels of Love shows JG's "deep sympathy with human emotions and especially with love beset by difficulties." His chief value as a novelist is the "power to portray emotions with art and with understanding." Resolution of *Beyond* is "too mechanical"; *A Saint's Progress* shows more artistic maturity than either *Beyond* or *The Dark Flower.*

1525 Galsworthy, Ada. "Preface," *The Forsyte Saga* (NY: Charles Scribner's Sons, 1933), pp. vii–x.

[A brief and informal note commenting on the gradual evolution and the favorable reception of *The Forsyte Saga.* The preface consists primarily of quotes from letters by JG, accompanied by Ada's flattering account of JG's sterling qualities as writer and human being.]

1526 Gerchunoff, Alberto. "John Galsworthy," CARAS Y CARETAS (Buenos Aires); rptd in REPERTORIO AMERICANO (San José, Costa Rica), XXVI:16 (1933), 241.

[A one-paragraph comment on JG's receiving the Nobel Prize.] [In Spanish.]

1527 Gretton, Mary S. "John Galsworthy," CONTEMPORARY REVIEW, CXLIII (March 1933), 319–25.

[This obit article focuses its praise on *The Forsyte Saga* and emphasizes JG's realism and verisimilitude.]

1528 Guyot, Edouard. "Diagnostic du Forsytisme" (Diagnosis of Forsyteism), REVUE ANGLO-AMERICAINE, X (1933), 290–300.

[An excerpt from his book, JOHN GALSWORTHY: LE ROMANCIÈR (John Galsworthy: Novelist), (Paris: Didier, 1933).] [In French.]

1529 Guyot, Édouard. JOHN GALSWORTHY: LE ROMANCIÈR (John Galsworthy: Novelist) (Paris: Didier, 1933).

JG is distinctively English. Pity is the source that in nourishing his sensibility allows him to maintain a middle path between a withering skepticism and an enthusiasm that might distort reality. There is nothing in JG of the philosophy of pity that one finds in Dickens's CHRISTMAS STORIES. Pity gives to JG's works a distinctive coloring; it makes his art different from that of a mere painter of social customs. One is reminded in some ways of Sterne. For JG pity involves the world of human affairs and that of animals; it is almost cosmic, and it develops an affective pantheism.

Shelton's character in *The Island Pharisees* is problematic. The question of how Shelton could for so long accept the Phariseeism of his class and rather suddenly change is troublesome. As a result of the harshness of the novel and its dogmatic rigor, which makes it a clear satire, the novel is rather unusual in JG's canon. *The Forsyte Saga* is not social history; for instance, there is nothing in the state of Soames's soul that would differentiate the England of George V from that of Victoria. Much of the time *Saga* is high comedy. Instead of using an individual, JG puts a family at the center of the work. There is throughout *Saga* no culminating point. Each character is developed to the extent necessary to reveal the character to the reader: the mystery which surrounds Timothy marks his place among the Shadows so well that his recommendation during the Boer War to conserve takes on almost superhuman proportions. Soames provides a continuity in *Saga*, and his various roles give to the work a certain richness of texture. [*The Freelands, Fraternity,* and *The Patrician* are also discussed.] [In French.]

1530 Gwynn, Stephen. "Ebb and Flow: A Monthly Commentary: Galsworthy's Nobel Prize," FORTNIGHTLY REVIEW, nsCXXXIII (Jan 1933), 110–13.

JG won the Nobel Prize rather than people like Shaw, Wells, Kipling, and Barrie because of his ability to analyze and "anatomise" the English, especially the upper middle merchant classes, in a way easily translatable by and understandable to Germans and Scandinavians. But his main appeal is the human appeal. JG depicts the English merchant as an "enjoying animal," with "more will than brains," for whom culture comes with possession of money. The theme of beauty, especially as seen in the unique, elusive quality of a woman's loveliness in Irene, is also characteristic. JG's two best character studies are in the short story "Old English," which is an expression of English will, and in Soames Forsyte (*The Forsyte Saga* and *A Modern Comedy*), who through many chapters and books rises from a disagreeable man to a "proper champion."

1531 Hamilton, Cosmo. "The Love of Life," PEOPLE WORTH TALKING ABOUT (NY: McBride, 1933), 51–60.

[This sketch of JG, originally read over the radio, is largely drawn from well-known comments by E. F. Benson, Joseph Conrad, Leon Schalit, and JG himself.]

1532 Harris, Frank. AUTOBIOGRAPHICAL LETTERS OF JOHN GALSWORTHY: A CORRESPONDENCE WITH FRANK HARRIS PREVIOUSLY UNPUBLISHED (NY: English Book Shop, 1933).

[Two brief letters to Harris from JG, dated 30 April 1921 and 23 May 1921, are printed.]

1533 Hedley, Rev. John. "Letter to John Galsworthy," in William Lyon Phelps, "As I Like It," SCRIBNER'S MAGAZINE, XCIV (July 1933), 42–45, espec 44–45.

[In a letter dated 27 May 1924, the Reverend Hedley wrote JG protesting that naming Fleur's dog Confucius (in *The White Monkey*) is a serious insult to the Chinese. JG's reply, dated 11 June 1924, is also rptd. JG changed the name to Ting-a-ling as a consequence.]

1534 Henderson, Ray. "Galsworthy in the Theatre," NEW YORK TIMES, 5 Feb 1933, Sec. 9, pp. 1, 3.

As Mrs. Jones in *The Silver Box*, Ethel Barrymore introduced JG the dramatist to American audiences. Winthrop Ames presented *Strife* on 17 Nov 1909. Two innovations (price and curtain time) began with *The Pigeon*. John Barrymore starred in *Justice*, 3 April 1916. Performances of JG's other plays are as follows: *The Fugitive*, Thirty-ninth Street Theatre, 19 March 1917; *A Bit O' Love*, Columbia Theatre, San Francisco, and in 1925 by Actors Theatre in NY; *The Little Man*, Maxine Elliott's Theatre, 12 Feb 1917; *The Mob* by Henry Jewett's Players, Copley Theatre, Boston, Oct 1920, and in the same season Neighborhood Playhouse in NY; *The Skin Game*, Bijou Theatre, 20 Oct 1920; *Loyalties*, Gaiety Theatre, 27 Sept 1922; *The Sun*, Triangle Theatre; *A Family Man*, Copley Theatre, Boston, and *The Eldest Son*, same theatre, 1922–23 season; *Windows*, Theatre Guild production at Garrick Theatre, Oct 1923; *Old English*, produced by Winthrop Ames at the Ritz Theatre, 20 Dec 1924; *The Foundations*, Lennox Hill Players, 1925; *Escape*, Booth Theatre, 26 Oct 1927; *The Roof* was presented later by Charles Hopkins. Over eight hundred performances made *Old English* JG's most successful play in America. JG's letter to Winthrop Ames [quoted] explains and corrects the journalistic error that *Escape* was to be JG's last play. One word summarizes JG's definite views about acting: "repression." In America JG wanted English actors to portray English characters.

1535 Héraucourt, Will. DIE DARSTELLUNG DES ENGLISCHEN NATIONALCHARAKTERS IN JOHN GALSWORTHYS FORSYTE SAGA: EINE PSYCHOLOGISCHE UNTERSUCHUNG (The Description of the English National Character in John Galsworthy's *Forsyte Saga:* A Psychological Study) (Marburg: N. G. Elwertsche Verlagsbuchhandlung, 1933).

[Making use of E. R. Jaensch's theory of psychological types, this study discusses the Forsytes as representatives of the English national character and arrives at a number of dubious generalizations.] [In German.]

1536 Holmes, John Haynes. "John Galsworthy," UNITY, CX (20 Feb 1933), 357–59.

[General appreciation and reminiscences about JG on his death. The man was greater than the artist.]

1537 Hutchison, Percy. "Galsworthy's Last Novel Closes the Forsyte Chronicle," New York Times Book Review, 8 Oct 1933, p. 3.

The relationship in *One More River* between Dinny and Dornford—"profound, unruffled confidence, dignity and peace"—are the characteristics to which JG attributes the greatness of England. The Clare and Jerry Corven divorce proceedings show JG at his legal best. *River* is not JG's best, but "for our own immediate time" it is inspiring, and JG has done great service for social historians in serving as "the humble camera man to an antic generation."

1538 Hutchinson, Percy. "Introduction," *The Forsyte Saga* (NY: Scribner's [Modern Standard Authors Series], 1933), pp. xv–xxxv.

JG's strength lay in his writing objectively and not in his using the methods of a psychological novelist or the method of the stream of consciousness.

1539 James, Stanley B. "A Contrast in Sagas: Sigrid Undset and John Galsworthy," Month, CLXI (1933), 520–26.

JG's *Forsyte Saga* deals with several generations of "the new aristocracy whose power rests on money," and it is his art which has won our sympathy for his Forsytes. The work of Sigrid Undset, however, contrasts with JG's in that she as a Catholic and as a woman focuses on the many generations of the family and its traditions of aristocratic pride. "In the Forsyte Saga it is wealth and social position which are inherited, but in these sagas of modern Scandinavia it is the inheritance of sins committed and spiritual victories won which count." Her realism is redeemed by her healthy-mindedness and her Catholicism.

1540 James, Stanley B. "John Galsworthy," Bookman (Lond), LXXXIII (1933), 473–79.

[This is a faulty citation found in EFT I:3 (1958), 18.]

1541 Jean-Aubry, G. "Souvenirs de John Galsworthy" (Memories of John Galsworthy,) Figaro, 18 March 1933, p. 6.

[Recalls his conversation with JG some eight years earlier on the idea of a gentleman. The first meeting between JG and Conrad on the *Torrens* (Autumn 1892) is described, and the fallacy that JG after reading Conrad's first MS encouraged Conrad to write is repudiated. JG was much troubled by the wave of modern cynicism; he believed it was especially difficult for the modern English novel to depict the changing, seething society of the present. The revival of interest in eighteenth-century theater (Sheridan, Congreve, Farquhar) seemed to JG an excuse which the English were using to explain their postwar cynicism. England, he felt, would of necessity have to believe in something again.] [In French.]

1542 "John Galsworthy," Die Literatur (Stuttgart), XXXV (1933), 332–333.

[Quotes from obit in the daily press.] [In German.]

1543 "John Galsworthy," NATION (NY), CXXXVI (15 Feb 1933), 163–64.
In the sense that he was the last to cultivate the Victorian form JG is "the last of the great Victorian novelists." He is not as radical as Shaw or Wells, and "he was a humanitarian rather than either a political or an economical radical." [An editorial.]

1544 "John Galsworthy," REVIEW OF REVIEWS (Lond), LXXXIII (Feb 1933), 11–12.
[Obit notice praising JG's "highmindedness" and sense of justice.]

1545 "John Galsworthy," SATURDAY REVIEW OF LITERATURE (NY), IX (11 Feb 1933), 421, 423.
Early in his career JG captured America's social conscience with his "aristocratic liberalism." Although dated, JG's social concern served as a transition between the "arrogant confidence" of the nineteenth century and the "radical reconstructions of society" of the twentieth. Americans are especially indebted to JG for his strong study of English personality and racial character. [A portrait of JG accompanies the obit essay.]

1546 "John Galsworthy mrtev" (Jchn Galsworthy Is Dead), PESTRÝ TÝDEN (Prague), VIII:7 (1933), 3.
[Photo of JG and a note commenting on his death.] [In Czech.]

1547 "John Galsworthy, proslulý anglicky romanopisec včera zemřel" (John Galsworthy, the Famous English Writer, Died Yesterday), ČESKE SLOVO (Prague), XXV:24 (1933), 1.
[Photo from JG's visit in Prague, showing him with T. G. Masaryk, president of ČSR.] [In Czech.]

1548 "John Galsworthy zemřel" (John Galsworthy Is Dead), ČESKE SLOVO (Prague), XXV:27 (1933), 8.
[Obit notice.] [In Czech.]

1549 K. "Smrt Jolyonova" (Jolyon's Death), ČESKE SLOVO (Prague), XXV:27 (1933), 4.
[A short note referring to a photograph on p. 1, presumably of JG.] [In Czech.]

1550 Kayser, Rudolph. "Zum Tode Galsworthys" (On Galsworthy's Death), NEUE RUNDSCHAU, XLIV (April 1933), 432.
Fame came late to JG, and now his fictional world is no longer the world of reality. Even his techniques of realism and non-Zolaesque naturalism have been replaced by other techniques. [In German.]

1551 Kummer, Herbert. "Amerikaner und Englaender erringen den literarischen Nobelpreis" (Americans and Englishmen Win the Nobel Prize for Literature), EISERNE BLAETTER (Munich), XV:1 (1933), 4–8.

Though JG may seem old-fashioned, he, rather than Huxley with his uprooted characters, deserves the Nobel Prize. As a writer of a class now belonging to the past, JG demonstrates restraint, a quality which Germans sadly lack. [In German.]

1552 Lane, James W. "John Galsworthy," COMMONWEAL, XVII (19 April 1933), 688.

[An obit notice.]

1553 "The Latest Galsworthy," TIMES LITERARY SUPPLEMENT (Lond), XXXII (5 Oct 1933), 666.

Dinny (*One More River*) is "all woman, and not an idea," one of JG's "most vigorous and complete imaginative creations." His constrained imagination limits the power of his writing. Compared with the greatest novelists, his works seem "a little prim and pinched and reserved," but it would be unfair to compare him with any less than the greatest. He will continue to be read for his "shrewd observation of changing times and manners, for his fine and deliberate art, and for his subdued but steadily burning love of freedom, justice and good will."

1554 Lehmkuehler, Wilhelm. "Die Vertreter der wohlhabenden Mittelklasse in Galsworthys *Forsyte Saga*" (The Representatives of the Upper Middle Class in Galsworthy's *Forsyte Saga*), PAEDAGOGISCHE WARTE (Osterwieck), Beilage zur Lehrerfortbildung, XIV (Dec 1933), 61–73.

[Assuming that JG's works are the best introduction to the English national character, Lehmkuehler describes the values of the Forsytes, calls Soames a tragic victim of his class and family background, and admits that after all JG has not only depicted Englishmen but universal types as well.] [In German.]

1555 Lindemann, Konrad. "Kolbenheyer—Galsworthy—Alverdes in konzentrationsmaessiger Behandlung auf der Oberprima" (The Teaching of Kolbenheyer—Galsworthy—Alverdes in Concentrated Readings in the Upper Sixth Forum), ZEITSCHRIFT FUER DEUTSCH-KUNDE (Leipzig), XLVII (1933), 494–96.

JG's "Quality," Kolbenheyer's WENZEL TIEGEL, and Alverdes's KILIAN portray eccentric shoemakers who are thinkers in the tradition of Hans Sachs and Jakob Boehme. The stories will help students to recognize the spirit of the German people. [In German.]

1556 "Das Literarische Echo: Echo der Zeitungen: John Galsworthy" (Literary Echo: Newspaper Pieces: John Galsworthy), DIE LITERATUR: MONATSSCHRIFT FUR LITERATURFREUNDE, XXXV (4 Feb 1933), 332–33.

[Four excerpts from German newspapers about JG are printed. According to Werner (D.A.Z. 52), JG's main theme, appearing in all his novels, "is the struggle between the individual and society."] [In German.]

1557 M., B. W. *"Strife,"* THEATRE WORLD (Lond), XIX (June 1933), 274.

Despite the passage of time there is still a "rich enough vein of human conflict" to make *Strife* palatable for all time. Even if industrial strife were to disappear, the play would remain an interesting commentary on life and on the way men's ideals "vanish into thin air from the breath of a newer generation."

1558 M., O. "The Saplings and the Oak," NEW STATESMAN AND NATION, VI (14 Oct 1933), 460–62.

JG struggles in *Over The River* to demonstrate that the English character—a combination of integrity and common sense—persists through economic disaster and social chaos into the younger generation of Forsytes. Typically Galsworthian are the dog, the death-bed scene, and the divorce case. "No jury could possibly believe" the divorce proceedings, yet the development of them in the novel is believable. JG was wise in choosing the chronicle form because, for *The Forsyte Saga*, his talent to observe society had adequate range, and the daily events of life sustained him. He is like Trollope in showing how individuals develop in the face of love and loss; but he is unlike Trollope in showing how the characters react "to prosperity, to war, to . . . the changing horizon of the age." *River's* politics are backwater politics, but Clare's apartment "breathes the air of 1932."

1559 MacAfee, Helen. "Outstanding Novels," YALE REVIEW, nsXXII (Winter 1933), xx.

[Brief comment announcing the publication of *Flowering Wilderness*. No critical insight.]

1560 [MacCarthy, Desmond.] "John Galsworthy," TIMES (Lond), 1 Feb 1933, pp. 11, 14; rptd in LIVING AGE, CCCXLIV (April 1933), 138–42.

JG cultivated his abilities to become a "sound artist in fiction and the drama, an essayist of some grace, and a poet above the negligible." Though some object to his pity for the unvalued woman and the underdog as sentimental, JG is nevertheless the greater for his moderation. Stylistically, he wrote "clean, sound, straight-forward English." [A photograph accompanies the obit.]

1561 McCarthy, Lillah (Lady Keeble). MYSELF AND MY FRIENDS (Lond: Thornton Butterworth; NY: E. P. Dutton, 1933), pp. 125, 146, 147, 148, 157, 182, 190, 191, 226.

JG was always "calm and serene." There were two JG's: (1) the "correct, well-groomed, quiet, reserved" and circumspect man; and (2) the adventurous JG who discovered Conrad. [Informal stage history and literary gossip. Reproduces a letter in JG's handwriting, p. 191.]

1562 Mackenzie, Compton. "Galsworthy, Bennett, and Wells," LITERATURE IN MY TIME (Lond: Rich & Cowan, 1933); rptd (Freeport, NY: Books for Libraries P, 1967), pp. 154–67.

The Man of Property marked the beginning of the new era in literature, expressing the revolt of youth against relics of the Victorian era. The passing of time has shown JG's faults to be lack of humor, lack of real experience with human nature, manipulation of scene suggesting theatricality, and suggestions of pomposity. The *Modern Comedy* trilogy makes one suspect that JG took types and dressed them with current events. The Continent likes JG because his characters fit their stereotype of what the English are like.

1563 McKown, Robert. "Galsworthy's Place in the Theatre," THEATRE WORLD (Lond), XIX (March 1933), 113.

JG's gift of realism makes him a great dramatist. Only JG of his generation filled his plays with men and women we meet every day. There are three causes for his success: (1) the reality of his characters; (2) his marvelous sense of theater; (3) his refusal to "write down" for popular success. There is nothing in English drama to surpass the last act of *Strife,* the auction scene in *The Skin Game,* the club scene in *Loyalties,* or the wordless scene in the third act of *Justice,* and he wrote perfect one-act plays: e.g., *The First and the Last, Hall-Marked,* and *Defeat.* Sybil Thorndike brackets *The Silver Box* with MACBETH and HIPPOLYTUS as one of the three perfect plays. Unlike most dramatists his first plays were his best and his last, his worst. Despite the debunking that has begun, there is among the dramatists who have brought the theater to its present height no one more honored or more deserving than JG.

1564 Marrot, H. V. "For a Life of Galsworthy," NEW REPUBLIC, LXXV (28 June 1933), 184.

[A request for information for the official biography.]

1565 Marrot, H. V. "Life of Galsworthy," NATION (NY), CXXXVI (3 May 1933), 505.

[A request for letters and information by and about JG for the official biography.]

1566 Matthews, T. S. "Fiction by Young and Old," NEW REPUBLIC, LXXVII (15 Nov 1933), 24–25.

JG constantly reminds the reader in *One More River* that life is a game that should be played by the rules.

1567 "A Memorial Edition of *The Forsyte Saga,* " NEW YORK TIMES BOOK REVIEW, 8 Oct 1933, p. 3.

[Brief notice of appearance.]

1568 Michel-Côte, P. "Parmi Les Livres: Galsworthy et le Traditionalisme Anglais" (Among Books: Galsworthy and English Traditionalism), LA REVUE HEBDOMADAIRE, nsXXIX (18 Feb 1933), 352–59.

JG's ideal is to be found in liberalism and in liberals such as Shelton, Courtier, and young Jolyon, men who are speculative, independent, sincere, and candid. JG belongs to a past culture, and there is a wide gap between his ideal and the ideal of the younger generation. [In French.]

1569 Michelena, Pedro Mourlane. "John Galsworthy y el patriciado inglés" (John Galsworthy and the English Patrician), EL SOL (Madrid); rptd in REPERTORIO AMERICANO (San José, Costa Rica), XXVI:16 (1933), 243.

JG follows George Moore in the journey of no return. As a classic writer JG will survive because of his clear style, neatness, and beauty, as well as for his logic and a sense of perfection ever present in the body of his work. [In Spanish.]

1570 "Mr. Galsworthy, O. M.," TIMES (Lond), 1 Feb 1933, p. 15.

JG, by aptitude and inclination a patrician, possessed a "curious idealism" and a workmanlike approach to the craft of fiction. He pitied the victims of circumstance and victims of their own character, often presenting social contrasts. His social philosophy tended to "eliminate responsibility from its humanitarian scale of values." [The essay contains some encapsulated comments about individual works.]

1571 Morisset, H. "La *Forsyte Saga* de Galsworthy" (*The Forsyte Saga* of Galsworthy), EUROPE: REVUE MENSUELLE, XXXI (15 Feb 1933), 270–73.

JG's method is very original; it consists of catching and isolating in the continuity of life certain privileged moments that reveal the soul. A gesture, a look, a word, an ordinary occurrence—these reveal the subterranean progress of the emotions and soul. Capturing the most complex and elusive impressions, these brief glimpses into the soul are juxtaposed without any apparent connection. Although such a minute and subtle art may seem fragmentary, one soon discovers that the details establish a unity which permits the reader to apprehend the souls of the characters. If JG has not achieved the instinctive and total revelation of the human soul in its most intimate profundities, as have the poet and the very greatest novelists, he has by this artistic accumulation of partial intuitions composed a painting of beings very complex, full, and delicate, and sometimes one of strength. [This is primarily a review of *The Forsyte Saga*.] [In French.]

1572 Moses, Montrose J. "John Galsworthy," NORTH AMERICAN REVIEW, CCXXXV (1933), 537–45; rptd in OPINIONS AND ATTITUDES IN THE TWENTIETH CENTURY, ed by Stewart Morgan and William Thomas (NY: Thomas Nelson, 1936), 210–20.

JG's strengths and his limitations are to be found in the distinctive qualities of his genius—"his sincerity, his fairness, his unperturbed contemplation, his orderly way of thinking, his neat, compact statement and arrangement of facts" and his sensitiveness, gentility, and benevolence. His beneficence detracted from the effectiveness of his observations, just as his irony was weakened by his lack of aggressive militancy. The workers in *Strife* are conventional; the scrubwoman in *The Silver Box* is a mere sketch, and one kept longing for an emotional outburst from Irene in *The Man of Property*. "There is a terrible meekness to Galsworthy's social criticism" because his realism is tinctured by his kindliness. His irony (poetic, true, touching) does not shake the soul. His lack of violence, his quiescent sincerity, and his gentleness will limit his appeal to newer generations of readers. In both his novels and his plays his technique was of the older generation. Each chapter "is in itself a cameo"; his manner is "episodic, yet complete." The power of *The Forsyte Saga* to survive will depend on its documentary value for the historian. His novels are patterned, neat, and sophisticated, but they are without "broad sweeps of passionate reaction. . . . and characters of pagan nakedness." Not being of the "earthy school of fictionists," his use of the emotional is inclined to be excessive and overemphasized, as in *The Dark Flower*. His gentleness, his compassion, and his humanitarianism "may turn out to be his undoing."

1573 Mottram, R. H. "John Galsworthy," NEW STATESMAN AND NATION, V (4 Feb 1933), 128–29.
[Personal reminiscences and an obit notice.]

1574 Murray, Gilbert, Henry W. Nevinson, and Sir William Rothenstein. "John Galsworthy as I Knew Him," BOOKMAN (Lond), LXXXIII (March 1933), 487.
[Reminiscences.]

1575 "New Books," CATHOLIC WORLD, CXXXVII (June 1933), 380.
[Brief notice of the publication of the "disappointing" *Candelabra*.]

1576 Nicholls, Edmund. "First Editions of John Galsworthy," BOOKMAN (Lond), LXXXIII (March 1933), 506–7.
[General and partial survey of JG first editions, with values of 1933. The essay is a part of BOOKMAN's tribute to JG on his death.]

1577 "Nositel Nobelovy ceny. Spisovatel Galsworthy zemřel" (Nobel Prize Winner. The Writer Galsworthy Is Dead), VEČERNÍ ČESKE SLOVO (Prague), XV:27 (1933), 2 [not seen].
[In Czech.]

1578 "Obituary Notes," PUBLISHER'S WEEKLY (NY), CXXIII (4 Feb 1933), 538–39.
[Obit summarizes JG's literary and social accomplishments.]

1579 *"One More River,"* A.L.A. BOOKLIST, XXX (Nov 1933), 79.
[Brief plot summary.]

1580 *"One More River,"* AMERICA, L (18 Nov 1933), 164.
One More River is an articulately plotted and technically good work; but JG's sympathy "blurs his intelligence." [Brief review.]

1581 *"One More River:* The Last to Be Crossed by John Galsworthy," SPRINGFIELD REPUBLICAN (Mass), 8 Oct 1933, Sec. E, p. 7.
The value of *One More River* rests in its interpretation of English life and human interests in general.

1582 Ould, Herman. "John Galsworthy and Music," SACKBUT, XIV (Sept 1933), 35–38.
JG, like old Jolyon, loved Beethoven, Mozart, Handel, Gluck, and Schumann. He generally cared little for opera, thinking it a "mongrel form," but his favorites were CARMEN, PAGLIACCI, and ORFEO. His favorite musician was Bach, but his works are relatively free of references to him; he also liked Brahms, who is likewise seldom mentioned. There are only two errors noticeable to professional musicians in all of JG's works—in *Beyond* and *The Patrician*.

1583 Ould, Herman. "John Galsworthy—Internationalist," BOOKMAN (Lond), LXXXIII (March 1933), 486.
JG's internationalism came from his devotion to English tradition and is typified by his presidency of the P.E.N. Club and his espousal of the aims of P.E.N.

1584 Pantling, Constance. "The Ideal of the 'Gentleman' in *Swan Song,*" REVUE DE L'ENSEIGNEMENT DES LANGUES VIVANTES (Paris), L (Dec 1933), 467–69; and LI (Jan 1934), 36–38. [Part of a lecture given at the British Institute in Paris.]
[Pantling analyzes the physical and moral qualities of the gentleman, JG's gentlemanly intentions, and then the two groups of characters in *Swan Song* who conform to the nineteenth-century code of the gentleman. Among the older people examined are the Marquess of Shropshire, Wilfred Bentworth, Sir Timothy Fanfield, Sir Lawrence Mont, Uncle Hilary, and Soames; among the younger people, Stainford and Val, Michael Mont, and Jon. JG "is the last of the eminent writers to introduce the 'gentleman' seriously into his novels. It is a distinction that smacks too much of social pretension and is therefore avoided: Huxley treats the type satirically; D. H. Lawrence dislikes and despises it. Only the moral foundation is accepted more or less by all."]

1585 Parvillez, Alphonse de. "Galsworthy, ou la revanche de l'ordre" (Galsworthy, or the Return of Order), ÉTUDES (Paris), 70th year, CCXV (20 May 1933), 477–92.
[This assessment of JG as an artist and thinker stresses such qualities as his psychological insight, his art of reticence, his irony, and his verisimilitude. JG's main themes are considered. His optimism reminds one of Rousseau; JG had an excessive distrust for institutions; he disliked the repressive moralism of both family and religion. The writer is worried by JG's criticism of marriage as an

institution and very nearly suggests that, at his death, JG would have rediscovered the virtues of Christianity.] [In French.]

1586 Paterson, Isabel. "John Galsworthy's Last Novel: A Completely Finished Work, Rounding Out the Career of the Charming Dinny Cherell," NEW YORK HERALD TRIBUNE BOOKS, 8 Oct 1933, p. 8.
One More River "has the courtesy of a farewell from a man of breeding who is a little tired but appreciative of this world's hospitality." Throughout the story, one senses an air of resignation and a loss of contact with his own creations.

1587 Patterson, Curtis. "A Literary Comedy of Manners," TOWN AND COUNTRY, LXXXVIII (15 March 1933), 48.
JG's biggest fault was in viewing contemporary society "through Edwardian clouds of glory." Especially faulty is his treatment of American speech and character. Yet he is an urbane and highly polished craftsman. [General comments serve as review on the American appearance of *Three Novels of Love* and *Candelabra*.]

1588 Phelps, William Lyon. "As I Like It," SCRIBNER'S MAGAZINE, XCIII (Feb 1933), 125–28.
JG's being given the Nobel Prize has met with general approval. In *The Forsyte Saga* JG "made what seems to be a permanent contribution to English fiction." Rolland's JEAN CHRISTOPHE and *Saga* are the "only two 'era' works of high distinction" of this century. JG would deserve the Nobel Prize for his plays alone. Only Barrie and Shaw have equalled him in drama among his contemporaries.

1589 Phelps, William Lyon. "As I Like It," SCRIBNER'S MAGAZINE, XCIII (April 1933), 257.
[Obit.]

1590 Phelps, William Lyon. "As I Like It," SCRIBNER'S MAGAZINE, XCIV (July 1933), 42–45, espec pp. 44–45.
[Prints the Reverend John Hedley's letter (dated 27 May 1924) to JG protesting the name Confucius for Fleur's dog in *The White Monkey* as a serious insult to the Chinese. JG's reply, dated 11 July 1924, expresses his regret and says that the name will be changed. JG changed the name to Ting-a-ling.]

1591 "Plays and Pictures. *Strife*," NEW STATESMAN AND NATION, nsV (27 May 1933), 687.
The theme of *Strife* is too complicated for JG's simple use of "parallels and dovetailings." [Brief reference to revival at the Little Theatre.]

1592 "Projev soustrasti presidenta republiky T. G. Masaryka vdově po Galsworthym" (Expression of Sympathy by the President of the

Republic, T. G. Masaryk, to the Widow of Galsworthy), NÁRODNÍ LISTY (Prague), LXXIII:33 (1933), 5 [not seen].
[In Czech.]

1593 R., G. R. B. "A Posthumous Message from John Galsworthy: His Latest Novel Deals with the Lives of His Personages with Whom We Are Familiar," BOSTON EVENING TRANSCRIPT BOOK SECTION, 21 Oct 1933, p. 1.
The value of *One More River* lies in its depiction of the ruling class's ability in postwar England to survive the onslaught of rising taxes and falling prices for the produce of their large estates.

1594 Radtke, Bruno. "Ein Brief Galsworthys über seinen Jugendroman *The Island Pharisees*" (A Letter of Galsworthy's Concerning His Early Novel *The Island Pharisees*), ARCHIV FÜR DAS STUDIUM DER NEUEREN SPRACHEN, CLXIV (1933), 72–74.
[Unable to locate the quotation, " 'The British nation . . . is defying Life to make it look at her,' " Radtke wrote to JG. JG's reply, dated 23 Aug 1927, is printed in full. In his letter JG remarks on the inaccuracy of the quotation and points out that the quotation refers to the British attitude to art shortly after the Boer War, that *The Island Pharisees* is satiric, and that the book does not present the whole truth. He also expresses his objection to the unscrupulous use that was made of this novel during the first World War.] [In German.]

1595 Reely, Mary Katharine. "A Selected List of Current Books: *Candelabra*," WISCONSIN LIBRARY BULLETIN (Madison), XXIX (March 1933), 82.
[Brief note on content of volume.]

1596 Reely, Mary Katharine. "A Selected List of Current Books: *One More River*," WISCONSIN LIBRARY BULLETIN (Madison), XXIX (Nov 1933), 240.
[Brief plot summary.]

1597 Reely, Mary Katharine. "A Selected List of Current Books: *Three Novels of Love*," WISCONSIN LIBRARY BULLETIN (Madison), XXIX (April 1933), 109.
[Brief notice of publication of the combined *The Dark Flower, Beyond,* and *A Saint's Progress*.]

1598 Rohmer, Charlotte. BUDDENBROOKS UND THE FORSYTE SAGA (BUDDENBROOKS and *The Forsyte Saga*). Published dissertation, University of Wuerzburg (Noerdlingen: C. H. Beck, 1933).
As realistic novels dealing with middle-class families, BUDDENBROOKS and *The Forsyte Saga* have much in common. But the attitudes of their authors are quite

different. Thomas Mann is a self-conscious individualist incapable of treating all his characters sympathetically. Unlike Mann, JG does not indulge in decadent themes; JG believes in life, love, and beauty. He has a sense of humor and is a typical representative of his class, an ideal gentleman. Of the two he is the healthier writer. [In German.]

1599 Rosati, Salvatore. "Comments and Reviews: 'English Literature,' " NUOVA ANTOLOGIA DI LETTERE, SCIENZE ED ARTI (Rome), LXVIII:1469 (1 June 1933), 473–74.

JG's *Maid in Waiting* [Italian translation *Ancella*] is a well-developed novel that depends precariously on a weak theme. The major strength of the novel is to be found in the characterization of Dinny and Jean; both are convincing portraits which are fully supported, as is true in all of JG's works, by the social setting. But all revolves around Hubert and his sensitivity to animal suffering, which drives him to kill a native who is maltreating the pack animals on an expedition in the Bolivian wilderness. In the subsequent criminal proceedings JG grotesquely exaggerates (even for an Englishman) the importance of animal protection in making Hubert a hero and a martyr to the cause of civilization. Although far from being his best novel, *Maid in Waiting* is part of the work of a distinguished English novelist, carefully translated with attention to stylistic subtleties by Mario Cassalino, and it does therefore merit attention. [In Italian.]

1600 S., E. "John Galsworthy," CHRISTIAN CENTURY, L (22 Feb 1933), 249–50.

JG, who interpreted life for postwar youth, was devoted to truth and compassion. More a stoic than a Christian prophet, he was always serious, with a dialectical bent of mind (seen notably in *Strife*). His characters were alive. It is a pity JG never embraced Christianity affirmatively—given his moral code that is consistent with the Gospels. [Obit.]

1601 Saurat, Denis. "Galsworthy," MARSYAS (Aigues-Vives), XIII (Jan 1933), 685–86.

The award of the Nobel Prize to JG is disappointing because we had hoped that Paul Valéry would receive it. It has been said that the Academy gave JG the prize out of repentance for overlooking Thomas Hardy, but Hardy was a third-rate novelist, and certainly JG is a better choice than the journalist Sinclair Lewis. Although *The Man of Property* has a certain literary value, it is not to be put alongside the works of Meredith, Trollope, or Kipling. JG's characters are wooden, his style is mediocre, and the story is banal. The milieu of the period is admirably reproduced. *The Man of Property* is a psychological offshoot of Meredith's EGOIST. Whereas Meredith persuades us of Sir Willoughby's monstrous egoism, JG fails to convince us that Soames is a monster. With each succeeding volume of the Forsytes JG came closer to the abyss of mob appeal and false sentimentality. His satire in *The Island Pharisees* served to indict the whole nation, and the resultant stereotyping was puerile; in *Saga* JG stereotypes Annette, Soames's French wife, as calculating, immoral, and repugnant. It is amusing to see intellectuals adopt the author of such puerile critiques as one of society's popular authors. But as one sees in the later volumes of *Saga* the English hypocrites (like Soames) have become sincere and pleasant persons. [In French.]

1602 Scott-James, R. A. "John Galsworthy," SPECTATOR, CL (3 Feb 1933), 145–46.
[Quotes from one of JG's letters and expresses respect for JG because he was disinclined to advocate anything and because he reacted away from his age rather than moving with it, as Shaw, Wells, and Bennett sometimes did.] JG was first an artist, and "propagandism . . . was thrust upon him." He was interested in Flaubert's and Turgenev's technique of detachment. His younger period is the more fruitful; he was "an active moving force in awakening the country from intellectual lethargy."

1603 Sekulić, Isidora. "Problem lepote u delu Dž. Golsvordija" (The Problems of Beauty in John Galsworthy's Work), SRPSKI KNJIŽEVNI GLASNIK nsXXXVIII (1933), 263–67 [not seen].
[In Serbo-Croatian.]

1604 "A Selection from the More Recent Titles: *Candelabra*," OPEN SHELF (Cleveland), March 1933, p. 7.
[Inconsequential review.]

1605 "A Selection from the More Recent Titles: *One More River*," OPEN SHELF (Cleveland), Dec 1933, p. 16.
[Inconsequential review.]

1606 Siegel, Paul. "Galsworthys *Strife* in der Mathematischen Oberprima" (Galsworthy's *Strife* in the Upper Sixth Form in Mathematics), NEUEREN SPRACHEN, XLI (Nov–Dec 1933) 387–409.
The gains for the classroom in teaching the play are that it familiarizes students with ordinary daily speech and the difficulties of slang; moreover, the intelligent design of the play and its clear technique enhance the use of the play. The central idea of the play is to be found in the struggle between Anthony and Roberts. The end of the play is a riddle, and it gives two answers to the problem raised: (1) the struggle between employers and laborers ends in a compromise, an armistice— this solution takes place in the objective business world; (2) when Anthony and Roberts face each other at the end of the play, they perceive their spiritual world. Anthony and Roberts are of the same kind, and they rise above all classes. This dualism makes *Strife* a great play. Characters like Anthony and Roberts are beyond the capabilities of a Bernard Shaw. [In German.]

1607 Smit, J. Henry. "John Galsworthy as Seen from the Vegetarian Point of View," VEGETARIAN NEWS, Jan 1933 [not seen]; rptd in THE SHORT STORIES OF JOHN GALSWORTHY (Rotterdam: D. Van Sijn, 1948), pp. 155–57.

[An inane series of quotations from JG illustrates his love for animals. Smit laments that JG was not really a vegetarian.]

1608 Soskin, William. "This Week: Shaw, Galsworthy and Some More Interesting Writers," NEW YORK EVENING POST, 25 Feb 1933, p. 7.

Candelabra's essays are pleasant but dated.

1609 Sparrow, John. "John Galsworthy," LONDON MERCURY, XXVIII (May 1933), 50–55.

JG is an artist of the second rank, competent, not great. There is "the impress of a common-place spirit" in his novels and plays. His work has the merit of photography. He creates external reality but fails to persuade the reader of the character's inner life. JG was more successful in his plays than in his novels. [The author acknowledges that he does not know JG's work well and he does not like what he knows.]

1610 Squire, J. C. "John Galsworthy," LONDON MERCURY, XXVII (March 1933), 388.

As a man JG deserved "every kind of public distinction," but his artistry is a different matter. He never equalled the "certain merit" of prose in *The Man of Property*. Most characters were "drearier than the living models." The "plays, however noble in intention, were false when new and date dreadfully now." His fame as "G. O. M. of letters" was made by the astute publication of *The Forsyte Saga* as the first of the cheap "omnibus books." If Trollope and Bennett be in the second class, then JG is "somewhat lower." "The odd thing is, that if he had let himself alone and been his own natural self, not overlaid by theories and duties, he might have been a much finer novelist. He always gave the impression of having a great deal pent-up." [Obit comment.]

1611 Stonier, G. W. "Selected Fiction," FORTNIGHTLY REVIEW, nsCXXXIII (1 Jan 1933), 134.

Flowering Wilderness "is written with care and dignity, but the 'pukka sahib' atmosphere here seems ludicrously unreal."

1612 Strong, L. A. G. "The Last of the Forsytes," SPECTATOR (Lond), CLI (6 Oct 1933), 454.

Over the River is typical JG. [Strong defends JG's value as a novelist, especially when JG attacks possession and "possessive jealousy."]

1613 Th. "John Galsworthy mrtev" (John Galsworthy Is Dead), NÁRODNÍ LISTY (Prague), LXXIII:32 (1933), 4 [not seen]. [Obit.] [In Czech.]

1614 *"Three Novels of Love,"* A.L.A. BOOKLIST, XXIX (May 1933), 277.
The novels reprinted under the title *Three Novels of Love* (*The Dark Flower, Beyond,* and *A Saint's Progress*) are unrelated except for the general theme of love. [Brief notice of publication.]

1615 *"Three Novels of Love,"* BOSTON EVENING TRANSCRIPT BOOK SECTION, 15 March 1933, p. 2.
The Dark Flower and *Beyond* are lasting stories of "adult emotional life"; *A Saint's Progress* is characterized by "artistic restraint and sensitivity to human emotion." [Brief review of the three novels bound into one volume.]

1616 *"Three Novels of Love,"* CHRISTIAN CENTURY, L (29 March 1933), 426.
[Brief, noncommittal notice of *The Dark Flower, Beyond,* and *A Saint's Progress.*]

1617 *"Three Novels of Love,"* COMMONWEAL, XVII (12 April 1933), 671.
"Deft characterizations, [and] scraps of moral insight" compensate for the effects of the passage of time in *The Dark Flower, A Saint's Progress,* and *Beyond.*

1618 V., E. M. "Clannish to the End," CHRISTIAN SCIENCE MONITOR, 2 Dec 1933, p. 7.
Characters in *One More River* are types without inner vitality or feeling; the novel is undistinguished except for the court scene, where JG as always is masterful.

1619 Véron, Jeanne. "John Galsworthy through French Eyes," CORNHILL MAGAZINE, LXXIV (April 1933), 385–88.
There is a mixture of "poetical sensualism and dry satire" in *Fraternity* that would appeal to the French. "The half-poetical, half-sordid descriptions of London, in *Fraternity,* are for me the most characteristic expression of Mr. Galsworthy's genius. . . . Even after trying seven times to translate *Fraternity,* my French words never conveyed the quality of realistic lyricism in the English of Mr. Galsworthy." *The Patrician* is an easier book for the French for several reasons: (1) the French take for granted that the English patrician is the model of all virtues; (2) the political situations in France and England since the war are similar; (3) the love story between a young man of promise and a married woman of no importance is universally understood. Although "A Man of Devon" and *The Island Pharisees* show a lack of composition, they also show "a directness and a strength of expression."

1620 Vidaković, A[leksandar]. "Džon Golsvordi, 1867–1933" (John Galsworthy, 1867–1933), SRPSKI KNJIŽEVNI GLASNIK, nsXXXVIII (1933), 267–69 [not seen].
[In Serbo-Croatian.]

1621 Walpole, Hugh. "John Galsworthy 1867–1933," THE POST VIC-
TORIANS, ed by William Ralph Inge (Lond: Ivor Nicholson & Watson,
1933), pp. x–xi, 173–85.

Unfortunately, JG's best works, *The Man of Property* and *The Silver Box*,
appeared early in his career; he shut himself off from the outside world through
spiritual isolation—he seemed austere and apart to those who knew him only
casually. He was shy, not replying to critical injustices to himself; rather he
replied only to the injustices to others. His work in essence was static in theme
and technique: that was JG's main fault because the social chronicler must be
aware of changing artistic and social scenes. His theme, stated early in *Property*
and followed throughout his other works, is his scorn for the "top-dog" and pity
for the "under-dog": yet it is usually the "upper-dogs" who win our sympathy
rather than the "under-dogs." JG could create human beings, but sentimentality
in relation to the under-dog usually creeps in: Irene is actually "callously
selfish," but her misery and Bosinney's "snarling unhappiness" are evident
throughout *Property*.

JG tried to give the novel a new technique in *Property:* "meticulous self-
conscious care" and a "vigorous and various" life—on the order of Turgenev and
Dickens. His characters have "London of the late '80's hung behind them like a
rich figured tapestry." The chapter "Drive with Swithin" is an example of
"perfect technical and emotional mastery." JG is best as a story-teller, but in
Soames Forsyte JG has created a universal character. JG's virtues are: "charm
and delicacy of detached scenes . . . narrative gift . . . Englishness . . . irony but
no humour . . . a passion for furniture, jewellery, clothes, and food, and the
eternally recurrent theme of unhappy and restless love." But his characters have
no spiritual life. JG is the most authentic painter of the age he depicted.

1622 Watson, E. H. Lacon. "John Galsworthy: The Novelist," EN-
GLISH REVIEW, LVII (1933), 308–12.

Most critics agree that JG was in the tradition of Thackeray and Trollope, and like
them he "loved his characters too well to part from them easily." *The Forsyte
Saga* overshadows all his other work by its length and abundance. JG was not
perhaps at his best in the short story. He was a humanitarian at a time when this
cult was unpopular. His work seemed too quiet, too unemotional to achieve great
commercial success, but *Saga* did achieve just that. His "was the most sympathetic of novelists," and his love for his fellowmen is "the real secret of his
popularity . . . the secret of his Nobel Prize, and his Order of Merit, and of the
lasting affection" of his readers.

1623 Watson, Ernest Bradlee, and Benfield Pressey (eds). FIVE
MODERN PLAYS (NY: Charles Scribner's Sons, 1933).

[Reprint of five plays and introductions from CONTEMPORARY DRAMA (NY:
Charles Scribner's Sons, 1931). A brief introduction to the play is followed by
the text of *Justice*.]

1624 Waugh, Arthur. "John Galsworthy as Novelist," BOOKMAN (Lond), LXXXIII (March 1933), 485.

JG was popular as a novelist because "he was consistent, well balanced in judgment, and immune from impatient moods and prejudices." Readers know that he will never let them down intellectually or sympathetically. His novels are testimony to his great strength of character.

1625 Weeks, Edward. "*One More River,*" ATLANTIC BOOKSHELF, Dec 1933, pp. 32, 34.

In *One More River,* Dinny Cherrell has pluck and integrity. There is also a "curious preoccupation with death." JG's "silk-smooth, keenly selective and sympathetic" style works best when he is portraying daily life. [Brief review.]

1626 "Where Galsworthy's Fame Lay," LITERARY DIGEST, CXV (11 Feb 1933), 40.

JG's fame was greater outside of England than in England because he had no solutions for its problems. [Obit.]

1627 Williamson, Hugh Ross. "John Galsworthy—Notes at Random," BOOKMAN (Lond), LXXXIII (March 1933), 473–79.

Soames's (or JG's) greatness is "due to the fact that the symbolism never subdues his individuality." *The Forsyte Saga* is a "modern morality," largely because of JG's sense of pity. Soames in part is Everyman. With Soames "the artist . . . [in JG] fought the moralist and the magistrate—and has won." JG insists that "the Christian paradox of gain only by voluntary loss is true of every spiritual value." The symbolic Irene is not satisfactory, "partly because, by equating her with Beauty, it becomes impossible at times to fit the novel and the allegory together." JG's work lives in part because it gives a "picture of epoch, and immortalizes a type." Of the dramas *Justice* perhaps is the most durable. *Strife* is unsatisfactory because JG does not recognize that the "real problem" in the play is political, not merely legal or moral. Some of JG's plays move because of moral fervor; others "compel admiration by his classic sense of tragedy." [A commemorative essay reprinting photographs of scenes in *Strife* and *Justice,* a facsimile of the last page of the MS "Indian Summer of a Forsyte," and a portrait by Coster.]

1628 Woodbridge, Homer E. "Last of the Cherrells," SATURDAY REVIEW OF LITERATURE (NY), X (7 Oct 1933), 159.

One More River is "decidedly thin"—the trilogy habit seems to have gotten to JG. The story cannot stand alone because it depends on the preceding novels.

1629 "The World and the Theatre," THEATRE ARTS MONTHLY, XVII (March 1933), 171–77.

While JG's lasting fame is as a novelist, he had a sense for good drama. His earliest plays are freest and best. Notable American performances of JG plays are Ethel Barrymore as the charwoman in *The Silver Box,* John Barrymore as Falder in *Justice* (1916), and Winthrop Ames's Little Theatre production of *Strife* (1909) and *The Pigeon* (1916). JG is associated with "some of the happiest and most hopeful days in the . . . American theatre." [A full-page photograph of Randall Davey's portrait is reproduced in this short obit essay.]

1934

1630 Adams, F. B., Jr. "A Letter from John Galsworthy," COL-OPHON, XIX (1934), No 10.
JG replies (13 March 1926) to a letter [see "Grove Lodge," CORNHILL MAGA-ZINE, No. 1033 (Autumn 1962)] from Rupert Croft-Cooke which asked for guidance and certainty. JG explains his religious, philosophic creed about the Principle of Unity and that of Variety and asserts his belief in the "gentleman." Human evil arises because men do not "balance rightly." [Probably Croft-Cooke prints a more accurate form of JG's reply.]

1631 Alevskii, M. "Angliiskie rant'e v romanakh Dzhona Golsuorsi" (English Rentiers in the Novels of John Galsworthy), KRASNAIA NOV', No. 8 (1934), 187–97 [not seen].
[In Russian.]

1632 Bab, Julius. "Abschied von Galsworthy" (Farewell of Galsworthy), DIE HILFE (Berlin), XL: 2 (1934), 43–46.
[Brief discussion of the posthumously published novels.] [In German.]

1633 Brewster, D., and A. Burrell. MODERN FICTION (NY: Columbia UP, 1934), pp. 8, 20, 69, 85, 200, 225, 249, 348.
[The references are slight, passing ones.]

1634 Cameron, Norman. "Music in Galsworthy," CHESTERIAN, XVI (Sept–Oct 1934), 6–10.
Old Jolyon Forsyte (*The Man of Property*) was an operagoer of the first order, who loved the older classics but thought that Wagner had ruined everything. But CARMEN was JG's favorite, as it was old Jolyon's—the "Habanera" especially, that "gypsy thing" that gave old Jolyon his abandon; that Fleur recalls when reminiscing about her honeymoon with the wrong man; that sets the tone for the heroine of *Flowering Wilderness* on a walk through Hyde Park—with the conclusion of the "Toreador's song." CARMEN is also the favorite of the cynical Wilfrid Desert. Soames's (*Property*) recognition of his inability to understand music illustrates JG's recognition of its power and what the lack of the ability to appreciate it means.

1635 Cantwell, Robert. "OUTLOOK Book Choice of the Month," NEW OUTLOOK (NY), CLXIV (Oct 1934), 53, 57–59.
[Brief notice of the beautifully bound—"but unreadable, uninspired, and belabored"—trilogy, *End of the Chapter.*]

1636 Colenutt, R. "The World of Mr. Galsworthy's Fiction," CORNHILL MAGAZINE, CXLIV (Jan 1934), 55–64.
Although JG's world of imagination is a large one, it is one limited in time and space. His plays always take place in "the present." The chief departure from the time limit is *On Forsyte 'Change.* This world is the world of JG's own era (ca. 1886–1930). The most noteworthy hiatus in time is the period of 1914–1918. Similarly, the scope of JG's world is also limited; his world is seen through the squire's eyes; his people have positions of dignity—it is the world of the gentleman. JG, however, brings his characters into collision with people of different standards, thereby gaining in conflict and suspense; or sometimes he faces his people with basic dilemmas involving standards of conduct. JG's method of "cross-references"—that is, characters from some of his works who appear also in other works—is "a device on the part of the author for increasing the reality of his world and helping us to feel that it has no particular limits as regards its inhabitants." The reader is taken into a crowd of people; some he knows well, some he's only met, and some are complete strangers—very much like the real everyday world. JG attains a clearness of definition by contrast, as can be seen in *Fraternity.* The stock response that *The Forsyte Saga* is JG's chief claim to fame errs in that it overlooks such first-rate works as *The White Monkey, The Silver Spoon,* and *Maid in Waiting.* JG's all-embracing sympathy gives breadth to his work.

1637 Davies, S. H. STUDIES IN THE ORIGINAL MANUSCRIPTS OF THE FORSYTE CHRONICLES; GALWORTHY THE CRAFTSMAN: FURTHER STUDIES IN THE ORIGINAL MANUSCRIPTS OF THE FORSYTE CHRONICLES; GALSWORTHY THE CRAFTSMAN: STUDIES IN THE ORIGINAL MANUSCRIPTS OF THE WHITE MONKEY AND THE SILVER SPOON; GALSWORTHY THE CRAFTSMAN: FINAL STUDIES IN THE ORIGINAL MANUSCRIPTS OF THE FORSYTE CHRONICLES (Lond[?]: pvtly ptd, 1934–35 [?]). [The first installment was received and dated by the British Museum "June 1934," the last part, "January 1935"].
[The study, based on JG's gift of *The Forsyte Saga* and *A Modern Comedy* MSS to the British Museum, reprints JG's own drawing of the home Bosinney created in *The Man of Property,* several photographs of JG's corrections in his MSS, and various incidents of JG revising the MSS, which generally illustrate JG's "avoidance of all but the relevant detail." Davies contends that JG is a careful critic of his own work. Altogether there are twenty-two pages of not very professional comment, examples, and illustrations. See also S. H. Davies, "Galsworthy the Craftsman," (1933).]

1638 Delattre, Floris. LE ROMAN SOCIAL DE JOHN GALSWORTHY (THE SOCIAL NOVEL OF JOHN GALSWORTHY). Extrait du BULLETIN DE L'ASSOCIATION FRANCE–GRANDE BRETAGNE, etc. 1934. 20 pp. [not seen].
[In French.]

1639 Dobrée, Bonamy. "Some Galsworthy Letters," SPECTATOR (Lond), CLIII (9 Nov 1934), 722.
JG's difficulty was in determining the "artistic limits of satire"—when to be a propagandist and how detached he should be. It is a pity that JG went more to the lyrical later in life, because he was more a satirist than a lyricist—lacking as he did the element of youth and understanding. [Review of Edward Garnett (ed), LETTERS FROM JOHN GALSWORTHY: 1900–1932 (Lond: Cape, 1934).]

1640 Edgar, Pelham. "John Galsworthy," THE ART OF THE NOVEL FROM 1700 TO THE PRESENT TIME (NY: Macmillan, 1934), pp. 206–16.
JG's fame as a novelist will depend on the fate of *The Forsyte Saga*. The first trilogy will last longer than *A Modern Comedy,* where the second, "ragged and unconvincing," is impeded by a too conscious sense of purpose. Soames Forsyte "seems capable of as many resuscitations as Sherlock Holmes." Marjorie Ferrar's trial scene is one of the best revelations of the later novels. Minor blemishes like the unconvincing death of Bosinney (*The Man of Property*) do not detract from the overall good characterization, dialogue, and description. Irene is an experiment with the Henry Jamesian technique of "indirect presentation," but Irene does not have the vitality necessary for her "destructive power." Especially good for a study of JG's art is the chapter "Drive with Swithin," with its "maximum of economy with the maximum of effect." Wells and Bennett might have a fuller sense of life, but JG "is the surer artist, and his report of human nature, if less wittily entertaining, is as reliable within its limits."

1641 Eishiskina, N. "Burzhuaznyi realizm na poslednem etape (*Forsaity* D. Golsuorsi)" (Bourgeois Realism at the Last Stage: J. Galsworthy's *Forsytes*), LITERATURNYI KRITIK, No. 5 (1934), 138–51 [not seen].
[In Russian.]

1642 Eishiskina, N. "*Grekhopadenie'* Golsuorsi" (*The Fall* by Galsworthy), LITERATURNAIA GAZETA, 22 Feb 1934 [n.p.] [not seen].
[Review of *The Fall* (?).] [In Russian.]

1643 "*End of the Chapter*," A.L.A. BOOKLIST, XXXI (Nov 1934), 95.
[The brief notice announces the appearance of the collected edition of *Maid in Waiting, Flowering Wilderness,* and *Over The River.*]

1644 "*End of the Chapter,*" CHRISTIAN CENTURY, LI (29 Aug 1934), 1095.

[Brief notice of publication in a single volume of *Maid in Waiting*, *Flowering Wilderness*, and *Over the River.*]

1645 Ervine, St. John. "John Galsworthy, 1867–1933," GREAT DEMOCRATS, ed by A. Barratt Brown (Lond: Ivor Nicholson & Watson, 1934), 277–95.
The character of Soames is the "acid test of Galsworthy's artistry," for although JG intended Soames to be unlikable, the reader's affection for him grows as *The Forsyte Saga* progresses. No one likes Irene—"that prig, with the cold, uncharitable heart and . . . venomous memory"; she brings misfortune on everyone. JG's laborers are without "moral force or high, unquenchable character, or irrepressible vigour." David Roberts (*Strife*) is JG's "most emphatic artisan," and he is merely an obstinate "man who mistakes contumacy for strength and supposes himself to be seeing visions when he is only seeing enemies." JG's knowledge of artists was as inadequate as his knowledge of artisans. He pitied mankind, but he did not love it. He "was of that order of Liberals and humanitarians who are eager to have ills removed so that they may not themselves be perturbed by their presence." Being innately noble, kind, and generous, JG was "bigger than his books and plays."

1646 Ford, Ford Madox. RETURN TO YESTERDAY (NY: Horace Liveright, 1934), pp. 269–74.
[Ford tells why he broke with JG in 1903 and refused ever to see him thereafter.] Even though JG and his friends were working to persuade butchers to adopt more humane methods of slaughter, they refused to use the argument, although true, that such methods would increase profits. The "humanitarians" believed this argument was unacceptable because greater humaneness "must be secured educatively. The moral sense of butchers must be worked on so that freely and without constraint they had mercy on their victims." Ford was so upset by this attitude that he wrote JG saying he could never see JG again.

1647 Galland, R. "Meredith et Galsworthy" (Meredith and Galsworthy), REVUE ANGLO-AMÉRICAINE, XII (Oct 1934), 47–48.
The following are striking similarities between BEAUCHAMP'S CAREER and *The Patrician:* (1) an aristocratic milieu hostile to the hero's ideas; (2) an independent champion of lost causes; (3) a married woman who offers herself to the hero and is finally renounced; (4) a description of an election; (5) a serious passion of the hero whose career means everything to those who love him. Further evidence of Meredith's influence can be seen in the way JG associates nature with crises in the characters' lives and in the use of chance, the accident which brings various personages together. [In French.]

1648 "Galsworthy and Friendly Critic," SPRINGFIELD REPUBLICAN (Mass), 8 Dec 1934, p. 10.
[Review of Edward Garnett (ed), LETTERS FROM JOHN GALSWORTHY, 1900–1932 (Lond: Cape, 1934).]

1649 "Galsworthy, John. *One More River,*" PRATT INSTITUTE QUAR-
TERLY BOOKLIST, Winter 1934, p. 35.
[Brief notice of publication.]

1650 "Galsworthy Letters," TIMES LITERARY SUPPLEMENT (Lond),
XXXIII (15 Nov 1934), 789.
[Brief review of Edward Garnett (ed), LETTERS FROM JOHN GALSWORTHY,
1900–1932 (Lond: Cape, 1934).]

1651 "Galsworthy's Trilogy: *End of the Chapter* His Last Three
Novels," SPRINGFIELD REPUBLICAN (Mass), 11 Nov 1934, Sec. E, p.
34.
End of the Chapter (*Maid in Waiting, Flowering Wilderness, One More River*)
continues the craftsmanship evident in *The Forsyte Saga.* The difference in
subject matter in part accounts for the loss of vitality.

1652 Garnett, Edward (ed). "Introduction," LETTERS FROM JOHN
GALSWORTHY, 1900–1932 (Lond: Cape; NY: Scribner's, 1934), 5–16.
JG "stands for the best of the upper-class Englishman of his period, ineradicably
English in his essential virtues and limitations." His compassion "informed his
finest work, such as the figure of Mrs. Pendyce in *The Country House,* and it was
the Achilles heel of his talent, as we may note in *The Fugitive.*" The *Country
House* is the finest of all his novels. Probably JG did not submit any of his work in
MS to me during the last twenty years of his life. Even before the war JG, like
Trollope, wrote too many books. "I do not speak here of Galsworthy's post-war
fiction and plays, which I have not critically studied." [These letters between JG
and his literary mentor provide significant information about JG as he learned the
discipline and craft of writing.]

1653 Gregory, Russell. "Theatre Notes: Embassy Theatre. *The
Roof,*" SATURDAY REVIEW (Lond), CLVII (30 June 1934), 774.
[Negative plot-summary review of *The Roof.*]

1654 Gregory, Russell. "Theatre Notes: Little Theatre. *The Little
Man,*" SATURDAY REVIEW (Lond), CLVII (30 June 1934), 774.
The Little Man is not worth seeing because characters are overdrawn and over-
acted.

1655 Honda, Kensho. "Some Topics from Galsworthy's Thoughts on
Art," STUDIES IN ENGLISH LITERATURE (Tokyo), XIV (1934), 380–88.
[The author introduces JG's artistic point of view by choosing three topics
(namely, "On Realism," "On Renaissance," and "On Criticism") from *The Inn
of Tranquillity,* a work which Mr. Honda has translated into Japanese.] [In
Japanese.]

1656 Hutchison, Percy. "Galsworthy's Letters to Edward Garnett,"
NEW YORK TIMES BOOK REVIEW, 16 Dec 1934, p. 6.

Throughout JG's letters there is a sense of refinement and a hatred of insincerity and sham. [Review of Edward Garnett (ed), LETTERS FROM JOHN GALSWORTHY 1900–1932 (Lond: Cape, 1934).]

1657 Hutchison, Percy. "Introduction," *The Forsyte Saga* (NY: Charles Scribner's Sons, 1934), pp. vii–xxxix.

JG was consummately honest, never sacrificing honesty for phrase and wit, even though there are clever phrases and wit aplenty in JG. *The Forsyte Saga* is really more ironic and comedy-of-mannersish than satiric, because the work is too realistic to create the distortions that satire requires. Soames is not the villain at the end of *The Man of Property* that some consider him to be: he has a "blind spot," a Nemesis "pulling from within" rather than the classical pulling from without, which alienates him from Irene. In the divorce proceedings, JG blames the "whole legal machine." The major irony of the *Saga* is the Jon-Fleur romance—a Romeo and Juliet situation. *A Modern Comedy* is "lighter, freer, more dancing" than *Saga*, "more nearly in the manner of out-and-out satire." JG treats minor characters (witness Timothy's aged family cook) and individual scenes (Old Jolyon going to the opera) with great artistry. [Hutchison apparently believes that JG can do no wrong.]

1658 Jopp, Gerhard. DIE MODIFIKATION DES VERBALBEGRIFFS BEI GALSWORTHY (The Modification of Verbal Concepts in Galsworthy). Published dissertation, University of Marburg (Marburg: Drukerei Bauer, 1934).

[This detailed study of JG's style in his formal language and his use of slang and dialect considers *The Island Pharisees, The Country House, The Forsyte Saga, A Modern Comedy, On Forsyte'Change, Castles in Spain, The Silver Box,* and *The Foundations.* Acoustical and visual impressions play a smaller role in JG's later work. Cites Bernhard Fehr (q.v., 1923) to the effect that JG changed from the artist of "consciousness." Increasingly JG concerned himself less with externals and more with the inner lives of his characters.] [In German.]

1659 Krause, Gerd. "Das Verhältnis der Menschen zum Besitz in Galsworthys *Forsyte Saga*" (The Relationship of Men to Property in Galsworthy's *Forsyte Saga*), NEUPHILOLOGISCHE MITTEILUNGEN (Helsingfors), XXXV (May 1934), 105–25.

Taine's theory that a work of literature reveals the psychology of a people is especially applicable to JG's works. His two major works, *A Modern Comedy* and *The Forsyte Saga,* involve, like JG's own life, two epochs, the Victorian era and its aftermath. In *Saga* Victorianism is shown in its time of full bloom, its decline, and its disintegration; moreover, Victorianism is subjected to detailed satire, treated with realism, and conditioned by humor. By portraying the Forsytes in their many-sidedness, JG creates not only individuals but also types of a class, representatives of a nation, and universal types. He uses the theme of a sense of property to illuminate his characters. [The thesis is supported by detailed discussion of the general characteristics of the Forsytes in relationship to ownership (pp. 107–14) and analyses of individual characters: Old Jolyon (115–17), Soames (117–25).] [In German.]

1660 Kreemers, R. M. J. DE NOBELPRIJSWINNER 1932 JOHN GALSWORTHY AS TONEELSCHRIVJER (John Galsworthy, 1932 Nobel Prize Winner, As Writer), 1934 [not seen].
[Listed in BRITISH MUSEUM CATALOGUE, No. 11856.a.32.] [In Danish.]

1661 Leggett, H. W. THE IDEA IN FICTION (Lond: Allen & Unwin, 1934), pp. 69, 75–76, 90, 92, 97–98, 149.
JG chose his characters to represent both sides of a question. Through Soames Forsyte he codified for literature the concept of the "sacredness of property." Interest is maintained in Soames throughout *The Forsyte Saga* by showing his reaction to the constantly changing world as the character of Soames himself develops over a period of years.

1662 "LETTERS FROM JOHN GALSWORTHY, 1900–1932," CHRISTIAN CENTURY, LI (26 Dec 1934), 1657.
The most interesting aspect of the JG-Edward Garnett letters is the early discussion of technique in fiction. [Review of Edward Garnett's collection (Lond: Cape, 1934).]

1663 "The Library of the Quarter," YALE REVIEW, nsXXIII (Winter 1934), vi.
[Paragraph plot-summary review of *One More River,* concluding that JG believes England is becoming second best.]

1664 Marriott, James W[illiam]. "John Galsworthy," MODERN DRAMA (Lond: Thomas Nelson, 1934), pp. 146–60.
JG's characters are interesting primarily as "social phenomena" rather than as people. His "architectural instinct for symmetry and poise" is too strong. The real villain of the restrained and realistic *Silver Box* is the judicial system. *Box* is a study in contrasts; *Justice* is straightforward, relentless narrative. *Strife* is developed by means of counterparts, ironically concluding with the compromise that was offered in the beginning. *The Little Man* with its mixed nationalities was courageously offered to the public in post-World War I England. JG's craftsmanship is indebted to Flaubert, Maupassant, Dostoievsky, and Chekhov in "close observation of details . . . economy of words," and detachment.

1665 "Mr. John Galsworthy, O. M.," DEVONIAN YEAR BOOK (Lond), 1934, pp. 41–42.
[Obit notice.]

1666 Mottram, R. H. "Galsworthy Letters," NEW STATESMAN AND NATION, nsVIII (10 Nov 1934), 665–66.
The value of the letters published in Edward Garnett's LETTERS FROM JOHN

GALSWORTHY consists in the autobiographical details about JG; in addition, the letters provide insight into the unorganized coterie of, among others, Joseph Conrad, W. H. Hudson, Hilaire Belloc, Thomas Seccombe, Ford Madox Ford, and Edward Garnett, the "unelected president and prime mover of this literary phenomenon."

1667 Ould, Hermon. JOHN GALSWORTHY (Lond: Chapman & Hall, 1934).

JG's method of characterization is usually elliptical; the reader is expected to draw his own conclusions about, for example, General Pendyce's (*The Country House*) nightly prayer to keep the Liberals out, or Viscount Harbinger's (*The Patrician*) limiting views on social reform. Although JG "habitually eschewed" symbolism, there are occasions when he used a kind of symbolism; "in *The Skin Game* the situation is worked out in such a way that frequently it runs parallel with the situation" of World War I. An example of JG's humor can be seen in *Fraternity*. When Stephen Dallison was unable to play golf on Saturday, he would, instead, go to his club and read the reviews; in both forms of exercise one went round and round. Despite his love of nature JG rarely resorted to irrelevant facts or descriptive setpieces. The roles of the gods in Greek tragedy are played by abstract forces and institutions like the Law, the Mob, Property, and the Land in JG's works. Some of his characters are too rigidly constructed: "there is not enough *give* in them—they are truer to themselves than anybody ever is!" In *The Freelands* he used the country "as a theme running contrapuntally . . . to the theme of the human characters, meeting it at appropriate points and . . . occasionally colliding with it and producing a significant discord." Except in his treatment of the poor, JG's use of pity is usually defensible and under control. The common misconception that JG's characters are weak and ineffective (this may result from considering *Justice* a typical JG drama) has overlooked numerous examples of very strong characters in his work who courageously face "the blind or malignant attacks" and remain unbroken even in defeat: Stephen More in *The Mob;* Michael Strangway in *A Bit o' Love;* and Roberts and Anthony in *Strife*. [This volume is largely based on personal reminiscences and an intelligent awareness of their significance and proper use; critical comments are scattered throughout.]

1668 Pellizzi, Camillo. IL TEATRO INGLESE (The English Theater) (Milano: Fratelli Treves, 1934); trans by Rowan Williams as ENGLISH DRAMA: THE LAST GREAT PHASE (Lond: MacMillan, 1935), pp. 115, 118–25.

JG treats the "symbolic individuality" of the "hostile forces of society and tradition." *Strife* and *The Mob* are JG's best dramas because he works best with the tragedy of society as a whole, emphasizing the sense of the "cruel, unjustifiable waste" of humanity. In the symbolic *Little Man,* the little man is the "indispensable and only hero of the new age." The conclusion to be reached from *Little Man:* "the modern middle classes . . . have built up all the moral and intellectual justifications of Communism." With JG, "middle-class realism" has gone beyond the tragic to the "elegaic and lyrical"; in his "perfect balance of contrasts," he goes "beyond drama" in his lyrical manner of expressing "contemplation and resigned sorrow."

1669 Polzer, V. "Galsworthy," GIESSENER ANZEIGER, FAMILIE BLATT, No. 11 (1934) [not seen].
[Listed in ANNUAL BIBLIOGRAPHY OF ENGLISH LANGUAGE AND LITERATURE (Cambridge: Modern Humanities Research Association, 1935).] [In German.]

1670 *"The Roof,"* NEW STATESMAN AND NATION, nsVII (2 June 1934), 848.
The Roof is awkward, crude, and insensitive, with occasional touches of comedy and charm. [Review of revival at the Embassy Theatre.]

1671 Skovgaard, Jes (annot). *Loyalties* (Engelsk Laesning for Gymnasiet I) (Copenhagen: H. Hirschsprungs, 1934; 4th ed., 1946).
JG's outstanding merit as a dramatist is his imparitality. [A teaching text with notes in English and Danish for high-school students.]

1672 Wells, H. G. "Digression about Novels," EXPERIMENT IN AUTOBIOGRAPHY (Lond: Gollancz & Cresset P, 1934), pp. 487–504; (NY: Macmillan, 1934), pp. 410–24, espec 418–19; rptd in HENRY JAMES AND H. G. WELLS . . . , ed by Leon Edel and Gordon N. Ray (Urbana: University of Illinois P, 1958), pp. 215–33, espec 226, 233.
Wells remarks that he knew of no satisfactory device "for exhibiting a train of reasoning in a character unless a set of ideas similar to those upon which the character thinks exists already in the reader's mind" and uses JG's Soames Forsytes as an example of one who "thinks along recognized British lines. He does not grapple with ideas new and difficult both for the reader and himself." *The Forsyte Saga* "is not so good and convincing as a group of untrammelled biographical studies of genteel successful types . . . might be."

1935

1673 Arns, Leo. GALSWORTHY UND DIE KRISIS DES INDUSTRIALIS-MUS (Galsworthy and the Crisis of Industrialism). Published dissertation, Bonn University, 1935 (Düren, Germany: n.p., 1935) [not seen]. [In German.]

1674 Bloor, R. H. U. THE ENGLISH NOVEL FROM CHAUCER TO GALSWORTHY (Lond: Ivor Nicholson & Watson, 1935), pp. 7, 242–46.
The Forsyte Saga and *A Modern Comedy* are the epilogue to the Victorian age.

These novels are more than mere adjuncts to history. Despite his merciless analysis of the Forsytes, it is clear that JG appreciates them and knows their worth. The theme of the novels is the disintegration of the Forsytes. Whereas an ordinary novelist would have focused on the love affair between Irene and Bosinney, JG kept the affair in the background, preserving its subservience to the main theme. It is probably true, as Dean Inge believes, that Irene is a "female cad," but "her character is not in question. She is a feminine force in this theme of disintegration." *Modern Comedy* is brilliant. JG's novels portray the fortunes of the possessive class, and the plays depict the victims of society who are caught in the social machinery. Plays like *Justice, The Silver Box, The Fugitive, The Pigeon,* and *Strife* show "life tearing life to shreds" not out of anger or hatred but simply because "we each move in our own limited sphere and cannot understand those in other spheres." The plays and novels complement each other and make a whole picture.

1675 Bodingbauer, Leopold. EINE STUDIE AN JOHN GALSWORTHY ÜBER DAS SOZIAL-VERHÄLTNIS OBERKLASSE-UNTERKLASSE (A Study in the Social Relationship between the Upper and Lower Classes in John Galsworthy). Unpublished dissertation, University of Vienna, 1935.
Because JG is a realist, his works offer an accurate view of the struggle between the upper and lower classes. He depicts the dried-up spirit of the reactionaries and the self-sufficiency of the bourgeoisie and criticizes their attitudes towards the lower classes from an individualistic point of view; he advocates social sympathy and denounces materialism. But since he extends his sympathies to individual members of the lower class and is solely interested in individual perfection, he cannot comprehend the masses and the need for a revolutionary change of the outdated capitalistic system. He remains, essentially, a conservative who works to preserve such values of the disappearing old order as beauty, dignity, a sense of service, and manners. Thus, he is opposed to the real forces of his time, represented by the worker and the technologist. [An amply documented study from a Fascist point of view.] [In German.]

1676 Brash, W. Bardsley. "John Galsworthy," LONDON QUARTERLY AND HOLBORN REVIEW, CLX (Oct 1935), 460–71.
JG's lasting quality is verisimilitude rather than creation of great characters. Other qualities are lightning-like satire, an "exquisite feeling for beauty, courage, and kindness." [A general discussion of JG's main works, adding no new critical insight.]

1677 Cecil, Lord David. "Dusting off the Gold Tops," SATURDAY REVIEW OF LITERATURE (NY), XI (19 Jan 1935), 430.
A twentieth-century Victorian novelist would have to be a composite of JG, Huxley, Woolf, Christie, and Wodehouse combined, because their individual fields of experience are narrow. [Photos of JG and the others mentioned are included.]

1678 Dukes, Ashley. "The English Scene," THEATRE ARTS MONTHLY, XIX (June 1935), 411–15.

Justice did some social good when it was first performed, but the current revival on stage is dated and not worth bothering with.

1679 Findeisen, Wilhelm. "Entwurf einer interrichtlichen Interpretation von Galsworthys *Strife*" (Proposal of an Interpretation of Conflicting Rights in Galsworthy's *Strife*), NEUPHILOLOGISCHE MONATSSCHRIFT, VI (1935), 140–43.

Strife deals not only with a social problem but also with an ethical one. The main interest is in the struggle between two opposed people representing two basic principles and not in the development of the strike. The struggle for principles, however, goes against nature, a god-determined order. Finally the masses who had at first shouted "Hosannah" will, when asked to endure struggle and hardship, shout "crucify him." [In German.]

1680 Flanner, Hildegarde. "A Warrior's Ghost," POETRY, XLVI (June 1935), 168–70.

The Collected Poems of John Galsworthy is a thoughtful and courageous volume, touching on many noble themes, but it is minor: JG's novels contain his best poetry.

1681 "Forsyte Origins: The Permanence of Galsworthy?" TIMES LITERARY SUPPLEMENT (Lond), 14 Dec 1935, p. 854.

H. V. Marrot's LIFE AND LETTERS OF JOHN GALSWORTHY could have been done more succinctly; unfortunately too few of JG's conversations are included.

1682 *"Forsytes, Pendyces and Others,"* A.L.A. BOOKLIST, XXXII (Dec 1935), 100–101.

[Brief notice of publication.]

1683 "Galsworthiana," SATURDAY REVIEW (Lond), CLIX (6 July 1935), 853–54.

[Brief notice of *Forsytes, Pendyces and Others,* without commentary.]

1684 "Galsworthy Bits: Group of *Forsytes, Pendyces and Others,"* SPRINGFIELD REPUBLICAN (Mass), 22 Dec 1935, Sec. E, p. 7.

Forsytes, Pendyces and Others "reveal the author's appreciation of nature and beauty, his concern for justice, and his kindly sensitive spirit."

1685 "Galsworthy Fragments," TIMES LITERARY SUPPLEMENT (Lond), XXXIV (13 June 1935), 377.

Forsytes, Pendyces and Others is inferior JG. Particularly unnoteworthy are his shallow comments on fellow writers.

1686 GALSWORTHY IN HIS HUMOUR (Lond: Duckworth, 1935).

[A series of snippets from JG's works on topics such as "Nation and Empire,"

"Human Nature, Liberty, Equality," "Manners," "The Press." For those who think JG is without a sense of humor, read one of his opinions of THE TIMES (Lond): "I'm always so sorry for people who read THE TIMES; such a very loud noise"—*The Winter Garden*. HUMOUR is included in this bibliography because the anonymous editor's title is misleading and the work is difficult to locate. The copy examined for this bibliography can be found in the British Museum.]

1687 Garnett, Edward. "A Representative Englishman," SPECTATOR (Lond), CLV (13 Dec 1935), 991.
[Review of H. V. Marrot, THE LIFE AND LETTERS OF JOHN GALSWORTHY (Lond: Heinemann, 1935).]

1688 Gassner, John (ed). "John Galsworthy," A TREASURY OF THE THEATRE (NY: Simon & Schuster, 1935); rptd (1940, 1950, 1951, 1960, 1967), pp. 597–98.
Only JG in England adopted the continental dramatic form of objective social drama and naturalism. In JG society equals the Greek Fate. The plays, penetrating and convincing rather than scintillating, employ "authentic dialogue" and are well organized. *Escape* shows the influence of the cinema. [Headnote to *Escape*.]

1689 Hammond, Lewis. "Last Fragments From Galsworthy: Varied in Type and in Quality, Some Unfinished, They Are Representative of the Author at Less Than His Peak," BOSTON EVENING TRANSCRIPT BOOK SECTION, 2 Nov 1935, p. 4.
The best stories in *Forsytes, Pendyces and Others* are "The Mummy," "Told by the Schoolmaster," and "The Smile." "The Doldrums," interesting for one character modeled after Joseph Conrad, is readable but lacks the polish of JG's later work. As a whole, the works are not stimulating.

1690 Henderson, Philip. LITERATURE AND A CHANGING CIVILIZATION (Lond: John Lane, 1935), pp. 126–27.
Although more popular than D. H. Lawrence, JG is ponderous and lifeless when compared to him. JG's gentle irony now produces idealization rather than adverse criticism of middle-class values.

1691 Hutchison, Percy. "Fragments and Remainders of Galsworthy's Writing," NEW YORK TIMES BOOK REVIEW, 27 Oct 1935, p. 2.
[Review consists of brief summaries of some of the tales in *Forsytes, Pendyces and Others*. Olive Eddis's photograph of JG is reprinted.]

1692 Kroener, Johanna. DIE TECHNIK DES REALISTISCHEN DRAMAS BEI IBSEN UND GALSWORTHY (Techniquess f Realistic Playwriting in Ibsen and John Galsworthy). Published dissertation, University of Munich, Beitraege zur englischen Philologie, XXVIII (Leipzig: Tauchnitz, 1935); rptd (NY: Johnson Reprint Co., 1967).
[This study compares Ibsen's and JG's use of language, soliloquies, dialogues,

pantomimes, stage directions, their techniques of characterization, and the structure of their plays. Avoiding the term *influence,* it shows some similarities between Ibsen and JG but points out that there are important differences because of JG's insistence on the social problems rather than the characters. A useful introduction to the techniques of JG.] [In German.]

1693 Linn, James W., and H. W. Taylor. A FOREWORD TO FICTION (NY: Appleton-Century, 1935), pp. 66, 69–70, 81–85, 193.
[A five-page analysis of the action of "The Apple Tree" suggests something of JG's superiority as a craftsman.]

1694 Marrot, H[arold] V[incent]. THE LIFE AND LETTERS OF JOHN GALSWORTHY (Lond: Heinemann, 1935; NY: Scribner's, 1936).
[This volume is the first full-length biography of JG. It is indispensable to any serious study of JG, despite such serious limitations as its being the "official life" done under Ada Galsworthy's supervision and its failure to provide critical comments of a literary nature about JG's work. Of the latter Marrot wrote, "Literary criticism as such forms no part of this life. . . ."]

1695 Millett, Fred B. CONTEMPORARY BRITISH LITERATURE. A CRITICAL SURVEY AND 232 AUTHOR-BIBLIOGRAPHIES (NY: Harcourt, Brace, 1935), pp. 234–39.
[Bibliographical list of JG's works and of some secondary works.]

1696 Millett, Fred B., and Gerald Eades Bentley. THE ART OF THE DRAMA (Lond & NY: Appleton-Century, 1935), pp. 13, 76, 147, 148, 153, 156, 187, 190.
JG and Ibsen are the most noteworthy "social-dramatic" reformers of 1875–1925. Falder in *Justice* represents a man who is led to crime through his own weakness rather than "viciousness," just as De Levis in *Loyalties* represents the modern Jew. JG's realism attempts to fuse scientific objectivity with social purpose and social criticism. Falder (*Justice*) is too weak to be a tragic figure, and the remorselessness of law does not help to make the "painful play" a tragedy. A sentimentalist to a certain extent, JG believes reform will come through developing man's "right feelings" toward himself rather than by reforming society.

1697 Moles, T. W. (ed). "Introduction," *Selected Short Stories by John Galsworthy* (Lond: Longmans, Green, 1935), pp. ix–xx.
JG portrays—in historical fiction similar to that of Fielding, Thackeray, and Dickens—the "religious, political, social and moral life" of a period in English history, recording the gradual disintegration of mid-Victorian attitudes and values. The "descriptive and narrative passages of high literary quality" of earlier novels change in the later ones to pages of "almost pure dialogue form . . . in keeping with the excitement of unrest which characterizes the life of the

modern world." JG, like other great novelists, was objective in his writing, with "definite self-revelation" foreign to his temperament; yet a "general interpretation" gives insight into his love of beauty, hatred of selfishness, and spiritual devotion to an ideal. The plays give more of his personality.

As a short story writer, JG was influenced by Turgenev and Maupassant. The usually trivial incidents of the tales are important insofar as they "unfold character or illustrate some inner conflict." [About half of the introduction is devoted to a general biographical and literary survey. A brief paragraph, usually stating the theme, is devoted to each of eleven short stories by JG. Pp. 183–89 contain notes and questions relating to the selections.]

1698 Osgood, Charles Grosvenor. THE VOICE OF ENGLAND (NY & Lond: Harper, 1935; rev ed, 1952), pp. 455, 563, 569, 573, 578–79. JG, the "master of stagecraft," develops theme with "consummate theatrical skill." [Passing references to JG.]

1699 Paterson, Isabel. "*Forsytes, Pendyces and Others:* By John Galsworthy," NEW YORK HERALD TRIBUNE BOOKS, 3 Nov 1935, p. 12. *Forsytes, Pendyces and Others* was "unfinished business," aggravated by various plots whose "main interest is associational." JG will continue to be read primarily for information he gives that relates to his own class.

1700 "PLAY PICTORIAL Interviews Mr. Wilfrid Lawson and Miss Ivy Tresmand," PLAY PICTORIAL (Lond), LXVI (June 1935), 10–11. Wilfrid Lawson, playing John Builder in Leon Lion's revival of *A Family Man*, stresses the humorous side of the play because the "heavy father of 1921 would not have seemed credible" in 1935. [The article is illustrated by four stills from the production.]

1701 R., G. R. B. "Some Letters from John Galsworthy: The Correspondence That Passed between the Novelist and His Friend Edward Garnett," BOSTON EVENING TRANSCRIPT BOOK SECTION, 12 Jan 1935, p. 2. [Review of Edward Garnett (ed), LETTERS FROM JOHN GALSWORTHY, 1900–1932 (Lond: Cape; NY: Scribner's, 1934).]

1702 Rabius, Wilhelm. DIE INNERE STRUKTURELLE VERWANDT-SCHAFT VON GALSWORTHYS "FORSYTE SAGA" UND DEN ISLAEND-ISCHEN SAGAS (The Relationship of Galsworthy's *The Forsyte Saga* and the Icelandic Sagas). Published dissertation, University of Marburg (Marburg: Kurhessische Verlagsdruckerei, 1935). [Compares the Icelandic sagas and *The Forsyte Saga* under such headings as family structure, relationship between fathers and sons, attitudes towards property, fate, religion, death, love, passion, and honor and concludes that the similarities are due to Nordic racial qualities.] [In German.]

1703 S., C. *"A Family Man,"* SATURDAY REVIEW (Lond), CLIX (8 June 1935), 724.
[Brief notice of revival of *A Family Man* at the Playhouse.]

1704 S., C. *"Justice,"* SATURDAY REVIEW (Lond), CLIX (20 April 1935), 503.
[Brief notice of the revival of *Justice* at the Playhouse.]

1705 S., C. *"The Skin Game,"* SATURDAY REVIEW (Lond), CLIX (11 May 1935), 605.
[Brief negative notice of revival of *The Skin Game* at the Playhouse.]

1706 Swinnerton, Frank. THE GEORGIAN LITERARY SCENE (Lond: Heinemann, 1935), pp. 199–207; as THE GEORGIAN SCENE (NY: Farrar, Rinehart, 1935).
JG is "the first genteel novelist of the Georgian scene and only the second genteel novelist in English literature"; his plays are "excellent but exceedingly narrow moralities." For modern youth JG is "either too wise or too tender."

1707 Wood, Frederick T. "Current Letters: New Series," ENGLISH STUDIES (Amsterdam), XVII (June 1935), 115–23, espec p. 121.
[Brief review of the ninety-odd *Collected Poems,* attesting to JG's mastery of "metre, atmosphere, and word-music" in poetry characterized by pity, sympathy, reverence for beauty and truth, and impatience with sham.]

1708 Zimmermann, Ilse. STILISTISCHER WERT DER PROGRESSIVEN FORM IN GALSWORTHY'S WERKEN (A Stylistic Study of the Progressive Form in Galsworthy's Works). Published dissertation, University of Marburg (Bochum-Langendreer: Poeppinghaus, 1935).
[This stylistic and linguistic analysis and commentary considers *The Island Pharisees, The Man of Property, The Country House, The Patrician,* "Indian Summer of a Forsyte," *In Chancery, To Let,* and *Swan Song.*] [In German.]

1936

1709 Beatty, Richmond Croom. "Galsworthy as Poet," SEWANEE REVIEW, XLIV (Jan–March 1936), 100–102.
From a reading of *The Collected Poems of John Galsworthy* it is clear that JG writes as a traditional poet; when his verse is measured against that of other traditionalists, it is just as clear that his work is "hopelessly disappointing."

1710 Collins, John E. "Social Background of Galsworthy's Novels." Unpublished dissertation, Boston College, 1936.

[Listed in COMPREHENSIVE DISSERTATION INDEX: 1861–1972 (Ann Arbor: Xerox University Microfilms, 1973), XXIX, 535.]

1711 Eaton, Harold Thomas. READING GALSWORTHY'S FORSYTE SAGA (NY: Charles Scribner's Sons, 1936).
[This fifty-page study guide of *The Forsyte Saga,* consisting primarily of a chapter-by-chapter outline of *The Man of Property, In Chancery, To Let,* and "The Awakening," is accompanied by an incomplete JG bibliography and a short list of "suggested supplementary readings."]

1712 Effelberger, Hans. "Galsworthys letzte Romane" (Galsworthy's Last Novels), DIE NEUEREN SPRACHEN, XLIV (1936), 123–26.
[A brief review of *End of the Chapter.*] [In German.]

1713 Ford, Ford Madox. "Galsworthy," AMERICAN MERCURY, XXXVII (April 1936), 448–59; rptd with minor changes in PORTRAITS FROM LIFE (Cambridge: Riverside, 1937), pp. 126–42; in MIGHTIER THAN THE SWORD (Lond: Allen & Unwin, 1938), pp. 166–89; in RUSSIAN LITERATURE AND MODERN ENGLISH FICTION, ed by Donald Davie (Chicago: University of Chicago P, 1965), pp. 54–71.
JG's presence suggested a "sort of fraility." Anger at the sufferings of the disadvantaged affected his spirit and robbed his later work of interest. His character has a "certain pixylike perversity . . . a certain . . . authentic gift." Turgenev was the great influence on JG. Even though Conrad never thought JG a great writer, JG had abilities that led to "technical, literary achievement." But JG's preoccupation with unhappy lovers and the helpless poor made him an "impassioned . . . aching" reformer rather than a "dispassionate artist." The change can be traced from the "sunlit quality" of *Villa Rubein* through the satirical *The Island Pharisees* to the reform-oriented *The Man of Property.* The novels suffer from a "dogged determination to find . . . ironic antithesis." JG was a better dramatist than novelist, bringing the state a "new temperament, a new point of view, a new and extraordinarily dramatic technique"—especially in the use of building antithesis. JG is unparalleled in modern drama in his combination of lofty mind, compassion, poetry, "occasional sunlight," and instinctive knowledge of dramatic stage technique.

1714 Gillett, Eric. "Galsworthy and the Edwardian Drama," LISTENER, XV (22 Jan 1936), 166.
In *The Silver Box,* JG's characterization is at its best; he later becomes more sentimental because the issue is "immediately personal." [Generalized excerpts are from a BBC program.]

1715 Gillett, Eric. "Galsworthy as Propagandist," LISTENER, XV (19 Feb 1936), 360.
From the beginning, playwrights like Aristophanes, Euripides, Shakespeare,

Molière, Shaw, and others have frequently written dramas for propaganda purposes. *Justice*, JG admitted, is propagandist; its impact was tremendous, and the practical results significant. In his plays, JG carefully pointed out "that the best of human nature, as we know it today, is not to be found in our existing penal code." Today the penal and legal codes again need reform, but there is hardly one person in a generation who has the ability and determination to help as did JG in *Justice*.

1716 Gillett, Eric. "Galsworthy's Place in the Theatre," LISTENER, XV (15 Jan 1936), 135–36.
[An appreciative overview of JG's work prompted by the recent publication of H. V. Marrot, THE LIFE AND LETTERS OF JOHN GALSWORTHY (Lond: Heinemann, 1935; NY: Scribner's, 1936).]

1717 Greenough, Chester Noyes. "John Galsworthy, 1867–1933," PROCEEDINGS OF THE AMERICAN ACADEMY OF ARTS AND SCIENCES, LXX:10 (1936) [not seen]; rptd in COLLECTED STUDIES BY CHESTER NOYES GREENOUGH (Cambridge: Harvard Cooperative Society, 1940), pp. 246–49.
JG's books "seem extraordinarily well fitted to endure."

1718 Henderson, Philip. THE NOVEL TODAY (Lond: John Lane, 1936), pp. 15, 24, 25, 103–9, 130.
JG's characters are primarily "museum pieces." The "artist remains the only symbol of escape from a conventional society set in a hard rigid mould." JG has "no very conspicuous imaginative honesty."

1719 Mark, Heinz. DIE VERWENDUNG DER MUNDART UND DES SLANG IN DEN WERKEN VON JOHN GALSWORTHY (The Use of Dialect and Slang in the Works of John Galsworthy). Dissertation, Berlin-Humboldt University; excerpts pub in SPRÄCHE UND KULTUR DER GERMANISCHEN UND ROMANTISCHEN VÖLKER, XXIII (Breslau: Verlod Priebatsch's Buchhandlung, 1936).
JG's use of Devonshire, Downs, and London dialects and slang places him in a tradition which began with the sixteenth-century dramatists, was continued by Fielding and Smollett, and was carried on in the nineteenth century by Scott, Dickens, Thackeray, Kingsley, Eliot, Hardy, and others. Except for Hardy no other major modern author is as closely tied to the land as is JG. The settings for most of his works are in the south of England. [Supportive evidence is provided by a detailed list of JG's use of dialect; words are grouped primarily under such subject headings as "Adjectives," "Adverbs," "Pronouns," and the like. The dialect section (pp. 1–101) is basically a word list of hundreds, emphasizing JG's attempts at dialectal spellings ("he didn't oughter," for example, in *The Country House*) or dialect words (such as "daverdy," meaning "languid," in *Captures*). Slang is handled in a comparable manner (pp. 102–37).] [In German.]

1720 Neville, Helen. "Galsworthy," NATION (NY), CXLII (1 Jan 1936), 26.
JG was "hopelessly overrated in his life, and one wonders how most of his work ever got into print." Artistic values are few, but he did have a bit of an imaginative faculty. [Brief notice of *Forsytes, Pendyces and Others*. Neville enthusiastically joins the anti-JG post-obit bandwagon.]

1721 Nicoll, Allardyce. THE ENGLISH THEATRE: A SHORT HISTORY (Lond: Thomas Nelson, 1936); rptd (Westport, Conn: Greenwood P, 1970), pp. 162, 194.
JG turned to the theater because in the early 1900s the play "seemed that kind of expression most suited to the ideals of the period."

1722 Pritchett, V. S. "John Galsworthy, A Forsyte to the Marrow," CHRISTIAN SCIENCE MONITOR WEEKLY MAGAZINE, 5 Feb 1936, p. 13.
[Review of H. V. Marrot, THE LIFE AND LETTERS OF JOHN GALSWORTHY (Lond: Heinemann, 1935; NY: Scribner's, 1936).]

1723 Reynolds, M. E. MEMORIES OF JOHN GALSWORTHY, BY HIS SISTER (Lond: Hale, 1936; NY: Stokes, 1937).
[This short biography, based on recollections, includes many letters and photographs. It is an important supplement to Marrot's official biography.]

1724 Schmitz, Wilhelmine. DER MENSCH UND DIE GESELLSCHAFT IM WERKE JOHN GALSWORTHYS (Man and Society in the Work of John Galsworthy) (Bochum-Langendreer: Verlag Heinrich Poppinghaus O. H-G, 1936).
[Schmitz examines in some detail JG's stratification of society in chapters ranging from ten to thirty-five pages on the following topics (each a chapter heading): "The Aristocracy," "The Forsyte Middle Class," "The Nouveau Riche," "The Philistine," "The Have-nots," and "The New Man and the New Society."] [In German.]

1725 Stinchcomb, LaFaye. "John Galsworthy's Sense of Justice." Unpublished master's thesis, Southern Methodist University, 1936.
[Considers JG's materials under the following headings: justice before the law—classes before the law, marriage and divorce, legal control of prisoners; feeling of responsibility for the weak—feeling of responsibility for the oppressed; feeling of responsibility for birds and beasts; responsibility of industry—labor and capital; relation between industry and the community; investments.]

1726 Woodbridge, Homer E. "Selections from a Writer's Workshop," SATURDAY REVIEW OF LITERATURE (NY), XIII (4 Jan 1936), 11.
Reading even bits and snippets from unpublished JG manuscripts, collected in *Forsytes, Pendyces and Others,* is refreshing—especially for the insight it gives into the method of JG at different stages in his career.

1727 Woods, George Benjamin, Homer A. Watt, and George K. Anderson. "John Galsworthy," THE LITERATURE OF ENGLAND. Two volumes. (Chicago: Scott, Foresman, 1936), II, 994–95.
JG is one of the most significant and substantial interpreters of industrial England. [Two pages of general comment are followed by the text of *Strife*. The play is dropped from subsequent volumes of the popular and still widely-used anthology; but JG's contribution to literature is mentioned briefly in later eds.]

1728 Woolf, Leonard. "The Mask of John Galsworthy," LONDON MERCURY, XXXIII (Feb 1936), 438–39.
H. V. Marrot's biography of JG fails to present "the psychological reality" of the man. JG's works are not art; at best they are social documents. They seem to have been written by a person without personality. "The story is good; the characters are good; the technique is masterly; the verbal economy is perfect; the moral is unimpeachable. . . . But they are mere verbal shells."

1937

1729 Burbiel, Erich. "Die Kunst der Charakterdarstellung in John Galsworthys *Forsyte Saga*" (The Artistry of Character Development in John Galsworthy's *Forsyte Saga*). Unpublished dissertation, Königsburg University, 1937.
[Listed in Lawrence F. McNamee, DISSERTATIONS IN ENGLISH AND AMERICAN LITERATURE (NY & Lond: Bowker, 1968).] [In German.]

1730 Connolly, Francis X. "Some Philosophical Problems in the Works of John Galsworthy." Unpublished dissertation, Fordham University, 1937.
[Listed in COMPREHENSIVE DISSERTATION INDEX: 1861–1972 (Ann Arbor: Xerox University Microfilms, 1973), XXIX, 535.]

1731 Curle, Richard. "A Remarkable Friendship: Conrad and Galsworthy," CARAVANSARY AND CONVERSATION: MEMORIES OF PLACES AND PERSONS (NY: Stokes, 1937), pp. 155–63.
The friendship between Conrad and JG was so strong that only death "was capable of breaking that friendship." "Their friendship . . . was based primarily on human affections and not on literary affinities."

1732 Cywiński, Stanisław. "Na Warsztacie Literatury. Galsworthy, Mauriac, Przesmycki, Kridl, Iwaszkiewicz, Parandowski, Segeń, Lukasiewicz" (Workshop in Literature . . .), DZIENNIK WILEŃSKI: rptd in NA WARSZTACIE LITERATURY. GALSWORTHY, MAURIAC, PRZES-

Mycki, Kridl, Iwaszkiewicz, Parandowski, Segeń, Lukasiewicz (Workshop in Literature . . .) (Wilno, 1937), 148 pp. [not seen]. [In Polish.]

1733 Galsworthy, Ada. Over the Hills and Far Away (Lond: Hale, 1937; NY: Scribner, 1938).
[Reminiscences by JG's wife of their life and travels. Important as a biographical supplement to Marrot's official life.]

1734 "John Galsworthy—Novelist and Playwright," Scholastic (Pittsburgh), XXXI (18 Sept 1937), 6.
[Brief biographical note that generalizes about the literary influence of Turgenev and Conrad on JG, but no evidence is cited to substantiate the generalization.]

1735 Kaufman, George S. [pseud]. "Justice in the Dock," Stage (NY), XIV (Aug 1937), 72.
[This issue of Stage is "The Fond Memories Number" and attempts to represent landmarks of the American theater over the past 120 years. Each review is presented "as if written by" George Jean Nathan, William Dean Howells, Henry James, George S. Kaufman, and others. This particular item is possibly based on Kaufman's "*Justice* Et Al," New York Tribune, 9 April 1916, p. 2, q.v.]

1736 Maxwell, W. B. Time Gathered: Autobiography (Lond: Hutchison, 1937; NY: Appleton-Century, 1938), pp. 261, 286, 332.
[JG was an acquaintance who talked Maxwell into supporting various committees. Maxwell believes that JG was probably regular in his working habits as an author.]

1737 Muller, Herbert J. Modern Fiction (NY: Funk and Wagnalls, 1937), pp. 232–40.
The Forsyte Saga warrants JG's "inclusion among the important writers of this age"; nevertheless, one finds that JG's art "is too refined to embrace the elemental conflicts and the terrible, turbulent emotions of great tragedy."

1738 Reimondo, Mary S. "The Ethics of Galsworthy." Unpublished dissertation, Niagara University, 1937.
[Listed in Comprehensive Dissertation Index: 1861–1972 (Ann Arbor: Xerox University Microfilms, 1973), XXIX, 535.]

1739 Watkin, E. I. "Galsworthy: In Darkness and the Shadow of Death," Men and Tendencies (Lond, NY: Sheed & Ward, 1937), pp. 18–28.
Wells and JG are "apostles of the new energetic humanism which is everywhere arising upon the ruins of liberalism to claim the place of God." JG could not "rise above the sphere of nature and humanity," because he lacked "the religious vision which alone could have shown him a supreme wisdom and love. . . . The

references to religion in his three final volumes display a pitiful ignorance of Christianity."

1740 Wissmann, Paul. "*The Skin Game* von Galsworthy als Primalektüre" (*The Skin Game* as Subject for Reading in the Senior Classes of High Schools), ZEITSCHRIFT FUR NEUSPRACHLICHEN UNTERRICHT (Berlin), XXXVI (1937), 369–76.
[Concentrates on the major characters and the social problems of the play and argues that this masterpiece will demonstrate important historical changes to German students.] [In German.]

1741 Wittko, Paul. "Galsworthy: Ein Kritiker des Englaendertums— Zu seinem 70. Geburtstag" (Galsworthy, A Critic of the English—For his 70th Birthday), DIE PROPYLAEEN (Munich, XXXIV (1937), 370–71.
JG's unbiased descriptions of the bourgeoisie and British imperialism will remain valuable for German readers. When visiting Germany, JG criticized prison conditions there. [In German.]

1938

1742 Balashov, P. "*Saga o Forsaitakh*" (*The Forsyte Saga*), LITERA-TURNOE OBOZRENIE, No. 5 (1938), 60–65 [not seen].
[In Russian.]

1743 Cruse, Amy. AFTER THE VICTORIANS (Lond: Allen & Unwin, 1938), pp. 96–97, 241, 242, 247, 249.
Even though the writers of the 1890s got involved and began using social questions in their writings, Edwardian readers disliked reading about poverty and misery unless the subjects were treated "in a humorous or a sensational fashion." Novelists who explored social questions usually did so in JG's way— presenting the evils and miseries of poverty while at the same time stating that there was no remedy to the problem—or H. G. Wells's way—recommending improved sanitation, cleanliness, order, and equal distribution of goods for the benefit of all.

1744 Frenz, Horst. "Die Entwicklung des Sozialen Dramas in En-gland vor Galsworthy" (The Evolution of Social Dramas in England before Galsworthy). Unpublished dissertation, Göttingen University, 1938.
[Listed in Lawrence F. McNamee, DISSERTATIONS IN ENGLISH AND AMERICAN LITERATURE (NY & Lond: Bowker, 1968).] [In German.]

1745 Friedrich, Hans E. "John Galsworthy," DIE CHRISTLICHE WELT (Marburg), XLIV: 18 (1938), 885–87.
Unlike Lawrence, JG is an analyst whose cold objectivity alienates the reader. Occasionally, however, the presence of a *dichter* or poet is felt. His observations in *The Forsyte Saga* apply to the upper middle class in Germany, too, if the differences in the national characters are disregarded. It is difficult to understand why some of JG's minor stories have been translated into German under the title *Die letzte Karte* (The Last Program). [In German.]

1746 Gese, Gertrud. "Galsworthy als Sozialer Kritiker und Reformer" (Galsworthy as Social Critic and Reformer). Unpublished dissertation, Greifswald University, 1938.
[Listed in Lawrence F. McNamee, DISSERTATIONS IN ENGLISH AND AMERICAN LITERATURE (NY & Lond: Bowker, 1968).] [In German.]

1747 Hobza, Jozef. "Svĕt Johna Galsworthyho" (The World of John Galsworthy), POSLEDNÍ KARTA (Prague: Melantrich, 1938) [not seen]. [In Czech.]

1748 Jerrold, Douglas. GEORGIAN ADVENTURE (NY: Scribner's, 1938), pp. 54, 297–98.
Aided by his "studied good form," JG in his heavy-handed tackling of social problems helped create the tense atmosphere of his time. The significance of his popularity is to be found in his avoidance of judgment and in the psychological need of a generation whose foundations were shattered—a need for "the comfortable relaxation afforded by the contemplation of an established society."

1749 Otis, William Bradley, and Morriss H. Needleman. A SURVEY HISTORY OF ENGLISH LITERATURE (NY: Barnes & Noble, 1938), pp. 581, 593.
[Brief list of important works by JG.]

1750 Radtke, Wilhelm. IRONIE UND HUMOR IN JOHN GALSWORTHYS FORSYTEZYKLUS (Irony and Humor in John Galsworthy's Forsyte Saga) (Lengerich i. W.: Lengericher Handelsdruckerei, [1938]) [not seen]. [In German.]

1751 Sitwell, Osbert. "The Modern Novel: Its Cause and Cure," in TRIO: DISSERTATIONS ON SOME ASPECTS OF NATIONAL GENIUS, by Osbert, Edith, and Sacheverell Sitwell (Lond: Macmillan, 1938), pp. 49–93.
JG's cautious pleading "so strictly unbiassed and wanting in any vulgar, melodramatic appeal, often, so far from attaining its object, persuades us to hope that the wealthy and careless wastrel, who leaves silver boxes about to tempt poor people, will prosper, and that the respectable and 'really-awfully-nice' charwoman, who has led so hard a life, will incur a severe and quite ummerited punishment for a theft she has never committed."

1939

1752 Baker, Ernest A. THE HISTORY OF THE ENGLISH NOVEL. Ten vols (Lond: Witherby, 1924–39), vol. X (1939); rptd (NY: Barnes & Noble, 1939); rptd (1960), pp. 288–344, esp 319–44.

Unlike Wells or Shaw, neither Arnold Bennett nor JG was a propagandist. With the possible exception of *Fraternity* JG did not "take a set of characters and then proceed to analyse their motives and behavior." All of his important characters bear "the trace of having been taken to pieces and then put together again; it is the peculiarity that stamps them as his. . . . Analysis, then synthesis; he was critical observer first, then portraitist or dramatist." JG created, "with a critical but tolerant art, a gallery of portraits from those classes who have got the very best out of life, *The Island Pharisees, The Man of Property, The Country House, The Patrician.*" The titles themselves are an indictment. A salient feature of JG's method "is that each person is seen through the eyes of the others. . . . The great triumph of his method is the enchanting figure of Irene" whose presence is felt even when she is absent. JG's characters always had to be "typical exemplars of some definite phase of social existence." *Fraternity,* a "satire on the fallacy of most humanitarian interference," and *The Dark Flower* have interest as psychological studies. He was not a born story-teller; his "definite vocation . . . was to exhibit a society and the types of people that make it, rather than to relate incidents and adventures." There is much about his characters that is "curiously reminiscent of that ancient species of fiction known as charactery."

1753 Bliumfel'd, M. "Romany Dzhona Golsuorsi" (The Novels of John Galsworthy), CHTO CHITAT', No. 6 (1939), 54–57 [not seen]. [In Russian.]

1754 Block, Anita Cahn. THE CHANGING WORLD IN PLAYS AND THEATRE (Bost: Little, Brown, 1939), pp. 10, 16, 17, 57–60, 68.

JG eloquently portrays the basic crime of poverty in his dramas of the underdog. In this he is "profoundly integrated with the modern age," like Ibsen, Hauptmann, Wedekind, and Shaw. For JG, like Ibsen, the "ultimate victim of bourgeois society" is woman (Falder's mate in *Justice;* Mrs. Jones in *The Silver Box*); Clare is the Galsworthian Hedda Gabler—"soft where Hedda is hard, gentle where Hedda is cruel, selfless where Hedda is selfish, passionate where Hedda is sensual"; but both are "helpless victims of the bourgeois tradition" that makes a woman a man's property. JG's concern is also evident in Irene in *The Forsyte Saga.* In *The Mob,* JG shows that the strongest man is he who can stand alone. JG appeals today as "a tender-minded playwright of meticulous skill": he failed "dismally" in his post-World War I novels to interpret the "lost" postwar generation.

1755 Daiches, David. THE NOVEL AND THE MODERN WORLD (Chicago: University of Chicago P, 1939), pp. 33–47; rptd without the Galsworthy material, rev ed 1960; rptd (Lond: Hogarth, 1960).

JG, a "worried humanitarian of the early twentieth century," wrote within the "propagandist tradition" of the Victorian novel. *The Island Pharisees, The Patrician,* and *The Freelands* "are rather wooden stories" that illustrate his criticism of the British upper middle class. He is neither a tragic writer nor an innovator. The interest of his work is to be found in his handling of the traditional materials in some ways which are perhaps a little more refined than those of his predecessors. There is "an effeminate streak" in his work deriving from the fact that some of his humanitarianism gets "in the way of the clarity of his observation." He is a realist, and his realism is more than that of the simple observer. At his best his realism "is based on a delicate response to detail—to the small but significant symbol." He emphasizes the symbolic aspects of his characters. The main weakness of *The Forsyte Saga* is his tendency to "overinsist." His "manner is neither better nor worse than the more specifically modern technique; but it is different and older." Works on a large scale—works like CLAYHANGER and JEAN CHRISTOPHE—tend to disintegrate into the episodic, but JG is fairly successful in *The Forsyte Saga* in avoiding this weakness. JG is the last of the "great Victorian novelists" because of the achievement of *Saga*. Expansiveness is part of JG's deliberate effect, and the charge of lack of economy is therefore irrelevant. Both "Indian Summer of a Forsyte" and "The Apple Tree" are examples of his "expansive realist-symbolic writing," and he succeeds to the extent that "he maintains the state of unstable equilibrium between convincing characterization and description on the realistic level and poetical-symbolic undertones and overtones." [In the rev ed of 1960 Daiches writes on page viii that he has omitted JG because JG "did not really belong to a book on the modern novel."]

1756 Ellis, G. U. TWILIGHT ON PARNASSUS: A SURVEY OF POST-WAR FICTION AND PRE-WAR CRITICISM (Lond: Michael Joseph, 1939). [Many references are made mentioning those who rejected JG.]

1757 Elwin, Malcolm. "Galsworthy and the Forsytes," OLD GODS FALLING (Lond: Collins; NY: Macmillan, 1939), pp. 10, 17, 31, 43, 44, 85, 106, 121, 158, 200, 276, 297, 330, 331, 333, 334, 345, 356, 358, 360, 363–90, 392, 395.

JG's satire is usually "tempered with a sardonic humour." He was conscientious in pursuit of "truest artistic expression." *The Man of Property* was revolutionary because it advocated a woman's right to live her own life. [Primarily biography and plot summary.]

1758 Gvozdev, A. ZAPADNO-EVROPEISKII TEATR NA RUBEZHE XIX I XX STOLETII. OCHERKI (The Western European Theater at the Turn of the Nineteenth and Twentieth Centuries. Essays) (Leningrad & Moscow: Iskusstvo, 1939), pp. 298–301 [not seen]. [In Russian.]

1759 Helsztyński, Stanisław. "John Galsworthy," OD SZEKSPIRA DO JOYCE' A (FROM SHAKESPEARE TO JOYCE) (Warsaw, 1939) [not seen]. [In Polish.]

1760 Kruschwitz, Hans. "Individuum und Gemeinschaft in Galsworthys 'Soames and the Flag' " (Individualism and Group Behavior in Galsworthy's "Soames and the Flag"), ZEITSCHRIFT FÜR NEUSPRACHLICHEN UNTERRICHT, XXXVIII (Aug 1939), 236–39. Individualism and communal interest are the two poles of this story. The story shows plainly to our youth the dangers that unbridled individualism can cause, but the story also points out that at appropriate moments in war the communal feeling awakens. [In German.]

1761 Popović, Vladan. "Golzvordi dramatičar" (Galsworthy the Dramatist), BERNARD SŎ I DRUGI ESEJI (Bernard Shaw and Other Essays), (Belgrade: K Mihailović, 1939) [not seen]. [In Serbo-Croatian.]

1762 Vočadlo, Otakar. "Uvod" (Introduction), *Jabloň (The Apple Tree)* (Prague, 1939) [not seen]. [In Czech.]

1940

1763 Dataller, Roger [pseud of A. E. Eagleston]. THE PLAIN MAN AND THE NOVEL (Lond: Nelson, 1940), pp. 64–65, 150–54. JG misrepresents the British workman.

1764 Dierlamm, G. "John Galsworthy als Dramatiker: Wilhelm Franz zum achtzigsten Geburtstag" (John Galsworthy as a Playwright: For Wilhelm Franz on His Eightieth Birthday), GERMANISCH-ROMANTISCHE MONATSSCHRIFT (Heidelberg), XXVIII (1940), 111–31. Despite the success of JG's novels in Germany, his plays are little known. This study attempts (1) to investigate the beginnings and development of JG as a dramatist, (2) to determine his masterpieces, and (3) to suggest the lasting accomplishment of JG as a dramatist. His interest in drama began when he was twelve. The thirty-year friendship with Conrad gave JG "world vision." It is probable that Hegel influenced JG's views regarding "perpetual conflict between opposing principles" and the "mysterious and everlasting reconcilement or Harmony."

JG's masterpieces in his first period are *The Silver Box* and *Strife,* and for the postwar era they are *The Skin Game, Loyalties,* and *Escape* [*Justice* and some of the other dramas are unfavorably criticized]. H. V. Marrot's explanation that JG's decline is due to the war is not convincing; the passing of Victorianism and the death of his father provide a better basis for understanding JG's decline. His work as a dramatist must be reconsidered in Germany. [See Walther Hoch, "John Galsworthy als Dramatiker in deutscher Beleuchtung" (1942).] [In German.]

1765 Gassner, John Waldhorn. MASTERS OF THE DRAMA (NY: Random House, 1940); 3rd ed rev and enlarged (NY: Dover, 1954), pp. 372, 616–18.

JG "took the problem play, divested it for the most part of preachment, strengthened it with objectivity, and steeped it in gentle irony"; but he was "too temperate and circumspect" to be a great dramatist. Along with his novels, JG has left "an impressive if hardly extraordinary collection" of dramatic work. [The most important plays receive several sentences of general comment.]

1766 Greene, Graham. "*Twenty-One Days,*" SPECTATOR (Lond), CLXIV (12 Jan 1940), 44.

[Brief, negative review of a cinema adaptation of JG's *The First and the Last.*]

1767 Niederstenbruch, Alex. "Rassische Merkmale in der Sprache von John Galsworthy" (Racial Characteristics in the Language of John Galsworthy), NEUPHILOLOGISCHE MONATSSCHRIFT, XI (1940), 299–308.

In his work JG utilizes the characteristics of three racial groups: Nordic, Western, and Eastern. Racial traits are borne out by his characters and in his use of sentence structure and word choice (for example, adverbs particularize places with which people are associated, and in turn these are related to racial traits). [In German.]

1941

1768 Edwards, H. "Galsworthy's Genealogical Error," MODERN LANGUAGE NOTES, LVI (1941), 619.

Val Dartie and Holly Forsyte were second cousins, not first cousins, as stated by JG in *To Let* (I, 5).

1769 Gettmann, Royal A. TURGENEV IN ENGLAND AND AMERICA (Urbana: University of Illinois P, 1941), pp. 178–80.

JG and Turgenev were very much alike socially, intellectually, and spiritually, but JG was much less successful in his use of pity. JG's admiration for Turgenev was strongly reinforced by the influence of Edward Garnett.

1770 Gillett, Eric (ed and intro). *Ten Famous Plays by John Galswor-thy* (Lond: Duckworth, 1941); rptd (1942; 1949; 1952), pp. viii–xviii. JG began writing drama at the suggestion of Edward Garnett, who felt JG was better suited for drama than for the novel. JG maintained the artistic integrity set out in "Some Platitudes Concerning Drama." *The Silver Box,* "with its complete lack of sensation and sentimentality, seemed uncontrived, almost casual"— many critics of the play were not prepared for his original treatment. A. B. Walkley of the TIMES (Lond), was an exception to the confused critics of *Joy* because he recognized JG's "naturalistic intentions." JG insisted twenty years after the first production that *Strife* is about "extremism or fanaticism" rather than about labor vs. capital. JG's naturalism and his essentially charitable view of human nature that is contrasted to a detestation "of a number of human institutions" are presented in *Justice.* JG was, as Conrad wrote, "a humanitarian moralist." [Introduction contains a biographical sketch and brief comments on the ten plays in the volume: *The Silver Box, Joy, Strife, Justice, The Skin Game, Loyalties, Windows, Old English, Escape,* and *The Roof.*]

1771 Gogeissl, L. "Das Bürgertum in England, Dargestellt nach Romanen von Thackeray, Dickens, und Galsworthy" (The Middle Class in England, as Presented in the Novels of Thackeray, Dickens, and Galsworthy). Unpublished dissertation, Nuremberg University, 1941.
[Listed in ANNUAL BIBLIOGRAPHY OF ENGLISH LANGUAGE AND LITERATURE (Cambridge: Cambridge UP, 1942).] [In German.]

1772 Hatcher, Harlan Henthorne (ed). "John Galsworthy," MODERN DRAMAS (NY: Harcourt, Brace, 1941); new ed (1944, 1948), pp. 69–72; rptd in MODERN DRAMAS, SHORTER EDITION (NY: Harcourt, Brace, 1941, 1944); new ed (1948), pp. 147–52.
JG's best plays have strong social interest because of his sense of fair play, humanity, and kindliness. JG practiced what he preached in "Some Platitudes Concerning Drama." *Justice* is tragedy in the early twentieth-century style, with machine justice destroying the pitiful Falder. It is naturalism at its peak, natural yet dramatic. Characters are alive; simplicity and restraint are classic; theme is disciplined, because JG tried to be impartial. JG truly presents the drama of social consciousness. [Headnote to *Justice.*]

1773 Monroe, N. Elizabeth. THE NOVEL AND SOCIETY: A CRITICAL STUDY OF THE MODERN NOVEL (Chapel Hill: University of North Carolina P, 1941), pp. 197, 250.
[Passing references to JG.]

1774 Short, R. W., and R. B. Sewall. "A Manual of Suggestions for Teachers Using SHORT STORIES FOR STUDY" (NY: Holt, 1941), pp. 27–29.

In his short story "Manna," JG, by his use of irony, "avoids the mystical issue and comments only upon the social effect of the traditional attitude, upon the rector and upon the villagers."

1942

1775 Dupont, V. JOHN GALSWORTHY: THE DRAMATIC ARTIST (Cahors: Imprimerie Typographique A. Coueslant, 1942); rptd (Paris: Henri Didier, [1942]; Folcroft Pa: Folcroft P, 1970).

JG believed that twentieth-century English drama could take one of two roads—naturalistic drama or poetic drama. JG tried both. He tended toward the sentimental and occasionally toward the melodramatic and sensational, working often with the themes of theft, forgery, and manslaughter. *The Silver Box, Strife, Justice,* and *Loyalties* are well-made plays; but in *The Foundations, The Forest,* and *The Roof,* plotting is feeble, held together often by the most superficial means. *The Skin Game* and *The Eldest Son* seem too crowded with incident for the good of the play. *The First and the Last* is complete melodrama. Only *Joy* and *The Foundations* of all JG's plays have happy endings. The melodramatic plots are often overshadowed by the "several depths of significance" in the plays, probing motives and consequences of events rather than exploiting the sensational, as in the case of melodrama.

JG's method is realistic and the plays serious, with the protagonist usually being caught up in the clash of conflicting forces such as: law and retribution in *Justice,* private charity and reform in *The Pigeon,* marriage in *The Fugitive,* family in *A Family Man,* national moods in *The Mob,* class problems in *Box* and *Skin Game,* caste in *Loyalties* and *Son,* and different generations in *Joy.* Despite this, the literary quality is never sacrificed for didactic purposes. JG's lesson was of pity and sympathy; his method was to present the importance of feeling in holding the plays together, especially with variations on the themes of love and pity. More often than not, his denouements unite a "double suggestion of triumph and overthrow," often concluding with an ambiguous ending, both in the plays and in the novels: Bosinney dying in the fog (*The Man of Property*) and the nature of Falder's death (*Justice*). More often than not, characters in the plays can be identified by their "psychological-keynote" and social significance. Except possibly for *Pigeon,* JG never really presents a complete character: his primary method is to reveal one aspect of the character or two complementary ones—without making him appear cramped or incompletely drawn.

Even though in *Joy* JG works within the strictures of the classical unities of time and place, the unities are not usually adhered to. Time elapsed in the plays, for example, runs from six hours to two and one-half years. The pattern of the action is often more complex than the episodic approach used in *Fugitive, Mob,* and *Escape*; this is especially true in the often used pattern of the parallel development of several lines of intrigue within one play. The plays generally are characterized by economy and restraint, with the *scène à faire* usually occurring in the last act. JG raised the level of esteem for the British stage and "made the work of more original playwrights more easy, by contributing to giving them more receptive audiences." [Originally a thesis. Despite the rather mechanical approach that Dupont uses to develop his argument, the study is one of the most comprehensive on JG's drama and avoids the usual tendency to emphasize theme at the expense of other aspects of drama. Most of the plays are discussed knowledgeably and in some detail, but only *Pigeon* is given a lengthy analysis (eight pages). Chaps 5–7, literally too crammed with material to be reduced meaningfully here, contain among others the following sub-headings: "Tension," "The Curve of Tension and the Development of the Action Units," "Exposition and Preparation," "Dialogue," "Stage Directions," "Comedy, Symbolism, Poetry," and "Shorter Plays and Experimental Ventures."]

1776 Frierson, William C. THE ENGLISH NOVEL IN TRANSITION, 1885–1940 (Norman, Okla: University of Oklahoma P, 1942); rptd (NY: Cooper Square Publishers, 1965), pp. 15, 131, 136, 139*n*, 142, 144, 148, 161–62, 163–66, 166–68, 211, 216, 219, 239, 247, 272, 277, 312, 320.
The two major influences that helped change the Victorian novel to its more modern focus were French naturalism and the impact of Dostoevsky and Tolstoy. JG's avowed masters were Maupassant and Turgenev. In his short stories and problem plays JG is a naturalist.

1777 Gerould, Gordon Hall. THE PATTERNS OF ENGLISH AND AMERICAN FICTION (Bost: Little, Brown, 1942), pp. 475–77.
JG's popular appeal derived from a combination of the "attitudes and mannerisms" of Thackeray and the "narrative method" of Hardy. The satiric conception of *The Man of Property* is Thackerayan, but the work is hampered by JG's superficial presentation of character and his inability to escape being partisan. JG learned from Hardy how to make "a smoothly running scene" and how to "enforce on scenes the mood he desired by highly emotionalized descriptions of nature." Because JG's purpose was representational and satiric, the result was frequently one of falsification. JG never quite succeeded because his was an "anemia of the imagination."

1778 Hoch, Walther. "John Galsworthy als Dramatiker in deutscher Beleuchtung" (John Galsworthy as Dramatist in a Germanic Inquiry), ZEITSCHRIFT FUER NEUSPRACHLICHEN UNTERRICHT (Berlin), XLI (1942), 61–67.
JG is not an individualist but a socialist. As a representative of democratic England he feels and suffers with the masses. *Strife* shows the defeat of fanatics and the victory of the majority, a solution which is genuinely English. It is only

on the continent that tyrants such as Napoleon and Lenin have been successful. *Justice* dramatizes the struggle of society against its enemies and the play contains forensic speeches of great power. *The Mob* is a better play than *Strife* because More's fight for the highest human ideals distinguishes him from such self-seeking heroes as Anthony and Roberts. [This article is chiefly a criticism of G. Dierlamm, "John Galsworthy als Dramatiker: Wilhelm Franz sum achtzigsten Geburtstag" (1940), q.v.] [In German.]

1779 Koziol, Herbert. "Arnold Bennett, John Galsworthy und J. B. Priestley ueber englische Demokratie" (Arnold Bennett, John Galsworthy, and J. B. Priestley Regarding English Democracy), DEUTSCH-LANDS ERNEUERUNG (Munich), XXVI (1942), 39–41.
Not only the Nazis but also such English writers as JG, Bennett, and Priestley have criticized democracy and the party system. [In German.]

1780 Kunitz, Stanley Jasspon, and Howard Haycroft. TWENTIETH CENTURY AUTHORS: A BIOGRAPHICAL DICTIONARY OF MODERN LITERATURE (NY: Wilson, 1942), pp. 510–12.
[Brief biographical and bibliographical sketch of JG.]

1781 Lehmkuehler, Wilhelm. "Englische Welt und Lebensanschauung in 'Galsworthys *Forsyte Saga*' " (British Weltanschauung in John Galsworthy's *The Forsyte Saga*), DIE MITTELSCHULE (Halle), LVI (11 Feb 142), 20–23.
In a war it is important to know one's enemies well. *The Forsyte Saga* may serve as an excellent introduction to the British national character. [Based on Lehmkuehler's article of 1933, q.v.] [In German.]

1782 Randall, David A., and John T. Winterich. "One Hundred Good Novels. Collations . . . and Notes . . . Galsworthy, John: *The Man of Property*," PUBLISHER'S WEEKLY, CXLI (21 Feb 1942), 898–99.
[Bibliographical description and collation of the first two distinct issues of *The Man of Property*, recording among other things three minor corrections (by JG himself) in the dedication copy; this is followed by a one-page biographical note, relating primarily to the publication of *Property*, but relying on information from H. V. Marrot's LIFE AND LETTERS OF JOHN GALSWORTHY (Lond: Heinemann, 1935).]

1783 Short, Ernest. "The Play of Ideas; John Galsworthy and Some Others," THEATRICAL CAVALCADE (Lond: Eyre & Spottiswoode, 1942; rptd Port Washington, NY: Kennikat P, 1970), pp. 74–78.
JG is the most characteristic of writers of intellectual comedy of his day. Concerned with British justice, his plays never "pillory" the individual members of the society he attacks. Society equals Greek Fate. JG did not write scenario: "plot was character and dialogue was character." He wanted actors to be less personal than Pinero's were because of his greater concern for social problems

than for individual characters. [Conventional plot summaries of *Justice, Strife,* and *Old English,* mentioning most of the prominent actors who appeared in the plays.]

1784 Titman, Lily. "John Galsworthy in Sussex," SUSSEX COUNTY MAGAZINE, XVI (Aug 1942), 227–28.
[Wistful reminiscences of JG's occupancy of Bury House near Pulborough, with references to several other JG associations in Sussex.]

1785 Wanderscheck, Dr. "Die Insel der Pharisaeer: Galsworthy über die Englaender" (The Island of the Pharisees: Galsworthy on the English), GESETZGEBUNG UND LITERATUR (Berlin), XXIII:1 (1942), 3–4.
Like Shaw JG has debunked British capitalism and imperialism, which are doomed to failure in the present war. [In German.]

1943

1786 Church, Richard. BRITISH AUTHORS: A TWENTIETH CENTURY GALLERY WITH 53 PORTRAITS (Lond & NY: Longmans, Green, 1943; new ed, 1948), pp. 48–50.
The straightforward morality and the love of serious tangibles fused and worked together in JG's work, and the consequence has been that his work has had great influence in forming foreign readers' views of English scene and character.

1787 Schalit, Leon. "John Galsworthy: Teacher and Prophet," CONTEMPORARY REVIEW (Lond), CLXIII (Feb 1943), 116–19.
JG in the 1920s was one of the few intelligent voices pleading for England to look to its future, especially in terms of a more productive agriculture at home and a self-sufficient British Empire on a larger scale. JG argued for international cooperation in such works as *Castles in Spain, The Silver Spoon,* and *The White Monkey* and in articles contributed to newspapers. Only through love and the cult of beauty can man save himself. JG was one of the kindest and "most balanced men who ever wrote."

1788 Wagenknecht, Edward. "Pity, Irony, and John Galsworthy," CAVALCADE OF THE ENGLISH NOVEL (NY: Holt, 1943; 1954), pp. 197, 232, 274, 373, 377, 436, 442, 460, 471, 477–93, 494, 495, 558, 575, 615–16.
The Island Pharisees is a remarkable prologue to his work, inasmuch as it contains every motif that JG would utilize in his work. Maturity came to his work with *The Man of Property,* and at about the same time *The Silver Box* signaled his arrival as a dramatist. Even though *A Modern Comedy* lacks the force of *The Forsyte Saga,* "it has gained in humanity" because of the presence of Soames and

Fleur, "the Beatrix Esmond of post-war fiction." JG's third trilogy, *End of the Chapter,* is something of an addendum to the Forsyte novels and is not satisfactory. His non-Forsyte novels can be divided into two groups: (1) four novels of social criticism—*The Country House, Fraternity, The Patrician,* and *The Freelands;* (2) three novels of passion—*The Dark Flower, Beyond,* and *A Saint's Progress.* Perhaps "no other novelist builds a book more artfully. . . . And perhaps none other makes us feel that we are more steadily in the presence of a fastidious intelligence." [Selected bibliography included.]

1789 Wagenknecht, Edward. "The Selfish Heroine: Thackeray and Galsworthy," COLLEGE ENGLISH, IV (1943), 293–98.

Fleur Forsyte, like Beatrix Esmond, is an example of the selfish heroine. It is Fleur's "constancy [to Jon]—not levity—that finally kills her father and nearly kills her." She made the mistake of marrying a man she did not love, and yet she did succeed in making Michael happy. Her appearances in *End of the Chapter* are not satisfactory, for she is too rigid in her self-control. "Beatrix's last years are a degradation redeemed only by her vitality; Fleur, like Gwendolen Harleth, though quite unemotionally, in her hard little post-war way, is saved, 'as by fire.' "

1790 Wolfbauer, Hildegard. "Die Objektivität in den Dramen John Galsworthys" (Objectivity in the Dramas of John Galsworthy). Unpublished dissertation, Erlangen University, 1943.

[Listed in Lawrence F. McNamee, DISSERTATIONS IN ENGLISH AND AMERICAN LITERATURE (NY & Lond: Bowker, 1968).] [In German.]

1944

1791 Eastman, Fred. "The Dramatist and the Minister," THE ARTS AND RELIGION, ed by Albert E. Bailey (NY: Macmillan, 1944), pp. 27, 142–50, 155.

Loyalties is a play about "social righteousness." De Levis, discriminated against and denied access to Gentile clubs because he is a Jew, "wants justice maintained, the truth vindicated, and the honor of his race upheld." JG's main interest is in "flesh and blood" characters; the stage serves as a "mirror of souls." Characters develop in crisis: De Levis evolves from the Jew who at first only wants money returned to a man who embraces the deeper standard of "his own integrity and loyalty to his race"; Jacob Twisden, the "fine old lawyer," changes loyalties to uphold the identity of his profession; Captain Dancy, who has "no standard of value beyond immediate self-interest," commits suicide. JG carefully employs conflict, suspense, climax, emotion, and thematic "spire of meaning"—the clash of loyalties. [JG is approached from the point of view of his usefulness in effective moral instruction and in the pastoral ministry. Lucid treatment of character trails off into imprecise comments about use of conflict, suspense, climax, and emotion.]

1792 Kain, Richard M. "Galsworthy, The Last Victorian Liberal," MADISON QUARTERLY, IV (1944), 84–94.

Seen in the light of modern power politics, demagoguery, and totalitarianism, JG's social criticism shows its affinity with Victorian liberalism and its three tenets—(1) the reliance upon scientific rationalism; (2) the reliance upon gradual legislative reform; (3) the reliance upon men of good will. Thomas Mann's awareness of "human irrationalism" helps account for the greater "depth of BUDDENBROOKS as compared to the *Forsyte Saga.*" Confronted with the gathering forces of war and its more brutal realities, JG "retreated to an academic humanism, a vague faith in lost cause." His was a "pale humanism, based upon a wishful faith in the innate decency of human nature."

1793 Lalou, René. LA LITTÉRATURE ANGLAISE DES ORIGINES À NOS JOURS (ENGLISH LITERATURE FROM ITS ORIGINS TO THE PRESENT) (Paris: Presses Universitaires de France, 1944), p. 120.

[Brief discussion of the "poetic and psychological elements" in *The Island Pharisees, The Forsyte Saga, Justice,* and *Fraternity.*] [In French.]

1794 [Morgan, Charles.] "Menander's Mirror: Irene Forsyte," TIMES LITERARY SUPPLEMENT (Lond), 4 Nov 1944, p. 351.

In time JG will take his proper place. The artistic flaw in *The Forsyte Saga* is Irene. JG mixed conventions by treating Irene as a goddess and as a woman on the realistic level. His deification of Irene destroys the effectiveness of her character in *Saga.* [Morgan did not reprint this essay in the first two series of his REFLECTIONS IN A MIRROR.]

1795 Stoll, Elmer Edgar. FROM SHAKESPEARE TO JOYCE (Garden City, NY: Doubleday, Doran, 1944), pp. 170, 298.

[JG is quoted in passing.]

1945

1796 Grove, Frederick Philip. "Morality in *The Forsyte Saga,*" UNIVERSITY OF TORONTO QUARTERLY, XV (1945–46), 54–64.

The Forsyte Saga is "too considerable an artistic achievement, if only in an architectonic sense," for a "wholesale condemnation" of it like Lawrence's to be valid. Of the six Forsyte novels only one, *The Man of Property,* if any, may survive. There is a moral confusion in JG's work "which affects the whole moral validity of the *Saga.*" Because he was in love with Irene, JG juggled and falsified moralities in *Saga*. The treatment of the Soames–Irene–Bosinney triangle (which D. H. Lawrence had rightly condemned but wrongly explained) is basic to a morally honest treatment of *Saga*, and here JG failed. [An important adverse criticism of JG's art.]

1797 Kilcoyne, Francis Patrick. "The Emergence and Growth of the Social and Political Expression in the Works of John Galsworthy." Unpublished dissertation, New York University, 1945.
[Listed in COMPREHENSIVE DISSERTATION INDEX: 1861–1972 (Ann Arbor: Xerox University Microfilms, 1973), XXIX, 535.]

1798 Murdoch, Walter. COLLECTED ESSAYS (Sydney & Lond: Angus & Robertson, 1945), pp. 119, 179, 367, 672.
[Passing references to JG, who encouraged Joseph Conrad and wrote about a "prosaic, unromantic, humdrum, unexciting world."]

1799 Obrzud, Zdzisław. "Dramat o strajku" (Play About a Strike), ODRA, No. 5 (1945), 6 [not seen].
[Review of *Strife*.] [In Polish.]

1800 Wilde, Arthur. "In John Galsworthy's Country," DEVONIAN YEARBOOK, XXXVI (1945), 66–70.
[A romanticized and effusive account ("It was a bit of paradise, here on earth") of Wilde's visit to JG's home at Manaton, Wingstone, in Devon.]

1946

1801 Clark, William Smith (ed). "Introduction to *The Silver Box*," CHIEF PATTERNS OF WORLD DRAMA (Bost: Houghton Mifflin, 1946), pp. 854–57.
The "Big Three" of English drama in the first half of the twentieth century were Shaw, Barrie, and JG. There is an obvious sociological message in all of JG's more significant plays. In characterization JG tended to use types rather than individuals. The realism of *The Silver Box* was so convincing that his later plays show "little more than minor variations in his dramatic pattern." His social problem plays qualify for a "permanent and notable place in world drama."

1802 Gray, James. ON SECOND THOUGHT (Minneapolis: University of Minnesota P, 1946), pp. 40–44, 57; rptd in German translation as HALBGOETTER AUF DER LITERARISCHEN BUEHNE (Munich: Desch, 1950), pp. 57–62.
The right of the ruling class to dominate the lives of lesser folk is the theme of all of JG's novels and plays. His trademark is "timorous good breeding." Although

he is better than the majority of the second-rate authors, JG remains a "facile second-rater" who lacked creative imagination. The award of the Nobel Prize to JG was "almost incredibly inept." He was essentially trivial; his distinguishing characteristics as a literary artist are "nervous apprehension and blank misgiving." The reason for his popularity was his cleverness—his mild criticisms flattered the comfortable security of those he criticized. In his own lifetime he was so overrated that he is certain to be underrated ever afterward. [These "second thoughts" consist of selected comments from his work as a newspaper reviewer of books for the ST. PAUL PIONEER PRESS AND DISPATCH.]

1803 LITERARY MANUSCRIPTS AND AUTOGRAPH LETTERS OF EMINENT AUTHORS (NY: Scribner Book Store [Charles Scribner's Sons], 1946), Catalogue No. 132.
[Offers for sale thirty-eight autograph letters, two typed letters, signed postcards, etc., from 1909 to 1930—all to Arnold Bennett; the original proof sheets of "Memorable Days" (Lond: pvtly ptd, Curwen P, 1924); the original typescript of "The Hondekoeter"; the final typescript with many autograph notes of JG of film scenario of *Loyalties* as prepared by C. Graham Barker and JG and produced in England in 1934 with Basil Rathbone as De Levis. The scenario differs greatly from the stage version.]

1804 McCullough, Bruce. REPRESENTATIVE ENGLISH NOVELISTS: DEFOE TO CONRAD (NY: Harper, 1946), pp. 320–35.
JG lacked a strong sense of character and therefore relied on his skill in constructing situations. There seems to be an inconsistency in Soames, the typical Forsyte, who while blind to spiritual values is completely possessed by Irene, and Irene is so totally a symbol that she can hardly be judged as an individual. Her possessiveness of Jon in *To Let* is as Forsytean as that of any Forsyte. JG shifted his position from one championing the rebels in *The Man of Property* to one championing family ties and motherhood in *To Let*. His chief weaknesses are his too-great insistence upon his meaning and his too-direct method of stating his meaning, losing thereby suggestiveness and a sense of spontaneity.

1805 Radziukinas, Helena. "Dusza Anglika w zwierciadle epopei mieszczańskiej" (Soul of an Englishman in the Mirror of a Middle-Class Epic), GAZETA LUBELSKA, No. 116 (1946), 6 [not seen].
[Discussion of *The Forsyte Saga*.] [In Polish.]

1806 Routh, Harold V. ENGLISH LITERATURE AND IDEAS IN THE TWENTIETH CENTURY: AN INQUIRY INTO PRESENT DIFFICULTIES AND FUTURE PROSPECTS (Lond: Methuen, 1946; NY: Longmans, 1948, 1950), pp. 19, 43–48, 99, 137.
JG's major achievements are the four novels *The Man of Property, The Country House, Fraternity,* and *The Patrician* and his three dramas *The Silver Box,*

326

Justice, and *Strife.* He developed in his plays "the dramatic possibilities of undramatic facts." His best art—diminishing as conscious humanitarianism took over—sprang from his own sufferings. Unfortunately he was too often careless or misinformed about realistic details, and he frequently lapsed into sentimentality. JG "is not sufficiently expert in human nature to earn a recurring revival. He sacrificed too much to the manners and moods of his own time."

1807 Siwicka, Zofia. "Sztuda, w której chciał grać Jaracz" (The Play in Which Jaracz Wanted to Star), ODRODZENIE (Lublin), No. 46 (1946), 5 [not seen].
[Review of a theater production of *The Roof.*] [In Polish.]

1947

1808 Bowen, Elizabeth. ENGLISH NOVELISTS (Britain in Pictures Series) (Lond: Collins, 1947), pp. 44–46.
JG's novels are noted for their "intellectual scrupulousness, sense of beauty, rather hopeless passion for social justice, and with regard to women, a serious but exotic sentimentality." Even though his portraits of men of property are "more searching than Thackeray's, more fastidious than Trollope's," they fail as major figures. He was perhaps "not ruthless enough." Because he could give "the fullest force to a scene," one remembers the scenes in his novels and therefore loses sight of their continuity.

1809 Burgum, Edwin B. THE NOVEL AND THE WORLD'S DILEMMA (NY: Oxford UP, 1947), pp. 53–55.
Both JG and Thomas Mann dealt with the "business-versus-art" theme. In *The Forsyte Saga* JG refused to take sides; Mann, in BUDDENBROOKS, concluded that bourgeois business morality purged of grossness and cruelty can complement an art purged of frivolity.

1810 Clark, Barrett H., and George Freedley (eds). A HISTORY OF MODERN DRAMA (NY & Lond: Appleton-Century, 1947), pp. 182–83, 184, 190, 730.
JG's "fetish" for impartiality limited his appeal because an audience likes to take sides. His thinking seems limited now but will perhaps find a proper critical climate in the future. "His fairness, pity, and irony are his strength and weakness as a dramatist." [Cursory dismissal of the plays with brief statements of theme in the major ones.]

1811 Durham, Willard Highley, and John W. Dodds (eds). BRITISH AND AMERICAN PLAYS: 1830–1945 (NY: Oxford UP, 1947), pp. 301–3.

[The introduction mentions briefly JG's passion for fairness and his principle of "the spire of meaning."]

1812 Eastman, Fred. "John Galsworthy," CHRIST IN THE DRAMA (NY: Macmillan, 1947), pp. 63–72.
[Eastman's point of view in relation to JG is to look "for a sincere interpretation of life by those who see it steadily and see it whole." The comments primarily summarize *Strife, The Pigeon,* and *Loyalties*—no religious or literary criticism, no insight, no Christ.]

1813 Jean-Aubry, Georges. VIE DE CONRAD (THE LIFE OF CONRAD) (Paris; Gallimard, 1947); trans by Helen Sebba as THE SEA DREAMER: A DEFINITIVE BIOGRAPHY OF JOSEPH CONRAD (Garden City, NY: Doubleday; Lond: Allen & Unwin, 1947), pp. 176, 191–92, 227, 230, 232, 235, 236, 246, 247, 248, 249, 254, 255, 257, 267, 282, 285.
[Various references to the Joseph Conrad-JG personal and literary friendship. See H. V. Marrot, THE LIFE AND LETTERS OF JOHN GALSWORTHY (Lond: Heinemann, 1935; NY: Scribner's 1936), for a more comprehensive treatment.]

1814 Liddell, Robert. A TREATISE ON THE NOVEL (Lond: Cape, 1947), pp. 125–26.
JG's method of delineating character by relying on externals is inadequate, for it fails to convey the reality of the mind or soul "with its complicated double and treble vision," a reality that one finds in the novels of Virginia Woolf.

1815 Narita, Narihisa. "J. Galsworthy's *Forsyte Saga,*" SENIOR ENGLISH (Japan), No. 9 (1947), pp. [?] [not seen].

1816 Nethercot, Arthur H. "The Quintessence of Idealism; or, the Slaves of Duty," PUBLICATIONS OF THE MODERN LANGUAGE ASSOCIATION, LXII (Sept 1947), 844–59, espec pp. 855–56.
In *Strife* and *Justice* JG views as destructive a wrong-headed but tenaciously held sense of duty. He also wrestles with society's dual standards in *The Eldest Son.*

1817 Smit, J. Henry. THE SHORT STORIES OF JOHN GALSWORTHY (Rotterdam: D. Van Sijn, 1947 [?], rptd (NY: Haskell House, 1966).
[A poorly written cursory treatment of the short stories. Chaps 1–4 (to p. 42) survey the history of the short story and well-known biographical aspects of JG's life. Chapter 5, "Construction," takes Wilson Follett's dicta and applies them superficially to the short stories; in fact, most of Smit's comments are applications of Follett, or of Ernest Baker, or of R. H. Coats, or of Leon Schalit. Other chapters with the titles "Portraits and Characters," ". . . Ancestry," "The Poetic Element," "Description and Setting," "Atmosphere," "Social Criticism," "Pessimism," "Sentimentality," "Impartiality," and "Humour" do little more than quote passages from various short stories to substantiate the opinions of others. An appendix reprints Smit's article, "John Galsworthy as Seen from the

Vegetarian Standpoint," that originally appeared in VEGETARIAN NEWS (Jan 1933).]

1818 Tindall, William York. FORCES IN MODERN BRITISH LITERA-TURE 1885–1946 (NY: Knopf, 1947; rev ed, NY: Vintage, 1956); rptd (Freeport, NY: Books for Libraries P, 1970), pp. 49–50, 115, 165, 175–76, 281, 301, 332.
[Brief statements of commonplace criticism.]

1819 Wiegler, Paul. "Galsworthy waere achtzig" (Galsworthy Would Be Eighty Now), SONNTAG (East Berlin), II (10 Aug 1947), n.p.
JG, who died on the day when the Nazis came to power, began as a radical, then became a somewhat melancholic chronicler of the decline of the bourgeoisie. When visiting Vienna in his sixties, he seemed to come from one of the houses of the Forsytes. [In German.]

1948

1820 "Bargain," TIME, LI (14 June 1948), 104.
The collection, ranging from classics to mediocrity, is pleasantly enhanced by the staying-power of JG's story of Swithin Forsyte in *Caravan*. It is "fast, matter-of-fact and honestly funny." [Review of Marshall McClintock (ed), THE NOBEL PRIZE TREASURY (NY: Doubleday, 1948).]

1821 Bartlett, Robert M. THEY DARED TO LIVE (NY: Association P, 1948), pp. 39–42.
[Anecdotal account of conversations with JG during JG's last visit to America (Dec 1930–April 1931) and of Bartlett's visit with Ada after JG's death. JG was a "deeply religious man."]

1822 Chew, Samuel C. "Modern Drama" and "The Modern Novel," A LITERARY HISTORY OF ENGLAND, ed by Albert C. Baugh (NY: Appleton-Century-Crofts, 1948; 2nd ed, 1967), pp. 1526–27, 1550, 1555–57.
[This brief statement of the themes of the dramas and novels is supplemented by an even briefer survey of unsympathetic critical opinions and concludes that, in drama, JG "in his desire to be just to the under-dog" was less than just to society. In the novel, as in the drama, JG lacks psychological depth; in the novel, JG mirrors Victorian society, and that is not enough.]

1823 Evans, Benjamin Ifor. A SHORT HISTORY OF ENGLISH DRAMA (Lond: Penguin, 1948; Lond: Staples P, 1950; rev ed, Lond: MacGibbon & Kee, 1965; Bost: Houghton Mifflin, 1965), pp. 172–76, 196.

Revivals of JG's plays have been infrequent, suggesting a lack of interest since his death. Yet his significance is greater than that of Jones and Pinero: his method, in awakening the social consciences of his audience, is to develop a single theme in a plot of simple design. *The Silver Box* has "mathematical precision," but it illustrates JG's central weakness: a single social theme leads to "rigidity of design," causing a lack of any independence of character. JG's best works are *Strife, Justice, The Skin Game, Loyalties,* and *Escape. Strife* illustrates JG's oversimplification of problem with a dash of sentiment.

1824 Faure, Françoise, "John Galsworthy et les Littératures Étrangères" (John Galsworthy and Continental Literatures), REVUE DE LITTÉRATURE COMPARÉE, XXII (1948), 84–102.

JG's present eclipse is temporary, for the growing interest in the Victorian period should help to renew interest in his work. Two signs of a revival are the BBC serial production of *The Forsyte Saga* in 1945 and the reprinting of *Saga* in 1947, despite the paper shortage. Among French influences on JG are Voltaire, Anatole France, Flaubert, and especially Maupassant and Zola. "The naturalists . . . have taught the English and Galsworthy in particular the importance of a critical attitude toward life." Russian influences on JG include Turgenev, Chekhov, and Tolstoy. French influences affect especially the intellect and technique; Russian influences affect the sensibility. JG's pity and his "inconclusiveness" are aspects of Russian influence. JG's categorical denial of Ibsen's influence is plausible, but Freud probably had some slight influence on JG's work in, for example, *Beyond* and *A Saint's Progress.* [In French.]

1825 Graham, Virginia. *"Escape,"* SPECTATOR (Lond), CLXXX (2 April 1948), 405.

[Favorable review of cinema version of *Escape,* starring Rex Harrison.]

1826 J., W. H. "Galsworthy, *The Forsyte Saga:* Odd Words," NOTES AND QUERIES, CXCIII (Sept 1948), 387.

The "odd words" are as follows: *gasper,* for cigarette; *Swan Song,* part I, chap 3: Jon Forsyte was "dabbing at hair, bright and stivery" (he made it stand up); *The Silver Spoon,* part I, chap 5: "Michael stivered his hair"; *Man of Property,* part I, chap 3: Irene's dress was not *daverdy* (soiled or withered); *Swan Song,* part II, chap 4: the portmanteau word *snoof* meaning "got no sense of smell to speak of."

1827 Lamm, Martin. "John Galsworthy," DET MODERNA DRAMAT: 1830–1930 (Stockholm: Bokforlaget Aldus, 1948; rev ed, 1964); trans by Karin Elliott as MODERN DRAMA (Oxford: Basil Blackwell, 1952; NY: Philosophical Library, 1953), pp. xv, 92, 147, 219, 285–92.

JG's plays are distinguished by "the English taciturnity of their characters," relying more than usual on gesture and facial expression. JG, unlike Shaw, does not laugh at himself and his audience; and he does not have Shaw's imagination:

he is a "fine and gifted dramatist . . . but no genius." The structure of his plays is often cut to a standard pattern and built on concrete situations. JG experienced no growth during his last fifteen years. [Primarily a brief biographical sketch with plot summaries of the most important plays.] [In Swedish.]

1828 Lewisohn, Ludwig (ed). AMONG THE NATIONS: THREE TALES AND A PLAY ABOUT JEWS (NY: Farrar, Straus, 1948; Toronto: Clarke-Irwin, 1948), pp. ix–xviii.

At last a Gentile (JG) has presented a Jew of "entire genuineness" because De Levis sees his false friends believing in the stereotype of the Jew. Acting in such a way as to confirm their suspicions and alienated from Jew (because he had abandoned his people, faith, and God) and Gentile alike, De Levis wanders homeless and desolate. [Text of *Loyalties* is reprinted.]

1829 Lion, Leon M. THE SURPRISE OF MY LIFE: THE LESSER HALF OF AN AUTOBIOGRAPHY (Lond: Hutchinson, 1948), pp. 96–100, 109, 116–31, 138, 155, 169, 179, 183, 185, 194, 212, 223, 237, 238, 243, 244, 250, 253, 256.

Lion the actor-manager was more influenced by JG than by any other dramatist. JG always followed two business practices with Lion: (1) JG accepted no advance fees but required a penalty clause if the play were not produced by a certain date, and (2) JG required Lion to pledge secrecy for any play offered him for production. JG insisted that no changes in his plays be allowed without his permission. Most changes in script during rehearsal originated with him, but JG was amenable to suggested changes, usually incorporating them. JG is the child of a "strong and splendid tradition" (Victorianism), yet he is the "fiercest of all rebels against it." One of JG's greatest theatrical devices is the "moral line" (in the Greek dramatic sense) at the curtain line and the doubling of its effect in the penultimate curtain line, as in *The Skin Game, Escape, Loyalties*—in all his plays, in fact, except *Exiled* and *The Roof*. The final scene in *Justice* is full of the Greek sense of pity and terror. [Lion's book contains some of JG's perceptive comments on the staging of his plays, especially pp. 122–25; gives occasional references to the stage history of JG dramas; reprints seventeen JG letters (some edited); and reproduces stills of Lion as De Levis and as the "Old Gentleman."]

1830 Morawski, Stefan. "Hardy, Lawrence, Galsworthy," TWÓR-CZOŚĆ (Warsaw), No. 5 (1948), 95–103 [not seen]. [In Polish.]

1831 Mosdell, D[oris]. "Film Review," CANADIAN FORUM (Toronto), XXVIII (Oct 1948), 162–63.
[Brief review of the Twentieth Century-Fox cinema adaptation of *Escape*.]

1832 "Unworthy Galsworthy," NEWSWEEK, XXXII (19 July 1948), 81.

Liberties taken with the stage version of *Escape* do not succeed in the Twentieth Century-Fox (Britain) film version. Only Rex Harrison's charm (as Matt Denant) sustains the action of the film.

1833 White, William. "Housman on Galsworthy: More Marginalia," REVIEW OF ENGLISH STUDIES, XXIV (July 1948), 240–41.
Housman's "slurs upon Galsworthy were private: abrupt statements to intimate friends, secret marginal defamation in books." Quite possibly Housman's reaction is more of a personal prejudice than a critical disapproval, though there is no evidence for any conjecture about the reason for such a prejudice. [Reproduces the five marginal comments made by Housman in his copy of *The Man of Property.*]

1834 Whitebait, William. "The Arts and Entertainment: The Movies," NEW STATESMAN AND NATION, XXXV (3 April 1948), 273.
Rex Harrison stars in this American production of *Escape,* which was filmed in England. "An argumentative, and to me boringly dated play, has been made into a moderately thrilling film."

1949

1835 Billing, Herbert S. *"The Man of Property,"* TIMES LITERARY SUPPLEMENT (Lond), 19 Feb 1949, p. 126.
The Man of Property "was composed and first went to press on January 26, 1906, and was reprinted on April 21, 1906, and again on July 8, 1906. We have no records of any variation in imposition between these reprints," and the file copies have been destroyed. Further reprints from type were on 16 August 1907, 3 October 1911, and finally 27 March 1915, "when we have a record that the imposition and signatures were altered." "Stereo plates were not made for a reprint until 1922." [Reply to *"The Man of Property,"* ibid., 22 Jan 1949, p. 64. See also, Tom Turner, ibid., 12 March 1949, p. 174.]

1836 Fenikowski, Franciszek. *"Srebrna szkatułka"* (*The Silver Box*), DZIENNIK BAŁTYCKI (Danzig), No. 106 (1949), 3 [not seen].
[Review of *The Silver Box,* produced by the Wybrzeże State Theater in Danzig.] [In Polish.]

1837 Fiszer, Edward. *"Srebrna szkatulka"* (*The Silver Box*), GŁOS WYBRZEŻA (Danzig), No. 104 (1949), 3 [not seen].
[Review of *The Silver Box,* produced by the Wybrzeże State Theater in Danzig.] [In Polish.]

1838 Goliński, Leszek. *"Srebrna szkatułka"* (*The Silver Box*), SLOWO POLSKIE (Wroclaw), No. 44 (1949), 3 [not seen].
[Review of *The Silver Box,* produced by the People's Theater, Wroclaw.] [In Polish.]

1839 Guseva, E. A. "Dve trilogii o Forsaitakh Dzhona Golsuorsi" (Two Trilogies on the Forsytes by John Galsworthy) (Moscow, IMLI im.M.Gor'kogo, 1949), 14 pp. [not seen].
[Abstract of an unpublished dissertation, Gorkii Universitet, 1949.] [In Russian.]

1840 Hudson, Lynton Alfred. LIFE AND THE THEATRE (Lond: George G. Harrap, 1949), p. 134.
JG's characters fight man-made economic and social systems, not cosmic or eternal forces.

1841 Jarosławski, Mieczysław. *"Srebrna szaktułka"* (*The Silver Box*), ODRA, No. 17 (1949), 4 [not seen].
[Review of *The Silver Box,* produced by the Wybrzeże State Theater in Danzig.] [In Polish.]

1842 Jones, W. S. Handley. "John Galsworthy and the Dilemma of Liberalism," LONDON QUARTERLY AND HOLBORN REVIEW, Jan 1949, pp. 223–32.
JG was uneasy with his stance of impartiality as seen in his frequent phrase of people who "want to make omelets without breaking eggs." His attitude toward the poor was "kindly but slightly Olympian." He distrusted popular movements, fearing mob rule. The root of his social philosophy is "Let sleeping dogs lie as long as possible, but when they do wake up give them a biscuit and take them for a run on the lead, lest they snap at you." Society is held together by the "moral cohesion of common virtues." Soames's change in the later Forsyte saga indicates that JG's "early attempts at moral crusading . . . petered out in the end." His main interest was in "human relationships," and a main theme is the "incursion of . . . alien influence in the life of a stolid family" (Bosinney, for example). Too inhibited by "fastidious moderation," JG gave the public a chronicle of the twilight of the middle class. [Jones's once-over-lightly essay has little substantial critical analysis.]

1843 Lamb, G. F. A COMMENTARY AND QUESTIONNAIRE ON THE SILVER BOX AND JUSTICE (GALSWORTHY) (Lond: Sir Isaac Pitman, 1949).
[A one-page general introduction is followed by "Analysis of the Play," which is in fact scene-by-scene summaries. Pp. 27–31 contain act-by-act questions about the two plays.]

1844 Lapter, K. "Wstep" (Introduction), *Walka (Strife)*, trans into Polish by J. Mondschein with stage adaptation by Tadeusz Zuchniewski (Warsaw: Kziazka i Wiedza, 1949) [not seen].
[In Polish.]

1845 Lutogniewski, Tadeusz. *"Srebrna szkatułka"* (*The Silver Box*), GAZETA ROBOTNICZA (Wroclaw), No. 46 (1949), 5 [not seen].
[Review of *The Silver Box*, produced by the People's Theater, Wroclaw.] [In Polish.]

1846 *"The Man of Property,"* TIMES LITERARY SUPPLEMENT (Lond), 22 Jan 1949, p. 64.
[This article provides a brief bibliographical analysis and description of what are claimed to be two variants of the first edition of *The Man of Property* and the relationship of these variants to a "second impression" of *Property* and *The Forsyte Saga*. See replies by Herbert S. Billing, ibid., 19 Feb 1949, p. 126; Tom Turner, ibid., 12 March 1949, p. 174.]

1847 N. *"Srebrna szkatułka.* Państwowy Teatr im. S. Jaracza, Olsztyn-Elblag" (*The Silver Box* at the S. Jaracz State Theater in Olsztyn-Elblag), ŻYCIE OLSZTYŃSKIE, No. 36 (1949), 4 [not seen].
[Review of a Polish theater performance of *The Silver Box*.] [In Polish.]

1848 Reynolds, Ernest Randolph. MODERN ENGLISH DRAMA: A SURVEY OF THE THEATRE FROM 1900 (Lond: George G. Harrap, 1949; Norman: University of Oklahoma P, 1951), pp. 52, 57, 133–37, 138, 150.
JG, like Shaw, represents the school of the drama of ideas. *Justice*, of all English plays, can most certainly point to the social action of prison reform, which helps to vindicate the cause of the drama of ideas. *Justice* best exemplifies JG's method: he manipulates "the sad puppet-show," with his "ironic pity" constantly breaking through. The audience can neither love nor hate Falder, nor anyone else in *Justice*. The characters are merely cogs in a great wheel. JG's impartiality "militates against real sympathy being aroused." In JG's plays, only man can remedy his wrongs in a setting filled with gloom and the "fog of social injustice." While lacking humor, JG plays are in the "well-made" tradition of Pinero, with coherent plots and poignant incidents. Characters are not memorable.

1849 S., J. M. *"Srebrna szkatułka"* (*The Silver Box*), TYGODNIK POWSZECHNY (Cracow), No. 25 (1949), 8 [not seen].
[Review of *The Silver Box*, produced by the Wybrzeże State Theater in Danzig.] [In Polish.]

1850 Short, Ernest Henry. INTRODUCING THE THEATRE (Lond: Eyre & Spottiswoode, 1949), pp. 43, 46, 62, 64, 68, 102, 201, 264, 305–6.
The Pigeon was the first modern play produced at the Birmingham Repertory

Theatre during the 1913–14 season. Falder's solitary cell scene in *Justice* is an excellent example of speechless drama. [Random comments about JG are drawn primarily from Short's THEATRICAL CAVALCADE (Lond: Eyre & Spottiswoode, 1942).]

1851 *"Srebrna szkatułka"* (*The Silver Box*), PRZEKRÓJ (Cracow), No. 205 (1949), 11 [not seen].
[Review of *The Silver Box*, produced by the People's Theatre, Wraclaw.] [In Polish.]

1852 *"Srebrna szkatułka*. Państwowy Teatr im. S. Jaracza, Olsztyn-Elblag"* (*The Silver Box* at the S. Jaracz State Theater in Olsztyn-Elblag), PRZEKRÓJ (Cracow), Nos. 209–10 (1949), 26 [not seen].
[Review of a theater performance, in Polish, of *The Silver Box*.] [In Polish.]

1853 Stevenson, Lionel. "Introduction," *The Man of Property* (NY: Scribner's, 1949), vii–xviii.
JG's novels and plays are characterized by "the tolerance, the almost inarticulate sympathy, which seems often to be in conflict with the ironical manner that he assumed." The emotional maturity evident in *The Man of Property* can be explained by the trials of JG in his affair with, and subsequent marriage to, Ada. Irene is presented objectively through the eyes of other characters rather than with penetrating psychological analysis, because she is governed by "emotional impulses rather than by clear thinking, and she is passive rather than dynamic." Her meetings with Bosinney add to the structural uncertainty of the situation which the readers as well as the Forsytes share. JG's purpose, after all, was to arouse pity for adversaries as well as for Irene—to show how all were caught in the web of convention. JG is masterful in presenting the large Forsyte family—especially in his use of the "key-phrase" to identify members. Young Jolyon is almost a portrait of JG; Soames emerges as the "most sympathetic and . . . heroic figure" in the whole saga. JG's London is "spacious, impersonal, and coldly cruel." In narrative technique, he shifts points of view, "making all the more conspicuous the exception of Irene and Bosinney, who are seen always from the outside." Other narrative techniques of *Property* are the "suspense of inevitability rather than surprise" and a style marked by irony and quiet understatement. JG and Trollope are similar, a similarity seen especially in the kinship of Soames and Irene with that of Plantagenet and Glencora Palliser in Trollope's "Parliamentary Series." *Property* is the last major work of the type of fiction that had been predominant since 1830.

1854 Strastil-Strassenheim, Edmund. "Die Kunst der Personenbeschreibung in Romanen John Galsworthys, W. Somerset Maughams und Graham Greenes" (The Art of Character Description in the Novels of John Galsworthy, W. Somerset Maugham, and Graham Greene). Unpublished dissertation, University of Graz (Austria), 1949.
[In German.]

1855 Turner, Tom. *"The Man of Property,"* TIMES LITERARY SUPPLE-MENT (Lond), 12 March 1949, p. 174.

[Remarks that a bibliographer once told him there were six variants of *The Man of Property*. Reports also that JG told him that there were only eleven copies of the dark green cloth issue of *The Island Pharisees* and that the text of the dark green cloth and the light green cloth editions of *Pharisees* varied. See also *"The Man of Property,"* ibid., 22 Jan 1949, p. 64; Herbert S. Billing, ibid., 19 Feb 1949, p. 126.]

1950

1856 Bates, H. E. EDWARD GARNETT (Lond: Max Parrish, 1950), pp. 15, 25, 26–28, 31, 41.

Bosinney (*The Man of Property*) is a portrait of Edward Garnett, who insisted on JG's changing Bosinney's death from suicide to accident. Late in his life Garnett "rather despised" JG, "in that waspish way . . . kept for his too successful protégés, for his universal Forsyte success." [There are passing references to JG in a book devoted to random comments on the literary career of Edward Garnett.]

1857 Downer, Alan S. THE BRITISH DRAMA: A HANDBOOK AND BRIEF CHRONICLE (NY: Appleton-Century-Crofts, 1950), pp. 311, 312, 315–17, 319, 330, 350, 367.

[Brief, general remarks about JG's relationship to the Court Theatre group; paragraphs of general comment are devoted to *Justice* and *Strife*.]

1858 Eaker, J. Gordon. "Galsworthy and the Modern Mind," PHILOLOGICAL QUARTERLY, XXIX (1950), 31–48.

JG legitimately turned the novel "to purposes of social criticism." Many of his novels and essays, the early ones in particular, consider various "aspects of the liberal idea" or liberalism: for example, in *The Silver Spoon* Michael Mont's program for reducing unemployment and overcrowding—emigration, the land, and the slums; in *The Island Pharisees, The Man of Property, The Country House, Fraternity,* and *The Patrician* the satiric attacks on British complacency and the different facets of upper-class society; in others, questions regarding the obligations of responsible management of limited liability companies to stockholders and employees; and another liberal theme concerns the emancipation of women. JG's treatment of the poor illustrates "his humanitarianism and common sense" and not his sentimentality. The value of his work lies in its portrayal of the period from late Victorian times to the era following World War I.

1859 Fenikowski, Franciszek. *"Gołębie serce"* (*The Dove's Heart* [*The Pigeon*]), DZIENNIK BAŁTYCKI (Danzig), No. 119 (1950), 5 [not seen].

[Review of the Wybrzeze State Theater's production of *The Pigeon* in Gdańsk-Gydnia-Sopot.] [In Polish.]

1860 Freeman, James C. "Whyte-Melville and Galsworthy's 'Bright Beings,' " NINETEENTH-CENTURY FICTION, V (1950–51), 85–100.
From the time of his undergraduate days at Oxford JG was intoxicated with the "bright beings" of Whyte-Melville's novels—Digby Grand, Daisy Walters, and the Honorable Crasher. "In the *Saga* and its sequels it was not the Forsytes but the Cherrels [*sic*] and the Monts who perpetuated the life of the class about whom Whyte-Melville wrote." Some of the representatives in JG's novels of Whyte-Melvillean society are the following: Shelton (*The Island Pharisees*), George Pendyce (*The Country House*), Lord Miltoun (*The Patrician*), George Forsyte, Montague Dartie, and Val Dartie (*The Forsyte Saga*), Johnny Dromore (*The Dark Flower*), Charles Clare Winton (*Beyond*), and Jack Muskham (*Flowering Wilderness*).

1861 "Galsworthy and Proust," TIMES LITERARY SUPPLEMENT (Lond), 8 Dec 1950, pp. 777–78.
There are some interesting artistic and biographical resemblances between JG and *The Forsyte Saga* and Proust and REMEMBRANCE OF THINGS PAST. The roles of the Forsyte uncles are similar to Swann's role in supplying materials of the past. Although JG attacks materialism, one suspects that he never entirely rejected it. His strong naturalism makes his improbabilities hard to accept. [This article is a review of *Saga* as illustrated by Anthony Gross and of REMEMBRANCE as illustrated by Philippe Jullian.]

1862 H[äusermann], H. W. "Brief Mention," ENGLISH STUDIES (Amsterdam), XXXI (1950), 206.
[A one-paragraph review of J. Henry Smit, THE SHORT STORIES OF JOHN GALSWORTHY (1947), which remarks that the analyses of JG's stories are superficial.]

1863 Horn, Wilhelm. "Sprachliche Kennzeichnung der Personen in Galsworthys Drama *Exiled*" (Linguistic Characteristics of Persons in Galsworthy's Drama *Exiled*), ARCHIV FUER DAS STUDIUM DER NEUEREN SPRACHEN (Brunswick), CLXXXVII (1950), 73–74.
[Different pronunications of the diphthong [ai] help to distinguish the speakers in JG's play.] [In German.]

1864 Kerr, Elizabeth M. BIBLIOGRAPHY OF THE SEQUENCE NOVEL (Minneapolis: University of Minnesota P, 1950), pp. 21–22.
[Lists the three trilogies of the Forsyte chronicles: *The Forsyte Saga, A Modern Comedy,* and *The End of the Chapter.*]

1865 Mirlas, Leon. [Reply], SUR, No. 189 (July 1950), 106–10.
[Answers point by point the criticisms raised by M. A. Olivera's review in SUR, No. 186 (April 1950), 67–72.] [In Spanish.]

1866 Nicoll, Allardyce. WORLD DRAMA FROM AESCHYLUS TO ANOUILH (NY: Harcourt, Brace, & World, 1950; Lond, 1951), pp. 664–67.
JG outdistances Pinero and Jones in dramatic power because of his "perfect mastery of naturalism . . . compassionate depiction of humanity . . . [and] fine humanitarianism of spirit." The prison scene in *Justice,* devoid of dialogue and having only literary stage directions, shocked his contemporaries and depicted JG's inventive power. [Nicholl makes paragraph comments about *The Silver Box* and *Justice* and mentions others briefly in passing.]

> **1867** Olivera, M. A. "John Galsworthy: *La Saga de los Forsyte*" (John Galsworthy: *The Forsyte Saga*), SUR, No. 186 (April 1950), 67–72.

[This review of a Spanish translation of *The Forsyte Saga* for Argentinian readers is broadly favorable, but at the same time it deals largely and in detail with sixteen mistranslated passages. See also L. Mirlas, SUR, No. 189 (July 1950), 106–10.] [In Spanish.]

> **1868** Perkins, Maxwell E. EDITOR TO AUTHOR: THE LETTERS OF MAXWELL E. PERKINS, ed by John Hall Wheelock (NY & Lond: Scribner, 1950), pp. 27–29, 38, 46, 63, 69, 185, 208, 270, 271.

[Concerning THE GREAT GATSBY, Perkins noted to F. Scott Fitzgerald that JG is "not really in sympathy with things today (1926)."] JG, "who never over-rated himself as a writer, but was one of great note in fact, always said that the most fruitful thing for a writer to do was quiet brooding."

> **1869** Święcicki, Józef Marian. "*Święty* Galsworthy'ego—apologia witalizmu" (Galsworthy's *Saint*—An Apology for Vitality), PRZEGLĄD POWSZECHNY (Cracow), CCXXX (1950), 229–49 [not seen].

[In Polish.]

> **1870** Ujević, Tin. "Bilješka o piscu" (A Note on the Author), in JABUKA ("The Apple Tree"), trans by Tin Ujević (Zagreb: Zora, 1950), pp. 123–28 [not seen].

[In Serbo-Croatian.]

1951

1871 Bax, Clifford. SOME I KNEW WELL (Lond: Phoenix House, 1951), pp. 100, 168–69.
At the turn of the century if one "wanted to find authors who assumed that men and women are spiritual beings involved in physical organisms," one had to turn to the two theosophical poets of Ireland—Yeats and AE. In England our

nourishment was Wells, with his "nineteenth-century science; Bennett, with his matter-of-fact mind; Shaw, with his brain-spun socialism; and Galsworthy with his sentimental humanitarianism." As a novelist JG had the "industry and the character-sense of a Victorian" and was less of a preacher than Wells and less of a reporter than Bennett. *The Forsyte Saga* will probably insure him a permanent place in literature in the company of Trollope. His dramas illustrate his power and his besetting weakness. The conflict between regard for justice and loyalty to a social class is so vitally handled in *Loyalties* that it may become "the most notable English play of our century's first quarter." Unfortunately, sentimentality often weakened his dramas: e.g., *Windows, The Little Man*.

1872 Belden, Albert D. "John Galsworthy—Novelist of Repentance," EXPOSITORY TIMES, LXIII (Nov 1951), 49–53.
JG is the "prophet of repentance" because he repeatedly suggests that the ideal does not become the real. His work illustrates the themes of strife between the creative and sterile elements in society and of the yearning that exceeds one's grasp. *The Island Pharisees* illustrates well the typical JG ideas of "British stolidity, insularity, conservatism," static society, and sacrifice of individual needs to demands of society. British society is limited by (1) inability to believe what is not flattering (*Pharisees*), (2) inability to part with one's possessions even if no longer desired (*The Man of Property*), (3) inability to "act outside" one's immediate environs (*The Country House*), and (4) inability to escape the predestination in one's blood (*The Patrician*). *Fraternity's* thesis is that only the affluent middle class has a social conscience: the working class has only "social need" and "economic appetite"; the aristocracy has "heredity" rather than social conscience. The plays *Justice* and *The Silver Box* continue the same themes. Soames (chromosomes, or heredity) Forsyte's (foresight on 'change') tragedy is that his possession (Irene) refuses to be possessed. *The Forsyte Saga* touches on two vital issues of 1951: the crime of an "unreflecting conventional loveless marriage" and the need for better laws of divorce. JG's "wistful belief in religion" is shown in the death of Old Jolyon in *Saga*. [This is the first in the series entitled "Vital Messages of Great British Writers."]

1873 Church, Richard. GROWTH OF THE ENGLISH NOVEL (Lond: Methuen, 1951), pp. 205–6.
JG's style is noteworthy for its combination of somber sensuousness, stoicism, deep sensibility, and quietness. His *The Dark Flower,* Wharton's ETHAN FROME, and Mackenzie's GUY AND PAULINE are akin artistically, and each has achieved a permanence in our literature. JG's work has similarities to the work of M. Baring, L. H. Myers, and C. P. Snow.

1874 Clark, Barrett H. "John Galsworthy," INTIMATE PORTRAITS (NY: Dramatists Play Service, 1951), xiii, 29–44, 141.
[A reminiscence about the visit of JG and Ada to the Dramatic Club of the University of Chicago during a visit to the United States in 1912, and again in

1919. Clark records some critical commonplaces about JG's dramatic works and emphasizes his shyness and reticence in conversation: Ada usually rescued him. Clark gives JG's explanation for the genesis of *Strife*.]

1875 Hudson, Lynton Alfred. THE ENGLISH STAGE: 1850–1950 (Lond: George G. Harrap, 1951), pp. 127, 132, 142–47, 149, 150, 154, 155, 161, 176–77, 187.

JG was the first dramatist to achieve "complete realism" (called "naturalism" by JG). The dramatist alone must create the "illusion of actuality." He wanted to evoke "participative empathy" and shorten the aesthetic distance between audience and stage. The problem in losing aesthetic distance is that the play might become an "exhibition of reality" rather than a play—as in the courtroom scene of *Justice* and the auction room of *The Skin Game*. Art becomes "Art for humanity's sake" rather than for art's sake, and "as nearly as possible it ceased to be art at all." JG's exact characters permit little interpretation; and his careful balancing of more than a single emotional appeal "exhausts the audience."

1876 Mottram, R. H. "The Edwardian Literary Landscape. II.— Galsworthy at Home," CHAMBERS'S JOURNAL, June 1951, pp. 339–40.
[A nostalgic look at JG's very pleasant, gentlemanly, and "unliterary" home at Wingstone.]

1877 Neill, S. Diana. A SHORT HISTORY OF THE ENGLISH NOVEL (Lond: Jarrolds, 1951), p. 267.
The Forsyte Saga is parochial and lacking in metaphysical qualities, but it is a fine study of English society.

1878 Schwab, William. "The Dramatic Art of John Galsworthy." Unpublished dissertation, University of Wisconsin (Madison), 1951.
[Listed in COMPREHENSIVE DISSERTATION INDEX: 1861–1972 (Ann Arbor: Xerox University Microfilms, 1973), XXIX, 535.]

1879 Voropanova, M. "Poslesl" (Foreword), *Ostrov Fariseev (The Island Pharisees)*, trans by T. Kudriavtsevoi (Moscow: Goslitizdat, 1951) [not seen].
[In Russian.]

1880 Wilson, A[lbert] E[dward]. EDWARDIAN THEATRE (Lond: Arthur Barker, 1951), pp. 10, 13, 83, 145, 173, 182–84, 194, 195, 201.
The Court Theatre venture of Vedrenne and Barker was largely responsible for giving JG his start as a playwright, helping to found a school of dramatists sympathizing with the underdog and attacking social problems without sacrificing dramatic form. [Wilson quotes from favorable reviews of *The Silver Box* and from some of JG's remarks at the censorship inquiry of 1909.]

1952

1881 Cohen, Walter, Jan Struther, and Lyman Bryson. [Discussion], INVITATION TO LEARNING, II (Spring 1952), 25–32.
[A generalized discussion of *The Forsyte Saga*.]

1882 Hamilton, Robert. "Galsworthy the Playwright," CONTEMPORARY REVIEW (Lond), CLXXXII (Oct 1952), 220–24.
JG's dramas suffer because they "embody a more explicit and self-conscious message" than the novels, often hovering "between a good story and a tract." JG "harrows" feelings rather than attempts a "genuine synthesis." [Brief discussions of *Strife* ("perhaps his best . . . play"), *A Family Man* (which contains all of JG's weaknesses), *Loyalties, Escape* (perhaps JG's "best theatre" piece), and a few others. The information is conventional.]

1883 Salomon, Albert. "Sociology and the Literary Artist," in SPIRITUAL PROBLEMS IN CONTEMPORARY LITERATURE, ed by Stanley R. Hopper (NY & Lond: Harper [The Institute for Religious and Social Studies], 1952), p. 17.
JG is a descendant of that line of writers from Cervantes through Goethe who portray society as the destiny of the individual. JG viewed society in its constructive aspect as the educator affording the individual a "chance to realize his potential."

1884 Siwek, Karl. "Das Urteil über das Ausland und den Ausländer im Epischen Werk John Galsworthys" (Judgment of Foreign Countries and Foreigners in John Galsworthy's Epic Work). Unpublished dissertation, Göttingen University, 1952.
[Listed in Lawrence F. McNamee, DISSERTATIONS IN ENGLISH AND AMERICAN LITERATURE (NY & Lond: Bowker, 1968).] [In German.]

1885 Voropanova, M. "Golsuorsi i russkaia literatura" (Galsworthy and Russian Literature) (Moscow: MGPI im. V. I. Lenina, 1952), 15 pp. [not seen].
[Abstract of an unpublished dissertation, MGPI im. V. I. Lenina, 1951.] [In Russian.]

1886 Worsley, Thomas Cuthbert. "Perfection," THE FUGITIVE ART: DRAMATIC COMMENTARIES 1947–1951 (Lond: John Lehmann, 1952), pp. 199–201.
The point of a JG play is not what the individual is but what social relations make the individual become. [A review of the production of *The Silver Box* at the Lyric Theatre, Hammersmith, concluding erroneously: "How well Galsworthy is beginning to revive!"]

1953

1887 Amend, Victor E. "The Development of John Galsworthy as a Social Dramatist," DISSERTATION ABSTRACTS, XIII (1953), 385. Unpublished dissertation, University of Michigan, 1953.

1888 Bennett, JoAnn Waite. "John Galsworthy and H. G. Wells," YALE UNIVERSITY LIBRARY GAZETTE, XXVIII (July 1953), 33–43.

With the recent additions of JG and Wells to the Yale collection, the Yale library now possesses "almost the entire body of each man's work." The Galsworthy collection is a combination of gifts, one from John Wesley Warrington, 1936, and the other (assembled by Jesse L. Moss, 1869) from two brothers, Professor Joseph C. Sloane and William Sloane. The JG collection includes first eds, inscribed copies, periodical publications, manuscripts, the typescript of *Strife,* and an advance copy of *A Bit o' Love.* The library possesses, in addition, an almost complete collection of JG's poems, essays, pamphlets, periodical publications, and some interesting letters.

1889 "Books Received," TIMES LITERARY SUPPLEMENT (Lond), 5 June 1953, p. 370.

[A brief review of R. H. Mottram's JOHN GALSWORTHY commenting on the close relationship between Mottram and JG.]

1890 Galsworthy, Ada. OUR DEAR DOGS (Lond: St. Catherine P, 1953).

[While mainly about the Galsworthys and their dogs, it does provide some biographical insights. There are many pictures.]

1891 Hamilton, Robert. "John Galsworthy: A Humanitarian Prophet," QUARTERLY REVIEW, CCXCI (Jan 1953), 72–80.

JG's major weaknesses were his inability to synthesize adequately his art and message and his tendency to sentimentalize his approach to problems of personality. Consequently, his work demonstrates the conflict between artist and prophet. He was also afflicted with an uncertainty of belief, due largely to his humanitarian and basically subjective approach to social problems. He was never extreme in anything: consequently his inspiration was inhibited. He was vague on religion, but in politics he favored the "benevolent application of wealth." His work is satisfying, "like a finely planned house," but it "never takes one's breath." Style is "simple, clear, and . . . readable," qualities that will endure when JG's designation as "humanitarian prophet" has faded.

1892 Italiaander, Rolf. "Begegnung mit John Galsworthy" (Meeting with John Galsworthy), NEUE LITERARISCHE WELT, IV:20 (1953), 3 [not seen].

[In German.]

1893 Jovanović, Ž. P. "Prilog bibliografiji Džona Golsvortija kod Srbija" (Introduction to Bibliography of John Galsworthy in Serbia), KŃIŽEVNOST (Belgrade), XVI (1953), 193–96 [not seen]. [In Serbo-Croatian.]

1894 Kent, George E. "Social Criticism in the Novels, Plays, and Representative Short Stories of John Galsworthy." Unpublished dissertation, Boston University, 1953.
[Listed in COMPREHENSIVE DISSERTATION INDEX: 1861–1972 (Ann Arbor: Xerox University Microfilms, 1973), XXIX, 535.]

1895 Kettle, Arnold. AN INTRODUCTION TO THE ENGLISH NOVEL. Two volumes (Lond: Hutchinson's University Library, 1953); (NY: Harper, 1960), II, 95–100.
JG's novels are examples of "middle-brow literature," an "inferior literature adapted to the special tastes and needs of the middle class." The "distinctive feature" of this literature is "not its quality but its function." Compared to his later novels, *The Man of Property* does have a "core of seriousness" and a "spark of genuine insight." "This spark is the theme of property and its effect upon the personal relationships of the Forsytes." But the satire of *Property* is not sustained. JG is too pusillanimous and afraid to let his characters develop. Robert Liddell's essay [q.v., 1947] misses the point of JG's method, but D. H. Lawrence's essay [q.v., SCRUTINIES 1928] is "the finest criticism" of JG. No one who has understood Lawrence "can ever return to Galsworthy quite seriously again."

1896 Longaker, Mark, and Edwin C. Bolles. CONTEMPORARY ENGLISH LITERATURE (NY: Appleton-Century-Crofts, 1953), pp. 11, 169, 173. 177, 178, 191–97, 318, 319, 389, 390, 392, 393, 409, 456, 458.
[Brief, conventional comments on JG's major works, concluding that his "zeal for causes often gets the better of his intelligence . . . and sense of humor" and that his "most dramatic moments are often suspect." JG was perhaps a finer gentleman than writer.]

1897 MacCarthy, Desmond. MEMORIES (Lond: Macgibbon & Kee, 1953; NY: Oxford UP, 1953), pp. 55–60.
The element of the unexpected is missing from JG's plays and novels. The struggle between Beauty (Irene) and Possessiveness (Soames Forsyte) would have been better had JG recognized its real nature—possessiveness versus sex. Although he had the power to rouse indignation and pity, he lacked the power to evoke tragic feeling and free comedy. He yielded to the temptation of thinking more "about the representative value of his characters than about character itself." *The Silver Box* and *The Pigeon* are two of his best plays. JG was, after all, "a very good writer of the second class who had the renown of a master, a genius, an artist." [This essay was written in 1933.]

1898 Maiskaia, E. L. "Leksiko-stilisticheskie sredstva kharakteris-

tiki personazhei v romanakh o Forsaitakh D. Golsuorsi" (Lexical-stylistic Methods of Characterizing Personages in John Galsworthy's Novels on the Forsytes) (Moscow: MGU im M. V. Lomonosova, 1953), 10 pp. [not seen].
[Abstract of an unpublished dissertation, MGU im M. V. Lomonosova, 1952).]
[In Russian.]

1899 Malany, Mary H. "Letters by Barrie to the Duchess of Suther-land," B[OSTON] P[UBLIC] L[IBRARY] Q[ARTERLY], V (1953), 38–47.
In a letter dated 9 March 1919, Barrie said of JG that "he would go to the stake for his opinions but he would go courteously raising his hat. The other day he was flung out of a hansom, and went as gracefully as if he were leaving his card. . . . He used to care for nothing but frivolity . . . and now so serious and would not put a pin in a butterfly."

1900 Mottram, R[alph] H[ale]. JOHN GALSWORTHY (Lond: Long-mans, Green [Writers and their Work: No. 38], 1953).
Ada is primarily responsible for JG's becoming a writer. JG's "legal thorough-ness" and "slightly ceremonious" nature kept him from being a Bohemian. The reading public took JG's *Island Pharisees* seriously to heart because he was a member of the upper class. In the "Wingstone Novels" (*Pharisees, The Country House, The Patrician, The Freelands*), JG wrote in a naturally feeling style "as if maintaining a running commentary." The "Addison Road" novels (*Fraternity, The Dark Flower, Beyond, A Saint's Progress*) suggest the brooding atmosphere of JG's London address. *The Man of Property* and *The Forsyte Saga* are in the tradition of Thackeray and Fielding rather than Dickens and Defoe. [The pam-phlet, a personal appreciation by one who knew JG well, contains a series of paragraph comments about the major works, and less about the minor ones. Mottram's—and the reader's plight—is underscored by his comment: "What can I say that is not usually known?"]

1901 Voropanova, M. "John Galsworthy a jeho román *Ostrov pok-rytcu. Předmluva*" (John Galsworthy and His Novel *The Island Pharisees*. Introduction), *Ostrov pokrytcu* (*The Island Pharisees*) (Prague: SNKLHU, 1953), p. 308 [not seen].
[In Czech.]

1902 Warnock, Robert. "John Galsworthy: *Loyalties,*" REPRESENTA-TIVE MODERN PLAYS: BRITISH (Chicago: Scott, Foresman, 1953), pp. 8, 268–76, 277–337.
From 1906 JG shared the leadership of serious drama in England with Shaw. JG developed a style of genteel naturalism, and his best and most characteristic features are a concern for social issues, a reforming zeal, a severely naturalistic technique, and a command of the well-made play. If *Loyalties* is one of his two or three most satisfying plays today, the explanation is that the theme remains timely and that *Loyalties* is one of his most dramatic works. JG's thesis is that

society is "shot through with needless and sometimes tragic conflicts that result from our traditional interpretation of loyalty to race, caste, family circle, or other social group as a virtue in itself." The play is without a villain or hero, and Dancy's death is not tragic. The play is a model of the well-made play. JG presents his material with scrupulous realism and masterful dramatic skill, and an analysis of the construction of the play is rewarding.

1903 Zelenskii, P. G. "Dramaturgiia Dzhona Golsuorsi" (John Galsworthy's Dramatic Composition) (Kiev: L'vovskii Gosudarstvennyi Universitet im. I. Franko, 1953), 15 pp. [not seen].
[Abstract of an unpublished dissertation, L'vovskii Gosudarstvennyi Universitet im. I. Franko, 1953).] [In Russian.]

1954

1904 Allen, Walter. THE ENGLISH NOVEL: A SHORT CRITICAL HISTORY (Lond: Phoenix House, 1954; NY: Dutton, 1955), pp. 310–12.
Of all JG's work only *The Man of Property* retains any interest today. JG's failure is "somewhat akin to Butler's in THE WAY OF ALL FLESH; it is the failure to establish an adequate compensating principle for what is being satirized." Irene never comes alive, and JG's defense against the Forsytes is sentimentality.

1905 Garnett, David. THE GOLDEN ECHO (NY: Harcourt, Brace, 1954), pp. 70–72.
[This anecdotal account suggests that JG drew Bosinney from Edward Garnett and that once JG was happily married to Ada he was finished as a serious writer.]

1906 Glasgow, Ellen. "Pages from the Autobiography of Ellen Glasgow," AMERICAN SCHOLAR, XXIII (Summer 1954), 281–93; rptd in THE WOMAN WITHIN (NY: Harcourt Brace, 1954), pp. 196–209, 267–70, 276–77.
JG "belonged, essentially, as his art belonged, to the rapidly disappearing era of the gentleman." *The Man of Property* is his finest novel. The quality of his later work "softened and thinned." In *The Forsyte Saga*, JG was a "superb novelist" as long as he treated Soames, but he later became preoccupied with the problems of the young girl and was "unable to divorce sex from sentimentality." [An account of a visit in 1914 at Capel House.]

1907 Gridina, E. "*Saga o Forsaitakh* D. Golsuorsi kak satira no angliiskuiu burzhuaziiu epokhi imperializma" (J. Galsworthy's *Forsyte Saga* as a Satire on the English Bourgeoisie of the Era of Imperialism) (L'vov: L'vovskii Gosudarstvennyi Universitet im.I. Franko, 1954), 14 pp. [not seen].

[Abstract of an unpublished dissertation, L'vovskii Gosudarstvennyi Universitet im.I. Franko, 1953.] [In Russian.]

1908 Heiney, Donald W. ESSENTIALS OF CONTEMPORARY LITERATURE (Great Neck, NY: Barron's Educational Series, 1954), pp. 33, 95–100.
[Brief biographical sketch and mini-plot summaries of some major works.]

1909 Maiskaia, E. L. "K voprosu o vzaimodeistvii avtorskoi rechi i rechi personazhei" (Po romanam o Forsaitakh DZH. Golsuorsi) (On the Interaction between the Author's Speech and the Speech of His Characters in John Galsworthy's Novels on the Forsytes), INOSTRANNAIA YAZYKI V SHKOLE, No. 4 (1954), 12–21 [not seen].
[In Russian.]

1910 Starrett, Vincent. "*The Forsyte Saga.* John Galsworthy," CHICAGO TRIBUNE, 1954, [not seen]; rptd in BEST LOVED BOOKS OF THE TWENTIETH CENTURY (NY: Bantam, 1955), 72–74.
The story that JG hurled a brick through a window to get material for *Justice* is untrue. *The Forsyte Saga* should have ended with *The Man of Property.* "With the slow passing of the original cast of characters, and the coming of the later generations, the Saga loses interest steadily . . . and becomes unconvincing and tedious in its later volumes as in its first great volume it was urgent and absorbing."

1911 Takahashi, Genji. STUDIES IN THE WORKS OF JOHN GALSWORTHY WITH SPECIAL REFERENCE TO HIS VISIONS OF LOVE AND BEAUTY (Tokyo: Shinozaki Shorin, 1954; 2nd ed, 1955; 3rd ed, rev and enlarged, 1971).
[Discusses JG's work from the standpoint of quixotism and pagan mysticism. Its chief value lies in its insights and in its sensitive appreciation of JG's nuances. Valuable bibliography studies eds and translations of JG in Japan.]

1912 Thienová, Inge. "John Galsworthy a *Ostrov pokrytcu*" (John Galsworthy's *The Island Pharisees*), ČASOPIS PRO MODERNÍ FILOLOGI (Prague), XXXVI:4 (1954), 244–47 [not seen].
[Review.] [In Czech.]

1913 Žeželj, Andra. "Umetnost Džona Golsvordija" (John Galsworthy's Art), *Jaca od Smrti* (*Beyond*) (Novi Sad: Matica srpska, 1954, 1959, 1964) [not seen]. [Pagination differs for each printing, but for the 1964 ed the article is found on pp. 285–88.]
[In Serbo-Croatian.]

1955

1914 "Books Received," TIMES LITERARY SUPPLEMENT (Lond), 29 April 1955, pp. 225–26.
[This one-paragraph review of Genji Takahashi, STUDIES IN THE WORKS OF JOHN GALSWORTHY WITH SPECIAL REFERENCE TO HIS VISIONS OF LOVE AND BEAUTY (Tokyo: Shinoza Shorin, [1954]) remarks on the careful and thoughtful study of JG's writing, his social background, and his character.]

1915 Edel, Leon. THE PSYCHOLOGICAL NOVEL 1900–1950 (Lond: Rupert Hart-Davis, 1955), p. 16.
The fictions of Richardson and Joyce are a "new kind of realism, unrelated" to those of Bennett, Wells, or JG. [A brief reference in passing.]

1916 Ervine, St. John. "Portrait of John Galsworthy," LISTENER, LIV (15 Sept 1955), 418–19.
[These personal impressions of JG see him as a Forsyte "to the backbone."]

1917 Ford, George H. DICKENS AND HIS READERS (Princeton: Princeton UP for University of Cincinnati, 1955), pp. 105*n*, 137–38, 191.
JG's dialogue, in contrast to Dickens's stylized dialogue, achieves with its naturalness "a drabness which finally becomes incredible."

1918 Fruehling, Jacek. *"Pojedynek"* (*The Duel [The Skin Game]*), OD A DO Z, No. 6 (1955), 2 [not seen].
[Review of *The Skin Game,* produced by Warsaw's Ateneum State Theater.] [In Polish.]

1919 Grodzicki, August. *"Pojedynek"* (*The Duel [The Skin Game]*), ŻYCIE WARSZAWY (Warsaw), No. 20 (1955), 6 [not seen].
[Review of *The Skin Game,* produced by Warsaw's Ateneum State Theater.] [In Polish.]

1920 Harkness, Bruce. "Conrad on Galsworthy: The Time Scheme of *Fraternity,*" MODERN FICTION STUDIES, I (May 1955), 12–18.
JG's main reason for focusing on time in *Fraternity* is to give literal accuracy to the plotting of calendar days from the last of April until 6 June 1907. Even though he has some contradictions and errors in the time scheme, JG's major problem is his inability to alter the tempo of the novel: he misses the mark in "Hilary's internal struggles, protracted through time." Conrad suggested that JG transpose the scene of Hughs's return from jail, which JG did. [Harkness develops the thesis that a good way to focus on the study of time in *Fraternity* is to compare Conrad's and JG's treatment of flashback, parallel time blocks, and general time.]

347

1921 Hoffman, Artur. *"Pojedynek" (The Duel [The Skin Game]),* DZIŚ I JUTRO, (Warsaw), No. 4 (1955), 7 [not seen].
[Review of *The Skin Game,* produced by Warsaw's Ateneum State Theater.] [In Polish.]

1922 Knickerbocker, Kenneth L., and H. W. Reninger. INTERPRETING LITERATURE (NY: Holt, 1955), pp. 106–18.
[A commentary on and an analysis of the short story "Quality."]

1923 Lennartz, Franz. "John Galsworthy," AUSLÄNDISCHE DICHTER UND SCHRIFTSTELLER UNSER ZEIT. EINZELDARSTELLUNGEN ZUR SCHÖNEN LITERATUR IN FREMDEN SPRACHEN (Stuttgart, 1955), pp. 215–22 [not seen].
[In German.]

1924 Marković, Vida E. "O romanu *Patricije* i njegovom piscu" *(The Patrician* and Its Author), *Patricije (The Patrician),* trans by Rada Priklniajer (1955), pp. 5–10 [not seen].
[In Serbo-Croatian.]

1925 Piaskowska, Janina. *"Pojedynek" (The Duel [The Skin Game]),* NOWA KULTURA (Warsaw), No. 5 (1955), 6 [not seen].
[Review of *The Skin Game,* produced by Warsaw's Ateneum State Theater.] [In Polish.]

1926 Podhorska-Okołow, Stefania. *"Srebrna szkatułka" (The Silver Box),* TEATR (Warsaw), No. 3 (1955), 7 [not seen].
[Review of the Polish Radio Theater production of *The Silver Box.*] [In Polish.]

1927 Purdom, Charles Benjamin. HARLEY GRANVILLE BARKER (Lond: Rockliff, 1955; Cambridge, Mass: Harvard UP, 1956); rptd (Westport, Conn: Greenwood P, 1971), pp. 59, 66, 70, 75, 76, 80, 89, 93, 96, 100–101, 103, 104, 110, 147, 152, 156, 158, 183, 190, 192, 229.
[Passing references to JG comment on performances of his plays and on his professional associations with Granville-Barker. A photograph of JG, Lillah McCarthy, and John Masefield faces p. 82.]

1928 Reinhardt, Waltraut. "CURRENT SYNTAX" BEI GALSWORTHY (Current Syntax in Galsworthy) [typescript]. Unpublished dissertation, University of Jena, 1955.
[Following a brief sketch of JG's views on the modern English language, the study deals systematically with the influence of modern syntax on JG's style. The study, based on an examination of almost all of JG's writings, is divided into twelve chapters (verb, article, noun, adjective, adverb, pronoun, preposition, conjunction, congruence, conversion, word order, sentence structure). Although he used modern constructions sparingly, JG was interested in the developments

of modern syntax. An appendix contains a survey of Americanisms in JG's writings and lists his opinions of American English.] [In German.]

1929 Rogalski, Aleksander. "Zwierciadła dekadencji. Zachodnio-europejksi świat mieszczański i kapitalistyczny w powieściach Tomasza Manna, Rogera Martin du Gard i Johna Galsworthy'ego" (Mirrors of Decadence. Western-European Middle Class and the Capitalist World in the Works of Thomas Mann, Roger Martin du Gard and John Galsworthy), ŻYCIE I MYŚL (Warsaw), Nos. 2–3 (1955), 166–89 [not seen].
[In Polish.]

1930 Šperling, Jaroslav. "*Ostrov pokrytcu*" (*The Island Pharisees*), STRAŽ LIDU (Cheb), XI:2 (1955), 4 [not seen].
[Review of *The Island Pharisees*.] [In Czech.]

1931 Thienová, Ingeborg. "Der kritische Realismus bei John Galsworthy" (Critical Realism in John Galsworthy's Works), ZEITSCHRIFT FUER ANGLISTIK UND AMERIKANISTIK (East Berlin), III (1955), 431–46.
Rather than writing museum pieces in memory of a decaying class, JG examined the bourgeoisie critically, especially in *The Man of Property,* his best work. He did not, however, establish contact with the progressive proletariat. His sympathy with the underprivileged was limited to mere pity; it did not enable him to describe them vividly and see in them more than "social cases." After the war the unbiased critical realist became a benevolent but passive and resigned observer of society and tended to regard the Forsytes as pillars of society. This change was not surprising, for JG never cut his ties with the upper middle class; he followed a Ruskin-like moral aestheticism that prevented him from judging society in terms other than its attitudes toward beauty and love. [In German.]

1932 Warmiński, Janusz. "Galsworthy w Warszawie" (Galsworthy in Warsaw), POLSKA (Warsaw), No. 2 (1955), 20–21 [not seen].
[In Polish.]

1933 Young, Ione Dodson. "The Social Conscience of John Galsworthy." Unpublished dissertation, University of Texas (Austin), 1955.
[Because of the impossibility of making an "accurate estimate of JG's achievements as a pure artist," this study investigates JG's aims and his attempts to realize these aims in an effort to discover what influence JG's social conscience had on his art. The chronological development of JG's social conscience considers JG's reactions to and involvements in such social problems as play censorship, prison reform, woman suffrage, divorce law reform, prevention of cruelty to animals, war work, and the P.E.N. Club. The manifestations of JG's social conscience are then categorized by exploring his treatment of caste or class

consciousness, justice, divorce, the land, war, and progress. There are three conclusions to this study: (1) JG is underestimated by present-day critics and readers; the judgment that his work is passé "seems frequently to result from prejudice and superficial knowledge"; (2) much of JG's work is based on social problems; (3) JG's social conscience aided rather than hindered his art.] [Listed in COMPREHENSIVE DISSERTATION INDEX: 1861–1972 (Ann Arbor: Xerox University Microfilms, 1973), XXIX, 535.]

1956

1934 Archer, William. "Extracts from a Lecture by William Archer on Galsworthy, Barrie and Shaw Delivered to the College Club, New York, in 1921," DRAMA, XLII (Autumn 1956), 29–36.
The emergence of JG, Barrie, and Shaw as playwrights and men of all-around intellectual power suggests that the day is past when "mere theatrical talent" could make a great playwright. JG's "immaculate correctness of speech" typifies his mental attitude. He transcends his upbringing as one of the "straitest sect of the Pharisees" through his love of humanity, which is the key to his genius. Characteristic of JG are straightforwardness without exaggeration or freakishness, staid and dignified humor, and idealism tempered by common sense.

1935 Babadzhan, E. M. "Nekotor'ye materialy nablydenii nad mnogoznachost'yu slov v sovremennom angliiskom yaz'yke (Po trilogii Dzh. Golsuorsi *Saga o Forsaitakh*)" (Some Material in Observation of the Multiple Meanings of Words in the English Language: On the Trilogy by J. Galsworthy, *The Forsyte Saga*) UCHENYE ZAPISKI (Moscow: Gosudarstvennyi Pedagogicheskii Institut), IX (1956), 41–62 [not seen].
[In Russian.]

1936 Buchanec, Jozef. "Pokrytci" (Pharisees), KULTÚRNY ŽIVOT (Bratislava), XI:33 (1956), 4 [not seen].
[Brief review of *The Island Pharisees*.] [In Czech.]

1937 Kovaleva, IU. B. "Vstup. stat'ia" (Introduction), *Drami i Komedii* (*Dramas and Comedies* [of JG]), trans by L. V. Khvostenko (Moscow: Iskutstvo, 1956) [not seen].
[In Russian.]

1938 "Milestones," TIME, LXVII (11 June 1956), 87.
[Thirty-five-word Ada Galsworthy obit notice.]

1939 Mottram, R. H. FOR SOME WE LOVED: AN INTIMATE PORTRAIT OF ADA AND JOHN GALSWORTHY (Lond: Hutchinson, 1956). [Although there is little critical analysis, this volume is useful for the many personal memories of one who was a lifelong friend of the Galsworthys.]

1940 Nenadal, Radislav. "John Galsworthy a jeho roman *Venkovské sidlo*" (John Galsworthy and His Novel *The Country House*), *Venkovské sidlo* (*The Country House*) (Prague: SNKLHU, 1956), pp. 251–58 [not seen].
[In Czech.]

1941 Phelps, Gilbert. THE RUSSIAN NOVEL IN ENGLISH FICTION (Lond: Hutchinson, 1956), pp. 112–25, 145–46, 153–54, 162, 176, 179. What JG meant by realism was different from what Virginia Woolf attributed to him. His realism was "in fact the kind of fiction that Turgenev wrote." The Tolstoyan challenge—"What do we live for?"—certainly affected JG's choice of themes: i.e., his exposure of the gap separating the abstract principle of justice and the reality of justice in human institutions. JG's treatment of upper-class life "undoubtedly derives some of its bite from Tolstoy." Tolstoy was influential in bringing about a "new frankness and realism in the treatment of domestic themes," and this new realism can be seen in JG's descriptions of the married life of Soames and Irene. There are some "Dostoyevskyan touches" in some of JG's early work; Turgenev, however, was the major Russian influence on JG.

1942 Poettgen, Heinz, and Karl Heinz Stader. "John Galsworthys 'The Man Who Kept His Form': Ein Beitrag zum Thema 'gentleman' und zur Gestalt der 'short story' " (John Galsworthy's "The Man Who Kept His Form": An Essay on the Theme of the Gentleman and the Form of the Short Story), DIE NEUEREN SPRACHEN (Frankfurt/Main), V (1956), 158–70. JG has created in Miles Ruding an excellent study of a man who is a gentleman and who lives by his code of good form: steady, capable, self-controlled, self-sufficient, limited by his uncreativeness. There is a nobility about him even when after the war he turns to work as a London cab driver. JG had begun working with the motif of the gentleman as early as 1908 in "A Portrait." Just as *doom* is a key word for Poe, *abyss* (*gouffre*) for Baudelaire, *mirror* for Cocteau, and *consciousness* for Henry James, so *balance, proportion,* and *form* are key words for JG. The story opens with a physical description of Ruding and progresses by means of varying motifs concerning Ruding's keeping his form so that a psychological portrait emerges. The tone of the story helps the reader become a listener to the narrator's tale. Following Poe's advice, JG chose each word for its contribution to the total effect. His use of understatement precludes false sentiment and exemplifies his use of the principle of balance. The very kernel of his aesthetics and a principle of life for JG is the principle of balance. [In German.]

1943 Pusiecki, Jan. "Piękno a własność" (Beauty and Property), KSIĄŻKA DLA CIEBIE (A BOOK FOR YOU), No. 9 (1956), 4–5 [not seen].

[Discussion of *The Forsyte Saga*.] [In Polish.]

1944 Řiha, Otakar. "*Strieborna tabatierka* Johna Galsworthyho. Doslov" (*The Silver Box* of John Galsworthy. Epilogue), *Strieborna tabatierka* (*The Silver Box*) (Martin, Osveta, 1956), pp. 63–68 [not seen].
[In Czech.]

1945 Rowell, George. THE VICTORIAN THEATRE: A SURVEY (Lond: Oxford UP, 1956), pp. 61, 135–36.
When JG became aware that there was a lack of passion in his plays, he "had recourse without compromising his beliefs" to *The Skin Game, Loyalties,* and *Escape;* these were plays with well-tried forms which were directed toward more positive effect.

1946 Scott-James, R. A. FIFTY YEARS OF ENGLISH LITERATURE, 1900–1950, WITH A POSTSCRIPT—1951 TO 1955 (Lond: Longmans, Green, 1956), pp. 42–46.
In perspective one recognizes that for ten years JG "was an active force in awakening Edwardian England" from intellectual lethargy. "More than any other then living man of letters he himself had become an English Institution."

1947 Swinnerton, Frank. BACKGROUND WITH CHORUS (NY: Farrar, Straus, & Cudahy, 1956), passim, espec pp. 101–3, 189–93.
JG's best work in the novel is in the "two or three early novels" in which he told "the only love story he knew." His plays are "too mechanical in their unresolved pros and cons to be vital." The decline in his prestige was due in part to the political hostility to "the class, which had lost its youth in Flanders," and in part to "what is thought to be his sentimental attitude towards it. In a Marxian period you cannot have gentility shown as anything but parasitic."

1948 Trifković, Risto. "Pogovor" (Afterword), PRVI I POSLEDNJI ("The First and the Last"), trans by Zlatko Gorijan (Sarajevo: Norodna prosvjeta, 1956), [n.p.] [not seen].
[In Serbo-Croatian.]

1949 [V., J. A.] "Vyznamny'anglický román" (An Outstanding English Novel), L'UD (Bratislava), 7 June 1956, [n.p.] [not seen].
[Review of *The Country House*.] [In Slovene.]

1950 Wilson, Angus. "Books in General: Reassessments—Galsworthy's *Forsyte Saga*," NEW STATESMAN AND NATION, LI (3 March 1956), 187.
By 1920 when *In Chancery* appeared, the split between the "serious" and the

"middlebrow" novel was clear, and JG belonged irrevocably with the latter. The most striking defect of *The Forsyte Saga* is "its complete failure in conflict." From the beginning JG "pulls his punches against the Forsytes," and their opponents—Bosinney and Irene—are "virtually nothing." The struggle between Soames and Irene lacks reality "because the sexual truth of passion" is absent. JG's failure can be seen in his failure with Soames. Soames's character is built up largely "of interior monologues, reflections on the changing ways of England." It is this formal failure that condemns JG; it reveals "his lack of values and the cold heart beneath his sentimentalism." Just as his sympathy for June is missing in *The Man of Property*, so, too, in the later Forsyte novels Annette and Jon "are never even realized as human beings."

1951 Zhantieva, D. "Preface," *The Forsyte Saga*. Three volumes (Moscow: Foreign Languages Publishing House, 1956) [not seen]. [Each volume of the trilogy—*The Man of Property, In Chancery, To Let*—is followed by an afterword. Listed in National Union Catalogue, NUC 63-11292.] [In Russian.]

1957

1952 F., D. C. "Galsworthy na plzeňśke scéně" (Galsworthy on the Stage in Pilsen), LIDOVÁ DEMOKRACIE (Prague), 18 Sept 1957, [n.p.] [not seen]. [A report on the production of *The Forest*.] [In Czech.]

1953 Gersh, Gabriel. "The English Family Novel," SOUTH ATLANTIC QUARTERLY, LVI (1957), 207–16. JG attacked the institution of the family in *The Man of Property*, especially male dominance of the woman. [Passing references.]

1954 Jungmann, Milan. "Druhy balicek knih" (Another Bundle of Books), LITERÁRNÍ NOVINY (Prague), VI:51–52 (1957), 5 [not seen]. [In Czech.]

1955 Krehayn, Joachim. "Chronist der Mittelklasse. Zu John Galsworthys neunzigstem Geburtstag" (Chronicler of the Middleclass. On John Galsworthy's Ninetieth Birthday), DER BIBLIOTHEKER (Berlin), XI:8 (1957), 809–16 [not seen]. [In German.]

1956 McCormick, John. CATASTROPHE AND IMAGINATION: AN INTERPRETATION OF THE RECENT ENGLISH AND AMERICAN NOVEL (Lond & NY: Longmans, Green, 1957), pp. 35–36, 161, 220. JG had the "wry honour" of composing the GÖTTERDÄMMERUNG for both the first and the second phase of the English novel. "His failure was proof . . . of the division of sensibility in the English novel in the years under scrutiny." His Forsyte novels read like those of a lesser Thackeray or a minor Trollope. They are readable only because JG perceived "the very cleavage in sensibility of his time, and took it for his theme." His inadequate technique and his inadequate imagination explain the slightness of his early work and the shoddiness of his later work. When his work "is not cheapened by obvious devices" it is dull.

1957 Marković, Vida E. "Predgovor" (Foreword), *Konac Dela* (*End of the Chapter*) (Belgrade: Prosveta, 1957); rptd (1968), pp. 7–19 [not seen].
[In Serbo-Croatian.]

1958 P[rochazka], J[aroslav]. "Galsworthy na česke scéně" (Galsworthy on the Czech Stage), SVOBODNÉ SLOVO (Prague), 18 Sept 1957, [n.p.] [not seen].
[Review of the production of *The Forest* at Pilsen.] [In Czech.]

1959 R., K. H. "John Galsworthy," WELTSTIMMEN (Stuttgart), XXVI (1957), 345–46.
Though a realist and a critic of society, JG had a sense of something beyond life and was a true, humane artist. He was better as a novelist than as a playwright. [In German.]

1960 Sanders, Charles R. LYTTON STRACHEY: HIS MIND AND ART (New Haven: Yale UP, 1957), pp. 61–62.
According to Strachey, JG's *Strife* was a failure because JG was unable to reconcile his purpose of showing the "class" struggle with his purpose of portraying conflicting persons.

1961 Š[ašek], V. "Anglický klasik v knihovně" (An English Classic in the Library), VEČERNI PRAHA (Prague), 25 Sept 1957, [n.p.] [not seen].
[A report on a "literary evening" devoted to JG at the City Library in Prague.] [In Czech.]

1962 Schloesser, Anselm. "John Galsworthys Bedeutung als Dramatiker" (John Galsworthy's Importance as a Playwright), ZEITSCHRIFT FUER ANGLISTIK UND AMERIKANISTIK (East Berlin), V (1957), 133–52.
Combining some of the best middle-class traditions with progressive ideas, JG wrote problem plays that are "compassionately satirical" (R. H. Coats) and are more important than the novels because as a dramatist JG is more interested in reforms and more effective as a craftsman. Though his views are thoroughly middle class, some of his plays are impressive as social criticism. If compared to Conrad and Lawrence, JG is a second-rate novelist, but in the field of drama JG's only contemporary rival was Shaw. [A detailed survey of the plays.] [In German.]

1963 Scott-James, R. A. "The Galsworthys," TIME AND TIDE (Lond), XXXVIII (26 Jan 1957), 101–2.
[Review of R. H. Mottram, FOR SOME WE LOVED (Lond: Hutchinson, 1956).]

1964 Sw[idzinski], F[rantišek]. *"Saga rodu Forsytu"* (*The Forsyte Saga*), OBRANA LIDU (Prague), 23 Nov 1957, [n.p.] [not seen].
[In Czech.]

1965 V., K. O. "Anglický dramatik no plzeňské scéně" (An English Playwright on the Stage at Pilsen), PRAVDA (Bratislava), XXXVIII:112 (1957), 4 [not seen].
[A report on the production of JG's *The Forest.*] [In Czech.]

1966 Weltmann, Lutz. "Der Gentleman in der Literatur: Erinnerungen an John Galsworthy" (The Gentleman of Literature: Remembering John Galsworthy), DEUTSCHE WOCHE (Munich), VII:33 (14 Aug 1957), 13.
JG, whose reputation has declined, was a tactful president of P.E.N. and sometimes too much of a gentleman as a writer. Unlike the plays, *The Forsyte Saga* will perhaps endure. [In German.]

1967 West, Rebecca. THE COURT AND THE CASTLE. . . . (New Haven: Yale UP, 1957), pp. 180, 197, 200, 208.
[Several brief, slight references.]

1968 Wood, J. D. "Social Criticism in the Forsyte Novels of John Galsworthy." Unpublished dissertation, University of Toronto, 1957.
[Listed in Lawrence F. McNamee, DISSERTATIONS IN ENGLISH AND AMERICAN LITERATURE, SUPP I, (NY & Lond: Bowker, 1969).]

1969 Wykes, Alan. "Galsworthy's Glossographer," SPECTATOR, CXCVIII (12 April 1957), 478.
[Wykes's tongue-in-cheek comments on his role as the editor of JG's plays who is sent to various countries of the Commonwealth. Ironic problems arise from preparing a glossary for outdated plays.]

1958

1970 Akhmechet, L. E. "*Ostrov Fariseev* i rannee tvorchestvo Dzhona Golsuorsi" (*The Island Pharisees* and the Early Works of John Galsworthy), SERIIA FILOLOGICHESKAIA, IAZYK I LITERATURA, No. 5 (1958), 329–44 [not seen].
[In Russian.]

1971 Bukolt, A. "Zestawienie filmów według Galsworthy'ego" (List of Films Based on Galsworthy's Works), EKRAN (Warsaw), No. 26 (1958), 11 [not seen].
[In Polish.]

1972 Conrad, Joseph. LETTERS TO WILLIAM BLACKWOOD AND DAVID S. MELDRUM, ed by William Blackburn (Durham, NC: Duke UP, 1958), pp. xvi, 100 and *n*, 109, 110, 117, 118, 122, 123, 151, 156, 157, 160, 162, 168, 184, 191.
[Recommending that Blackwood publish JG's *A Man of Devon*, Conrad notes that JG "has the making of a stylist in him, with a well balanced temperament and a poetical vision." JG, in turn, offers to be a guarantor of a loan Conrad wishes to negotiate.]

1973 Chicherin, A. "Peresmotr suzhdenii o Forsaitovskom tsikle (K izucheniu tvorchestra Dzh. Golsuorsi v sovetskom literaturovedenii)" (Review of Opinions on the Forsyte Cycle: On the Study of J. Galsworthy's Work in Soviet Literary Criticism), VOPROSY LITERATURY (Moscow), No. 1 (1958), 152–66 [not seen].
[According to abstractor in ABSTRACTS IN ENGLISH STUDIES, I:9 (Sept 1958), this is largely a defense of *A Modern Comedy* against such critics as D. Zhantiyeva, M. Nersessova, L. Zonina, and others who rank these novels as inferior to the other Forsyte books.] [In Russian.]

1974 Daiches, David. THE PRESENT AGE AFTER 1920 (Lond: The Cresset P, 1958), pp. 92, 112, 149, 163, 172, 246–48, 267.
JG has not lasted as a novelist because of his inability to give a consistent "vision of men in fully realized concrete particulars." Irene is "not a character but a piece of arty nonsense." The Forsyte novels "document an era with perceptiveness and intelligence," but JG's art is superficial: humanity and "powers of social observation" exceed artistic powers.

1975 DZHON GOLSUORSI (JOHN GALSWORTHY) (Moscow: Vsesoiŭzaia gosudarstvennaĭa biblioteka inostrannoi literatury, 1958).
JG, one of the twentieth century's greatest critical realists, is penetrating, sensitive, and full of life. Often using deeply sociological and psychological images, he paints a true picture of the crisis of bourgeois Victorian England. Unfortunately, the bourgeois limitation of the author and the conservatism of his sociopolitical views are clearly expressed in many of his works. This limitation in turn negatively affects his creativity and decreases the possibilities of his realism—especially for readers in the last half of the twentieth century.

In *Strife*, JG clearly and graphically paints the two poles of modern society: the stubborn and insistent exploiter Anthony is contrasted to Roberts, the leader of the striking workers. The pointedness of the drama is dulled because of JG's desire to soften the extreme views and to show the fruitfulness of sensible compromise. *The Freelands* (1915), which ends the most radical period of JG's works, explores the deep injustice and inhumanity in the relationships of English bourgeois society, the sad fate of simple people in England, and the searching and doubting of the more conscientious intelligentsia. In the years of crises and revolution after World War I, JG became remarkably more cautious in his criticism of bourgeois society, trying to idealize the older generation as representing firm moral values, stability, and equilibrium, qualities which he thinks are lacking in postwar bourgeois youth. The social significance of *The Forsyte Saga* is in depicting the process of collapse of family and government—in presenting the passing away of the era of the presumably indestructible Forsytes. JG is the subject of many articles and dissertations dedicated to his novels, dramas, and stylistic peculiarities in the Soviet Union and is of great interest to Russian literary critics. [The work is basically a chronological listing of JG items discussed primarily through plot summary, pp. 4–19. Pp. 19–48 give an extensive bibliography: 20–24, a chronological list of works published in England; 36–42, translations into Russian; 44–46, Russian criticism of JG.] [In Russian.]

1976 Fricker, Robert. DER MODERNE ENGLISCHE ROMAN (THE MODERN ENGLISH NOVEL) (Goettingen: Vandenhoeck & Ruprecht, 1958; rev ed, 1966).
[Passing references.] [In German.]

1977 Oguri, Keizo. "Galsworthy's Technique—'Italicized Emphasis,' " THE HUMANITIES (Journal of the Yokohama National University), Sec. II, No. 7 (Sept 1958), 30–41.
JG's habit of using italics for emphasis can be helpful to non-English speaking students of English pronunciation (accent and intonation) who manage to acquire correct word stress with the aid of dictionaries but who might be at a loss as to the correct sentence stress and proper intonation. JG's dramas and novels with their many printed marks and hints of pronunciation may serve as excellent textbooks of spoken English. [This paper attempts to analyze and interpret JG's technique of "italicized emphasis" with a view to learning the correct way to speak English.] [In Japanese.]

1978 P[óltorzycka], Dz[ennet]. "Nad książkami Johna Galsworthy'ego" (Reading John Galsworthy's Books), RADIO I TELEWIZJA (Warsaw), No. 16 (1958), 20 [not seen].
[In Polish.]

1979 Řiha, Otakar. "John Galsworthy tentoraz ako dramatik" (John Galsworthy, This Time as a Dramatist), FILM A DIVADLO (Prague), II:6 (1958), 14 [not seen].
[In Slovene.]

1980 Ross, Woodburn O. "John Galsworthy: Aspects of an Attitude," in STUDIES IN HONOR OF JOHN WILCOX, ed by A. Dayle Wallace and Woodburn O. Ross (Detroit: Wayne State UP, 1958), pp. 195–208. Some of the reasons for the continuing decline in JG's reputation are as follows: (1) his being a late Victorian; (2) his being a sentimentalist; (3) his resistance to extremist positions; and (4) his being mislabelled a social critic. "His work is highly personal, it is intelligent, it is moving. But it is limited in scope." In his crude, early story "Dick Denver's Idea," found in *From the Four Winds,* JG first used a pattern that was "to be fundamental to a large number of his subsequent works": "a gallant man falls in love with a married woman; the woman's husband is a brute; the marriage constitutes no genuine spiritual union." The story asks such questions as whether a marriage based on "barren law instead of love" is entitled to respect. *Jocelyn* is "a surprising improvement" in its treatment of the theme and probably was "somewhat better than the average novel written then." In *Villa Rubein* "conditions within the social organization which keep the young lovers apart are attacked." JG learned how to turn the facts in his own case "to a criticism of qualities of human character and of certain aspects of society" in *The Man of Property. The Country House* is essentially *Property* in a new locale and with some change of action. With *Fraternity* in 1909 JG completes his development and afterwards "had nothing significantly new to say. . . . and the fresh variations, though frequently vigorous and probing, represented no fundamental new development." JG's limitations were the "limitations of imagination." "He learned principally—not exclusively—to create modifications of three characters—Arthur, the unwanted husband; Ada Cooper, the beautiful and suffering wife; and himself, the gallant lover." In his limited area JG was at home and did well.

1981 Sharenkov, Viktor. "John Galsworthy. 25 godini ot smurtta mu" (John Galsworthy. 25 Years Since His Death), SEPTEMVRI (Sofia?), II (1958), 158–63 [not seen].
[In Bulgarian.]

1982 Tracht, Jan. "Maly rozhover s Jánom Trachtom, překladatel'om Galsworthyho *Ságy rodu Forsytu"* (A Short Conversation with Jan Tracht, the Translator of Galsworthy's *Forsyte Saga*), KULŤURNY ŽIVOT (Bratislava), XIII:49 (1958), 4 [not seen].
[In Slovene.]

1983 Trewin, John Courtenay. THE GAY TWENTIES: A DECADE OF THE THEATRE (Lond: MacDonald, 1958), pp. 10, 15, 19, 39, 56, 64, 74, 85, 86–87, 117.
[Trewin refers in passing to appearances of JG's plays in the 1920s.]

1984 Wells, H. G. [Letter to Henry James], in HENRY JAMES AND H. G. WELLS: A RECORD OF THEIR FRIENDSHIP. . . . ed by Leon Edel and Gordon N. Ray (Urbana: University of Illinois P, 1958), p. 141. JG's "cold, almost affectedly ironical detachment" cannot attain the depth of Conrad's method.

1985 Wittkopp, Wilhelm. "Galsworthys Forsyte Saga: Ein Bild der absterbenden englischen Bourgeoisie" (Galsworthy's Forsyte Saga: An Image of the Dying British Bourgeoisie), FREMDSPRACHENUNTER-RICHT (Berlin), II (1958), 511–23. Though a critic of the bourgeoisie, JG remained a member of the middle class. Unlike Thomas Mann he was not a provincial; he recognized that the fate of the Forsytes was linked to the development of imperialism. A study of his works will be encouraging to students in socialist countries. [In German.]

1986 Zhantieva, D. "On A. Chicherin's Article," VOPROSI LITERA-TURY (Problems of Literature) (Moscow), No. 7 (July 1958), 170–78. [Reiterates the position that despite JG's forceful realism in the two trilogies— The Forsyte Saga and A Modern Comedy—some of the conservative elements in The Man of Property are extended into Comedy. This is a reply to A. Chicherin, 1958, q.v.] [In Russian.]

1959

1987 Baines, Jocelyn. JOSEPH CONRAD: A CRITICAL BIOGRAPHY (Lond: Weidenfeld & Nicolson, 1959; NY: McGraw-Hill, 1960); rptd in paperback (NY: McGraw-Hill, 1967). [Various references to JG, especially a biographical note on pp. 129–31, supplemented by quotations from letters of Conrad to JG. The letters are more extensively presented in H. V. Marrot, THE LIFE AND LETTERS OF JOHN GALSWORTHY (Lond: Heinemann, 1935; NY: Charles Scribner's Sons, 1936).]

1988 Božidar, Borko. "John Galsworthy in njegovo dels" (John Galsworthy and His Work), Zadnje Poglavlje (End of the Chapter), trans by Janez Gradišnik (Ljubljana: Cankerjeva založba, 1959), rptd (1967; 1969), pp. 777–83 [not seen]. [In Slovene.]

1989 Karl, Frederick R., and Marvin Magalaner. A READERS GUIDE TO GREAT TWENTIETH-CENTURY ENGLISH NOVELS (NY: Noonday P, 1959), pp. 8, 13, 15, 44, 45, 129, 173, 222. [Brief, passing references to JG are made as the works of Conrad, Lawrence, and

Virginia Woolf are discussed. JG is classified as belonging with other conventional and outmoded realists like Bennett and Wells.]

1990 Kot, Jozef. "Doslov" (Epilogue), *Forsytovska sága* (*The Forsyte Saga*) (Bratislava, 1959), p. 837 [not seen].
[In Czech.]

1991 "Literary Relations: John Galsworthy," THE GARNETTS: A LITERARY FAMILY: AN EXHIBITION (Austin: Humanities Research Center, University of Texas, 1959), 9.
[This exhibition included some first eds of JG's work, an early draft of "Censorship and Plays," and six holograph letters, JG to Edward and Constance Garnett.]

1992 Marković, Vida E. "Pogovor" (Afterword), *Tamni Cvet* (*Dark Flower*), trans by Aleksander Vidaković (Belgrade: "Rad," 1959, 1961, 1963, 1965), [n.p.] [not seen].
[In Serbo-Croatian.]

1993 Pallette, Drew B. "Young Galsworthy: The Forging of a Satirist," MODERN PHILOLOGY, LVI (Feb 1959), 178–86.
In *The Man of Property* despite Irene's statements to the contrary, there is little evidence that she really tried to make her marriage with Soames work. And in *To Let* her interference in the love match between Fleur and Jon seems terribly self-centered. Although JG's personal involvement warped as well as directed the satire in *Property*, JG achieved an impact and power in this novel that he did not attain again. Throughout his career "his memory of personal emotion continued to be his strength," and he is most effective when he deals with personal or domestic situations as when Soames worries about his father or his daughter. The lack of rapport between JG and D. H. Lawrence probably helps explain the "note of personal antagonism" that is found in Lawrence's famous attack on JG.

1994 Perrine, Laurence. STORY AND STRUCTURE (NY: Harcourt, Brace, 1959), pp. 83–84.
[Analytical questions for JG's "The Japanese Quince" are provided.]

1995 Voropanova, M. I. "Tema oblicheniia angliiskogo burzhuaznogo obshchestve v tvorchestve Golsuorsi perioda 1905–1917 godov (Po roman *Bratstvo*)" (Exposure of English Bourgeois Society in the Work of Galsworthy during the Period 1905–1917: Based on the Novel *Fraternity*), UCHENYE ZAPISKI (Krasnoiarsk. Gosudarstvennyi pedagogicheskii institut), XIII (1959), 223–60 [not seen].
[In Russian.]

1996 Wilson, Asher. "Oscar Wilde and *Loyalties*," EDUCATIONAL THEATRE JOURNAL, XI (Oct 1959), 208–11.

Parallels between the actual events of Oscar Wilde's trial in 1895 and the sequence of events in JG's play *Loyalties* (1921) suggest that JG identified himself with Wilde. Like Wilde JG was "under the ban of morals of the period as well as the law of the land" because of his love affair with his married cousin Ada.

1997 Zumwalt, Eugene E. "The Myth of the Garden in Galsworthy's 'The Apple Tree,' " RESEARCH STUDIES (State College of Washington), XXVII (Sept 1959), 129–34.
In his conception of the modern garden in "The Apple Tree," JG combines pagan and Judaic ideas. Ashurst is both Hercules who wrests the golden apples from the Garden of Hesperides and the modern man in the Judaeo-Christian tradition who rejects the pagan love of Megan.

1960

1998 Bache, William B. "*Justice:* Galsworthy's Dramatic Tragedy," MODERN DRAMA, III (Sept 1960), 138–42.
Although Falder "is not grand in the way that Lear, Hamlet, and Macbeth are" and although Falder is "spiritually unbowed" at the end, *Justice* can still be read as a tragedy if one keeps in mind JG's statement "Justice is a machine," by means of which JG "was both pointing out the design of the play . . . and suggesting the dimensions of its spire of meaning." To be sure Falder is defeated, but, ironically, we realize that "the prosecutors and the executors of justice have been ruthlessly crushed or are being ruthlessly crushed—a more subtle annihilation than that of Falder and Ruth, but just as certain—by the machine, justice." JG said in the preface to the Devon Edition that society " 'stands to the modern individual as the gods and other elemental forces stood to the individual' " in the Greek world. [Using JG's article "Some Platitudes Concerning Drama" and his "Preface" to the Devon Ed (I, xi), this article carefully analyzes, on an act-by-act basis, *Justice*.]

1999 Blair, Thomas Marshall Howe (ed). FIFTY MODERN STORIES (Evanston, Ill: Row, Peterson, 1960), p. 657.
"The First and the Last" is a masterpiece of dramatic narrative, with a "searching treatment of character and a well-managed plot." The atmosphere of London is vividly portrayed. [Prefatory note to "The First and the Last."]

2000 Bogataj, Katarina. JOHN GALSWORTHY. UMETNOST IN KULTURA, 8 (Arts and Culture Collection, 8), (Ljubljana: Prosvetni servis, 1960) [not seen].
[In Serbo-Croatian.]

2001 Buckstead, Richard Chris. "H. G. Wells, Arnold Bennett, John Galsworthy: Three Novelists in Revolt against the Middle Class," DISSERTATION ABSTRACTS, XX (1960), 4652–53. Unpublished dissertation, State University of Iowa (Iowa City), 1960.

2002 Carrington, Norman T. (ed). TWO MODERN PLAYS (Lond: James Brodie, [n.d.]), pp. 7–35, 70–71; rptd in *Strife* (Lond: James Brodie [Notes on Chosen British Texts Series], 1960).
[A student's guide to *Strife,* accompanied by the text of the play. A biographical sketch is followed by discussions of topics in a study-guide format, concluding with review questions. The important theme of *Strife* is "extremism of fanaticism" rather than industrial unrest, emphasizing that "violence recoils upon the violent." *Strife* develops by parallelism and contrast, giving a realistic portrayal of life. Characters are not psychologically complex; rather, JG individualizes types.]

2003 Choudhuri, Asoke Dev. "Galsworthy's First Play," VISVABHARATI QUARTERLY, XXVI:1 (Summer 1960), 21–23.
JG's low standing at present is justified at least in part by the fact that he said nothing "original or startling." He was just the man to fill the vacuum created by the inane comedies of the day. *The Silver Box* did not call for social revolution (as did Shaw's plays), nor did it display elemental human passions, as did Barker's WASTE. *Box* is important because it was JG's first work to vindicate clearly his sympathies for the underdog and to show his concern for social justice. *Box* is a milestone in the development of JG's artistic conscience.

2004 Daiches, David. A CRITICAL HISTORY OF ENGLISH LITERATURE. Two volumes (NY: Ronald P, 1960); rptd (1970), pp. 1109, 1132.
Although JG's dramas ("humanitarian fables of social and moral worry") evoke respect and sympathy for their technical competence and humane feeling, these qualities do not make a great dramatist. His Forsyte novels "document an era with perceptiveness and intelligence," but his art is a surface one. JG remained unaware of the novel as "anything more than a social commentary."

2005 D'iakonova, N. DZHON GOLSUORSI: 1867–1933 (JOHN GALSWORTHY: 1867–1933) (Leningrad & Moscow: Iskusstvo, 1960).
JG's writings were affected by concern for the fate of England, the gradual weakening of bourgeois power, and the suffering of the poor and oppressed. Although he could not solve these problems, he did focus attention on them, thus taking part in the great fight against evil and injustice in the bourgeois world. Even though he condemned the cruelty of the capitalistic leaders and foresaw the coming destruction of the old order, he was often content simply with sentimental expressions of dissatisfaction and sympathy. His abstract demand for social justice was characteristic of his creative activity. JG did not occupy himself with politics: he looked at it with distrust. After the great October revolution divided

the world into two camps, he wrote many articles asking for international solidarity among artists, financiers, and craftsmen. He refers to the solidarity of the masses with obvious apprehension, characteristically considering the Russian Revolution one of the consequences of war, not an active force in history. JG's works are contradictory: he believes that social problems can be solved within the frames of the existing social structure under conditions of mutual kindness and tolerance among the representatives of the various classes. But in his works reconciliation does not occur; serious class struggle is compounded because of the complete failure of the upper class to help the lower class.

JG devoted more than twenty years to the stage. His dramatic legacy was not uniform—it included great successes like *The Silver Box,* as well as serious failures like *Exiled.* With few exceptions, all his better plays were written during the first period of his creative life when the author acutely felt the pernicious influence of the bourgeoisie. But in the second period, when the storms of war and revolution forced him to feel more strongly his allegiance to the proprietary class, his works visibly deteriorated. From the beginning of his activity as a writer, even during the time of his greatest radicalism and sharp social criticism, his main aim was to instill in the ruling classes a line of reasonable conduct that might save England from the revolution.

In Russia, JG's plays are less known than his novels. Before the revolution only *Joy* was translated. In the first years after the revolution *Strife* was translated and successfully performed in Petersburg and Moscow. There were later some performances of *Box* and *The Skin Game.* It is obvious that the Soviet public did not have a chance to see his best works on the stage. [In Russian.]

2006 [K., Š.] "Láska spaľujúca" (Burning Love), KULTÚRNY ŽIVOT (Bratislava), XV:43 (1960), 4 [not seen].
[Review of *The Dark Flower.*] [In Slovene.]

2007 Murgaš, Emil. "John Galsworthy: *Forsytovská Sága"* (John Galsworthy: *The Forsyte Saga*), SLOVENSKÉ POHĽADY (Bratislava), LXXVI:4 (1960), 432–34 [not seen].
[Review of *The Forsyte Saga.*] [In Czech.]

2008 Murgaš, Emil. "Na okraj genézy a odkazu Galsworthyho diela" (On the Genesis and Legacy of Galsworthy's Works), ĽUD (Bratislava), 1 Oct 1960 [not seen].
[Review of *The Dark Flower.*] [In Slovene.]

2009 Natan, L. N. "An Unnoticed Application of 'Inner Monologue' in *The Forsyte Saga,"* PHILOLOGICA PRAGENSIA (Prague), III (1960), 15–22.
After JG the use of "inner monologue" in the tradition of Jane Austen, George Eliot, and Meredith is discontinued, and writers like Joyce and Woolf use instead

"stream of consciousness." An analysis of the speech of Soames Forsyte, in particular the use of "inner monologue," will enable one to grasp more clearly the characterization of Soames. Analysis of Soames's speech shows that his language is "neutral," "unobtrusive," and "colorless." His syntax is grammatical, word order is direct, and there are almost no inversions or ellipses. In contrast, Bosinney's speech has many inversions and unfinished sentences. Soames avoids abstract nouns, whereas Bosinney uses many abstract nouns. JG failed in his intention to condemn the English upper middle class ("Irene and Bosinney were meant . . . to represent progressive tendencies in English society") because he came to admire the bourgeoisie. A comparison of Soames's "direct speech" and "inner monologue" in *The Man of Property* shows that both are pretty much the same except in the final chapters where Soames gets rather emotional in the inner monologues. As JG worked on the later novels he faced the problem of developing Soames's character so that his unpleasant personality (found in *Property*) would become more and more admirable as the Forsyte chronicles continued. The method JG used was Soames's inner monologues; in the later novels the Soames of "direct speech" is not the same as the Soames of the inner monologues. JG vainly tried to make the reader accept the change as a profound change in Soames's nature and psychology, but there is an artificiality in the later inner monologues, and the reader is not deceived.

2010 Otten, Kurt. "Die Überwindung des Realismus im Modernen Englischen Drama" (The Victory of Realism in Modern English Drama), DIE NEUEREN SPRACHEN, No. 6 (June 1960), 265–78.
JG is the only realistic dramatist whose work fits Yeats's derogatory definition, given in various writings. Yeats's definition fits in part because JG, unlike Ibsen, did not have enough genius to allow the inner meaning to emerge through the banal surface. [In German.]

2011 Petkovová-Kresáková, Zora. "*Tmavý kvet.* Doslov" (*The Dark Flower.* Epilogue), *Tmavý kvet* (*The Dark Flower*) (Bratislava: Slovenské vydavateľstvo krasnej literatury, 1960). pp. 303–8 [not seen].
[In Czech.]

2012 Priestley, J. B. LITERATURE AND WESTERN MAN (NY: Harper, 1960), pp. 354–55.
Even though JG still identified himself, perhaps unconsciously, with the upper middle class, he challenged its pretensions and limitations.

2013 Steinberg, M. W. (ed). ASPECTS OF MODERN DRAMA (NY: Henry Holt, 1960), pp. 79–80.
[A brief biographical note accompanies the text of *Strife*.]

2014 Tarselius, Rut. "You Dance a Treat," ACTA UNIVERSITATIS

STOCKHOLMIENSIS (Stockholm Studies in Modern Philology), nsI (1960), 132–34.
[JG's use of the phrase "a treat" is referred to.]

2015 Žiak, D. "Galsworthyho *Tmavy kvet*" (Galsworthy's *Dark Flower*), PRÁCA, (Bratislava), 26 August 1960, [n.p.] [not seen]. [In Slovene.]

1961

2016 Bednár, Alfonz. "Doslov" (Epilogue), *Moderná Komédia (Modern Comedy)* (Bratislava, 1961, 1970), pp. 821–84 [not seen]. [Afterword to *A Modern Comedy.*] [In Czech.]

2017 Choudhuri, A. D. GALSWORTHY'S PLAYS: A CRITICAL SURVEY (Calcutta: Orient Longmans, 1961).
Characteristic aspects of JG's novels are humane treatment of human psychology, poetic fancy, tact, and subtlety. His dramatic world is "colored in a grey monotone" because of emphasis on naked realism, where society takes the place of the Greek Nemesis. Rejection of noble and spiritual aspirations and the subconscious aspect of life combined with the absence of the comic spirit limits JG's artistic scope. His earnestness begets monotony and gloom; his sentimentality occasionally cloys. Although he analyzes the structure of modern society, he seldom goes beneath the surface. His early dramas are characterized by articulate craftsmanship; but in his later plays JG became more amorphous, while at the same time he began to compromise his social criticism. Throughout his dramas the dialogue, in "complete harmony" with characterization, is written with a remarkable precision and presents colloquial English at its best. Dramatic irony is often present. While JG does not have the intellectual vitality of Shaw, his "keen sensibility and delicacy of observation" demonstrate a good grasp of modern society, of the architectural quality of dramatic craftsmanship, and of moral vitality. [Choudhuri discusses JG's dramas thematically in two lengthy chapters: "Social Problems" (*The Silver Box, Strife, Justice, The Foundations, The Skin Game, The Forest, Exiled*) and "Society and the Individual" (*The Eldest Son, The Mob, Old English, A Family Man, Loyalties, The Show, Escape*). The brief chapter "A Variety of Playlets" (*The Little Dream, The First and Last, The Little Man, Hall-Marked, Defeat, The Sun, Punch and Go*) emphasizes JG's whimsicality, "charity of humour," and technical experimentation. Choudhuri's discussion, synthesizing plot summary and critical comment, is one of the most copious commentaries available—though occasionally repetitious and with touches of dissertationese. The biographical chapter "The Journey" gives no new insight into JG's life and works; the discursive twenty-eight-page chapter

"Galsworthy, Shaw and Barker" has so little information about JG (and much of that is repetitious) that it is hard to justify inclusion in the study. An appendix, "Contemporary Theatre-Climate," surveys briefly the significant movements of late nineteenth- and early twentieth-century drama.]

> **2018** Ford, Boris (ed). THE MODERN AGE. THE PELICAN GUIDE TO ENGLISH LITERATURE, Vol. VII (Harmondsworth: Penguin Books, 1961; 2nd ed, 1963; rev ed, 1964), pp. 60, 61, 212, 216, 257, 258, 284, 372, 539.

[Passing references to JG, indebted to the strictures of Virginia Woolf and D. H. Lawrence, q.v.]

> **2019** Garnett, David. "Some Writers I Have Known: Galsworthy, Forster, Moore, and Wells," TEXAS QUARTERLY, IV (Autumn 1961), 190–202; rptd with slight modifications as "E. M. Forster and Galsworthy," REVIEW OF ENGLISH LITERATURE (Leeds), V (Jan 1964), 7–18.

As a person JG had little humor, tried very hard, and "was rather rigid, with good intentions." He was not subtle and naturally disliked anything equivocal. He loved dogs but preferred to idealize women. Both Forster and JG appealed to the intelligentsia because they "attacked British complacency, smugness, conventionality, respectability, and love of money." JG was an angry young man whose writing declined in quality when his father died and he could marry Ada, his cousin's wife. JG surveyed his own class in *The Island Pharisees* and found them wanting. His best book is *The Man of Property,* and the character of Bosinney in it is modelled upon Edward Garnett [author's father]. Edward Garnett, who was the first unconventional and unambitious Englishman whom JG "got to know well," was JG's mentor, and it was his objection to Bosinney's suicide that resulted in JG's changing the incident in the novel. In *A Country House* JG fell in love with his own class in the person of Mrs. Pendyce. Although Courtier in *The Patrician* was modelled on H. W. Nevinson, the character is unreal. After his marriage when he was no longer an angry, bitter young man, he could no longer do first-rate work. There will in all likelihood be a revival of interest in JG's novels, as there was a Trollope revival in the 1930s; "the Forsytes will soon acquire a period charm." People like "bad novels," and they like characters that reappear in several novels.

> **2020** Hallman, Ralph J. PSYCHOLOGY OF LITERATURE: A STUDY OF ALIENATION AND TRAGEDY (NY: Philosophical Library, 1961), pp. 188–92.

The irony in *Justice* is that law, the force that sustains Falder economically, destroys his chances for freedom. Desiring to assert himself, Falder rebels, consequently yielding his freedom. His tragedy is his belief in eternal and fixed laws. Falder's noble and "sacred" love for Mrs. Honeywill impels him to action and thus to defeat, which arises from his need to violate conventional norms. When Falder realizes after his prison sentence that his "sacred love" is a common prostitute, he knows that life has no meaning. Falder needs "personal law," capable of mercy, but he gets nothing but abstract law, personified by the judge who believes that justice to mankind has been achieved. [Hallman uses his discussion of *Justice*, which concludes a chapter entitled "Freedom: The Great Deception," to prove the point made in the title of the chapter.]

2021 Harding, Joan N. "John Galsworthy and the Just Man," CONTEMPORARY REVIEW (Lond), CXCIX (April 1961), 198–203.
JG's novels and plays give essentially the same view of human nature, in which man is perhaps best described as a "litigious creature," dominated by a "will to survival which is indivisible from the will to power"—with a self-interest, however, in a system that ostensibly tries to protect the weak from the strong. On the whole JG's characters are interested in the "orthodox machinery of the law in action, and the results it produces." In the various lawsuits, JG shows both the active and the passive sides of arbitration. The just man in JG is he who, perhaps like young Jolyon (*A Modern Comedy*) can find a "zest in living for its own sake without any ulterior expectation, and accepting his fellow-beings as they are." JG suggests that modern man's "will to love" is being sapped by repudiation of faith and "the surfeiting of his appetite by material acquisitions." JG in his last trilogy (*The End of the Chapter*) seems to suggest that the discipline of a belief, in this case Catholicism, is necessary.

2022 Karl, Frederick R[obert]. A READER'S GUIDE TO THE CONTEMPORARY ENGLISH NOVEL (NY: Farrar, Straus & Giroux, 1961, 1962, 1971; rev ed, 1972) pp. 4, 63, 83, 146, 313.
C. P. Snow follows JG in technique and manner and in use of the novel for moral comment.

2023 Khoshimukhamedova, I. O. "O nekotorykh osobennostiakh frazeologii v romane Golsuorsi *Sobstvennik*" (Certain Phraseological Peculiarities in Galsworthy's Novel *The Man of Property*), UCHENYE ZAPISKI, SERIIA FILOLOGICHESKAIA (Dushanbe: Gosudarstvennyi pedagogicheskii institut), XXIX:13 (1961), 114–20 [not seen].
[In Russian.]

2024 Masur, Gerhard. "Culture and Society," PROPHETS OF YESTERDAY (NY: Macmillan, 1961; Lond: Weidenfeld & Nicholson, 1963), pp. 237, 240, 245–49, 250.
JG's main aim is to portray English society, not to solve problems or to "provoke immediate reforms." [Primarily a brief sociological look at *The Forsyte Saga*, with an intriguing comment about Irene's beauty: she is "as much a child of the bourgeoisie as is Soames. . . . she lives by means of her beauty as others live by means of their work or their wit." The thought is not developed.]

2025 Priestley, J. B. "I Had the Time. . . . The Great Panjandrums," SUNDAY TIMES (Lond), Magazine section, 2 July 1961, pp. 21–22.

The great panjandrums of the 1920s were Shaw, Wells, and Bennett. Charles Evans of Heinemann was in all probability the man responsible for JG's getting the Order of Merit and the Nobel Prize, for it was Evans "who thought of reprinting several Galsworthy novels in one volume and calling it *The Forsyte Saga.* It was no more a saga than its author was a Norse pirate." [Personal reminiscences concerning Wells, Bennett, Shaw, JG, and Hugh Walpole.]

2026 Rein, David M. " 'The Apple Tree' and the Student Reader," CEA CRITIC, XXIII (1961), iii, 10–11.
Students react favorably to this story because they associate with Ashurst. They recognize and accept his rejection of Megan and his subsequent marriage as a necessary, realistic compromise of a romantic ideal.

2027 Shanthaveerappa, S. N. "A Critique of *The Silver Box,*" HALF-YEARLY JOURNAL OF THE MYSORE UNIVERSITY (Mysore), XX (March 1961), 39–45.
[Conventional criticism is presented in a negative and poorly written and constructed essay.]

2028 Weales, Gerald. RELIGION IN MODERN BRITISH DRAMA (Phila: University of Pennsylvania P, 1961), pp. 16–17, 46, 51, 52–53, 54, 280, 281, 283.
JG liked to create a character embodying "Christian charity and to examine the consequences." Cases in point are (1) *The Pigeon,* where a befriended wastrel comments: "I saw well from the first that you are no Christian. You have so kind a face"; and (2) *The Little Man,* which approaches the theme of the fool as Christ. In *The Little Dream,* the soul searches a mystery that it cannot understand and which perhaps does not exist. *A Bit o' Love* attempts to "grasp an essentially amorphous idea of love and religion" that, although sounding Christian at times, seems to reject Christianity. In *Strife* and *Justice,* which are "more ethical than mystical," JG shows man's potential in a negative way.

2029 Zhukova, L. K. "K voprosu o frazeologicheskikh razobshcheniiakh v romane Golsuorsi *Belaia obez'iana* (Sokr. doklad na I Mezhdurespb. konferentsii po voprosam frazeologii). Sent. 1959 g." (Phraseological Dissociations in Galsworthy's Novel *The White Monkey:* Brief Report at the First Inter-Republican Conference on Problems of Phraseology. September, 1959), TRUDY (Samarkand. Universitet), No. 106 (1961), 207–12 [not seen].
[In Russian.]

1962

2030 Bobyleva, L. K. "O nekotorykh formakh epiteta v iazyke Golsuorsi" (On Certain Forms of Epithet in J. Galsworthy's Language), UCHENYE ZAPISKI (Vladivostok: Dal'nevostochnyi gosudarstvennyi universitet), No. 5 (1962), 99–105 [not seen].
[In Russian.]

2031 Croft-Cooke, Rupert. "Grove Lodge," CORNHILL MAGAZINE, No. 1033 (Autumn 1962), 50–59.
[The author wrote JG asking for guidance and certainty (see F. B. Adams, "A Letter from John Galsworthy," 1934). JG in his reply attempted to explain certain aspects of his philosophy (see F. B. Adams). In this article Croft-Cooke summarizes his personal reminiscences of his annual tea with the Galsworthys at Grove Lodge. At their first meeting the author noticed that Lubbock's CRAFT OF FICTION was beside JG, and they discussed Lubbock's work. JG was quite enthusiastic about Belloc's work. The occasions were quite formal, and despite his efforts to unbend, JG remained rather stiff and reserved. Mrs. Galsworthy's charm helped relieve the strain. Croft-Cooke's discovery "that four out of five parts of *The Forsyte Saga* and a great many of the short stories end with a line of metrically faultness blank verse" (count only the last ten syllables) caused JG some dismay. JG remarked that he had written these lines unconsciously. "It is noteworthy that none of the five parts of *A Modern Comedy* on which he was working, ends with a line of blank verse."]

2032 Elektorowicz, Leszek. "Galsworthy jako nowelista" (Galsworthy as a Short Story Writer), ŻYCIE LITERACKIE (Cracow), No. 34 (1962), 5 [not seen].
[In Polish.]

2033 Fisher, John C. "Mythical Concepts in 'The Apple Tree,'" COLLEGE ENGLISH, XXIII (May 1962), 655–56.
In "The Apple Tree" JG successfully fuses images into symbols "for the opposition of pagan and Christian myths." Megan as Aphrodite's handmaiden represents pagan myth, and gold, a favorite color of Aphrodite, is used frequently throughout the story. Silver is the symbol for Stella (chastity, Artemis), and she rescues Ashurst from a "pagan love." Ashurst is not able to break completely with Megan, Aphrodite's handmaiden, until his swim out to sea when he realizes that "the red cliffs symbolize . . . distance from shore, and fertility."

2034 Jovanović, Slobodan A. TRI OGLEDA: IBSEN, GALSWORTHY, COLETTE (Three Essays: Ibsen, Galsworthy, Colette) (Kruševac: Bajdala, 1962), pp. 29–68 [not seen].
[In Serbo-Croatian.]

2035 Knight, G. Wilson. THE GOLDEN LABYRINTH (NY: Norton, 1962; Lond: Phoenix House, 1962; Lond: Methuen, 1965), pp. 119, 309, 321, 336.

JG's plays preserve with integrity the major dramatic instinct to accept and balance opposites and to work with the theme of justice in a properly judicial tone.

2036 Mirković, Ljiljana. "Pogovor" (Afterword), *Vila Rubein (Villa Rubein)*, trans by Aleksandar Kostić (Belgrade: Narodna knjiga, 1962), pp. 181–87 [not seen].
[In Serbo-Croatian.]

2037 Molkhova, Zhana. "Galeriiata na Forsaitovtsi" (The Gallery of the Forsytes), RODNA RECH, X (1962), 28–32 [not seen].
[Literary and critical sketch of *The Forsyte Saga.*] [In Bulgarian.]

2038 Molkhova, Zhana. "Observations on the Language and Style of John Galsworthy. *The Forsyte Saga* and *A Modern Comedy,* Part I," ANNUAIRE. SOFIA UNIVERSITET. FILOLOGICHESKI FACULTET, V, Book 2 (1962), 719–82.
[Résumé and bibliography.] [In Bulgarian.]

2039 Pira, Gisela. "The Juryman (Versuch einer Interpretation)" ("The Juryman" [A Proposed Interpretation]), DIE NEUEREN SPRACHEN, nsXI (April 1962), 164–68.

JG deviates from the classical form of the short story in "The Juryman" by emphasizing " 'the living moment' " and by giving to the story a conclusion that points into the future. Through the deserter, Mr. Bosengate perceives his own incompleteness in his life and marriage. The first phase of the story ends with Bosengate's "I must go to work" and his wife's "And I to weep." Clearly, man is bound to his fellowman, and without this relationship life is empty. The second phase shows the vain heart conquering its own weakness. By understanding the deserter's reasons, Bosengate gains new insight into his own heart. Although he fails to convey these feelings to his wife, he has discovered a greater significance to his own life. [In German.]

2040 Pira, Gisela. "Ultima Thule (Versuch einer Interpretation)" (Ultima Thule [Attempt at an Analysis]), DIE NEUEREN SPRACHEN, XI (1962), 521–23.

The story dramatizes the conflict between the normal and the ideal world. The genuine Ultima Thule dies with Thompson. [In German.]

2041 Styan, J. L. THE DARK COMEDY (Lond: Cambridge UP, 1962; 2nd ed rev, 1968), p. 125.

Unlike the dialectal plays of Shaw, JG's drama satisfies the playgoer's conscience with his treatment of theme.

2042 Tewari, R. L. A CRITICAL STUDY OF LOYALTIES (GALSWORTHY) (Moussoorie, India: Saraswati Sudan, 1962).
JG's basic qualities as a dramatist are naturalism, objectivity, sympathy, deep reverence for all of life, impartiality, and irony. His forte as a dramatist is characterization—primarily by assigning to each a "dominant idea" and by creating dramatic conflict. The theme of *Loyalties* is "casteism," with each character a "perfect egoist," disregarding others. JG does not have faith in the "efficacy of politics"; and he believes that organized religion is useless. Like Shaw, JG is antiromantic, mystical, and realistic; they differ in that, where Shaw is intellectual, JG is "analytic and synthetic." [The bulk of Tewari's work, designed for "degree and post-graduate classes" in Indian universities, consists largely of plot summary and character study without psychological depth. Introductory chapters on characteristics of twentieth-century drama, JG's life, and summaries of JG plays follow the general pattern of study guides designed for uninspired undergraduates.]

2043 Zhantevoi, D. "Vstup. stat'ia" (Introduction), *Dzhon Golsuorsi: Sobranie Sochinenii* (John Galsworthy: Collected Works), trans and ed by M. Lorie. Sixteen volumes (Moscow: Pravda, 1962), I, 3–30.
[In Russian.]

2044 Zhantieva, D. "O Golsuorsi-Kritike" (On Galsworthy as a Critic), INOSTRANNAIA LITERATURA (Moscow), No. 7 (1962), 196–97 [not seen].
[In Russian.]

1963

2045 Barker, Dudley. THE MAN OF PRINCIPLE: A VIEW OF JOHN GALSWORTHY (Lond: Heinemann, 1961); rptd (NY: Stein & Day, 1963, 1969).
[This volume reconsiders JG's life and his achievements as a writer. Its greatest value derives from the many details, e.g., the name of JG's first love, Sybil Carr; these details make possible a fuller knowledge of his life. The book displays a definite animus against Ada Galsworthy.] Ada became a woman who was "self-centered, possessive and impatient of others"; she became increasingly neurotic, and she used her hypochondria and her insistence upon extensive traveling as ways of escaping from society. JG's rebellion against the moneyed class was not a true rebellion; he would not have been a rebel if his own class had not cast Ada out. [Barker's description of Professor Stone's masterpiece in *Fraternity* as a "masterpiece of satiric philosophy" is misleading.] When JG added "Indian Summer of a Forsyte" to *The Man of Property,* he betrayed his

own purpose by blunting the satire and giving a "happy" ending to the Forsyte story. With *In Chancery* JG changed in attitude from an animosity toward the Forsytes to a "gentle anger." His career as an important writer ended with the death of Soames Forsyte.

2046 Berezowski, Maksymilian. "Najniebezpieczniejszy człowiek Anglii" (The Most Dangerous Man in England), TRYBUNA LUDU (Warsaw), No. 110 (1963), [n.p.] [not seen].
[In Polish.]

2047 Blanke, Gustav H. "Aristokratie und Gentleman im Englischen und Amerikanischen Roman des 19. und 20. Jahrhunderts" (The Aristocracy and the Gentleman in English and American Novels in the Nineteenth and Twentieth Centuries), GERMANISCH-ROMANTISCHE MONATSSCHRIFT, nsXIII (July 1963), 281–306.
[There are several references to JG, H. G. Wells, and D. H. Lawrence concerning the new social movements in late nineteenth- and early twentieth-century England: the new concern with the middle class and the class consciousness of the upper class.] [In German.]

2048 Borinski, Ludwig. "Galsworthys *Forsyte Saga*" (Galsworthy's Forsyte Saga), MEISTER DES MODERNEN ENGLISCHEN ROMANS (MASTERS OF THE MODERN ENGLISH NOVEL) (Heidelberg: Quelle & Meyer, 1963), 82–105, et passim.
[Concentrates on the social background of the novels and emphasizes JG's atmospheric descriptions, his use of the interior monologue, and the vagueness of his world view.] [In German.]

2049 Christian, R. F. "An Unpublished Letter by Maksim Gor'ky," SLAVONIC AND EAST EUROPEAN REVIEW, XLII (Dec 1963), 189–90.
[Reprints a letter by Gorky giving a delayed and graciously negative response to JG's invitation to visit London for a P.E.N. award and welcome. The letter is in the University of Birmingham collection.]

2050 Currie, A. W. "The Vancouver Coal Mining Company. A Source for Galsworthy's *Strife*," QUEEN'S QUARTERLY (Ottawa), LXX (Spring 1963), 50–63.
JG's grandfather was an original investor in the Vancouver Coal Mining Company, and JG's father played an active role in its operation. Parallels with *Strife:* John Anthony acts much like JG's father; directors are preoccupied with shares and payment of dividends. [The essay is primarily a detailed study of the activities of JG's father in the affairs of the coal mining company.]

2051 Elektorowicz, Leszek. "Wstęp" (Introduction), *Karawana* (*Caravan*), trans into Polish by Izabela Czermakowa and Wanda Kra-

gen (Poznań: Wydawnictwo Poznańskie, 1963; 2nd ed, 1966), [n.p.] [not seen].
[In Polish.]

2052 Fricker, Robert. "John Galsworthy: *Justice,*" in Horst Oppel (ed.), DAS MODERNE ENGLISCHE DRAMA: INTERPRETATIONEN (Berlin: Erich Schmidt, 1963; 2nd ed rev, 1966), 107–23.
[This thorough and important analysis of the play as a study of human justice and as a tragedy praises the effectiveness of JG's rhetoric of understatement but is aware of his limitations as a playwright.] [In German.]

2053 Gupta, Prakash Chandra. THE ART OF GALSWORTHY AND OTHER STUDIES (Allahabad, India: Vidyarthi Granthagar, [1963?]), pp. 1–74.
JG's work has two contending strains: social criticism and lyric creation of beauty. While they worked well together early, the lyrical aspect gained the upper hand. *Villa Rubein* is the first novel containing the distinctive JG themes of "a haunting sense of the beauty of nature" and "love entering . . . the world of philistinism and throwing it into turmoil and disorder." *The Island Pharisees,* in the writing of which JG underwent his period of severest literary training, opened his war on the gods of property. The war continued in *The Man of Property.* Whereas the waters of *The Forsyte Saga* are deep and turbulent, the waters of *A Modern Comedy* are more "bubble and froth": JG's mature, impressionistic technique makes more effective the picture of the inconsequences and restlessness of modernity. JG is at his best in describing youthful passion.

JG's plays have a "pretence of judicial impassivity" with too much reserve and understatement—too many tones of grey in the sad spectacle of life. JG, like Ibsen and Shaw, uses the drama to criticize middle-class life. In *The Skin Game,* sympathy is with the dying upper middle class. Especial concerns are the contrast of old aristocracy and the new rich (*The Skin Game, Loyalties*), and the individual victims of social tyranny (*The Mob, The Foundations, A Bit o' Love*). Distinct character types can be seen in Builder, Barthwick, Bastaple, Strood, Strangway, and Clare Desmond. His plays are built on common incidents; his dialogue is clever; he is a master at presenting crowds on the stage; and his dramatic tone is that of a "pervasive sense of pity and indignation."

JG's short stories, characterized by a sense of brooding and introspection and written with economy and restraint, deal with basic aspects of life such as love, hate, beauty, war, and hunger.

The critical writings demonstrate an Epicureanism, with vision and balance. All art must have a "spire of meaning"—a social and moral purpose. But this purpose must not be superimposed—it must grow organically. JG's method is to present life and character, without fear or prejudice. Vitality of life and of art is of great importance; but he does not practice art for the sake of experiment. [Gupta's most important contribution in the four chapters devoted to JG is the one entitled "The Aesthetics of Galsworthy," which quotes significant passages from JG's critical and aesthetic writings and attempts to put his work into aesthetic perspective. The other three chapters, devoted to the novel, play, and short story, are filled with commonplace JG criticism. The study is full of typographical errors and is poorly organized, especially chaps 1–3.]

2054 Lawrence, T. E. TO HIS BIOGRAPHERS, ed by Robert Graves and Liddell Hart (NY: Doubleday, 1963), I, 144.

[JG is included in a list of Lawrence's preferences in reading, a group of authors whom Lawrence calls "easy men."]

2055 Pędziński, Zbigniew. "Epik zdejmuje maske" (An Epic Writer Takes Off His Mask), TYGODNIK KULTURALNY (Warsaw), No. 19 (1963), [n.p.] [not seen].

[Review of Polish edition of *Caravan*.] [In Polish.]

2056 Pilashevskaia, E. "Obraznye frazeologizmy o romane Golsuorsi *Sobstvennik*" (Figurative Phraseologisms in Galsworthy's Novel *The Man of Property*), UCHENYE ZAPISKI (Kishinev. Universitet), L (1963), 27–37 [not seen].

[In Russian.]

2057 Pritchett, V. S. "Sensitive Toff," NEW STATESMAN, LXV (22 Feb 1963), 273–74.

[In what is nominally a review of Dudley Barker, MAN OF PRINCIPLE (Lond: Heinemann, 1963), Pritchett focuses on what for him is the essential JG, who "slaved away, like a Forsyte at the office, until he attained a non-stop facility which was his personal triumph and, in the end, his downfall." His weaknesses fitted him for the stage: "his simple, sentimental view of the class situation, his feeling for moral melodrama, his eye for the short scene, his topical sense of justice and reformist temper made acceptable by dialogue done in off-hand remarks. . . . Actors gave life to what, in his novels, was really lifeless." In *The Forsyte Saga* Irene is in effect a victim who illustrates the preceding comments. JG was a gentle and "moral toff" to the end.]

2058 Roberts, Sir Syndey Castle. EDWARDIAN RETROSPECT (Lond: Oxford UP, 1963), pp. 9–10.

[Overview of the Edwardian age that emphasizes JG's humorless dedication to drama portraying poverty, unemployment, and the struggle of the underdog in such works as *The Silver Box, Strife,* and *Justice.*]

2059 Stevens, Earl E. "A Study of the Structure of John Galsworthy's *The Forsyte Saga,*" DISSERTATION ABSTRACTS, XXIV (1963), 2489.

Unpublished dissertation, University of North Carolina (Chapel Hill), 1963.

2060 Swinnerton, Frank. FIGURES IN THE FOREGROUND: LITERARY REMINISCENCES, 1917–1940 (Lond: Hutchison, 1963; Garden City, NY: Doubleday, 1964) rptd (Freeport, NY: Books for Libraries P, 1970), pp. 16, 24, 26, 27, 35, 36, 46, 75, 103, 148, 154, 158, 168, 192, 252, 259. JG said all he had to say in the novel form in *The Man of Property;* he did not allow his characters to grow or to change. Virginia Woolf's reference to JG as " 'that stark man' shows ignorance" that could have been corrected had Woolf's contacts with men of letters been wider. [Passing references to JG.]

2061 Turapina, E. N., and R. G. Borisova. "Sravnitel'nyi analiz perevodov nekotorykh frazeologicheskikh edinits s angliiskogo iazyka na russkii po romanu Dzh. Golsuorsi *Sobstvennik"* (Comparative Analysis of Translations of Certain Phraseological Units from English into Russian Based on J. Galsworthy's Novel *The Man of Property*), UCHENYE ZAPISKI (Kuibyshev. Gosudarstvennyi pedagogisheskii institut), No. 43 (1963), 169–87 [not seen]. [In Russian.]

2062 Wilson, Asher Boldon, Jr. "John Galsworthy's Letters to Leon Lion," DISSERTATION ABSTRACTS, XXIII (1963), 4366. Unpublished dissertation, Stanford University, 1962. Pub as JOHN GALSWORTHY'S LETTERS TO LEON LION (The Hague: Mouton, 1968; Atlantic Highlands, NJ: Humanities P, 1968), q.v.

2063 Zaworska, Helena. ". . . lubujemy się skrycie w romantyce?" (. . . Do We Secretly Enjoy Romanticism?) NOWE KSIĄŻKI (Warsaw), No. 11 (1963), 557–58 [not seen]. [Review of *Caravan.*] [In Polish.]

1964

2064 Allen, Walter. TRADITION AND DREAM: THE ENGLISH AND AMERICAN NOVEL FROM THE TWENTIES TO OUR TIME (Lond: Phoenix House, 1964); pub in the United States as THE MODERN NOVEL IN BRITAIN AND THE UNITED STATES (NY: E. P. Dutton, 1964; Harmondsworth: Penguin, 1965), pp. 1, 71. JG's best work was done before 1914.

2065 Bartholomew, Raymond E. "The Tooth of Time: John Galsworthy's Critical Reputation." Unpublished dissertation, Western Reserve University, 1964.
[Listed in COMPREHENSIVE DISSERTATION INDEX: 1861–1972 (Ann Arbor: Xerox University Microfilms, 1973), XXIX, 535.]

2066 Day, Martin S. HISTORY OF ENGLISH LITERATURE. 1837 TO THE PRESENT (Garden City, NY: Doubleday, 1964), pp. 285–86, 367–68.
[This college course guide gives brief plots and statements of theme for five plays and summarizes the plots of *The Forsyte Saga*. No critical insight.]

2067 Duncan, Barry. THE ST. JAMES'S THEATRE: ITS STRANGE AND COMPLETE HISTORY: 1835–1957 (Lond: Barrie & Rockliff, 1964), pp. 219, 288, 310.
[Mentions in passing that JG's *The Silver Box* was in the repertory of 1913, and that in 1929 *The Skin Game* transferred from Wyndham's to St. James's with Edmund Gwenn and Mabel Terry-Lewis in starring roles.]

2068 Fricker, Robert. DAS MODERNE ENGLISCHE DRAMA (Modern English Drama) (Goettingen: Vandenhoeck & Ruprecht, 1964), pp. 26–29.
JG's plays present problems clearly and implicitly offer solutions. They were effective in their time but seem to date quickly. Exceptions are *Justice, Loyalties,* and *The Pigeon.* [In German.]

2069 Hampden, John (ed). "*The Silver Box,*" MODERN PLAY SERIES (Lond: Duckworth, 1964), pp. 84–104.
[Hampden emphasizes the revolutionary and "often resented" aspect of the play of ideas, the type JG writes. Brief biographical note precedes *The Silver Box,* which in turn is followed by a series of questions.]

2070 Ku[likowska], K[rystyna]. "Frajer *Gołębie serce*" (Frajer, *The Dove's Heart* [*The Pigeon*]), RADIO I TELEWIZJA, (Warsaw), No. 5 (1964) [n.p.] [not seen].
[Review of the Polish Television Theater production of *The Pigeon.*] [In Polish.]

2071 Nowell-Smith, Simon Harcourt (ed). EDWARDIAN ENGLAND, 1901–1914 (Lond: Oxford UP, 1964), pp. 98, 134, 141, 309–10, 315, 395, 396–97, 402, 405.
[Passing references to JG in political, economic, and literary contexts. No critical comment.]

2072 Petrović, Miluton. "Golsvordi kao pripovedać" (Galsworthy Story Writer), ZBORNIK FILOZOFSKOG FAKULTETA U PRIŠTINI, II (1964–65), 279–85 [not seen].
[In Serbo-Croatian with an English summary.]

2073 Pritchett, V[ictor] S[awdon]. "The Forsytes," THE LIVING NOVEL AND LATER APPRECIATIONS (NY: Random House, 1964), pp. 282–88.

JG's imagination was lukewarm: he gave thumbnail sketches of people with "jog-trot realism"—always blurring things when a question of feeling arose. JG codified the English: property is the English passion—inconvenient emotions were controlled by convention. He rebelled from his own class for chivalric rather than deeply principled reasons. But he was (after the scandal with Ada had died down) indignant about cruelty within the system. The Soames–Irene–Bosinney triangle in *The Man of Property* indicates JG's sentimental "high-minded evasion of facts" and his unwillingness to face the deeper consequences of this evasion. JG was most fitted for the stage, because actors could give life to his lifeless writing. JG was an ingenious theatrical craftsman, hitting upon the idiom of his era.

2074 Scrimgeour, Gary J. "Naturalist Drama and Galsworthy," MODERN DRAMA, VII (May 1964), 65–78.

JG's desire to reflect contemporary life on the stage has defeated his prospects for permanence. There are a number of weaknesses in his work that explain why he has failed to win "an enduring audience for his plays": (1) he owed too much to his predecessors; (2) he was uneasy with symbolism; (3) his method of dramatic compactness depended "on common signals no longer received by the audience"; (4) his drama is trapped in staginess; and (5) his philosophy is "trapped in dubious theory."

2075 Waugh, Evelyn. "Introduction," *The Man of Property,* illus by Charles Mozley (NY: Limited Editions Club, 1964), pp. v–viii; rptd in *The Man of Property* (NY: Heritage P, 1964).

Gilbert Murray's comment to JG in a 1922 letter discussing *The Forsyte Saga*—"I believe you have a queer poetical method which simulates realism in order to attain beauty"—contains "profound criticism." In *The Man of Property,* the "old or middle-aged" characters of 1886 were seen with JG's nineteen-year-old perception and "described sixteen years later when they have become the embodiment of the frustration of his [JG's] love." The Forsyte's obsession with "urban commercial matters" and with Soames's house—he builds "an expensive villa in the purlieus of London on a modest plot of ground which he does not even freehold"—does not ring true. *Property,* written in the "heyday of security . . . is a tragedy in the Greek fashion where Nemesis is inescapable, and Nemesis is property itself." The novel ends as it does because JG "had set out to write a tragedy, not a comedy of manners. The victims had to be duly sacrificed . . . to . . . the ineluctable God of . . . [JG's] creation—Forsyteism. . . . That was the law of life as [he] . . . saw it in the harrowing uncertainties" of his nine-year ordeal with Ada and the unsympathetic Galsworthy family. In other matters, Bosinney is guilty of professional impropriety; JG's fairness of mind is evident in the judge's summing up; and the principle theme of *Property* is the "representation of a class." [Waugh's short essay is more intriguing and stimulating than fully developed. Its primary value is in refocusing attention on Gilbert Murray's perceptive comment and on opening to reconsideration the interrelationship between JG's life and Soames's travail.]

2076 Wierzewski, Wojciech. "Frajer *Gołebie serce"* (Frajer, *The Dove's Heart* [*The Pigeon*]), EKRAN (Warsaw), No. 5 (1964), 14 [not seen].
[Review of the Polish Television Theater production of *The Pigeon.*] [In Polish.]

1965

2077 Campos, Christophe. THE VIEW OF FRANCE FROM ARNOLD TO BLOOMSBURY (Lond: Oxford, 1965), pp. 10, 205, 207, 239.
Though JG was steeped in a French atmosphere, he did not describe France. French colloquial phrases are "sprinkled" through JG's novels by "aristocrats, artists, and lovers," especially in *Villa Rubein, To Let,* and *The Dark Flower.* Irene in *The Forsyte Saga* goes to Paris to free herself from moral ties.

2078 Carlson, Marvin. "A Selected Bibliography of Bibliographies," MODERN DRAMA, VIII (May 1965), 114.
[Two bibliographies of JG are listed: H. V. Marrot, A BIBLIOGRAPHY OF THE WORKS OF JOHN GALSWORTHY and Alice Thurston McGirr, "Reading List on John Galsworthy," BULLETIN OF BIBLIOGRAPHY, VII (1913), 113–15.]

2079 Chiari, J. LANDMARKS OF CONTEMPORARY DRAMA (Lond: Herbert Jenkins, 1965), p. 31.
Followers of Beckett, Brecht, and Porter in the 1960s who rely primarily on mood and social excitement as ways for creating drama are in effect going back to the naturalism of JG, Zola, and Becque.

2080 Chmelová, Elena. "Doslov" (Epilogue), *Koniec Kapitoly* (*The Man of Property*) (Bratislava, 1965, 1971), [n.p.] [not seen].
[In Czech.]

2081 Dillenbeck, Marsden V., and Marian L. Warren (eds). *The Man of Property and Indian Summer of a Forsyte.* (NY: Charles Scribner's Sons, 1965), pp. ix–xiii, 361–430.
[Introduction and study guide contain critical comment and apparatus adapted for use in secondary school teaching.]

2082 Dreyer, Artur E. *"Gesellschaft* von John Galsworthy" *(Loyalties* by John Galsworthy) ZENTRALBLATT FUR GESAMTE FORSTWESEN (Wien), X (1965–66), 183–84 [not seen].
[Elusive citation listed in INTERNATIONALE BIBLIOGRAPHIE DER ZEITSCHRIFTEN-LITERATUR (Leipzig: Felix Dietrich, 1967).] [In German.]

2083 Gordan, John Dozier. "An Anniversary Exhibition. The Henry W. and Albert A. Berg Collection 1940–1965, Part II," BULLETIN OF THE NEW YORK PUBLIC LIBRARY, LXIX (Nov 1965), 597–608.
[A biographical headnote accompanies announcement of a corrected typescript of *Escape*. In the Berg Collection there are some two dozen MSS and typescripts of plays and novels; in addition, there are about 120 letters.]

2084 Gordan, John Dozier. "Novels in Manuscript: An Exhibition from the Berg Collection, Part II," BULLETIN OF THE NEW YORK PUBLIC LIBRARY, LXIX (June 1965), 396–413.
[A brief biographical note, pp. 402–3, announces the display of a corrected typescript of *The Country House.*]

2085 Hagopian, John V., and Martin Dolch (eds). INSIGHT II: ANALYSES OF MODERN BRITISH LITERATURE (Frankfurt Am Main: Hirschgraben-Verlag, 1965), pp. 141–47.
[Includes a discussion of JG's *The Skin Game,* which is abstracted separately under the author's name (1965): Arvin R. Wells.]

2086 Molkhova, Zh. "S predg" (Foreword), *Sobstvenikut (The Man of Property)*, trans by Neviana Rozeva (Sofia: Narodna Kultura, 1965), [n.p.] [not seen].
[In Bulgarian.]

2087 Ross, Robert H. THE GEORGIAN REVOLT, 1910–1922: RISE AND FALL OF THE POETIC IDEAL (Carbondale: Southern Illinois UP, 1965), pp. vii, 4, 7, 8, 9, 81.
[Passing references of no critical significance.]

2088 Wells, Arvin R. *"The Skin Game,"* INSIGHT II: ANALYSES OF MODERN BRITISH LITERATURE, ed by John V. Hagopian and Martin Dolch (Frankfurt Am Main: Hirschgraben-Verlag, 1965), pp. 142–47.
JG's work relies on sociological realism to depict the society of the late Victorian and Edwardian periods. For the most part his work is dated, as can be seen in *The Skin Game:* the dialogue is commonplace; the characters are blatant social types; and the primitive dramatic machinery is adequate to sociological truth. JG used the literary convention that the gentleman's lady (Mrs. Hillcrist) is more realistic and ruthless than the gentleman. [Followed by questions and explanations for students.]

1966

2089 Chichirin, A. V. "Cennost' *Forsaitskogo* cikla" (The Value of *The Forsyte Chronicles*), IZVESTIIA AKADEMII NAUK S.S.S.R.: OTDELENIE LITERATURY I JAZYKA (Moscow), XXV (1966), 481–88 [not seen].
On the basis of a careful examination and study of JG's major works, especially the two Forsyte trilogies which make up *The Forsyte Chronicles*, one discovers that JG did not personify abstract categories or defend the bourgeois world. Instead, he gave in *Chronicles* (they make up the "epic novel of English critical realism") "a complete, realistic depiction of the 40-year flowering and decline of the proprietary (free-enterprise) ideology in England." [Based on the abstract, no. 2195, found in ABSTRACTS OF ENGLISH STUDIES, XI (1968), 352–53.] [In Russian.]

2090 Dawood, M. K. "John Galsworthy, A Study of His Plays." Unpublished dissertation, Trinity (Dublin), 1966.
[Listed in Lawrence F. McNamee, DISSERTATIONS IN ENGLISH AND AMERICAN LITERATURE, SUPP I (NY & Lond: Bowker, 1969).]

2091 Efremova, T. Ya. "Golsuorsi i Turgenev" (Galsworthy and Turgenev), K PROBLEMAM TEORI I ISTORII LITERATURY (On Problems in Literary Theory and History) (Stavropol, 1966) [not seen].
[Listed in ANNUAL BIBLIOGRAPHY OF ENGLISH LANGUAGE AND LITERATURE, XLI (Cambridge: Modern Humanities Research Association, 1968).] [In Russian.]

2092 "The Forsytes," TIMES (Lond), 23 March 1966, p. 13.
Although *The Forsyte Saga* "is not among the great masterpieces of literature," the news that the BBC is going to televise it is pleasing. There are many who have an affection for *Saga*. The period it covers is "one of the most attractively picturesque periods of our social history," and there is an eagerness to see realized some of the memorable scenes from *Saga*.

2093 Goldberg, Jonathan J. "A Well-Arranged Museum: The World of John Galsworthy's Novels," DISSERTATION ABSTRACTS, XXVII (1966), 772A–73A. Unpublished dissertation, New York University, 1966.

2094 Hamilton, Robert. *"The Forsyte Saga,"* QUARTERLY REVIEW, CCCIV (Oct 1966), 431–41.
JG's background (Forsyte to the marrow) and his affair with Ada led him inexorably to become a great writer in the limited and personal field of Forsyteism. The quality of his character gave the patience, and his family income the

time, for JG to develop the technical mastery to become a writer. Protest against his own class softened in direct proportion as that class accepted Ada—this can be traced through the gradual change of Soames in *The Forsyte Saga. Swan Song* and the interludes "A Silent Wooing" and "Passers By" actually comprise the fourth volume of *Saga; The White Monkey* and *The Silver Spoon* are primarily separate entities. Thus *Saga* is divided into two parts: 1880–1901 and 1920–1926. Part one ends with the divorce of Soames and Irene and their later marriages to Annette and young Jolyon. Fleur's seduction of Jon at moonrise in the coppice of Robin Hill (*Swan Song*) culminates with poetic justice the act that began the whole saga: the "forcible intercourse which Fleur's father had with Jon's mother." Fleur's frustration over Jon's termination of the liaison leads to the fire in Soames's art gallery and subsequently to his death. *Saga* has many such symbolic "confidences," especially in the increasing presence of the moon symbolism.

Contrary to popular critical opinion, the younger generations of Forsytes—June and Winifred and Fleur and Jon—as well as Michael Mont, are as skillfully drawn as, if not better drawn than, the oldest generation. Soames's "clipped speech," natural for the dry and reserved person that he is, makes a virtue of the "rather flat elements of . . . [JG's] literary style" and prevents the Galsworthian sentimentality that appears in other works. Soames is a unique person in literature not because he is "great, powerful, strange, or peculiar" but because he is "himself": this JG accomplishes with "high art." While the basic tragedy of *Saga* is in family conflict, the deepest conflict lies in the "hidden egoism" of Soames and Irene: thus the "final tragedy . . . is the nemesis of pride." [Hamilton's essay is important because it is one of the few critical comments in the last two decades that attempts a critical analysis of the text of *Saga*. He has enough sense of his own critical abilities not to feel it necessary to follow—or even to give lip service to—the strictures of D. H. Lawrence and Virginia Woolf on JG. One leaves the article unconvinced, however, that *The White Monkey* and *The Silver Spoon* can be omitted from a study of the structure of the whole Forsyte series.]

2095 Madison, Charles A. "OF MEN AND BOOKS/'Writers and Publishers,' " AMERICAN SCHOLAR, XXXV (Summer 1966), 531–41. [This article surveys the author-publisher relationship between Charles Scribner and JG, Edith Wharton, George Santayana, F. Scott Fitzgerald, Ernest Hemingway, Thomas Wolfe, and others. The personal and business relationships between JG and Charles Scribner were most felicitous (pp. 531–33).]

2096 O[strowski], A[dam]. *"Pierwszy i ostatni"* (*The First and the Last*), RADIO I TELEWIZJA (Warsaw), No. 15 (1966), 24 [not seen]. [Review of the Cracow Television Theater production of *The First and the Last*.] [In Polish.]

2097 [Sowińska, Beata]. *"Pierwszy i ostatni"* (*The First and the Last*), ŻYCIE WARSZAWY (Warsaw), No. 74 (1966), 5 [not seen]. [Review of the Cracow Television Theater production of *The First and the Last*.] [In Polish.]

2098 Viedemanis, Gladys. *"The Man of Property,"* ENGLISH JOURNAL, LV (May 1966), 627–28. [Review of the novel and study guide, ed by Marsden Dillenbeck and Marian L. Warren (NY: Scribner's, 1965).]

2099 West, Herbert Faulkner. "A Few Random Thoughts on Modern First Editions," AMERICAN BOOK COLLECTOR, XVI (April 1966), 8–9. Although JG's reputation is currently in a period of decline, he will make a comeback; consequently now is the time to buy collector's editions of his works.

2100 Wroncki, Jan. *"Pierwszy i ostatni"* (*The First and the Last*), EKRAN (Warsaw), No. 15, (1966), 14 [not seen]. [Review of the Cracow Television Theater production of *The First and the Last*.] [In Polish.]

1967

2101 Ahlström, Gunnar. "La 'Petite Histoire' de l'attribution du prix Nobel à John Galsworthy" (A Brief History of the Award of the Nobel Prize to John Galsworthy) in John Galsworthy, *Le propriétaire* (*The Man of Property*), trans by Cammile Mayran (Paris: Presses du Campagnonnage [Collection Guilde des bibliophiles. Sér. Collection des prix Nobel de littérature], 1967), pp. 7–12. In 1932 various candidates were considered for the Nobel Prize in literature. The long-time disregard of English writers suggested that it was time to make amends, inasmuch as Yeats and Shaw were considered Irish and only Kipling, in 1908, had received the prize. There were many illustrious Edwardians— Chesterton, Bennett, Wells, Galsworthy, and Forster. JG's greatest rival was H. G. Wells, who was clearly superior intellectually as well as in terms of his social message. JG's strengths were the artistic finish of his work, the fact that he was a gentleman, and his work as president of the P.E.N. Club, for giving him the prize would also give recognition to the literature of internationalism, which he had served with such perfect urbanity. Thus he was awarded the Nobel Prize for 1932 for "the noble art of narration which attained its perfection in *The Forsyte Saga.*" [In French.]

2102 Auchincloss, Louis. "Afterword," *The Man of Property* (NY: New American Library, 1967), pp. 293–99.

In the 1960s JG's reputation dropped to the point that "he is more forgotten than denigrated." Because of the success and apparent ease he enjoyed in his lifetime, it seems "almost only fair" that he has since been forgotten. Among the Forsyte novels *The Man of Property* is his best, but JG works too hard to make Soames unpleasant. JG's contention that Irene embodies the disturbing effect of Beauty is not persuasive. Irene "is purely and simply a beautiful woman. . . . who never in the least disturbs their Forsyte values." As *In Chancery* and *To Let* get into the fourth generation, "the family theme is fatally diluted" because the second and third generations are the only generations in which a "family" really exists. The love stories of the later volumes could do very well without the family connection, as there is "a curious flavor of mild incest." In the later Forsyte books "the trouble is that his material . . . seems to have taken control" of JG.

2103 Bănkova, Neli. "Realistat Golsuarti Po slucaj 100 godini ot rozdenietoni pisatelja" (Galsworthy, the Realist. On the Occasion of His 100th Anniversary), LITERATUREN FRONT, No. 34 (17 Aug 1967), [n.p.] [not seen].
[Listed in ANNUAL BIBLIOGRAPHY OF ENGLISH LANGUAGE AND LITERATURE (Cambridge: Modern Humanities Research Association, 1967).] [In Serbo-Croatian.]

2104 Bryden, Ronald. "The Wife and the Dark Flower," OBSERVER (Lond), 8 Jan 1967, pp. 14–15.
The accepted view that JG was a rebel who after his marriage became a defender and champion of Forsytes should be modified by the publication of Margaret Morris's story of her brief relationship with JG. Her story, while showing him as a man of honor, makes him more human and less stuffy than the accepted view of him. [A brief summary of the relationship is given.]

2105 Bufkin, E. C. THE TWENTIETH CENTURY NOVEL IN ENGLISH: A CHECKLIST (Athens: University of Georgia P, 1967), pp. 42–43.
[Titles of JG's novels are listed.]

2106 Chakravorty, Sukharanjan. "Galsworthy: A Critic of His Age," MODERN REVIEW (Calcutta), CXXII (Oct 1967), 254–55.
[Brief essay filled with critical clichés, typographical errors, and wretched grammatical constructions.]

2107 Corrigan, Robert Willoughby (ed). MASTERPIECES OF THE MODERN ENGLISH THEATRE (NY: Macmillan, 1967), p. 212.
Loyalties illustrates some of JG's faults as a dramatist: impartiality, some sentimentality, and too many clues and clichés. Its importance lies in treatment of theme. [Biographical note accompanies text of *Loyalties* and "Some Platitudes Concerning Drama."]

2108 Downes, J. Cyril. "The Religion of John Galsworthy," LONDON QUARTERLY AND HOLBORN REVIEW, July 1967, pp. 237–42.

JG's religious beliefs are seen in terms of "nobility of character . . . compassion for the weak and fallen . . . concern for social justice . . . [and] passionate love of beauty." Christianity for JG was "impractical, unattainable, unreal." On the whole the clergymen in his works are portrayed unsympathetically. Other religious aspects in JG are belief in determinism and "a kind of Nature-mysticism."

2109 Evans, D. W. (ed). CATALOGUE OF THE COLLECTION: JOHN GALSWORTHY (Birmingham: University of Birmingham Library, 1967). The collection of 2,049 items of Galsworthiana at the Birmingham University Library (listed in this catalogue) has been loaned to the library for twenty years by the Galsworthy trustees through R. H. Sauter. The collection contains MSS, letters, and memorabilia.

2110 Evans, T. F. "Notes From London," INDEPENDENT SHAVIAN, V (1967), 38.
The BBC's twenty-six-week serialization of the Forsyte novels is part of the centenary celebration of JG's birth. It is to be hoped that other works of JG, his plays especially, will be reconstructed; although his plays will never be very popular, "their concern with serious issues, craftsmanship, their sincerity and their restraint might add to the present-day theater some elements that it has temporarily put on one side."

2111 Fuller, Roy. "Saga Pudding," NEW STATESMAN, LXXIII (20 Jan 1967), 92.
[A denigrating overview of *The Forsyte Saga* occasioned by the Penguin eds of *The Man of Property, In Chancery,* and *To Let,* and the BBC-TV serial. Fuller takes issue with, among other things, D. H. Lawrence's essay on JG and JG's purported legal expertise. JG's language is repetitious, and his decline as a writer in the years marking the beginning and the end of the first trilogy is typified by his "degenerate Meredithian rhetoric" and by his "jerky, 'contemporary' style" that compensates for his "increasing ignorance." The TV serial hides many of JG's deficiencies.]

2112 Gale, John. "Galsworthy: The Gilt-edged Rebel," OBSERVER (Lond), 8 Jan 1967, pp. 4–6, 8–13.
[An interview with Donald Wilson, the producer of the dramatization of *The Forsyte Saga* for BBC 2.]

2113 GALSWORTHY CENTENARY EXHIBITION: CATALOGUE. HELD IN THE HESLOP ROOM, THE MAIN LIBRARY, UNIVERSITY OF BIRMINGHAM, 19 MAY–3 JUNE 1967 (Birmingham: The University Library, 1967), 16 pp.
The Centenary Exhibition shows some 289 of the collection of over 2,000 items of Galsworthiana given by the Galsworthy trustees through R. H. Sauter in 1962 to the Birmingham library. The collection contains almost all of JG's MSS and typescripts except for the British Museum holograph of *The Forsyte Chronicles*.

The collection also includes letters to and from his famous contemporaries and some personal items such as his Order of Merit and the Nobel Prize Medal.

2114 "Galsworthy: Küsse im Taxi (Galsworthy: A Kiss in a Taxi)," DER SPIEGEL (Hamburg), XXI:33 (Aug 1967), 83–84.
[An article in the manner of TIME magazine commenting on the enormous success of the BBC production of *The Forsyte Saga* and on three new books about JG: D. Barker, THE MAN OF PRINCIPLE; Rudolf Sauter, GALSWORTHY, THE MAN; Margaret Morris, MY GALSWORTHY STORY.] [In German.]

2115 Goetsch, Paul. DIE ROMANKONZEPTION IN ENGLAND, 1880–1910 (THE CONCEPT OF THE NOVEL IN ENGLAND, 1880–1910) (Heidelberg: Carl Winter, 1967).
[Passing references.] [In German.]

2116 Hamerliński, Andrzej. "Wizerunek mieszczańskiego świata. 100-lecie urodzin Johna Galsworthy" (A Picture of Middle Class Life. The Centennial of John Galsworthy's Birth), NOWINY RZESZOWSKIE (Rzeszow), No. 209 (1967), [n.p.] [not seen].
[In Polish.]

2117 Hulban, Horia. "John Galsworthy," IASUL LITERAR (Bucharest), XVIII:10 (Oct 1967), 75–77 [not seen].
[Centennial essay of appreciation. Listed in ANNUAL BIBLIOGRAPHY OF ENGLISH LANGUAGE AND LITERATURE (Cambridge: Modern Humanities Research Association, 1967).] [In Rumanian.]

2118 Johnson, Pamela Hansford. "Speaking of Books: *The Forsyte Saga*," NEW YORK TIMES SUNDAY REVIEW OF BOOKS, 12 March 1967, pp. 2, 36.
JG's reputation seems to be on the rise again, thanks to the televised version of *The Forsyte Saga*. His popularity in England declined for two main reasons: (1) JG "represented *fin de siècle* snobbery at its worst"; and (2) the audience cannot really identify with anyone in the novels, with the possible exception of the "unfortunate Soames"—and with him only occasionally. Irene is a female cad who is largely responsible for wrecking the lives of Jon and Fleur. Bosinney is a "Bohemian fake . . . consistently rude . . . consistently dishonest . . . just the thin creature who would have attracted a thin-soulled Irene: all gas and gaiters." Irene and Fleur betray JG because they get out of hand, seeming to control JG rather than vice versa. Actually, *The Man of Property* is very like ANNA KARENINA: Karenin, Soames; Anna, Irene; Vronsky, Bosinney; June, Kitty Levin. *Saga* is "dead at the core," despite some profound social insight and "patchy psychological insight." Yet the novel, perhaps alone among novels, can be read "against the spirit of the author's intent" and still make psychological sense.

2119 Kertman, L. "Ottsy i deti (*Saga o Forsaitakh*. Golsuorsi i vlianie na nee russkogo klassicheskogo romana)" (Fathers and Sons: J. Galsworthy's *The Forsyte Saga* and the Influence on It of the Classical Russian Novel), UCHENYE ZAPISKI (Perm. Universitet), No. 157 (1967), 254–93 [not seen].
[In Russian.]

2120 Klein, John W. "Galsworthy and Bizet," MUSICAL TIMES, CVIII (Aug 1967), 700–701.
[Klein primarily covers material gone over before but emphasizes that JG's translation of CARMEN has "rather wordy sentimentality" and an "occasional lack of humor."]

2121 Lambert, J. W. "The Galsworthy Saga," SUNDAY TIMES WEEKLY REVIEW (Lond), 8 Jan 1967, pp. 21–22.
JG's strongest point is his comic irony. Although not one of the greatest writers, JG "did indeed make a world with his pen." Virginia Woolf's dismissal of JG does not hold up, for in his best work he has captured life. A modest epitaph might be, "He was the noblest Forsyte of them all." [This recapitulation of biographical highlights was prompted by the première of the BBC television series on *The Forsyte Saga*.]

2122 Las Vergnas, Raymond. "La Vie et l'oeuvre de John Galsworthy" (Life and Work of John Galsworthy), in John Galsworthy *Le propriétaire* (*The Man of Property*), trans by Cammile Mayran (Paris: Presses du Campagnonnage [Collection Guilde des bibliophiles. Sér. Collection des prix Nobel de littérature], 1967), pp. 23–42.
There appears in "Salvation of a Forsyte" more fully developed than before the interior conflict within JG between responsibility, legality, conformity, and the bohemian spirit. A remarkable characteristic of *The Man of Property* is the breadth of the novel as it encompasses the various branches of the Forsytes. *Property* and *The Country House* are particularly noteworthy for their character studies. In *Fraternity*, on the other hand, the various events in the novel and matters of technique are more important than the portraits of the various characters themselves. [A brief standard survey of JG's life and works.] [In French.]

2123 Marina, Joaquina González. "John Galsworthy y su mondo" (John Galsworthy and His World), INSULA (Madrid), XXII (Nov 1967), 13.
JG's work is not great, but the work has lasting merit, primarily because he described the England that he knew. [A general article relating JG's life to his work.] [In Spanish.]

2124 Martin, Wallace. THE NEW AGE UNDER ORAGE: CHAPTERS IN

ENGLISH CULTURAL HISTORY (Manchester: Manchester UP; NY: Barnes & Noble, 1967), pp. 34, 78, 83–84, 97, 102, 129, 242.
[Incidental references to JG.]

2125 "Memories of Galsworthy," LISTENER, LXXVIII (10 Aug 1967), 166.
[Comments by R. H. Mottram, St. John Irvine, Frank Galsworthy, and Rudolph and Viola Sauter transcribed from a 1959 broadcast and presented on the one hundredth anniversary of JG's birth. The influence of JG's family on characters in *The Forsyte Saga* is emphasized.]

2126 Mertner, Edgar, and Ewald Standop. ENGLISCHE LITERATUR-GESCHICHTE (ENGLISH LITERARY HISTORY) (Heidelberg: Quelle & Meyer, 1967) [not seen]; rev (1971), pp. 557, 565–69, 574, 586–87, 593, 623, 629, 641.
[Brief discussion of JG as a novelist and dramatist.] [In German.]

2127 Morris, Margaret. MY GALSWORTHY STORY INCLUDING 67 HITHERTO UNPUBLISHED LETTERS, intro by Marjorie Deans (Lond: Peter Owen, 1967).
[JG taught Margaret to appreciate Dostoevski, Turgenev, Chekhov, and others; and he and Ada were instrumental in getting her to start a school to train children in her style of dancing. JG did not, however, encourage her in suffragette activities, nor in her growing love for him. When JG told Ada about the growing intimacy between them, Ada wrote an understanding note; but JG never met Margaret alone again and never even saw her after January 1912, though the correspondence continued until JG's necessary but quite untypical short note suggesting that Morris not write again. Perhaps in part because of the break, Margaret's stage career was interrupted, JG stopped writing drama for a time, and eventually Margaret married the artist Ferguson. The volume is especially valuable for the letters of JG, giving insight into his attitude to the Morris episode, for the lengthy letters describing his reactions to America in 1912, for reinforcing the knowledge that JG was intellectual, "invariably courteous, lovable and kind," and also that personally he was "dynamic and deeply passionate . . . spontaneous and full of joy." Morris's comments, while true, often tend toward the melodramatic. Marjorie Deans' introduction gives brief general biographies of John and Ada Galsworthy and of Margaret Morris, emphasizing the importance of JG's legal training in the development of his novels, his rebellion from his family as a result of collecting rents from his father's London slum property, and the presentation of the John-Ada love match in *The Dark Flower*. Morris's record and letters from JG cover a period of her three-year close—but, she emphasizes, never sexually intimate—association with JG beginning in 1910, after her successful choreography for Gluck's OR-PHEUS AND EURYDICE.]

2128 Morris, Margaret, and Peter Ross. "Bohemia Revisited: Margaret Morris Talks to Peter Ross," LISTENER, LXXVIII (10 Aug 1967), 166–67.

JG was a passionate man, but his honor was greater than his passion; consequently he did not pursue his relationship with Morris any further than that described by Morris in MY GALSWORTHY STORY (Lond: Peter Owens, 1967). In addition, he did not want to make Ada suffer. [This was originally given on the BBC program "Woman's Hour."]

2129 Österling, Anders. "Discours de réception prononcé par Anders Österling lors de la remise du Prix Nobel de littérature à John Galsworthy, le 10 Décembre 1932" (Formal Speech Given by Anders Österling Presenting the Nobel Prize for Literature to John Galsworthy, 10 Dec 1932), in John Galsworthy, *Le propriétaire* (*The Man of Property*), trans by Cammile Mayran (Paris: Presses du Campagnonnage [Collection Guilde des bibliophiles. Sér. Collection des prix Nobel de littérature], 1967), pp. 13–21.

From *The Island Pharisees* on, the fundamental trait of JG's work will be his satire against Pharisaism. His two trilogies—*The Forsyte Saga* and *A Modern Comedy*—are almost unique in contemporary literature, as he pursued his chronicles across three generations. It is instructive to watch JG's evolution in his novels as they change from being radical critiques of society to becoming works that are objective and impartial works that are purely human. JG's irony is particularly distinctive. There are several varieties of irony—negative irony, laughing irony, and an irony that challenges the evils of the world. At times JG successfully utilizes nature—winds, clouds, fragrances, and cries of birds—in his irony as he awakens the reader's imagination. [In French.]

2130 Parrinder, Patrick. "Pastiche and After," CAMBRIDGE REVIEW, LXXXIXA (4 Nov 1967), 66–67.

[The review article of Angus Wilson's NO LAUGHING MATTER suggests a "neat 'modern' reversal" of *The Forsyte Saga*.]

2131 Sauter, Rudolf. GALSWORTHY THE MAN: AN INTIMATE PORTRAIT (Lond: Peter Owen, 1967).

[This portrait is essentially one of Galsworthiana. The intention is to present a personal, intimate account so that the reader will know about JG the man rather than be exposed to a certain number of facts about him and his work. Those who are interested in JG will find that the volume provides some additional information, but it will probably not advance JG's stock or increase a serious interest in his work.]

2132 Severikova, N. M. "K 100-letiyu so dnya rozhdeniya Dzhona Golsuorsi (1867–1933)" (The 100th Anniversary of the Birth of John

Galsworthy), SREDNEE SPETSIAL'NOE OBRAZOVANIE (Moscow), VII (1967), 49–51 [not seen].
[Listed in ANNUAL BIBLIOGRAPHY OF ENGLISH LANGUAGE AND LITERATURE (Cambridge: Modern Humanities Research Association, 1969).] [In Russian.]

2133 Skuratovs'ka, L. I. "Proza Golsuorsi i traditsii Dikkensa" (Galsworthy's Prose and the Traditions of Dickens), RADYAN'SKE LITERATURNAVSTSVO (Kiev), IX (1967), 42–50 [not seen].
[Listed in ANNUAL BIBLIOGRAPHY OF ENGLISH LANGUAGE AND LITERATURE (Cambridge: Modern Humanities Research Association, 1967).] [In Russian.]

2134 Smith, Godfrey. "The New Forsyte Saga," SUNDAY TIMES WEEKLY REVIEW (Lond), 11 June 1967, p. 45.
[Announcing that a continuation of *The Forsyte Saga* called *Last Quartet of the Forsyte Saga* has just been discovered, Mr. Smith continues the history of the Forsytes into the 1960s.]

2135 Stepanov, St. "Vera v cheloveka. V kn.: Golsuorsi, D. Khristianin" (Belief in Man. In the book: Galsworthy, J., *A Saint's Progress*), POLITIZDAT (Moscow), 1967, pp. 51–54 [not seen].
[In Russian.]

2136 Stevenson, Lionel. YESTERDAY AND AFTER (NY: Barnes & Noble, 1967), vol. XI to THE HISTORY OF THE ENGLISH NOVEL, by Ernest A. Baker. Ten volumes (NY: Barnes & Noble, 1930); rptd (1960), pp. 42, 47, 49, 60, 96, 105, 175, 184, 207, 223, 237, 258, 259, 267, 274, 285, 298, 299, 313, 323, 350, 351.
Trollope's practice of using a character through several novels was revitalized by JG. The "new woman" figured in the novels of Wells, Bennett, Lawrence, and JG. JG and his contemporaries Wells and Bennett were at the apex of their fame in the 1920s. [Passing references to JG linking him to such writers as Wells, Hueffer (Ford), Forster, Woolf, and Joyce who recognized that English society was self-indulgent and facing collapse.]

2137 Szamuely, Tibor. *"Saga o Forsaitakh" (The Forsyte Saga)*, SPECTATOR (Lond), CCXVIII (2 June 1967), 645.
The Forsyte Saga has found its greatest popularity in Bolshevik Russia. One reason is that *Saga* is in the tradition of the classical Russian novel, and Russians primarily are conservative. The main reason, however, is that the Soviet reader looks to Western and to prerevolutionary Russian writers as escapist literature. This opens the "window on reality" of the outside world, which Russians are barred from: JG painted a "realistic picture of a way of life utterly, and alluringly, dissimilar" to Russian life, presenting people who are secure, stable, propertied, and assured in the present and confident in the future. *Saga* is about ordinary people, not the aristocrats of earlier Russian literature; and the Russian government allows the works of JG to be published.

2138 Taylor, John Russell. THE RISE AND FALL OF THE WELL-MADE PLAY (Lond: Methuen; NY: Hill & Wang, 1967), pp. 9, 115–19, 127, 137, 144, 161.

In JG's plays, decency and fair play reign supreme. In at least six plays JG avoids the traps of oversimplification and overt didacticism. The best plays are characterized by "prosaicness and down-to-earthness." JG's early masterpiece is *Strife. Loyalties* in effect sounded the death knell for "old-time craftsmanship" of the well-made play tradition. [Specific comments on the plays are primarily plot summary.]

2139 Tugusheva, M. "100-letii yubilei Golsuorsi" (Galsworthy's 100th Anniversary), VOPROSY LITERATURY, I (1967), 215–17 [not seen]. [Listed in ANNUAL BIBLIOGRAPHY OF ENGLISH LANGUAGE AND LITERATURE (Cambridge: Modern Humanities Research Association, 1968).] [In Russian.]

2140 Vočadlo, Otakar. "Návrat Forsytu" (Return of the Forsytes), LIDOVÁ DEMOKRACIE (Prague), 13 August 1967, p. 5 [not seen]. [Comment on the BBC-TV *Forsyte Saga* and MY GALSWORTHY STORY, by Margaret Morris.] [In Czech.]

2141 Waterman, Edith French. "THE GALSWORTHY READER," LIBRARY JOURNAL, XCII (15 Dec 1967), 4504. [Brief notice of Anthony West (ed), THE GALSWORTHY READER (NY: Scribner's, 1967).]

2142 West, Anthony (ed). THE GALSWORTHY READER (NY: Charles Scribner's Sons, 1967), vii–xxi.

JG was the least literary of the literary men of his time, detached from the mainstream of its intellectual life, living a life of "amazing sanity" as he became increasingly detached from the intellectual milieu of contemporary writers. When Ada became JG's mistress, he was set on the path of becoming a writer whose mission was to give "expression to the secret fears and anxieties that revolution" caused to his class. Much of JG's writing is strongly influenced by the Arthur–Ada–John Galsworthy affair, as in Soames (Arthur), Bosinney (JG), and Irene (Ada) in *The Man of Property,* with sympathy focused primarily on Soames. Death and atonement are themes related to the guilt of Bosinney-Irene and of JG-Ada. *The Dark Flower* reflects JG's association with Margaret Morris. JG's self-denigration is strong in *Fraternity,* and the Ada figure dominates *Beyond.* Bryan Summerhay (in *Beyond*) is JG's better self. Sexual guilt is in several fantasies—as in *A Saint's Progress*—about young women who "brought grief to their fathers and to the men who truly loved them" by their physical rather than social needs and obligations. The same theme is the basis of *A Modern Comedy.* The scene of Fleur "raping" Jon is remarkable for its "reversal of the traditional masculine and feminine roles." Soames's death in *Swan Song* (which reemphasizes the death-as-punishment theme so prominent in JG) results from his collection of art as property; Fleur (who is indirectly responsible) will carry "the burden of guilty responsibility" with her: "the great attack on bourgeois possessiveness and hardheartedness" becomes a "lament for the greediest and coldest representative of the enemy," because of the sympathy JG builds for Soames.

Justice today is not seen as the brutal realism it was in 1909 but as an "almost naïve piece of infantile fantasy." The psychic function of *Justice* is related to the "universality of the fantasy of vengeance by self-destruction." JG never learned the need for dramatic construction; his best two plays, *Justice* and *The Silver Box*, are essentially amateurish; and his most successful, commercially speaking—*The Skin Game*—now seems a parody. JG was, for his class, a master story teller. [West examines JG's works primarily from the point of view of inadvertent self-revelation and, given these limitations, makes perceptive comments.]

2143 Wilson, Donald. "*The Forsyte Saga* on Television," LISTENER, LXXVIII (30 Nov 1967), 697.
[A brief discussion of some of the aspects of producing *The Forsyte Saga* for television, with special emphasis given to the necessity of supplying some material not originally in JG's work, such as the development of the Forsyte family history in early episodes and the development of the characters Annette and Winifred.]

2144 Zhantieva, D. "Muzhestvo dobroty" (The Courage of Goodness) LITERATURNAIA GAZETA, XXXIII (16 Aug 1967), 7.
The living images of JG remain at the time of his centennial celebration. The main characters of *The Forsyte Saga* are vivid in the Russian memory. JG attacked the bourgeois society that had become paralyzed by complacency and privileged stability, overcoming interdictions and conditions that had tied down English literature. In "Writer's Credo," JG confirms his loyalty to the fundamental principles of critical realism, avoiding didacticism. Overcoming Forsyteism himself, JG showed what people can be, rebelling against naturalism and against the aesthetic impassivity that he contrasted to the creative principles of Dickens. [In Russian.]

1968

2145 Bailey, L. W. "Holmes and Soames," BAKER STREET JOURNAL, XVIII (Dec 1968), 195–200.
[Centennial appreciation indicating what might have happened if Sherlock Holmes had become involved in investigating the twelve years between the Irene-Bosinney affair and the Irene-Soames divorce (*The Forsyte Saga*). Should

be read in conjunction with Evelyn Herzog's "IRENE! (gasp!) IRENE!" BAKER STREET JOURNAL, XVIII (Dec 1968), 201–7.]

2146 Egmond, Peter van. "Naming Techniques in John Galsworthy's *The Forsyte Saga*," NAMES, XVI:4 (Dec 1968), 371–79.

There are three basic naming techniques in *The Forsyte Saga:* (1) the "allegorical" naming of characters suggestive of Dickens—e.g., a Rollhard automobile, Caramel and Baker's (a confectionery), Mr. Gathercole who danced with "Miss Pink, a blushing wallflower"; (2) the naming of many of the major characters with names that are etymologically significant—Roger and his umbrella, as his name means "famous with the spear"; Timothy means "honoring God," and Timothy's God is Mammon; (3) the giving of typical English names to many of the minor characters—Warmson, a butler; Cook, a servant. In *Saga* JG is a conscious artist and his names are a "conscious part of his literary craftsmanship."

2147 "Galsworthy, John: 1867–1933 (Též výňatek z dila)" (John Galsworthy: 1867–1933, including an Excerpt from His Work), FRIENDSHIP, II:4 (1968/69), 4–5 [not seen].
[In Czech.]

2148 "THE GALSWORTHY READER. ed. Anthony West," A.L.A. BOOKLIST, LXIV (1 April 1968), 900.

The book is "a purely elective acquisition for sizable libraries and middle-aged and older users who remember" JG "nostalgically or students of English literature needing to sample his work." West's introduction emphasizes biographical interest in the works, mentioning JG's limitations and the dated appeal of his writing. [Reviewer spent more time reading West than JG.]

2149 Hamer, Douglas. "The Connotation of 'Saga,' " NOTES AND QUERIES, nsXXX (Jan 1968), 30–31.

For two hundred years scholars have recognized that Icelandic sagas were stories of families, not dynasties. Thus JG, who followed Hall Caine's example in THE BONDSMAN: A NEW SAGA (1890), had precedent in using "saga" to describe several generations in the history of a family.

2150 Harris, Wendell V. "Molly's 'Yes': The Transvaluation of Sex in Modern Fiction," TEXAS STUDIES IN LITERATURE AND LANGUAGE, X (Spring 1968), 107–18.

The Forsyte Saga "ambiguously and diffidently" presents sexual desire as the antithesis to the nineteenth-century conservative mind: "although the sexual relationship is barely alluded to . . . the increasing subordination of all other values to . . . sexual love is clear enough." As such *Saga* is in the mainstream of the movement toward sexual love as a dominating force in modern fiction.

2151 Herzog, Evelyn. "IRENE! (gasp!) IRENE!" BAKER STREET JOURNAL, XVIII (Dec 1968), 201–7.

[A BAKER STREET JOURNALesque view of the possible relationship between Irene Forsyte (*The Forsyte Saga*) and Irene Adler (who perhaps cavorted with Sherlock Holmes) in an intriguing detective mystery designed to help solve the problem of what Irene really did in the twelve years between the two Forsyte husbands Soames and Jolyon. A study not for the injudicious, the narrow-minded, or those with a Jamesian will-to-believe. Should be read in conjunction with L. W. Bailey's "Holmes and Soames," BAKER STREET JOURNAL, XVIII (Dec 1968), 195–200.]

>   **2152** Holloway, David. JOHN GALSWORTHY (Lond: Morgan-Grampian Books [International Profile Series], 1968; Capetown: Nasionele Boekhandel, 1969).

The current revival of interest in JG can be attributed largely to the cause of his loss of esteem shortly after his death: he is an "exact social chronicler" of his life and times. Readers of the 1960s like him because he did not propagandize in the Forsyte Chronicles. Satire of the "plush, convention-ridden world" of *The Man of Property* mellowed some in the later works because JG liked less what was taking their place. JG did not think it "reasonable" to apply Freudian analysis to Soames and Irene. A man of "solid worth and decent achievement . . . not a man of genius but a professional craftsman," JG was the "head of his profession," with a strong sense of social purpose in his novels and dramas. [Holloway's semi-scholarly biography capitalizes on the success of the BBC-TV production of *The Forsyte Saga,* with ten pages of photographs from the series, other photos taken while JG was alive, and a copious selection of stills from various stage productions. This brief biographical treatment (92 pp.) of JG contains some plot summaries and short comments about his works. It is sloppily written and laced with graduate school generalities (i.e., "Every writer has a best period, when the work he produces is of a higher quality than at any other time"). The material is covered more carefully and in much greater detail in other JG biographies. Holloway speculates that JG resumed the novels about Soames—and treated him with greater kindness than in *Property*—because of what he considered a personal insult from David Lloyd George, who was thinking of conscripting him (JG) for duty in World War I: JG must have realized he was not being fair to Soames, because Soames's generation was superior to the generation following. The text has not been carefully proofread, and Holloway seems to have confused *A Bit o' Love* and *The Fugitive*. Pages 89–91 contain a useful chronology of JG's life.]

>   **2153** Karl, Frederick R. "Conrad-Galsworthy: A Record of Their Friendship in Letters," MIDWAY (Chicago), IX (Autumn 1968), 87–106.

JG preferred Conrad the Victorian and moralist to Conrad the "modern, anguished victim of his own perceptions." There is "a general misunderstanding of or general defensiveness about each other's work that runs through" their entire friendship, "accompanied by a personal tolerance that has no relationship to the artistic standards of either." [The letters and text cover familiar ground, emphasizing that early in their relationship Conrad wanted JG to write more symbolically.]

2154 Kertman, L. "Anglichanin na rendez-vous. (Russkii klassicheskii roman i *Saga o Forsaitakh* D. Golsuorsi)" (An Englishman at a Rendezvous: The Russian Classical Novel and J. Galsworthy's *The Forsyte Saga*), UCHENYE ZAPISKI (Perm. Gosudarstvennyi universitet), No. 193 (1968), 232 ff. [not seen].
[In Russian.]

2155 Lambert, J. W. "The Galsworthy Saga," HORIZON, X (Autumn 1968), 106–11.
[Popular essay recalling well-known biographical aspects of JG's life, in part instigated by Margaret Morris's MY GALSWORTHY STORY. Draws parallels between the life of JG and that of the people of *The Forsyte Saga*. JG perhaps had too much pity to be a great artist. "Time is steadily making nonsense of Virginia Woolf's dismissal of him" as a writer about "unimportant things," because the Forsytes are still alive, with "grey unmoving eyes hiding their instinct with its hidden roots of violence"; and the novels are full of "the extraordinary pulse of sexual energy that drums" through all his best work.]

2156 Mi [Pohorský, Miloš]. "John Galsworthy, *Saga rodu Forsytu*" (John Galsworthy's *The Forsyte Saga*), IMPULS (Prague), III:3 (1968), 203–4 [not seen].
[In Czech.]

2157 Miller, J. William. "John Galsworthy," MODERN PLAYWRIGHTS AT WORK. Two volumes (Lond: Samuel French, 1968), I, x, 204–29, 392, 398, 401, 408–10, 443.
JG, a master of naturalism, tended in his life as in his plays to observe rather than to involve himself in others' lives. By 1910, with the success of *The Silver Box, Strife,* and *Justice,* JG was recognized as a leader of English playwrights. [A good overview of JG's dramatic method for the person beginning a study of JG's drama. Miller relies heavily on JG's own comments about drama and dramatic technique, and on H. V. Marrot's LIFE AND LETTERS OF JOHN GALSWORTHY (Lond: Heinemann, 1935) and Dudley Barker's THE MAN OF PRINCIPLE (NY: Stein & Day, 1963).]

2158 Nicoll, Allardyce. ENGLISH DRAMA: A MODERN VIEWPOINT (Lond: George G. Harrap, 1968), pp. 113–14, 170.
JG is really more Brechtian than Brecht because JG "honestly designed to stimulate thought" and at the same time to show his personal indignation a the horrors of society. JG deserves to be studied by contemporary dramatists. "He was a revolutionary fired by no self-interest, driven . . . by no feeling of personal injustice, and, even when . . . moved to indignation, [preserved] his sense of

balance." [A brief but refreshing reappraisal of JG's worth as dramatist after a generation of neglect.]

2159 Salerno, Henry F. ENGLISH DRAMA IN TRANSITION: 1880–1920 (NY: Pegasus, 1968), pp. 341–44.
In his dramas, JG presented life as it is, leaving the public to draw whatever conclusions seem valid, avoiding "theatricality and cheap sensationalism," constructing simple plots by following the devices of the well-made play, writing life-like and often humorless dialogue, and believing that "men lived among men in a disharmonic . . . perpetually ironic state." Despite the too-obvious use of coincidence in *The Silver Box*, it is "tightly and powerfully constructed," has "hard-hitting" dialogue, "generates ironic power," and sustains interest today. [Headnote to *Box*.]

2160 Salerno, Henry F. "The Problem Play: Some Aesthetic Considerations," ENGLISH LITERATURE IN TRANSITION: 1880–1920, XI:4 (1968), 195–205.
Characteristics of the well-made play in JG's *The Silver Box* are the coincidences of parallel thefts, of the policeman seeing the silver box on the bed, and of Mrs. Jones being employed by the family whose silver box was stolen. Aspects of the well-made play explore dual standards of justice, illuminating in doing so the "operation of social institutions in their management of individuals within . . . society."

2161 Savchenko, S. "Literaturnye vzglyady Dzhona Golsuorsi v dooktyabrskii period ego tvorchestva" (John Galsworthy's Literary Views in the pre-October Period of His Career), NAUCHNYE TRUDY FILOSOFSKOGO FAKUL'TETA KIRGISZKOGO UNIVERSITETA, XIV (1968), 68–74 [not seen].
[Listed in ANNUAL BIBLIOGRAPHY OF ENGLISH LANGUAGE AND LITERATURE (Cambridge: Modern Humanities Research Association, 1969).] [In Russian.]

2162 Temple, Ruth Z. (ed). TWENTIETH CENTURY BRITISH LITERATURE: A REFERENCE GUIDE AND BIBLIOGRAPHY (NY: Frederick Ungar, 1968), pp. 164–65.
[Bibliography contains thirty-seven articles that mention JG's name.]

2163 Voropanova, M. I. DZHON GOLSUORSI. OCHERK ZHIZNI I TVORCHESTVA (John Galsworthy: An Essay on His Life and Work) (Krasnoiarsk: Knizhoe isdatel'stvo, 1968). 550 pp.
[In Russian.]

2164 Wilson, Asher Boldon. JOHN GALSWORTHY'S LETTERS TO LEON LION (The Hague: Mouton, 1968).
JG believed that the action of drama arose from the interplay between character and circumstance; Granville-Barker concurred with JG in this belief, and

Barker's productions of JG's earlier plays "are still considered definitive." From 1906 to 1914 JG wrote eight full-length plays, five of which—*The Silver Box, Strife, Justice, The Pigeon,* and *The Fugitive*—were critical successes. Following the war JG wrote ten full-length plays, and there were three successes—*The Skin Game, Loyalties,* and *Escape.* One reason for JG's decline in reputation as a playwright was "his failure to find in the post-war theatre a producer for his plays of the calibre of Granville Barker." The planning for the Grein-Lion revivals of 1921–22 "tended to be hasty or haphazard"; the shortage of funds hampered their efforts; and the plays were under-rehearsed. Even JG's concern for careful casting could not by itself bring the productions up to the standards of the original productions. The popular successes JG had after the war came at a price; there was a "decline in the power of the moral or argument in the post-war plays, and a concomitant increase in dependence upon plot device to sustain the audience's interest." JG's greatest power in the theater had been his ability to evoke this "sense of moral certainty through an illusion of reality." The range of problems covered by his plays is "not exceeded by any playwright of his period." A. R. Skemp remarked that JG was a Platonist, and "it is from Socrates' definition of love that Galsworthy draws the morals or arguments of his plays." The variousness of the critics in their assessments of JG's plays "can be reconciled only through granting the essentially ironic nature of the majority of Galsworthy's plays." [Three essays—"Galsworthy in the Pre-War London Theatre," "Galsworthy in the Post-War London Theatre," and "The Playwright's Development" serve as an excellent introduction to this annotated ed of JG's letters to Leon Lion covering the period from 25 July 1921 to 2 November 1932.]

1969

2165 "As the Victorian World Turns," TIME, XCIV (3 Oct 1969), 84. The television version of *The Forsyte Saga* differs from PEYTON PLACE and SECRET STORM primarily in "its distinguished origins and its careful preparation." The production is "stylish . . . fast-paced . . . gripping, dramatic . . . highly believable . . . totally entertaining."

2166 Ausmus, Martin Russey. "Some Forms of the Sequence Novel in British Fiction," DISSERTATION ABSTRACTS, XXX (1969), 1975A. Unpublished dissertation, University of Oklahoma, 1969.

2167 Bobok, Jozef. "Úvaha nad Ságou" (Reflection on the Saga), PRAVDA (Bratislava), 1 Dec 1969, p. 5 [not seen]. [In Slovene.]

1969: 2165–2174

2168 Boor, Ján. "John Galsworthy," *Forsytovska sága* (*Forsyte Saga*) (Bratislava, 1969, 1970), pp. 949–58 [not seen].
[Afterword to *The Forsyte Saga.*] [In Czech.]

2169 Burgess, Anthony. "Seen Any Good Galsworthy Lately?" NEW YORK TIMES MAGAZINE, 16 Nov 1969, pp. 57, 59, 60, 62, 64.
JG belongs to the "conservative, somewhat slipshod range of late-Edwardian, quinto-Georgian British writers who cared less about words than what lay behind the words." While he influenced Thomas Mann and was read seriously in Russia, British intellectuals spurned him. His plays, "somewhat melodramatic sermons," are too old-fashioned for today's theatergoers. *The Forsyte Saga's* style, full of "old rhythms, clichés, the easy way out," more concerned with "contrivance" than with "direct observation of life," is well adapted to television as a "superior soap opera," a "leisurely, middlebrow television serial."

2170 de Berker, Patricia. "Oedipal Odours—Patricia de Berker on the Forsytes," LISTENER, LXXXI (27 Feb 1969), 270–71.
In *The Forsyte Saga* JG wrestles with his confusion "between the sexual and the maternal woman." Irene is the only "alive" woman in *Saga*. JG is most effective when evoking "the dream-like atmosphere with which sentimentalists tend to clothe their earliest memories." Speaking oedipally, Irene becomes involved with Jolyon after a platonic affair with old Jolyon; and the last "seduction" by Irene is of her own son Jon "in all but the most literal sense of the word." JG's "illogicalities tumble over each other" in his determination to make Irene's attitude plausible. Jon's relation to Irene is seen before the trip to America as one of "filial infatuation" rather than "filial devotion." [The article was inspired by the BBC-TV production of *The Forsyte Saga.*]

2171 Green, Philip. "They Wrote for Fame and Fortune: John Galsworthy," WRITER (Lond), (1969), pp. 13–15.
[In response to the success of the BBC television production of *The Forsyte Saga,* this note provides a very brief survey of JG's career. The critical estimate is favorable.]

2172 Hergešić, Tvo. "Književnice nobelovci" (Nobel Prize-Winning Authors), Žagreb, Radio-televizija Žagreb, "Mladost," št. "Štampa," (Šibenik), (1969), pp. 71–81 [not seen].
[In Serbo-Croatian.]

2173 Leonard, John. "Soap Opera for Highbrows: *The Forsyte Saga,*" LIFE, LXVII (21 Nov 1969), 21.
[Brief, whimsical review of BBC-TV's *The Forsyte Saga.*]

2174 Marković, Vida E. "Pogovor" (Foreword), *Na Berzi Forsajta* (*On Forsyte 'Change*), trans by Olivera Glišić and Miloš Nešić (Belgrade: "Rad"; Ljubljana: "Delo," (1969), pp. 91–94 [not seen].
[In Serbo-Croatian.]

2175 Marković, Vida E. THE REPUTATION OF GALSWORTHY IN EN-GLAND, 1897–1950 (Belgrade: Filoloski Fakultet Beogradskog Univerziteta, 1969).

During the period 1897–1914 JG wrote many of his social novels and became a leading playwright of the Repertory Movement. Until 1914 he enjoyed the reputation of being a great writer. The years 1915–1923 cover the second stage of his career. He maintained his reputation as a leading author despite the growing influence of the more modern writers and the vogue for D. H. Lawrence. Two of his greatest commercial successes for the theater—*Loyalties* and *The Skin Game*—were produced during this period. By 1924 JG was openly attacked by the moderns, who henceforth ignored him almost entirely. After his death he remained popular with the general reader, but the growing tensions of the prewar years turned readers' interests in other directions. Literary circles continued to ignore his works during the period 1933–1950. Even in this period the general verdict would acknowledge that he was a good author of the second class. JG will survive as the author of *The Forsyte Saga,* a work which added a new theme and another character to English fiction.

2176 Müllenbrock, Heinz-Joachim. "Gesellschaftliche Thematik in E. M. Forster's Roman HOWARDS END" (Social Themes in E. M. Forster's Novel HOWARDS END), ANGLIA, LXXXVII (1969), 367–91, espec pp. 388–90.

[In a study devoted primarily to E. M. Forster, Müllenbrock argues that JG, whose works are important for cultural history rather than for literary merit, calls for social compromise in *Strife* and exposes the narrowness of the inflexible principle of authority in *The Patrician.*] [In German.]

2177 Pike, E. Royston. "John Galsworthy and His Forsytes," HUMAN DOCUMENTS OF THE AGE OF THE FORSYTES (Lond: Allen & Unwin, 1969), pp. 7–12.

[Pike's introductory chapter justifies this collection of original documents from 1880–1902. He emphasizes the permanence of JG's record, the relation of JG's actual life to the Forsytes, and the need to present those aspects of the last of the Victorian Age that JG did not really write about with the precision and truth he devoted to the Forsyte class. This is followed by an excellent selection of original documents drawn from various sources.]

2178 Osawa, Mamoru. ("London and *The Forsyte Saga,*") TRAVELS IN AMERICA AND ENGLAND (Kanazawa: Hokkoku Shuppan-sha, 1969), pp. 339–62.

JG's literary fame peaked in 1933 and has continued to decline ever since. *The Forsyte Saga* is an amalgamation of two opposite forces: one is a satirical, critical view, and the other is a romantic, sensitive one. JG's romanticism, which is idealistic in the first part of *Saga,* becomes nostalgic in the latter part. That his realism is neither exact nor strict enough is the fundamental weakness of *Saga.*

There are two main lines of story in *Saga*. The first consists of a critical attack on Forsyteism, and the second develops the process of transforming the main force of Forsyteism (Soames) into its opposite. This transformation becomes complete in *To Let; To Let* is, thus, "anti-climactic" and thereby weakens the whole theme. The cause of this weakness is to be found in JG's very ambiguous treatment of Bosinney's death at the end of *The Man of Property*. *Saga* is not a critical analysis of Victorianism because it does not present a true criticism of that society; instead, it is a vast chronicle of the Victorian age which describes its transformation and decline. [Professor Osawa writes that the title of this article might better have been "Enantiodromy in *The Forsyte Saga*."] [In Japanese.]

> **2179** Savchenko, S. "*Etyudy o strannostyakh* Dzh. Golsuorsi kak satira na angliiskoe dekadentstvo" (John Galsworthy's *Studies in Extravagance* as a Satire on English Decadence), NAUCHNYE TRUDY (Kirigizskii. Universitet. Filologicheskii Fakultet), XV (1969), 121-30 [not seen].

[Listed in ANNUAL BIBLIOGRAPHY OF ENGLISH LANGUAGE AND LITERATURE (Cambridge: Modern Humanities Research Association, 1970).] [In Russian.]

> **2180** Shraibman, A. M. "Vnutrennii monolog kak sredstvo psikhologicheskogo analiza v *Saga o Forsaitakh* Dzhona Golsuorsi (Uchebnoe posobie)" (Internal Monologue as a Means of Psychological Analysis in John Galsworthy's *Forsyte Saga*. A Textbook) (Kishinev, 1969) [not seen].

[In Russian.]

> **2181** Stessin, Lawrence. "The Businessman in Fiction," LITERARY REVIEW, XII (Spring 1969), 281-89.

JG's presentation of Soames (*The Man of Property*) perpetuates the tradition in literature that treats the businessman harshly.

> **2182** Thody, Philip. "The Politics of the Family Novel: Is Conservatism Inevitable?" MOSAIC, III (Fall 1969), 87-101.

[This study uses Zola's LES ROUGON-MACQUART as the basis for a study of the following family novels: JG's *The Forsyte Saga*, Thomas Mann's BUDDENBROOKS, Roger Martin du Gard's LES THIBAULT, and Georges Duhamel's CHRONIQUE DES PASQUIER. The essay considers the question whether these family novels are conservative or apolitical because their authors were seeking to perpetuate the values of the nineteenth century or whether there is something in a particular genre such as the family novel that leads the authors "to defend the values of stability and order."] Irene faces the crisis of Fleur and Jon's falling in love in *A Modern Comedy* by succeeding in keeping them apart. Earlier Irene had argued that marriages without love are meaningless, but she has become less flexible and open in views than Soames. That there is continued popular interest in the writings of these authors may have political implications: "most people do not want a revolution."

2183 Watts, Marjorie. "Galsworthy and the P.E.N.," TIMES LITERARY SUPPLEMENT (Lond), 28 Aug 1969, p. 955.
[This letter to the editor corrects misinformation circulating that JG founded the P.E.N. Club. Actually, JG was first president: it was founded by Mrs. C. A. Dawson-Scott.]

1970

2184 Bandyopadhyay, Sarit Kumar. "Trends in Modern Bengali Drama," INDIAN WRITING TODAY, IV (July–Sept 1970), 149–55.
The viability of the "Shaw-Galsworthy-Granville Barker tradition" of realistic-naturalistic plays can be seen in the *Bohurupee* theater group, founded by Mr. Sambhu Mitra.

2185 Bergonzi, Bernard. THE SITUATION OF THE NOVEL (Lond: Macmillan; Pittsburgh: University of Pittsburgh P, 1970), pp. 150, 151, 153.
The television serialization of *The Forsyte Saga* and the desire to escape the present have brought about a rebirth of interest in JG's novels.

2186 Chapple, J. A. V. DOCUMENTARY AND IMAGINATIVE LITERATURE: 1880–1920 (Lond: Blandford P [History and Literature Series]; NY: Barnes & Noble, 1970), pp. 30, 54, 134–37, 155, 221, 339.
[Brief, conventional comments about *The Silver Box, Strife, The Foundations, Justice, The Man of Property, In Chancery, To Let, The Country House,* and *The Patrician* within the context of a chapter entitled "The Search for Values" and concluding that JG is "decent, humanitarian and concerned, but not revolutionary."]

2187 Conrad, Borys. MY FATHER: JOSEPH CONRAD (Lond: Calder & Boyars, 1970), pp. 15–17.
[Borys Conrad comments briefly on JG's visits to Joseph Conrad and reprints JG's character sketch of Conrad. The H. G. Wells photo of JG is reproduced facing p. 64.]

2188 Cook, Bruce. "After *Forsyte Saga,* More Good Reads on TV?" NATIONAL OBSERVER, 2 Feb 1970, p. 19.
The Forsyte Saga is a "good read," middle-class fare, which makes it ideal for television. [The article is essentially an appeal for more "middle brow" adult entertainment like *Saga* on television.]

2189 Dooley, D. J. "Character and Credibility in *The Forsyte Saga,*" DALHOUSIE REVIEW (Halifax), L (Autumn 1970), 373–77.

The Forsyte Saga, which most critics denounce, has proved its lasting appeal once again in the phenomenal success on BBC-TV. [The subject of the title is not developed in depth.]

2190 Freedman, Richard. "26 Sunday Nights with the Forsytes," BOOK WORLD (Chicago TRIBUNE), 8 Feb 1970, p. 6.

[Freedman, like most of the rest of the world, has been hooked on the televised *Forsyte Saga* because of the pleasure of encountering "real writing, real acting, and even real 'production values.' "] But perhaps most important is the sense of continuity of life as *Saga* traces the decline of Victorian life into the modern world, contrasting the "stuffy materialism of the older generation" to the freer world of the 1920s. The television series perhaps surpasses the novels in the part devoted to the 1920s because of television's ability to give a more consistent tone through historical perspective than JG was able to do while living and writing in the 1920s. The series is a "sumptuous visualization" of JG's work and of a world that we have lost.

2191 G., K. *"Saga rodu Forsytów"* (*The Forsyte Saga*), FILIPINKA (Warsaw), No. 21 (1970), [n.p.] [not seen].
[Review of film adaptation of *The Forsyte Saga.*] [In Polish.]

2192 Hawkes, Carol A. "Galsworthy: The Paradox of Realism," ENGLISH LITERATURE IN TRANSITION, 1880–1920, XIII:4 (1970), 288– 95.

Realism to the Victorians meant "a vivid rendering of ordinary experience as opposed to the exotic imagination of romanticism"; reality for them involved a consensus to which right-thinking people subscribed. This consensus has been challenged by twentieth-century novelists, and the new realism is a paradoxical realism that questions even the "revulsion from the values" of the Victorian world. In his social fiction before World War I JG's work is pivotal because it "prepares the way for an alienated generation a half-century younger than his own." His first two novels—*Jocelyn* (1898) and *Villa Rubein* (1900) and his first two collections of short stories are romantic, but with *The Island Pharisees* (1904) JG emerges "as both a realist and an alien in his world." In dramatizing Shelton's pursuit of reality, JG "most clearly departs from the conventions of nineteenth-century realism." Shelton's disgust with his own class and his rejection of the social outcasts lead him to the "dark." Human nature repels him, and he casts off all allegiances until he is destitute: "Alone in the dark and musty rooms, he fixes his eyes on the night 'as one lost man might fix his eyes upon another' " (Pt. II, Ch. xxxiii). Following *Pharisees,* JG entered the second stage of his development as a realist, a stage of detachment so complete "that it scrutinizes action and value alike." The "image of reality" that JG creates in the next four social novels—*The Man of Property, The Country House, Fraternity,* and *The Patrician*—is the image of "the living dead." Instead of violent rebellion, "alienation remains in an eternal stalemate with the established order."

401

Death—either physical or spiritual—occurs in every novel, and "the poor are as susceptible to corruption as the rich." The mortal sin of his waste land is complacency. Always using the techniques of traditional realism, JG analyzes "economic complacency" in *Property*, "social complacency" in *House*, the "complacency of the artistic-intellectual Establishment" in *Fraternity*, and "political complacency" in *Patrician*. In *Fraternity* the penalties for those "who transgress the limits by extending their human sympathies" are harsh: "desolation for Hilary Dallison, defeat for young Thyme, madness for Sylvanus Stone." In portraying the slum world, JG's "balance of [its] vices and inadequacies precludes proletarianism." Both worlds—that of the Dallisons and that of the little model—are mean, and both are dead. In *Patrician* the controlling image is dryness.

"D. H. Lawrence's criticism that Galsworthy fails to make passion a redemptive force" is beside the point, because Lawrence's view "requires a mystique of love [which is] inadmissible in the context of Galsworthy's world. Galsworthy's lovers exist within the established order because that order is real, and no one can flout reality and escape disaster." The "ultimate step in the rejection of reality by reality" is to be seen in his lovers like Irene and Bosinney, George Pendyce and Helen Bellew, Hilary Dallison and the little model, Miltoun and Audrey Noel, who forget reality. JG was "attempting to carry an uncompromising realism, philosophical as well as technical, as far as it would go." Such an attempt could only lead to nihilism, and JG was not a nihilist. After *Property* he retreated to an "irony incidental or verbal," and his work moved from the satiric to the lyrical. The way that JG solved the problem of the paradoxical realism of *Pharisees* was to return to the manner of the Victorians, and it is in these later works in the Victorian manner that one can see the justice in Woolf's remarks about their "incompleteness." Nevertheless, JG's contribution to modern realism is genuine.

2193 Marchant, Peter. "*The Forsyte Saga* Reconsidered: The Case of the Common Reader Versus Literary Criticism," WESTERN HUMANITIES REVIEW (Salt Lake City), XXIV (Summer 1970), 221–29.
JG wrote trash, with "flabby prose," absurd imagery, clumsy exposition, and soap opera melodrama and characterization. Reasons for the survival of *The Forsyte Saga* are its obvious sexuality: JG's "weak satire and repetitious didacticism" do not destroy "the sensual pleasure they attempt to condemn." Sexual lovers (Soames, Bosinney, Jon) are punished; lovers who "transform sexual passion into the worship of aesthetic Beauty are rewarded." Male lovers in the Saga are sexually immature. "The enduring vitality of *The Forsyte Saga* . . . lies . . . in the ultimate validity of its unconscious meaning." Paradoxically, JG lacked an ironic sense, but "what he says is profoundly ironic because of his very inability to perceive that it is."

2194 Michalski, Czesław. *"Saga rodu Forsytów"* (*The Forsyte Saga*), GAZETA ZIELONOGÓRSKA (Zielona Gora),, No. 243 (1970), [n.p.] [not seen].
[Review of film adaptation of *The Forsyte Saga*.] [In Polish.]

2195 Michener, James A. "A Hit—In Any Language," TV GUIDE (30 May–5 June 1970), pp. 4–6, 8–9.
[This "background" article on the television production of *The Forsyte Saga* points out the enormous success of the series in fifty-five countries.] The novels themselves, except for *The Man of Property*, which was a fine piece of work, are ordinary, and the last four are very bad. Probably there were at least two dozen writers in English who could have done better: e.g., Ernest Hemingway, Edith Wharton, and Thomas Hardy. The brilliance of the television series "does not stem from the books" but from the way the series was produced—(1) the leisurely pace of the story; (2) the serious treatment of the material; and (3) excellent casting.

2196 Razumovskaia, T. F. "K probleme tvorcheskoi vzaimosviazi L. N. Tolstogo i D. Golsuorsi (Struktura kharakterov v romanakh ANNA KARENINA i *Sobstvennik*)" (The Creative Relationship Between L. N. Tolstoi and J. Galsworthy: Character Structure in the Novels ANNA KARENINA and *The Man of Property*), UCHENYE ZAPISKI (Gorkii. Universitet), No. 120 (1970), 80–90 [not seen].
[In Russian.]

2197 Razumovskaia, T. F. "Nasledie D. Golsuorsi—v sovetskoi kritike" (The Legacy of J. Galsworthy in Soviet Criticism), UCHENYE ZAPISKI (Gorkii. Universitet), No. 120 (1970), 139–42 [not seen].
[Listed in ANNUAL BIBLIOGRAPHY OF ENGLISH LANGUAGE AND LITERATURE (Cambridge: Modern Humanities Research Association, 1970).] [In Russian.]

2198 Razumovskaia, T. F. "*Villa Rubein* Golsuorsi i turgenevskaia traditsiia" (Galsworthy's *Villa Rubein* and the Turgenev Tradition), UCHENYE ZAPISKI (Gorkii. Universitet), No. 120 (1970), 66–79 [not seen].
[In Russian.]

2199 Robson, William Wallace. MODERN ENGLISH LITERATURE (Lond: Oxford UP, 1970), pp. xiii–xv, 36, 41–43, 102, 153.
JG was a genuine, if not great, artist. At their best the Edwardian realists are impressively truthful. D. H. Lawrence's criticism of JG is the best; he accused JG of selling out human values to social ones. JG's personal quarrel with society prompted *The Island Pharisees* and *The Man of Property*. His sympathies for the oppressed are shown in his dramas. JG "wears the blinkers of an English

gentleman" and lacks the "ruthless honesty" needed for great writing. Like all popular novelists JG has narrative power. [A disorganized set of biases owing more to the influence of D. H. Lawrence's 1928 essay in SCRUTINIES than to Robson.]

2200 Rybakova, N. I. "K probleme narodnosti romana D. Golsuorsi" (The National Character of J. Galsworthy's Novels), UCHENYE ZAPISKI (Gorkii. Universitet), No. 120 (1970), 193–203 [not seen].
[In Russian.]

2201 "Saga," NEW YORKER, XLV (10 Jan 1970), 15–17.
[Urbane and witty statistics-jammed article on the onslaught of the televised *Forsyte Saga*. Examples: the TV script has 300,000 words and 120 speaking parts; more than 1,300,000 JG volumes have been sold in England since the TV series began.]

2202 Savchenko, S. "Povest'Dzh. Golsuorsi *Pylaiushchee kop'e* kak satira na dzhingoism" (John Galsworthy's Tale, *The Burning Spear,* as a Satire on Jingoism), NAUCHNYE TRUDY (Frunze. Universitet. Filologicheskii Fakultet), No. 16 (1970), 131–41 [not seen].
[In Russian.]

2203 Schonbaum, S. SHAKESPEARE'S LIVES (NY: Oxford UP, 1970), p. 602.
JG declared that Looney's SHAKESPEARE IDENTIFIED (1920) was " 'the best detective story' which ever came his way."

2204 Smith, Philip Edward, II. "John Galworthy's Plays: The Theory and Practice of Dramatic Realism," DISSERTATION ABSTRACTS, XXX (1970), 4465A–66A. Unpublished dissertation, Northwestern University, 1969.

2205 "Soames Forsyte and Pornography," NATIONAL OBSERVER, 18 May 1970, p. 10.
[Editorial comments on the masterful treatment of the rape of Irene by Soames Forsyte, "one of the most uptight individuals in literary history," in the BBC-TV production *The Man of Property;* he then contrasts that to the growing interest in pornography and concludes by arguing that, as the *Forsyte Saga* episode demonstrates, pornography is unnecessary for art.]

2206 Sprusiński, Michał. *"Saga rodu Forsytów" (The Forsyte Saga)*, PERSPEKTYWY (Warsaw), Nos. 51–52 (1970), 55 [not seen].
[Review of film adaptation of *The Forsyte Saga.*] [In Polish.]

2207 Takada. Mineo. "The Difficulties Lie in His Englishness: A

Study of John Galsworthy" ANNUAL REPORTS OF STUDIES (Kyoto: Doshisha Women's College), CXXII (1970[?]), [n.p.] [not seen].
[Cited in PMLA BIBLIOGRAPHY, 1971, item 6327.]

2208 Taxner, Ernó. "John Galsworthy," AZ ANGOL IRODALOM A HUSZADIK SZÁZADBAN (ENGLISH LITERATURE IN THE TWENTIETH CENTURY), ed by Lázló Báti and István Krestó-Nagy (Budapest:Gondolat, 1970), pp. 139–56.
[A general and conventional study of JG's contributions to literature, with emphasis on *The Forsyte Saga*.] [In Hungarian.]

2209 VIEWER'S GUIDE TO THE FORSYTE SAGA (Owings Mills, Md: Maryland Center for Public Broadcasting, [1970]).
[A guide containing background information about the television series, the cast, the Forsyte family tree, six photos of the staff, and synopses of the twenty-six television episodes.]

2210 W., J. "*Saga rodu Forstyów*" (*The Forstye Saga*), POMORZE (Bydgoszez), No. 22 (1970), [n.p.], [not seen].
[Review of film adaptation of *The Forsyte Saga*.] [In Polish.]

2211 West, Anthony. "The Real Scandal behind *The Forsyte Saga*," VOGUE, CLV (May 1970), 206–7, 264, 266, 274.
The Forsyte Saga's success as a television serial is largely a result of the appeal to middle-class and upper-middle-class tastes, which heretofore have largely been neglected on television. *Saga* is a period piece. Forsytes of the older generation had barely made it in society, thus giving their children the "appearance, but not the substance, of membership in the leisured élite," in effect forcing them to live as "imposters." "The children's dismal and anxiety-ridden charade is what the . . . *Saga* is all about." [West repeats much of the information about JG–Ada– Arthur that he presented in his introduction to THE GALSWORTHY READER (NY: Scribner's, 1968).]

2212 Williams, Raymond. THE ENGLISH NOVEL FROM DICKENS TO LAWRENCE (NY & Oxford: Oxford UP, 1970), pp. 120, 124, 127–28, 133, 182, 183.
The Wells–Bennett–JG approach to literature shows how "narrow . . . unimaginative . . . upholstered and materialistic the English . . . had become" in the early twentieth century. JG's self-critical writing develops from within the "centre's limits" of society. D. H. Lawrence's criticism of JG as "too much aware of objective reality" accurately captures JG's world.

1971

2213 Bellamy, William. THE NOVELS OF WELLS, BENNETT AND GALSWORTHY: 1890–1910 (Lond: Routledge & Kegan Paul; NY: Barnes & Noble, 1971), pp. 1, 2, 3, 7, 11, 12, 15, 16, 19, 20, 21, 22, 23, 27, 29, 32, 36–37, 41, 42, 44, 46, 47, 48, 65, 84, 88–102, 105, 106, 107, 111, 112, 118, 145, 148, 157, 159, 160, 165–204, 205, 206, 211–16, 219, 232. The study seeks to "establish a line of continuity in the English novel, arguing that the release and consolidation of the self in modern times has depended upon a gradually developing ability to confront the post Darwinian crisis of consciousness." JG, Wells, and Bennett were "consciously or unconsciously" depicting themselves in a "post-cultural crisis" similar to that of today. Criticism of JG by the "cultural revisionists" Virginia Woolf and D. H. Lawrence addressed itself as much to their predicaments and crises as to JG's work. Our generation, in turn reacting to the "Modernism" of Woolf, T. S. Eliot, and Lawrence, "returns with fascination to the predicament of Soames Forsyte." JG's fiction of the 1890s is a "literature of offence," "defined most accurately in terms of its rendering of the symptomatic nature of subjective experience." His "post-1900 fiction . . . perhaps [responds] . . . too directly to sensed crisis to be 'great art' or even 'art' at all." JG, like Wells and Bennett, provided the "dialectical transition from art for art's sake to art for life's sake" that was necessary for the emergence of "cultural revisionism" in the 1920s.

Jocelyn, a musical novel of the Ford Madox Ford "Sonata-form" variety, portrays "2 selves in post-cultural crisis," finally curing themselves in "fevered consciousnesses, in . . . erotic reunion with the cosmos." In *Jocelyn,* JG is more "concerned with the pathology of temperament" than with love or moral experience. The death of Irma and the abandonment of Nielsen are "ruthless Darwinism." Irma's suicide disrupts existentially rather than morally. "The empty desert at the end of *Jocelyn* is a model of the post-cultural universe in process of cosmic repletion."

The narrator's stance in *The Man of Property* is much like the relation between a psychoanalyst and his patient. Soames Forsyte is "caught between the old culture and the new order," with Irene polarized against a "newly conscious Forsyte, in cultural crisis." Soames is "inexplicably despised," with feelings of guilt and alienation, occasionally desiring to be free of "inherited morality." Social criticism is given focus through Soames's diagnostic individual self-consciousness. Hilary, "an existential sentimentalist," plays a focal role in *Fraternity,* a novel in which the "elements are always . . . on the point of breaking away from the centre." "The Freudian tension of the erotic scenes reinforces the fine représentation of class tension" in *Fraternity,* just as Cecilia's "existential insecurity" at the beginning of the novel represents much of the insecurity of the Edwardian age. *"Fraternity* untendentiously analyses the corruption of consciousness in terms of post-cultural crisis." In conclusion, JG, like Wells and Bennett, "helped to institutionalize the therapeutic imagination of modern man." [Much of Bellamy's discussion of JG's works is conceived in terms of Philip Rieff's THE TRIUMPH OF THE THERAPEUTIC (1966). Bellamy's analysis demonstrates the limitations of such an approach. The main value of the volume is in challenging the pronouncements of Virginia Woolf and D. H. Lawrence that have become clichés in JG criticism. In trying so hard to place JG in trends of Rieffian psychology and such philosophical movements as neo-Vitalism, however, Bellamy over-reacts and is guilty of the same kind of faulty critical appraisal that he accuses Woolf and Lawrence of. To compound this, Bellamy has neither the grace of Woolf's style nor the challenging effrontery of Lawrence's to make his book readable. Phrases such as "continuity in the dialectal effort," "cosmic repletion," "emergent crises," "para-Freudian," "commitment therapy," and "post-Darwinian repletion" become clichés themselves rather than viable focal points for criticism. *The Country House,* for example, "is characterized by its fictional presentation of a conflict of therapies." *Fraternity* is analysed in similar terms.]

2214 Bellamy, William. "Wells, Bennett, and Galsworthy," TIMES LITERARY SUPPLEMENT (Lond), 23 July 1971, p. 861.
[Bellamy reacts in self-justification to the reviewer of THE NOVELS OF WELLS, BENNETT AND GALSWORTHY (Lond: Routledge & Kegan Paul, 1971) in "Hurray for the End of Culture," TIMES LITERARY SUPPLEMENT (9 July 1971), thanking the reviewer for including Bellamy in the "vanguard of a new school of anti-literary criticism."]

2215 Eaker, J. Gordon. "Galsworthy as Thinker in *The Forsyte Saga,*" PHI KAPPA PHI JOURNAL, LI (Winter 1971), 10–20.
JG writes to "preserve the rules of the road" of the Western tradition in his later works. A case in point is *Flowering Wilderness,* where Wilfred Desert converts to Mohammedanism at gunpoint: the English with their interlocked value system feel that if one value goes, all go—thus Wilfred is rejected. The early novels present different aspects of the "liberal idea": (1) complacency *(The Island Pharisees, The Man of Property, The Country House,* and *The Patrician),* which JG fought in his desire to liberate the spirit; (2) the liberation of women (Irene in *The Forsyte Saga)* and divorce laws *(In Chancery);* (3) the limited liability company, where wealth is detached from the land and from responsible management *(Strife);* and (4) the general items associated with industrialism, such as low-cost housing (Hilary Charwell in *Swan Song),* poverty (Bicket in *The White Monkey),* and the two scales of justice *(The Silver Box).* But JG was primarily concerned with the disintegration of moral standards *(Monkey, The Silver Spoon,*

Swan Song). Such ideas were presented in the works primarily through JG's method of the clash of ideas. "Quality" partly sums up JG's philosophy: to take pride in one's work and to find the golden mean. [A comprehensive and general overview.]

2216 Elwin, Malcolm. "Wells, Bennett and Galsworthy," TIMES LITERARY SUPPLEMENT (Lond), 23 July 1971, p. 861.
[Elwin asserts that, contrary to what the TLS reviewer of William Bellamy's THE NOVELS OF WELLS, BENNETT AND GALSWORTHY (Lond: Routledge & Kegan Paul, 1971) contends, Wells, Bennett, and Galsworthy were probably first grouped as a "triumvirate" by Ford Madox Hueffer in THE CRITICAL ATTITUDE (Lond: Duckworth, 1911), and not by Virginia Woolf.]

2217 Fréchet, Alec. "Galsworthy Hier et Aujourd'hui" (Galsworthy Yesterday and Today), ÉTUDES ANGLAISES (Paris), XXIV:2 (1971), 171–82.
Yesterday JG was thought to be a significant spokesman for his period, his class, and literature; today, the accepted view is the opposite. JG was never lucky with his critics, whether favorable or unfavorable; they were never of superior quality. Because much of Galsworthian criticism is biased, it is necessary to distinguish between his friends and his enemies. The critical neglect JG suffered from in 1914–1928 became more pronounced during the period 1930–1950. The enormous success of the BBC television series on the Forsytes and the renewed interest in his works indicate that there is a universality in his work and that there is something alive in it. The recent works by Rudolf Sauter and Margaret Morris are useful. The sound scholarship of Asher B. Wilson's edition of JG's letters to Leon Lion is a sign of the times. The critiques of JG are getting more numerous; the criticism is changing; it is becoming diversified, less querulous, more objective. There is still a great deal that needs to be done; it must distinguish the good from the bad in his works; it must extract from his works that which is always true and even new. [In French.]

2218 Fréchet, Alec. "Le Secret de Galsworthy" (The Secret of Galsworthy), ÉTUDES ANGLAISES (Paris), XXIV:2 (1971), 152–61.
To his contemporaries JG's secret was his ten-year affair with Ada, his cousin's wife, a secret that was unknown until the publication of Marrot's LIFE AND LETTERS. Knowing of this affair helps us to understand the obsessive theme of a woman who marries without love. A second though less important secret, revealed in 1967, was JG's relationship with Margaret Morris. The third secret and the focus of this paper concerns those aspects of his personality revealed in his diary and in *The Burning Spear*. In this third crisis he suffered a prolonged neurosis of despair. Thinking about the war and what his duty should be, JG recognized that Ada paralyzed him; he could face neither separation from her nor

a full commitment to duty. Ada was an enigma, and JG exaggerated her being the causes of his irresolution and misfortune. Insights into this third crisis are found in the treatment of the themes of love, war, and madness in *Spear*.

In almost all his works JG shows poor taste in treating love; there are unpleasant forms of eroticism as, for example, in *Spear* Lavender's senile sensuality and the sentimental description of Blink, Lavender's dog. The eroticism borders on the abnormal. The theme of dementia is found in the following: (1) from *The Island Pharisees* on, JG calls stupid or mad all who do not respect the traditions of the group; (2) he gives to Blink, Lavender's bitch, the same kind of madness as his own dog Dick exhibited; (3) he makes Lavender look stupid or idiotic while affirming that Lavender is not, and yet Lavender does become demented and delirious; (4) Lavender falls into comas and has visual hallucinations; (5) he allows Isabel to mock Lavender's illness; (6) he shows a pathological hatred for the press and for war. Finally, war makes everything absurd, for one's principles are inevitably sacrificed, and he (Lavender, JG) is conquered by despair. The pathological conditions abound (suicide, for example, is in almost all of JG's works). The buffoonery of *Spear* does not explain away the absurd, the despair, the abnormal, and Lavender's powerlessness. The work itself is ominous, confused, obscure, and clearly a failure.

When conditions after 1920 became favorable, JG overcame his depression and became quite prolific; even the quality of his work improved. His detractors called him sentimental, and sometimes his sentimentality is irritating. Yet one should not confuse sentimentality with emotionalism. JG was an emotional person with anxieties. He bore his troubles secretly and saved himself by action. He was a bourgeois who decided to work intellectually. His intensity, sympathy, sincerity made of him a practical man capable of discerning the ills of the world ahead of his contemporaries. His experience of life was rich and varied. [In French.]

2219 Friebe, Freimut. " 'Che farò' bei George Eliot und John Galsworthy: Der englische Gentleman und die Musik im 19. Jahrhundert" ("Che farò" in George Eliot and John Galsworthy: The English Gentleman and Music in the Nineteenth Century), LITERATUR IN WISSENSCHAFT UND UNTERRICHT (Kiel), IV (1971), 251–64.
George Eliot in "Mr. Gilfil's Love Story" accurately portrays the role of the musician and the place of music in upper-class society in the late eighteenth century in England. Caterina is treated as a domestic in Sir Christopher's household, and music serves as a passing after-dinner entertainment. For JG in "Indian Summer of a Forsyte" the place of the musician and the function of music are much different. Irene is the benefactor, and old Jolyon is dependent on her for her beauty and music. Music for old Jolyon embodies Beauty. [In German.]

2220 Groot, Roy Andries de. "A Holiday Feast at the Forsytes," ESQUIRE, LXXV (Jan 1971), 130–33, 164, 167.

A primary appeal of the BBC television series of *The Forsyte Saga* was nostalgia; another ingredient that helped hold the attention of viewers was the "running thread of concentration on food and wine." Accordingly, an elaborate meal based completely on the various references to food and wine throughout *Saga* was planned and executed by Maurice Chantreau, executive chef of New York's Four Seasons Restaurant. [The various restaurants here and abroad that would prepare this feast are listed at the end of the article.]

2221 Hamerliński, Andrzej. "Nad *Saga rodu Forsytów*" (On *The Forsyte Saga*), ZIELONY SZTANDAR (Warsaw), No. 9 (1971), [n.p.] [not seen]. [In Polish.]

2222 Kermode, Frank. "The English Novel, circa 1907," in TWENTIETH-CENTURY LITERATURE IN RETROSPECT, ed by Reuben A. Brower (Cambridge, Mass: Harvard UP [Harvard English Studies, 2] 1971), pp. 45–64.

A study of the relationship between the changing times and the condition of England question—and the changing techniques of fiction—is instructive. Three popular works of fiction in 1907 that illustrate the pressures of the times are William de Morgan's ALICE-FOR-SHORT, Florence Barclay's THE ROSARY, and Elinor Glyn's THREE WEEKS. Serious and increased interest in the techniques of fiction in the period are largely due to Henry James's fiction and his prefaces. The "new" novel not only demanded an increased awareness on the part of the reader, but it also broke away from the "closed endings" and the "expectation-satisfying devices" of the older novel. JG's *The Country House* should have been a Ford Madox Ford novel in its concern about preventing a divorce, but the novel is lacking because of its "social falsity"—"there is no sorrow like that of the rich"—and because of its failure of tone. JG solves the problem of the New Amoral Woman and divorce by the novelist's trick of having dull Mrs. Pendyce succeed because she *is* a lady in persuading the New Woman's husband to drop the divorce proceedings. Conrad's THE SECRET AGENT is the best novel of 1907, and it is "new"; and G. K. Chesterton's THE MAN WHO WAS THURSDAY (1908) is another illustration of "the old" kind of fantasy.

2223 Mikhail, E. H. JOHN GALSWORTHY THE DRAMATIST: A BIBLIOGRAPHY OF CRITICISM (Troy, NY: Whitston Publishing, 1971).

[Lists a number of references to criticism of JG's dramatic works.]

2224 Molkhova, Zhana. "Observations on the Language and Style of John Galsworthy. *The Forsyte Saga* and *A Modern Comedy,* Part II," ANNUAIRE. SOFIA UNIVERSITET. FILOLOGICHESKI FAKULTET, XIV, Book 2 (1971), 331–94.

[Résumé and bibliography.] [In Bulgarian.]

2225 Otten, Kurt. "John Galsworthy," in Rudolf Suehnel and Dieter Riesner (eds.), ENGLISCHE DICHTER DER MODERNE: IHR LEBEN UND WERK (Modern English Writers: Their Lives and Works) (Berlin: Erich Schmidt, 1971), pp. 129–48.

JG's plays, of which *Strife* is the best, are more complex than they seem, but they have dated more than the novels. All his works reflect the very positivism and materialism that he criticizes. [A good introduction.] [In German.]

2226 Prorok, Leszek. "*Saga rodu Forsytów*" (*The Forsyte Saga*), ŻYCIE LITERACKIE (Cracow), No. 15 (1971), 10 [not seen].
[Review of film adaptation of *The Forsyte Saga*.] [In Polish.]

2227 Ramsey, Roger. "Another Way of Looking at a Blackbird," RESEARCH STUDIES, XXXIX (June 1971), 152–54.

Laurence Perrine's analysis of "The Japanese Quince" [LITERATURE: STRUCTURE, SOUND, AND SENSE (NY: Harcourt Brace & World, 1970), p. 105, and Perrine and Margaret Morton Blum, INSTRUCTOR'S MANUAL FOR LITERATURE: STRUCTURE, SOUND, AND SENSE (NY: Harcourt Brace & World, 1970), p. 6] leaves the story static and almost inert. To interpret the blackbird "as part of the tree symbol" is inadequate. "But there is another way of looking at this blackbird and consequently at the action of the story." In the first paragraph Mr. Nilson "cannot judge the value difference between the tree and the temperature"; both make for a pleasant spring day. By the end of the story, however, the quince tree "seemed more living than a tree." There has been a dramatic change in Mr. Nilson's perceptions. "The bird at the heart of the branches of the tree can then be identified with the unusual feeling Mr. Nilson has 'just under his fifth rib,' " and its song is a plea for attention, a call to life, a call to the darker places of the heart. "Although Mr. Nilson rejects the call, he can no longer ignore it; he has been tempted," just as earlier he had been tempted by Mr. Tandram to establish a meaningful human social relationship. The blackbird, Mr. Tandram, and the empty feeling in Mr. Nilson's heart "are all one. They call Mr. Nilson to life." In addition to the blackbird there is the use of the color black; the darkness of the heart's recesses, the bird's blackness, and the black frock coat worn by Mr. Tandram imply the world of unknowns; perhaps there is even the suggestion of a nothingness comparable to Conrad's "destructive principle." And finally the "reader is left with the pathos of life missed, life here understood as dark, mysterious, dangerous, not quite proper." Mr. Nilson's failure to immerse himself in the "destructive element" makes him almost nostalgic.

2228 Sarbu, Aladár. "A *Forsyte Saga* mai szemmel" (*The Forsyte Saga* Viewed with Modern Eyes), ÉLET ÉS TUDOMÁNY (Budapest), XXVI:5 (1971), 203–7 [not seen].
[Listed in ANNUAL BIBLIOGRAPHY OF ENGLISH LANGUAGE AND LITERATURE (Cambridge: Modern Humanities Research Association, 1971).] [In Hungarian.]

2229 Shatsky, Joel Lawrence. "Shaw, Barker and Galsworthy: The Development of the Drama of Ideas," DISSERTATION ABSTRACTS, XXXI (1971), 4180A. Unpublished dissertation, New York University, 1970.

2230 Smith, Frank Glover. D. H. LAWRENCE: THE RAINBOW (Lond: Arnold [Studies in English Literature, No. 46], 1971), pp. 7, 22, 23, 61, 62.

For THE RAINBOW Lawrence used the "pattern of generations" as used by Mann in BUDDENBROOKS and by JG in *The Forsyte Saga*. Lawrence rejected the method of characterization that Bennett, Wells, and JG relied on; he believed that JG's characters existed only as social beings; they lacked inner reality. The themes—"changes in society" and "the emancipation of women"—are ones that Lawrence shared with JG, Wells, and Bennett. JG's observation that THE RAINBOW was a " 'failure as a work of art' " is wrong, for the novel is clearly one of the really important novels in English.

2231 Stern, Faith Elaine Bueltmann. "John Galsworthy's Dramatic Theory and Practice," DISSERTATION ABSTRACTS, XXXII (1971), 986A. Unpublished dissertation, George Washington University, 1971.

2232 Terlecki, Olgierd. "*Saga rodu Forsytów*" (*The Forsyte Saga*), ŻYCIE LITERACKIE (Cracow), No. 2 (1971), [n.p.] [not seen]. [Review of film adaptation of *The Forsyte Saga*.] [In Polish.]

2233 Vančura, Zdeněk. "*Sága po šedesáti letech. Doslov*" (The *Saga* After Sixty Years: Epilogue), *Saga rodu Forsytu* (*The Forsyte Saga*) (Prague: Odeon, 1971), pp. 797–99 [not seen]. [In Czech.]

1972

2234 Akhmechet, L. I. "Golsuorsi i Turgenev" (Galsworthy and Turgenev), UCHENYE ZAPISKI BASHKIRSKOGO UNIVERSITETA (Ufa), No. 51 (1972), pp. 308–21 [not seen]. [Listed in ANNUAL BIBLIOGRAPHY OF ENGLISH LANGUAGE AND LITERATURE (Cambridge: Modern Humanities Research Association, 1972).] [In Russian.]

2235 Carroll, LaVon Brown. "John Galsworthy: The Making of an Edwardian Novelist," DISSERTATION ABSTRACTS, XXXII (1972), 6416A–17A. Unpublished dissertation, University of Utah, 1972.

2236 Cockburn, Claud. BESTSELLER. THE BOOKS THAT EVERYONE READ 1900–1939 (Lond: Sidgwick & Jackson, 1972), pp. 2, 3.
Although one speaks of Bennett, Shaw, and JG as the writers of middle-class England in 1900–39, the real best sellers, like Robert Hichens (THE GARDEN OF ALLAH), and H. deVere Stacpoole (THE BLUE LAGOON), and others of their ilk served a need and were highly popular.

2237 "The Forsytes Return," NEW ZEALAND LISTENER, LXIX (31 Jan 1972), 2–3.
[A brief background piece noting that the television version of *The Forsyte Saga* is going to be shown again.]

2238 Gesner, Carol. "Galsworthy's 'Apple Tree' and the Longus Tradition," STUDIES IN THE TWENTIETH CENTURY, No. 9 (Spring 1972), 83–88.
JG clearly casts a Greek mood over "The Apple Tree" and amplifies this mood by using various details of the pastoral tradition: e.g., at Megan's home Ashurst receives the "traditional pastoral offerings of cream, cakes, and cider, bathes in the stream, and thinks of Theocritus." The plot structure of the traditional pastoral plot as utilized by Longus in DAPHNIS AND CHLOE is modified by JG to suit twentieth-century realism.

2239 Gill, Richard. HAPPY RURAL SEAT: THE ENGLISH COUNTRY HOUSE AND THE LITERARY IMAGINATION (New Haven & Lond: Yale UP, 1972), pp. 14, 97, 98, 99, 113, 115–25, 131, 147, 239, 274–75.
JG, who was at home in country houses, found much to criticize in the lifestyles that JG himself could not avoid living. Three novels look at different strata of society in relationship to the country house: *The Man of Property* (the middle class), *The Country House* (the gentry), and *The Patricians* (the aristocracy). The building of Robin Hill in *Property* gives the "narrative backbone" for character and theme, and by the time of *In Chancery,* Robin Hill kindles a sense of continuity; but the symbolic aspect of Robin Hill is beclouded in *To Let.* Unfortunately, JG did not fully grasp the potential symbolic significance of Robin Hill.

2240 Hart, John E. "Ritual and Spectacle in *The Man of Property,*" RESEARCH STUDIES, XL (March 1972), 34–43.
The story of the Forsytes is the saga of mankind, the allegory of man's needs to follow ancient forms and tribal patterns. JG uses "ritual or family celebrations as an integral part of his allegorical technique": June's engagement, the death of Aunt Ann, Swithin's dinner party, the dance at Roger's. Central to the story is the organic metaphor of growth, blossoming, and decline. Part I opens with June's engagement at the summit of Forsyte efflorescence and ends with Aunt Ann's death in the autumn; in Part II the planning and building of Robin Hill coincides with the springtime of Irene and Bosinney's love which perishes in the autumn;

Part III focuses on the trial and ends with Bosinney's death in the November fog. Soames is a "man of property" and so is Bosinney. "Money is important to Bosinney, because it provides artistic opportunity." Soames's recourse to law "is the method society provides and approves for protecting its tribal members in a civilized manner." By the end of the novel Soames "has become a creature of habit, a victim of certitudes that no longer function." The reason for the decline in JG's reputation seems to lie more with changing tastes and fashions "than with the meaning and structure of his vision."

> **2241** Horkay, Laszlo. "A *Forsyte Saga* magyar vonatkozásu nyitánya" (Hungarian Reference in the Opening of *The Forsyte Saga*), FILOLOGIAI KOZLONY (Budapest), XVI:3–4 (1972), 519–20 [not seen]. [Listed in ANNUAL BIBLIOGRAPHY OF ENGLISH LANGUAGE AND LITERATURE (Cambridge: Modern Humanities Research Association, 1972).] [In Hungarian.]

> **2242** Kurowska, Elżbieta. "*Saga Rodu Forsyteów' w Polsce Lat Trzydziestych*" (*The Forsyte Saga* in Poland in the Nineteen Thirties), PRZEGIĄD HUMANISTYCZNY (Warsaw), XVI:5 (1972), 49–56.

Translations of JG's work achieved little critical notice or popularity in Poland until the publication of *The Forsyte Saga* in 1930. In the 1930s Polish literary magazines published a dozen or more important articles about JG. Roman Dyboski and Stanislaw Helsztyński were two of the major Polish reviewers of the period. Dyboski emphasized in particular the strengths and virtues of British civilization and culture, even though he was quite aware of England's postwar problems. Emphasizing the biographical aspects of JG as an upper-class gentleman, Helsztyński focused on the ideal representatives of the upper class in JG's work and found in JG's social criticism elements of "Marxist" or "socialist" ideology. Some critics felt that JG's work analyzed the changes which had taken place in England from 1886 to 1926 and depicted the history of a social class and the annals of several generations of a family with common psychic foundations. The theme of *Saga* and *A Modern Comedy* for these critics is the disintegration of the bourgeoisie. Critics like F. Turynowa, Dyboski, and Helsztyński treated Irene symbolically. Although most Polish critics were unanimous in their praise, Waclaw Borowy perceived internal contradictions in *Saga:* JG not only satirized property; he also wrote in praise of possessiveness; Irene is a real woman, not a symbol, who is frightened when weak and spiteful when strong; Soames changes from an unsympathetic to a sympathetic character.

In 1930 Helsztyński argued that *Comedy* was more radical than *Saga; Comedy* concerns broader social and political issues like unemployment, housing, and population, which had developed as part of the aftermath of World War I. In contrast to *Saga,* which is static, *Comedy* is dynamic.

Interest in JG's work declined after 1933; the only excellent article on JG is one on *Saga* and *Comedy* in 1935 by Andrzej Tretiak. Tretiak explores specifically the essence of the English psyche, collectively and individually, in JG's work.

Tretiak saw that sentimentalism was an element of JG's "Englishness." The vignettes in *On Forsyte 'Change* do not represent real life; they· are Victorian constructs which are seen through sentimental prisms. JG's escape to historicism enabled him to avoid confronting and solving problems. The value of *Saga* is that it documents the changes and growth in "Englishness" over a number of years. JG's last trilogy, *End of the Chapter,* did not arouse much response in Poland. For Dyboski *Chapter* is "elegiac lyricism." In 1936 Helsztyński remarked that *Over the River* showed JG's withdrawal from the war generation and the consequent loss of a critical outlook on English society.

A particularly serious problem in appreciating JG's works for Polish readers is the bad quality of the translations. The translations of *Saga, Comedy,* and *Chapter* were assigned to ten persons, and not surprisingly there were many inaccuracies and inconsistencies of style. In some instances the translator seemed unaware of English idiom and English society. As a writer JG was seen as an English realist in the tradition of Fielding, Smollett, and Dickens. Dyboski saw a relationship in JG's work to Zola's Rougon-Macquart series and to Mann's BUDDENBROOKS.

After 1935 Polish critics of JG held that he was a secondary classic writer, but as World War II drew nearer JG's ideology and the "Englishness" of his work seemed inappropriate. Newer writers with newer techniques—Conrad, Huxley in POINT COUNTERPOINT, Proust, and Joyce—became relevant. [In Polish.]

> **2243** Pedchenko, E. D. "Vvod pryamoi rechi v avtorskoe povestvo-vanie. Po romanutrilogii Dzh. Golsuorsi *Konets glavy* " (The Introduc-tion of Direct Speech into the Author's Narration. Based on J. Galswor-thy's Novel-Trilogy, *The End of the Chapter*), UCHENYE ZAPISKI KISHINEVSKII UNIVERSITET (Kishinev), No. 115 (1972), pp. 129–37 [not seen].

[Listed in ANNUAL BIBLIOGRAPHY OF ENGLISH LANGUAGE AND LITERATURE (Cambridge: Modern Humanities Research Association, 1972).] [In Ukranian.]

> **2244** Shraibman, A. "Problemy khudozhestvennogo stilia v *Saga o Forsaitakh* D. Golsuorsi" (Problems of Literary Style in J. Galswor-thy's *The Forsyte Saga*) (Leningrad, 1972), 19 pp. [not seen].

[Abstract of an unpublished dissertation.] [In Russian.]

> **2245** Urbánek, Zdeněk. "Forsytove v nove úloze. Doslov" (The Forsytes in a New Part: Epilogue), *Moderní komedie* (*A Modern Com-edy*) (Prague: Odeon, 1972), [n.p.] [not seen].

[In Czech.]

1973

2246 Biswas, Anima. "Galsworthy and Ibsen," MODERN REVIEW, CXXXII:5 (May 1973), 392–95.

Both Ibsen and JG are realists in the sense that a realist is one who uses "words and actions," so that they "cross the limits of their apparent meaning . . . and acquire varied nuances or symbolic dimensions." Ibsen was the founder of "modern realist drama," and JG, despite his assertions that Ibsen did not influence him, nevertheless absorbed "the motifs and techniques introduced by Ibsen" that had helped to mold the "new Drama" in England from the 1890s on. And like Ibsen, JG used symbolism "to heighten the picture of reality."

2247 Goetsch, Paul. "Das englische Drama seit Shaw" (British Drama since Shaw), in Josefa Nuenning (ed.), DAS ENGLISCHE DRAMA (Darmstadt: Wissenschaftliche Buchgesellschaft, 1973), pp. 403–507.

Unlike Granville-Barker, JG too frequently depends on the form of the well-made play and on structural symmetry (Scrimgeour). His plays rarely transcend the topical problems they raise. [*Strife, Justice,* and *The Silver Box* receive special attention.] [In German.]

2248 Nicoll, Allardyce. ENGLISH DRAMA 1900–1930: THE BEGINNINGS OF THE MODERN PERIOD (Cambridge: Cambridge UP, 1973), pp. 2, 129, 132, 180, 218, 276, 333, 335, 338, 396, 399–407, 408, 420, 439.

JG seems to place himself beside his stage people in his dramas of ideas, which are filled with "warm humility and compassion." Whereas Shaw's wit arouses laughter, JG's sympathy arouses people to reconsider the meaning of life. Yet the dramas lack complete success because of JG's "triple bafflement" of himself, humanity, and "limitations of the dramatic form." JG was more a man of "sympathetic conviction" than of principle, feeling that the world needs the rule of justice and sympathy: his lack of the "arrogant mind" and the "stylistic precision" of the good satirist kept him from presenting the clear vision that captures the imagination of the audience. Because he lacks a sense of comedy, he tries to surmount the tedium of ordinary commonplace scenes by resorting to melodrama. He also tries—unsuccessfully at times—to express emotions not suitable for commonplace dialogue by wordless episodes: consequently, stage directions occasionally end a scene, as in *Strife* or *The Fugitive* or *The Mob.* JG ultimately was thwarted by the effects of the style that he had chosen to write in. [Nicoll presents a handlist of JG plays on p. 660.]

2249 Seymour-Smith, Martin. GUIDE TO MODERN WORLD LITERATURE (Lond: Wolfe; NY: Funk & Wagnalls, 1973), pp. 186, 200.

In contrast to H. G. Wells, JG's talent is "drab." *The Man of Property* is JG's best work. In later works he remained a "courteous, considerate, and conscientious man," but his work is by no means major: JG did not understand the postwar generation, he manipulated his characters to suit his emotions, and in general, the characters are "flat and lifeless." The dramas, especially *The Silver Box, Strife*, and *Justice*, are "well made, restrained, and display a genuine passion for social justice." [Heavily indebted to D. H. Lawrence's strictures (SCRUTINIES, Lond: Wishart, 1928) and to the often patronizing critical comment that resulted from the televised *Forsyte Saga*—i.e.: "He cannot hope to achieve more than his recent enshrinement as author of the original script (so to speak) of the (for ever?) current soap opera of *The Forsyte Saga*."]

2250 Stevens, Earl E. "John Galsworthy," BRITISH WINNERS OF THE NOBEL LITERARY PRIZE, ed by Walter Kidd (Norman: University of Oklahoma P, 1973), pp. 8–9, 130–67, 269–70.

JG extended the objective realism of Balzac and Maupassant to social documentation of his era and to candid criticism of "Victorian shortcomings and social ills." During the period of his life from the publication of *The Island Pharisees* (the first distinctly Galsworthian work) through *The Man of Property*, JG was constantly striving to improve his technique. By the time *Property* was finished, JG was in full control of his art, characteristics of which he presented in "A Novelist's Allegory" (1908). To JG the role of the artist is to "present life as he honestly [sees] . . . it," because art "attains its purpose of revelation and delight when it is able 'to alter or enlarge a point of view over life, a mood of living' or when it increases the reader's 'power to see.' " To avoid the element of propaganda, JG adopted the "negative method" of presenting art. *Property*, which develops two main plots to convey the theme of "the impact of beauty and passion on the Forsyte world," shows him in effective command of his material, especially in his use of satire and the omniscient-narrator convention.

During the period 1906–1910, which marked a growing recognition of JG as a novelist and as a playwright of stature in such plays as *The Silver Box, Strife*, and *Justice*, JG devoted himself to a four-fold task. The first of these was, in the novel, to "explore through character rather than story 'the utter disharmony of the Christian religion with the English character,' " by focusing satirically on four sections of upper-class English society. This was accomplished, after a generalized attack on upper-class society in *Pharisees*, by *Property*, an analysis of the propertied, professional class; *The Country House*, the landed gentry; *Fraternity*, the intelligentsia; and *The Patrician*, the aristocracy. The second task, in the drama, was to use the "brickwork technique" that "refused to take any liberty with perfect naturalness and actuality of expression" to "create an 'intensely exact and actual reproduction of people talking, and the room or what not in which they talk.' " *Strife* and *Justice* are cases in point. Third was the "corrosive quality" of JG's writings, evident especially in *Fraternity*, that "haunts the reader's memory" as JG presents the antithesis of life in his often too balanced and artificial way. The fourth aspect of JG's development was the stylistic shift evident most clearly in his later work as he moved from the satiric to the lyric form in his art: *The Forsyte Saga* shifts from satiric novel (*Property*), to lyric interlude ("Indian Summer of a Forsyte"), to satiric novel (*In Chancery*), to lyric interlude ("The Awakening"), back to satiric novel (*To Let*). The same pattern is followed in *A Modern Comedy*.

Unlike most important novelists, JG has not had the rebirth of critical interest that one normally expects after the inevitable hiatus following a writer's death. Reasons for this are: (1) a reaction to the overinflated value that he had as a novelist during his lifetime; (2) his reputation primarily as a sociological critic, a reformer, and a "disturbing chronicler of the contemporary"; (3) his technically old-fashioned style, working primarily within the traditions of the Victorian novel; (4) his old-fashioned philosophy based on humanitarian ideals; and (5) his limited range and subject matter—primarily the milieu of the upper classes. A proper critical perspective, when it evolves, will recognize him as the last important Victorian novelist. [This essay emphasizes JG's consistent artistic development through *Saga* and is especially valuable as a corrective to many studies that gloss over the artistic craftsmanship of JG. The essay also provides brief but cogent critical commentary on plot, theme, and structure of the major novels and several of the plays, while at the same time recording JG's rightful place as humanitarian and philanthropist. The case for the need to reevaluate JG critically is convincing.]

> **2251** Tugusheva, M. P. DZHON GOLSUORSI: ZYTCHI I TVORZESTVO (JOHN GALSWORTHY: LIFE AND WORKS) (Moscow: Izdatelstvo Hayka, 1973) [not seen].

[In Russian.]

1974

> **2252** Banerjee, Jacqueline. "Galsworthy's 'Dangerous Experiment,'" ANGLO-WELSH REVIEW, XXIV (1974), 135–43.

In all of JG's work "indulgence in the passions is always regarded as something 'dangerous' . . . and as such it is, ultimately, to be abandoned." For him, "passion recedes further and further beyond the bounds of social propriety and 'the sense of property' (on which, as young Jolyon (*The Forsyte Saga*) sees, the marriage tie is based) instead of evolving as a positive force in opposition to it; and from an inadequate portrayal of it, Galsworthy progresses towards a basic loss of faith in it." In abandoning the " 'dangerous experiment' of passion" and replacing it "with half-hearted convictions about the powers for good of the propertied class," JG diminished his stature as a writer. Because of JG's failure, it has been left "to others to carry on the 'dangerous experiment,' to vindicate and explore the passions, so as to reveal their positive value in the attainment of individual fulfilment."

2253 Core, George. "Author and Agency: Galsworthy and the Pinkers," LIBRARY CHRONICLE OF THE UNIVERSITY OF TEXAS, VI (1974), 61–73.

The career of James B. Pinker as a literary agent is remarkable, and the correspondence (approximately twelve hundred letters) between JG and the Pinker agency is valuable for the insight it provides into "recent publishing history and literary relations in England and the United States." Besides representing writers like Conrad, Lawrence, and Joyce, Pinker also handled popular writers like Wells, Bennett, Maugham, and JG. JG's relationship with the Pinker agency began in 1906 and continued until JG's death in 1933. Although the correspondence provides no new critical insights into JG's work, it does reveal that JG was "little more than a hack who was worried only by the mechanical aspects of writing another manuscript and seeing it through the press." As a writer JG had a good but crude sense of plot; his characterization was poor; his style was "undistinguished at its mediocre best"; the dialogue was forced, and there is a lack of dramatic development. He could not develop a scene. That JG was more concerned with his profits than with his art and that the Pinker agency was a very effective one help to explain why a popular writer like JG could achieve such an impressive reputation. [Implicit in this article is the questionable notion that a really good writer's letters to his agent should be concerned more with matters literary and less with matters practical.]

2254 Wootton, Carol. "The Lure of the Basilisk: Chopin's Music in the Writings of Thomas Mann, John Galsworthy and Hermann Hesse," ARCADIA, IX (1974), 23–38.

Writers like Mann, Hesse, and JG utilized Chopin's music for its *fin-de-siècle* mood of melancholic yearning and its aestheticism. For Old Jolyon in "Indian Summer of a Forsyte" Chopin's music becomes associated with Irene; Old Jolyon's sympathetic responses indicate "an awareness of the changing spirit of the age with the intrusion of aestheticism into England towards the turn of the century."

1975

2255 Gillie, Christopher. MOVEMENTS IN ENGLISH LITERATURE: 1900–1940 (Lond: Cambridge UP, 1975), pp. 92, 165.

JG brought the "social substance" of his novels to his plays but failed to understand that drama requires a different "shape of experience." [Brief comments of dismissal about *The Forsyte Saga* and *Strife*.]

2256 Farris, Erdmuthe Christiane. "John Galsworthy and the Drama of Social Problems," DISSERTATION ABSTRACTS, XXXV (1975), 7301A. Unpublished dissertation, Columbia University (NY), 1974.

2257 Gindin, James. "Ethical Structures in John Galsworthy, Elizabeth Bowen, and Iris Murdoch," FORMS OF MODERN BRITISH FICTION, ed by Alan Warren Friedman (Austin: University of Texas P, 1975), pp. 5, 15–41, 166, 204, 220.

In MR. BENNETT AND MRS. BROWN, Virginia Woolf argued for the kind of fiction that was metaphysical, that transformed ordinary experience, and that assumed an essential core of personality. In her view only fiction that satisfied these criteria could be considered great. But there is "another well-established line of fiction" that is "more concerned with relationships between personalities than with an essence of human personality." Frequently such fiction is concerned with ethical questions, speculations, and judgments. Central to this kind of fiction is "what man *does* to himself and to others." The central focus of JG's work is ethical, not metaphysical. In *The Forsyte Saga* the struggle is between property and beauty, and it is the artist "who can appreciate beauty, who can create because he is able to understand and to avoid imposition." In JG's terms, not all artists are worthy: e.g., Bosinney. Young Jolyon exemplifies the artist who fully appreciates beauty and yet "on matters other than art" his limitations on "ethical questions that surround his role as father" are self-evident. In *A Modern Comedy,* "the public ethical focus shifts away from the artist to the man involved in politics and society, Michael Mont." In *End of the Chapter,* JG's "ethical focus on political issues involving England in a changing world" continues. The particular issues may seem trivial but JG's point is that in a civilized society the various issues—political, religious, and sexual—must be judged within the terms of a wide social context. Although colonialism may be implicitly endorsed in *Flowering Wilderness*, it is not endorsed in *Maid In Waiting*. In JG's work the ethical perspective is always intelligent and sympathetic, for he "never advocates the intensity of cores or metaphysical truths." Other writers who have involved themselves in ethical fiction are the early Hemingway, the later Fitzgerald, Elizabeth Bowen, Saul Bellow in such works as HERZOG and MR. SAMMLER'S PLANET, and Iris Murdoch.

2258 Scheick, William J. "Chance and Impartiality: A Study Based on the Manuscript of Galsworthy's *Loyalties,* TEXAS STUDIES IN LANGUAGE AND LITERATURE, XVII (1975), 653–72.

A contrast of the first and last versions of the manuscript of *Loyalties* gives insight into JG's stylistic techniques and meaning. Of particular interest is the way revisions of the manuscript change "dialogue, dramatic tension, characterization and structural detail." JG's final version of the opening scene, for example, uses more concise diction than the original version to mute the theme of racial prejudice and to change Winsor from a "two-dimensional caricature of his social class" to a more complex character. In a later version, Dancy's suicide note is changed from a "self-pitying, unconvincing in its self-conscious irony, unrealistically long" statement to one that is "realistically elliptical and understated. . .untainted by self-pity. . . . Melodrama yields to artistic control."

Changes are also made to emphasize the theme of chance, which JG considers the "fundamental reality of the postwar world." In revising the initial and final scenes of the play, JG worked for "impartiality in his point of view" to transform his audience into sensitive yet helpless bystanders." [This study is one of very few to address itself to JG's conscious artistry.]

1976

2259 Dupré, Catherine. JOHN GALSWORTHY: A BIOGRAPHY (Lond: Collins; NY: Coward, McCann & Geoghegan, 1976).
The young JG, a product of typical Victorian upbringing of the newly rich middle class, was greatly influenced by the closeness of the relationships within the Galsworthy family, especially the "small intellectual world which [the Galsworthy children] created for themselves, and which had already begun to criticize so sharply the values of their parents." JG's writing career developed concurrently with his relationship with Ada. Ada had neither JG's vision nor "the generosity to let his spirit rove where hers could not follow": this led inexorably to the diminishing of JG's creative ability. *Jocelyn* is the story of Ada and John, written when their affair "must still have been most painful and poignant"; it has "passages . . . as accomplished as any its author ever wrote," in part because JG explores his own suffering and in part because he explores the relationship between Ada and her mother. Likewise, the story of Irene in *The Man of Property* is obviously the story of Ada. JG is too obsessed throughout his works "with the state of the unhappily married woman," a theme which "becomes both the wealth and poverty of his writing." *Property*, JG's first "social novel," was so filled with parallels to the Galsworthy family that JG's sister Lilian questioned the wisdom of publishing it. *Villa Rubein* tells of Lilian and of her marriage to the painter Georg Sauter. The protagonist Hilary in *Fraternity*, another novel about an unhappily married woman, is the most autobiographical and complex character that JG created; had he continued in this line of development, JG would be held in higher esteem today than he is. Ferrand speaks for JG in *The Island Pharisees*, a novel in which JG demonstrates his "most unguarded and explosive mood against society." *The Country House*, a "mellower and gentler book" than *Property*, does for the country what *Property* does for the town.

"The object of nearly all of [JG's] work is . . . to moralize," but the plays, especially *The Silver Box, Strife, Justice, The Mob,* and *The Skin Game* are more didactic than his novels. With *Box,* JG's name became associated with Shaw in the "new theatre of ideas." *Strife* is JG's first decidedly social treatise.

JG's strength was sapped by the war years. *Beyond* records the effect: JG the man was involved with the problems of World War I, while JG the artist wrote unsuccessfully "of love and of trite romance." *Beyond,* like *The Patrician,* is "romantic and mentally undemanding." After he chose not to follow the pattern set for Hilary in *Fraternity,* his work became less concerned with the inner life of his characters at a time when the mainstream of literary talent was becoming more and more involved in exploring the inner life.

Returning to the Forsytes after the war, JG believed that he had reached the "shores of permanence," not for "tremendous depth or intellectual insight" but for the story of his uncles who are portrayed so vividly in *The Forsyte Saga. In Chancery* reveals JG's "sense of despair about the futility of life, the inevitable snuffing out of death." *Chancery* and *To Let* owe their success to the fact that JG "gauged exactly the mood of the day . . . [in novels that are] nostalgic . . . well-written, undemanding and easy to read." *The Silver Spoon* is filled with "trivial adventures," and *Swan Song* demonstrates that JG is beginning to lose his power as a writer. The *End of the Chapter* is "a poor piece of work"; despite the final idealized woman Dinny Cherrell, *Maid in Waiting* is "weak and meandering"; *Flowering Wilderness* is filled with "emptiness and despair"; and *Over the River* speaks ultimately of what JG recognized as "his own tragedy as a creative writer": "It might be said of [me] that I create characters who have feelings which they cannot express."

In his final years, JG was an "isolated figure in the literary world," turning more to family and community while drifting apart from literary friends. Becoming more and more a conformist and feeling at the same time that he was essentially "unfulfilled as a writer," JG died fearing that he had not created the truly great works that he had envisioned.

2260 Patterson, Alice C. "Cyril Povey: The Emblem of Social Change," ENGLISH LITERATURE IN TRANSITION: 1880–1920, XIX:4 (1976), 248–64.
[Passing references, especially pp. 262–66, suggest that Bosinney (*The Man of Property*), like George Ponderevo (Wells, TONO-BUNGAY) and Cyril Povey (Bennett, THE OLD WIVES' TALE), is implicitly an emblem of the "new order," providing "the bridge between the Victorian world and the modern world." JG, Wells, and Bennett create human characters who, in their "existential stance," can evaluate the Victorian era while presaging the modern world.]

2261 Stevens, Harold Ray. "Galsworthy's *Fraternity:* The Closed Door and the Paralyzed Society," ENGLISH LITERATURE IN TRANSITION, XIX:4 (1976), 283–98.
JG's representation of upper-middle-class life with Hilary and Bianca Dallison and Stephen and Cecilia Dallison suggests "that marital harmony or the lack of it distinctly correlates to one's ability to live meaningfully in the larger social context." Hilary and Bianca are unable and unwilling to come to terms with their

married life; Stephen and Cecilia have been able to come to terms with themselves in a relationship that is "uninspired and innocuous." In this uptight world JG uses "the metaphor of the closed door . . . to symbolize both the surface frustration and the inner turmoil that forecloses on the possibility of happiness." Hilary and Bianca live in " 'married celibacy' " and speak to each other through strained, compressed lips. In contrast, the life of the poor on Hound Street is "open and matter-of-fact." In both worlds, however, the metaphors JG uses suggest "strained frustration." The motif of the "open and closed door" is complemented by the image of "open and closed—or partially open and closed—lips."

The paradox that Hilary recognizes—"social conscience results from comfort and security and comfort and security destroy the power of action"—is illustrated by the novel itself. The Dallisons continue on in their various ways, unchanged but liberal; the poor remain, and like the Hughses they have no means of escape. The only suggested solutions are Martin's work as a sanitist to improve the sanitation facilities and Mr. Stone's preaching of Universal Brotherhood; and Mr. Stone's sermon "is the message of an old man crying out in senile-accented frustration from his wasteland."

The major problem with JG as a prose stylist "is that he was so entrapped by the standards of the Dallisons and the Forsytes that he was unable to write independently of them." Instead of presenting his characters' inner feelings as Joyce might have Molly Bloom do, JG "supplies parallels, often impressionistically, to allow the reader to associate what he as writer is reluctant or unable to treat more maturely and explicitly." Like the Dallisons JG compresses his tight lips "because of his difficulty in formulating succinctly that overt actions often are motivated by suppressed psychological pressures"; he often uses various metaphors to suggest some of these inner realities: e.g., the metaphor of the pale glow of the gas street lamps—the streetwalker, the lamppost, and the halo from these lamps that envelops London; other metaphors are drawn from animal behavior—cats and dogs on the prowl and honey bees gathering nectar. JG's message is clear despite the fact that "his Victorian stylistic predilections and Edwardian upper middle class temperament" kept him from using "a more mature stream of consciousness style about the interplay of sexual frustration and of social ills."

1977

2262 Mitgang, Herbert. "Publishing: A Hindsight Saga," NEW YORK TIMES, 28 Jan 1977, p. C20.

The American publication of *Jocelyn*, JG's first novel, is scheduled for this spring. The novel was first published in English in 1898 with a printing of 750 copies, but JG withdrew the novel because, according to Catherine Dupré, JG's latest biographer, it was too revealing of his intimate, passionate, and illicit romance with Ada. The most famous and most successful use by JG of the theme of two lovers who are not free to marry is, of course, *The Man of Property*.

Index

AUTHORS

Included here are authors of articles and books on Galsworthy, editors and compilers of works in which criticism on Galsworthy appears. Editors and translators are identified parenthetically: (ed), (trans). Numbers after each name refer to the item(s) in the bibliography where the name occurs.

425

Index

TITLES OF SECONDARY WORKS

Titles of articles in periodicals and chapters in books are in quotation marks; book titles are in upper case; translations of article titles originally appearing in a foreign language are in parentheses, without quotation marks, and in lower case; translations of book titles originally appearing in a foreign language are in parentheses and in upper case. Numbers after each title refer to the item in the bibliography where the title appears.

437

JOHN GALSWORTHY

441

445

JOHN GALSWORTHY

John Galsworthy

Index

PERIODICALS AND NEWSPAPERS

Included here are periodicals and newspapers for which entries occur in the bibliography. Numbers after each title refer to the number(s) of the item in the bibliography where the title appears.

469

Index

FOREIGN LANGUAGES

Included here are the languages in which articles and books listed in the bibliography originally appeared. Numbers under each language refer to the items in the bibliography where the foreign-language title is given. English language items are not listed.

Index

PRIMARY TITLES

Included here are all titles by Galsworthy occurring in titles of articles or books or in the abstracts. Numbers after each title refer to the item in the bibliography where the title appears. Titles of individual novels in the trilogies (*The Forsyte Saga, A Modern Comedy,* and *End of the Chapter*) are not always cited in the abstracts; consequently users of this index should consult both the specific novel and the appropriate trilogy.

479

956, 960, 963, 965, 982, 992, 997, 1051, 1054, 1058, 1066, 1071, 1127, 1188, 1266, 1311, 1329, 1506, 1533, 1590, 1636, 1787, 2029, 2094, 2215

Windows: 739, 742, 747, 765, 771, 781, 785, 809, 812, 821, 832, 835, 850, 855, 862, 863, 865, 867, 872, 877, 880, 884, 894, 896, 971, 1018, 1153, 1182, 1310, 1483, 1508, 1534, 1770, 1871

"The Winter Garden": 1686

The Annotated Secondary Bibliography Series on English Literature in Transition 1880–1920 *was designed by John B. Goetz of Chicago, Illinois. This volume was typeset by Weimer Typesetting Co. of Indianapolis, Indiana. The text is set in Times Roman; the display face is Perpetua. The book was printed by Kingsport Press of Kingsport, Tennessee, on Warren #50 Olde Style wove paper.*